Making The Most of Your Money Now

By the Editors of MONEY Magazine

Edited by Junius Ellis

MONEY STAFF

Frank Lalli
managing editor

executive editors Caroline Donnelly, Tyler Mathisen
assistant managing editors Lynn Crimando, Richard Eisenberg, Frank Merrick
senior editors Joseph Coyle, Eric Gelman, Joanna Krotz, Kevin McKean, Eric Schurenberg
Wall Street editor Michael Sivy
associate editors Denise Topolnicki, Walter Updegrave
Washington, D.C bureau chief Teresa Tritch
senior writer Jerry Edgerton
staff writers Gary Belsky, Elizabeth Fenner, Carla Fried, Beth Kobliner, Lani Luciano, Elizabeth MacDonald, John Manners, Ruth Simon, Marguerite Smith, Penelope Wang
statistics editor Jersey Gilbert
art director Rudy Hoglund
associate art directors Traci Churchill, Helene Elek
designers Nadia Maryniak, Mimi Maxwell
picture editor Deborah Pierce
deputy picture editor Miriam Hsia
assistant picture editor Leslie Yoo
chief of reporters Katharine Drake
senior staff Holly Ketron, Prashanta Misra
staff Lesley Alderman, Mark Bautz, Susan Berger, Kirsten Chancellor, Judy Feldman, Jillian Kasky, Roberta Kirwan, Sheryl Nance-Nash, Vanessa O'Connell, Elif Sinanoglu, Kelly Smith, Ellen Stark, Amanda Walmac, Daphne Mosher (mail)
editorial manager Mark Giles
copy chief Patricia Feimster
editorial systems manager Andrew Schwartz
systems engineer Al Criscuolo
senior coordinator Sukey Rosenbaum
staff Kathleen Beakley, Nigel Killikelly, Jeanne McGough, Bill O'Connor, Sarah Plant, Suzanne Riggio, Judith Ryan, Eve Sennett
editorial production manager Karen Diaz
staff Sally Boggan
editorial finances manager Michael Terry
assistant to the managing editor Arlene Lemanski
staff Leslie Fields, Marianne Nardone, Darlen Obertance, Samantha Welsh
contributing editors Steve Gelman, Pauline Tai
contributing writers Anthony Cook, Ken and Daria Dolan, Echo Garrett, Marlys Harris, Andrea Rock, Suzanne Seixas, Clint Willis
Wall Street correspondent Jordan Goodman
chief of correspondents Sian Ballen
Atlanta: Mary Bounds
Boston: Paul Katzeff
Chicago: Lynn Adkins
Denver: Stephen Marsh
Detroit: Ami Walsh
Honolulu: Kathy Titchen
Houston: Gary Taylor
Los Angeles: Laura Meyers
Miami: Elizabeth Roberts
Minneapolis: Nancy Stesin
New Orleans: Janet Plume
Orange County, Calif.: Dorothy Jean
Phoenix: Kathy Shocket
Portland, Ore.: Jeff Wuorio
St. Louis: Carol Shepley
San Diego: Sylvia Tiersten
San Francisco: Stephen Bloom, Tim Turner
Seattle: Nancy Way
Stamford, Conn.: Karen Daugherty

ISBN: 0-376-01915-8
Manufactured in the United States of America
First Printing 1994

To order MONEY magazine, call Customer Service at 800-633-9970 or write to MONEY, P.O. Box 60001, Tampa, Florida 33660-0001.

Published by MONEY Books
Time Inc. Home Entertainment
1271 Avenue of the Americas
New York, NY 10020

Making the Most of Your Money Now

editor: Junius Ellis
designer: Melissa Tardiff Design
Melissa Tardiff, Corinne Myller

New Business Development

director: David Gitow
assistant director: Mary McGrade
production director: John Calvano
operations director: David Rivchin

Contents

Where to Put Your Money in 1994

Investment strategists differ greatly about when today's aging bull markets in stocks and bonds are likely to peak. Predictions range from as early as this spring to as late as spring 1995. In contrast, most experts agree on how the end will actually unfold. With the economy gathering strength after three years of listless recovery, inflation will creep up, pushing interest rates high enough to suck investors' money out of stocks and send share prices tumbling. In the worst scenario, investors could lose 15% or more on stocks and at least 10% on bonds.

MONEY doesn't buy that pessimistic forecast. In fact, we're mildly optimistic about the markets in 1994. While we agree that stocks may peak early this year and fall 10% or more before bouncing back, we think savvy investors can still make money in stocks and bonds. The trick will be to diversify your holdings cleverly to minimize your risk of losses. Here's what we see ahead for 1994:

Gross domestic product will show solid growth of more than 3%, up from 2.8% in 1993.

Inflation will advance to 3.2% by December, up from last year's 2.7% rate. For 1994 as a whole, inflation will average 3%.

Short-term interest rates could gradually increase to 3.7%, up from last year's 3.2%.

Long-term interest rates could rise to 6.8% from last year's 6.2%, hitting holders of long-term bonds with principal losses of 5% or more.

Tax-exempt municipal bonds, however, could appreciate as more investors seek shelter from the Clinton Administration's steeper taxes.

Blue-chip stocks will underperform. Even after adding in their average 2.7% dividend yields, such shares may return little more than 4%.

Small-company stocks will sprint past blue chips with annual returns averaging 8%.

Foreign stocks will be stars, returning about 10% overall, especially if the North American Free Trade Agreement helps to boost world trade.

You will find our financial outlook reflected throughout this chapter and book. We not only spell out your best investment strategies now but also suggest smart moves for other areas of your financial life, from ducking painful new tax bites (Chapter 2) to picking the best health insurance coverage (Chapter 3) and financing a secure retirement (Chapter 4). For most people, however, managing their portfolio successfully will be this year's most demanding task. In looking ahead, start by setting aside the comforting statistic that Standard & Poor's 500-stock index has returned an average of 10% a year since 1926. You generally earn that much only when stocks are cheap, relative to such fundamentals as earnings and dividends, rather than the increasingly pricey market of late. Look instead at the market analysis by the Leuthold Group in Minneapolis (see the chart on page 8). Leuthold researchers found that when stocks begin the year with price/earnings ratios averaging more than 20—as was the case in early 1994—share prices are likely to lose 1.6% over the following four quarters.

"When stocks are this high, you usually get below-average returns because P/Es can't move up much further," says Leuthold Group senior analyst Jim Floyd. "You occasionally get a real disaster like the 1987 stock market crash." On the basis of his research, Floyd sees a better than even chance of a 10% to 15% stock price decline during the year. We disagree, however. We think stocks are more likely to manage a small gain.

What should investors do now? In a word, diversify. You could improve your odds by putting at least 25% of your stock portfolio into shares of smaller companies with revenues of $500 million or less. While such issues would be hurt worse than big stocks in a market decline, they could outperform blue chips by an impressive four percentage points or so if stocks continue to advance, as we expect.

Small stocks typically trade at lower P/Es than blue chips do during recessions and then rebound to above-average P/Es as the economy revives, explains Claudia Mott, director of small-company research at Prudential Securities in New York City.

With the current recovery already three years old, she thinks small stocks are 5% cheaper than they would normally be at this point in the economic cycle. Adds Mark Tincher, manager of the Vista Growth & Income fund: "Over an eight-year period, small stocks as a group outperform big stocks an average of roughly 35%. We haven't come close to that."

Also consider putting as much as 25% of your stock portfolio into foreign companies. "Unlike the U.S., European markets probably will benefit from falling rates in 1994," says Larry Jeddeloh of the *Institutional Strategist* in Minneapolis. Moreover, "Europe is still cheaper than Tokyo or New York," says Jean-Marie Eveillard of the SoGen International fund. (See the table on page 9.) Overall, we expect diversified international stock funds to gain about 10% this year.

A half point rise in short-term interest rates should be seen as an early warning of a possible U.S. stock slump. Such rates lately were basically even with inflation. That's unusual; short rates typically are at least half a point higher. If inflation speeds up to 3.2%, as we expect, short rates could climb to around 3.7%. An increase of that magnitude could easily knock down the stock market averages by 5% or more.

Yields on long-term bonds recently were only about three percentage points above inflation.

MONEY's Financial Forecast

While 1994 will be a difficult year for investors, you can boost your profits by buying foreign stocks, shares of small U.S. companies and mutual funds specializing in such securities.

	1994	Average*
U.S. blue chips	4.0%	14.4
U.S. small stocks	8.0	27.3
Foreign stocks	10.0	11.1
Money funds	3.4	4.2
Long-term Treasuries	2.0	11.8
Long-term munis	4.0	11.2
Utilities	6.0	3.8
Real estate investment trusts	6.0	27.0

*Average annual return from Jan. 1, 1991 to date

They normally are in a higher range than that. "With a stronger economy and a couple of bad inflation numbers, bond yields could move back into the middle of the range," says Joseph

McAlinden of brokerage Dillon Read in New York City. That could mean yields of 6.8% or more and principal losses on bonds of 5% to 8.5%. Thus we think holders of bonds with maturities of 10 years or longer will be lucky to earn 2% in 1994.

As an income producing alternative to bonds, you might want to consider dividend-driven shares of utilities and REITs (real estate investment trusts), which could provide total returns of 6% or so. For more on utilities and REITS, see "Safe Ways to Earn Steady 5% Returns" on page 23.

The optimum portfolio mix for 1994.
Overall, your best investment strategy this year is to reduce your core holding of U.S. blue chips to 30% or less, and increase small-company shares to at least 15% and foreign stocks to 15% or more. Cut back your holdings of long-term bonds to a minimum. And keep as much as 10% in intermediate issues (maturing in fewer than 10 years), 10% in utilities, REITs or other high-yield stocks and 20% in cash reserves. That portfolio is likely to earn you a total return of 6% to 8%.

If you're a fairly conservative investor, you probably should skip small stocks. Still limit your holdings in U.S. blue chips to 40% and put 20% in top-quality foreign stocks, 10% in bonds of short or intermediate terms and 30% in cash. That combination could lower your likely annual return to around 5%. But you'll slash risk to a minimum and still outpace inflation in the difficult year ahead.

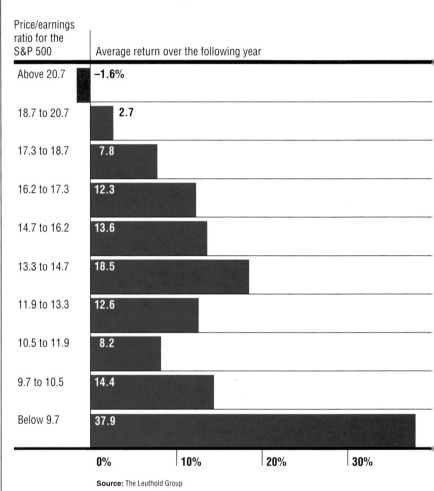

U.S. Blue Chips Are Vulnerable

Since 1926, when stocks' P/E ratio rose above 20.7, as it did recently, the S&P 500 has lost an average of 1.6% within 12 months.

Price/earnings ratio for the S&P 500	Average return over the following year
Above 20.7	−1.6%
18.7 to 20.7	2.7
17.3 to 18.7	7.8
16.2 to 17.3	12.3
14.7 to 16.2	13.6
13.3 to 14.7	18.5
11.9 to 13.3	12.6
10.5 to 11.9	8.2
9.7 to 10.5	14.4
Below 9.7	37.9

Source: The Leuthold Group

Foreign Stocks Look More Promising

Stocks are cheaper in many foreign countries than they are in America, based on fundamental financial measures that relate share prices to earnings, dividends and the cash flow generated by businesses. The table on the right compares average share prices on nine of the world's largest stock markets, starting with Spain's Bolsa, where prices recently appeared to be the least expensive. Many U.S. investors prefer to choose among the roughly 1,000 overseas stocks that conveniently trade on Wall Street as ADRs (American depositary receipts) as described in detail in "Your Best Foreign Investments Now" beginning on page 16. Another option for small investors is to select one or more international mutual funds.

Small Stocks Still Have Vroom to Advance

Small stocks are trading well below their peak historical prices and therefore have the potential to out-pace blue chips in 1994. This chart shows that over the past 14 years, small stock P/Es have ranged from 21% below those of the S&P 500 to 27% above. Lately, small stocks had P/Es only 6% higher than those of big stocks, giving them plenty of room to move up if the recovery continues.

Premium or discount

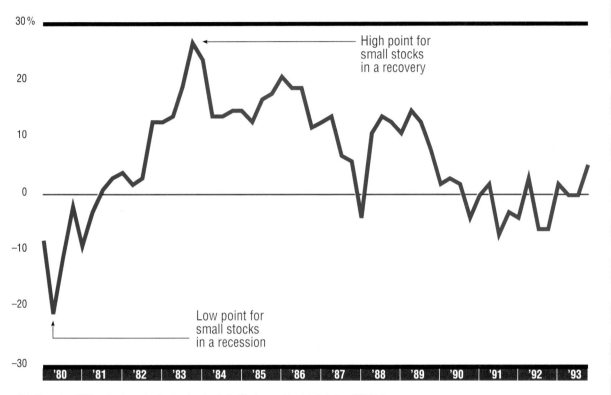

Note: The small-stock P/Es are based on analysts' projected earnings for the following year of the stocks in the Russell 2000 index
Source: Frank Russell Co., Prudential Securities

Country	Overall rating	P/E ratio	Price/cash-flow ratio	Dividend yield
Spain	17	16.6	5.8	3.6%
Canada	12	N.M.	12.0	2.6
United Kingdom	12	21.0	11.6	3.8
France	9	25.6	7.5	3.0
Italy	4	N.M.	4.8	1.9
Switzerland	1	18.6	10.9	1.6
Germany	0	25.0	5.2	2.7
Japan	−1	73.3	10.5	0.8
United States	**−1**	**21.5**	**10.1**	**2.8**

Notes: Ratios are based on earnings, cash flows or dividends for the most recent 12-month period. The overall rating is a proprietary score that reflects those ratios and data on economic growth, interest rates and inflation. **Source:** Institutional Strategist

Short-Term Interest Rates Could Rise

Yields on money funds and T-bills, which usually float half a percentage point or more above inflation, could bounce higher than inflation in 1994.

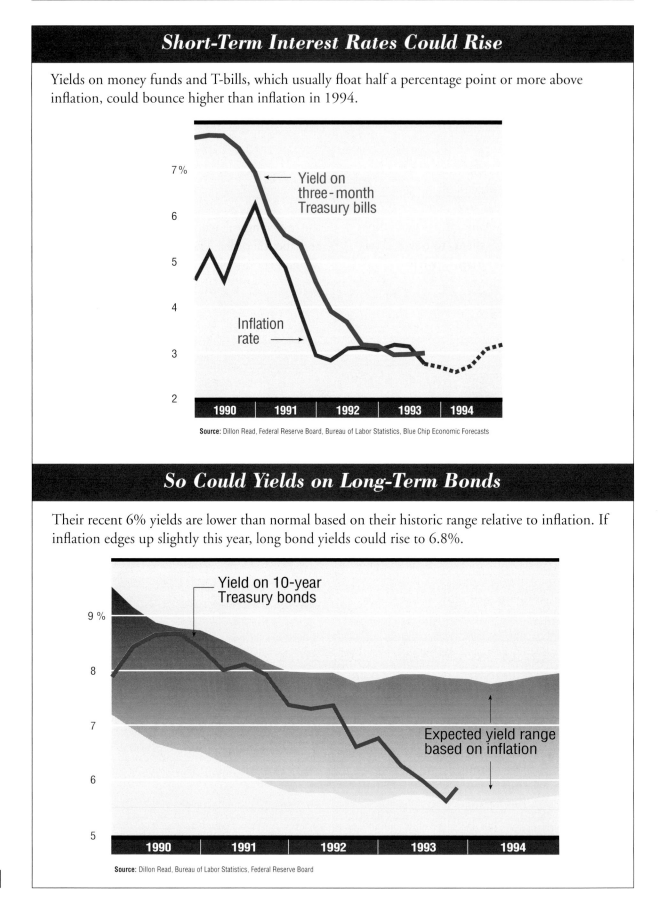

Source: Dillon Read, Federal Reserve Board, Bureau of Labor Statistics, Blue Chip Economic Forecasts

So Could Yields on Long-Term Bonds

Their recent 6% yields are lower than normal based on their historic range relative to inflation. If inflation edges up slightly this year, long bond yields could rise to 6.8%.

Source: Dillon Read, Bureau of Labor Statistics, Federal Reserve Board

Top Picks by Our All-Star Brokers

The 10 members of our A Team reveal their favorite stocks for a fickle 1994.
Their buys have the potential for heady 33% profit gains by year-end.

Here are three questions that are sure to intrigue both bulls and bears in today's increasingly pricey stock market. Who are the best stockbrokers in America? What companies are they urging their clients to buy and sell this year? And, most importantly, why?

For answers, check out the 30 stock picks and pans offered by our All Star lineup of 10 of the nation's top brokers for 1994. Their buy recommendations as a group figure to deliver earnings growth—the most reliable gauge of a stock's future appreciation—averaging a bustling 33% this year. That's more than double the 14% profit increase forecast for the companies in the S&P 500. Yet the All Stars' buy list is priced in line with the market's price/earnings multiple, recently 16 based on most analysts' projections for 1994.

In choosing our A Team, we first sought referrals from a number of prominent money managers and brokerage executives, who were asked to nominate exemplars at firms other than their own. To be considered, candidates had to be willing to take new accounts of $150,000 or less (a minimum that disqualified some heavy hitters) and to have a pristine record of professional conduct. This point was confirmed by submitting each name to the National Association of Securities Dealers, which keeps track of disciplinary actions that have been taken against brokers.

In making our final selection, we focused on the key attributes of accountability and independent thinking that set All Stars apart from journeymen. Our 10 stars customarily:
• Base their recommendations on their own research as well as that of analysts.
• Own the stocks on their buy lists—a show of confidence rare among brokers.
• Avoid most brokerage products whose fat sales and management fees can weigh down returns.
• Give regular customers sizable commission discounts amounting to 20% to 25% in many cases.

You no doubt will glean other insights from the following All Star cameos, which appear in alphabetical order. They feature the brokers' overall market outlook (bullish, bearish or simply anxious) plus three stock recommendations that each believes will handily beat the market in 1994.

Robert Anning

FIRM: Merrill Lynch, Cincinnati, 800-234-2099. AGE: 53. ROOKIE YEAR: 1967. CLIENTS: 300. MINIMUM ACCOUNT: $150,000. AVERAGE: $1.2 million. OUTLOOK: Anxious.

RESUME: Native of Cincinnati; graduate of Trinity College; former Navy intelligence officer on Adm. Thomas Moorer's staff

CLIENT PROFILE: Wealthy Midwest families

PHILOSOPHY: "Traders rarely retire rich," says Anning, who credits skills honed during his four-year Navy hitch with helping him discern when Wall Street scuttlebutt is credible. "I strive to remain fully invested in stocks whose superior profit growth greatly reduces the risk of losing money over time," he adds. Accordingly, Anning thinks each of his picks is capable of three-year earnings gains of 20% annually, roughly triple the norm. The stocks are also heavily owned or controlled by corporate insiders (average stake: 48%).

PICKS: Buy **Shaw Industries** (New York Stock Exchange, lately $25). Anning says the world's largest and most efficient carpetmaker, with annual sales of $2.3 billion, is profiting handsomely from mortgage holders' rush to refinance, which frees up money for remodeling. Buy $2 billion **Coca-Cola Amatil** (its American depositary receipts trade over the counter, $15), an Australian bottler that's developing franchises in Coke-thirsty Indonesia and Eastern Europe. And buy $1 billion

Sunbeam-Oster (NYSE, $22), a restructured consumer products firm whose net profit margins have soared 50%, to 8% over the past two years.

Sherri Carfi

FIRM: Chicago Corp., Chicago, 800-621-0686. AGE: 44. ROOKIE YEAR: 1971. CLIENTS: 175. MINIMUM: $100,000. AVERAGE: $1 million. OUTLOOK: Anxious.

RESUME: Native of Chicago; career broker who worked her way up from secretary to broker

CLIENT PROFILE: Owners of successful companies and professional money managers, who account for more than 80% of her business

PHILOSOPHY: "I look for smaller companies whose earnings seem destined to accelerate faster than most analysts have forecast," says Carfi. But she buys only stocks whose senior managers candidly field her questions or those of her 75 institutional clients. "My livelihood depends on trust," she says. "I can deal with mistakes. But I won't tolerate management that tries to cover them up." That's never been an issue for Carfi's three picks, which as a group figure to expand earnings a heady 25% annually over the next three years.

PICKS: Buy $258 million **Integrated Health Services** (NYSE, $28), a 68-unit chain whose mostly post-op patients are stable enough to leave a hospital's intensive care unit, slashing the cost of convalescing by 20% to 60%. Buy $240 million **SEI Corp.** (OTC, $26), a top provider of data processing services to booming investment management firms and bank trust offices. And buy $65 million **DiMark Inc.** (American Stock Exchange, $12), a marketing agency that's thriving in two traditionally hard-selling sectors, managed health care and financial services.

Joan Getsinger

FIRM: Donaldson Lufkin & Jenrette, San Francisco, 800-227-4492. AGE: 49. ROOKIE YEAR: 1980. CLIENTS: 300. MINIMUM: $100,000. AVERAGE: $250,000. OUTLOOK: Bullish.

RESUME: Native of Bloomfield Hills, Mich.; graduate of the University of Michigan; began her career in 1972 and rose from secretary to junior

partner of a prominent broker; went solo in 1983

CLIENT PROFILE: Conservative investors, many of whom were referrals from two brokers who retired in the mid-1980s

PHILOSOPHY: "The key to my success was having a solid base of clients when I went out on my own," says Getsinger. "Instead of making cold calls, I built up my Rolodex of investment contacts." Her networking lately has been focused on finding bargains in three sectors that she believes will stage unexpectedly strong rebounds this year: electronic components, farm equipment and California banks.

PICKS: Buy $3.5 billion **AMP Inc.** (NYSE, $63), the world leader in electronic connectors used in computer and phone networks. "AMP is a low-risk way to play today's hot information highways theme," says Getsinger. Buy $6.2 billion **Deere** (NYSE, $74), the world's top maker of farm machinery. "Midwest farmers have lots of extra cash from flood claims and decade-old equipment that's wearing out," she explains. And buy **BankAmerica** (NYSE, $46), the nation's No. 2 bank, with $184 billion in assets, after Citibank. "BankAmerica's concentration in California makes it a terrific proxy for the state's resurgent economy beginning this year," predicts Getsinger.

Richard Gottfred

FIRM: William Blair & Co., Chicago, 800-621-0687. AGE: 47. ROOKIE YEAR: 1970. CLIENTS: 150. MINIMUM: None. AVERAGE: $300,000. OUTLOOK: Bullish.

RESUME: Native of Chicago; graduate of Valparaiso University; career broker

CLIENT PROFILE: Executives who have built businesses and understand market risks

PHILOSOPHY: "Like my firm, I'm particularly partial to smaller firms with growing but glamourless franchises that generate lots of repeat business," says Gottfred, a partner in Chicago's carriage-trade brokerage, founded in 1934.

PICKS: Buy $176 million **Department 56** (NYSE, $27). Gottfred expects three-year earnings to compound 20% annually on sales mostly to collectors of the firm's ceramic figures and model villages (average price: $40 per piece) evoking nostalgic Christmas scenes. Buy $135 million drugmaker **Elan Corp.** (ASE, $42). Its projected 40% annual growth rate through 1996, he says, is fueled mainly by recurring royalties from drugs owned by other firms but reformulated by Elan to improve their efficacy. And buy startup drug researcher **ProCyte Corp.** (OTC, $14). He's counting on regulatory approval, and huge profits, starting in 1995 for its drug Iamin for treatment of common (and currently incurable) foot ulcers that afflict 600,000 diabetics in the U.S.

Malcolm Lowenthal

FIRM: Wertheim Schroder, New York City, 800-992-9876. AGE: 58. ROOKIE YEAR: 1962. CLIENTS: 200. MINIMUM: None. AVERAGE: $200,000. OUTLOOK: Anxious.

RESUME: Native of Waterbury, Conn.; graduate of Cornell; career broker who works with partner Roy Alexander, 51

CLIENT PROFILE: Seasoned investors who buy stocks that appear cheap and also sell short those that seem unduly dear

PHILOSOPHY: "There are always two sides to a stock story," says Lowenthal. "I talk to the bulls and bears, try to separate fact from fiction and invest accordingly." His search for value—and the lack of it—has lately turned up two recommended buys and one short sale.

PICKS: Buy $2 billion **McGraw-Hill** (NYSE, $68) for its thriving Standard & Poor's division (financial services now account for half the parent's profits) and multimedia assets including textbooks and TV stations. Buy **Cardiovascular Imaging** (OTC, $8). Its $9 million annual sales represent half the market for a promising new technology—tiny probes that transmit ultrasound snapshots of patients' clogged arteries, thus greatly helping doctors control costs by tailoring treatments to the condition.

PAN: Sell short $32 million **ReSound Corp.** (OTC, $20), a hearing aid maker whose share price has held up despite a patent infringement suit by deep-pocketed 3M and substantial stock sales by a number of senior corporate insiders.

Peter Slocum

FIRM: A.G. Edwards, Carefree, Ariz., 800-688-3123. AGE: 53. ROOKIE YEAR: 1966. CLIENTS: 250. MINIMUM: None. AVERAGE: $500,000. OUTLOOK: Bullish.

RESUME: Native of Boston; graduate of Columbia (A.B. and M.A.); began career at Merrill Lynch in London; worked abroad for 15 years before settling in Carefree (pop. 1,600), where he heads a three-broker team that includes son Josh, 32

CLIENT PROFILE: Corporate executives and money managers in both the U.S. and overseas

PHILOSOPHY: "My clients expect me to bring them ideas that aren't shopworn on Wall Street," says Slocum. He recommends three high-growth but unheralded stocks with average P/Es well below the market's.

PICKS: Buy $617 million poultry producer **WLR Foods** (OTC, $19), which figures to increase earnings 20% annually through 1996, thanks to consumers' waning appetite for red meat. Buy the A shares of $164 million furnituremaker **Bush Industries** (ASE, $31). It's a likely 25% grower, says Slocum, powered by torrid demand for Bush's affordable, ready-to-assemble home entertainment centers beloved by couch potatoes. And buy tiny $21 million **Orthomet** (OTC, $8), an innovator in artificial knee and finger joints that he's betting can grow 45% in the current fiscal year, then 30% annually over the next three.

Steven Spence

FIRM: Paine Webber, Portland, Ore., 800-245-0900. AGE: 46. ROOKIE YEAR: 1971. CLIENTS: 350. MINIMUM: None. AVERAGE: $250,000. OUTLOOK: Bearish.

RESUME: Native of Pasadena; graduate of San Diego State; career broker

CLIENT PROFILE: Executives who typically own stakes in their companies

PHILOSOPHY: "I'm a diehard value investor," says Spence, who looks for low-profile firms selling at bargain prices relative to cash flow and book value. Such cheapos are so scarce now, however, that he's urging clients to stash half their cash in riskless short-term Treasury bonds. Still, Spence is upbeat about two Northwest firms he's discovered and one cyclical papermaker.

PICKS: Buy $72 million **In Focus Systems** (OTC, $15). This Portland firm is 20% owned by $16 billion Motorola and, says Spence, "is about to revolutionize the $4 billion market for color LCD screens in portable computers." How soon? Early this year, he expects Apple and Compaq to start receiving the first samples of In Focus' sharper, less costly screens. Both PC makers are also big buyers of keyboards made by $123 million **Key Tronic** (OTC, $8). The Spokane concern is a buy on the strength of a cost-cutting campaign that promises to double profits in the next fiscal year. The same rationale applies to downtrodden $4.7 billion papermaker **James River** (NYSE, $19), where post-restructuring earnings could spurt tenfold in 1994 and up to 72% in 1995.

George Stark

FIRM: Burnham Securities, Houston, 800-669-5905. AGE: 49. ROOKIE YEAR: 1967. CLIENTS: 35 families. MINIMUM: $150,000. AVERAGE: $1.5 million. OUTLOOK: Bullish.

RESUME: Born in pre-Castro Havana; raised in Paris; graduate of Cornell and France's Insead (M.B.A.); career broker who teamed up with the Burnham family (who once ran Drexel Burnham) to launch their four-year-old brokerage firm based in New York City

CLIENT PROFILE: Monied clans in Texas, the Southwest, Latin America and Europe

PHILOSOPHY: "My steady growth and income style of investing mirrors that of our Burnham Fund," says Stark. He sits on the investment committee of the $124 million fund (3% load; 800-874-3863) and notes that its recent 12-month return of 15% edged the S&P 500's 13%.

PICKS: Buy $1.3 billion **Hilton Hotels** (NYSE, $61) for its shrewd move in the next two years to export its booming Las Vegas gambling operations via casinos in other sun 'n' fun spots like Australia and Greece. Buy $67 billion **AT&T** (NYSE, $53) for the long-term growth potential of its pending acquisition of $2 billion McCaw Cellular, the

nation's largest mobile-phone network. And buy $426 million software house **ASK Group** (OTC, $13) for a dramatic earnings surge from a penny a share in fiscal 1993 to, projects Stark, about 70 cents in 1994 in response to new management and faster upgrades of the firm's database programs for big corporate clients.

Stanley Trilling

FIRM: Paine Webber, Los Angeles, 800-344-3786. AGE: 54. ROOKIE YEAR: 1969. CLIENTS: 250. MINIMUM: None. AVERAGE: $1 million. OUTLOOK: Bullish.

RESUME: Native of Los Angeles; graduate of the University of California at Berkeley; formerly a marketer at Hoffmann La Roche

CLIENT PROFILE: Entrepreneurs and money managers who demand fresh ideas and fast service from his five-broker boutique

PHILOSOPHY: "Emerging growth stocks, our specialty, will remain hot for a while after the Dow finally peaks above 4000 sometime this year," predicts Trilling. He recommends two such firms, both of which promise to double their earnings in 1994, plus one big-name short sale as a "prudent precaution in a toppy market."

PICKS: Buy $33 million **Special Devices** (OTC, $8), a leading maker of the triggering gizmo in auto air bags. By 1996, Trilling expects the firm's current 10% share to vroom to 40% of the U.S. market. Also buy $24 million **Veterinary Centers of America** (OTC, $6), a rapidly expanding chain of 22 clinics with a cash cushion of $2.10 a share partly from the proceeds of selling a large 10% stake to H.J. Heinz over a year ago.

PAN: Sell short $3.7 billion newspaper magnate **Times Mirror** (NYSE, $33). The reason: "In my view there's no end in sight to the regional recessions battering its flagship *Los Angeles Times* and Long Island's *Newsday*," says Trilling.

Monk White

FIRM: Smith Barney Shearson, Dallas, 800-527-5814. AGE: 52. ROOKIE YEAR: 1966. CLIENTS: 100. MINIMUM: $150,000. AVERAGE: $500,000. OUTLOOK: Bullish.

RESUME: Native of Fort Worth; graduate of the University of Texas and Wharton School (M.B.A.); career broker

CLIENT PROFILE: Wealthy Dallas/Fort Worth families and dealmakers including Richard Rainwater, who made his first $100 million managing the Bass brothers' billions

PHILOSOPHY: It's no coincidence that Smith Barney often serves as an investment banker to ventures put together by the enterprising Rainwater, whose friendship with White dates back to their days at the University of Texas. "We both share an interest in finding growth stocks with a special competitive edge that's still not fully appreciated by most investors," says White.

PICKS: Buy $2.5 billion YPF (NYSE, $26), Argentina's recently privatized oil monopoly. White says drastic pruning of YPF's bloated payroll will boost its earnings 68% in 1994 and 35% annually in the next three years. Buy $2.1 billion **United Healthcare** (NYSE, $76), one of the nation's largest, lowest-cost chains of HMOs that, he maintains, is capable of sustaining annual growth of about 30% over the next three years. And buy $38 billion capital goods giant **General Electric** (NYSE, $105), among the biggest beneficiaries of the long-awaited global economic recovery that White believes will commence this year.

How You Rate as an Investor

You know your salary and the amount of your last raise. But you may not have a clear grasp of what you are earning on your investments. With a regular performance checkup, you can see whether your investments are on track and make necessary adjustments to meet your goals.

This worksheet will help. Use it to determine the returns on one investment, a portion of your holdings such as stocks or bonds, or your entire portfolio. To account for irregular contributions and withdrawals, the worksheet employs a shortcut devised by John Markese of the American Association of Individual Investors. "For brief periods, the difference between this averaging technique and exact calculations is insignificant," he explains. Individual investors like you earned an average of 11% over a recent 12-month period, according to MONEY's Small Investor Index. Investors' gains came mainly from stocks (42% of the typical portfolio), which surged 18%. Bonds (20%) climbed 10% and cash (37%) crept up a mere 3%. If any portion of your portfolio is lagging, consider shifting some money into better performing choices. See the main text for recommendations of stocks and mutual funds that are expected to excel this year.

Beginning value. Enter the value of your investment at the beginning of the period you are examining.

A. _____

Net additions. Add up any additional money you put into the investment during the period. From that total, subtract any withdrawals you made. (If you took out more than you put in, the figure will be negative.) Enter the result.

B. _____

Adjusted beginning value. Multiply line B by 0.5 and add the result to the figure on line A. (If the figure on line B is negative, you will subtract it.) Enter the result.

C. _____

End value. Enter the value of the investment at the end of the period plus any interest, dividends or capital gains that you have taken as cash rather than reinvested.

D. _____

Adjusted end value. Multiply line B by 0.5 and subtract the result from line D. (If the figure on line B is negative, you will add it.) Enter the result.

E. _____

Total return. Divide line E by line C and subtract 1 from the result. (If the result is less than 1, your return is negative.) Multiply that number by 100. Enter the result

F. _____ %

Your Best Foreign Investments Now

Here are stocks of 21 overseas companies plus six international funds that could deliver some of the the world's strongest returns this year.

American investors, it seems, are finally overcoming their smug detachment from the rest of the world. Last year stock funds invested solely overseas took in a record $5.4 billion in a single month. That was *triple* their previous monthly record and fully 45% of all the money that flowed into stock funds in the period. The impetus to get offshore: the much higher returns abundant abroad. Consider:

• International stock funds as a group returned 39% in 1994, reports fund ranker Micropal, compared with U.S. stock funds' average 13% return. Leading the rout overseas were funds invested primarily in companies of the Pacific Basin (up an average of 64%), Latin America (57%), Canada (34%) and Europe (26%).

• The 335 U.S. stocks in Morgan Stanley's world index of 1,515 firms gained just 7% as a group last year. That return proved to be dead last behind the stocks of 22 overseas markets, which collectively climbed 31% in dollar terms. (Note that a weaker dollar inflates returns earned abroad, while a stronger dollar deflates those returns.) Pacing the bull runs of major foreign markets was Hong Kong (up 110%), followed by Singapore (66%), New Zealand (63%), Switzerland (44%), Sweden (36%) and Germany (34%). Even the bear-mauled Japanese stock market staged an impressive 25% comeback for the year.

• One of the world's hottest stocks during the period, says Morgan Stanley, was Hong Kong electronics firm Applied International (up 510%). Applied, like many global companies, dotes on U.S. investors. Its shares conveniently trade here as ADRs (American depositary receipts), as do about a thousand other foreign stocks. Its ADR administra-

tor, the Bank of New York, even mails out Applied's financial statements on request (telephone 212-815-2122). What about the world's biggest duds? Six of the globe's 20 worst stocks hailed from Wall Street, including U.S. Surgical (down 67%), Chemical Waste Management (down 60%) and Apple Computer (down 51%).

If you're keen to broaden your profit horizons abroad, begin by weighing the advice of the accomplished foreign stock pickers introduced below. They will not beguile you with travelogues of faraway bourses. To the contrary, they know that U.S. stocks have been the world champs over the past five years, with the S&P 500 index returning 99%, vs. just 28% for Morgan Stanley's Europe index and a negligible 4% for its Pacific index. Over the next five years, however, overseas markets seem destined to outperform. One reason, argues Peter Lynch, ex-skipper of Fidelity Magellan, is that "stocks outside the U.S. tend to be not as well covered and more undervalued." Today's booming foreign markets also reflect mounting optimism that the global slump in industrial countries will soon be history, unleashing even more capital investment in rapidly modernizing regions like Southeast Asia and Latin America. Thus developing economies should continue to be the most exciting destinations for investors, given those countries' projected real growth of 4% to 8% this year, vs. the 2% to 2.5% recoveries hoped for in Europe, Japan and the U.S.

Where to begin? Mutual funds are ideal if you lack the resolve to become fluent in foreign markets. But direct ownership is gaining popularity among seasoned U.S. investors. At MONEY's request, seven professionals combed their portfolios to recommend 21 top stocks drawn from four timely investment themes. Seventeen of the picks trade as ADRs in the U.S., in most cases over the counter. The four exceptions can be bought on overseas exchanges via big brokers like Merrill Lynch. It has the broadest global research, on over 400 foreign firms, among retail brokerages. Commissions are comparable to those on U.S. stocks. (Merrill Lynch often imposes a $25,000 minimum on such orders.) The four themes:

The mother of bull markets. Hong Kong's sizzling stock market is widely viewed by international investors as the best proxy for mainland China's torrid fling with capitalism. Proclaims Barton Biggs, Morgan Stanley's influential global guru: "In the next few years China will have the mother of all bull markets. Not only will prices rise several thousand percent, but the supply of stock will double year after year." But foreigners eager for a stake in China's blistering 13% annual economic growth can now buy only the thinly traded B shares in 30 of the 113 companies listed on the fledgling Shanghai and Shenzhen exchanges (locals own the A shares). Therein lies the allure of Hong Kong's diversified trading companies, among the biggest venture capitalists in China despite the political risk inherent in the British colony's return to mainland rule in mid-1997.

Some noted Asia strategists don't share Biggs' fervor (see below). But one who does is Robert Howe, Hong Kong-based co-manager with Benny Thomas of **T. Rowe Price New Asia**, which returned 79% last year. The fund's three-year return of 33% annually is among the best for hot Pacific region funds, up 17% a year as a group. Even with the Hong Kong market's recent surge, argues Howe, prices of his pet trading companies still don't fully reflect the huge profit potential of their numerous mainland ventures. He recommends four with ADRs from his Hong Kong holdings. As a group they figure to grow earnings 22% this year—the key gauge of a stock's future appreciation—or roughly triple the norm for U.S. stocks. Yet the foursome lately was priced at 12 times earnings, on average, vs. the U.S.'s 16 earnings multiple. They are **Hutchison Whampoa** (ADR ticker symbol HUWHY, recently $25 a share),

a $2.7 billion conglomerate that's building port facilities in southern China; $1.6 billion **New World** (NEWDY, $26), active in real estate development in the Yangtze River port of Wuhan, the Chicago of China; $5 billion **Swire Pacific** (SWIRY, $18), which controls airline Cathay Pacific and a new Coca-Cola franchise on the mainland; and $570 million **Wharf Holdings** (WARFY, $48), a developer that's also big in Wuhan.

Many such deals, however, are threatened by Beijing's inability to douse rampant speculation, corruption and inflation, lately 22%, warns Michael Bunker of Global Asset Management in London. He's also the manager of GAM **Pacific Basin**, up 51% last year and among the leaders in its class with a five-year return of 18% annually, vs. 7% for his peers. "The government, like the economy, is basically out of control," says Bunker. Since there's no apparent successor to aged leader Deng Xiaoping, 89, Bunker fears investors could soon be blindsided by a power struggle as well as an economic hard landing.

The urge to splurge. Asia's historically high savings rate and dawn-to-dusk work ethic are the envy of the world. What's often not appreciated, says Bunker, is the fast-growing demand for such middle-class trappings as spacious houses, new cars, vacations and the like. Among the earliest beneficiaries are banks offering consumers their first mortgages, auto loans and credit cards. Bunker's favorite among ADRs is **Development Bank of Singapore** (DEVBY, $31). The prosperous island nation's richest bank, with $38 billion in assets, is capable of boosting earnings about 20% this year, as are his two other picks. He thinks Malaysia's $630 million **Genting Berhad** (GEBEY, $14) is a buy both for its Resorts World casino, the country's only legal one, and housing developments. And Bunker recommends direct purchase on the Jakarta exchange of $210 million **Hero Supermarkets**, Indonesia's dominant chain of modern food stores.

There's also huge pent-up consumer demand from wannabe burghers in neocapitalist Eastern Europe, adds John Horseman, manager of GAM

Five Signs of a Market Top

For more than a year, stock prices have been so high that the market has looked risky. But if you really want reasons to worry about how long this aging bull market will continue, consider:

Mutual funds are being sold via ATMs. The automated teller machines at Wells Fargo Bank enable customers to buy, switch and redeem fund shares at more than 1,700 locations. "It won't be long before investors can buy fund shares with Visa or American Express," jokes James Stack of investment advisory newsletter *InvesTech Market Analyst* in Whitefish, Mont. It's a Wall Street truism that a bull market ends when there are no buyers left because they've already invested all their money. If that's so, then what additional cash will be available to drive stocks higher once everyone with a bank account is fully invested in the market?

Diehard bears seem to be turning bullish. Michael Murphy of the newsletter *Overpriced Stock Service* in Half Moon Bay, Calif. has long specialized in spotting overextended stocks that investors can sell short (in the hope that they will profit because the shares' prices go down). Now Murphy has helped launch a new mutual fund that can own, as well as sell short, shares of small high-tech companies. Moreover, the Feshbach Bros. investment firm in Palo Alto formerly ranked among the nation's most active short sellers. Recently, however, Joe, Kurt and Matt Feshbach have reportedly been buying more stocks. When even such skeptics as Murphy and the Feshbachs are willing to jump into a rising market, how many other people are likely to remain with uninvested cash that can push share prices higher in the future?

Wall Street is shoveling out new stock issues. Firms that underwrite new stocks are quick to capitalize on the torrent of money that is pouring into the market. Individuals are adding $11 billion to $12 billion a month to stock funds, while initial public offerings are running at a monthly rate of more than $10 billion. Nearly half of the money small investors are putting into stock funds is going into overseas issues. Conclusion: "The supply of new U.S. stock far outweighs the amount of new money going into the U.S. market," says Charles Biderman of *Individual Investor Trim Tabs* in Santa Rosa, Calif. In all markets, when supply outruns demand, prices have to fall.

Dividend growth is perilously puny. The rate, in fact, recently was the lowest it has been since the 1973-75 recession. Over the past year, dividends paid by industrial companies that make up the S&P 400 index have actually fallen 5% as restructuring corporate giants such as General Motors and IBM have slashed their payouts 50% or more. "If dividend payments continue to slow, stocks will get hammered by investors," says Stephen Leeb of the *Big Picture* market newsletter in Alexandria, Va. "And if dividend growth speeds up as a result of a faster economy, interest rates will probably increase, setting off a market correction."

A stronger economy is also a threat. Once investors see interest rates starting to move up, the deluge of dollars fleeing money funds and bank CDs for the stock market will begin to slow. So small investors should keep a close eye on three-month Treasury bill yields. If they climb to 3.5%, up from a recent 3.1%, money market and CD investors are going to start rediscovering the discreet charm of cash. Then flows into stocks will diminish, and not long after, share prices will start to decline.

International in London. He credits his fat returns of 80% in 1993 and 19% annually over five years partly to spotting bargains among European consumer-spending stocks that are too provincial to have ADRs. Horseman recommends three such stocks capable of sterling profit growth averaging 24% this year. Hungary's leading supermarket chain, $215 million **Julius Meinl**, recently traded on the Vienna exchange at a forecast P/E of around 15. And you'll pay only about 12 times earnings on the Zurich exchange for $515 million ceramic tile maker **Keramik** and nine times earnings for $280 million roofing firm **Sarna**, both prime suppliers to the rush rebuilding of East Germany's run-down housing stock.

And don't overlook bargains south of our border, says James Conheady, co-manager with Jeffrey Russell of **Smith Barney International** (up 53% in 1993) in New York City. Conheady says timely 1990 bets on Mexican consumer stocks like $1.7 billion retailer Cifra—an almost 1,200% profit realized in 1992—helped fuel the fund's superb three-year return of 28% annually, vs. 15% for its peers. Among his Mexican holdings, he recommends three with ADRs that figure to deliver five-year profit growth averaging 23% annually. He likes $560 million soft-drink bottler **Coca-Cola Femsa** (recently $33 on the NYSE), a new joint venture of Coke USA and Mexico's beer baron that aims to expand across Latin America. Another pick: Mexico's top commercial TV/cable network, $1.4 billion **Televisa** ($70, NYSE), which owns the world's largest Spanish language video library. And check out the B stock of $456 million **Maseca** (GIMBY, $15), a superefficient maker of corn flour that's raised its share of Mexico's tortilla market from 55% in 1988 to 72% today.

Revenge of the Japanese consumer. The Bank of Japan's easy money policies last year sparked a 25% rebound in Japanese stocks. But a rock-bottom prime lending rate of 3.4%, vs. 6% in the U.S., failed to restart an economy stalled by the strong yen abroad and weak demand at home, says Stephen Silverman, manager of **Merrill Lynch Pacific** (up 33% in 1993) in Princeton, N.J. Over

a recent 10-year stretch, his fund's sumo-size 530% return was the second best performance in the U.S. after Ken Heebner's hot-handed growth fund, CGM Capital, which rose 546%.

Silverman predicts that Japan's new populist government will soon opt to stimulate growth by deregulating the economy and making the consumer king. "But only the strongest, most cutthroat companies will benefit initially," he says. Silverman recommends three with ADRs from his hefty Japanese holdings. They are $24 billion **Ito-Yokado** (IYCOY, $184), a general retailer and owner of Seven-Eleven Japan that's the bane of traditional mom-and-pop stores; $6.1 billion **Toyo Seikan** (TOS, $265), Japan's dominant maker of bottles and cans; and insurer **Tokio Marine & Fire** (TKIOY, $55), with assets of $38 billion, a leader in auto coverage cushioned by an undervalued investment portfolio.

Banking on the old world. You don't need an M.B.A. to grasp the profit potential of many European banks, says Richard King, manager of **Warburg Pincus International** (up 51% in 1993) in New York City. In Europe, King sees a lucrative replay of U.S. banking in recent years. Falling short-term interest rates fatten net margins (the difference between the rates banks pay and charge for funds) and prod bankers to put bad debt behind them. He recommends two traded on the NYSE: **Banco Santander** (STD, $47), Spain's third largest with $61 billion in assets, and Britain's **National Westminster** (NW, $56), No. 2 in Europe's fastest-reviving economy.

Seconding this thesis is Joseph McNay, head of Essex Investment Management, a Boston firm serving many prominent institutions and families (including Bill and Hillary Clinton). McNay has bet on German behemoths with ADRs: **Deutsche Bank** (DBKAY, $522 a share), **Dresdner Bank** (DRSDY, $27) and **Commerzbank** (CRZBY, $46). Why? He says these banks are major shareholders in, as well as lenders to, German industry, another beneficiary of lower rates. "If you buy and hold them for a couple of years," adds McNay, "these stocks are bound to be big winners."

Stock Funds Poised to Outperform

We identify ten portfolios that figure to profit most in three promising
fund groups this year—value, domestic growth and international.

Despite the storm gathering over U.S. markets, this is no time to abandon stocks. True, most analysts regard a market retreat of 10% to 15% increasingly likely. The typical stock lately traded at three times the value of its company's assets and about 35 times its dividend. That's the priciest levels since just before the October 1987 crash.

Wary or not, you can't afford to bail entirely out of stocks if you have investment goals more than five years away (e.g., paying your kids' college bills or financing your retirement). History shows that the market eventually will reward you handsomely for hanging in there. In the past 67 years, stocks have fallen at least 10% in the space of a month seven times, only to rebound 20% or more within six months, reports research firm Ibbotson Associates. Moreover, even in a sinking market, savvy investors can find plenty of opportunities to make money.

Three investment themes and corresponding types of stock funds look most promising this year. We particularly like so-called value funds, which invest in out-of-favor businesses with unrecognized potential, and domestic growth funds that have shored up their portfolios against a market downturn. We are also high on international funds that can capitalize on fast growing or recovering economies abroad. (Most of our recommendations appear in the previous section, "Your Best Foreign Investments Now," beginning on page 16.)

It's a vintage year for value hunters. Stock pros figure that value-minded funds will outperform their growth rivals, which buy stocks with rapidly expanding earnings. The rationale: value funds characteristically hold stocks that many investors have already given up on. Thus these funds typically fall 33% less than growth funds as a group

when the market sinks, reports the Boston research firm Trinity Investment Management.

Value investors' favorite stocks come in all sizes. One fund feasting on the giants among them is **T. Rowe Price Equity-Income** (up 15% in 1993). Managed by Brian Rogers, the fund has been heavily invested in such wounded behemoths as American Express, whose stock fell 48% in the two years to December 1991. The financial services giant is now remaking itself, having sold its brokerage unit, Shearson Lehman, to Primerica and its trust company, Boston Co., to Mellon Bank. And the stock? It recently was up 39% from its 12-month low. Rogers expects the tough 1994 market to force many other ailing companies to go through similar makeovers to pump up their stock prices. "Shareholders and boards are less tolerant of poor performance," he says. "That trend should be good for the types of companies we invest in." Rogers also has bought a number of limping drug stocks, including Bristol-Myers Squibb, Eli Lilly, SmithKline Beecham, Upjohn and Warner Lambert. He thinks their prices, driven down 30% to 40% on average from their highs over the past two years, will rebound once investors' fears about health care reform prove to be unfounded.

Two value-seeking proponents of smaller stocks, Charles Royce and Tom Ebright, have produced consistently superior returns as managers of **Pennsylvania Mutual** (up 11% in 1993). That popular fund is closed to new investors, but Royce and Ebright follow the same investing style with their two-year-old **Royce Premier** (up 19% in 1993). The fund owns about 50 stocks, vs. the 450 held by Pennsylvania Mutual. "Of the small companies that we own, these are the ones we are most confident will realize above-average returns," says Royce. One example: Willis Corroon Group, an insurance broker headquartered in London that's big in the U.S. and expanding market share in Europe and the Far East. "We're convinced this is going to be one of the world's top three insurance brokers in profitability," Royce says.

Few fund managers are better at ferreting out values that others have overlooked than Mario Gabelli. His **Gabelli Asset** fund (up 22% in 1993) specializes in stocks with unrecognized earnings potential as well as those priced cheaply relative to the value of their assets. About 35% of the fund is invested in stocks that Gabelli jokingly calls his Interactive Couch Potato portfolio (telephone, cellular, cable, broadcast, entertainment and publishing firms). Gabelli thinks a stronger economy this year could also lift the prices of the fund's industrial holdings, such as Caterpillar, General Motors and Navistar.

Another small-stock connoisseur, Mark Tincher of **Vista Growth & Income** (up 13% in 1993), is not strictly a value investor. Instead, he takes an eclectic approach that attempts to measure both values and earnings momentum and singles out whatever shares, growth or value, are most promising. The fund's disciplined approach partly explains its enviable consistency. In each year since the fund's launch in 1987 (Tincher took over in 1991), it has ranked in the top 4% of funds in its growth and income category. And Vista's 29% annual return over the period was more than double that of the S&P 500 index.

Favor growth funds with good defenses. Even in a high-risk market, it still makes sense to invest for the long term in growth funds. True, investors' rosy expectations for many glamourous growth companies have pushed their share prices to dizzy heights. These stocks could get clobbered if their earnings fall short, a possibility in the slow-growth economy that we foresee this year. Thus the best growth funds to buy now are those that possess big cash cushions or own stocks that have already taken a pasting and are now on the mend.

Jim Craig has adopted both defenses as manager of the high-profile **Janus Fund** (up 11% in 1993). "Three years is old for a bull market," he explains. "And with so many smart people in the market, it's picked over." Craig has been keeping about a quarter of the giant fund's $9 billion of assets in cash. Besides serving as a buffer against a market tumble, the cash allows him to pick up first-rate growth stocks if their prices drop to more attractive levels. For example, Craig has repurchased Wal-Mart and Gillette, two 1980s meteors that he sold before they fell to earth in 1993. He also likes telecommunications stocks with a twist. While other pros have chased the latest media merger or small companies with new technologies, Craig bought long-distance carriers AT&T and MCI. "Most people don't realize that half the price of a long-distance call goes to pay for access to the regional carriers," says Craig. As technology improves, he adds, "the cost of obtaining that access will go down big time, and AT&T's and MCI's profit margins will expand."

Last year investors shunned two groups of traditionally steady growers—brand-name food stocks and health-related issues—because of concerns about consumers' increasing price consciousness and health care reform. That gives you a rare opportunity to buy well-run funds loaded with stocks that may not be unfashionable for much longer. Take Parker Hall and David Fowler, managers of **Vanguard U.S. Growth Portfolio** (down 1% in 1993). They held once high-revving firms such as Wal-Mart and WMX Technologies (formerly Waste Management) after they stalled out in 1993, as well as depressed drugmakers like Pfizer and Abbot Laboratories. "Our big growth stocks have underperformed," admits Fowler, "but we're encouraged that they're down to historically low prices compared with the market."

Another star manager down on his luck, Roger Engemann, runs **Pasadena Growth** (down 6% in 1993). The fund buys shares of companies that are growing about twice as fast as the norm and stays with them until their growth rates slow. Most of the fund's assets are in what Engemann considers high-quality growth stocks, such as Coca-Cola and Wal-Mart, that many investors dumped to buy cyclical issues that profit most from the economy's recovery. "My stocks had a rotten year," says Engemann. "But their earnings are growing 15%

annually, and they're selling at market P/Es." In effect, he says, buyers like him are getting some of the best companies in America at also-ran prices.

Mark Goldstein of **Neuberger & Berman Manhattan** (up 10% in 1993) buttresses his growth approach with elements of value investing. Goldstein figures his stocks' profits can expand about 25% this year, compared with roughly 14% for the S&P 500 companies. Yet his stocks' as a group lately were priced in line with the S&P 500's earnings multiple, based on analysts' estimates for 1994. His favorites have included drugmakers such as Pfizer, gambling stocks such as Circus Circus and retailers such as Tops Appliance City, an appliance discounter in metropolitan New York. "The company enjoys the highest sales per square foot of any discounter," he says. "And it plans to double the number of its stores over the next 18 months."

Broaden your profit horizons overseas. With domestic funds scrambling to squeeze profits out of pricey U.S. stocks, the year's most successful portfolios may be those that invest abroad. The Pacific Rim economies are growing furiously. Europe, which is climbing out of recession, is a value investor's paradise. And the stock markets of newly liberalized Latin American countries are euphoric over passage of the North American Free Trade Agreement.

If, however, the idea of investing in hot foreign markets makes you nervous, you're an ideal candidate to own the worldly but conservative **Tweedy Browne Global Value** fund (launched in June of 1993). The management team of Chris Browne, Will Browne, John Spears and James Clark invest wherever they find good companies bargain priced relative to earnings or assets. And when they say cheap, they mean it. About a third of the portfolio, which is heavily weighted with European names, is stashed in stocks selling at less than half the value of their assets. Take Franco Tosi, an Italian manufacturer of paper and plastic packaging material. By Clark's calculation, the stock lately was selling at 59% of the company's net assets and about 10 times earnings. Furthermore, Franco Tosi's dividend yield exceeded 5%. Clark expects the firm to recover as the European recession eases.

Doubts on Dollar-Cost Averaging

MONEY and legions of financial advisers have long recommended dollar-cost averaging. That's a technique in which you regularly put the same amount of money into a mutual fund or other investment, regardless of market swings, thus reducing your average cost per share. We think dollar-cost averaging is still a wise way to invest out of a weekly paycheck. But two new studies suggest it can be costly if you have a pension payout or lump sum to invest.

An analysis by Cincinnati investment adviser James Gore illustrates the problem. By keeping most of the money in a low-yielding money fund (while feeding it into an investment by installments), you can shave your annual returns by 2.2 percentage points relative to

investing a sum all at once. And a statistical study by two Wright State University professors found that you'll make more money plunking the whole sum into the market about two-thirds of the time. "Because the market trend is usually up, you are almost always better off investing the entire sum at once," says one of them, Richard Williams.

Since the odds of a market correction are increasing, however, many investment advisers recommend against investing a lump sum all at once right now. Instead, they typically urge clients to put half of their principal into a conservative stock fund, such as value-minded **Gabelli Asset** (see page 21), and invest the rest gradually over the next six to 12 months.

Despite rebounds in many European markets, these stocks generally are still cheaper than most American ones, says Will Browne. "Europe's markets remind me of the U.S. in 1973-74 and 1982, when everyone was depressed," he says. An investor who bought at the end of those down years would have posted 12-month gains of 37% and 22%, respectively. In what figures to be a lean year for investors, any fund that promises that kind of return is definitely a keeper.

Safe Ways to Earn Steady 5% Returns

Income-oriented investors who aim much higher than that with fixed-income securities could be exposing themselves to unreasonable risk.

For income investors, this will be the year to say good-bye to easy money. We forecast that long-term interst rates will rise another half percentage point to about 6.8% by late 1994. "People have been spoiled by the fixed-income returns of the past decade," warns Chicago money manager Gary Brinson. "It's going to be very difficult to get 6% or 7% on bonds this year, let alone the double-digit returns investors have grown accustomed to." A more realistic goal for conservative investors this year is 4% to 5%, about what you can expect from a boring but prudent portfolio of cash, intermediate bonds and a few high-yielding stocks.

Some bond funds promise higher returns. But their managers often take more chances than they acknowledge. Fund managers can quietly extend their portfolios' maturities, buy low-quality bonds or venture into foreign bonds. A more worrisome tactic is to load up on complex financial instruments known as derivatives. For example, some funds tripped up last year on a form of derivative known as interest-only STRIPS. These treacherous securities amount to a high-stakes bet that interest rates will rise. When rates fell instead during the first nine months of 1993, these supposedly low-risk funds suffered small losses relative to the 8% average return for taxable bond funds overall.

That's why the core of your income portfolio should be the low-yielding but safe investments known on Wall Street as cash. Cash includes money-market funds (recently yielding 2.7%), six-month CDs (2.8%) and even Uncle Sam's Series EE savings bonds, which pay at least 4% if held for six months or more. To add a slightly higher potential gain for only a little more risk, you might consider putting as much as 40% of your income investments in a mix of intermediate-term bond funds or Treasuries (yielding 4.8%), a foreign bond fund (5.6%) and high-yielding stocks. If your top marginal tax bracket is 28% or above, you may also want to consider tax-free municipal bonds or a muni bond fund (4.1%). But you should resist the temptation to chase high yields. "The hard fact is that no investment now yielding more than 5% will perform well if interest rates rise by half a point," says James Stack of investment newsletter *InvesTech Market Analyst*. Here's a look at your best income options, starting with the safest. You will find representative yields, returns and (if applicable) costs in the table on page 25.

Series EE savings bonds. Conservative short-term investors can't beat savings bonds. Backed by the U.S. Government, the bonds pay a guaranteed 4% if held six months or more. After five years, you'll get either 4% or a rate roughly equal to 85% of the yield on five-year Treasuries over the period you've owned the bond, whichever is higher. Two added benefits: interest income is exempt from state and local taxes, and you defer federal taxes until you redeem the bonds. "There's no other way to earn 4% risk free," says Glen Parker of the investment advisory *Income & Safety*. "You should buy savings bonds and hold for six months to see if something better comes along."

Money funds and six-month CDs. With yields of 4% or less, these ultrasafe investments won't keep you far ahead of taxes and 1994's forecast 3% inflation. But in a dangerous year they have a welcome attribute. Even if rates leap, you'll run virtually no chance of losing money. If you happen to be in the 28% tax bracket or higher, tax-exempt money funds' 2% yield is your best bet. The average taxable fund pays just 2% after taxes to investors in the 28% bracket and even less to those burdened with higher rates.

Before investing in any money fund, check the prospectus to see whether the manager has boosted the yield by temporarily waiving some expenses. Once the waiver expires, your return will drop by the amount the manager had been absorbing. Also look for a fund that's part of a large fund family. That way, the manager can dip into corporate money to make up losses if an investment defaults. No true money fund has ever lost shareholders' money. Yet two years ago, John Nuveen, Evergreen and other families had to rescue their tax-free funds from losses after the failure of insurer Mutual Benefit Life, which backed some of their holdings.

If you can't stomach even a remote chance of loss, you can park spare cash in a CD or bank money-market deposit account, both of which are backed by the Federal Deposit Insurance Corporation to a maximum of $100,000 per person at any single institution. "Even now you can often beat your neighborhood bank by one to 1.5 percentage points, although it may mean going out of your local area," says Hugo Ottolenghi of newsletter *100 Highest Yields*. Provided you stay within the FDIC limit, your money will be just as safe as if it were in the bank across the street.

Intermediate-term bond funds. For a little more return without a lot more risk, consider bond funds that own intermediate maturities of five to 10 years. You'll collect roughly a percentage point more interest than you would on six-month CDs,

and chances are you'll still wind up in the black even if rates rise. If you have more than a few thousand dollars to save, invest directly in U.S. Treasury notes and spare yourself the expenses of a bond fund. You can buy Treasuries in denominations of $1,000 to $5,000 (depending on maturity) through your bank or broker for a $30 to $50 commission. Or you can buy them commission-free through the government's Treasury Direct program. An application can be obtained from any Federal Reserve bank or branch or by calling 202-874-4000.

Despite the gloomy outlook for interest rates this year, some analysts believe intermediates may be a better choice than short-term bonds. That's because these experts expect short rates to climb faster than those on longer term bonds. According to Thomas Steffanci, Fidelity's head of fixed-income investing, you'll fare better with intermediates if short rates rise half a point more than intermediate rates do.

Municipal bonds and bond funds. Soon after high-income investors pay President Clinton's tax hikes, they're all but certain to consider buying munis. Even investors in the great middle-class bracket of 28% might give munis some thought. Thanks to a large supply of new issues, munis recently yielded 87% as much as Treasuries before taxes, compared with the usual 80% or so. To match the average muni fund's 4% yield after taxes, a taxable fund would have to pay close to 6% to someone in the 28% bracket and 7% to someone in the new 39.6% bracket.

Where there's higher yields, however, you'll usually find higher risks. And muni bonds aren't an exception to the rule. Mutual funds now hold an estimated 28% of all munis. Some fund groups, such as Franklin, often scoop up all the bonds of a specific maturity in a municipal issue. That raises the question of who will buy if funds suddenly need to unload bonds, as they would if enough shareholders cashed in their shares during an interest rate spike. "As bond prices fell and the funds come around to sell $20 million or $50 million blocks of bonds, the traders would simply

Where the Top Yields Are for 1994

Load up your income portfolio this year with secure money funds, savings bonds and other securities. The picks below are either top performers in their category or highly recommended by investment pros.

	% yield[1]	% compound annual total return to Nov. 1			Average maturity (years)	Annual expenses (% of assets)	Minimum initial investment	Telephone
		1993	Three years	Five years				
Certificates of deposit								
Six-month: So. Pacific Thrift & Loan (Calif.)	4.0	N.A.	N.A.	N.A.	Six months	None	$5,000	310-204-2913
Six-month: First Deposit Natl. Bank (N.H.)	3.7	N.A.	N.A.	N.A.	Six months	None	10,000	800-821-9049
Money-market deposit accounts								
First Deposit National Bank (N.H.)	3.1	3.3	4.9	6.4	N.A.	None	5,000	800-821-9049
Key Bank, U.S.A. (N.Y.)	3.0	3.3	4.9	6.3	N.A.	None	2,500	800-872-5553
Money-market funds								
Fidelity Spartan Money Market Fund	3.0	3.1	4.9	N.A.	71 days	0.30	20,000	800-544-8888
Vanguard Money Market Reserves–Prime	2.9	3.0	4.8	7.1	59 days	0.32	3,000	800-662-7447
Tax-exempt money-market funds								
Evergreen Tax-Exempt Money Fund	2.4	2.5	3.9	N.A.	65 days	0.29	2,000	800-235-0064
Vanguard MuniBond	2.4	2.4	3.6	5.0	75 days	0.17	3,000	800-662-7447
U.S. Government securities								
Series EE savings bonds	4.0	4.2	5.0	6.5	N.A.	None	25	800-487-2663
Five-year Treasury notes	4.8	10.4	11.6	10.3	5.0	None	1,000	202-874-4000
Intermediate-term bond funds								
Columbia Fixed-Income Securities	4.9	11.4	13.4	11.4	7.3	0.65	1,000	800-547-1707
Vanguard Fixed-Inc. Intermed.-Term U.S.	4.9	12.1	N.A.	N.A.	6.6	0.29	3,000	800-662-7447
Tax-exempt intermediate-term bond funds								
Dreyfus Intermediate Municipal Bond	4.4	10.6	10.9	9.2	10.0	0.71	2,500	800-645-6561
Fidelity Limited-Term Municipals	4.6	10.7	10.7	9.1	9.6	0.60	2,500	800-544-8888
Global bond funds								
Scudder International Bond	5.1	15.0	15.7	14.9	9.9	1.25	1,000	800-225-2470
T. Rowe Price International Bond	6.4	18.1	13.1	10.2	5.6	1.02	2,500	800-638-5660
Income stock funds								
Invesco Industrial Income	2.6	14.9	22.7	17.7	9.6	0.98	1,000	800-525-8085
T. Rowe Price Equity-Income	3.1	13.8	21.8	11.5	10.1	0.95	2,500	800-638-5660

[1]Definitions of yield: bank accounts—return after compounding interest; money-market funds—annualized seven-day yields; bond funds—SEC 30-day yields; savings bonds—annual percentage yield compounded semiannually, assuming bonds are held six months or more; Treasury notes—yield to maturity; stock funds—12-month distribution rate **Sources:** Department of the Treasury; *100 Highest Yields; Money Fund Report*, Ashland, Mass.; Morningstar Mutual Funds; Salomon Bros.

fade into the woodwork," says James Lynch of newsletter *Lynch Municipal Bond Advisor*. To cut potential losses, you should definitely stick to funds with average maturities of approximately seven to 10 years. Compared with longer-term funds, munis in that maturity range are generally less vulnerable to losses if interest rates decline.

Foreign bond funds. With Europe and Japan still looking ahead to economic recovery, many analysts think foreign bonds are trading at attractive levels. "In Europe, yields were lately between 6% and 8.5%," says Arthur Micheletti of the Bailard Biehl & Kaiser International Fixed-Income Fund. "A slow economy and low inflation there are putting pressure on central banks to bring rates down." That means investors can expect capital gains in addition to high interest payments.

The price of those high potential returns, however, is the risk of currency fluctuations. In the first quarter of 1991, for instance, foreign bonds returned an average of 4.5% in local currencies, according to J.P. Morgan Bank. But over the same period the dollar appreciated against overseas currencies by an average of 8%. The greenback's rise shrank the dollar value of foreign-denominated bonds, so that investors who redeemed their shares at the end of the quarter walked away with a 4% loss measured in dollars. "More than half of U.S. investors' gains or losses in international bonds are attributable to currency moves," says James Stack of *InvesTech*. "Investors should view these bonds not as an income alternative but rather as a combination of income and capital risk."

Unless you relish risk, you should stay away from funds that specialize in bonds issued in emerging markets such as Brazil and Mexico. Instead, you should consider funds that invest mainly in the established markets of Europe and Japan. Even if Latin American economies benefit big from increased trade with the U.S., bond funds that play in those markets are very risky. "The low quality of these bonds really reflects questions about whether they'll pay up," says Moody's analyst Steve Schoepke. "I've seen portfolios in which the bonds have already defaulted."

Other high-income options. If you are willing to take on some stock market volatility, consider a stake in so-called equity income funds that hold stocks paying fat dividends. "Equity income funds are often a good substitute for bond funds because they have the crucial ability to increase capital and dividends over time, allowing you to keep pace with inflation," says John Rekenthaler of fund bible *Morningstar Mutual Funds*. In a bull market, many high-dividend stocks are no longer bargains. So stick with funds that are proven, low-volatility performers such as T. Rowe Price Equity Income and Invesco Industrial Income.

If you prefer to invest part of your income portfolio directly in yield stocks, you might start with a foundation of carefully chosen electric utility companies such as those discussed on the right. Analyst Jim Floyd of the Leuthold Group, a Minneapolis money manager, also suggests investments in undervalued big-name consumer companies such as drugmaker **Upjohn** (recent yield: 4.7%), oil giant **Exxon** (4.4%) and **Jostens** (4.5%), a marketer of class rings and yearbooks. "Some of these companies have been beaten up pretty badly," he says. "You can get fairly good yields right now, plus the opportunity for higher dividends and prices in the future."

Convertibles are another alternative. Although they pay fixed interest like conventional bonds, converts can be traded for a specified number of shares of the issuer's stock. Thus convertible prices rise and fall with the price of that stock, although the convertible tends to be 40% to 60% less volatile. Investment advisor Richard Young, editor of *Richard Young's Intelligence Report*, is particularly keen on convertible preferred stocks such as **Ashland Oil** (recent yield: 5%) and **Burlington Northern Rail** (4.6%).

To round out your income portfolio, consider real estate investment trusts (REITs), which invest in portfolios of commercial properties. At Alex. Brown, analyst Robert Frank expects the trusts to return 12% to 15% annually over the next three years as recovering real estate prices boost earnings and dividends. (We're forecasting returns of 6% for 1994.) He advises sticking to seasoned REITs such as **Health Care Properties** (recent yield: 6.2%) and **Weingarten Realty** (5.5%). Just remember, however, that REITs have already run up 70% from their lows in late 1990. And when they fall, they can land hard.

That kind of caution figures to pay dividends in 1994 not just for prospective REIT buyers but also for all income-oriented investors. In what is shaping up as a rather difficult year for fixed-income securities, success is likely to be a matter of accumulating lots of small victories and avoiding those big principal-depleting losses.

Sturdy Utilities for a Shaky Market

With interest rates and competition on the rise, only the most financially solid and efficiently managed companies like these will thrive.

If you're expecting electric utilities to meander through 1994 as the reliable old dividend machines they've always been, you're in for a shock. Like bonds, shares in utilities will take a pratfall if interest rates climb. And a two-year-old federal law that weakens electric companies' status as local monopolies will force many utilities to do something they've never done before—compete.

"Utilities that can't deliver power cheaply risk losing big industrial and municipal customers, who can either generate electricity themselves or go to more efficient utilities," warns analyst Craig Lucas of the New York City brokerage Oppenheimer & Co. The bond rating agencies Moody's and Standard & Poor's take the risk so seriously that both will consider downgrading as many as half of all electric companies in the next five years.

Are utilities still worth owning? You bet. For starters, their yields recently averaged 6.1%. That's almost three percentage points more than Treasury bills, a margin nearly two points higher than the norm over the past decade. And utilities retain a unique advantage over a bond in that their dividends can grow. This distinction could prove cru-

Top Electrics Can Light Up Your Cash Flow

All nine utilities boast yields above 5% and figure to boost dividends over the next five years.

	Recent yield	Recent price	Projected annual dividend growth	Projected five-year total return	Payout ratio	P/E ratio	Financial strength	Regulatory climate
Minnesota Power & Light (Midwest)	6.4%	$31.00	2.5%	37.6%	82%	14.1	A2	Average
Baltimore Gas & Electric (Mid-Atlantic)	6.2	23.75	3.5	64.1	84	14.3	A1	Average
Ipalco (Midwest)	6.1	33.50	4.0	37.1	80	13.5	Aa2	Good
KU Energy (South)	5.7	28.25	3.0	35.2	78	14.0	Aa2	Average
Dominion Resources (Mid-Atlantic)	5.5	44.75	3.5	49.0	78	14.9	A2	Average
LG&E Energy (South)	5.5	37.75	3.5	44.0	79	14.8	Aa2	Average
Wisconsin Public Service (Midwest)	5.4	32.25	2.5	39.5	68	13.3	Aa2	Very good
Southern Co. (Southeast)	5.3	42.50	3.0	31.3	73	14.4	A3	Average
Wisconsin Energy (Midwest)	5.1	26.75	4.0	39.7	79	16.3	Aa2	Very good

Sources: Merrill Lynch, Moody's Investors Service, Oppenheimer & Co., G.R. Pugh & Co., *Value Line Investment Survey* **Notes:** Dividend growth projections are from *Value Line.* Total returns are MONEY estimates based on Oppenheimer earnings projections. Payout ratio as of second quarter 1993. Price/earnings (P/E) ratios are based on trailing 12-month earnings. Regulatory climate ratings are based on Merrill Lynch opinions.

cial in helping you defend the purchasing power of your income against inflation.

For example, with consumer prices expected to rise a little over 3% a year, the payout of $48 annually on a five-year Treasury note will lose 16% of its value by the time the bond matures. By contrast, the typical utility is expected to raise its dividend 2% to 2.5% annually over the next five years, which means that its income payout would erode by only 3% to 5%. Most of the stocks recommended in the table on the previous page figure to increase dividends by at least 3%, which would halt the erosion of your purchasing power entirely. And if share prices keep pace with projected annual earnings growth of 2% to 3%, our recommended utilities' total return could average 7.3% to 8.2% yearly through 1998.

Utilities may fall short of that pace this year; our forecast for 1994 returns is 6% or so. But the nine power suppliers cited on the previous page are equipped to handle the worst that this year is likely to offer. We chose them with the help of G.R. Pugh & Co., an industry research firm in Cranford, N.J. Among their main attributes:

- **Competitive advantage.** We wanted only efficient energy providers that are more likely to take business from regional rivals than to lose it. All of our picks generate power more cheaply than the average cost for utilities in their regions.
- **Reasonable yields.** We ruled out utilities yielding more than a point above the recent 6.1% industry average because high dividends typically indicate financial problems.
- **Low payout ratios.** A subpar ratio of dividends to available earnings signals that a utility isn't straining to maintain its dividend. Our picks' ratios are below the industry average of 85%.
- **Good relations with regulators.** Since state and local commissions set caps on utilities' charges and profit margins, staying on the regulators' good side is essential. "I can't think of a case where a regulator's action didn't play some role in a utility's dividend cut," says Roger Conrad of investment newsletter *Utility Forecaster* in Alexandria, Va. Merrill Lynch analysts publish quarterly ratings of each utility's regulatory climate, based on their evaluations of past rate cases. Only companies that were rated average or better made our cut.

How to Check Out Hot Stock Tips

Sometimes a sizzling suggestion can pay off. Other times, you fry.
Here's how to tell the good from the bad and the downright ugly.

Whether the tidbit comes at the water cooler or in a taxi, from your best friend or from a cold-calling broker, you're bound to hear a stock tip every now and then. More likely now than then, with the Dow setting one dazzling record after another. But putting your money where someone else's mouth is is far more likely to be risky than rewarding unless you follow the tip up with some research. Here's the right way to do just that.

If you're like many investors, your first instinct upon hearing a plausible dinner-party argument for a stock is to bounce the idea off your broker the next morning. Fair enough. But to make the conversation a more intelligent one, head for your public library first. Start by looking up the company in the *Value Line Investment Survey* or *Standard & Poor's Stock Guide*. Value Line covers 1,700 mostly large corporations; S&P covers 5,500 outfits. So chances are you'll find information on the firm that interests you in one or maybe both of the publications. Pay particular attention to how the share price has fluctuated lately. If a stock is being touted or is in the news, it may be a good time to look. But it's probably the wrong time to buy, since the news may already be reflected in the price. Here is a sampling of various types of stock pitches you may be tempted to swing at:

The old new product scenario: "There's finally a cure for baldness, and only HairWeGo Inc. has it." Who can resist betting on a fresh new company that has just pioneered (or so you hear) a major scientific breakthrough or is on the forefront of a new technology? Well, maybe you should. While everyone wants to get in on the ground floor of the next biotech or software star, buying the stock of such a cutting-edge company can be especially tricky. The business or product is likely to be difficult to understand. And standard stock analysis is complicated if, as is often the case, the company has yet to earn a dime.

Still, investors are far from helpless. Michael Murphy of the *California Technology Stock Letter* says researching the product or technology is not the way to start. Whatever business it's in, Murphy determines the value of a development-stage company by comparing its total market value (the number of shares outstanding times the price) with how much it has spent on research and development over the past five years (this is data that can be gleaned from company financial reports). Murphy's law: stick with firms sporting a ratio of market value to R&D of less than 10 to 1. If it's higher than that, the stock is overpriced.

The unbelievable bargain stock story: "GigaMart is a steal at $25. If the company were split up, the sum of its parts would fetch $50 a share."

Not so fast. The textbook way to see whether a stock is undervalued is to weigh its price as a multiple of earnings or book value. Any stock trading at less than one times book value (the company's net worth per share) or below the market's earnings multiple is a potential bargain. But don't make the beginner's mistake of merely comparing your little hotshot's P/E to the market's and concluding that the shares are cheap or too high priced. Instead, check out a stock's annual relative P/E ratio, available in *Value Line*, to see whether the company usually trades at a discount or premium to the market. Zero in on the strength of the

What Munis Pay You Now

With higher tax rates retroactive to January 1, 1993, tax-free investments become even more appealing. This worksheet, illustrated with the example of a Philadelphia resident who pays federal tax at the 28% rate, state tax at 2.8% and city tax at 4.96%, will show you how much a taxable investment would have to pay you to match the after-tax yield of a bond or fund paying a triple-tax-free 4.9%. (If you pay no city income tax, enter zero in the appropriate space in step one.) As the result in step five demonstrates, a fully taxable investment would have to yield at least 7.4% to net more after-tax income than the triple-tax-free choice.

1. **Total your state and city tax rates, expressed as a decimal number.**

	+		=	
0.028 (Pa.)	+	0.0496 (Phila.)	=	0.0776

2. **Multiply the result by 1 minus your federal tax rate.**

	× (1–	)	=	
0.0776	× (1–0.28)		=	0.0559

3. **Add the result to your federal tax rate.**

	+		=	
0.0559	+	0.28	=	0.3359

4. **Subtract the sum from 1.**

1–	=	
1–0.3359	=	0.6641

5. **Divide the result into the tax-free yield, expressed as a decimal.**

	÷		=	
0.049	÷	0.6641	=	0.0738

firm's finances. You should start by looking at S&P's investment quality or *Value Line*'s financial strength ratings and think twice before investing in a company with less than a B+ grade from either source. Then you should scrutinize how much debt the company has and stick with outfits where debt is no more than 40% of capital.

The high-dividend dazzler: "Forget 3% CDs. Here's a Fortune 500 company paying 7%, and you can't lose with a yield like that." Oh yes you can. Just ask investors who bought troubled IBM at $70 a share in fall 1992 when its yield was almost 7%. Since then, the computer giant has sliced its dividend 79% and the stock's price has slid to the mid-$50s. In truth, an ultrahigh yield is often a sign of financial trouble and always a call for further study. Compare the yield with that of other companies in the same industry. If it's two to three percentage points higher than the industry benchmark, figure that the dividend is ripe for pruning. To find out whether the dividend will get the ax any time soon, scrutinize the so-called payout ratio, or dividends as a percent of earnings. You can find it in *Value Line* or calculate it by dividing the annual dividend by the past 12-months' earnings per share. The lower the payout ratio, the more cushion the company has to maintain the dividend if earnings drop. For an industrial company, conservative investors should look for a ratio of 50% or less (70% in the case of a utility).

The earnings growth grabber: "Blastoff Inc.'s profits are going to explode over the next year. It's the next Microsoft." Since stock prices tend to track prospects for earnings growth, everyone loves a company capable of 20% profit increases year after year. Two telltales will help you gauge how profitable a business is. Look for an above-average return on equity (ROE), or what the company is earning on the shareholders' stake. Coupled with low debt, a high ROE can predict superior earnings growth, assuming the company reinvests profits in the business. An ROE above 12% merits attention; above 15% suggests a solid grower; and 20% or more means you have a potential scorcher. But since an ROE is merely a snapshot of the company's profitability, look for signs that a company can sustain such a torrid return. Also favor firms with high, and expanding, profit margins. This indicates the concern maintains pricing flexibility or is reducing its costs. Either way, that's good.

The turnaround teaser: "Comput-O-Matic has finally turned the corner. You'll be reading all about this stock two years from now." Maybe so. But probably not if the same managers who steered a losing company into trouble in the first place are still running the show. Before swallowing the hook on such a story, search newspaper articles for reports of executive changes or consult the company's latest annual reports. Also look in *Value Line* to see whether cash flow (how much net cash the business generates) has moved into the plus column. Such a turnaround can be a sign that earnings will follow suit, and Wall Street simply loves positive earnings reversals. And check whether company insiders are really optimistic about their firm. Look up insider buying behavior in *Value Line.* Just as more insider selling than buying over recent months could signal a problem, increased buying may be a sign that the stock is poised to take off.

Money Helps

Q. Why do stocks split, and what's in it for investors? I own shares in Textron, which split a while back. Now the price has climbed to nearly its pre-split level.
—Ray Scarcello, Canyon Country, Calif.

A. A company divides its stock to make it cheaper and thus more attractive to small investors, usually after the price has risen sharply and may go even higher. While you get more shares, you don't benefit immediately because each share's value declines proportionally. Still, investors regard a split as a sign of good times to come. In contrast, when a company does a reverse split (combining shares to prevent their price from falling into penny stock land), that is seen as a bad omen. Textron was priced at about $58 a share before a two-for-one split in May 1987 dropped its price to $29. The stock recently had appreciated back to around $57. That works out to a respectable return of 11% annually.

CHAPTER

2

Your Best Tax-Saving Strategies

After two major tax increases in three years, many taxpayers hold two articles of faith that are probably wrong. Article 1: neither President Clinton nor Congress has the gall to ask us to pay more tax anytime soon. Article 2: there is precious little left that any middle-income American can do to shrink his overall tax bill, which could top the 40% level after adding in state and local taxes.

The sad fact is that new taxes are coming, perhaps this year. But with a few well-chosen strategies, you can still cut your taxes by thousands of dollars. Indeed, by making the moves outlined in this chapter, you could reduce your total tax bill by 30% or more. And that doesn't even account for the fact that the smartest federal tax-cutting moves often reduce your state and local income tax as well because most states and localities peg their tax to the income you report on your 1040. (Turn to page 40 for our 50-state ranking of the local tax bill for a typical family of four in the same income bracket as MONEY readers.)

Moreover, today's most effective tax-reduction techniques tend to be long-range tactics rather than quick fixes at filing time. So you'll be able to keep those tax savings rolling in year after year. Just be careful to sidestep the IRS's most common audit traps, discussed later in this chapter.

Sure Ways to Slash Taxes 30% or More

With new tax brackets in effect and higher taxes ahead, a tough tax-cutting program is your best defense. Start with these ways to tame your 1040.

Noting that federal spending is scheduled to increase18% in the next five years, many Washington insiders say that taxes almost certainly will have to rise again. The nation's highest earners have already taken their lumps, with the new 36% rate for couples with taxable incomes above $140,000 ($115,000 for singles) and 39.6% for incomes over $250,000. The most politically palatable way for the feds to proceed is to avoid a highly visible income tax hike on the middle class but to continue snipping away at write-offs. Last year, for example, Congress made permanent the provision that clips your deduction for mortgage interest, state and local taxes and miscellaneous expenses by 3% for every dollar earned in adjusted gross income above $111,800.

Many experts believe that swipe is a prelude to further cuts. Likely ones include raising the percentage by which your itemized deductions are trimmed to 5% from 3%; shrinking the amount of home mortgage debt against which you can claim an interest deduction from the current $1 million to $500,000; and phasing out the deduction for personal property taxes. What's more, Social Security payroll taxes are likely to rise. In 1994, inflation alone will boost the wage base on which employees pay the 6.2% Social Security tax to $60,600 from $57,600, for a hike of $186 to total $3,757. Beyond that, Congress could well pass a law to raise the Social Security tax rate and the wage cap. Such options could prove irresistible as spending outstrips revenue and retiring baby boomers strain the Social Security trust fund.

Thus it's more important than ever to take advantage of the tax-trimming strategies still available. Get started with the winners, discussed below, that fall into the categories of your family, your investments and your retirement.

Transfer money to your child's custodial account.
For starters, his or her standard deduction shields the first $600 of investment income in 1994. Earnings from $600 to $22,750 this year are taxed at just 15%—as long as your child is at least age 14—a bracket that's almost certainly far lower than yours. The best way to funnel income to

your kids is to put taxable income-producing assets such as cash or dividend-paying securities into a custodial account that you open in your child's name at a bank, brokerage or mutual fund. You can give as much as $10,000 a year without incurring a gift tax ($20,000 if you and your spouse make the gift). The funds belong to your child but are managed by a custodian—you or someone you appoint—until the child reaches age 18 or 21, depending on your state's law.

Say your 15-year-old son's custodial account earns $5,000 and he has no other income. The federal income tax on the account would come to $660. He might owe a negligible amount of state taxes on the funds too. Your tax on the same amount, assuming a 35% combined federal and state tax rate, would be more than 2.5 times that amount, or $1,750. If your child is under age 14, however, don't keep more than approximately $50,000 in the custodial account this year. That's because the so-called kiddie tax requires him or her to pay tax at your top rate on investment earnings above $1,200, which is the amount $50,000 would likely earn in a bank money fund.

Emphasize investments geared for growth. The new tax law kept the top capital gains rate at 28% for investments held more than a year. So if your tax rate is 31%, 36% or 39.6%, you might want to take advantage of the spread by investing in growth stocks or growth mutual funds whose profits come mainly from capital appreciation. There are two caveats, however. Never base any investment decision primarily on taxes. Your investments have to make sense in terms of your goals and tolerance for risk. And don't venture into growth investments unless you plan to hold them for several years. You may need to stay in the market long enough to ride out periodic downturns. For investment ideas, refer back to Chapter 1, "Where to Put Your Money in 1994."

Stash cash in tax-free municipal bonds. If you're in the 28% tax bracket ($38,001 to $91,850 for married joint filers; $22,751 to $55,100 for single filers) or higher, you can get better after-tax returns

Software for Your Tax Return

If you're willing to invest the time, it makes sense to do your own return with the help of a computer rather than hire a tax pro. But pay attention when a program says you should consult a professional. It means that experience and extra knowledge are called for. MONEY reviewed three of the most popular tax preparation programs. You can get big discounts by buying directly from a manufacturer using the toll-free numbers listed in the reviews. Note that there are IBM and Macintosh versions available for each of these three programs.

Kiplinger TaxCut ($40, 800-365-1546). This program is the popular *Andrew Tobias' TaxCut* (see below) improved with additional information prepared by the tax editor of *Kiplinger's Personal Finance Magazine*. The extra guidance puts even complicated issues within reach of the tax-timid. For example, the Kiplinger advice makes the calculations required to figure tax on a lump-sum distribution from a retirement account eminently understandable. In addition to 86 IRS forms, schedules and worksheets, the package includes a copy of Kiplinger's tax guide.

Andrew Tobias' TaxCut ($30, 800-284-3694). *TaxCut's* smooth question-and-answer format communicates clearly and purposefully as you move through the forms and schedules of your tax return. For instance, the questions that deal with capital gains lead you to a warning that mutual fund shares are handled differently from other types of assets. *TaxCut* also makes it easy to jump from your 1040 to another form, such as Schedule A for itemized deductions, and back again.

TurboTax ($50, 800-964-1040). This package offers just as many forms and worksheets as *TaxCut*, but its overall tax advice is somewhat less crisp. One plus: the type on *TurboTax's* screen display is easy on the eyes, a real boon when you are working on a complicated return.

on high-quality munis and muni bond funds than on comparable taxable bonds or bond funds. Topnotch munis rated A or better with maturities under 15 years are your best buys today given the likelihood of a half point rise in interest rates this year. If rates moved up that much, long-term munis generally would drop in value almost twice as much as intermediate-term munis. Such bonds recently yielded around 4.3% to 4.9% free of federal and usually state and local income taxes if you live in the state where the bonds are issued. That's equivalent to taxable yields of 6.7% to 7.7% for a New York City investor in the 28% federal bracket. Comparable taxable corporate bonds recently yielded about 5.5% to 6.1%.

Invest in rental real estate. Now is an opportune time to take advantage of the tax breaks of owning rental properties. With the housing market on the upswing, single-family rental houses and small apartment buildings could provide annual returns of 15% or more if held for five years or more. The impetus is a combination of appreciation, tax benefits and rising rents. The tax angle? If your adjusted gross income is $100,000 or less and you actively manage your property, you can deduct as much as $25,000 of rental losses against your other income. Since a large portion of any rental loss is likely to come from depreciation, the deduction may actually exceed your operating costs. The $25,000 maximum allowable loss ratchets down by 50 cents for every dollar of AGI above $100,000 and disappears at $150,000. At an AGI of $125,000, for example, you could write off $12,500 in losses against ordinary income.

Fully fund tax-deferred retirement plans. If you feel you can't afford to stoke your company-sponsored 401(k) with the maximum amount your plan allows, you should reassess how much you spend and save. Your aim is to determine whether you can use the earnings on any other savings and investments for daily expenses, thus freeing up more of your salary for 401(k) contributions. Say you're single and make $40,000 a year and now put 4%, or $1,600, in your 401(k). Also assume

you earn and reinvest about $100 a month from investments. If you used that money for your everyday cash outlays, you could painlessly bolster your 401(k) contribution to 6% a year, the maximum allowed under many plans. That's an $800 increase to $2,400. The payoff: you would reap another $224 in federal income tax savings, assuming you are in the 28% bracket. And you probably would earn $400 more in employer matching funds because most supplement employees' 401(k) contributions by 50%. With a 7% return, your principal would grow by $7,200 after five years and by $52,400 after 20 years.

If you're self-employed, you can make tax-deductible contributions of as much as 20% of your net self-employment earnings, up to $30,000. Start out by fully funding a profit-sharing Keogh, which you may be able to open free of charge at a bank, brokerage or mutual fund. You're allowed to make a deductible contribution of as much as 13% of your self-employment income but can alter the size of your contribution each year. Then, as your earnings stabilize, you could also begin funding a money-purchase Keogh with 7% of your income. This plan requires you to set aside the same percentage every year.

Reduce the bite on retirees' Social Security. The new tax law deals its sharpest blow to many retirees through a change effective this year. The number to focus on is your so-called provisional income—adjusted gross income, plus your tax-exempt income, plus half of your Social Security benefit. Once that figure exceeds $44,000 (for couples) and $34,000 (for singles), as much as 85% of your Social Security is taxed, compared with a maximum of 50% under the old law. One countermeasure is to defer income into 1995 or later by moving out of some investments that generate cash you don't need currently and into ones that let you delay reporting the income. With U.S. Series EE savings bonds, for instance, you can invest as much as $15,000 a year ($30,000 for couples) and earn a guaranteed minimum annual rate of 4% if you hold the bonds for at least six months. You do not have to include the interest in your income until you redeem the bonds, which could be as long as 30 years after you buy them.

You can also trim the tax you owe on your benefits by investing in munis even though tax-exempt interest is counted when calculating whether you owe tax on Social Security. Here's how. Let's say you and your spouse are in the 28% bracket and take the standard deduction for persons over 65. Also assume you collect $20,000 in Social Security benefits and have provisional income of $56,000, of which $6,000 is interest from taxable bonds and $40,000 is from taxable pensions. If you replace the taxable bonds with munis or a muni fund, you'd need to earn interest of only $4,320 to pocket as much as you would on the taxable bonds after tax. (You could do that with a $100,000 portfolio of munis yielding 4.3%.) And only $4,320, rather than $6,000, would be added to your provisional income to determine how much of your Social Security benefit is taxable. As a result, you would shield from tax an additional $1,428 of your Social Security benefit, for a tax savings of $400 a year. This strategy works best if your provisional income is not too far above the new 85% thresholds. So even though it won't work for every retiree, the potential savings make it worth running the numbers.

Put your nanny on the books. Even if you never want to be Attorney General, pay Social Security taxes on the wages of any household employee, such as a nanny, that you hire this year. Paying Social Security taxes on his or her wages isn't just the law. Compliance could also cut your income tax bill and prevent you from owing some ugly tax penalties. By putting your nanny on the books, you will be able to claim the child care credit. That's worth as much as $480 a year for one child and $960 for two or more. You can have your accountant set up your books and handle all your tax forms for employing household help. But you'll pay about $500 a year for the service.

Should you fail to pay the taxes and get caught by the IRS, you will be liable for double the amount of overdue Social Security taxes, plus interest and penalties. For example, if you paid

Social Security's New Bite

Will you be among the 13% of Social Security recipients hit by the higher taxes that kick in this year? This worksheet holds the answer and, if it's yes, here's how much you'll owe[1].

1. Estimate your household's 1994 Social Security benefits. _____

2. Estimate your 1994 adjusted gross income (excluding taxable Social Security) and add 50% of the amount on line 1, plus all your tax-exempt income. _____

3. Subtract $32,000 from line 2 ($25,000 if single). _____

4. Subtract $44,000 from line 2 ($34,000 if single). _____

If line 4 is zero or less, you will not have to pay additional taxes on your benefits, and you can leave the rest of the worksheet blank.

5. If line 3 is greater than line 1, enter line 1 times 0.50. _____

6. If line 3 is less than line 1, enter line 3 times 0.50. _____

7. Enter line 1 times 0.85. _____

8. Enter line 4 times 0.85, plus the lesser of **a)** $6,000 ($4,500 if single) or **b)** line 5 or line 6 (one should be blank). _____

9. The lesser of line 7 or line 8 is the amount of your benefits that will be taxed this year:
Taxable Social Security benefits: $ _____

To find out how much more the new tax law is adding to your bill:

10. Subtract line 5 or line 6 (one should be blank) from line 9. _____
Additional benefits taxed: $ _____

11. To calculate how much additional tax you'll owe on your benefits, multiply line 10 by your anticipated tax rate. For example, you will be in the 28% bracket this year if your taxable income is between $38,001 and $91,850 ($22,751 to $55,100 for singles).

Additional tax: $ _____

[1]If any of these computations result in negative numbers, write in zero. Source: Price Waterhouse

your employee $5,000 a year under the table for the past five years, the tab for getting nabbed would be around $6,110, plus another $2,000 or so for federal and state unemployment taxes (the exact amount depends on the state you live in). Whether your employee is new or has been working for you off the books, to start paying the nanny tax, call the IRS at 800-829-3676 and request an employer identification number and Package 942, which contains the necessary forms. Also ask your state tax department about meeting any local requirements.

If you've been paying your nanny under the

Money Helps

Q. My wife and I are in the market to buy our first house, and my parents want to give us $50,000 toward a down payment. My folks would then live with us in the house. Is there any way for them to avoid gift tax on the money?
—**Mark Knudson, Skokie, Ill.**

A. Your generous folks can give you and your wife $40,000 right off the bat. That's because the tax code allows any person to pass as much as $10,000 a year to any other person without paying tax. So your dad can give you $10,000; your mom can give you $10,000; and then Dad and Mom can each give $10,000 apiece to your missus. As for the remaining $10,000, your parents could go ahead and give it to you anyway. But then they must subtract that amount from the $600,000 that they can pass tax-free to their heirs after death. (They'll have to file Form 709 with their tax return.) Or they could lend it to you at some reasonable market rate and then forgive the loan in future years by converting it to a gift. That last plan has one flaw, however. They could always call the note if they don't like your taste in drapes.

---

table and you want to confess, you will be liable for all the back taxes, interest and penalties. The IRS has said, however, that it will arrange a payment plan if you need one and will not prosecute you if you come forward voluntarily. But don't make the move before consulting a tax lawyer.

Adjust your 1994 withholding. If you expect to get a tax refund for your 1993 taxes, you're letting the IRS take a bigger than necessary bite out of your paycheck each week. Worse, if you have been elevated into a higher tax bracket but fail to adjust your withholding this year, you may be courting an underpayment penalty. To match your withholding more closely to your tax liability, complete a 1994 Form W-4 withholding certificate, which is available at your company payroll office. If less tax will be withheld from your paycheck as a result, resolve to invest your newfound cash. For example, you could arrange with a mutual fund family to transfer the additional sum from your bank to one of its funds every month.

Maintain better tax records. With deductions squeezed, you can't afford to lose any because of poor documentation. For example, this year each gift to a charity of $250 or more must have written notification from the organization, dated no later than the time you file your return, acknowledging your donation and stating whether you received anything in exchange. And if you did get something, a description and estimate of its value must be included with the notification.

Tax pros recommend using an accordion file to sort your tax records. Be sure to save records for any transactions with tax implications. If you're not sure about the tax angles of a financial move, check with your tax preparer. For most taxpayers, these files are a must: brokerage and mutual fund statements; business travel and entertainment receipts; documentation of charitable contributions; income statements, such as W-2s and 1099s; records of interest paid; receipts for medical expenses not covered by insurance; records of miscellaneous deductions; and records for property taxes and estimated tax payments.

Audit Red Flags You Should Avoid

Each tax season, the IRS hands its examiners a list of the most common errors—both intentional and otherwise—that taxpayers make on their returns. Their mission is to audit every return that has at least one of these red flags. MONEY was given an early peek at the top audit instigators for tax year 1993, described below. If your return might be open to question by the IRS, use the strategy we suggest.

Overstating deductions. You are more likely to be audited if your deduction is huge relative to your income—say your medical write-off is $20,000 and you earn only $50,000. The IRS also looks hard for excessive write-offs on hobby and gambling losses. Read IRS Publication 529 for a list of legitimate write-offs. If you intend to claim any miscellaneous deductions on Schedule A, list the type and amount of each, attaching an explanatory statement if you have especially large deductions.

Padded entertainment breaks. Taxpayers can deduct 80% of their unreimbursed expenses for business meals and entertainment on their 1993 returns. But that limit dropped to 50% this year. The IRS will be checking carefully for undocumented expenses and for people writing off 100% of their T&E costs. On Form 2106, list the date of every meal or event, its location, the amount spent, your business benefit and your client's name and occupation.

Undocumented charitable deductions. This flag is likely to turn fire-engine red in 1994 because the new tax law demands even more proof for claiming any charitable contribution worth $250 or more. Here's your strategy for 1993 returns. For property contributions over $500 but not more than $5,000, attach Form 8283 listing the charity's name and address, a description of the donation, the date of your contribution and its fair market value. Attach an appraisal for property worth $5,000 or more.

Questionable property and theft losses. The IRS will be prowling for taxpayers who overstate such losses or report them without documentation. Attach Form 4684 to your return to explain your loss. Disaster victims should attach copies of appraisals of their property made both before and after the casualty, any police or fire department records, plus photographs of the damage. If you were robbed, note the date and time of the theft and staple any police reports to the form. For personal property, remember to reduce your deductions by your insurance reimbursement plus 10% of your adjusted gross income (AGI) and $100 for each casualty.

Poorly documented child care credits. The IRS will boot this break right off your return if you don't list your babysitter's tax ID, which is his or her Social Security number. In 1993, the IRS rejected $1.2 billion worth of such write-offs. So list your babysitter's name, address, Social Security number and the total amount you paid for the service on Form 2441 in order to get the maximum $480 credit for one child ($960 for two or more).

Miscellaneous deductions on Schedule C. Because there is a floor of 2% of AGI for Schedule A miscellaneous deductions, Schedule C (for business write-offs) attracts a swarm of personal deductions. Claim only allowable business write-offs that appear in IRS Publication 334.

Cheesy home-office deductions. The IRS says a large number of the 1.6 million taxpayers who deduct their home-office expenses don't attach the required Form 8829. What's more, many who send along the form fail to fully describe their home-office space. Others take the write-off even though their home is not their most important place of business. Don't bother going for this deduction unless you use your home office solely for business or you perform important business functions at home. Follow instructions to the letter on Form 8829.

How to Tame State and Local Taxes

Rising property taxes are more than making up for the lag in state tax hikes.
Use these strategies to keep both kinds of taxes as low as possible.

At long last the voice of the taxpayer has been heard in state capitols all across the country. "Voters are just in a bad mood, and state officials are reluctant to risk their wrath by raising taxes," says Steven Gold, director of the Center for the Study of the States in Albany, N.Y. Christie Whitman, New Jersey's new governor, won at least partly on a promise to cut income taxes 30% over three years. Indeed, our 50-state forecast for state tax increases in 1994 and 1995 (see page 40) shows only Michigan, Vermont and the District of Columbia as all but certain to hike taxes in the next two years. And, even then, the net effect of Michigan's anticipated tax increase may be a wash for many residents. It may merely replace the $6 billion in school-related property taxes that the state legislature abolished last year. For fiscal 1994, state legislatures have enacted just $4.1 billion in new taxes—a fourth the size of the giant $16.2 billion tax blitz of 1992. But this trend probably won't last for long. Here's why:

New cutbacks in federal deductions mean higher state taxes. That's because states typically require residents to compute their state income taxes based on their federal return. For example, you can claim only 50% of unreimbursed business travel and entertainment expenses, vs. 80% before the new law. Thus your federal and state income tax bills could well be higher than they would otherwise be. Rhode Island, however, reduced its top state income tax rates in 1993 to offset the federal increases for a year.

Property tax increases are accelerating. One impetus is that, since 1991, local governments have lost more than $1 billion in state and federal funds as a result of various austerity measures. For the second quarter of 1993, total U.S. property taxes rose 5.7% from the same period in 1992, vs. a 4.6% rise in state income taxes. What's more, problems such as soaring education and health care expenditures persist at the state level. Thus the states are unlikely to continue their moderation throughout the 1990s.

To counteract looming state and property taxes, first familiarize yourself with the unique rules governing your state and local tax codes. Buried in the instruction booklet for your state tax return is a trove of tips designed to reduce both your income and property taxes. Here's one small comfort. If you itemize on your federal tax return, you are allowed to deduct on your 1040 form your state income and property taxes. That's especially helpful for residents of places like Wisconsin, Rhode Island and New York where the state income tax rate is unusually steep. For specific tax-cutting moves, you should follow these strategies:

Seek out all broad state tax breaks. For instance, taxpayers in nine states (Alabama, Iowa, Louisiana, Missouri, Montana, North Dakota, Oklahoma, Oregon and Utah) can write off at least some of their federal income tax on their state returns. If your health care bills are high, you should keep in mind that Alabama, Arizona, New Jersey and Wisconsin let you deduct a larger share of your medical bills than the expenses exceeding 7.5% of adjustable gross income that you are permitted to deduct on your federal 1040.

Dig deep for special allowances. Certain groups of taxpayers can reap more state benefits than others—if they know to take them. Married working couples should consider filing separate state returns, for example. If you earn substantially more than your spouse, the effective state income tax rate you'll pay by filing jointly may be higher than if you file separately. In the District of Columbia and 13 states, married couples can file separately even if they will file joint federal returns. The states: Alabama, Arizona, Arkansas, Delaware, Hawaii, Iowa, Kentucky, Mississippi, Montana, Pennsylvania, Tennessee, Virginia and West Virginia. So work out your state taxes both ways to see whether you come out better filing separately or jointly.

Most parents should file separate state returns for their children. Under the so-called kiddie tax rules, if your child is under 14, any investment income above $1,200 a year would be taxed by Uncle Sam at your higher rate. All states except California and Hawaii, however, blessedly tax your kids at their rates regardless of their income as long as you file separate returns for them. To take advantage of this deal, you must also file separate federal returns for each of your children. For example, if you live in New York State and your daughter's investment income is $4,500, you could save about $200 on your state return by filing separately for her.

Under another special break, retirees don't have to pay state income taxes on Social Security benefits in the following 26 states: Alabama, Arizona, Arkansas, California, Delaware, Georgia, Hawaii, Idaho, Illinois, Indiana, Kentucky, Louisiana, Maine, Maryland, Massachusetts, Michigan, Minnesota, Mississippi, New Jersey, New York, North Carolina, Ohio, Oklahoma, Oregon, Pennsylvania and Virginia. That's particularly welcome news this year when as much as 85% of the benefits will be taxed by Uncle Sam, up from 50% in 1993. Furthermore, any type of pension is exempt from taxation in Hawaii, Illinois and Pennsylvania. Private pension benefits are partially deductible if you live in one of the following 17 states: Alabama, Arkansas, Colorado, Delaware, Georgia, Louisiana, Maryland, Michigan, Mississippi, Montana, New Jersey, New Mexico, New York, North Carolina, Oregon, South Carolina and Utah.

Consider investing in Treasuries. That's because interest from Treasury bills, notes and bonds is exempt from state and local tax if you live in Washington, D.C. or one of the 43 states with its own income tax on unearned income. But U.S. Government bond funds such as Vanguard Intermediate Term U.S. Treasury Portfolio and Strong Government Securities, despite their names, are not 100% exempt from state taxes because they aren't fully invested in Treasuries. What's more, California, Connecticut, New Jersey, New York, Pennsylvania and Vermont have special guidelines that limit your ability to exclude Treasury interest from funds. If you live in one of these states, ask the fund to supply you with your own state's precise rules, as well as the percentage of the fund's holdings and income that are derived from Treasuries.

Look into munis issued in your home state. They can be a triple-tax boon if you're in the 28% tax bracket or above and live in a state with a steep income tax. The interest they pay is exempt from all federal, state and local taxes. But you should shun munis maturing beyond 15 years if you believe, as MONEY does, that interest rates are likely to rise by as much as half a percentage point this year. The scant additional yield that you would get for choosing a bond with a longer maturity is not worth the added potential risk of principal loss. If you don't have enough money to buy a portfolio of munis, shop for a mutual fund that invests only in tax-exempt bonds issued by your state.

Grab all available property tax breaks. Every state except Connecticut, Indiana, Massachusetts, New Jersey, Pennsylvania and West Virginia lets homeowners deduct or get a credit for at least some of their property taxes on their state income tax returns. In 18 states (and Washington, D.C.) you can avoid even owing taxes on a certain dollar amount of your home's value. The states are Alabama, California, Florida, Georgia, Hawaii, Idaho, Illinois, Indiana, Iowa, Louisiana, Massachusetts, Minnesota, Mississippi, New Mexico, Oklahoma, Texas, Wisconsin and Wyoming. Among the most generous are Florida, which offers a maximum $25,000 exemption, and

Hawaii, where exemptions can run from $40,000 to $120,000, depending on the county and your age. Many states also offer property tax breaks for individuals with physical disabilities, veterans and senior citizens.

Don't hesitate to appeal your assessment. More than half of the people who challenge their assessments succeed in reducing them, reports Gene Baroni, national director of multistate tax services for the accounting firm Coopers & Lybrand. The average reduction was about 10%. Say you live in Pittsburgh, where property taxes are a steep 2.5% of fair market value. If your $200,000 home's assessed value is reduced by 8%, you would save nearly $400 a year.

The most successful appeals show that your home's assessment is too high compared with similar properties, says David Keating of the National Taxpayers Union based in Washington, D.C. By combing through lists of recent sales in your local assessor's office, you can find out what comparable homes in your area have sold for in the past six months. Lowering your assessment today can pay off in reduced property taxes for years to come. It also sends the message that the voice of the taxpayer can be accompanied by swift action.

Local Levies in 50 States

Taxes vary by 650% from Alaska to New York

Alaska and New York occupy the polar extremes in our ranking of state and local tax burdens. A typical prosperous two-income family of four that subscribes to MONEY pays only $1,694 in Alaska, while the New York bill is nearly seven times as high at $11,020.

The table lists all the tax loads of the family, who earned $75,634 in 1993, plus $4,908 in investment income. They spent $36,657 on food, clothing, prescription drugs, household goods, a new car and other items.

The states are ranked by the typical family's total tax bill for state and local income, sales, property and gasoline taxes.

The third column grades the state's odds of imposing an increase in 1994 or 1995, according to tax experts:

A – No major tax hikes expected (20 states)
B – Moderate chance (18)
C – Strong possibility (10)
D – Nearly sure thing (two and D.C.).

Sources: All state income tax estimates were provided by the state and local tax group of Ernst & Young, the international accounting and management consulting firm. Other sources: Vertex Inc.; Lundberg Survey Inc.; *A Far Cry From Fair* (1991) by Citizens for Tax Justice and the Institute on Taxation and Economic Policy.

Notes: 1 – Additional local income tax may also be assessed. **2** – Local income tax calculated on state return. **3** – None means state imposes no death tax, 0 means no tax applies to a spouse or child heir. **4** – Tax rates are for couples filing jointly in 1993.

	STATE	Total annual tax on typical household	Grade for risk of future tax hikes
1	Alaska	$1,694	A
2	Wyoming	3,456	A
3	Nevada	3,775	B
4	Florida	4,039	C
5	South Dakota	4,293	A
6	Tennessee	4,469	B
7	Texas	4,843	B
8	New Hampshire	4,978	C
9	Washington	5,070	A
10	Alabama[1]	5,487	C
11	North Dakota	5,611	B
12	Mississippi	5,934	A
13	Louisiana	6,010	C
14	Missouri[1]	6,067	A
15	Delaware[1]	6,304	B
16	New Mexico	6,529	A
17	West Virginia	6,541	B
18	Arkansas	6,571	A
19	Arizona	6,871	A
20	South Carolina	6,919	A
21	Indiana	7,017	B
22	Kentucky[1]	7,110	C
23	New Jersey	7,274	A
24	Pennsylvania	7,292	B
25	Oklahoma	7,352	A
26	Illinois	7,517	C
27	Kansas	7,527	A
28	Virginia	7,547	B
29	North Carolina	7,648	A
30	Colorado	7,669	B
31	Iowa[1]	7,717	A
32	Georgia	7,732	B
33	Michigan[1]	7,885	D
34	California	8,065	B
35	Idaho	8,128	A
36	Utah	8,272	A
37	Ohio	8,362	B
38	Vermont	8,442	D
39	Hawaii	8,579	C
40	Nebraska	8,634	A
41	Montana	8,648	B
42	Minnesota	8,811	B
43	Connecticut	8,821	A
44	Massachusetts	8,830	B
45	Maine	8,885	C
46	Oregon	8,959	C
47	Rhode Island	8,997	B
48	Maryland[2]	9,025	B
49	Wisconsin	9,351	A
50	District of Columbia	10,181	D
51	New York[1]	11,020	C

| Tax on earned income | | | | Sales tax | | | Death tax[3] on | | |
For singles earning $35,000	For two-income married earning $50,000	For two-income married earning $75,000	For two-income married earning $100,000	Statewide rate	Highest combined state and local	Property tax	$600,000 estate left to spouse	$600,000 estate left to child	Comments[4]
0	0	0	0	0.000%	7.000%	$1,539	None	None	Most tax revenue from the oil and gas industry
0	0	0	0	4.000	6.000	1,561	None	None	Most tax revenue from oil company and sales taxes
0	0	0	0	6.500	7.000	1,306	None	None	Most tax revenue from sales, gambling and gas taxes
0	0	0	0	6.000	7.000	1,924	None	None	Most tax revenue from sales, use and admissions taxes
0	0	0	0	4.000	6.000	2,484	0	$41,250	Primary source of tax revenue: sales and gas taxes
0	0	0	0	7.000	8.750	1,238	0	0	Certain interest and dividend income taxed at 6%
0	0	0	0	6.250	8.250	2,387	None	None	Revenue mainly from sales and oil company taxes
0	0	0	0	0.000	0.000	4,346	0	0	Dividends and interest over $2,400 taxed at 5%
0	0	0	0	7.000	8.200	2,155	None	None	Revenue mostly from sales, property and corporate taxes
$1,251	$1,272	$2,157	$2,991	4.000	10.000	693	None	None	Top rate: 5% on taxable income over $6,000
751	627	1,519	2,519	5.000	6.000	2,080	None	None	Top rate: 12% on taxable income over $50,000
1,185	1,178	2,453	3,728	7.000	7.000	1,111	0	0	Top rate: 5% on taxable income over $10,000
895	1,005	1,765	2,505	4.000	10.500	1,014	0	17,050	Top rate: 6% on taxable income over $100,000
1,168	1,220	2,227	3,278	4.225	7.725	1,303	None	None	Top rate: 6% on taxable income over $9,000
1,812	1,935	3,893	5,856	0.000	0.000	1,289	0	31,250	Top rate: 7.7% on taxable income over $40,000
1,319	1,213	2,968	4,931	5.125	6.875	984	None	None	Top rate: 8.5% on taxable income over $41,600
1,260	1,697	3,230	4,855	6.000	6.000	590	None	None	Top rate: 6.5% on taxable income over $60,000
1,694	1,549	3,191	4,909	4.500	7.500	1,018	None	None	Top rate: 7% on taxable income over $25,000
1,271	1,091	2,226	3,498	5.000	8.500	1,949	None	None	Top rate: 7% on taxable income over $300,000
1,733	1,694	3,436	5,177	5.000	6.000	1,485	None	None	Top rate: 7% on taxable income over $10,800
1,496	2,024	3,124	4,224	5.000	5.000	1,733	0	24,950	Rate: a flat 3.4% of AGI, with modifications
1,841	2,146	3,708	5,271	6.000	6.000	1,227	0	45,350	Top rate: 6% on taxable income over $8,000
750	965	1,784	3,234	4.000	4.000	3,972	0	0	Top rate: 7% on taxable income over $150,000
1,330	1,900	2,850	3,800	6.000	7.000	2,246	$35,880	36,000	Rate: a flat 2.8% on a broad base of taxable income
1,885	1,620	4,148	6,153	4.500	9.500	1,193	0	17,725	Top rate: 7% on taxable income over $21,000
1,020	1,380	2,130	2,880	6.250	8.750	2,529	None	None	Rate: a flat 3% of taxable income
1,630	1,047	2,638	4,273	4.900	7.150	2,250	0	21,750	Top rate: 6.45% on taxable income over $60,000
1,537	1,805	3,271	4,737	4.500	4.500	2,255	None	None	Top rate: 5.75% on taxable income over $17,000
1,915	1,963	3,747	5,532	6.000	6.000	1,332	0	7,000	Top rate: 7.75% on taxable income over $100,000
1,319	1,483	2,785	4,033	3.000	9.000	2,044	None	None	Rate: a flat 5% of modified federal taxable income
1,875	1,747	3,319	4,981	5.000	6.000	2,233	0	39,825	Top rate: 9.98% on taxable income over $47,700
1,682	1,724	3,254	4,784	4.000	6.000	1,797	None	None	Top rate: 6% on taxable income over $10,000
1,513	1,914	3,064	4,214	4.000	4.000	3,042	0	34,200	Rate: a flat 4.6% of all taxable income
1,468	854	2,750	5,121	7.250	8.750	2,132	None	None	Top rate: 11% on taxable income over $424,760
2,108	1,940	3,957	6,048	5.000	7.000	1,684	None	None	Top rate: 8.2% on taxable income over $40,000
1,834	1,936	3,548	5,127	6.000	7.250	1,855	None	None	Top rate: 7.2% on taxable income over $7,500
1,766	2,337	2,648	4,153	5.000	7.000	1,652	2,100	30,100	Top rate: 7.5% on taxable income over $200,000
833	1,234	3,162	5,512	5.000	5.000	2,997	None	None	Top rate: 34% of federal income tax above $13,100
2,729	2,484	5,002	7,552	4.000	4.000	1,128	None	None	Top rate: 10% on taxable income over $41,000
1,424	1,515	3,159	4,941	5.000	6.500	3,073	0	5,850	Top rate: 6.99% on taxable income over $46,750
2,035	2,262	4,810	7,612	0.000	0.000	2,558	0	0	Top rate: 11% on tax. inc. over $59,400; 4.7% surtax
2,045	1,969	4,011	6,015	6.500	7.500	2,202	None	None	Top rate: 8.5% on taxable income over $83,300
1,419	1,176	3,039	4,500	6.000	6.000	3,415	0	37,895	Rate: a flat 4.5% of taxable income
1,584	2,420	3,878	5,339	5.000	5.000	2,878	25,000	57,000	Rate on earned income is 5.95%; unearned, 12%
878	1,541	3,770	6,108	6.000	6.000	2,488	None	None	Top rate: 8.5% on taxable income over $33,000
2,469	2,533	4,825	7,120	0.000	0.000	3,159	None	None	Top rate: 9% on taxable income over $10,000
818	1,185	2,895	4,919	7.000	7.000	3,342	None	None	Top rate: 32% of modified federal tax liability
2,295	2,480	4,392	6,305	5.000	5.000	2,222	5,000	6,000	Top rate, with local surtax: 9% over $150,000
1,954	2,140	3,867	5,327	5.000	5.500	3,167	None	None	Top rate: 6.93% on taxable income over $20,000
2,504	2,690	5,113	7,536	6.000	6.000	2,390	None	None	Top rate: 9.5% on taxable income over $20,000
1,927	2,202	4,210	6,218	4.000	8.500	3,467	0	25,500	Top rate: 7.875% on taxable income over $26,000

Getting Over Mutual Fund Tax Hurdles

Funds stop being convenient investments when it comes time to calculate your taxes.
Here's how to avoid shelling out more than your due.

Most of the time, mutual funds simplify investors' lives. But not at tax time. That's partly because tax law requires funds to pay out, or distribute, virtually all their income from interest, dividends and net capital gains each year. That means that you often owe taxes on capital gains from your fund even if you didn't sell any shares. In fact, you may owe taxes even if you didn't make any money. That happened to shareholders of USAA Mutual Aggressive Growth in 1992. Although the fund shed 8.5% of its value that year, it paid out $2.14 per share in taxable capital gains distributions because it unloaded some holdings at a profit during the year.

Things get more confounding when you do sell shares. If you're like most investors, you have your funds reinvest your distributions. From a tax standpoint, each reinvestment counts as a separate purchase. Thus you're confronted with a mess when you sit down to calculate your taxable gains. Included might be a large clump of shares you bought at one price (your initial investment); dozens of tiny lots acquired at different prices (shares purchased with reinvested distributions); and a further raft of small chunks each bought at yet another price (the regular purchases you made). Each lot you bought produces a different capital gain or loss, which means that much extra calculator punching to figure out what you owe Uncle Sam. Here are tips that can spare you some headaches on this year's tax return.

Don't buy fund shares at the wrong time. Most stock funds distribute capital gains once a year, usually in December, and some total return funds pay out income quarterly. (To learn your fund's distribution dates, call its 800 number.) If you're contemplating a purchase close to a distribution date, you shouldn't act until after the date passes.

Otherwise, you'll receive a taxable payout of all the capital gains or income the fund booked since its last payout even if you've owned your stake for only a week. In effect, the fund hands you back part of your principal in the form of a distribution. But now you have to pay income tax on it.

Check gains and losses on the fund's books. When you're considering whether to buy a fund, check the changes in net assets in the fund's annual report. The number to look for is the "change in unrealized appreciation on investments." That represents capital gains embedded in the fund's portfolio. When the fund sells its winners, those gains must be distributed to shareholders. To judge how big the payout could be, you should divide the unrealized appreciation by the fund's net assets. A result of more than 0.2 suggests that a walloping big payout is possible. While the potential for a big distribution shouldn't by itself rule out your purchase of a promising fund, it could decide a close call between competing funds. In contrast, realized losses are a plus for new investors. The fund can use prior years' losses to offset current gains for as long as eight years. Look for "tax-loss carry-forward" as a footnote in the annual report's financial statement.

Take advantage of your own losses. If one of your funds is down for the year, you should consider selling and taking the tax write-off. The loss can offset capital gains plus as much as $3,000 of other income. In fact, it often makes tax sense to move out of a losing no-load fund temporarily even if you still like its prospects. The IRS will disqualify the loss if you repurchase your shares within 31 days. But nothing prevents you from hopping into a similar no-load portfolio for a little longer than that and then switching back.

Consider selling out in the same year. While you don't want to overrule your investment sense just to streamline your taxes, here's something to think about. If you sell a fund's shares over a number of years, you have to keep records of each sale and decide which of the four IRS approved accounting methods yields the lowest tax. If you sell all at once, all four methods will give you the same tax. So you can use the simplest method, called average cost, single category. It allows you to figure the average cost of all your shares, regardless of when you bought them. And that work will be automatically done for you if the fund you're selling belongs to one of the growing number of families that calculate tax costs for redeeming shareholders

(among them Vanguard, T. Rowe Price, Putnam and IDS). Keep in mind, though, that if you're not unloading all your shares, the single category method may cost you more in taxes than the three other alternative methods described below.

Figure the most tax-efficient method. Unless you elect otherwise when you sell only some of your fund shares, the IRS assumes that the shares you sell first are the ones you bought first. That method is called first in, first out. It's fine if your fund has been a loser. But the oldest shares typically have the biggest gains. So they're the ones on which you're better off postponing taxes. You can do that by using a method known as specific iden-

Tax Shelters Are Back

Back in the early 1980s, brokers and financial planners urged wealthy clients to get into high-write-off tax shelters, many of which crashed and burned after tax reform erased their advantages in 1986. These days the pitch is tax credits on limited partnerships that buy or build housing for low-income renters. For example, Merrill Lynch and Paine Webber have joined forces on the American Tax Credit Trust (minimum investment: $5,000).

Tax credits are more enticing than deductions, of course. Credits directly reduce your taxes because you subtract them from your tax liability. The partnerships are in vogue for two reasons. First, the credits, which had previously been temporary, were made a permanent feature of the tax code with the 1993 tax law. Second, with the top bracket raised to 39.6%, the write-off is more attractive to upper-income taxpayers. An investor in the 28% bracket who puts up $5,000, for example, might reduce his tax bill by about $700 a year for 10 years. Someone in the 39.6% bracket who invests $60,000 might subtract $9,900 (usually the maximum credit) from his tax bill each of those years.

Promoters like to say the 15-year partnerships will return 14% or more annually, counting tax

breaks. But that assumes the properties appreciate, so you will get capital gains at the end of the period. Partnership sponsors estimate you will earn 10% to 12% a year if there are no gains.

Those returns sound fabulous in today's low-rate environment. But the deals have many catches. The potential for capital gains may be remote. In fact, some low-income properties are completely worthless after 15 years. And it's tough to get your money back before the 15 years are up without getting clobbered because there is not much of a secondary market for the partnerships. If a project fails to meet strict federal rules every year, you could lose future tax credits plus a portion of those you've already claimed. You might also lose credits if your tax bracket drops over the next 10 years. And you usually cannot claim a credit for any year in which you take the maximum $25,000 loss on rental real estate or pay the alternative minimum tax.

Still interested? Be sure to consult your tax adviser for guidance. Analysts say the safest buys are through large players like Boston Capital, Boston Financial Group and Related Capital. And make sure the partnership will hold at least 25 properties across the country, for adequate diversification.

tification. It permits you to sell whichever shares will minimize your taxes. For example, you might pick only shares on which you have a loss, thereby offsetting gains from a different investment.

The fourth method is called average cost, double category. It requires you to distinguish between shares you've held for more than a year and those you bought more recently and to calculate a separate average cost for each. That way you can take advantage of the now substantial difference in tax rates on long-term and short-term gains. Long-term gains (on shares held more than a year) are taxed at a maximum rate of 28%. Short-term gains are taxed as ordinary income, which could mean a rate as high as 39.6%.

Here's a final caveat. Once you use either single or double categories for a given fund, you're stuck with that method for the fund. You can't change the tax treatment without written permission from the IRS. And don't hold your breath for that.

Fight the Feds in Tax Court and Win

It's not easy to outgun the IRS in a legal battle. If you follow these tactics, however, you will increase your chance of winning.

Challenging the IRS in Tax Court over an alleged tax deficiency can be a struggle. On average over the past six years, the court decided just 10% of cases in favor of taxpayers and issued split decisions 37% of the time. The IRS won the rest. The agency prevails so often because in Tax Court you bear the burden of proof. As unfair as it seems, the IRS is presumed correct when it issues a deficiency notice. The only way you can win is to prove to one of the 41 Tax Court judges that the IRS was wrong.

Nonetheless, the Tax Court can be a helpful ally when the IRS demands taxes you don't owe. Despite its name, the court is independent of the IRS. Unlike the equally independent U.S. District Court and the U.S. Court of Claims—the other federal courts where tax cases are heard—you can go to Tax Court without paying the disputed tax in advance. And the Tax Court will come to you. Judges travel to 79 locations around the country to hear disputes. If you decide to take on the IRS, following the tactics described in detail below will improve your chances of winning in court:

Don't be cowed by the IRS. Your ticket to court is an official IRS notice of deficiency. The government outlines the back taxes and penalties it says you owe. It also informs you of your right to petition the Tax Court within 90 days if you want to fight back without paying up first. At last count, the IRS annually issued more than 1.6 million deficiency notices to taxpayers who had disagreed with the results of an audit or hadn't responded to a demand for more taxes. If you have legitimate grounds to contest the tax, you can turn to the court. File the petition promptly by registered mail, so you will have a receipt to prove that it was sent during the 90-day window. If you're not fully confident about the merits of your case, get a second opinion from your tax pro while you're waiting for the petition papers to arrive. Expect to pay about $100 to $225 for an hour's consultation.

Don't overpay for Tax Court counsel. A tax lawyer or C.P.A. admitted to practice before the court can give you an estimate of your case's potential cost up front. A quick settlement without a trial might run $1,500 to $2,000, but fees for representation in a full-blown trial can easily exceed $15,000. You can probably navigate Tax Court without a lawyer if the alleged deficiency is $10,000 or less for each year at issue. With such relatively low sums at stake, you can elect on your petition to have your case heard as a small case, the Tax Court equivalent of a small-claims court proceeding. Each year a third of the 30,000 Tax Court petitioners opt for small-case status. About 90% are settled before the judge weighs in, but taxpayers only win 10% of the cases that go to trial.

In a small case, your petition comes as a simple preprinted form. You just fill in the blanks. Moreover, if the IRS doesn't settle the case beforehand, you won't be held to arcane rules of evidence in the relatively informal trial. Instead, the judge will accept most any documents or testimony you think is relevant and will often help you develop your case by eliciting facts. Thanks to these procedures, most small-case taxpayers are able to complete their own petitions, perhaps with coaching from a tax pro, and represent themselves in court. Small-case is especially appropriate when you have facts that can be readily explained. If your case turns on a complicated point of law, you will probably need to hire a professional.

Larger cases follow formal rules of courtroom practice and procedure. They are no place for an amateur. Says Lapsley Hamblen, chief judge of the Tax Court: "Unlike in small cases, the judge in a regular case exercises less discretion to bend the rules of evidence to help out a taxpayer. So it's preferable to have counsel."

Check out court-sanctioned legal clinics. If you live near one of the 14 legal clinics approved by the Tax Court, you can seek free legal advice from law students who work under the supervision of a professor who has been admitted to practice before the court. The clinics are located at American University in Washington, D.C.; University of Bridgeport in Connecticut; University of Denver; Georgia State University in Atlanta; Illinois Institute of Technology Chicago-Kent College of Law, and Loyola University, also in Chicago; Loyola University in New Orleans; University of Minnesota in Minneapolis; University of New Mexico in Albuquerque; New York Law School and Yeshiva University, both in New York City; Southern Methodist University in Dallas; Villanova College in Philadelphia; and Widener University in Wilmington, Del.

Go for a settlement. When you send your petition to the Tax Court, a clerk forwards it to the IRS, where it is automatically routed to one of its appeals officers for a possible settlement. If you already tried settling after your audit, the petition is sent to an attorney who must prepare the case for trial. Even IRS lawyers settle disputes, however. With some 30,000 Tax Court petitions filed each year and a backlog of more than 40,000, it's imperative that the IRS settle because the agency doesn't have the resources to try all cases.

If your petition is sent to an IRS appeals office, you'll get a call or letter asking you to visit to discuss your case. You or your tax pro can attend. Let your adviser decide. Many pros want to handle the conference alone because issues can be broached more dispassionately in your absence. Unlike auditors, IRS appeals officers take into account the hazards of litigation when considering whether to proceed with your case. "The IRS doesn't want to risk an unfavorable decision in court that might encourage other taxpayers to exploit the tax law's ambiguity," says Frederick Daily, a San Francisco tax attorney and author of *Stand Up to the IRS* (Nolo, $20). "If the IRS thinks you have a chance of winning, it will often try to settle."

The cases the IRS is likeliest to settle are ones in which the facts are in dispute. Take Barbara Wolfe of Keyport, N.J. In 1988, she received a deficiency notice for $116,857, five years of taxes and penalties on income that the IRS said her husband, who worked on oil pipelines, had failed to report. The notice went to Wolfe because neither she nor the IRS could locate her husband, from whom she had been separated since 1986. In her Tax Court petition, Wolfe claimed she was an "innocent spouse." This designation absolves one spouse of taxes allegedly incurred by the other, if the first spouse can prove that he or she had no way of knowing about the understatement. One fact in her favor: Wolfe's husband had worked out of the country for two of the five years in dispute. The day before the case was set for trial in 1991, the IRS' lawyer offered to reduce the bill 65% by knocking off two years' worth of the tax and all penalties. Wolfe accepted. "I wanted to fight on," she says. "But when I considered the cost of going to court and the possibility of losing, it wasn't worth the risk."

Be cooperative in pretrial preparation. Before a judge hears your case, you and the IRS attorney must agree to as many facts as possible and present them to the court. You must also swap the evidence that each side plans to offer. If you don't cooperate, you run the risk of angering the judge and could face restrictions on the evidence you can present. "Many taxpayers feel mistreated by the IRS and carry their ill will over to the court system," says Tax Court judge Peter Panuthos. "They only end up compromising their own cases."

Present the strongest argument you can. As in an

audit, your best records are receipts, canceled checks, invoices or an original diary to verify your expenditures. If your record keeping became sloppy because of an illness, get a letter from your doctor attesting to the affliction. Your oral testimony is crucial too. Woody Rowland, a former IRS attorney now in private practice in San Rafael, Calif., once tried a Tax Court case for the IRS involving a woman who raised breeding horses. The IRS had disallowed her losses of some $75,000, claiming that the business was a hobby. "Her losses were so great for so many years that it was hard to believe she was in a business," says Rowland. Surprise! "At the trial, the woman explained what it was like to stay up all night with the mares when they were foaling and how much effort the horses required. I knew I had lost as soon as I heard her."

Give More to Your Kids, Less to IRS

Prudent parents should be familiar with the Tax Theory of Relativity—it's better to give to your real relatives than to your Uncle Sam.

If some members of Congress had their way, you would be able to pass on such assets as brown eyes, prematurely gray hair and little else. In their quest to cut the federal budget deficit, legislators have been studying a variety of ways to increase estate and gift taxes. (For more on estate planning, see "How to Take Care of Your Heirs," page 85.) Possible changes include restricting the annual maximum amount of tax-free gifts and lowering the $600,000 lifetime exemption from federal estate taxes. So now may be the time to establish a gift giving program. You will save by shifting income-producing assets to family members in lower tax brackets. And you'll reduce the size of your estate, and thus your estate taxes. Here are the best ways to give to your kids, starting with the easiest:

Outright gifts. You and your spouse may each give annual tax-free gifts of up to $10,000 ($20,000 if

you make the gift together) to as many recipients as you wish. There is no limit on gifts for a relative's tuition or medical expenses. But the money must be paid directly to the school or health care provider. Giving money to your kids isn't the tax saver it was before the 1986 tax reform law. Now if your child is under 14 and has annual investment income above $1,200, it is taxable at your higher rate. But the strategy of shifting income to your child does make more sense with the new top tax rate of 39.6%. If you shifted $1,100 to your child and you are in the top bracket, you might save $165 in federal taxes.

Custodian accounts. They are the simplest way to transfer legal title to an asset to a young child who's too young to manage it. You establish the account through either the Uniform Gifts to Minors Act (applicable in 20 states) or the Uniform Transfer to Minors Act (in the other 30 states and Washington, D.C.). You open a bank or brokerage account in your child's name and appoint a custodian to administer it until the youngster reaches age 18 or 21, depending on your state's law. Transfers of property into these accounts qualify for the $10,000/$20,000 annual gift tax exclusion.

Favor stocks or mutual funds with growth potential for these accounts. By handing over a growth stock worth $20,000 today, you could be removing $100,000 from your future estate. And don't name yourself custodian of your own gifts. If you do and die before your child becomes an adult, the value of your gift will be taxed as part of your estate. Name your spouse as custodian instead. If you and your spouse will make the gift jointly, consider a third party custodian.

Children's trusts. Only two types of trusts, called a minor's and a Crummey, qualify for the annual gift tax exclusion. In a minor's, or 2503(c) trust, the trustee (normally you) controls the income and principal until your child turns 21. A Crummey trust is more tight-fisted. Your child owns the principal at age 21 but can't take the money and run. Instead, he or she can withdraw a limited amount each year. The sum is determined by you when you create the trust. If your child dies before 21, the funds go to his or her estate. More than likely, you will need a lawyer to set up a trust. Thus it may not be worthwhile to spend an estimated $1,000 to $1,500 in legal fees to establish a trust unless you plan to transfer assets of more than $50,000.

Interest-free loans. These are useful if you want to make a gift to your adult child and get the principal back without the legal acrobatics of a trust. No-interest loans of $10,000 or less are exempt from gift tax unless used to purchase income-producing property, such as rental real estate. The same is true for interest-free loans totaling up to $100,000 if your child's net investment income for the year is $1,000 or less. If your loan doesn't meet either of these criteria, the forgone interest on it is subject to gift tax. Forgone interest is the amount you would have collected if you had charged a market rate monitored by the federal government. Make sure you have all the loan's terms in writing or the IRS may treat the entire transaction as a gift.

Special trusts called GRITs. A grantor retained income trust (GRIT) makes sense if your and your

---

Money Helps

Q. When I was getting ready to buy my first home, I read in Charles Givens' *More Wealth Without Risk* that I could borrow money for a down payment from my 401(k) and secure the loan via a second mortgage note on my house. That way, the interest would be tax deductible. I called the IRS to check, and the agent I talked to laughed at me. She said that the loan would be secured by funds in the 401(k) and is therefore not deductible. Can you tell me who is right?
—Samuel Sim, Yucaipa, Calif.

A. Under law, interest is deductible as mortgage interest if a house is collateral for a loan. Thus accountant Gary Case, who did research for the Givens book, argues that if you give your employer a piece of paper saying that the loan is a second mortgage on the house, then you're okay. But Howard Golden of benefits consultant Kwasha Lipton points out that "no employer would agree to become the holder of your mortgage." Doing so would violate federal law governing the handling of pension funds. Besides, the loan is already secured. With a 401(k) loan, you can borrow only as much as 50% of your funds. If you default on the loan, your employer will take what you owe from the balance. At the IRS, spokesman Henry Holmes states in no uncertain terms that you can forget the Givens strategy. "If you try it and we identify it, we're going to challenge it," declared Holmes.

How Congress Does its Taxes

Like most taxpayers, Clay Shaw of Fort Lauderdale finds the tax code almost incomprehensible. "It is a rat's nest," he says. "I'm a C.P.A. and a lawyer. I had the highest grade in taxation at law school. Yet I don't prepare my own income tax return." Not shocked by this admission? You will be when you discover that Clay Shaw is also a Republican U.S. representative and a senior member of the House committee that helps to write the very tax laws that he finds so unintelligible.

In fact, the majority of the senators and representatives on Congress' two tax-writing committees don't fill out their own returns. And those who do their own taxes can get all the first-rate advice they want—you guessed it—for free. They can consult either experts employed by Congress or the specialists in two offices that the IRS maintains on Capitol Hill from February 1 to April 15 each year. The cost to taxpayers of the IRS handholding is as much as $100,000 annually.

Members of Congress, including those on the tax committees, have every right to hire preparers. That's what 46% of their taxpaying constituents do, including two out of three MONEY subscribers. Americans pay tax pros $30 billion a year, up 80% since 1982. Moreover, some extremely wealthy senators and representatives would be foolish not to consult tax professionals. But the overwhelming reason cited by legislators for relying on tax pros is the complexity of the law, not of their personal tax situations. Amended almost every year since 1980,

the tax code now consists of more than 2,000 pages of basic statute, 10,000 pages of IRS regulations and 200,000 pages of IRS and court interpretations of the law's provisions.

No wonder that flummoxed lawmakers call on tax pros for help. All members of Congress, as well as their Capitol Hill employees, are entitled to special assistance from the IRS. The agency assigns a taxpayer service specialist to the Senate's Dirksen Building and another to the House's Cannon Building. Every business day during tax season, the specialists answer questions, review tax returns or even prepare them at no charge. Explains a former chief counsel at the IRS: "The IRS offices on the Hill are basically another perk. But the agency views them as a political necessity because Congress determines the IRS' budget and oversees its activities. Nobody is interested in alienating Congress."

If tax law were simplified, the extra help wouldn't be needed. And the feds would take in more money. That's because complexity encourages cheating. Representative Bill Archer, a Texas Republican, sits on the House Ways and Means Committee. He recently predicted that tax simplification just isn't going to happen until members of Congress have to fill out their own tax returns. When the National Taxpayers Union, a fiscally conservative lobbying group, suggested that Archer draft a measure requiring just that, he declined. An aide to Archer responded that such a proposal is impractical because there's no way to enforce it.

---

spouse's estates together exceed $1.2 million (your combined lifetime exemption). You can put your home in an irrevocable GRIT, reserving the right to live there for, say, 10 years. When the trust ends, your child gets the house. If you don't want to move when the GRIT expires, your child could then rent the home to you at a market rate. What makes a GRIT so appealing is that the transfer is valued at only a fraction of what your home is worth because your child has to wait to get it. For

example, if you put your house, now worth $350,000, in a 10-year GRIT and you are 50 years old, its present value according to IRS tables is $172,165. By making the transfer, you will use up only that much of your lifetime exemption, instead of $350,000. Expect to pay an estate lawyer $1,500 to $2,000 to set up a GRIT. If you move out or die before the trust ends, the assets automatically will be included in your estate. Then your heirs will just have to grit and bear it.

Your Stake in Health Care Reform

Some version of Bill and Hillary Clinton's 1,342-page health reform bill probably will come to a vote late this year. But don't expect the revamping of the current system to improve your life any time soon. Even if legislation passes, any mandated changes would be years away. In the meantime, most employers will continue their rush to scale back medical coverage and shift more of the expenses onto employees. And they may even begin to step up the pace. "It's easier for companies to cut benefits now that the Administration says it's going to straighten out the health care mess," explains Lance Tane of benefits consultant Kwasha Lipton in Fort Lee, N.J.

There eventually will be universal coverage in this country. The public strongly favors a health system that guarantees care for all and eliminates the worry that losing a job could expose you to staggering medical bills. But Americans can't count on that kind of security for at least another three years. Until that day, you should expect health coverage to become more restrictive, expensive and, for the 37 million without it, harder to find. The goal of this chapter is to help you help yourself, starting now, before the possibly painful reality of medical reform is thrust upon you.

What to Do Until Health Reform Comes

While the debate rages on in Washington, your employer will likely keep reducing coverage and raising your costs. Here's how to cope now.

The facts basically tell the story. Today only about 65% of employees can choose traditional indemnity insurance that allows them to select any doctor they please, compared with 89% in 1988. Families are being asked to pay 25% of the cost of their premiums for indemnity coverage, vs. 21% three years ago. Or they pay 29% of premiums for health maintenance organizations (HMOs) that limit patients' choices of doctors and hospitals, vs. 24% three years ago. And some insurers have stopped offering individual indemnity coverage altogether.

To help you manage your health care costs while you wait for reform, check out these strategies for four types of people: 1) those who have coverage through an employer, 2) those who buy their own insurance, 3) those who lack coverage and 4) the retired.

Your coverage is subsidized by an employer. You will have to make do for now with the choices that your company currently offers. These often include both a traditional fee-for-service indemnity plan and a managed care plan (detailed later in this chapter). If you pay premiums and think you might incur a number of medical bills, you'll probably save money going with managed care. Your share of the premium may be higher than with a conventional plan (figure about $108 a month for family HMO membership, compared with $96 a month for indemnity coverage). But you should come out ahead because managed care usually has no annual deductible and minimal $5 to $15 out-of-pocket costs for each doctor visit, if any charge at all. On the other hand, if you are under 30, in good health and rarely see a doctor, you may save money by choosing the indemnity plan. Note, however, that the Clintons want to eliminate the ability of an employee to make pretax contributions to cover his or her portion of insurance premiums.

Everyone covered by indemnity plans should look for ways to hold down their doctors' bills. Reason: 20% or more of the money they spend comes straight out of their pockets. So before choosing a physician, inquire about his or her fee schedule and then call two or three other doctors to compare. Studies show that fees can vary by

633% from one doctor to another in the same city. Take St. Louis, where an office visit ranges from $15 to $110, according to Medirisk, a health care database in Atlanta. Also ask the local medical society whether there are any publications that offer comparisons of fees in your area. A new telephone service, Health Care Cost Hotline, can give you the median fee for any of 7,000 health services in any U.S. zip code. Average cost: $6 a call (800-383-3434).

Whatever type of plan you choose, take advantage of any wellness programs your company may offer. Some 2,200 employers now provide training to help workers change habits by, say, quitting smoking and eating right. About 4% of firms with wellness plans throw in financial sweeteners, such as a $100 yearly bonus for participants or a 10% discount in their health premiums. Does your company offer a flexible spending account, or FSA? It can be a significant tax saver because it lets you put aside pretax cash from your paycheck to meet medical expenses. Benefits consultant Foster Higgins estimates a single employee with adjusted gross income of $50,000 can save $249 a year in taxes by using an FSA to pay medical bills.

You buy medical coverage on your own. You can cut your premiums by raising your deductible. A major medical policy for a 35-year-old couple with two kids might run $3,708 a year with a $500 deductible. The policy costs 50% less, or $1,896, if you raise the deductible to $2,500. You can help defray the extra expenses you'll face if you get sick by banking the $151 monthly savings. You can also save by joining an organization that lets you obtain low group insurance rates. The self-employed can check into trade, professional or fraternal groups. If you're a professional woman, you could get 8% off the individual rate on major medical insurance from Mutual of Omaha by joining the National Association of Female Executives ($20 a year; 800-927-6233). Business owners and self-employed people may be able to pare their costs 30% by joining the Small Business Service Bureau (800-222-5678), a national insurance-buying coalition with annual dues of $125.

At the very least, solicit comparative quotes on premiums to make sure you're getting the best deal. For $15, Quotesmith (800-556-9393) will scan 150 insurers and provide a price list for at least 30 different policies suited to your needs.

You currently have no medical insurance. Until reform makes coverage available universally, you need to get insurance on your own even if it means scrimping elsewhere in your budget. After all, one costly illness can wipe you out. Look into an HMO if you use medical services heavily. A family in Boston might pay about $410 a month in HMO premiums, compared with around $489 for a typical indemnity plan. If you're about to lose coverage because of a layoff, investigate extending your benefits for 18 months by assuming the insurance costs yourself under the federal COBRA rules (the name stands for the 1986 Consolidated Omnibus Budget Reconciliation Act). Don't accept the coverage automatically, however, because your employer's policy may be more expensive than those offered by other insurers. Again, it pays to shop around.

You are in your retirement years. Health reform will probably improve your coverage but raise your medical costs. Later this decade Congress is likely to add prescription drug coverage to Medicare (the federal health insurance program for people 65 and older). The price: your annual Medicare premium, lately about $440 a person, might well rise by $130 or so to pay for these benefits. And health care experts think that Congress and the Clinton Adminstration will probably raise Medicare premiums for households with incomes exceeding $90,000, though by less than the White House's proposed 200% maximum increase.

For now, however, if you're over 65 you should have a supplemental private Medigap insurance policy to cover bills that Medicare doesn't. There are now 10 federally standardized Medigap policies available, each with varying amounts of coverage. The least expensive run about $340 a year for bare-bones insurance when you're 65. The most costly are about $3,600 a year at age 80 and cover prescription drugs, home health care and doctors' fees exceeding Medicare's limit for physicians in your area. The most expensive Medigap plan with the broadest coverage may not be the best one for you. For instance, if your doctor's fee is not above Medicare's limit, you don't need to buy excess-fees coverage. Make sure that you sign up for Medigap around the same time that you apply for Medicare. A 1991 law gives new Medicare recipients a six-month window during which they cannot be turned down for Medigap insurance.

If you're an early retiree in your fifties or early sixties without coverage from your former employer, insurance will continue to be a problem until health reform arrives. Insurers routinely charge people over 50, even those who are healthy, two or three times what they charge those under 30.

Worse, if you have a chronic condition such as diabetes or heart disease, coverage may not be available unless you live in one of the 28 states that have high-risk pools. In such an arrangement, an individual might have to pay $10,000 or more a year for insurance.

The White House proposal calls for early retirees to get their insurance coverage through government-run health alliances. Premiums would not be set by age, and the government would pick up 80% of the average tab for retirees with incomes below $90,000. But such generosity could cost $12 billion over three years starting in 1998. Thus many experts think it will have a difficult time getting through Congress. So early retirees need to explore every cost-cutting strategy, from joining HMOs to raising their deductibles.

Your Checkup on Managed Care

Reformers hope to cure soaring medical expenses with HMOs and kindred plans that limit patients' choice of doctors and hospitals. Here's our diagnosis.

Managed care is a catchall term for a style of delivering health services that's touted as the best remedy for curbing medical price inflation. True or not, managed care is here to stay. Insurers and company health plans have already stampeded into utilization review, a process in which an expert must approve many treatments in advance. Increasingly popular are HMOs, preferred provider organizations (PPOs) and plans called point of service (POS). All aim to shave costs by managing care and are defined on the right.

While these arrangements differ in detail, they're all based on the premise that treatment decisions are no longer up to you and your doctor alone. Instead, your choices are subject to approval by others whose mission is to curtail costs. Selection of doctors or hospitals often is limited too. Already 93% of all health plans employ utilization review, and more restrictive forms of managed care are growing rapidly. The share of insured

people covered by an HMO, PPO or POS rose from 27% in 1987 to 49% last year. Notes Michael Herbert of the American Managed Care and Review Association, a trade group: "People better get used to managed care because, in a few years, that may be all there is." Later in this chapter we provide advice on various ways that you can get the most out of the system.

The goal of managed care is to abolish the estimated 20% to 30% of treatment that may not be effective or necessary. Utilization review companies try to do this by requiring patients to notify them upon entering a hospital. If the review firm disapproves of the hospital stay, the patient can appeal. If the appeal is denied, the patient pays the bill. HMOs and the like practice more comprehensive cost control. The employer, or sometimes the patient, pays a flat or discounted fee for health care from a network of doctors and hospitals. Nonemergency treatment outside the network is

The ABCs of Managed Care

Plan	How it works	What you pay	Benefits
HMO	A specified group of doctors and hospitals provide the care. And a gatekeeper must approve all services before they are performed.	There isn't a deductible. The nominal fees generally range from nothing to $15 a visit depending on the service performed.	Virtually all services are covered, including preventive care. Out-of-pocket costs tend to be lower than any other managed care plan.
PPO	Network care comes from a specified group of physicians and hospitals. You can pay extra to get care from outside the network. There generally isn't a gatekeeper.	The typical yearly family deductible is $400. The plan pays 80% to 100% for what's done within the network but only 50% to 70% for services rendered outside it.	Preventive services may be covered. There are lower deductibles and copayments for care within the organization than for outside it.
POS	POSs combine the features of HMOs and PPOs. Patients can get care in or out of the network, but there is a gatekeeper who must approve all services.	In addition to a deductible, there is a flat $5 to $15 fee for network care, and you pay 20% to 50% of the bills for care you get outside the network.	Preventive services are generally covered. And there are low out-of-pocket costs for the care you get in the network.

only partially covered, or not covered at all, unless the network approves it. While treatment decisions are nominally up to doctor and patient, the network can overrule them. And the network often has an incentive to hold down costs, since that builds profits.

Supporters and critics of managed care agree the system usually brings cost savings when it is first implemented. A Congressional Budget Office review of the research literature concluded that HMOs that pay doctors a flat salary or a flat rate per patient provide care for 15% less than traditional insurance does. Employees get a break too, often paying no deductible and fees of just $5 to $15 per doctor visit including preventive care.

The evidence is mixed, however, on whether managed care can hold down the rate of price escalation once the system is in place. Backers of managed care say the system would contain costs better if only more people were enrolled in it. But critics counter that extending managed care's reach undermines its advantage for two reasons.

First, traditional plans tend to suffer from what's known as adverse selection. That means they attract older, sicker patients who need more care and have longstanding relationships with doctors who aren't in managed care networks. If managed care took on those high-cost patients, they say, its expenses would go up. Second, when managed care and traditional plans exist side by side, doctors and hospitals who accept lower fees for managed care patients may make up the difference by charging everyone else more. At first glance, it would seem that bringing all patients under managed care would end this practice. But doctors can, and often do, find other ways to prop up their incomes. At Southern California Edison, for example, managed care cut annual increases in health costs from 18% a year to only about 9% a year when first introduced in 1989. But the firm expects price hikes to return to 15% or so within five years. One reason: some doctors seem to be encouraging employees to see them more often so as to make up for low fees.

Managed care firms argue that, since they target only wasteful spending, they do not imperil the quality of care. Take, for example, the Baystate Medical Center in Springfield, Mass. Its managed care patients typically leave the intensive care unit two days earlier and the hospital five days sooner than do other patients with traditional insurance coverage. What's more, those managed patients are no more likely to die or to be readmitted later. But critics of managed care point to an inherent weakness of plans that rely on a limited list of doctors. Medical care has become so diverse that it's practically impossible for one HMO or PPO to include all specialties. The result: sometimes the sickest patients get the worst care.

Tim and Jana Devine of Santa Barbara may be victims of this problem. They say none of the pediatricians in Tim's HMO would agree to be the principal doctor for their year-old son Scott, who was born with a severe diaphragmatic hernia, because his care would be so complex and time

consuming. Thus Blue Cross of California, which pays bills for the HMO, refused to pick up any of the $750,000 cost of the nine operations Scott has had. Blue Cross's rationale was that no HMO physician had recommended the operations. Jana's traditional health insurance paid the bills instead, even though Tim's HMO was primary insurer.

Owing to a quirk of law, people wronged by such plans often have limited recourse. That's because almost all employer-paid health plans fall under the federal Employee Retirement and Income Security Act (ERISA), which allows workers to sue for lost benefits but not to collect damages. The Fifth U.S. Circuit Court of Appeals, in throwing out a patient's complaint because of ERISA, called on Congress to reevaluate the law because "bad medical judgments will end up being cost-free to the plans that rely on [utilization review] companies to contain medical costs."

How to Choose the Best Managed Plan

Whether it's a routine exam or major surgery, some managed care providers perform better than others. Here's what you need to know to spot a winner.

If you are one of the millions of Americans who would sooner take out your own appendix than join a managed care plan, prepare for a surprise. Supervised health care, the type provided by HMOs and other big medical networks, has actually provided high-quality care for millions of families during the past 20 years. That fact may fly in the face of stories you have heard about managed care being synonymous with first-degree hassles and second-class treatment. On average, the doctors and hospitals working under the managed care umbrella deserve good marks for their brand of health care, according to medical data and patient surveys.

Every industry, of course, has its lemons. By the end of this decade, an estimated 75 million Americans are expected to join today's 100 million enrolled in medical networks. Thus the challenge

for you is to separate the quality providers from the rest. The good news is that you can. Armed with some smart questions, it is possible to do a head-to-toe checkup on any plan you may be asked to consider. And you'll probably need to size up more than just one. Roughly half of all employers currently offer two or more managed care options including HMOs. Before you begin your research, you may need to jettison these widely held misconceptions:

Myth: Many doctors join managed care plans because they are too poorly qualified to attract patients on their own. On average, network medical staffs are 70% board certified. That means the physicians have completed three to seven years of hospital residency in their specialty and passed rigorous tests administered by medical specialty boards. Among all doctors who are practicing in the U.S. today, only 48% are board certified.

Myth: Quality of care often is secondary to cost savings in medical networks. "Not true," says Alan Hillman, director of the Center of Health Policy at the University of Pennsylvania. "Virtually every study that's looked at the quality of treatment has found network care to be as good as or better than treatment by doctors outside of managed care plans." Still, those studies deal with the averages. There are managed care plans that don't live up to the high standards advocates claim for them. Each year, HealthPlan Management Services, an Atlanta consultant, rates over 400 HMOs on 29 measures of price and quality. Their *HMO Buyers' Guide,* sold only to employers for a fee of $5,500, gives 109 HMOs top marks for high quality at a reasonable price. Scraping the bottom, however, are 114 plans that ranked low in quality but high in price. (On the following page, we present our ranking of the top 10 plans in America.)

How do you make sure you wind up in a plan that offers quality care? You may not have the choice, of course. If your employer is more dazzled by low price than high quality, the plans you are offered will show it. In most cases, however, workers have the option of sticking with traditional fee-for-service indemnity insurance, albeit at higher out-of-pocket cost. Thus knowing how to evaluate a plan's quality can help you avoid a costly, even catastrophic mistake.

Start with your employee benefits department. In screening competing providers, your employer may have gathered most of the information you'll want. If you can't get the facts you want from your employer, phone the managed care plan directly. Be aware that most plans don't field many tough questions from consumers, so you may get the runaround at first. You should persist, however. A first rate plan will try to give you all the information you seek, even if it means you must take your questions to the plan's medical director. Here are the three areas you should focus on:

How good are the plan's doctors? To begin evaluat-

ing the quality of its medical staff, get the doctor directory for the plan you're considering and see whether you or anyone you know can spot a physician you trust. Then call that doctor and ask what he or she thinks of colleagues in the plan. If the impression is favorable, you'll hear about it instantly. If it isn't, get ready for an indirect response that can speak volumes. If you get one, look elsewhere for a health care provider.

Money Helps

Q. Under my health insurance at work, I pay 20% of the cost of services outside of a medical network designated by the company. The insurer picks up the other 80%. I have been told that when doctors and hospitals bill an insurer, they often charge less than the full "retail" price. So on a $100 medical bill, I might get billed for $20 while my insurer pays the health care provider only $60. Does that sound like an 80-20 split to you?
—David Williams, W. Bloomfield, Mich.

A. Hardly. Many insurers have contracts with hospitals and medical groups that let them buy health care at a discount. But if your insurer gets a price break, says Bob Eicher of benefits consultant Foster Higgins, you are legally entitled to the same percentage reduction on your portion of the bill. Lots of mistakes are being made, however, because of the complexity of the new types of medical networks. So sometimes insurance companies fail to pass on the discounts. There is a clever way, however, to make sure you are getting a fair shake. Ask the medical service provider to bill you for the full amount and forward the bill to your insurer for payment of its share. The insurer will send you a confirmation showing exactly how much it paid the provider and how much you owe.

The 10 Best HMOs in America

	HMO	Location	Number of people enrolled	Comment
1.	Kaiser Foundation Health Plan	San Francisco	2,437,117	Started in 1945. Rated No.1 for past four years. A full 99% of children in the plan are immunized.
2.	Kaiser Foundation Health Plan	Los Angeles	2,258,328	Excels in programs for children. Also relies on extensive patient database to monitor its care.
3.	Harvard Community Health Plan	Boston	545,000	Pioneered usage of computerized medical record keeping system for quick access to patient data.
4.	Group Health	Minneapolis	327,000	An impressive 95% of network doctors are board certified, well above the 70% HMO average.
5.	TakeCare Health Plan	San Francisco	366,681	Emphasizes personal attention; no automated phone response, just live operators.
6.	HMO PA-U.S. Healthcare	Philadelphia	660,000	Strong advocate of preventive medicine. For example, promotes immunization and mammograms.
7.	Group Health Cooperative	Seattle	478,000	Among the most consumer-oriented HMOs, its board of trustees is elected by members.
8.	PacifiCare of California	Los Angeles	767,472	Has affiliations with 291 hospitals, the largest number among the top 10.
9.	Pilgrim Health Care	Boston	265,000	Independent surveys of patients show 96% satisfaction, well above average.
10.	MedCenters Health Plan	Minneapolis	251,260	A leader in measuring medical outcomes; patients are asked to rate the results of their care.

Note: Both Group Health (No. 4) and MedCenters (No. 10) are managed by HealthPartners, their parent company. Source: HealthPlan Management Services.

You'll also want to find out the percentage of network doctors who are board certified. You can get that information in the physician directory or from the plan. One that falls short of the 70% network average for board certification is probably not setting high enough standards. A caveat: there are over 100 self-styled medical boards that offer membership with little or no testing requirements. Be sure the certification a doctor claims reflects membership in one of the 24 boards recognized by the American Board of Medical Specialties (as do the boards counted in the 70% average cited above). If you have any lingering doubts, you should check the certification of a physician by calling the ABMS at 800-776-2378.

Other valuable bits of information can be gleaned from the forms doctors must fill out to join the plan, which plan sponsors should furnish to consumers without hesitation. Any reluctance to do so may signal that the network is less probing than it ought to be. Besides education and training, the form also should ask for the doctor's malpractice insurer. Ask whether the application information is verified and how often it's updated. The best plans check everything and update every two years. If a plan doesn't, think twice about using it. Beyond the application information, you should ask the plan whether it has obtained a copy of each doctor's current profile in the National Practitioner Data Bank. This federal file tracks malpractice suits and other disciplinary actions that have been taken against doctors.

Will cost take precedence over care? There's no proof that the cost consciousness of most medical networks cuts the quality of care. Yet doctors, like most people, may find it difficult to keep money entirely out of their minds when doing their jobs. "It's just human nature not to do the work if you're not going to earn any additional money," says San Francisco physician Daniel Hartman, who gets 60% of his patients via managed care. Such plans use several different payment schemes for doctors. But all place some restraints on their income, and some may even penalize them for ordering up a lot of patient services. Each doctor responds to these influences differently. While it is impossible to scrutinize quality based on how (and how much) a plan pays doctors, you should make a personal assessment after you join. If the doctors seem unmotivated or uninterested, you can always vote with your feet.

The most important test of quality, of course, is whether the patient gets well and stays that way. All plans keep track of utilization—that is, patients' use of services such as office visits, lab tests and hospital days. But the best ones also monitor outcomes—how the care affects patients. Ask the network how many unplanned surgeries patients had last year, not just how many operations were performed overall. This research shows whether doctors are doing an adequate job of anticipating the need for surgery. Also ask how many hospital admissions were actually cases of re-admission within 30 days of discharge. That's a suggestion doctors are discharging patients too soon. The point isn't for you to analyze the answers—most will be too complicated for a lay person to decipher. It's to test whether the plan collects the data you need to evaluate it.

One way managed care plans cut costs is to restrict patients' access to specialists or at least discourage it. To this end, most have so-called gatekeepers—doctors who must authorize any consultations you have with specialists. If it's important to you to see a specialist on your own initiative, pick a plan with no gatekeeper. Also ask about preventive services. Some plans leave it up to you to get preventive care or not. Others keep individ-

ual records on patients and follow up with letters or phone messages if, say, a patient is overdue for a mammogram. You should ask the plan you're investigating how it makes sure patients get preventive services. While you may consider personal contacts a nuisance, they do indicate that a plan is serious about your health.

Ask about accreditation. Although some state insurance departments monitor HMOs and PPOs for solvency and sometimes mediate consumer complaints, they don't review the quality of medical care. And the federal government qualifies HMOs to receive payments from Medicare or Medicaid. But quality standards are not very rigorous. Two voluntary accrediting agencies, however, have begun certifying managed care plans on more stringent measures than before. The National Committee for Quality Assurance, which evaluates HMOs, has accredited about 50 of the 546 plans in the U.S. since it began work in 1991. The American Accreditation Program has vetted about 120 of the estimated 500 PPOs since 1990. Don't subtract points from a plan that lacks accreditation. Instead, favor one that does because accreditation offers an extra assurance of quality.

How satisfied will you be? Top-quality medical care is the surest guarantor of a happy patient. But it's not enough. A chaotic waiting room or a phone system operated by computers instead of people may drive you wild. If so, ask the plan's representative about both. Find out how long you'll have to wait for an appointment. The average for an urgent visit to an HMO physician is about three days. The wait for a routine visit averages four weeks. How much time with the doctor is allotted per patient? The average is 15 minutes.

You may also want to ask about demographics. Is your age group in the majority or minority of the plan's members? Being in the majority often means that more services and attention will be directed to your concerns. Find out whether the plan compiles a patient satisfaction survey and, if so, ask for a copy. Most HMOs and some PPOs do, and it is an indication that the plan wants to keep subscribers happy. You should ask whether doctors are formally rewarded with raises or bonuses for good reviews from patients. Again, it shows that patients' views really count.

One of the more traumatic things that can happen to you in a plan is to lose the doctor who has been treating you. Turnover rates in networks range from 5% to 15% a year, depending on the type of contracts doctors sign. Some plans will allow you to continue with a doctor who has left, at the plan's expense, until treatment is completed. Others will require you to switch. Be sure to ask

about a plan's policy, especially if you have a condition that may require lengthy treatment.

Ask how you and the plan would resolve disputes over care. The best method is a formal grievance procedure with a panel of medical reviewers. Worst is an ad hoc approach, with no systematic response to these problems. Also ask what percentage of disputes were resolved within one month. It should be 75% or more. Otherwise, the plan is either inefficient at resolving problems or, worse, generating serious problems you should avoid.

Health Reform's Winners and Losers

Will efforts to rein in runaway medical costs help or hurt you? Here are answers for 11 situations, one of which probably mirrors your own.

Senator John Rockefeller IV of West Virginia calls the health care revolution "the largest undertaking in our social history." If anything, that's an understatement. Such reform proposes to: 1) curb escalating health care spending, an estimated $940 billion last year; 2) guarantee full care to everyone, thereby adding as much as $90 billion a year to Americans' tax bills; 3) change dramatically the practice and delivery of medicine; and 4) find common ground among hundreds of interest groups, including doctors, drugmakers, hospitals, insurers and employers.

This sea change mostly will affect middle-income workers who are neither rich enough to afford independent specialists nor old enough to qualify for Medicare nor poor enough to be eligible for Medicaid. The following profiles of people like you should serve to explain who figures to win under reform, who probably will lose and who's currently too close to call.

Reform's Likely Winners

Employed but buys own coverage. Debbie Brown, the San Diego Chamber of Commerce's special-

events coordinator, pays her employer $245 a month (8% of her salary) for her husband's and kids' insurance. The Chamber puts up $196 a month for hers. "We're in an HMO," says Debbie, "and we don't get coverage for vision or dental care." Last year she paid $400 for eyeglasses, but decided she couldn't come up with $1,500 for braces for one of the kids. These expenses are more affordable now that Debbie has opened an employee flexible spending account, which will allow her to pay $5,000 a year of medical bills with salary set aside before taxes.

Prognosis: "Everyone buying their own health insurance—whether employed or self-employed—will get the same type of policy for 15% to 20% less after reform," says Robert Blendon, a professor of health policy at Harvard. "Many people will get more comprehensive coverage for what they pay now for a bare-bones policy." That's because giant health care cooperatives will bid for low-cost coverage for individuals as well as employees of small businesses. Such small businesses often don't provide company-paid insurance.

Self-employed with soaring premiums. Pat and

David Coggins, antiques store owners based in Marblehead, Mass., have watched their annual Blue Cross/Blue Shield premiums jump 173% to $3,000 over the past decade. And the bill rose 22% to $3,660 this year. They have a $2,500-per-person deductible and Pat says: "Heaven help us if something happens to both of us at once."
Prognosis: When health reform is in place, the Cogginses' costs will probably plateau at around $4,000 a year for a much broader policy with possibly no deductible. The couple will be covered for visits to doctors, prescription drugs, annual checkups and other preventive care—items that they currently pay for themselves.

Out of work and in poor health. Robert Ruggles was a customer service manager at Tandem Computers in Santa Ana, Calif. for 14 years until his job was eliminated in late 1990. Since then, he and his wife Edith have been unable to find affordable insurance, largely because of pre-existing conditions. Robert has the skin disorder lupus, which is in remission, and he and Edith both have high blood pressure. Blue Cross of California says that they might be accepted into a high-risk plan with premiums up to $800 a month. But that's out of the question. The couple live on investment income of $2,000 a month in addition to the $800 each earns monthly from part-time work.
Prognosis: Rules on pre-existing conditions will change, predicts Ed Howard of the Alliance for Health Reform, a nonpartisan advocacy group in Washington, D.C. Insurers won't be allowed to reject people like the Ruggleses, and less costly policies will be available.

Senior citizen with Medicare and Medigap. Agnes Ranseen of Evanston, Ill. is unhappy with her health care coverage, and she doesn't believe reform will make it any better. The retired social studies teacher has annual pension and Social Security income exceeding $13,000. Every month she pays $17 for Medicare (after receiving a rebate from her pension fund) and nearly $45 for a Blue Cross/Blue Shield hospitalization policy with a

Money Helps

**Q. I want my husband to purchase some disability insurance because he is the major breadwinner for our family of four. He's 31 and had an intestinal condition that was corrected three years ago. His employer provides disability insurance that would replace 40% of his income after six months but only up to a maximum of $100 a week. Quotes I've received from other companies are astronomical. Are there any good low-cost insurers?
—Kandi Speegle, Tulsa**

A. Most group disability policies like the one provided by your husband's employer cover 40% of salary. He could also receive as much as $1,375 a month in Social Security disability benefits—but only if he can hold no other job and is disabled for more than one year. So your conclusion that you need extra coverage is correct. Insurance experts tend to be coy about quoting prices. It all depends, they say, on the age and income of the individual, whether there would be cost-of-living adjustments and so on. Fee for Service (800-874-5662), a Tampa-based national network of salaried (no commission) insurance brokers, offers one disability policy underwritten by John Alden. Coverage that would pay $2,250 a month after 90 days of disability runs about $500 a year. That cost is 15% to 20% less than those of other policies, according to Fee for Service spokesperson Judith Maurer. The hitch is your husband's past medical problem. If it is the kind of condition that could recur, insurers may refuse to sell him a disability policy or else charge him a higher premium. So you should start beefing up your savings now. Then you won't be so dependent on your husband's income.

The Lowdown on Dental HMOs

If you work for a company with 100 or more employees, chances are your dental bills don't have much bite. That's because nearly 90% of such companies provide dental plans that pick up 50% to 100% of your cost and let you choose any dentist you please.

This comfortable scenario is likely to change under health care reform. If the Clinton Administration's broad package of benefits is enacted, warns Bob Eicher of consultant Foster Higgins in New York City, many companies will pay more for coverage. A likely place to save is dental care, which "the Clintons' plan provides for children but not for adults except in some emergencies." Thus many companies may drop their conventional dental insurance and only offer employees managed dental plans similar in structure to HMOs.

Dental HMOs limit you to seeing dentists enrolled in the plan but charge premiums that can cost 30% less than those of an unrestricted plan. There's usually no deductible, compared with $25 to $50 a year under a conventional plan, and the dental HMO pays 100% of the cost of preventive and routine services instead of 50% to 80%. Both types of plans provide roughly equal maximum annual payments of $1,000 or so for orthodontics.

If your company offers a choice between a traditional plan and a dental HMO, as some 10% of employers now do, should you try managed care? You should, says Donald Mayes, a Hershey, Pa. expert on dental benefits, provided that the answer is yes to these four questions:

• Do the plan's general dentists belong to the American Academy of General Dentistry and are specialists board eligible or board certified by appropriate dental groups?

• Does the plan hold expenses to no more than 15% of budget, leaving enough for patient care?

• Are preventive services such as exams and cleanings covered at no out-of-pocket cost?

• Does the wait for nonemergency dental care from the plan average four weeks or fewer?

$500 deductible. "Hardly any of my bills are covered," she complains. "I'll use the doctor only if I'm critically ill. I think that's a foolish way to take care of myself." Even so, she opposes managed care: "I hate the idea of not being able to choose my own doctor."

Prognosis: With prescription drugs likely to be covered early in the reform process and some coverage for long-term care phased in later, the twin terrors of the elderly will be tamed. Most other retiree medical expenses would be covered too, with the probable exception of dental care. Perhaps by the year 2000, say experts, Medicare will be folded into the reformed system and recipients will join big regional plans. The result: lower cost but, as Ranseen suspects, less choice.

A pair of country doctors. Catherine McGinnis and husband James Allen, both physicians, work in a group practice in Hutchinson, Minn. (population 11,500). Like most country doctors, McGinnis worries most about how managed care would work in an area where competition is impractical and the nearest rival clinic is 45 minutes away in Waconia. "Rural doctors and hospitals are already reimbursed at lower rates than those in urban areas, so it's hard to think we'll have further cuts," she says.

Prognosis: Harvard's Blendon points out that, as the Clintons of Arkansas well know, pure cutthroat managed competition won't work in isolated rural areas. For this reason, reform will bring less change there—including fewer HMOs—than anywhere else. Moreover, he says, "there will be an effort to pay rural doctors more to attract practitioners to the country."

Reform's Likely Losers

Divorced Mom with A+ coverage. To Karen Long of Tacoma, Wash., health care heaven is spelled Weyerhaeuser. As project manager for internal communications at the giant forest-products company, Long pays $30 a month to cover herself and her three children. Her plan requires her to pay a $500 yearly deductible before she's reimbursed for 80% of bills but caps her out-of-pocket costs at $3,000. And she has total freedom to choose her doctors. "We have great preventive-care coverage for dental checkups and cleaning, screenings like mammograms and good prescription drug coverage," she says.

Prognosis: "Families with superior coverage and low premiums will either pay more or get less coverage," says Ed Howard of the Alliance for Health Reform. If employers wind up losing their tax deduction for what they spend to provide coverage over a certain level—a possibility under reform—many might "opt for the bare minimum package of benefits," says Bill Gradison, president of the Health Insurance Association of America in Washington, D.C.

Too young to afford coverage. Vida Petronis, a freelance copy editor in New York City, doesn't think she needs health coverage. Nor does she think she can afford it. She rejected a bare-bones Blue Cross/Blue Shield policy with no deductible that would have cost her $1,200 a year (6% of her more than $20,000 income). Her fear is that reform will force her to buy unnecessary coverage. "I'm young and healthy and take very good care of myself," she says. "The standard package is likely to have more benefits than I need or want. Putting everybody in the same risk pool means that I'll have to subsidize people with bad health habits. I don't really think that's fair."

Prognosis: Like it or not, Petronis and other

healthy young people will have to pay for coverage. Uwe Reinhardt, a health care economist at Princeton, estimates that people at Petronis' income level or above could end up paying a mandatory $1,800 a year, making the $1,200 policy she rejected seem like a bargain. One small consolation is that premiums would almost certainly be tax deductible for the self-employed, trimming Petronis' cost by $270.

A big-city medical specialist. New Orleans radiologist Edward Soll fears that reform will severely squeeze physicians' incomes. But as director of Diagnostic Imaging Services, an outpatient radiology business, he believes he and his two partners will do just fine. DIS has a payroll of $3.5 million and serves about 100,000 patients a year at fees ranging from $95 for mammograms to $895 for magnetic resonance imaging. About two-thirds of Soll's business comes from Medicare, Medicaid and contract services like HMOs. After reform that figure could push inexorably toward 100% by the end of the decade, making it impossible to shift costs onto private patients. Still he says, "I'm not worried. We'll get more business under reform, albeit at generally lower fees."

Prognosis: Some specialists like Soll may be able to pump up their patient volume after health care reform. But most probably will see their fees contract and their incomes fall.

Too Close to Call

A victim of catastrophic illness. Jane Hawley of Phoenix is dying of AIDS. "I discovered I had it in 1990 when it was full-blown," she says. "I think I got it in 1979 or 1980 from a lover." With perhaps a year to live, she is too weak to work. She is not eligible for Medicaid under Arizona's strict rules; her $484 monthly Social Security disability income exceeds the state's $267 maximum. But her disability does qualify her for Medicare, which pays 80% of her doctor bills. And under the federal Ryan White Act, her income is low enough to qualify her for free antiviral drugs like AZT and

DDC. But for the six other medicines she needs, she taps the AIDS underground, which retrieves drugs left by the deceased and distributes them illegally to the needy. "I've stockpiled as many drugs as I can find, maybe four months' worth, because I know I'm getting weaker by the day," she says. "I'll have to move in with my parents pretty soon, and they can't go looking for drugs for me." **Prognosis:** Reform almost certainly will come too late to help Jane Hawley. But it will be a boon to

---

Money Helps

Q. My 22-year-old daughter graduates from college soon. She plans to travel in Europe for a year or so, doing odd jobs and hoping to land a permanent spot. My group health policy covers her only if she is a student, though. How can I insure her until she finds a full-time job?
—**Michael Conway, Littleton, Colo.**

A. You are in a Catch-22. Most individual U.S. policies will not cover her abroad. And most European policies won't protect her if she returns to the U.S., which she might do on holidays. European countries sometimes provide medical service free to each other's citizens. But visiting Americans usually aren't eligible for more than emergency care. To be safe, buy two policies. For protection abroad, choose one like International Lifeline from British United Provident Association in London ($644 a year; 44-71-353-5212). It pays hospital bills up to $288,000 and out-patient fees up to $1,440 anywhere except the U.S. and Canada. And for home, get a U.S. policy like MedFlex Major Medical from Mutual of Omaha ($1,228 a year; 303-755-0357), which covers her for as much as $1 million in hospital and outpatient expenses. With those premiums, of course, you may have to take an odd job yourself.

AIDS patients, as well as to many others made dependent on costly drugs by illnesses. That's because there's a strong chance Congress will put some prescription drug coverage into the basic package of benefits it passes. And every benefit in that package will go to Medicaid recipients as well.

Spouse needs long-term care. Jack McClenaghan, a retired corporate controller in Portland, Ore., was diagnosed with Alzheimer's in 1984. The disease has progressed to the point where Jack "walks, breathes, feeds himself—and that's about it," says wife Mary Lou. He has not been able to talk for years and generally recognizes no one but his wife, not even his children. Medicare covers 80% of Jack's doctor bills but none of his living expenses. He is now in foster care, which costs Mary Lou $1,650 a month (more than half of the couple's $3,000-a-month income from family savings, Jack's pension and Social Security). Jack's otherwise robust health ("He has the blood pressure of a 12-year-old," says Mary Lou) indicates that he will live for many more years. Although his wife hopes that reform will bring her some relief, she says: "I'm worried we may have too much income to be eligible for long-term-care benefits."
Prognosis: Most health care experts agree that some long-term care coverage will be included in the basic reform package. But it may not be phased in until the end of the decade.

A businesswoman doesn't cover employees. Laurie Neuse and partners at restaurant Spaghettini in Seal Beach, Calif. have dropped HMO coverage for their 80 employees, including a number of parents who had worked for them since 1988. "We could no longer afford it," says Neuse. Over the three years the insurance was in force, costs jumped from $3,500 to $5,000 a month.
Prognosis: What's good for employees is not so great for employers. Many small businesses struggle financially, one reason why a third offer no health plans to employees. Princeton's Reinhardt predicts that businesses with 100 or fewer workers will be awarded government subsidies, probably when health expenses exceed 8% of payroll.

Cut Your Spiraling Drug Costs

*Prescription prices have doubled over the past decade. Here's how you
can realize significant savings starting today.*

Nobody needs to remind consumers that drug prices soared six times faster than inflation from 1980 through 1992, up 128% on average. As part of the Clintons' health reform package, Congress is likely to include voluntary price caps such as a proposal by the Pharmaceutical Manufacturers Association (PMA) to impose a ceiling on average annual price increases. Although that may not happen this year, there are steps you can begin taking today to keep your pill bills low. Here are reasons why drug prices went out of sight and four ways to cut your prescription costs by as much as 70%:

How Prices Spun Out of Control

Drug companies often cite these self-serving industry arguments to justify their pricing.

● **The industry line:** Drug companies need to recoup their research-and-development outlays, which have doubled since 1987. **The reality:** Though R&D costs are substantial and have mounted, some drugmakers broaden the definition of research to include marketing expenses. That practice can artificially inflate R&D figures by as much as 25%, says economist Steven Schondelmeyer at the University of Minnesota. PMA spokesman Dave Emerick disputes that finding, however, saying that there's no hard data on market research.

● **The industry line:** The pharmaceutical business is high risk. The PMA now estimates that only one in five new medications gets approved by the U.S. Food and Drug Administration. Thus prices must be high enough to reward shareholders for taking risks. **The reality:** Even so, it is hard to justify recent price hikes. Since 1986, drugmakers' profits

have risen about four times faster than those of the average Fortune 500 company. And drug companies have substantially reduced their risks. One strategy they've pursued is to focus on "me too" drugs at the expense of riskier breakthrough medicines. The idea is to grab a share of a lucrative market by creating a costlier drug that essentially duplicates a competitor's product while being just different enough in chemical composition to warrant its own patent.

● **The industry line:** Marketers contend that me toos offer key advantages, such as formulations that pack the effectiveness of three pills into one. **The reality:** Over the past 12 years, more than 80% of all new drugs were rated by the FDA as offering little or no therapeutic gain over existing drugs. Even when a newer drug is proved to be only slightly more helpful than an older one, the price difference can be heart-stopping. For example, a recent study shows that a cardiac drug called t-PA is 1% more effective than Streptokinase. But t-PA costs $2,200 per treatment, or six times more than Streptokinase.

● **The industry line:** A drug must be priced high so its maker can recoup R&D costs before the 17-year patent expires, exposing the company to competition from cheaper generics. **The reality:** Drug companies typically raise prices when a drug's patent expires, so increased revenues can partially offset losses in sales. In fact, price inflation is often greatest on medications that have been sold for decades. For instance, Wyeth-Ayerst hiked the cost of Premarin, an estrogen replacement pill sold since the 1950s, almost 15% annually from 1987 to 1992, vs. a 4% annual rise in inflation during the same period. Spokesman Audrey Ashby counters that the company had to spend money on recent clinical trials that found additional uses for Premarin, such as reducing risk of heart disease.

If the industry's excuses had validity, drug prices would have always soared. But prices took off in the late 1970s, when the industry found a way to create almost unlimited demand for some drugs by marketing them directly to patients. Until then, drug companies assumed that demand for a drug could not be stretched beyond the need determined by physicians. In August 1977 the FDA announced its approval of Tagamet, a revolutionary antiulcer drug from SmithKline that eliminated the need for surgery for most ulcer sufferers. The Tagamet approval brought a whirlwind of publicity. The drug was featured on network news, and pharmacies were bombarded with orders. The industry realized that "if this kind of publicity could generate this kind of demand with one drug, it could be made to happen with others," former drug company spokesman David Jones told FDA officials.

Industry analysts estimate that 22% of drug company revenues is spent on advertising and marketing, compared with less than 10% of revenues for other heavily promoted products such as beer and detergents. Most of the marketing dollars go toward persuading doctors and hospital pharmacy directors to prescribe or buy a company's offerings. The drugmakers send over their 50,000 sales representatives, advertise heavily in medical journals and employ many clever promotional schemes. Pharmaceutical promotional efforts in recent years have ranged from sending doctors on exotic vacations under the guise of continuing medical education to even awarding frequent-flier miles for every prescription a doctor writes for a given drug.

The promoters are so good at what they do that doctors don't always realize they're being hustled. Frederick Fenster, an internist at Seattle's Virginia Mason Center and a professor at the University of Washington, recalls a presentation at his hospital by a visiting professor who advocated using new drugs to treat elderly patients with high blood pressure. "His talk made it seem like you were guilty of malpractice if you didn't use the newer medications," says Fenster. "Soon after I switched a few patients to them, they practically attacked me because the new drugs cost 10 times what they were paying." It wasn't until later that Fenster learned the professor was paid by a drug company to make his presentation.

How You Can Fight Back

Ask for a generic version of the drug. If available, generics can save you as much as 70% of the price of brand-name prescription drugs. For instance, 20 capsules (500 mg each) of the generic form of the antibiotic Keflex cost about $16, a saving of nearly $40 over the brand name's standard $55 price. Switching to a generic may not be advisable if you need a drug requiring precise adjustments of dosage, as is common with antiepileptic drugs or some cardiac and asthma medications.

Comparison shop at pharmacies. For example: Charles Yahn of Rockford, Ill. takes Mevacor, a cholesterol-lowering drug. He has found the price of his prescription ranges from $43 for 30 tablets (20 mg) at Wal-Mart to $53 at a local discount drugstore, a 24% difference. One reason: chains typically charge less than independent pharmacies because chains get bigger volume discounts.

Consider mail-order pharmacies. A recent Health Insurance Association of America survey found that people over 65 can save approximately $120 a year by purchasing prescription drugs for chronic conditions from mail-order houses. Three large ones: Action Mail Order (P.O. Box 787, Waterville, Maine 04903; 800-452-1976); Family Pharmaceuticals (P.O. Box 1288, Mount Pleasant, S.C. 29465; 800-922-3444) and Medi-Mail (871-C Grier Dr., Las Vegas, Nev. 89119; 800-331-1458).

Ask your benefits office about discounts. A growing number of large and medium-size companies now offer savings of as much as 10% to 25%. Some have programs that let employees buy drugs at a discount at participating drugstores, and others have arrangements with mail-order plans.

CHAPTER

4

The New Realities of Retirement

Like many Americans, you probably are determined to provide for your family and then retire, perhaps well before the traditional exit age of 65, without drastically reducing your standard of living. Achieving that goal won't be easy. Lots of today's retirees successfully called it quits without a plan, cruising on autopilot, kept aloft by generous company pensions, Social Security and the fabulous price appreciation of houses bought decades earlier. No longer. The generation facing retirement in the next 10 or 20 years is bucking powerful downdrafts. With baby boomers' hunger for housing largely satisfied, the value of most families' biggest asset probably won't grow more than 4% or so a year. And as the population bulge moves into retirement age, the vast numbers will force cutbacks in public and private retiree benefits, most drastically in medical insurance coverage.

What all this means is that if you expect to retire comfortably, you could have to make some hard sacrifices starting now. You might, for example, have to tell your kids to set their sights on first-rate public colleges rather than expensive private schools. And once you retire, you may be forced to switch from your family doctor to an HMO for affordable care. Assistance abounds, fortunately. Several financial services firms, including mutual fund sponsors Fidelity, T. Rowe Price and Vanguard, have developed software programs that can help you estimate how much you need to save for retirement (refer to "The Top Retirement Software" later in this chapter). A more rigorous though costly approach to consider is to seek the help of an experienced financial planner (typical cost: $600 to $800). But even if you follow this path, be assured that the heavy lifting, as well as the delicious payoff, will still be yours.

How to Retire Sooner with More

To retire with all the money you will ever need, you must know where to put your savings now and how to handle your medical bills later.

Seven years ago, Jim and Shirley Kelley, then 56 and 55, fled from Raleigh, N.C. for the Caribbean breezes of St. Thomas, where they now dock their retirement home, the 46-foot sloop Whimsey. While the Kelleys' life may sound like a fantasy, it actually was the product of careful planning. In 1987, Jim, a marketing manager at IBM, took an early-out offer that sweetened his pension by 25%, to $33,000 a year. He then landed a job teaching data processing at the University of the Virgin Islands through an IBM program that, for two years, paid him 35% of his final salary. In 1989 he turned that appointment into a faculty position that now pays $38,000 annually, plus medical benefits. Today, he teaches four days a week, which leaves plenty of time for long weekend cruises with Shirley. In addition, to offset the Whimsey's $8,000 annual bill for maintenance

and repair, Shirley leads cruises and offers instructional classes in scuba diving. "People say we were lucky," says Jim. "But we put ourselves in the position to be lucky by exploring options and checking out what we could do in retirement."

Whether you dream of sailing the Caribbean or simply gardening in the backyard, a successful early retirement can be yours if you plan for it aggressively. A recent MONEY survey found that 55% of Americans hope to retire before 65. But many will be disappointed unless they boost their saving today. Baby boomers typically save only about a third of the amount they will need to maintain their pre-retirement standard of living, according to a study for Merrill Lynch by Princeton University economist Douglas Bernheim. This means that you have to resolve several key issues to make early retirement a reality.

What you need to set aside. Deciding to retire early demands the right temperament as well as enough money. (To gauge the former, take the quiz "Are You Ready for Early Retirement?" later in this chapter.) After all, a lot of people say they expect to retire between ages 50 and 64. If so, they will likely live another 18 to 29 years on average. The most content early retirees are people who developed outside interests while working; their identities were not wedded to their careers. "If you can't come up with 30 things you like to do, you're not a good candidate for early retirement yet," says Robert Atchley of the Scripps Gerontology Center at Miami University.

Once you decide you're cut out for early retirement, you must determine whether you can swing it financially. (For estimates of the costs and savings involved, fill out the worksheets beginning on pages 70 and 76.) Expect that your post-career expenses will still equal roughly 70% to 80% of your pre-retirement income. Next, figure how much you can safely expect from Social Security and your company pension. Social Security now replaces an average of 38% of pre-retirement income, with the percentage falling as your salary climbs above roughly $35,000. About 60% of retirees get company pensions, which replace an average of 40% of pre-retirement income. Pension formulas typically are based on your years of service and your salary for the last five years on the job. Ask your benefits department for an estimate of the pension you can expect at age 55 and at your company's normal retirement age, usually 65. Some employers will also calculate your pension starting on the date you hope to leave work.

How to structure your nest egg. Chances are that your retirement portfolio needs an overhaul in 1994 to compensate for today's sky-high markets and equally lofty income tax rates. Let's start with bonds and bond funds. Your problem here may be that you have too much money in them. When interest rates dropped 1.6 percentage points in 1993, bond portfolios made sharp gains. So you may need to trim the fixed-income portion of your savings back to where you really want it to be.

And with long-term rates poised to rise half a percentage point this year, you may want to tilt your bond holdings toward shorter maturities to protect against price declines.

As for stocks, remember that you're dealing with your retirement funds, the longest of your long-term investments. That means establishing broad allocations of your retirement portfolio based upon your age. In your twenties and thirties, stocks or stock funds should make up as much as 70% to 80% of the mix, with the balance in bond investments. As you approach early retirement you will want to start gradually reducing the stock portion until it hits a still sizable 50% at retirement. Why? With inflation and the long life expectancy of retirees, you need growth in your portfolio.

Given the steep new top tax brackets of 36% and 39.6%, choosing the most tax-advantaged and cost-efficient vehicles for your retirement needs will also help your nest egg grow faster. Someone setting aside $4,000 a year for 35 years in a company-sponsored 401(k) plan earning 8% on average will have $744,409 at retirement, compared with only $301,042 if he or she had put the same amount in taxable investments. (See page 73 for an overview of such tax-deferred savings plans.)

Why your company plans are so crucial. With capital gains still taxed at 28%, upper-income investors with portfolios outside their sheltered retirement plans might put income-oriented investments into the plans and keep stocks that produce only capital gains outside. But your first retirement savings dollars should go into workplace plans such as 401(k)s. "What's important for retirement is putting money away early," says accountant Andrea Markezin of Ernst & Young, "and funding your 401(k) is a real no brainer." Contributions this year of up to an estimated $9,235 are automatically taken out of your paycheck in pretax dollars, giving you the discipline of enforced savings and a tax cutter at the same time. Better yet, 86% of companies offering 401(k)s match at least part of your contribution, producing an automatic gain. If you work for a nonprofit organization or a school, your employer may offer a 403(b) pension plan or a tax-sheltered annuity in which you can stash up to $9,500 pretax this year.

If you are self-employed, you can shelter much more. Some sole proprietors find a simplified employee pension (SEP) is the easiest solution. The maximum 1994 contribution is 13% of net business income, or $22,500, whichever is less. A business owner nearing retirement can sock away the most, however, via a special type of defined-benefit Keogh that can be funded this year with an estimated annual benefit of up to $118,737.

A small-business owner setting up a plan for employees as well may want to opt for a profit-sharing Keogh, whose annual contribution limit for the business owner is the same as a SEP's. The employer contributes to employees' accounts according to a formula based on their income. A profit-sharing Keogh is more flexible than a SEP, enabling you to vary contributions to employee accounts using such factors as age or length of service. If you want to invest even more for retirement for you and your staff, you should consider combining a profit-sharing Keogh with a money-purchase Keogh and put away an additional 7% of net earnings. But you'll have to commit to a set contribution level every year.

What about IRAs and annuities? Since tax reform cut the full deductibility of Individual Retirement Accounts, they have been overlooked by many investors. Yet IRAs should still be the second place for your retirement savings after completely funding company plans. You'll qualify for a full or a partial IRA deduction if you don't have a company pension or if your adjusted gross income falls below $50,000 for a married couple or $35,000 for singles. Even if you don't get the write-off, you can still put up to $2,000 into a nondeductible IRA every year and profit from its tax-deferred earnings. Be forewarned, however, that there are paperwork hassles associated with nondeductible IRAs. Solution: hold your deductible and nondeductible IRAs in separate accounts.

Variable and fixed annuities are also marketed as retirement vehicles because their investment earnings are tax deferred too. Variable ones let you put money into portfolios of stocks, bonds or cash; fixed annuities pay a flat rate of interest, lately 5% or so. (For more details and five-year performance data on variable annuities, see "A Buyer's Guide to Annuities" later in this chapter.) But unless you've already fully funded your workplace plans and IRA and are sure you will stay invested at least 10 years, think twice before putting money into these commercially sold annuities. First, you must put in after-tax dollars. You'll also be clobbered by surrender fees of as much as 8% of the amount you withdraw if you take money out within the first eight years, not to mention a 10% tax penalty on your accrued earnings if you want out before 59.5. And annual fees average slightly above 2%, vs. the 1.5% average expense ratio of stock funds.

How to handle future medical bills. Even after the Clintons' health care reform, medical expenses are likely to consume 15% to 20% of your income in retirement, says William Custer of the Employee Benefit Research Institute. To ease the pain, try to obtain comprehensive health insurance that will cover you from the day you retire until you turn 65 and qualify for Medicare. If you're among the most fortunate early retirees, your employer will let you keep your current coverage. (Warning: Unless you are protected by a union contract or a personal employment contract, there may be little you can do if your employer ever decides to cut retiree health benefits.) Or, under the federal COBRA law, you can buy medical coverage through your company's group policy for as long as two years at your employer's cost.

Before your coverage runs out, look into joining your local Blue Cross/Blue Shield plan or an HMO if it has a so-called open enrollment period (typically one month each year when it must accept all applicants). Also look for affordable private coverage, which is often cheaper than Blue Cross if you're in good health. You can cut your premiums 20% to 50% by opting for a high annual deductible of, say, $2,500. That may sound like a lot. But it's really a fairly small price to pay for achieving your dream of early retirement.

Are You Ready for Early Retirement?

What will it be? St. Thomas in January with daiquiris at the 19th hole and a pile of dividend checks waiting for you back at the villa? Or a part-time job at the local mall, macaroni four nights a week and a mailbox stuffed with mounting bills? To learn whether you have the temperament and financial wherewithal to retire early, take this quiz prepared with the assistance of Helen Dennis, a retirement consultant at the Andrus Gerontology Center, University of Southern California. Circle as many answers as you find appropriate. The scoring for the quiz is explained at the end.

1. To assure adequate income in retirement, you have
A. Identified the income and benefits you expect from your employer and Social Security
B. Calculated your anticipated retirement income
C. Estimated your retirement expenses
D. None of the above

2. To save for retirement, you put aside money every year in
A. An IRA, a Keogh or a SEP
B. A 401(k) or 403(b) plan
C. Stocks, bonds, mutual funds or investment real estate
D. None of the above

3. If you stopped working today, you would
A. Feel financially secure
B. Enjoy not having to work
C. Lose some self-esteem

4. If you have a free week, you
A. Have fun with friends
B. Catch up on chores
C. Take a trip
D. Are often eager to get back to work

5. You are currently a
A. Volunteer
B. Member of a club, society or organization
C. Participant in a group activity outside of work
D. None of the above

6. To stay healthy, you
A. Exercise regularly
B. Maintain a low-fat, high-carbohydrate diet
C. Manage stress well
D. None of the above

7. To find out what it's like to retire early, you have
A. Discussed it with more than one person who has done so
B. Not talked with anyone who has retired early

8. You plan to cover medical expenses until you turn 65 and become eligible for Medicare
A. Through insurance from your employer
B. By buying health insurance on your own
C. Don't know

9. To earn income in retirement, you
A. Plan to develop new skills before retiring
B. Have a hobby that you can turn into a job
C. Will do the same type of work you do now, but on your own schedule
D. Don't know

10. Your spouse or partner
A. Thinks it would be great if you could afford to retire early
B. Is looking forward to spending more time with you during your retirement
C. Would probably be climbing the walls if you retired early

Scoring: The first two questions are critically important; you can't retire early unless you have enough money to live on. Award yourself two points for answers A, B or C but no points for D. For all other questions, give yourself one point for each circled answer, except for the last one in each set, which gets zero.

1 to 13 points: Either early retirement isn't right for you or you need to start saving and preparing for it immediately.

14 to 22 points: You are a reasonably good candidate for early retirement. Just keep saving, and try to stay healthy.

23 points or more: You're an excellent candidate for early retirement, and you probably can swing it both financially and emotionally.

Adding Up Your Costs in Retirement

While nearly everyone looks forward to retirement as a time of doing exactly as one pleases, there are as many ways to pursue your pleasures as there are people. That's an important retirement planning point, because the stuff of your post-working-life dreams—be it Caribbean cruises, relocating to the sunbelt or simply working on your golf score—helps determine how much money you should be putting toward those goals now. The rule of thumb among financial planners and benefit consultants is that you will need an annual retirement income amounting to roughly 70% to 80% of your family's current earnings.

Whatever the life style you envision, the best way to ensure that you can pay for it is to plan as far ahead as possible. The first step is to determine what your annual expenses are likely to be. The worksheet on the facing page is specifically designed to help you do that. Despite the diversity in retirement living, financial planners surveyed by MONEY note at least some similarities in spending patterns after age 65. For example, most retirees spend about the same amount on food, gifts, charitable contributions and personal care as they did while working. Medical and dental bills, on the other hand, are significantly higher, depending on how generous your company's retirement coverage is. Here are some general guidelines to help you fill out the worksheet on the right.

Line 1: If you pay off your mortgage and take care of all necessary maintenance problems before you retire, housing costs should drop by as much as 25% to 30%. Count on even more shrinkage if you sell your house and buy a smaller one. Condominium owners and renters should factor in maintenance-fee and rent increases. And anyone who plans to spend more time at home should anticipate higher utilities charges.

Line 2: Financial planners estimate that if you are moving from business suits to jeans, you can expect to reduce clothing expenses by 20% to 35%.

Line 4: Scratch commuting costs. Other transportation expenses will increase if you intend to be very active. Planners recommend that two-car couples keep both autos during retirement, especially if both are fairly active.

Line 6: Most people keep giving the same amounts to charitable, political and educational institutions, as well as to family members outside the immediate household. But the overall figure drops, usually by the amount you used to give at the office.

Line 7: If your kids will be grown by the time you retire, you can eliminate education expenses, unless you plan to help pay your grandchildren's college bills. And if you intend to return to school yourself, check into reduced tuition costs for senior citizens.

Line 8: There will be little change in your payout for property, liability and auto insurance, but retirees can generally reduce their life insurance coverage by at least 50% or, if their spouses are fully provided for under their pension plan, eliminate it altogether.

Line 9: If you are currently covered by a company health plan, expect medical and dental costs to spurt by about 50% because of increased illnesses combined with reduced insurance coverage. Medicare pays part of doctors' fees and hospital bills. Check your company's coverage for retirees.

Line 10: You should plan to be debt-free by the time you retire, thereby eliminating loan repayment expenses.

Line 12: How much you spend for entertainment depends on how active you are. Expect such expenditures to rise an average of about 20% during your retirement.

Line 13: Budget for higher veterinary bills if you will have an aging dog, cat or other pet.

Line 14: While your contributions to pension plans cease at retirement, many financial planners encourage clients to continue setting aside about 10% of their income as a hedge against inflation.

Line 15: If you don't work, it's farewell to Social Security (FICA) taxes. Also check laws in your state because some don't tax income from retirement plans. The conventional wisdom that you will be in a lower tax bracket after retirement is no longer true for high earners. You will be taxed on up to 50% of your Social Security benefits if the total of your adjusted gross income, nontaxable interest, and half your Social Security benefits exceeds $25,000 ($32,000 if you are married). If that total is over $34,000 ($44,000 for couples), you'll owe tax on up to 85% of benefits.

Line 16: With more adult kids expecting financial help from Mom and Dad and Americans' increasing longevity, you could be contributing to the down payment on a child's first house while paying for a parent's nursing home.

Total current expenditures should equal 100% of your current before-tax income. By dividing your total expenditures at retirement by your current gross income, you will arrive at the percentage of your current income that you will need in retirement.

EXPENDITURES	At retirement	Current year
1. Housing. Rent, mortgage, property taxes, utilities (gas, oil, electricity and water), telephone, home furnishings, household services, maintenance, improvements	_____	_____
2. Clothing. Purchases and cleaning	_____	_____
3. Food. (including tobacco and alcohol)	_____	_____
4. Transportation. Car repair and maintenance, installment payments, gas, commuting costs, other	_____	_____
5. Gifts.	_____	_____
6. Contributions.	_____	_____
7. Education.	_____	_____
8. Insurance. Life, medical, auto, property, liability	_____	_____
9. Medical and dental care. Premiums, deductible and out-of-pocket costs	_____	_____
10. Loan repayment costs.	_____	_____
11. Personal care. Grooming, health club, other	_____	_____
12. Entertainment. Vacations, dining out, movies, plays, concerts, sports events, cable TV, videocassettes, entertaining, sports, hobbies, other	_____	_____
13. Pet expenses.	_____	_____
14. Investments and retirement savings. Contribution to company plans, IRAs, Keoghs, SEPs and other investments	_____	_____
15. Taxes. Federal, FICA, state, local	_____	_____
16. Support of relatives.	_____	_____
TOTAL EXPENDITURES. (add lines 1 through 16)	_____	_____
TOTAL CURRENT EXPENDITURES DIVIDED BY CURRENT GROSS INCOME.	_____	_____
TOTAL EXPENDITURES AT RETIREMENT DIVIDED BY CURRENT GROSS INCOME.	_____	_____

Beat Five Threats to Your Future

Whether you will wind up living the retirement of your dreams or of your nightmares depends on whether you avoid these major pitfalls.

1. You may not receive a traditional pension.

For those lucky enough to get one, the monthly pension check can replace as much as a third of pre-retirement income. These days 29% of retirees collect private pensions, compared with only 9% in 1962. But if current trends continue, the heyday of the traditional pension is past. Reason: companies, particularly small ones, are shunning such defined-benefit plans in favor of less expensive to administer defined-contribution plans such as 401(k)s. The number of defined-benefit plans dropped 25% from 1983 to 1989, while the number of defined-contribution plans climbed 40%.

Under a defined-benefit pension, employees are guaranteed a fixed monthly payout for life and usually are not required to make contributions of their own. By contrast, defined-contribution plans are funded primarily by employees, who also assume all investment risk. With a traditional pension, you can simply sit back and watch your employer's contributions to the plan grow into a rich source of retirement income. A defined-contribution plan, however, may never amount to much if you fail to contribute enough to it or if you mismanage your investments. In short, you become even more vulnerable to other threats, such as inflation and your own shortcomings as a saver, discussed below.

Advice: Try to get a job at a big company that offers both a pension and a 401(k). If you can't achieve that ideal, you'll need to increase your savings to make up for the loss of the money that a pension would provide. A 35-year-old earning $50,000 a year who can count on Social Security, a 401(k) and a pension needn't save a cent more to enjoy a worry-free retirement, assuming that he or she contributes 6% of pre-tax pay to the 401(k) and the employer kicks in the customary 50 cents for each dollar. Take away the pension, however,

and the employee must save an additional 9% of after-tax income to retire just as comfortably.

2. Medical benefits will be cut or canceled.

Bills for doctors, drugs and hospitals can wreck even the best retirement plans. Employer-sponsored medical coverage is especially crucial for early retirees who are too young to qualify for Medicare, the government insurance program for those age 65 and older. But company coverage is also valuable because it covers most of the costs that Medicare doesn't.

Today only a third of all retirees get free or low-cost health insurance from their former employers—and that figure is declining fast. Employers are scaling back because, starting last year, they must report the cost of future retiree health benefits on their balance sheets, thereby reducing profits. According to a survey of 2,400 firms, 7% have ended or plan to end benefits for future retirees, 30% have raised premiums for current retirees and 26% have hiked deductibles or co-payments for current retirees. Some who've suffered cutbacks have sued former employers to reinstate promised benefits. But courts so far have ruled that employers have the right to change or terminate such plans as long as documents describing employee and retiree benefits make that position clear.

Advice: People who plan to retire soon but are over age 65 don't have it too bad. At worst, they'll have to buy a private Medigap policy costing up to $3,000 a year if their employer eliminates its supplemental medical insurance. But if you are contemplating early retirement, make sure you can afford to buy health insurance on your own. Individual coverage is usually expensive, costing between $3,500 and $12,000 a year, depending on the overall health of both you and your spouse.

How the Plans Stack Up

Plan	Available to	Best for	Maximum contribution	Tax break on contributions/ earnings	Matching contributions	Charges/fees	Early withdrawal[6]	Number of investment options
401(k)	Employees of for-profit businesses	Everyone who qualifies	15% of salary, up to $9,235[1] in 1994	Yes/Yes	Anywhere from 0% to 100%,[3] but typically only up to 6% of salary	Depends on plan/annual expenses of 1% to 1.5% of assets[4]	Only in case of hardship	Three to 10, typically, depending on your employer's plan
403(b)	Employees of nonprofit organizations	Everyone who qualifies	20% of gross salary or $9,500, whichever is less	Yes/Yes	Generally not available	Depends on plan/annual expenses of 1% to 3% of assets	Only in case of hardship and employee contributions only	One to 10, typically, depending on your employer's plan
IRA	Anyone with earned income	Those who don't have company pension plans or who have put the maximum into their company plans	100% of wages up to $2,000; $2,250 if joint with spouse	Sometimes/ Yes	None	Depends on investment/ zero to $50 annual fee	Always permitted	Nearly everything except real estate, collectibles and other hard assets
SEP	The self-employed and employees of small businesses	Self-employed person who is a sole proprietor	13% of net self-employment income, or $22,500, whichever is less[2]	Yes/Yes	None	Depends on investment/ $10 to $30 a year	Always permitted	Same as IRA
PROFIT-SHARING KEOGH	The self-employed and employees of unincorporated small businesses	Small-business owner who is funding a plan for himself and employees	Same as SEP[2]	Yes/Yes	None	Depends on investment/ $500 to $2,000 in annual administrative expenses	Always permitted	Unlimited
MONEY-PURCHASE KEOGH	Same as profit-sharing Keogh	Small-business owner who wants to shelter more than allowed by profit-sharing Keogh	20% of net self-employment income, or $30,000, whichever is less[2]	Yes/Yes	None	Same as profit-sharing Keogh	Always permitted	Unlimited
DEFINED-BENEFIT KEOGH	Same as profit-sharing Keogh	Self-employed person nearing retirement who needs to set aside a high percentage of income	Maximum needed to fund $118,737[1] annual benefit, or three years' average income, whichever is less[2]	Yes/Yes	None	Depends on investment/ $2,000 to $4,000 annual expenses	Always permitted	Unlimited
VARIABLE ANNUITY	Anyone	Someone who has put the maximum into other plans and won't need the money for 10 years	None	No/Yes	None	6% to 8% surrender charges[5]/ annual expenses of 2% to 2.2% of assets	Always permitted	Anywhere from one to 22, but typically nine
FIXED ANNUITY	Anyone	Someone who has put the maximum into other plans and shuns risk	None	No/Yes	None	Surrender charges of 6% to 8%[5]	Always permitted	One

Notes: [1]Estimate [2]Small-business owners fund the SEPs and Keoghs of their employees. [3]Percentage of employee's contribution [4]Some plans charge $20 to $30 annual administrative fees. [5]Surrender charges last six to eight years and typically decline by 1% a year. [6]All plans are subject to 10% income tax penalty, except in case of death or disability.

3. Social Security benefits will shrink.

This squeeze has already begun. The new tax law enacted in 1993 increases the portion of your Social Security payments subject to federal income tax. You will owe tax on up to 50% of your Social Security benefits if the total of your adjusted gross income, nontaxable interest, and half your Social Security benefits exceeds $25,000 ($32,000 if you are married). If that total is more than $34,000 ($44,000 for couples), you owe tax on up to 85% of benefits. The age at which you can collect full Social Security benefits, now 65, is already scheduled to rise to 66 in 2005 and to 67 in 2022. And experts believe Congress will keep nibbling away at Social Security. The retirement age might be further advanced, all benefits may be taxed and cost-of-living adjustments may even be scaled back or frozen for a while.

Advice: Face up to the fact that Congress is making the Social Security system even more progressive, meaning that lower-paid employees get the most out of it. For instance, Social Security now replaces 58% of lower-paid workers' wages but only 25% of higher-paid employees' salaries. That's why a 35-year-old couple earning $150,000 a year should save 12% of their after-tax income, vs. 5% for a couple earning $30,000.

4. Inflation will slowly erode your savings.

Even at a gentle 3% a year, inflation cuts the value of a traditional pension in half in 23 years. While Social Security benefits are still adjusted for cost-of-living increases, most private pensions are not. Between 1984 and 1989, the latest period for which statistics are available, the U.S. Department of Labor reports that only 24% of all pension plans gave retirees one or more cost-of-living increases. Inflation can also stunt the growth of your retirement savings if you rely too much on bonds and other fixed-income investments. From 1926 to 1992, the average annual rate of return on riskless Treasury bills worked out to 3.8%, compared with 3.2% for inflation.

Advice: Don't be afraid to put part of your retirement savings into stocks. According to Ibbotson Associates, a Chicago investment con-

sulting firm, the average rate of return for the S&P 500 index from 1926 to 1992 was a healthy 12% annually, well above the inflation rate. Yet a Bankers Trust survey of 401(k) plans revealed that when employers offered a guaranteed investment contract (GIC), which is similar to a bank CD, employees put 47% of their new contributions into it. They put only 19% into stock funds. By contrast, many financial planners urge clients under age 45 to sink up to 80% of their retirement savings into stocks or stock funds and gradually decrease the stock percentage as they get older.

5. You will eventually sabotage yourself.

You, like most Americans, are the single most potent threat to your prosperous retirement. The danger is that you won't put enough aside or that you will squander your savings. The U.S. personal savings rate has stood at around 4% since the late 1980s, half what it was in the 1970s and a scandal compared with other nations. The Japanese save at three times our rate, the Germans double. And despite an increased tendency to retire solo, many singles spend like they expect to retire on someone else's savings. On average, married couples put away 5% of their pre-tax pay, single men save 3% and single women save less than 2%. More unsettling, most people tend to blow their retirement savings while they are employed. One study found that only 11% of workers who received lump-sum distributions from a tax-deferred retirement account rolled the entire amount over into a similar account, while 34% spent the entire payout.

Advice: Stop living only for today and make a lifetime commitment to your 401(k) account, or Keogh if you are self-employed. Studies suggest that, on average, employees who do save through 401(k)s put in 5% of their compensation each year. Doing this from age 22 to 65 builds principal that figures to earn roughly 35% of your income just before you retire. If you are a typical retiree, that will pay for just half of your needs. But if you were to set aside the maximum allowable contribution for most plans (usually 13% of compensation) for the same amount of time, you would replace a whopping 91% of your final pay.

Sidestep the 20% Withholding Trap

The feds want to hold back a fifth of any lump-sum payout, whether you're retiring or just changing jobs. Here are six ways to beat the bite.

A bitter surprise awaits many of the workers who have lost their jobs recently, along with other employees who have chosen to leave their companies. Under an obscure law effective last year, the government requires employers to withhold 20% from certain lump-sum cash distributions to departing employees. Uncle Sam bites any time that the money is not directly transferred by an employer from either a 401(k), pension, employee stock plan or profit sharing account to another retirement account. You previously could take the check directly and use the money without any withholding for as long as 60 days before rolling the sum over into an IRA or another employer's plan. But no more. In all, the feds pocketed an estimated $2 billion last year under the new law. Besides disrupting some 2 million lives, the complex law could cause smaller firms to drop their pension plans to avoid the new fiduciary liability and costs involved.

Taxpayers who fail to ask their employers to make a direct transfer to, say, an IRA must not only be satisfied with a check for 80% of their money but must also come up with the missing 20% for the IRA within 60 days. If they don't have the 20%, that amount is taxed as income, and an early 10% withdrawal penalty is tacked on for taxpayers under the age of 55 if they're leaving their job that year, or under 59.5 otherwise. Then they must either wait 12 months or more to get the 20% back after they file their tax return the following year or recapture the money slowly by adjusting the withholding on their paychecks. If they wait until they file the following year, they'll get back only 62% of their withheld money because of taxes and penalties, assuming they're in the 28% bracket. Those who do put the missing 20% into the IRA within 60 days simply get that money back when they file for a refund the following April 15.

Despite a mushroom cloud of complaints from taxpayers, there is little chance Congress will budge other than possibly to permit exemptions for, say, 401(k) distributions used to pay for medical bills. The result: new retirees could inadvertently lose chunks of their nest egg.

Here's how. If you don't replace the withheld 20%, you face a triple whammy—federal and state taxes, the 10% penalty for those under age 59.5 plus loss of interest on the amount withheld. Say, for example, you're owed $50,000 in a lump sum. You get a check for $40,000 with $10,000 withheld. You can't afford to replace the $10,000 so you forfeit $500, assuming you would have invested the $10,000 at 5% the first year. The 10% penalty slices off another $1,000, and combined federal and state income taxes could easily come to $3,500. Total shrinkage works out to about $5,000, or 10% of your life savings.

But all is not lost. There are six ways to avoid being snared in the 20% trap, starting with the simplest and most accessible.

Have your employer transfer money to an IRA.

Under law, your company must do what you say. To execute the transfer, ask your employer in writing either to wire the funds or to write a check payable to the trustee of the new plan, with the memo line reading, "Direct rollover." Also have a separate check made out to you for any after-tax contributions you have made to your 401(k). That money isn't subject to the 20% and can't be rolled into another tax-sheltered account. Once the company transfers the money to your IRA, a loophole in the law allows you to do what you used to be able to do. You can pull your money out the next day without having 20% withheld. But you may do so only once a year, and then you must roll over the entire balance within 60 days to another

IRA to avoid paying income tax plus an additional 10% penalty if you're under age 59.5.

Keep the money in your old employer's plan. Some employers will try to push you to cash out. If the value of any account is $3,500 or more, however, you have the right to stay put until you reach the plan's retirement age or 62, whichever is later. Your money will continue to grow tax deferred and can later be moved to a new employer's plan or an IRA. One warning: if you're over the plan's retirement age or 62, the company may give you a payout without your consent. That's because most plans like to cut back on administrative costs. Such distributions would probably be subject to the 20% withholding penalty.

Take your lump-sum in company stock. In another loophole in the law, the 20% penalty does not apply to stock distributions. But you will owe income tax and a 10% penalty if you're under age 59.5. In addition, loading up on company stock exposes you to a potentially ruinous risk of any future collapse in the stock's value. So if you take stock to avoid the 20% withholding, it may be wise to cash out quickly and put the money into an IRA. Do it within 60 days, or you'll owe taxes plus an early-withdrawal penalty on it.

Transfer the money to your new employer's plan. Be warned that this tactic does not always work. According to one survey of 401(k) plans, 72% of them accepted rollovers from another employer's accounts. But only 58% allowed direct transfers.

Park the money temporarily in a conduit IRA. If you have to wait to get into your new employer's plan and don't want to leave your funds with your old employer, get your old boss to transfer your retirement balance to a conduit IRA. This is simply a regular IRA used specifically for rollovers to keep them separate from other IRA funds. If you commingle those assets, the law says you cannot roll any part of them into an employer's plan. To be safe, set up a conduit IRA at a financial institution other than the one where you have your present

How Much Should You Save?

The worksheet at right will tell you approximately how much you need to start saving now to hold on to your standard of living in retirement. The multipliers used in lines 7, 9 and 11 allow for inflation by assuming your investments will grow at three percentage points over the inflation rate, before and after retirement. This keeps all figures in today's dollars.

Line 3: You and your spouse can ask your local Social Security office to estimate the annual benefits you each have earned. You can also calculate them yourself with the help of a Social Security fact sheet called *How Your Retirement Benefit is Figured.* For a rough estimate of your benefit, fill in $13,000 if you make $42,000 or more. If you make between $20,000 and $42,000, enter between $8,700 and $13,000.

Line 4: Your company benefits department may be able to estimate your pension. Make sure the estimate assumes that you continue working until your retirement age at your current salary. That will somewhat understate your likely eventual payout but will keep the figure in today's dollars.

Line 7: The multipliers in column A incorporate the cautious assumption that men will live to 90 and women to 94—longer than 85% of them do now. Single men should use the multiplier under "men." Women and married couples should use the one under "women," since wives usually outlive their husbands.

Line 8: Your personal retirement portfolio includes any investments you have specifically earmarked for retirement, aside from your IRA or Keogh. For your employer-sponsored savings plans, check the most recent statement from your 401(k), profit-sharing, thrift or stock ownership plan and total your vested balance in each.

Line 12: Consult the most recent annual statement from these plans to find the amount your company contributed on your behalf to each of the plans last year. Enter the total.

AGE AT WHICH YOU EXPECT TO RETIRE	MULTIPLIER A	
	men	women
55	22.1	23.5
56	21.8	23.2
57	21.4	22.8
58	21.0	22.5
59	20.6	22.1
60	20.2	21.8
61	19.8	21.4
62	19.3	21.0
63	18.9	20.6
64	18.4	20.2
65	17.9	19.8
66	17.4	19.3
67	16.9	18.9

TIME UNTIL YOU EXPECT TO RETIRE	MULTIPLIER B	MULTIPLIER C
1 year	1.03	1.000
3 years	1.09	.324
5 years	1.16	.188
7 years	1.23	.131
9 years	1.30	.098
11 years	1.38	.078
13 years	1.47	.064
15 years	1.56	.054
20 years	1.81	.037

1. Current gross income _____

2. Annual income needed in retirement, in today's dollars (70% of line 1) _____

3. Annual Social Security retirement benefits _____

4. Annual pension benefits _____

5. Guaranteed annual retirement income (line 3 plus line 4) _____

6. Additional retirement income needed (line 2 minus line 5) _____

7. Capital required to provide additional retirement income (line 6 times multiplier from column A at left) _____

8. Amount you have saved already

_____ + _____ + _____ = _____

| personal retirement portfolio | IRA/Keogh | employer-sponsored savings plans | total savings |

9. What your current investments will have grown to by the time you retire (total from line 8 times multiplier from Column B at left) _____

10. Additional retirement capital required (line 7 minus line 9) _____

11. Total annual savings still needed (line 10 times multiplier, column C at left) _____

12. Annual employer contributions to your company savings plans _____

13. Amount you need to set aside each year (line 11 minus line 12) _____

Companies with the Best Benefits

Though beleaguered, IBM is No. 1 on our annual ranking of the 10 major corporations that provide the most generous employee benefits in America. Despite red-ink-stained balance sheets, a 55% cut in its dividend, huge lay-offs and a change in chief executives, the computer maker left its benefits largely untouched. IBM employees still enjoy such enviable perks as free family medical and dental coverage. (An IBM spokesman refused to comment on what might happen to benefits this year.)

Like IBM, our other top 10 companies sparkle with spectacular benefits, including extensive medical coverage, generous pension and profit sharing plans, and lengthy vacations. For example, Hewlett-Packard, No. 7, rewards workers with no fewer than four separate retirement plans—a pension, a company matched savings plan, a stock purchase program and profit sharing awards. But even these companies have done some trimming. Nine, including IBM, required workers to pay a greater share of their health insurance costs, mainly by raising premiums or deductibles. IBM hiked its deductible on hospital stays from 40% of the first night's cost to 100% and added a dental care deductible of $40 a person.

Three companies added new medical benefits even as they pared others.

| COMPANY | INSURANCE | | |
Number of U.S. employees	**Medical**	**Dental**	**Life and disability**
1 IBM 158,000	No cost. Deductible: 0.3% of salary with a $150 minimum; hospital deductible: 100% of first night. Reimbursement: 80%; surgical, 100%. No out-of-pocket maximum.	Deductible: $40 per person. Reimbursement: set amount for each procedure, based on prevailing local charges. Lifetime maximum: $8,500 per person.	Life: up to $50,000, based on length of service, plus survivor's benefit equal to three years' salary. Short-term disability: 52 weeks at full pay. Long-term disability: 67% of pay.
2 Procter & Gamble[1] 47,600	Cost: $27 a month. Deductible: in P&G network, none; out of network, $350. Reimbursement: in network, 100% after set fee; out of network, 80%. Out-of-pocket max.: $3,150.	Deductible: preventive, none; other, $75. Reimbursement: 50% of prevailing local charges. Maximum annual benefit: $1,600 per person.	Life: one year's salary. Short-term disability: 67% of pay for 52 weeks. Long-term disability: 50%.
3 Johnson & Johnson[1] 39,000	Cost: $43 to $51 a month. Deductible: 0.25% of pay up to $600; hospitalization, $375. Reimbursement: 80%; major, 100%. Out-of-pocket maximum: 2.5% of pay up to $6,000.	Deductible: routine, none; major, $150. Reimbursement: routine, 60%, increasing to 90% after three years; major, 60%. Annual limit: $1,000 per person.	Life: one year's salary. Short-term disability: 75% to 100% of pay for 26 weeks, based on service. Long-term disability: employee can buy; cost based on pay and amount of coverage.
4 Xerox[1] 56,000	Cost: $137.83 a month. Deductible: 1% of pay. Reimbursement: 80%. Out-of-pocket maximum: 4% of salary up to a total of $4,000.	Cost: $8 a month. Deductible: 0.25% of salary. Reimbursement: basic, 100%; major, 50%. No annual limit.	Life: up to six years' salary, based on age and service. Short-term disability: up to five months at full pay. Long-term disability: 60% of pay.
5 Eastman Kodak[1] 77,100	Cost: $240 a year. Deductible: $750. Reimbursement: 80%. Out-of-pocket maximum: $3,000.	Cost: $60 a year. No deductible. Reimbursement: preventive, 80%; major, 50%. Annual maximum: $1,000 a person for preventive and restorative.	Life: six months' pay. Short-term disability: full pay for 26 weeks (less than 15 years' service) or 52 weeks (more than 15 years'). Long-term: 55%.
6 Citicorp[1] 41,000	Cost: $41 a year. Deductible: 2% of annual salary. Reimbursement: 80%. Out-of-pocket maximum: 5% of salary.	Cost: $244 a year. Deductible: $75. Reimbursement: preventive, 100%; basic, 80%; major, 50%. Maximum annual benefit: $2,500 per person.	Life: one year's salary. Short-term disability: 67% of pay for six months. Long-term disability: 50%.
7 Hewlett-Packard 56,462	Cost: $111 a month. Deductible: $450. Reimbursement: 80%; hospital, 90%. Out-of-pocket maximum: $2,500.	Cost: $21 a month. Deductible: $150. Reimbursement: 80% on most procedures. Maximum annual benefit: $1,500 per person.	Life: $50,000 after three years of service. Short-term disability: 75% of pay for 39 weeks. Long-term: 75% of first $3,000 of monthly pay; 50% of pay from $3,000 to $18,500.
8 AT&T[1] 230,000	Cost: $50 a month. Deductible: $150 to $450. Reimbursement: 80%; hospital, 100%; surgical, 95% to 100%. Out-of-pocket max.: $1,000 a person.	No deductible. Reimbursement: preventive, 100%; major, 60% to 65%. Maximum annual benefit: $1,250 per person.	Life: one year's salary. Short-term disability: up to 100% for 52 weeks, based on years of service. Long-term disability: 50%.
9 Merck[1] 20,500	Deductible: 0.5% of salary with a $300 minimum. Reimbursement: 90%. Out-of-pocket maximum: 2.5% of annual pay with $1,500 minimum.	Deductible: routine, none; major, $25 a person. Reimbursement: preventive and basic, 100%; major, 50%. Max. annual benefit: $1,500 a person.	Life: one year's salary. Short-term disability: 100% of salary for up to 26 weeks, based on years of service. Long-term disability: 60%.
10 Quaker Oats[1] 11,000	Cost: $60 a month. Deductible: $595. Reimbursement: 85%. Out-of-pocket maximum: $3,000.	Cost: $8 a month. Deductible: $100 lifetime. Reimbursement: preventive, 90%; basic, 80%; major, 50%. Maximum annual benefit: $1,375.	Life: one year's salary. Short-term disability: 67% to 100% of pay for up to 50 weeks, based on length of service. Long-term disability: 50%.

Notes: 1 – Company offers a flexible benefit plan.

THE NEW REALITIES OF RETIREMENT

Johnson & Johnson and Hewlett-Packard began paying for routine checkups and tests for infants, while AT&T launched a prenatal care program. And under the first phase of Xerox's LifeCycle Assistance plan, employees earning less than $50,000 are eligible for annual grants of $2,500 (minus 5% of their base pay) for child care expenses. Their lifetime limit: $10,000.

To compile the honor roll, we asked 11 leading benefits specialists to nominate large U.S. companies known for outstanding plans. Of the 44 corporations the experts cited, we eliminated 19 whose plans did not cover at least 10,000 workers. We ranked the finalists according to a computer model

that weighed various components, including some not shown here.

At companies where employees choose among several levels of coverage, we evaluated the most popular medical and dental plans and the basic levels of life and disability insurance. Premiums and deductibles shown for medical and dental insurance are for families unless otherwise noted. Vacation is the maximum available; all companies offer two weeks to start unless otherwise noted. The cost figures for flexible benefit plans are what an average employee would pay above his or her allotted credits. Pensions are based on a final five-year average salary of $50,000.

RETIREMENT PLAN

Time off	Pension	Savings and stock purchase plans	Extras
Vacation: five weeks after 20 years. Twelve holidays. Personal leave: three years with benefits.	$19,223 at age 65 or after 30 years. $16,039 at 60 after 25 years. $11,570 at 55 after 20 years. Free lifetime health insurance for retiree and family with 15 years of service.	Company match: 30% on up to 5% of pay. Maximum pretax contribution: 9%. Stock-purchase plan: 15% discount on up to 10% of salary. Company contributes 2% of salary to personal retirement account.	$500 for vision care and other health costs not covered under main plan. One year paid leave for community service.
Vacation: six weeks after 25 years. Twelve holidays. Parental leave: up to one year, with benefits for three months.	No pension plan. Retiree pays $12.60 a month for health insurance. Retirees with more than 25 years' service receive $12,500 of life insurance.	No savings plan. Profit sharing: fixed percentage that increases gradually from 5% of pay to 25% after 20 years of service.	Bonus credits that may be used for such purposes as vision care, long-term-care insurance, fitness equipment or child care.
Vacation: one week, growing to six after 30 years. Eleven holidays. Parental leave: one year with benefits.	$19,194 at age 65 after 30 years. $14,759 at 60 after 25 years. $9,324 at 55 after 20 years. Retiree pays an average of $9 a month for health insurance.	Company match: 75% on up to 6% of salary, 25% of which is paid in company stock. Maximum pretax contribution: 10%.	Well-baby care. Child-care centers at three sites, plus fitness centers at 65 sites.
Vacation: six weeks after 25 years. Ten holidays. Personal leave: one year, with benefits for three months.	$21,000 at age 65 after 30 years. $13,125 at 60 after 25 years. $7,000 at 55 after 20 years. Retiree pays $69.33 for spouse's health care.	No company match. Maximum pretax contribution: 18%. Profit sharing: up to 10%, based on company performance (5% in 1992). Stock-ownership plan: 2% of pay.	Up to $10,000 (lifetime) for child care. One year paid leave for community service.
Vacation: six weeks after 35 years. Ten holidays. Family leave: 17 weeks with benefits. Personal: one year.	$20,523 at age 65 with 30 years. $17,103 at 60 after 25 years. $6,841 at 55 after 20 years. Free health insurance for retiree and family.	No company match. Maximum pretax contribution: 15%. Profit sharing: 5% to 15% of pay; employee can take the cash or put it into a tax-deferred account.	Up to 40 hours a year paid time off for community service. Long-term care at group rates.
Vacation: five weeks after 25 years. Ten holidays. Parental leave: 12 weeks with benefits. Personal: two years.	$23,400 at age 65 after 30 years. $20,640 at 60 after 25 years. $11,640 at 55 after 20 years. Company pays portion of retiree health insurance, based on service.	No company match. Maximum pretax contribution: 18%. Bonuses of 3% of pay can go into a tax-deferred account, where company matches 100%.	Prenatal care. Fitness centers at 10 locations. Child care available at three sites.
Vacation: three weeks, growing to six after 30 years. Eleven holidays. Parental leave: four months. Personal leave: up to one year.	$19,100 at age 65 after 30 years. $13,400 at 60 after 25 years. $9,200 at 55 after 20 years. Free health insurance for retiree with 30 years' service.	Company match: 33% on up to 6% of salary. Stock-purchase plan: company match of 50% on up to 10% of salary. Maximum combined pretax contribution: 12%. Profit sharing: 5% to 6% of pay.	Universal life insurance at low rates. Well-baby care.
Vacation: five weeks after 25 years. Ten holidays. Parental leave: one year with benefits.	$20,487 at age 65 after 30 years. $17,162 at 60 after 25 years. $13,838 at 55 after 20 years. Free health insurance for retiree and spouse.	Company match: 67% on up to 6% of salary. Maximum pretax contribution: 16%.	Fitness centers at 20 locations. Free legal consultations and hotline.
Vacation: six weeks after 27 years. Twelve holidays. Parental leave: 18 months with benefits.	$24,000 at 65 after 30 years. $20,200 at 60 after 25 years. $11,960 at 55 after 20 years. Free health insurance for retiree and family.	Company match: 50% on up to 5% of salary. Maximum pretax contribution: 15%.	Fitness centers at two locations. Child-care centers at two sites. Leave of up to one year for job-related activities.
Vacation: five weeks after 25 years. Eleven holidays. Personal leave: six months with benefits.	$20,619 at age 65 after 30 years. $16,125 at 60 after 25 years. $10,393 at 55 after 20 years. Retiree pays $2.20 a month for health insurance.	No company match. Maximum pretax contribution: 7% of salary. Stock-ownership plan: approximately 10% of pay.	Company contributes up to $600 to flexible spending accounts. Bonus credits for healthy lifestyles.

IRA. That way you'll avoid having a clerk accidentally mix it with other IRA monies.

Start periodic withdrawals from the old plan. You also can avoid the 20% trap by annuitizing. That means asking your old employer to spread your disbursements out over a lifetime series of equal payments or in 10 or more annual installments. This is a good idea for retirees who need money to live on. You must pay tax on the distributions, however. And if you opt for the 10 or more payments and you're under age 59.5, you'll owe the 10% penalty. If you already have an arrangement whereby you're getting fewer than 10 annual payments, 20% of what you expected in 1994 (and in subsequent years) will be withheld. To avoid this process, ask your plan administrator to transfer the payment to an IRA. You can then set up a payout schedule for that IRA, regardless of the number of payments, without any withholding.

A Buyer's Guide to Variable Annuities

Use our rankings of these popular tax-deferred retirement accounts to pick ones with a superior record and minimal drag from steep fees.

What do you call a retirement savings account that crosses an insurance contract with a mutual fund to produce gains that are turbocharged and tax-free? Answer: red-hot variable annuities. Or so you may already have heard from the legion of insurance agents, financial planners, stockbrokers and even bankers who are touting such products. Sales of variable annuities are zooming partly because so many investors are trying to escape today's high tax rates. Last year investors poured a record $40 billion into variables, up from $29 billion in 1992, and some experts think the annual inflow could hit $60 billion this year.

A variable annuity is essentially an investment, sold by an insurance company, that lets you put your money into a choice of portfolios called subaccounts that often are run by established mutual fund companies such as Dreyfus, Fidelity and Neuberger & Berman. Some of the portfolios are even modeled on well-known funds. The Hartford Putnam Capital Manager annuity, for instance, includes a Voyager subaccount that closely mimics Putnam's highly regarded Voyager aggressive growth fund. Since insurance investments are shielded from taxes, the money you put in grows tax-free until you withdraw it, just as it would in a 401(k) plan. And there's no limit on how much you can invest each year, as there is with most retirement plans. You simply make deposits—albeit in after-tax dollars.

Reaping the benefits of variables isn't as easy. Many of them have onerous fees that can turn a high-performance savings program into an investment lemon. For people in the 28% federal tax bracket or higher who are willing to tie up their money for 10 to 15 years, annuities can be a valuable supplement to other retirement accounts. In additon to outlining variables' pros and cons, we name the best performers among those tracked by Morningstar, the mutual fund research firm. The table beginning on page 82 lists the 20 best annuities overall. On the right we also identify the annuities whose funds were recently the top gainers in their investment categories.

How these hybrid investments work. The insurance component of a variable doesn't amount to much more than a death benefit. It promises that when you die your beneficiaries will receive at least the principal you put into the annuity over the years. Most variable annuities also give you the option of annuitizing. This allows you to convert the value of your account to a monthly income stream that the insurer guarantees to pay for a specified period, typically the rest of your life.

What you're really buying with a variable annuity is access to the subaccounts—essentially tax-deferred mutual funds. The typical annuity offers seven of them. You can easily divvy your balance up among several accounts, each pursuing a different strategy such as investing for growth, total return or income. You can also switch money from subaccount to subaccount. Your investment income is sheltered from taxes. So are any capital gains you may realize as you meander among the portfolios.

Unfortunately, these benefits can be blunted by annuities' steep fees. Variables usually carry a surrender charge that's akin to a back-end load on a mutual fund and can nip you for as much as 9% of your principal if you bail out within the first seven to 10 years. (The surrender charge starts out at the maximum and declines by a percentage point or so each year.) Even if you don't withdraw your money, variables come saddled with a so-called insurance charge that averages 1.3% or so annually. Although variables' prospectuses state that this levy covers such costs as providing the death benefit, more than half of it usually goes to pay sales commissions and other marketing expenses. Add in the cost of managing the portfolios, and an annuity's total charges can exceed a hefty 2% a year.

The limits on an annuity's tax shelter. You'll owe ordinary income tax on the account's earnings when you withdraw them, plus a 10% penalty if you bail out before age 59.5. If you needed to cash out your annuity to meet emergency expenses, for example, taxes, penalties and the surrender charge could wipe out the entire benefit of tax deferral. What's more, the new tax law pushed the top rate on income (39.6%) well above that on capital gains (28%). The change could penalize high-tax-bracket investors who seek shelter in annuity stock funds. Reason: capital gains in an annuity, as in a 401(k) or IRA, are taxed at the ordinary income rate when they're withdrawn, not at the lower capital gains rate. Since it can take 10 to 15 years of

tax deferral to offset that disadvantage, deposits to such accounts should be money that you will not need for a long time.

Assuming you are a good candidate for an annuity, our rankings can help you choose from among the best. To be considered for our list, an annuity had to offer a minimum of one fund with at least a three-year record in each of three broad investment categories—growth, total return and bonds. We then graded each subaccount on its performance relative to its peers and averaged those grades to award the overall performance scores that are the basis of our rankings. We did not consider the performance of fixed-rate and money-market subaccounts because their earnings are too low to contribute much to your invest-

Best Bets for Specific Aims

These annuities lead four investment categories, though some—like Pacific Mutual—did not make our top 20 (see next page).

	PHONE	SCORE[1]
GROWTH		
1. Pacific Mutual Select	800-800-7681	100
2. Phoenix Home Life Big Edge Plus	800-843-8348	94
3. Kemper Advantage III	800-621-5001	91
4. Connecticut Mutual Panorama	800-234-5606	89
5. Fidelity Retirement Reserves	800-544-2442	88
TOTAL RETURN		
1. MONYMaster	800-487-6669	100
2. Connecticut Mutual Panorama	800-234-5606	97
3. Templeton Investment Plus	800-243-4840	94
4. IDS Flexible Annuity	612-671-3131	91
5. Kemper Advantage III	800-621-5001	88
BONDS		
1. Great American Maxiflex VA	317-571-3700	97
2. Phoenix Home Life Big Edge Plus	800-843-8348	92
3. WRL Freedom Variable Annuity	800-443-9975	91
4. Connecticut Mutual Panorama	800-234-5606	87
5. CIGNA Investors Var. Annuity	800-925-6000	87
INTERNATIONAL GROWTH		
1. Templeton Invest. Plus Annuity	800-243-4840	94
2. John Hancock Independ. Annuity	800-422-0237	92
3. Scudder Horizon Plan	800-225-2470	88
4. Hartford Putnam Capital Manager	800-521-0538	85
5. Prudential VIP-86	800-346-3778	81

Note: [1]Score is for category only, not overall score of annuity

The Top 20 Variable Annuities

Though its range of investments is limited, Connecticut Mutual Panorama soared to the top of our list of best-performing annuities thanks to solid returns by its three main portfolios over the past five years. These rankings are based on an overall score that reflects the investment performance of each annuity's subaccounts relative to their competitors (for details, see the footnote, lower right). The numbered boxes give general information about the annuity. Below each box, we list the subaccounts upon which its rank was based (we excluded money-market and fixed-rate accounts). Some subaccounts appear more than once. For example, Fidelity Growth can be bought through either Ameritas Overture II or Fidelity Retirement Reserves. Their performances may vary because the annuities impose different costs.

SUBACCOUNT NAME	TYPE[1]	EXPENSE RATIO[2]	RISK RATING[3]	% ANNUALIZED RETURN[4]		SUB-ACCOUNT SCORE
				THREE YEARS	FIVE YEARS	

1 CONNECTICUT MUTUAL PANORAMA   800-234-5606
Overall score: 91   Total funds: 4   Minimum initial investment: $500
Annual insurance cost: 0.73%   Top surrender fee/expires: 5%/11th year

Panorama Growth	G	0.76%	2	25.6	17.6	89
Panorama Total Return	B	0.68	2	19.5	14.4	97
Panorama Income	CB	0.77	3	13.2	10.4	87

2 PHOENIX HOME LIFE BIG EDGE PLUS   800-843-8348
Overall score: 82   Total funds: 7   Minimum initial investment: $1,000[5]
Annual insurance cost: 1.25%   Top surrender fee/expires: 6%/7th year

Big Edge Growth	G	0.50%	2	25.8	20.0	94
Big Edge Total Return	B	0.50	2	17.3	13.6	85
Big Edge Bond	CB	0.50	2	15.0	10.4	92
Big Edge International	IS	1.50	4	8.7	—	58

3 AMERITAS OVERTURE II   800-634-8353
Overall score: 75   Total funds: 14   Minimum initial investment: $2,000
Annual insurance cost: 1.45%   Top surrender fee/expires: 6%/8th year

Overture II/Fidelity Growth	G	0.75	4	27.0	15.8	83
Overture II/Fid. Equity-Income	GI	0.65	2	24.1	10.9	63
Overture II/Fid. Asset Man.	B	0.91	1	18.4	—	90
Overture II/Fidelity Overseas	IS	1.14	4	6.3	9.1	59
Overture II/Fid. High Income	HY	0.67	2	25.0	11.5	79

4 FIDELITY RETIREMENT RESERVES   800-544-2442
Overall score: 73   Total funds: 9   Minimum initial investment: $2,500
Annual insurance cost: 1%   Top surrender fee/expires: 5%/6th year

Retirement Reserves/Fidelity Growth	G	0.75	4	27.3	16.1	88
Retirement Reserves/Fidelity Equity-Income	GI	0.65	2	24.4	11.2	69
Retirement Reserves/Fidelity Asset Manager	B	0.91	1	18.7	—	93
Retirement Reserves/Fidelity Overseas	IS	1.14	4	6.6	9.3	74
Retirement Reserves/Fidelity High Income	HY	0.67	2	25.3	11.8	87
Retirement Reserves/Fidelity Investment-Grade Bond	CB	0.76	2	10.7	—	29

5 IDS FLEXIBLE ANNUITY   612-671-3131
Overall score: 73   Total funds: 7   Minimum initial investment: $2,000
Annual insurance cost: 1%   Top surrender fee/expires: 7%/7th year

IDS Flex. Ann. Cap. Resource	G	0.70	3	20.0	14.1	49
IDS Flex. Ann. Managed	B	0.71	2	18.3	14.3	91
IDS Flex. Ann. Spec. Income	CB	0.71	3	14.7	10.0	78

SUBACCOUNT NAME	TYPE[1]	EXPENSE RATIO[2]	RISK RATING[3]	% ANNUALIZED RETURN[4]		SUB-ACCOUNT SCORE
				THREE YEARS	FIVE YEARS	

6 SCUDDER HORIZON PLAN   800-225-2470
Overall score: 72   Total funds: 7   Minimum initial investment: $2,500
Annual insurance cost: 0.70%   No surrender charge

Horizon Plan Capital Growth	G	0.63	3	25.5	14.8	71
Horizon Plan Balanced	B	0.75	3	15.2	10.8	46
Horizon Plan Intl.	IS	1.31	3	10.4	12.7	88
Horizon Plan Bond	CB	0.63	3	13.2	10.3	84

7 SECURITY BENEFIT VARIFLEX   800-888-2461
Overall score: 72   Total funds: 8   Minimum initial investment: $500
Annual insurance cost: 1.20%   Top surrender fee/expires: 8%/9th year

Variflex Growth	G	0.86	3	21.5	14.4	59
Variflex Income-Growth	B	0.86	4	17.3	13.3	83
Variflex High Grade Income	CB	0.86	3	12.9	10.1	74

8 MANULIFE ACCOUNT 2 ANNUITY   800-387-2728
Overall score: 72   Total funds: 7   Minimum initial investment: $1,000
Annual insurance cost: 1.50%   Top surrender fee/expires: 8%/9th year

Annuity Common Stock	G	0.50	3	17.3	13.4	33
Annuity Emerging Gro. Eq.	AG	0.50	5	40.3	25.6	98
Annuity Balanced	B	0.50	2	14.4	11.6	56
Annuity Real Estate Securities	SP	0.50	2	30.6	16.3	100
Annuity Capital Growth Bond	CB	0.50	3	11.2	9.5	45

9 KEMPER ADVANTAGE III   800-621-5001
Overall score: 66   Total funds: 7   Minimum initial investment: $2,500
Annual insurance cost: 1.30%   Top surrender fee/expires: 6%/7th year

Kemper Adv. Equity	G	0.64	3	26.5	18.1	91
Kemper Adv. Total Return	B	0.60	4	17.6	14.3	88
Kemper Adv. Gov. Securities	GB	0.62	4	9.4	—	14
Kemper Adv. High Yield	HY	0.64	2	26.6	10.6	71

10 METROPOLITAN LIFE PREFERENCE PLUS   800-638-2704
Overall score: 66   Total funds: 7   Minimum initial investment: none
Annual insurance cost: 1.25%   Top surrender fee/expires: 7%/8th year

Preference Plus Agg. Growth	AG	0.75	5	35.9	—	90
Preference Plus Growth	G	0.25	3	20.9	—	53
Preference Plus Diversified	B	0.25	3	16.4	—	67
Preference Plus Stock Index	GI	0.25	2	17.2	—	55
Preference Plus Income	CB	0.25	3	12.2	—	65

11 GUARDIAN INVESTOR   800-221-3253
Overall score: 65   Total funds: 8   Minimum initial investment: $500[6]
Annual insurance cost: 1.15%   Top surrender fee/expires: 6%/8th year

Investor/Guardian Stock	G	0.55	2	27.9	—	99
Investor/Value Line Centurion	G	0.54	4	24.8	—	75
Investor/Guardian Real Estate	SP	—	4	(7.1)	—	7
Investor/Value Line Strat. Asset	B	0.55	4	26.0	—	99
Investor/Guardian Bond	CB	0.56	3	11.3	—	44

12 PRUDENTIAL VIP-86[7] 800-346-3778

Overall score: 63   Total funds: 13   Minimum initial investment: $1,000
Annual insurance cost: 1.20%   Top surrender fee/expires: 8%/9th year

SUBACCOUNT NAME	TYPE[1]	EXPENSE RATIO[2]	RISK RATING[3]	THREE YEARS	FIVE YEARS	SUB-ACCOUNT SCORE
VIP-86 Common stock	G	0.53	3	23.3	14.9	69
VIP-86 Aggress. Managed Flex	B	0.67	3	17.8	13.0	84
VIP-86 Conservative Managed	B	0.62	1	13.1	10.7	28
VIP-86 High Dividend Stock	GI	0.57	1	21.4	13.9	90
VIP-86 Natural Resources	SP	0.72	2	14.2	12.9	74
VIP-86 Real Property Account	SP	4.47	1	0.4	2.5	15
VIP-86 Stock Index	GI	0.46	2	17.1	12.6	73
VIP-86 Global Equity	IS	1.87	4	11.1	—	81
VIP-86 Bond	CB	0.47	3	11.4	9.7	54
VIP-86 Gov. Securities	GB	0.53	4	12.3	—	86
VIP-86 High Yield Bond	HY	0.70	2	23.0	9.4	36

13 LIFE OF VIRGINIA COMMONWEALTH 804-281-6000

Overall score: 60   Total funds: 23   Minimum initial investment: $5,000
Annual insurance cost: 1.35%   Top surrender fee/expires: 6%/7th year

SUBACCOUNT NAME	TYPE	EXPENSE RATIO	RISK RATING	THREE YEARS	FIVE YEARS	SUB-ACCOUNT SCORE
Commonwealth/Fidelity Gro.	G	0.75	4	27.1	16.0	85
Commonwealth/Opp. Cap. App.	AG	0.54	4	31.6	18.1	62
Commonwealth/Opp. Gro.	G	0.61	2	15.5	10.9	16
Commonwealth/Fid. Eq. Inc.	GI	0.65	2	24.2	11.0	65
Commonwealth/Fidelity Asset	B	0.91	1	18.5	—	91
Commonwealth/Com. Stock	GI	1.03	3	21.7	12.1	74
Commonwealth/Total Return	B	0.98	3	17.4	11.0	58
Commonwealth/Neu. Bal.	B	0.95	4	13.3	—	20
Commonwealth/Opp. Multi-Strat.	B	0.55	2	13.7	9.9	23
Commonwealth/Fid. Overseas	IS	1.14	4	6.4	9.2	66
Commonwealth/Fid. Hi. Inc.	HY	0.67	2	25.1	11.6	83
Commonwealth/Gov. Securs.	GB	0.90	4	11.6	8.8	42
Commonwealth/Opp. Bond	CB	0.56	1	12.1	10.2	73
Commonwealth/Opp. Hi. Inc.	HY	0.73	1	23.9	15.5	87

14 HARTFORD PUTNAM CAPITAL MANAGER 800-521-0538

Overall score: 59   Total funds: 9   Minimum initial investment: $1,000
Annual insurance cost: 1.40%   Top surrender fee/expires: 7%/8th year

SUBACCOUNT NAME	TYPE	EXPENSE RATIO	RISK RATING	THREE YEARS	FIVE YEARS	SUB-ACCOUNT SCORE
Capital Manager Voyager	AG	0.75	3	29.1	18.7	63
Capital Manager Gro. & Inc.	GI	0.69	1	16.4	12.0	47
Capital Manager Global Asset Allocation	B	0.79	2	14.1	9.8	23
Capital Manager Global Growth	IS	0.85	3	11.3	—	85
Cap. Mgr. Gov./Hi. Qual. Bond	CB	0.70	4	12.1	9.9	64
Capital Manager High Yield	HY	0.71	2	25.4	10.7	73

15 MFS/SUN COMPASS 3 800-752-7215

Overall score: 59   Total funds: 8   Minimum initial investment: $300[5]
Annual insurance cost: 1.40%   Top surrender fee/expires: 6%/8th year

SUBACCOUNT NAME	TYPE	EXPENSE RATIO	RISK RATING	THREE YEARS	FIVE YEARS	SUB-ACCOUNT SCORE
Compass 3 Capital Appreciation Variable Acct.	G	0.80	4	21.2	16.3	74
Compass 3 Managed Sectors Variable Account	AG	0.92	4	25.8	18.1	40
Compass 3 Total Return Variable Account	B	0.86	1	16.4	11.4	62
Compass 3 World Govs. Variable Account	IB	1.15	5	9.4	9.6	65
Compass 3 Gov. Securities Variable Account	GB	0.62	3	10.7	9.3	58
Compass 3 High Yield Variable Account	HY	0.93	2	24.1	10.0	52

16 MONYMaster 800-487-6669

Overall score: 58   Total funds: 7   Minimum initial investment: $2,000
Annual insurance cost: 1.25%   Top surrender fee/expires: 7%/9th year

SUBACCOUNT NAME	TYPE	EXPENSE RATIO	RISK RATING	THREE YEARS	FIVE YEARS	SUB-ACCOUNT SCORE
Equity Portfolio	G	0.79	1	20.6	13.7	47
Small Cap Portfolio	AG	0.86	2	28.9	16.5	31
Managed Portfolio	B	0.69	3	27.0	18.9	100
Intermediate Term Bond	CB	0.53	1	9.6	8.3	15
Long Term Bond	CB	0.51	4	14.7	11.6	95

17 FRANKLIN VALUEMARK 800-342-3863

Overall score: 56   Total funds: 18   Minimum initial investment: $2,000[8]
Annual insurance cost: 1.40%   Top surrender fee/expires: 5%/6th year

SUBACCOUNT NAME	TYPE	EXPENSE RATIO	RISK RATING	THREE YEARS	FIVE YEARS	SUB-ACCOUNT SCORE
Equity Growth	G	0.62	3	13.5	—	4
Income Securities	B	0.67	1	22.9	—	97
Precious Metals	SP	0.69	5	8.4	—	33
Real Estate Securities	SP	0.69	2	24.1	—	73
Utility Equity	SP	0.55	1	15.5	—	67
Global Income	IB	0.67	5	8.3	—	38
High Income	HY	0.68	1	19.8	—	26
Investment Grade Bond	CB	0.68	3	9.3	—	11
U.S. Government Securities	GB	0.59	2	10.9	—	52
Zero-coupon 1995	GB	0.25	4	10.5	—	38
Zero-coupon 2000	GB	0.25	5	16.6	—	93
Zero-coupon 2005	GB	0.25	5	21.0	—	97
Zero-coupon 2010	GB	0.25	5	23.1	—	100

18 NEW ENGLAND ZENITH ACCUMULATOR 800-333-2501

Overall score: 55   Total funds: 10   Minimum initial investment: $300[5]
Annual insurance cost: 1.35%   Top surrender fee/expires: 6.5%/11th year

SUBACCOUNT NAME	TYPE	EXPENSE RATIO	RISK RATING	THREE YEARS	FIVE YEARS	SUB-ACCOUNT SCORE
Accumulator Capital Growth	G	0.70	4	21.4	14.1	55
Accumulator Managed	B	0.54	2	13.6	10.5	29
Accumulator Stock Index	GI	0.35	2	17.0	12.4	62
Accumulator Bond Income	CB	0.44	3	12.7	10.2	75

19 UNION CENTRAL LIFE CARILLON ACCOUNT 800-999-1840

Overall score: 53   Total funds: 6   Minimum initial investment: $50
Annual insurance cost: 1.45%   Top surrender fee/expires: 7%/9th year

SUBACCOUNT NAME	TYPE	EXPENSE RATIO	RISK RATING	THREE YEARS	FIVE YEARS	SUB-ACCOUNT SCORE
Carillon Equity	G	0.72	3	26.5	10.3	42
Carillon Capital	B	0.88	2	16.1	—	65
Carillon Bond	CB	0.66	2	11.8	9.6	53

20 FORTIS BENEFITS OPPORTUNITY ANNUITY[9] 800-800-2638

Overall score: 50   Total funds: 7   Minimum initial investment: $500[5]
Annual insurance cost: 1.35%   Top surrender fee/expires: 5%/6th year

SUBACCOUNT NAME	TYPE	EXPENSE RATIO	RISK RATING	THREE YEARS	FIVE YEARS	SUB-ACCOUNT SCORE
Fortis Growth Stock	G	0.76	4	21.9	17.0	79
Fortis Asset Allocation	B	0.60	1	14.6	12.0	64
Fortis Diverse Income	CB	0.67	2	10.7	9.3	35
Fortis U.S. Gov. Secs.	GB	0.57	4	9.6	—	21

Methodology: To be ranked, an annuity had to be widely available, accept periodic investments and offer at least one subaccount with a three-year track record in each of three broad categories: growth (including growth and aggressive growth accounts), total return (including balanced, growth and income and specialty accounts such as real estate and natural resources) and fixed income (including corporate, government and high-yield bond accounts). If an annuity had international stock or bond accounts, we considered them too. We then asked Morningstar Inc. of Chicago (800-876-5005) to assign each subaccount a score from 0 to 100 based on its percentile performance compared with other subaccounts that have the same investment objective during the three years to Nov. 1 or a weighted average of the three- and five-year periods to that date. Finally, we averaged the scores of individual subaccounts to produce each annuity's overall score and rank.

Notes: Annual insurance charge includes costs for death benefit and expenses, but not annual contract fees that typically run $25 to $40 a year. [1]AG: aggressive growth; B: balanced; CB: corporate bond; G: growth; GI: growth and income; GB: government bond; HY: high-yield bond; IB: international bond; IS: international stock; SP: specialty fund. [2]Annual subaccount expenses as a percentage of assets [3]Morningstar risk ratings range from one (the lowest risk) to five (the highest) and measure a subaccount's volatility as compared with that of others in its category [4]Total returns are net of all fees except surrender charges and annual contract fees. [5]Minimum initial investment can be spread over the course of a year. [6]$1,000 in New York [7]The company offers a similar annuity with the same investment choices but slightly different terms under the name Prudential Discovery Plus. [8]$5,000 in New York and Pennsylvania [9]The company offers a similar annuity with the same investment choices but slightly different terms under the name Fortis Benefits Masters Annuity.

ment goals. And we eliminated from consideration annuities that were not available in most states and those that require you to invest your money in one up-front payment. Such single-premium annuities are unsuitable for most people because the accounts build up their savings gradually. Connecticut Mutual Panorama grabbed the No. 1 spot for overall performance, propelled by the outstanding record of its growth and balanced funds over the three years that ended November 1, 1993. Cruising into second place was Phoenix Home Life Big Edge Plus. And third went to Ameritas Overture II, which narrowly edged out Fidelity Retirement Reserves even though Fidelity manages the investment portfolios for both. Before you rush out to buy one of these top performers, however, consider the following advice from the experts that we consulted.

Buy annuities that suit your investment style. Top-ranking Connecticut Mutual offers only four basic subaccounts—a growth, balanced, corporate bond and money-market fund. And Phoenix Home Life offers just six. If you want to invest in specialized sectors or diversify broadly, you should consider annuities that scored lower on overall performance but provide a wider array of options. Even if your preferences are plain vanilla, you shouldn't automatically go with our overall top rankers. If you plan to stick mostly to one style such as growth or total return, then consider an annuity from our list of top performers by investment category.

Don't become obsessive about annuity fees. Sure, they can dampen performance. Let's assume that an annuity and a mutual fund both earn 10% a year but the annuity's expenses are one percentage point higher than the fund's. It may take 15 years for the annuity to amass the same total after-tax earnings as the fund even with its tax advantages. Yet superior performance can minimize this difference. If both investments earned 12%, for example, the annuity could surpass the fund in only 10 years. Since stock accounts are the most likely to generate such lofty returns, you should tilt your annuity investment mix toward them. In general,

you should be wary of annuities with total expenses that exceed 2% annually. But it would be foolish to avoid an annuity with strong investment performance simply because its fees are a bit above this industry benchmark.

Go for performance, not glitzy features. To separate themselves from the competition, some annuities are offering gimmicky extras such as a so-called step-up feature. This resets the death benefit after six years to the higher of the account's market value or what you paid in. The death benefit is then reset again every six years to the higher of market value or the previous reset. The Franklin ValueMark II annuity even guarantees that your heirs will receive at least your original investment compounded at 5% a year. But look closer. The guarantee is only a benefit if you happen to die when your account balance is down from the last reset (or when the average annual earnings in your account are below 5% in the case of Franklin ValueMark II). Such gimmicks can also add to the annuity's annual cost and erode your return. But if a top-performing annuity offers a reset, as does second-ranked Phoenix Home Life Big Edge Plus, there's no harm in grabbing it.

Beware the clone fund pitch. A salesman often will tout an annuity because it has a subaccount that is akin to a popular mutual fund. But watch out. Even if the subaccount has the same name and manager as a fund, that doesn't mean the returns would be equal. "Rarely are they exactly the same portfolios," says Morningstar's Jennifer Strickland. "In most cases, they're fraternal rather than identical twins." For example, in the Nationwide/Best of America IV annuity, the TCI Growth subaccount has averaged a 13% annual return over the past five years, a full five points a year less than the 18% annual gain for its better-known mutual fund cousin, Twentieth Century Growth. Why? Although the same portfolio managers run both the fund and the subaccount, the advisers take a slightly less aggressive approach in managing the annuity. So you should strive to buy an annuity for its performance, not for what it imitates.

How to Take Care of Your Heirs

No need to doze over those turgid tracts on wills, trusts and death taxes.
Here's our concise guide to establishing a lasting legacy.

It's strange but true: about seven of 10 adults have life insurance, but only a third have wills. The most plausible explanation for such faulty forward planning is that insurance is sold and wills are not. Since lawyers don't hawk their wares door to door, you will just have to motivate yourself to provide a secure financial future for your family. Consider the possible consequences if you decide to do nothing:

Thy will won't be done. Should you die without a will, your heirs' inheritances will be determined under state laws of intestacy, which may not match your own notion of who should get what. In most states, your assets are apportioned among your spouse and children, often with half to two-thirds going to your kids.

The tax man grabbeth. Even if you write a will, your estate may not escape taxation. By using trusts, however, a married couple can pass as much as $1.2 million to their heirs free of federal estate tax with its grim-reaper rates as high as 55%.

Suffer ye children. A solid estate plan will protect and preserve property you leave to children or disabled heirs. You can also spare your heirs the inconvenience of probate, the legal process in which your will is proved valid and your assets are inventoried in court.

To accomplish all of this, you will need the help of an attorney who's an expert on estate planning. Finding one may be difficult. Ask your friends, relatives, accountant or financial planner for recommendations, or call your city's bar association and ask for the telephone number of the local estate planning council. You will be able to communicate more effectively with your lawyer if you understand the fundamentals discussed below.

Preparing a simple will. Many people never get around to writing a will for fear of confronting their own mortality. Others figure they don't need one if they own all of their assets jointly. But their survivors eventually learn that joint ownership is no substitute for a well-drafted will. And the peace of mind that it provides comes at a modest price. Simple wills for a husband or wife cost around $150 each. A more elaborate will might cost considerably more, depending on the complexity of your family and finances.

Assume, for example, that an elderly widow puts her son's name on her bank account, making him joint owner of the balance, so he can deposit checks for her. She may tell him to divide the money equally with his siblings after she's gone, but what if he decides to keep the cash? His brothers and sisters can sue, but litigation is costly and time consuming and may not be worthwhile unless a large amount of money is at stake.

Married couples shouldn't rely solely on joint ownership either. If a childless couple were involved in an accident in which the husband was killed while the wife survived for another day, the husband's half of the couple's joint property would automatically pass to his wife. But unless she managed somehow to scribble a will as she lay on her deathbed, all of the couple's assets would go to the wife's relatives after her death, leaving his family with nothing. Couples with minor children also need wills, despite the fact that their jointly held property will go to their children under state laws of intestacy if they die together. It's in a will that you nominate guardians to care for your children and manage their inheritances. If you don't name

The Top Retirement Software

Reviewers assembled from *Computerized Investing* magazine and MONEY have graded the most popular retirement planning software programs for their overall ease of use and the quality of their advice. Leading the winners: Vanguard's inexpensive $17.50 package and Calypso's $103 program.

SOFTWARE	GRADE	PRICE	HARDWARE REQUIREMENTS	COMMENTS
Vanguard's Retirement Planner 800-876-1840	A	$17.50	IBM PC or compatible with 1MB of hard disk and 512KB of random access memory (RAM); DOS 3.0	The most user-friendly program of the bunch, Vanguard automatically computes your Social Security benefits and lets you adjust investment returns and taxes both before and after retirement.
Retire ASAP by Calypso Software 800-225-8246	A	103.00	IBM PC or compatible with 1.5MB of hard disk and 640KB of RAM; DOS 3.0	Though the most expensive of the five programs, ASAP is ideal for determining the most suitable asset allocations for your current stage in life. Like Vanguard, software shows you how much you stand to lose in Social Security benefits by taking early retirement.
Harvest Time by Computer Lab 800-397-1456	A–	54.00	IBM PC or compatible with 1.5MB of hard disk; DOS 3.3	While versatile, Harvest Time scores low on the ease-of-use test. For instance, though its charts can be displayed on-screen, you can't print them out. Best feature: tables that let you track your contributions and the investment growth in all your retirement plans.
Fidelity's Retirement Planning Software 800-457-1768	B	17.50	IBM PC or compatible with 6.5MB of hard disk and 640KB of RAM; DOS 4.01	It's especially worthwhile for explaining key terms such as dollar-cost averaging and for recommending general investment strategies based on your finances. The program also graphically shows the devastating effects of delaying saving. But it doesn't calculate tax rates, either before or after retirement.
T. Rowe Price Retirement Planning Kit 800-541-1472	B	15.00	IBM PC or compatible with 640KB of RAM; DOS 2.1	The least helpful of the three fund-family programs, Price's doesn't offer specific retirement planning charts or compute your Social Security benefits. But it does put you through a clever three-stage risk/reward drill before recommending portfolio allocations among asset classes.

Note: Prices include shipping and handling but not local taxes. None of these programs is available for the Apple Macintosh. **Source:** American Association of Individual Investors' *Computerized Investing;* 312-280-0170.

caretakers for your kids, the probate judge will appoint guardians of his or her own choosing for the children and their assets.

You also nominate the executor of your estate in your will. It is his or her responsibility to pay your debts, file tax returns and disburse assets to your heirs after you are gone. (See "Advice for Executors" later in this chapter.) If you already have a will, examine it periodically to make sure it still reflects your wishes.

When to review your will. The sour old Scrooge who revises his will weekly to avenge every slight

may have a point. Most people seldom bother to review their wills at all, passing up the chance to make necessary changes. You and your lawyer should review your will every three years or so, but examine it sooner if you've grown much richer or suffered a serious financial setback. You should also review your will after the birth of a child or the death of a spouse or other beneficiary. An examination is also in order after tax law changes. And bear in mind that your will may be partially invalidated if you marry or divorce after writing it. If you move to another state, ask a local lawyer to make certain your will complies with your new state's statutes. He or she can also tell if you've done all you can to diminish state death taxes.

You needn't tear up your old will and begin anew to make minor changes. For example, you can add or remove a beneficiary, change the amount of someone's bequest or replace an executor or guardian by asking your attorney to draft an amendment to your will called a codicil. Like wills, codicils must be signed and witnessed. After you've added a couple of codicils, draw up a fresh will to avoid possible confusion. Whatever you do, don't alter the original copy of your will yourself. If you do, its validity can come into question.

Moreover, you shouldn't stash the original in your safe-deposit box; banks in many states will seal boxes until a court orders them opened. If you include burial instructions in your will, your survivors may not get to read them before your funeral. Leave the original copy of your will with your lawyer, who may store it in his office or, better yet, with other wills in a bank vault. Or you can file your will at your county probate court for a small fee. If you wish, you can give your executor a copy of your will. To make reviewing it easy, keep copies in your safe-deposit box as well as at home.

Keeping it in the family with trusts. If your heirs are very young, disabled or simply disinclined to manage money, you will shortchange them if you do nothing more than write a rudimentary will. Say that you and your spouse die and leave your assets to your minor children. The guardian of their property named in your will must report expenditures and investments on the children's behalf to a judge. This may prevent the guardian from stealing or dissipating the children's inheritances. But it also gives a judge who is unfamiliar with your financial goals and philosophy power over how your legacy is managed.

That's one reason why it's advisable to create a trust in your will to hold your children's inheritances. If you do, you needn't name a guardian of your children's assets because a trustee you select will follow instructions that you set down in your trust document. Another advantage of creating a trust is that you can keep the trust principal out of

your children's hands until you think they will be mature enough to manage money. If you leave property to your children in your will, they can claim their inheritances when they reach the age of majority, which is 18 in most states.

Many people shy away from trusts because they associate them with the superrich. In reality, a married couple might pay as little as $250 to establish trusts for their children. Trusts are quite flexible, and a lawyer can draft yours to fit your family's particular needs. Before you read about types of trusts, it may be helpful to understand just how trusts work.

A trust is a legal device that holds property placed in it by a person called the grantor for the benefit of one or more beneficiaries. The grantor sets forth instructions for the management of the trust and the disbursement of its income and principal in a document, called the trust agreement, drawn up by an attorney. The grantor also chooses a trustee to carry out his wishes.

There are two basic types of trusts, testamentary and living (sometimes called inter vivos). A testamentary trust is created in your will and takes effect upon your death. A living trust operates during your lifetime. Living trusts may be either revocable or irrevocable. With a revocable trust, you continue to control the trust property, meaning you can change the trust's provisions, terminate it or even serve as trustee. Once you establish an irrevocable trust, however, you cannot control assets in it or tinker with its provisions.

As a result, property in an irrevocable trust isn't included in your estate for the purpose of calculating estate taxes. (You may incur gift tax when you put property into an irrevocable trust.) Assets in a revocable trust are part of your taxable estate. A testamentary trust for your minor children that becomes irrevocable upon your death is included in your taxable estate because you controlled the property during your lifetime.

A trust is only as effective as the trustee you choose. The ideal trustee is financially savvy and has your children's best interests at heart. Your relatives and friends will probably agree to serve without any compensation. Institutional trustees

Duck This Pension Pitch

Life insurance agents and financial planners have come up with a novel new pitch to peddle policies. The basic spiel: use the tax-shelter benefits of your coverage to build your own private pension plan. If you salt away, say, $1,000 a month or more for 20 years into a universal or variable life insurance policy, the salesman explains, the investment portion of the policy (called the cash value) would grow by as much as 12% a year. Then, when you need income for retirement, you could stop paying premiums, withdraw what you've paid in and begin borrowing against the policy through the insurer's free or low-cost loans, which don't have to be repaid. The outstanding loan balance and any interest would be deducted from the death benefit when you die. And the loan proceeds escape income taxes.

Sounds good. But these private pension pitches can be dangerously misleading, warn retirement experts. "In the real world you're taking a lot of risk," cautions Mark White, president of Direct Insurance Services, a San Diego Insurance agency. If interest rates drop—or in the case of variable life if the stock market falls—so would the policy's return. Then your pile for retirement might never materialize. The tax-free loans could also backfire, since borrowing big could so erode the cash value that you would have to pay more premiums just to keep the policy in force. If the policy lapses, all loans in excess of the premiums you've paid plus any remaining cash value in the policy would become taxable. So if you plowed in $12,000 a year for 20 years, then borrowed $40,000 annually for 20 years, and the policy lapsed, you would owe taxes on at least $560,000. That's a $156,800 bill for someone in the 28% tax bracket. Our advice? Pass on these private pensions and stash your savings in IRAs, 401(k)s and variable annuities.

such as banks and trust companies will generally levy annual fees of about 1% of a trust's assets up to $1 million. After that, the larger the trust, the smaller the trustee's percentage.

Sidestepping estate taxes. If you fail to draw up an airtight estate plan, the IRS may claim a more than generous share of your estate. The top rate is currently 55% on taxable estates of more than $3 million. In addition, state death taxes range from zero to 30%. Still, with proper planning, most estates can escape federal and state taxation. Your $600,000 exclusion from federal taxes includes the sum of taxable gifts you make while you are alive as well as the estate you leave when you die. You can make tax-free gifts up to $10,000 a year each to as many people as you like; married couples giving jointly may bestow as much as $20,000 annually per recipient. You can also make unlimited tax-free gifts to charity and payments to health care and educational institutions to cover a relative's or friend's bills.

In addition, you may make gifts of any size and leave an estate of any value to your spouse tax-free. If your spouse is not adept at money management, you might want to leave assets to him or her in a trust that qualifies for the marital deduction, meaning that its contents aren't subject to estate tax. There are two basic types of marital deduction trusts. With a general power of appointment trust, your spouse decides which heirs get the trust's assets after he or she dies. With a QTIP trust (for qualified terminable interest property), you choose your spouse's eventual heirs.

If you leave everything to your spouse, however, you may succeed only in postponing estate taxes until his or her death. As a result, more complicated tax planning may be necessary. You can eliminate or at least reduce estate taxes by removing assets from your estate. This is accomplished by making tax-free gifts during your lifetime, including charitable contributions in your will and placing property in trusts.

A married couple can pass as much as $1.2 million to their heirs tax-free if both spouses fully utilize their $600,000 exemptions. Take, for example, a couple with revocable bypass trusts (sometimes called family or credit-shelter trusts). If the husband dies or becomes unable to manage his financial affairs, assets he owns of up to $600,000 go into his trust. His wife will receive income from the trust and is entitled, say, to as much as 5% or $5,000 of the principal, whichever is greater, each year. In addition, the trustee has the discretion to give her the principal that she needs to support herself or pay medical bills. After her death, the couple's children become the trust's beneficiaries. No estate tax will be due because the trust isn't included in the wife's estate and the amount contributed to it by her husband was within his $600,000 exemption. If the wife dies or becomes incapacitated first, her trust is funded in a similar way for her husband's benefit.

You can also trim your tax liability by placing property in an irrevocable living trust. The hitch: few people can afford to relinquish control of real estate, securities or other assets years before their death. Many people, however, can afford to transfer the ownership of their life insurance policies to an irrevocable life insurance trust. Upon your death, your life insurance proceeds go into such a trust untaxed. Your spouse typically receives income from the trust for life and can tap its principal if necessary. After he or she dies, the assets go to heirs named in your trust agreement.

There's one catch, however. If you die within three years of establishing an irrevocable life insurance trust, the insurance proceeds are included in your taxable estate. For that reason, attorneys often include a clause in the trust agreement stating that should you die within three years, the insurance will go directly to your spouse or into a trust for his or her benefit. The trust is included in his or her estate.

Why it pays to be charitable. You can also remove assets from your taxable estate by making gifts to charity during your lifetime or in your will. If you give during your lifetime, you can be a philanthropist at wholesale prices because you get an income tax deduction and remove the property from your estate. You can also experience the joy of giving, which you cannot do if you leave money to a charity in your will. Another option: you can even give assets to a charity and keep on getting income from them by establishing a trust or buying an annuity from the charity. Of course, because you retain income from your gift, the tax deductions you receive will be smaller than what you might have gotten with an outright gift.

If you establish a charitable remainder unitrust, for example, you receive an amount determined annually by multiplying a fixed percentage that you select when you create the trust—typically 7% to 9%—by the market value of the trust's assets. After your death, payments end or a beneficiary that you name can continue to receive the income from the trust. When he or she dies, the trust's property passes to the charity. In general, charities welcome only sizable remainder unitrusts that are worth $25,000 or more.

Charitable remainder annuity trusts work much like unitrusts but pay out a fixed amount each year, usually 7% to 9%. Appreciated property producing little or no income makes the best gift. If you sold it and reinvested the proceeds for higher income, you would incur a taxable capital gain. But if a charitable trust sells the property, no tax is due. For smaller donors, some charities offer pooled income funds that operate much like mutual funds. Many such funds accept initial donations as small as $5,000.

Altruists whose hearts are bigger than their bank accounts should also consider charitable gift annuities. Many tax-exempt organizations issue these contracts for contributions as small as $1,000. In exchange for your donation, the charity pays you a fixed amount each year for life. The younger you are when you buy the annuity, the lower your return. For example, a 50-year-old would receive 6.5% for life while a 90-year-old would collect 14%. You would receive more income if you bought an annuity from an insurance company, but you would not get any income tax deductions or an estate tax break.

One last point: it's crucial to leave a liquid estate. If yours is loaded with real estate or fine art, your heirs may be forced to sell your assets at fire-sale prices to satisfy the tax man. Your survivors will not face a liquidity crisis if you leave them enough life insurance to pay the estate taxes. Also, insurance proceeds are not subject to probate, so your executor will be able to get his or her hands on cash fast.

Advice for executors. So your father wants you to serve as the executor of his estate. No doubt you won't think of this honor again until he dies. But you will be able to settle his estate more economically if you prepare for the task in advance. First, you must discuss your father's financial affairs and intentions with him. Ask him to maintain an up-to-date inventory of his assets and liabilities, which he can leave in a specified place. He doesn't have to give you a copy of the will, but he should tell you where the original is and who prepared it.

When you file the will in court, a judge will appoint you executor of the estate. The court may require you to post a bond—the size is typically

---

Money Helps

Q. My husband and I plan to leave money to our son and daughter, and we want to place our daughter's share in a trust. I have found two trust companies. But how should I choose between them?
—Dorothy Havens, Rio Rico, Ariz.

A. Start by getting such basic information as the minimum amount the company handles (usually $100,000) and its fees (from 1% to 2% of assets per year). Then request the performance figures (over one, three and five years) of its stock and bond portfolios and compare them with those of similar mutual funds. You might also encourage your daughter to interview several trust officers to find one with whom she feels most comfortable. After you are gone, the two of them will have to negotiate a number of important matters concerning her use of your legacy.

---

equal to the value of an estate's cars, furnishings and other personal property—to safeguard the financial interests of other heirs, unless your father waived the bond in his will. The bond premium is paid out of the estate.

Your first duty is to identify and determine the value of the estate's assets. Then, with an attorney's aid, you must shepherd the estate through probate proceedings. You needn't hire the lawyer who prepared your father's will. But you may want to do so if he or she is familiar with your father's financial affairs. Fees for attorneys, appraisers and accountants come out of the estate. If your father rented a safe-deposit box, you may have to inventory its contents under the watchful eyes of a state tax collector. It's also your responsibility to file claims for any life insurance or veterans' and Social Security benefits that are due. If your father died in an accident or because of medical malpractice, see to it that any necessary lawsuits are filed.

In the meantime, you must invest and protect the estate's assets, perhaps seeking advice from a broker, investment adviser or bank trust officer. Finally, you must pay your father's outstanding debts, file any required income, federal estate and state death tax returns and distribute what's left over to your father's heirs. It's your prerogative to determine which assets to sell to raise cash to pay debts, taxes and bequests. Throughout, you must keep careful records because most courts require a detailed accounting of all money received, spent and held by the estate.

Your load may be lightened considerably if your father has named a bank or trust company as co-executor. The institutional executor will make investment decisions and file tax returns, relying on you to interpret your father's wishes. But don't count on such assistance unless your father's estate is both large and complicated. Most banks and trust companies won't handle estates of less than $75,000. An institutional executor's fees range from 2% to 5% of the estate's total value.

What's in it for you? Your commission, which may be set by state law or the probate court, is 1% to 5% of the estate. But you can waive the fee, accepting instead the gratitude of your fellow heirs.

Should You Work After Retirement?

Career switching and part-time jobs are big among retirees seeking an escape from the paralyzing boredom afflicting so many of their peers.

Chances are there's another job in your retirement, even if you won't need the pay. What with longer, healthier lives and earlier, richer retirements, Americans face a prospect that would have startled their parents and left their grandparents incredulous: decades of active, useful living after they receive the golden handshake. What sensible person whose life has largely been defined by work would want to laze through so many potentially fruitful years? Here are no-nonsense answers to some of the first questions you are apt to ask yourself about that next big step.

Why should I work after I retire? To begin with, you may have no choice. Inflation, poor planning and an inadequate pension may force the issue. And even if you don't need a job to make ends meet, you may decide you want one just to keep active and healthy—benefits that become more crucial as you get older.

Does it pay to keep working? If you're well off, you could wind up losing money by working. Social Security and tax code provisions penalize people who earn too much in retirement. For example, if you go back to work between the ages of 62 and 64, you will lose one dollar of Social Security benefits for every two dollars you earn above certain income limits. Between 65 and 69, you give up one dollar of benefits for every three dollars earned over specified limits. Once you reach age 70, you can earn as much as you like without penalty. In addition, you are taxed on up to 50% of your Social Security benefits if the total of your adjusted gross income, nontaxable interest, and half your Social Security benefits exceeds $25,000 ($32,000 if you are married). If that total exceeds $34,000 ($44,000 for couples), you owe tax on up to 85% of your benefits. If you keep working past

65, your benefits will rise by a certain percentage each year until age 70. These increases range from 3% to 8% depending on the year of your birth.

When and how should I begin planning my retirement career? Start as soon as you can—certainly well before you call it quits at your present job. If you want to change fields, begin planning at least five years before you retire. This will give you time to take classes and meet people in your field of interest. Even if you want to stay in the same field, it's a good idea to research potential employers a year before your planned retirement.

What's the best way to find a job? Most career counselors answer this question with the buzz word *networking*. Make a list of everyone you know—friends, relatives, business relations, old school chums, even distant acquaintances—who may be able to help you find a job, whether it is in your old field or a new one. You can often make useful contacts at career seminars or by joining professional organizations. If you don't know anyone at a company you are interested in, try to find out the name of the person who has the power to hire you. Look in the *Reference Book of Corporate Managements* or *Standard & Poor's Register*, available at most libraries. Or phone the personnel department at the company. Then write a letter to that executive detailing your skills and interests. After a week or so, follow up with a phone call. Be cordial but persistent. Typically, you will have to be interviewed by 20 to 30 people, and it may take anywhere from three months to a year before a job offer materializes.

Will I be offered a lower salary because I am receiving a pension? The practice still exists at many companies, but habits are changing. Federal law protects older job seekers from arbitrary hiring and salary discrimination. And employers are coming to appreciate that older workers are usually well worth full pay. If you are asked your salary expectations, be assertive. To protect yourself from being shortchanged, find out what the average salary is for the position you want. Career counselors or library research can help. Should you meet the job qualifications for a position in your old field, it's only fair that you should request the middle to high end of the salary range. If you are changing fields and need additional training, you should expect your salary to be at the low end of the scale.

Should I prepare for conflicts with younger colleagues?

The best preparation is the confidence of knowing that you're probably more experienced and more reliable than younger workers. If you feel someone is treating you unfairly because of your age, discuss the matter in a friendly, professional manner. If your troubles continue, complain to your superior. If you are at least 40 years old and the person causing your difficulties is in a higher position, go to your local Equal Employment Opportunity Commission office. The commission will investigate to determine whether your accusation has merit. If the EEOC probers find your grievance valid, they typically will try to resolve it by conciliation before taking an employer or individual to court. You can also sue independently, but that can take months.

Should I consider starting my own business?

Probably not. While independence sounds exhilarating, don't forget that 66% of small businesses fail within five years, often because of poor planning or lack of funds. Before you embark on what could be a financially and emotionally devastating experience, ask yourself the following questions (more than one or two nays should give you pause). Do I have a product or service that's really needed? Do I have financial backing or money of my own that I can afford to lose? Am I happy working alone? Most telling, do I consider myself a risk taker? Someone who's been a middle manag-

er at the same company for 30 years may not have what it takes to become an entrepreneur. If you are convinced that you are one, seek advice from people who have started their own businesses. The Service Corps of Retired Executives, sponsored by the Small Business Administration, provides free advice on starting your own business. Look for SCORE's address in your telephone directory under U.S. Government/SBA/SCORE.

Where can I go for job training and placement?

Your first and best source is your present employer. More and more companies offer job planning and counseling. Another option is to call your state job training or employment service (look in the telephone book under State Government Offices). Many have listings for older workers or can at least direct you to placement services in your area. Private career counselors provide occupational testing, one-on-one counseling and training in job-search skills. But if your employer doesn't pay the fees for you, be prepared for charges that can run into the thousands. Another excellent source of help is the growing number of nonprofit organizations set up to assist older workers. The American Association of Retired Persons sponsors AARP Works, an employment planning program available in more than 100 locations. For information, write to AARP Works, AARP Fulfillment, 601 E Street, N.W., Washington, D.C. 20049. You can also write for nonpaying consulting work to the National Executive Service Corps (257 Park Avenue South, New York, N.Y. 10010), a volunteer placement service for retired executives. Small and medium-size businesses often recruit through its Senior Career Planning & Placement Service.

How can I try out a new career?

If you don't need to work for money, by all means explore the field of volunteering. Often this can later turn into a paid job. There's a big advantage to starting this way. You can set your own schedule and contribute your time to a cause that may give you great satisfaction. Volunteer opportunities abound in hospitals, day care centers, libraries, schools and other community or charitable organizations.

Take Charge of Your Family's Finances

If you ask an American family how it's doing these days, you're likely to hear a tale of woe. College graduates can't find suitable work; managerial jobs are being slashed at even profitable companies. So most Americans will be astonished to hear that they're probably much better off than their folks were at the same stage of life. A recent study by the Congressional Budget Office reveals that baby boomers, who were born between 1946 and 1964, earn more money and have accumulated considerably more assets than their parents had in the early 1960s. Boomers ages 35 to 44 had a median net worth of $54,200 in 1989, the latest year for which complete statistics are available, compared with $29,300 (in 1989 dollars) for their counterparts in 1962.

Moreover, lifestyles are richer in many ways. For example, our houses are bigger, with a new home averaging almost 2,100 square feet, vs. 1,535 in the mid-1960s. But that doesn't mean we don't want even more, according to a Gallup poll that asked adults which of 10 indulgences they would most likely acquire if money were no object. The greatest portion of respondents (52%) said they wanted a vacation home, something that only 3% of all U.S. families now enjoy. Nearly half would like to take annual vacations to foreign countries. Fortunately, those dreams may be within reach. Interest rates are at or near record lows and inflation is dormant, paving the way for stronger economic growth and income gains in the years ahead. The advice and charts presented in this chapter will help you find out where your family stands in the uncertain 1990s and tell you how you can improve your position, starting with the increasingly important topic of job security.

How to Keep Your Career on Track

The recession is over, but America's employers continue to lay off people.
Here are smart strategies for keeping your career moving forward.

About a decade ago, people who lost their jobs could at least take comfort in the fact that the American economy, the world's great employment machine, would soon need their services again. Now, however, the recession has run its course, and many working people still have reasons to wake up in a cold sweat. Consider:

• While earlier recessions harmed mostly blue-collar employees, the latest layoffs hit more white-collar and professional workers than before. They made up 11% of unemployed during this recession, vs. less than 8% in the 1981-82 slump.

• Many of the lost jobs won't be coming back. After the 1981-82 recession, some 90% of laid-off workers found positions with comparable pay and benefits within nine months, according to Columbia University Business School professor Warren Boeker. "Today only 10% do," he says.

• Wages are only keeping pace with inflation, and salaries for many individual jobs are actually dropping. Architects lost 8% in real wages between 1983 and 1991, and economists 11%.

The main reason for continuing concern is that the economic rebound has been so halfhearted. This glacial recovery has generated barely enough jobs to cover the new workers entering the labor force, never mind the millions who are unemployed. Against that backdrop, President Clinton's vow to create as many as 500,000 additional jobs by the end of this year seems overly optimistic. And while hiring has ticked up recently, dropping the national unemployment rate to 6.4%, much of that job growth was in the form of part-time and temporary slots.

While these conditions were accelerated by recession, the forces that set them in motion,

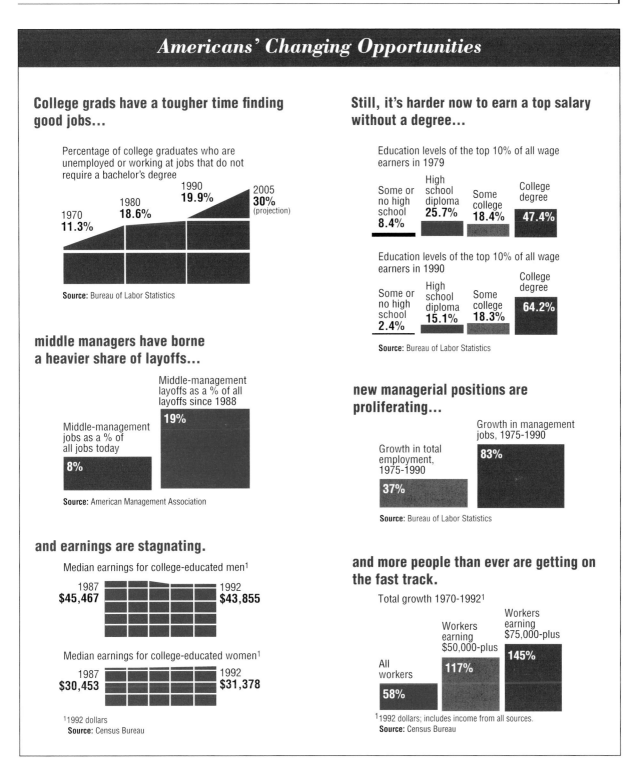

Americans' Changing Opportunities

College grads have a tougher time finding good jobs...

Percentage of college graduates who are unemployed or working at jobs that do not require a bachelor's degree

1970
11.3%

1980
18.6%

1990
19.9%

2005
30%
(projection)

Source: Bureau of Labor Statistics

middle managers have borne a heavier share of layoffs...

Middle-management layoffs as a % of all layoffs since 1988
19%

Middle-management jobs as a % of all jobs today
8%

Source: American Management Association

and earnings are stagnating.

Median earnings for college-educated men[1]

1987
$45,467

1992
$43,855

Median earnings for college-educated women[1]

1987
$30,453

1992
$31,378

[1]1992 dollars
Source: Census Bureau

Still, it's harder now to earn a top salary without a degree...

Education levels of the top 10% of all wage earners in 1979

Some or no high school
8.4%

High school diploma
25.7%

Some college
18.4%

College degree
47.4%

Education levels of the top 10% of all wage earners in 1990

Some or no high school
2.4%

High school diploma
15.1%

Some college
18.3%

College degree
64.2%

Source: Bureau of Labor Statistics

new managerial positions are proliferating...

Growth in total employment, 1975-1990
37%

Growth in management jobs, 1975-1990
83%

Source: Bureau of Labor Statistics

and more people than ever are getting on the fast track.

Total growth 1970-1992[1]

All workers
58%

Workers earning $50,000-plus
117%

Workers earning $75,000-plus
145%

[1]1992 dollars; includes income from all sources.
Source: Census Bureau

including fiercer global competition and rapid technological change, still persist. But you can overcome them to find a new job, or buttress your current career standing, with these strategies.

Stay on the lookout for a new job. The sad fact is that no position is completely safe these days. Average job tenure in corporate America has shrunk almost 50% over the past decade to fewer than seven years, calculates the outplacement firm Challenger Gray & Christmas. And even such traditional safe havens as the government no longer guarantee a sinecure. Fully 40% of U.S. municipalities have cut their payrolls in recent years, partly through attrition but mostly via pink slips.

Your next job need not be at another company. Pay attention to the special skills of people newly hired or recently promoted by your current employer. That will give you an indication of what talents are valued so you can upgrade your skills and re-invent your job to make sure it stays relevant to your company's needs. And get yourself noticed. Volunteer for projects and be ready to seize opportunities to show your leadership, even if only by running the United Way drive or the office softball team.

Think total compensation, not perks. In the boom years of the 1950s and 1960s, company-paid insurance and pension plans became so common that many workers came to regard them as a given. No more. With benefits shrinking as they become more expensive, you need to look at total compensation when negotiating a raise or considering a job offer. You should ask a prospective employer for a copy of its benefits handbook, and calculate your out-of-pocket costs for medical and life insurance. If you have young children, find out whether the company is among the 6% that underwrite the cost of child care. And thoroughly scrutinize its pension plan. In many cases, you'll come out ahead with a defined-contribution plan such as a 401(k) rather than a conventional defined-benefit pension. Reason: defined-contribution plans often require you to ante up your own money (sometimes matched by an employer). But you don't lose what you've saved when you leave the company. With a defined-benefit plan, on the other hand, you must stick around for five to seven years to become entitled to a benefit. That can be difficult in a volatile job market.

Approach small ponds with caution. Almost everyone who's worked for a big corporation has dreamed of moving to a smaller company, where there is more autonomy. And finding such jobs is relatively easy. Firms with fewer than 500 employees generate 51% of new jobs, according to a

study by James Medoff, James Hamilton and Charles Brown. But their research, published in *Employers Large and Small* (Harvard University Press, $22), concluded that the same small firms were responsible for an even larger fraction (53%) of job losses. "Unlike large companies, which lay off workers, small firms frequently go out of business," explains Medoff. Moreover, large firms pay salaries that average 30% more than the smaller ones and spend two to 10 times as much on benefits. Moral: if you insist on being a big fish in a small pond, try to pick a pond with good pay, decent benefits and bright prospects.

Broaden your horizons overseas. In 1987, 20 of the world's 50 largest companies were based in the U.S., compared with 28 in Europe or Japan. At last count, Americans could claim only 15 firms on that list, while the Europeans and Asians had expanded their share to 34. As trade barriers drop and companies compete abroad, you'll boost your chances for advancement at U.S. and foreign firms alike if you become more of a world citizen. To make yourself more attractive to international employers, you might start by brushing up your foreign languages or learning a new one. Also seize opportunities to travel abroad, whether for business or pleasure.

Actually working in another country is the best experience of all. That's why John Summers and his wife Marjorie lobbied his company for the chance to move to Tokyo. Summers, an application engineering manager for a Boston-based maker of assembly line equipment, wanted to learn more about Japan's highly advanced robotics industry. Marjorie, an attorney, hoped to become a cultural adviser to Asian and American firms. "Japan is the technology center of the universe and a huge part of the world market," says Summers, who, along with Marjorie, plans to soak up as much of the language and culture as he can.

Try working under contract. There's at least one respect in which a corporate staff reduction increases opportunity. Companies that have gone through a layoff often hire temporary help—not just clerical workers but consultants and managers—to handle specific, short-term assignments. Given the high cost of benefits, such as federally mandated family leave, it's cheaper than committing to a permanent employee. "As business picks up, many companies then fill staff jobs by trying out someone working on contract first," says David Lord of *Executive Recruiter News*, a trade magazine for the recruiting industry. The publication's list of search firms that place temporary managers in finance, human resources and other fields has doubled to 100 in recent years (you can order a copy for $15 by calling 800-531-0007).

Maintain your own employment file. If you have worked for many years and command a high salary, you may feel especially vulnerable to a layoff. Age discrimination is hard to prove. But you can challenge a layoff on grounds such as breach of faith and fair dealing if you document your performance beforehand. Keep a file including memos of praise and details of successes. Someday such evidence could help you win higher severance

pay, contract work or even second thoughts by your boss about letting you go.

Keep a lid on your personal spending. Since you can't be sure what your salary or benefits will be a year from now, it's risky to spend with only the present in mind. Thus many financial planners urge salaried clients to put away 10% of their pay. Equally important is to avoid working for the same company as your spouse, since you risk suffering a double whammy if your company gets into trouble and lays off the two of you. Pat and Elizabeth Farrell of suburban Houston beat that hazard twice, when they worked together at Dow Chemical and then at Lockheed. But after hard times hit their latest employer, computermaker Compaq, she lost her $50,000-a-year job as an accountant and Pat would have been out of his $80,000 post as a facilities manager except for Compaq's policy of not laying off two spouses at once. "We'd have been cooked," says Elizabeth, who has opened a monogramming shop. Few employers would have been so enlightened.

Where to Find Today's Best Jobs

According to our comprehensive survey, career prospects appear brightest in the booming sectors of computing and health care and in the nation's capital.

Susan Laubert's career path shows the benefits of being in the right place and the right field. Over the past 12 years Laubert, a computer systems analyst, has seen four jobs disappear in corporate downsizings and cutbacks. Yet in each case she secured a new position at higher pay before she was through the door of the company she was leaving. The latest entry on her resume is RMS Technologies, where she supervises analysts who process data from a NASA satellite.

What's her secret? For one thing, as a computer analyst, Laubert is in the field that tops the Bureau of Labor Statistics list of the fastest growing white-collar jobs. Demand for systems analysts

remained strong throughout the past recession, even at many companies that were laying off other workers. What's more, Laubert is lucky enough to be plying her trade in the Washington, D.C. area, the nation's hottest job market. The capital region grew steadily during the 1980s and continues to add jobs faster than any other metropolitan area. Government spending acts as a magnet for everything from corporate lobbyists to law firms.

People who want to plant their careers in similarly fertile soil should consult the two sets of tables that follow on the next four pages. We identify the 50 managerial and professional occupations that will produce the most new jobs by year

Careers With the Best Prospects

The best opportunities belong to analysts (of computers and organizations) and therapists (for minds and bodies), according to our ranking of professional-managerial occupations that promise to show the greatest percentage employment gains by 2005. The figures in the second, third and fourth columns give a sense of what you can expect to earn pursuing each career. They are based on data from the Economic Research Institute, a compensation specialist in Newport Beach, Calif. The starting salary is an average of what people are generally paid in their first year. The median salary is at dead center; half the people

	CAREER (% increase expected by 2005)	Starting salary	Median salary	Typical top salary	Ratio of men to women	Tips and comments
1	Computer systems analyst (79)	$27,788	$38,821	$52,462	66/34	Those who understand how organizations work are in greatest demand.
2	Physical therapist (76)	19,168	25,807	34,375	22/78	Private practices are creating opportunities outside of hospitals and institutions.
3	Operations analyst (73)	20,521	29,654	50,047	57/43	Railroads and airlines are among the biggest employers.
4	Psychologist (64)	28,007	39,607	84,069	41/59	Worker training and computerized learning are hot specialties.
5	Travel agent (62)	14,250	23,817	37,563	40/60	Agencies that specialize in cruise bookings are expanding.
6	Computer programmer (56)	20,120	30,806	51,918	68/32	Businesses need programmers familiar with local area network technology.
7	Occupational therapist (55)	25,800	29,284	38,750	10/90	Experience treating back and repetitive motion injuries is valuable.
8	Management analyst (52)	18,147	30,992	110,600[9]	69/31	Many of these consultants serve as expert witnesses in business litigation.
9	Respiratory therapist (52)	27,614[2]	34,344	44,952	40/60	With gerontology experience you'll breathe easier about your future.
10	Marketing, advertising or p.r. manager (47)	23,261[3]	39,190	76,638	69/31	Having a thorough understanding of product development will promote your career.
11	Hotel manager or assistant manager (44)	32,283[4]	55,438	80,934	76/24	An ability to deal with benefits and personnel is a fast way in.
12	Registered nurse (44)	28,773	31,463	62,488	5/95	Nurses are needed at outpatient facilities and to treat patients at home.
13	Health services manager (42)	45,723	51,677	91,381	33/67	Medical groups and clinics are looking for people with marketing skills.
14	Broker/financial service representative (40)	26,269[5]	27,432	42,770	71/29	Financial firms need people to sell retirement savings plans to employers.
15	Accountant (34)	20,366	30,314	50,765	48/52	Women now represent more than half the profession.
16	Biologist (34)	21,221	33,485	56,503	58/42	Funding for AIDS studies has created renewed demand for biomedical researchers.
17	Counselor (34)	13,365	18,869	34,962	39/61	In 38 states and D.C., drug, family and other counselors must now be licensed.
18	Data processing manager[1] (34)	26,752	45,938	87,066	80/20	Develop a specialty such as database management or telecommunications.
19	Electrical/electronic engineer (34)	26,047[6]	41,896	68,768	91/9	Designers of microprocessors for artificial intelligence applications are in demand.
20	Lawyer (34)	31,632[7]	51,111	121,718	81/19	The President, his wife and most of the Cabinet are lawyers.
21	Physician (34)	60,787[8]	110,573	266,220	80/20	Family practitioners will find it easier to start careers in HMOs or rural practices.
22	Pilot (34)	21,845	33,887	62,835	97/3	Two years as a flight instructor helps you qualify for high-paying airline positions.
23	Property manager (34)	30,676	51,684	74,697	54/46	Employers prefer that you have real estate sales experience as well as a college degree.
24	Secondary school teacher (34)	18,768	28,737	49,104	45/55	Mainstreaming of special-ed students makes special-ed training a plus.
25	Social worker (34)	13,797	17,943	33,169	31/69	Rural areas continue to need more of these professionals.

Sources: Bureau of Labor Statistics, Economic Research Institute **Notes:** Top salaries do not reflect earnings of supervisors or managers unless otherwise noted. **1** – BLS growth projections include scientific and engineering managers. **2** – Starting salary is for therapy aide; other salaries are for therapy managers. **3** – Salaries are for advertising managers. **4** – Salaries are for hotel managers. **5** – Brokers' earnings depend on commissions; salaries are for financial sales representatives. **6** – Salaries are for electrical engineers. **7** – Salaries are

in the field make more than that, half make less. Typical top salaries reflect wages that someone would receive after eight to 12 years of service in that position. All these figures are based on national samples; there are considerable differences from region to region. In the fifth column is the ratio of men to women pursuing each career, as reported in the most recent Census. Despite the gains made by women over the past decade, striking imbalances remain in such male-dominated fields as engineering and architecture.

	CAREER (% increase expected by 2005)	Starting salary	Median salary	Typical top salary	Ratio of men to women	Tips and comments
26	Speech pathologist (34)	$19,651	$26,457	$45,239	12/88	Bilingual practitioners are especially sought after.
27	Construction or project manager (33)	28,797[10]	49,452	92,194	98/2	Look for jobs on industrial projects, and be prepared to relocate.
28	Human resources specialist (32)	20,595	31,952	43,930	43/57	Small companies need people who know everything from benefits to job safety.
29	Restaurant or food service manager (32)	19,808	32,744	43,740	39/61	Requirements now include computer literacy at many establishments.
30	Visual artist (32)	23,814	26,960	51,488[16]	48/52	Be able to work with several graphics software programs.
31	Veterinarian (31)	29,591	41,847	77,120	73/27	The number of women vets has tripled since 1980.
32	Civil engineer (30)	29,123	41,188	66,227	94/6	Expertise in constructing pollution-control facilities will ensure employment.
33	Inspector/ compliance officer (30)	15,697	22,419	39,966	77/23	The growth of government regulation creates boundless opportunity.
34	Adult education teacher (29)	15,718	22,192	39,360	60/40	Look for jobs at community colleges and mid-size companies.
35	Financial manager (28)	25,098[11]	42,284	81,106	55/45	Talk your way into the expanding global investing field with foreign language skills.
36	Interior or industrial designer (26)	18,875	27,275	46,830	47/53	Make sure your training fits the licensing requirements in your state.
37	Writer or editor (26)	12,930[12]	18,048	62,927	49/51	Technical writers have the best employment prospects.
38	Architect (24)	28,084	41,066	86,019	83/17	Historic restoration and building renovations are the hot specialties now.
39	Insurance underwriter (24)	19,967	28,853	48,963	36/64	Actuaries tend to get the highest-paying entry-level jobs.
40	Mechanical engineer (24)	29,125	41,190	66,228	95/5	The three big specialties are robotics, robotics and robotics.
41	Nutritionist/ dietitian (24)	17,000[13]	27,300	36,000	6/94	Food-processing firms need help coping with new federal labeling regulations.
42	Project cost estimator (24)	20,917	28,503	42,796	73/27	Best prospects are in industries like biotech, where the manufacturing process is evolving.
43	School administrator (24)	29,830[14]	41,524	66,163	45/55	It helps if you have a background in business administration as well as education.
44	Administrative manager (23)	26,057	41,920	68,833	42/58	Many are setting up their own firms to handle clerical work for large companies.
45	Employment interviewer (23)	21,412	31,309	42,708	24/76	Agencies that supply temporary office workers need interviewers.
46	Primary school teacher (23)	19,440	28,935	48,912	12/88	The fastest-growing student populations are in sunbelt states.
47	Purchasing agent (23)	16,481[15]	17,692	64,695	55/45	Telecommunications companies offer the best prospects for advancement.
48	Budget analyst (22)	23,712	32,305	43,468	40/60	Besides accounting skills, you need the ability to make effective presentations.
49	Clerical supervisor (22)	16,596	25,795	35,471	9/91	You usually need to start by doing the kind of work that you want to supervise.
50	Geologist (22)	30,866	45,943	64,503	89/11	Consulting firms need ground-water experts to help plan cleanup projects.

for corporate lawyers. **8** – Salaries are for general practitioners. **9** – Salary is for partners in consulting firms. **10** – Salaries are for construction superintendents. **11** – Salaries are for accounting managers. **12** – Starting and median salaries are for writers; top salary is for editors. **13** – Salaries are from 1990 BLS data. **14** – Salaries are for principals and headmasters. **15** – Starting and median salaries are for agents; top salary is for purchasing managers. **16** – Top salary is for commercial artists.

America's Top Job Markets

The smaller cities have the most favorable employment climates. These areas will thrive as companies continue to take advantage of the lower taxes and operating costs that can be found away from the older trade centers like New York and Chicago. We identified the nation's most promising job markets by first looking for the metropolitan areas where employment would be growing faster than the projected national average rate of 3.6% a year. (Forecasts are by Woods & Poole

METROPOLITAN AREA (total new jobs by 1995)	Fast-growing occupations	Typical salary	Purchasing power
1 Washington, D.C. (118,200)	Purchasing manager	$43,800	$35,600
	Computer programmer	34,600	28,100
	Accountant	34,000	27,600
2 Anaheim, Calif. (108,800)	Sales manager	45,000	34,000
	Financial service rep	33,000	24,900
	Photographer	33,500	25,300
3 Atlanta (104,600)	Operations analyst	31,600	32,000
	Physical therapist	27,500	27,800
	Psychologist	42,000	42,500
4 Phoenix (92,000)	Travel agent	23,000	23,100
	Computer systems analyst	37,500	37,700
	Financial manager	40,900	41,100
5 San Diego (77,100)	Psychologist	42,600	36,600
	Sales manager	40,800	35,100
	Medical services manager	59,900	51,400
6 Tampa-St. Petersburg (76,300)	Management analyst	29,500	30,400
	Computer programmer	29,300	30,200
	Computer systems analyst	37,500	38,600
7 Orlando (70,300)	Civil engineer	39,700	40,400
	Travel agent	22,700	23,100
	Primary school teacher	27,600	28,100
8 Dallas (69,300)	Computer systems analyst	39,200	39,800
	Financial service rep	27,800	28,200
	Operations analyst	30,000	30,500
9 Riverside, Calif. (67,700)	Sales manager	39,400	35,300
	Designer	28,300	25,300
	Accountant	31,500	28,200
10 Minneapolis-St. Paul (64,700)	Writer	18,700	18,600
	Psychologist	41,700	41,500
	Chemical engineer	52,400	52,200
11 Charlotte, N.C. (53,100)	Pilot	35,200	34,900
	Operations analyst	30,500	30,200
	Sales manager	39,800	39,400
12 Seattle (50,900)	Technical writer	39,800	34,900
	Computer systems analyst	42,300	37,200
	Financial service rep	29,800	26,200
13 Columbus, Ohio (48,300)	Management analyst	32,200	32,000
	Computer programmer	32,000	31,800
	Chemist	37,000	36,700
14 San Jose (47,900)	Computer systems analyst	44,200	34,400
	Technical writer	41,500	32,300
	Mechanical engineer	46,900	36,500
15 Oakland (46,600)	Computer programmer	36,100	30,500
	Physical therapist	30,300	25,500
	Computer systems analyst	45,000	38,000
16 Fort Worth (45,700)	Property manager	49,600	51,600
	Accountant	28,900	30,000
	Computer programmer	29,400	30,500
17 Sacramento (45,500)	Management analyst	34,600	30,900
	Purchasing agent	20,100	17,900
	Accountant	33,800	30,200

METROPOLITAN AREA (total new jobs by 1995)
18 Cincinnati (44,500)
19 Raleigh-Durham, N.C. (44,000)
20 Portland, Ore. (43,200)
21 Indianapolis (42,100)
22 West Palm Beach (40,100)
23 Fort Lauderdale (39,200)
24 Greensboro-Winston-Salem, N.C. (37,500)
25 New Brunswick, N.J. (33,500)
26 Las Vegas (32,700)
27 Milwaukee (32,700)
28 Nashville (32,100)
29 Grand Rapids (29,200)
30 Greenville, S.C. (28,100)
31 Rochester, N.Y. (27,800)
32 Austin (26,800)
33 Providence (25,300)
34 Memphis (23,900)

Economics, a research firm in Washington, D.C.) To fill out each city's employment picture, we cite three jobs that are especially hot in the area, along with representative salaries. We calculate the buying power of each salary by adjusting it for the local cost of living. A computer programmer earns more in Washington, D.C. than in Fort Wayne. But the nation's capital is more expensive, so the programmer's paycheck will go further in the Hoosier State.

Fast-growing occupations	Typical salary	Purchasing power
Computer systems analyst	$38,500	$38,500
Management analyst	30,900	30,900
Public relations specialist	29,900	29,900
Computer programmer	29,100	29,900
Chemist	34,700	35,600
Economist	30,900	31,700
Management analyst	31,600	29,800
Technical writer	37,100	35,100
Physical therapist	26,300	24,800
Insurance underwriter	27,800	28,700
Property manager	50,400	52,000
Computer programmer	29,700	30,600
Financial service rep	26,500	26,600
Property manager	50,900	51,100
Lawyer	50,300	50,500
Travel agent	22,700	20,300
Medical services manager	54,400	48,600
Primary school teacher	27,500	24,600
Computer systems analyst	36,800	38,000
Designer	25,300	26,100
Registered nurse	29,200	30,100
Operations analyst	30,200	26,300
Accountant	30,900	26,900
Architect	41,800	36,300
Property manager	57,200	56,600
School administrator	46,000	45,500
Lawyer	56,600	56,000
Management analyst	31,000	29,900
Computer systems analyst	38,600	37,300
Medical services manager	56,000	54,000
Property manager	51,300	55,100
Management analyst	30,600	32,800
Primary school teacher	28,500	30,600
Industrial designer	29,700	29,400
Accountant	31,900	31,600
Registered nurse	33,100	32,800
Electrical engineer	38,700	40,700
School administrator	38,300	40,300
Mechanical engineer	38,000	40,000
Computer systems analyst	42,200	39,100
Civil engineer	44,800	41,500
Designer	30,100	27,800
Property manager	51,000	54,900
Computer programmer	30,100	32,400
Electrical engineer	41,100	44,200
Psychologist	39,300	31,400
Human resources specialist	31,900	25,400
Computer programmer	30,700	24,500
Health services manager	53,900	56,400
Pilot	32,500	34,000
Financial service rep	26,300	27,600

METROPOLITAN AREA (total new jobs by 1995)	Fast-growing occupations	Typical salary	Purchasing power
35 **Oxnard-Ventura, Calif.** (23,000)	Computer systems analyst	$41,500	$33,700
	Lawyer	54,100	44,000
	Accountant	32,800	26,600
36 **Tucson** (23,000)	Property manager	50,700	50,000
	Interior designer	23,900	23,600
	Social worker	18,600	18,300
37 **Albany-Schenectady, N.Y.** (19,400)	Psychologist	43,400	37,900
	Social worker	19,900	17,400
	Public relations specialist	33,500	29,200
38 **Wilmington** (18,900)	Computer systems analyst	43,200	39,000
	Financial manager	46,600	42,000
	Real estate agent	21,200	19,100
39 **Fort Myers, Fla.** (18,300)	Social worker	17,400	17,500
	Registered nurse	30,000	30,200
	Accountant	28,900	29,100
40 **Lake County, Ill.** (17,700)	Computer systems analyst	36,500	31,200
	Management analyst	28,900	24,800
	Chemical engineer	47,200	40,400
41 **Knoxville** (17,600)	Financial manager	37,000	39,800
	School administrator	36,300	39,100
	Registered nurse	27,300	29,400
42 **Harrisburg, Pa.** (15,500)	Operations analyst	30,200	29,600
	Computer systems analyst	39,800	38,900
	Social worker	18,700	18,300
43 **Allentown-Bethlehem, Pa.** (15,100)	Computer programmer	32,000	31,300
	Chemist	37,400	36,400
	Registered nurse	32,700	31,800
44 **Worcester, Mass.** (15,100)	Computer systems analyst	39,800	36,100
	Electrical engineer	42,800	38,700
	Accountant	31,300	28,300
45 **Santa Rosa-Petaluma, Calif.** (15,000)	Accountant	29,700	27,400
	Lawyer	51,500	47,500
	Physician	110,800	102,200
46 **Fort Wayne** (14,800)	Sales manager	37,900	40,800
	Computer programmer	30,900	33,300
	School administrator	41,600	44,700
47 **Portsmouth, N.H.** (14,800)	Accountant	31,900	27,500
	Real estate agent	19,600	17,000
	Pilot	34,600	29,800
48 **Columbia, S.C.** (14,700)	Management analyst	28,000	29,400
	School administrator	37,900	39,200
	Social worker	17,100	17,600
49 **El Paso** (14,700)	Primary school teacher	25,100	26,400
	Physician	107,500	112,800
	Registered nurse	27,300	28,700
50 **Syracuse** (14,300)	Computer systems analyst	39,900	38,600
	Psychologist	40,800	39,400
	Computer programmer	31,700	30,700

Sources: Bureau of Labor Statistics, Claritas/NPDC, Economic Research Institute, Woods & Poole

2005. Such service careers as computing, health care, teaching, counseling, marketing, accounting and management dominate our rankings. And no wonder, since the service sector is expected to account for nearly 19 of 20 new jobs over the next decade or so. We also name the metropolitan areas with the most promising job outlooks.

Economists point to two encouraging developments for job seekers. Service sector wages will continue to rise, thanks mainly to improvements in office technology that let each person accomplish more. And competition for jobs will ease a bit. The annual increase in the number of people looking for work will slow from the 2% or 3% of the postwar period to just 1.3% as the baby-bust generation increasingly enters the labor force.

Advice for New Grads

If job hunting were baseball, Steven Froot would have gone down swinging. Strike one came when the 1990 Florida State graduate sent his resume to the new Florida Marlins team in July 1991. He received a form rejection letter. Strike two followed three months later when Froot answered a Marlins employment ad and scored another form rejection. Six months later he spotted another Marlins ad in a week-old paper. He called, only to learn that the deadline for submitting applications had passed. But Froot, a finance major and lifelong ball fan, wouldn't be benched. He convinced a secretary to let him submit his resume by fax. And he beat out 500 other applicants to become the team's $25,000-a-year manager of ticket operations. Says Froot: "It's the next best thing to being on the team."

With a sluggish employment market producing only six new entry-level slots for every 10 graduates, you'll need Froot's persistence and then some to get a hit. Here are some tips:

Get your foot in the door. If the company you're interested in won't give you the job you want, consider taking another position to demonstrate your skills, style and commitment. Dara Metz, a 1991 art history graduate of the University of Arizona, set her sights on working for New York City's prestigious Pace Gallery as a registrar, a person who keeps track of an artwork's ownership history. Pace said no. When the interviewer mentioned a temporary secretarial position at the gallery, Metz jumped at it. Today she earns around $20,000 in her position as assistant registrar. Says Metz: "I was here, knowledgeable and eager, so they let me move up."

Intern or volunteer. After graduating from the University of California at Riverside in 1992, Amy Klabunde spent three months as an intern at a Department of Energy lab. While doing research, she learned a lot about environmental policy. That made it possible for her to snag a $28,000-a-year job at a San Diego environmental engineering firm.

Network. "The No. 1 job-search tactic is making connections," says Jerry Houser, director of the University of Southern California's career center. He suggests calling alumni for leads. To meet people, join professional organizations such as the Junior Chamber of Commerce and attend workshops, seminars and charitable events. "The more visible and active you are, the sooner you'll find a job," says Houser.

Be flexible. Don't be rigid about where you live, what you earn or your hours and duties. Darren Gordon, a 1990 Syracuse University graduate, hated his first job selling Grolier encyclopedias door to door in suburban New Jersey. But he saw the position as a first step in a sales and marketing career. Sure enough, after six months, he found a sweeter spot at Hershey Foods, where he earns $31,000 a year selling Reese's Peanut Butter Cups and Kit Kats to supermarkets located in the same general area as his old encyclopedia route.

A Quiz You Can Really Bank On

This cram course in banking facts can save you money as institutions invent more ways to raise fees. Turn to the end of the quiz for the answers.

1. Which method of calculating your credit card balance is better if you sometimes pay your bill in full and sometimes don't?

A. The "average daily balance" method

B. The "two cycle" method

2. You need to deposit $9,000 in your bank account by writing a check on your out-of-town money market fund. What's the quickest way to get the funds to clear?

A. Deposit one $9,000 check.

B. Deposit two $4,500 checks on successive days.

C. It doesn't matter.

3. You write 120 checks a year. Should you choose a free checking account that requires a $3,000 minimum balance, or an account that charges 50 cents per check but requires a $500 balance?

A. Free account

B. 50 cents-per-check account

4. Ads for bank CDs often warn of a penalty for early withdrawal. How much will you typically pay if you completely cash out of a one-year CD before it matures?

A. One to three months of interest

B. One to three months' interest plus 1.5% of principal

C. Just 1.5% of principal

5. Where are you likely to find the best interest rate on a car loan?

A. A bank

B. A thrift

C. A credit union

D. A car dealership

6. If you use an ATM at a bank other than your own, that bank cannot charge a fee unless your bank routinely charges for the use of ATMs.

A. True

B. False

7. Which of the following products sold at banks are covered by federal deposit insurance?

A. Annuities

B. Money-market funds

C. Money-market accounts

D. All of the above

8. If your real estate agent finds you a mortgage through his or her computerized loan origination system, you can be reasonably sure of getting the best possible terms.

A. True

B. False

9. If someone uses your lost or stolen ATM card to take cash from your account, for what amount are you responsible?

A. No more than $50 if you tell the bank within two business days of finding the loss

B. No more than $500 if you tell the bank with in 60 days of getting your statement

C. An unlimited amount

D. All of the above

10. You can often get the annual fee on your credit card reduced or eliminated if you have a good credit history.

A. True

B. False

11. Choose an adjustable rate mortgage over a fixed rate one when:

A. Interest rates are rising.

B. Interest rates are falling.

C. You plan to stay put for at least four years.

D. You plan to move within four years.

E. Either A, C or both

F. Either B, D or both

12. Even after the S&L crisis, some banking institutions are still not covered by federal insurance.

A. True

B. False

13. Which of the following entries can hurt your creditworthiness?

A. You moved in the past two years.

B. You changed jobs in the past two years.

C. Your credit report shows a number of recent inquiries.

D. You don't currently have any credit cards.

E. All of the above

14. As a mortgage holder, you can retire your loan at any time simply by paying the outstanding principal.

A. True

B. False

Answers

1. A. With the two-cycle average daily balance method, used by the Discover card among others, you incur extra finance charges during any month where you fail to pay all your balance after being fully paid up the month before. For such months, interest accrues from the date of purchase or posting, not from the end of the cycle.

2. B. If you deposit more than $5,000 in a single day from a bank outside your Federal Reserve district, your bank can hold the funds in excess of $5,000 for up to 11 business days. Deposits of less than $5,000 must be made available within five business days.

3. B. You'll pay $60 in checking fees, but if you park the $2,500 difference in required balances in a five-year CD, you'll earn about $128 in interest, for a pre-tax profit of $68.

4. A. But if your bank charges a penalty of three months of interest, and you cash out after one month, the other two months' interest will be subtracted from your principal.

5. C. Auto loan rates at credit unions average as much as two percentage points lower.

6. B. Even if your bank offers free ATMs, you can be hit for up to $2 per shot to use another bank's ATM.

7. C. For guidance, you should get the free booklet *Your Insured Deposits* from the FDIC. Request one from the agency's Office of Consumer Affairs, 550 17th St. N.W., Washington, D.C. 20429.

8. B. Before you agree to use a broker's mortgage origination system, which can cost $250 or more, be sure it includes data from the majority of institutions making loans in your area.

9. D. The longer you wait, the greater your liability, and after 60 days it is unlimited.

10. A. The card business is so competitive that banks will often drop their fees to keep your business if you threaten to leave for a free card.

11. F. ARMs are best when rates seem likely to fall or when you plan to move soon.

12. A. Nearly 1% of banks and S&Ls and about 7% of credit unions still lack such coverage. You should check your bank or thrift for a notice saying it's a member of the FDIC. At credit unions, look for a National Credit Union Administration (NCUA) sign.

13. E. If you are ever denied credit for one of these common reasons, you can often clear up the problem by writing a letter of explanation.

14. B. Some banks charge a prepayment penalty of up to 2% of the outstanding loan balance for retiring a loan within the first three years.

Scoring

If you got 11 or more questions right, you either work at a bank or have mastered the system. With eight to 10 correct, you're a savvy bank customer. With five to seven right, you need a refresher course. With zero to four right, better watch your wallet.

Ways to Ride Today's Housing Recovery

Whether you plan to buy, sell or renovate, now is a terrific time to be in the resurgent housing market. Here's how to make all the right moves.

The housing market has something for everyone this year. If you are a would-be home buyer, stable and affordable prices make 1994 an ideal time to snag a house. If you are looking to sell, rising demand will allow you to unload the old homestead in a reasonable period of time. And if you are staying put, you can enhance your home by financing a remodeling project at today's bargain interest rates. You can also profit by trading in your current mortgage for a new low-rate loan.

Housing analysts predict that mortgage interest rates are unlikely to climb more than half a percentage point this year. Meanwhile, anemic job growth will keep house prices in most parts of the country from moving up much faster than inflation. The combination of low rates and low prices will keep houses affordable and spur sales to near-record levels. Last year the National Association of Realtors' Housing Affordability Index hit 135%, its highest point in 20 years, and is expected to remain at a lofty level. (The index measures the ease with which median-income households can buy the median-priced home in the U.S.) The trade group forecasts 1994 home sales reaching nearly 4.9 million, the most in any year since 1979, when 5 million homes changed hands.

It is difficult to generalize about the housing market, however, because home prices tend to move in response to the local economy. For an idea of prices in your area, refer to the table on page 106, which projects median house prices for the nation's 50 largest metropolitan areas. Two sunbelt states, Florida and Texas, boast six of the 10 hottest housing markets with prices that are expected to beat inflation by one to nearly two percentage points. The No. 1 market for forecast appreciation is Orlando, where housing with a median price of $92,100 should rise 5%.

The outlook in California remains gloomy. Rebuilding after January's killer earthquake and the autumn 1993 fires that destroyed more than 840 homes could boost the local economy in some areas. But that spurt won't be enough to help home prices in cities such as Los Angeles, where the median price is 14% below its May 1991 peak of $229,070. Whether the market in your area is torrid, tepid or thawing out, here are some tips to help you make the best moves:

You are ready to buy. You should negotiate hard for the lowest price. With appreciation in many markets crawling along at 2% to 3% annually, it could take three to five years for you just to break even if you overpay by 10%. And that excludes the typical 6% seller's commission you'd also have to recoup. Don't use the seller's asking price as a starting point, but learn the prices that comparable houses have sold for during the past three to six months. You should ask your agent for a comparative market analysis, which can show you whether prices are trending up or down.

If values appear flat or declining slightly, try to get a price 5% to 10% below the most recent comparables. If, however, values are rising at the rate of inflation or better, you should generally be willing to match the price of recent sales. In either case, your offer should be only a few percentage points lower than what you are prepared to pay—and not so low that the seller dismisses it as not being serious. Also have a lender pre-approve your mortgage application and issue a mortgage commitment letter. This shows you have the wherewithal to close on the sale, and can give your offer the edge even over higher bids.

You are ready to sell. This is no time to be greedy. You want to price the house to sell within 45 days

Torrid and Tepid Housing Markets

With Orlando's 5.1% increase leading the way, house price gains will be modest in the 50 largest metropolitan areas this year. Only 27 will see median prices meet or beat the country's expected 3.2% inflation rate, according to Regional Financial Associates, the forecasting firm that prepared this analysis for us. There's good news in Florida, where Orlando and Tampa promise the highest gains in the nation. At the bottom of our list is Detroit, where an anemic job growth rate and a declining population will drive down prices. And California's housing market will continue to struggle. Six of the state's metro areas rank among the 10 places with the gloomiest 1994 outlooks.

Rank	Metropolitan area	Median price	Projected gain or loss in 1994	Rank	Metropolitan area	Median price	Projected gain or loss in 1994	Rank	Metropolitan area	Median price	Projected gain or loss in 1994
1	Orlando	$ 92,100	5.1%	18	Fort Worth	$ 84,200	3.9%	34	Pittsburgh	$ 85,200	2.6%
2	Tampa	76,900	4.9	19	Chicago	145,900	3.9	35	Cleveland	96,200	2.6
3	Portland, Ore.	107,700	4.7	20	Milwaukee	104,100	3.8	36	New York City	176,500	2.6
4	Atlanta	93,200	4.6	21	Memphis	90,600	3.7	37	Northern N.J.[3]	193,200	2.5
5	Salt Lake City	88,400	4.6	22	Nashville	91,300	3.7	38	Oakland	232,800	2.4
6	Fort Lauderdale	105,100	4.5	23	Cincinnati	95,100	3.6	39	Boston	176,900	2.2
7	Dallas	95,800	4.5	24	Kansas City	84,900	3.5	40	Long Island, N.Y.	158,700	2.2
8	San Antonio	79,400	4.5		**U.S. median**	**108,400**	**3.5**	41	Newark	191,900	2.1
9	Phoenix	90,200	4.4	25	New Orleans	77,000	3.4	42	Sacramento	129,900	1.9
10	Houston	81,800	4.3	26	Columbus, Ohio	92,900	3.4	43	Riverside, Calif.[4]	135,500	1.8
11	Miami	99,100	4.3	27	Philadelphia	122,500	3.2	44	San Diego	177,200	1.5
12	Charlotte, N.C.	108,800	4.2	28	S. Central N.J.[1]	136,100	3.1	45	Rochester, N.Y.	86,500	1.4
13	Denver	105,000	4.1	29	Hartford	134,800	3.0	46	Los Angeles	196,300	0.8
14	Minneapolis	96,600	4.1	30	Baltimore	118,900	2.9	47	Anaheim, Calif.[5]	221,300	0.5
15	Indianapolis	87,600	4.1	31	N. Central N.J.[2]	170,700	2.9	48	San Jose	230,600	0.4
16	Norfolk	101,500	4.1	32	St. Louis	86,700	2.8	49	Seattle	151,300	0.2
17	Washington, D.C.	161,200	4.0	33	San Francisco	258,700	2.7	50	Detroit	87,400	−0.1

Notes and sources: 1 – Monmouth and Ocean counties   **2** – Middlesex, Somerset and Hunterdon counties   **3** – Bergen and Passaic counties   **4** – Includes San Bernardino   **5** – Includes prices for Orange County, Calif.   **Median prices** from the National Association of Realtors are for existing homes sold in the quarter that ended Oct. 31, 1993. **Price projections** are by Regional Financial Associates.

of its listing. When a house sits on the market longer than that, shoppers begin to wonder what's wrong with it. To sell quickly, it is advisable to set an asking price close to what you will accept, rather than starting high with lots of room for haggling. If you know that sellers in your area are attracting multiple offers, you might consider asking 5% or so higher than the market. But if prices are still heading down, as has been the case lately in Southern California, go 3% to 5% lower.

You are just sitting tight. Whether you've already refinanced your mortgage, check to see how much you can cut your monthly payments by trading in your mortgage for a loan at current bargain rates. Many lenders are now offering no-points mort-

A Real Estate Pro's Advice

These days, without brisk price appreciation to bank on, buying and selling a home successfully depends on how well you know your market. For professional advice on scoping out your local real estate scene, we spoke with Richard Loughlin, president of Century 21 Real Estate, the nation's largest network of real estate brokerages. Here are excerpts from that interview:

Q. How should home buyers and sellers respond to today's sluggish appreciation?

A. Buyers should plan on owning a home for at least five years. Otherwise, becoming a homeowner probably won't make financial sense given today's modest price gains and a real estate agent's normal sales commission of about 6% or so. The key for sellers is setting a price that attracts buyers and agents. Pricing a house at more than 5% to 7% above what comparable homes have been selling for really turns off buyers and agents. You want to sell the house within 45 days of when you put it on the market. After that, a house can take on the feeling of used merchandise, and agents grow less interested in showing it.

Q. How can you tell whether your market is getting hotter or colder?

A. For starters, you should look at how long the "for sale" signs are staying on front lawns. If the same signs have been up for three to six months, you know properties aren't moving. For a more precise diagnosis, you should get a comparative market analysis from an agent.

He or she should be willing to tell you exactly how many homes are on the market in your price range, how long such homes tend to remain on the market before they are sold, and how sales prices compare with asking prices. Moreover, the agent can tell you how those figures have changed over the past three to six months.

Q. How do you find the right agent?

A. Whether you're a buyer or a seller, you want to work with an agent and a real estate office that do at least 50% of their business in your immediate area and in your price range. They know your market the best. Interview three agents from different offices, and ask each for a written market analysis to see whose work seems most useful. If you want help selling your home, you'll typically be obligated to work with an agent for three to six months. Before signing a contract, you should call a few of the agent's recent clients. Then you should ask them how responsive the agent was to their phone calls and how attentive to details he or she was during the closing process.

gages, and a few will even pick up most other closing costs. By reducing your interest rate as little as half a point on a 30-year $150,000 loan, you could save roughly $600 a year. (Later in this chapter we provide more advice on lowering the costs of mortgages and other loans.) With money available at such alluring rates, 1994 can also be a fine year for renovating. "Many homeowners are finding that they can borrow to remodel their home, refinance their mortgage, and often keep their monthly house payments the same," says Wendy Jordan, editor of *Remodeling* magazine. What's more, business is still sluggish for many remodelers, so you should bargain with contractors for price discounts of 5% or so. But beware of those willing to cut their price much lower.

Your Best Debt-Defying Moves Now

The days of falling interest rates are coming to an end. So don't wait too long to lighten up your borrowing load and interest expenses.

This year's big news for borrowers is that you can no longer bank on declining interest rates. A warming economy has already pushed the 30-year fixed rate mortgage from a low of 6.8% last October to over 7%. The news isn't all glum, however. The opportunities for bargain-basement borrowing that prevailed during 1993 haven't disappeared overnight. And while mortgage rates have blipped up, rates on home-equity lines (HELs) are expected to hold steady. Credit card rates should actually fall a bit further as purveyors of plastic vie for a spot in your wallet. Still, if you are in the market to borrow money, there's no time like the present. Here are three deft debt-related moves that you can make right now:

Refinance your mortgage. About 8 million homeowners still hold 30-year fixed mortgages with rates above 9.5%, or more than two points higher than recent levels. Experts say you will save money if you lower your rate by only one-half of a percentage point. So even if you were one of the alert homeowners who refinanced in late 1992 or early last year, you need to pull out the calculator again.

The basic rule of thumb is that you must stay put long enough to recover the expense of refinancing (including any up-front points and closing costs) through lower monthly payments. To determine how long that will take, subtract the monthly payment on the new mortgage from your current monthly payment. Next, you should divide the refinancing costs by the monthly savings. The number you come up with is roughly how many months it will take to break even. For example, if you pay $3,000 in points and closing costs to lower your monthly payments by $200, it will take 15 months to recoup.

Part of your decision to refinance involves choosing between an adjustable and a fixed rate loan. Homeowners who are sure they will move within the next four to five years can keep monthly payments to the absolute minimum by choosing an adjustable rate mortgage (ARM). The smart move is to steer clear of the most common type, one that adjusts annually. Despite temptingly low teaser rates of 3.5% or so, one-year ARMs leave you too vulnerable to rising rates. Instead, consider an ARM that adjusts every three years, called a 3/3. Its recent rate averaged around 6%. Thus if the rate jumps the standard maximum of two points, the most you'll pay for years four through six is 8%. That means your total costs with the 3/3 ARM are certain to be lower than with a fixed rate for the first five years of your loan.

Instead of refinancing to lower your monthly payments, you can choose to shorten the term of your loan. The popularity of 15-year mortgages has tripled during the past three years, mainly because borrowers like the idea of paying off the loan more quickly and saving thousands in interest costs. As appealing as that sounds, it usually makes sense only for homeowners who want to retire all their mortgage debt before they retire, or before they face a major obligation such as college for the kids. Otherwise, the traditional 30-year loan is better, says Frazier Bell, a mortgage lender in Charlottesville, Va. and author of *How to Get the Best Home Loan* (John Wiley & Sons, $15). For one thing, the longer term means lower payments. At recent rates, the difference on a $100,000 loan is about $200 a month. That gives you more cash for everyday living, emergencies or investing. And if you're eager to reduce your indebtedness and find yourself with some extra cash on hand, just send in the money. Making just one extra monthly payment a year will enable you to polish off a 30-year loan in 24 years, thereby saving $34,516 in interest costs on a $100,000 loan at 7.2%.

Open a home-equity credit line. Such loans have several things going for them this year. For one, most lines are pegged at 1.5 to two percentage points above the prime lending rate, lately 6%. Bankers were slow to drop their prime rates even as other rates fell during 1993. And industry analysts believe bankers will keep the prime at its current level even if other rates rise slightly. That means today's 7.5% HEL rate should hold fairly steady throughout the year. Another plus: interest payments on HELs of $100,000 or less are usually tax deductible. And President Clinton's income tax increases have made deductions more valuable now than at any time since the Reagan tax cuts of 1986. Deductibility widens the advantage of a 7.5% HEL rate over the nondeductible average credit-card rate of 18%.

Thanks to fierce competition among banks, you should be able to find a lender willing to waive the typical HEL up-front costs of $600 to $700. Financial planners recommend taking advantage of a free offer to set up a home-equity line of credit, even if you don't need any cash now. Once you have a credit line, however, be careful how you use it. Avoid borrowing more money than you will be able to pay back within three years or so. The rate on your HEL will rise whenever the prime rate does, with no annual cap and a lifetime ceiling of 18% to 24%. While the prime isn't expected to be a big mover in 1994, you don't want to be caught with a large HEL balance during an upward interest-rate spiral down the road.

Switch to a low-rate credit card. Even if other lending rates climb, the outlook is for credit card rates to continue the slow decline that last year saw rates fall from an average of 18.5% to just under 18%. (For more on credit cards, turn the page.) Robert McKinley of RAM Research in Frederick, Md. expects that average to fall a full point in 1994. And he believes more cards will be available at 10% or below. But don't wait for your rate to drop. Find a low-rate card now. If you are one of the cardholders who carry a monthly balance ($2,200 is typical) and you pay the average 18% rate, your annual interest bill is $396.

Switch to a card with a 10% rate and you'd save $176 a year. The catch: some issuers set higher credit requirements for low-rate cards. For $5, the Bankcard Holders of America (703-481-1110) sells a pamphlet that discusses the qualifying standards that low-rate issuers use. For example, lenders frown on applicants who are carrying over monthly balances on more than four credit cards. Therefore, you may want to pay off some of your high-rate balances before you apply for a new card.

Money Helps

Q. Within four weeks of buying my new house, I noticed water leaking from the master bathroom shower to the crawl space under the house. Two plumbers told me the problem had surely existed for more than a year and would cost $3,500 to fix. Do I have recourse against the house's previous owner or the firm I paid $700 to inspect the home?
—Shahid Malik, Rye, N.Y.

A. In New York, as in most states, if you don't ask the seller about a specific house defect, he or she is not obliged to volunteer it. (Only Arkansas, California, Kentucky, Maine, New Hampshire and Wisconsin require sellers to reveal "known defects.") Even if you did ask about leaks, and the previous owner lied, you would have to hire a lawyer to prove that in court. As for inspection firms, these guys are covered or they'd be in court day and night defending themselves against angry buyers. Most firms have disclaimers in their contracts for inaccessible parts of the house, like crawl spaces. And they won't refund more than the fee you paid. But call to complain anyway and have your lawyer send the seller a letter demanding reimbursement. Maybe they'll pay for some of the repairs to make you go away.

Credit Cards That Pay You Back

It used to be easy to figure out which credit card would cost you least. If you were among the 70% of people who carried a balance month to month, you could hold down the finance charges by choosing the card with the lowest interest rate. If, on the other hand, you conscientiously paid your monthly bill in full, you could avoid card-related expenses altogether by picking one with no annual fee.

These days you can do much better than that. In fact, competition among card issuers is so hot that some will pay you as much as $250 a year to use their plastic. These payments are often in the form of discounts on specific purchases, such as a ticket on a particular airline or a certain brand of car. But sometimes they are made in cash. Moreover, finding a card that offers a discount on something that you want is getting easier. Shell has a MasterCard that offers as much as $70 worth of free gasoline each year if your credit card charges hit $3,500. With other cards, you can snag free travel on American, Continental or United airlines, as well as discounts on everything from General Motors and Ford automobiles to GE refrigerators.

Folks who pay their monthly bills in full get the most value, of course. As the table at the right shows, they would do better with any rebate card than with a typical no-fee card. But those who carry balances can come out ahead using rebates too. When you add up the annual fee and usual interest charge for each card and then subtract the value of its rebate, the airline and auto cards are all better bargains

than the best conventional plastic. If, however, you don't use the discounts, rebate cards are bad deals. They carry interest as high as 20% and annual fees of as much as $60 a year. Here's a rundown of the various types of rebate cards recently available:

Airline cards. These are terrific deals for frequent fliers or people who charge at least $10,000 to $15,000 in purchases yearly. Most programs give you one mile for every dollar you spend. But you need 20,000 miles or so to get a free round-trip ticket in the U.S. American and some other carriers require you to use your miles within three years. So unless you are a big spender, you should consider using an airline card to supplement the miles you accumulate by flying. Frequent fliers may also want to check out American Express' Membership Miles program (800-274-6453), which credits miles to your choice of five airline frequent-flier programs.

Auto cards. Ford has the better deal in standard cards, letting you earn $700 in credits each year, compared with GM's $500. But GM offers a gold card (annual fee: $39, vs. no fee for its standard card) that lets you accumulate $1,000 in credits a year.

Other cards. If you pay your balance in full, cards sponsored by GE, Shell and other companies still work in your favor. But if you carry a balance, their high rates and relatively low rebates make them poor values, compared with an ordinary low-rate bank card.

Card	800 number
AMERICAN AADVANTAGE	359-4444
UNITED MILEAGE PLUS	537-7783
CONTINENTAL	446-5336
GM	947-1000
FORD	374-7777
ARKANSAS FEDERAL	477-3348
SHELL	373-3427
GE REWARDS	437-3927
DISCOVER	347-2683
H&R BLOCK	934-0101
US WEST	872-2699
START	955-7010

Even if you don't always pay your bill in full, credit-card freebies can save you plenty. We computed the total yearly cost for each of 11 giveback cards and one low-rate conventional card (Arkansas Federal), including annual fees and finance charges for monthly revolving debt of $1,100 and annual expenditures of $2,200, both national averages. Then we subtracted the rebates and ranked the cards by how much they paid you—or cost.

What you get	Interest rate	Annual fee	Total cost before rebate	Rebate	Cost (or payback) per year	Comments
One frequent-flier mile for each dollar you charge	15.4%	$50	$219	$303[6]	($84)	You need 20,000 miles for a round-trip domestic ticket; miles must be used within three years.
One frequent-flier mile for each dollar you charge, up to 10,000 miles a month, 50,000 miles a year	15.9[1]	$60	$235	$271[6]	($36)	You need 20,000 miles for a round-trip domestic ticket; miles must be used within three years.
One frequent-flier mile for each dollar you charge, plus a 5,000-mile sign-up bonus	19.95	$45	$264	$249[6]	$15	You need 20,000 miles for a round-trip domestic ticket; no deadline for when miles must be used.
A credit equal to 5% of your charges good toward buying or leasing any new GM car or truck except the Saturn	16.4[1]	None	$180	$110	$70	Maximum rebate is $500 a year for as many as seven years, or $3,500 total.
A credit equal to 5% of your charges good toward buying or leasing any new Ford, Lincoln or Mercury	15.4[1]	$20	$189	$110	$79	Maximum rebate is $700 a year for as many as five years, or $3,500 total.
Nothing; this is a conventional low-rate card.	7.75[1]	$35	$120	None	$120	This card costs less than all the giveback cards except those issued by airlines and automakers.
A credit equal to 3% of Shell gasoline charges and 2% of all other charges good toward purchase of Shell gasoline	16.4[1]	$20	$200	$56[7]	$144	Maximum rebate for most customers will be about $70 a year; annual fee waived if you sign up by April 30, 1994.
A $10 "rewards check" for every $500 in charges, good at 27 retailers including Macy's, K Mart and Pier 1	16.9[1]	None	$186	$40	$146	You get coupons for additional discounts on specific goods; all discounts expire after three months.
An annual cash rebate rising from 0.25% of charges under $1,000 a year to 1% of charges over $3,000	14.9[1,2]	None	$164	$9	$155	The rebate is not generous, but at least it's cash instead of a merchandise discount.
A $5 credit toward tax preparation for every $500 charged; must be used for the tax year in which credits are earned	15.9[1]	$9	$184	$20	$164	The full rebate, or a portion, can be used by any immediate family member.
An annual cash rebate rising from 0.25% of charges under $2,000 a year to 1% of charges over $6,000	16.9[1,3]	None	$186	$6	$180	Rebate is doubled on long-distance calls with any carrier; maximum rebate is $500 a year.
A quarterly rebate, paid either in cash or deposited in a tax-deferred annuity in $100 increments, equal to 1% of your charges	15.9[1,4]	$35[5]	$210	$22	$188	Rebate rises as high as 7% for purchases at 20 vendors, including Eddie Bauer, Spiegel and Hertz.

Notes: [1]Variable interest rate. [2]Based on at least $1,000 in annual purchases and no late payments; 16.9% if purchases are between $500 and $900 or 19.8% if below $500. [3]8.9% for the first six months 46% until March 31, 1994 [5]$25 for first year; later fees waived if you charge more than $2,000 a year. [6]Value of frequent-flier miles is figured by multiplying the miles earned from $2,200 in annual purchases, by the cost per passenger mile for each airline. [7]Based on average fuel used by a two-car family **Sources:** Bankcard Holders of America and card issuers

Questions to Ask About Life Insurance

The road to purchasing a life insurance policy can be pocked with potholes.
Get answers to these crucial questions before you buy.

Last year more than 12 million Americans spent an estimated $10 billion in premiums on newly issued life insurance policies. It's a fair bet that most of those buyers don't really know what they are buying, or why. Consumers must contend with a maze of policy types, indecipherable jargon and often arcane calculations. And they need to stay away from weak or terminally ill insurers. To avoid tripping up when you shop for coverage, get answers to these questions from a carefully selected agent recommended by friends or advisers you trust.

What type of life insurance is best? The basic choices are term or permanent life. With term, the insurance company agrees to pay your survivors a death benefit if you die while the policy is in force. The cost of term insurance typically rises annually as you age. A 35-year-old male who doesn't smoke might pay $300 a year for $250,000 of term coverage, but by age 55 the policy could cost him about $2,000. Ask for a policy that guarantees you'll be able to keep it regardless of changes in your health. With permanent insurance, which includes whole life, universal life and variable life, a portion of your annual premium goes into a tax-deferred savings fund known as the cash value account. Your cash value earns interest at a rate that's generally tied to yields on high-grade long-term bonds. Rates on variable accounts fluctuate with the stock and bond markets. Permanent premiums generally don't rise after you buy the policy. The downside: premiums are four to nine times higher than initial premiums for comparable term contracts. That's because you're funding the savings account and the commissions are steeper. Permanent insurance offers some estate planning advantages. But the purpose of life insurance is to protect your family from a loss of income.

How much life insurance do I need? You ought to have enough coverage so your beneficiaries can pay their bills, both for living expenses today and college costs in the future. One rule of thumb is to buy life insurance worth about five to seven times the gross salary you are insuring. But that's merely a starting point. Subtract from that figure the income your survivors would receive from life insurance you have at work and your investments. For more tips, request the free *Consumer's Guide to Life Insurance* published by the American Council of Life Insurance (800-942-4242).

What's the insurer's financial strength? Experts suggest that safety conscious shoppers stick with companies that get upper-deck ratings from at least two of the four major grading agencies. That's an A++ from A.M. Best; AAA or AA+ from Duff & Phelps; AAA, AA+ or AA from Standard & Poor's; and Aaa, Aa1, Aa2 or Aa3 from Moody's Investors Service. The insurer also should not have any grade below A+ from Best, AA from Duff & Phelps, AA- from S&P, or A1 from Moody's. More than 80 companies pass this test, including such giants as Metropolitan Life, New York Life and Northwestern Mutual.

How are policy illustrations calculated? The policy illustration is a key sales tool for agents recommending cash value policies. A computer printout shows the potential value of the policy's savings component in, say, 20 years. Quiz the agent about the assumptions in the calculations to determine whether the illustrations are realistic. For example, ask the agent to verify that the interest rate figures are net of expenses, since that's what you'll really earn. Tell the agent to show you what would happen to your cash value if the insurer earned two percentage points less than anticipated, just to be

Beware Bank Fund Pitches

Regulators are increasingly alarmed by the ways that banks are selling mutual funds, both their own and those run by other companies. These products are riskier than traditional bank offerings in two respects. They are not insured by the FDIC, and they can fall in value. Federal regulators have issued voluntary guidelines meant to ensure that banks alert customers to these risks. And some banks certainly do. At Wells Fargo Bank in San Francisco, investment advisers have large placards on their desks reminding customers of the distinction between bank accounts and investments. At the same time, other banks seem to be encouraging customers to think of these investments as safer than they are. Witness:

• A Colorado bank recently mailed its depositors an investment pitch that asked "Tired of low interest rates?" before going on to tout a "strategic income fund" as "both a safe and a high yield investment." According to Colorado state securities commissioner Philip Feigin, the letter described investments in the fund as "deposits" but nowhere did it mention that the "strategic income fund" was in fact a fund invested in junk bonds.

• When a Maine retiree's $62,000 in CDs came due, his bank's manager urged him to visit the investment section of the bank, according to Stephen Diamond, that state's securities administrator. A sales representative told the retiree that he could earn 10% to 12% annually in an asset-allocation fund (one that invests in stocks

and bonds). The customer took the bait. His first statement showed a loss, but the sales rep assured him that the investment needed to decline before it went up. Three months later, the account was down to $50,000. The customer complained to the bank branch manager, who helped him get a refund for the full $62,000, plus interest of $1,440.

• Crestar Bank in Richmond calls its line of mutual funds CrestFunds, and NationsBank in Charlotte, N.C. sells Nations Fund. They do so in blatant disregard of the federal guidelines that discourage banks from using names similar or identical to the banks' on their uninsured products. "The bank's name has traditionally been associated with federal deposit insurance, and when you put it on a mutual fund you get a carryover effect," says Michael Vargon, deputy director of the New Mexico Securities Division. A Crestar spokesman points out that CrestFunds are sold in separate offices, not bank branches, and that signs in the office make it clear that the funds are not bank deposits. Robert Gordon, director of marketing for the NationsBank Mutual Fund Group, says that brochures and salespeople make customers "aware of what they are buying and the risks and rewards involved."

• To avoid being misled by banks' sales practices, be disciplined in your hunt for higher yields. Designate a portion of your cash for investing and a portion for savings. Put the savings into money-market funds or other types of vehicles where there is little or no risk to your principal.

safe. Also get a worst-case scenario—what the cash value buildup would be if the insurer ends up paying the mere guaranteed rate, typically 4% to 5%.

How will premiums fluctuate over time? If you're interested in a term policy, make sure the agent shows you its projected annual cost five, 10 and 20

years into the contract and the maximum charge in each case. A policy with the lowest initial premium may cost more as the policy ages than a similar policy with a higher initial charge. Your agent may recommend a level term policy with set premiums for an extended period, such as 10 years. Since the premium is basically an average of the cost for the entire period, you'll pay more in the early years of a level policy than with the traditional annual renewable term. So it's generally advisable to go for level term only if you expect to keep the coverage for the entire period.

As for premiums on permanent policies, agents may tell you that you can make them vanish after just five or 10 payments by tapping your cash value to pay for them. What you may not hear is that this vanishing act will occur only if the insurer's expectations for your cash value's growth come true. Make sure that the agent explains how many extra premiums you'll need to pay if your savings account doesn't grow as quickly as forecast.

Insurance You Can Do Without

Dropping these types of overpriced policies could cut your insurance premium costs by 10%. Better yet, don't buy them in the first place.

Failing to protect yourself and your family against serious financial loss is a huge mistake. But this doesn't mean you should overinsure—the cost of buying both a belt and suspenders can really add up. Insurance analysts estimate that Americans waste about 10% of the $180 billion that they spend on insurance coverage annually. Here are types of policies to avoid, and two basic rules to follow: 1) don't cover yourself against small losses that you could handle by tapping your savings, and 2) shun narrowly drawn policies that insure you for just one risk such as contracting a specific disease or dying in a plane crash. Rely instead on comprehensive health or life coverage against a variety of scenarios.

Credit insurance. You hear it just about every time you get a loan at a bank, car dealership or finance company. The pitch: check this box for credit life and disability insurance, and you can rest easy knowing your loan payments would be made if you became disabled or died. Don't do it. Credit insurance is generally too expensive for the risk involved. Instead of buying credit insurance for a small debt, simply expand your savings enough to handle several months of payments. For a large debt, increase your basic life and disability coverage.

Term life for a child. Insurance agents position term policies for children as a guarantee that a child can remain insured even if he or she contracts a disease someday. Forget that, and forgo paying up to $200 a year. The overriding reason to insure a person's life is to protect dependents against a loss of income, which won't apply unless you're one of actor Macaulay Culkin's parents.

Cancer insurance. Every day, it seems, the newspapers report that something else you eat, drink or breathe could give you cancer. That's why cancer insurers say you should buy their policies, which pay benefits if you turn out to be the one person out of three who gets cancer during your lifetime. But look again. Comprehensive major medical coverage can insure you against all types of maladies at roughly the same cost.

Hospital indemnity policies. You've probably noticed ads with this come-on: for just pennies a day, we'll give you up to $75 for every day you're in the hospital. Problem is, the average hospital stay runs $750 a day. Besides, a comprehensive health policy, covering major expenses in or out of the hospital, should make such a policy unnecessary.

Mortgage protection insurance. Since no job is secure these days, you may be tempted to get a policy that will make your mortgage payments for six to 12 months if you are laid off. If you do, you'll find yourself paying a lot of money for rela-

Finding a Financial Planner

Plenty of people who call themselves financial planners do work that ranges from incompetent to fraudulent. A good way to begin your search for a trustworthy practitioner is to request the free publication, *Consumer Guide to Comprehensive Financial Planning*, from the International Association for Financial Planning (800-945-4237). Then follow this process to weed out the phonies and find the right planner for you.

Identify reputable planners in your area.
The best sources of references are friends and business associates. If you don't know anyone who has a planner, call the Institute of Certified Financial Planners (800-282-7526) for the names and phone numbers of C.F.P.s in your area. Once you have the names of three local planners, telephone them to set up initial meetings, which should be free of charge.

Subject prospects to tough interviews.
Use this session to learn how the planner is compensated and whether he or she has any potential conflicts of interest. This is also the time to assess the adviser's expertise and to see if the two of you hit it off. From a compensation standpoint, there are three types of planners. With fee only, you pay about $80 to $125 an hour plus an annual fee of 1% to 2% of your portfolio. Fee based get similar fees plus commissions on investments and insurance they sell, amounting to 3% to 5% of your portfolio annually. And commission only are paid only when you buy investments or insurance from them, again, about 3% to 5% a year.

If the planner accepts commissions, ask what type of investments he or she tends to sell. If you hear a one-product pitch, you are dealing with someone more interested in selling than planning. Also find out about the planner's experience and clients. Ask for a description of the income levels, portfolio sizes and jobs of typical clients. You want to work with a planner who deals with people whose finances are like yours and is experienced in issues you face. Thus you should ask to inspect one of the adviser's actual plans, with the client's name deleted for privacy. Make sure that you find it easy to understand and that its recommendations are specific.

Check the planner's record with regulators.
Call your state securities department and the federal SEC in Washington, D.C. (202-272-7450) to see whether the planner has been the subject of disciplinary actions by either of these agencies. If the adviser's firm belongs to the National Association of Securities Dealers, phone the NASD (800-289-9999) to see whether there have been any judgments against the planner, if complaints have resulted in arbitration awards to the complainant, or if there are any pending disciplinary proceedings.

---

tively puny coverage. Premiums tend to amount to 3% to 4% of your annual mortgage payment.

Home warranties. These contracts, which protect you against major home defects, are offered by real estate agents or builders. But don't be quick to sign up. Warranties are pricey and frequently filled with exclusions. New home warranties are espe-

cially chancy, since their guarantees are only as strong as the builders standing behind them. More than 12,000 builders have gone out of business since 1988, according to Dun & Bradstreet. Instead of a warranty, you would be smarter to spend $170 to $300 for a home inspection.

Collision coverage on old cars. Here's a quick and

cost-effective way to cut your auto insurance by 20% to 40%. Drop your collision coverage if your car is more than, say, five years old and the collision portion of your premium exceeds 10% of the car's market value. Just figure on buying another car if the one you've got gets wrecked. Check the National Automobile Dealers Association's *Official Used Car Guide* for an estimate of your road-weary model's value.

Extended service contracts. Right after your dealer tells you what a honey you bought, he hands you off to another guy pushing a service contract for when the car breaks down. Just say no. The big-ticket items covered by such contracts rarely give trouble during the first few years of ownership.

Flight insurance. There you are at the airport, trying to remain calm before you get on a plane. You see the vending machine that can sell you a policy on the spot covering you for as much as $500,000 if you die or lose any limbs in a crash. Pass it by. You don't increase your insurance every time you get in a car. Yet you are 56 times more likely to be killed in a car accident than in a plane.

Trip cancellation insurance. Are you worried that an unforeseen emergency will force you to scrap your vacation? You could buy a contract from your travel agent costing $5.50 per $100 of coverage. But insurers usually won't pay out if you cancel because an old ailment flares up. Most airlines will let you simply buy a new ticket for a $25 fee.

Rain insurance. Property insurance agents might say this is just the ticket if you're worried about rain spoiling your garden party. But the premium for a rain insurance policy ranges from 5% to 10% of your party's tab. Save your money. You can always give your guests a rain date or shift the festivities indoors.

Wedding insurance. No, these types of policies are not designed to reimburse the father of the bride in the event the groom doesn't show up at the altar. Instead, they offer coverage for nonrefundable expenses incurred by canceling the wedding due to injury and for personal liability protection if someone is hurt, say, dancing at the reception. You may already be insured, perhaps by the wedding or reception site's liability policy or your homeowners policy. Besides, the possibility of any of these things happening at your wedding is so small, it's like playing the lottery.

Software For All Your Financial Needs

Selecting and mastering the right computer programs can make minding your money a breeze. Our reviewers pick the best.

When homemaker Sue Muff of suburban Seattle pays the monthly bills, she doesn't waste time writing out checks by hand while pecking at a calculator to figure her balance. These and other annoyances are just memories, now that Sue and her physician husband Nicholas handle their finances by computer. Using a simple $29 program named *Quicken*, Sue prints checks and envelopes in which to mail them, keeps track of expenditures by category and, at tax time, pro-duces a list of deductible ones with the press of a button. "Our accountant loves it," she says, "and he charges us about $400 less as a result."

The Muffs are among a growing number of Americans who are using personal finance software to make their lives easier. In fact, software in the personal finance category now ties database managers (essentially electronic file cabinets) for fourth place in overall sales. The first three are word processors, spreadsheets and games. And no wonder. Today's money management programs are gigabytes ahead of the clunky ones that gathered dust on dealers' shelves back in the early 1980s. Now you can find nifty packages that will keep your balances, pay your bills electronically, plan your budget, help you select the right mix of stocks, bonds and mutual funds and then buy or sell them for you. But with more than two dozen programs to choose among these days, which one do you really need?

The answer depends in part on what computer you own or plan to buy. If your machine is an older IBM or compatible with 640 kilobytes of random access memory (RAM), you're probably limited to software that runs on Microsoft's venerable MS-DOS (or DOS) operating system. Most programs are available in DOS versions. If you own a newer machine, or are shopping for one, you can choose the more user-friendly software designed for Microsoft's Windows (for IBMs and compatibles) or Apple's Macintosh.

To help you decide which program to buy, we analyzed many of the best-selling packages in three categories: banking and record keeping, financial planning, and portfolio management. (Refer back to page 33 for a review of new tax software.) Unless otherwise indicated, all programs come in versions for DOS, Windows and Macintosh. Prices are those you would pay at a discounter or software chain like Egghead or CompUSA. While two of the entries (*WealthBuilder* and *Smart Investor*) were created with MONEY's help, our team of reviewers strived to treat all programs impartially.

Banking and record keeping. If you only want help with basic financial chores like bill paying and budgeting, then any of these three programs will do the job. All keep a running record of spending by category, letting you see at a glance what you are shelling out each month for food, gas, entertainment or any other purpose. All can share this information with popular tax programs and track a simple mutual fund or stock portfolio. But only *Quicken* and *MoneyCounts* can obtain stock price quotes from data services like America Online, CompuServe and Prodigy (fee: $10 to $15 per

month). And all either print checks and envelopes for you or offer access to services that pay your bills by transferring funds from your bank account (cost: $10 for 20 checks a month).

Quicken ($29). The granddaddy of personal finance software has been updated continually since its 1984 release and remains this category's best buy. The latest version, for example, offers a Quicken Gold Visa card that lets you retrieve by modem your list of charges each month, separated by expenditure type. That saves you from having to enter each transaction manually to maintain a complete detailed record of your spending for, say, tax or budget purposes.

Microsoft Money ($29, Windows only). This program resembles a stripped-down *Quicken* but lacks the ability to get on-line market updates. Thanks to clear instructions and attractive graphics, however, it remains a good choice for beginners who don't need to track investments.

MoneyCounts ($19, DOS only). Though it doesn't have snazzy graphics, this inexpensive DOS program does some things the others don't. It lets you create one-key commands, for example, that accomplish what would otherwise take a series of keystrokes. And you can maintain large mailing lists and automatically address envelopes or labels.

Financial planning. With the exception of *WealthBuilder*, the packages in this category handle the same basic record-keeping chores as those above. But these programs go further. You can define a goal, like saving for retirement, and then figure out how much you need to save, all with the guidance of on-screen advice similar to what you might get from a financial planner. You can select a portfolio of stocks or funds and follow its performance. And you can handle such miscellaneous tasks as analyzing your life insurance needs or calculating payments on a mortgage.

Managing Your Money ($49). This pioneering program features helpful advice from personal finance guru Andrew Tobias and is updated every year or so. The new Windows version includes spiffy graphics that make it easy to use. To see your checking or savings account balance, for example, you simply click on a picture of a bank. The Windows program isn't able to summon stock prices by modem, as the DOS and Mac versions do. If that matters to you, stick to those programs, choose another product, or wait for the modem-capable Windows edition later this year.

CA-Simply Money ($49, Windows only). With sophisticated graphics and full modem powers, this newcomer by Computer Associates is probably the best buy for people using Windows. The commentary, by *Kiplinger's Personal Finance Magazine*, covers roughly the same topics as that of *Managing Your Money* but is frequently clearer and more lively.

WealthBuilder ($70, DOS and Mac only). The program doesn't include check writing and doesn't do household accounts. But it does enable you to construct a more thorough financial plan than others in this category do. *WealthBuilder* begins by asking for basic information such as your age, income and number of dependents. Next the program assesses your investment risk tolerance by asking questions like, "What would you do if you won $500 on a bet?" (If you choose "go for double or nothing," you're a risk taker.) Then it recommends strategies for such goals as buying a house, paying college bills or retiring comfortably. To select stocks or funds, use the companion *Smart Investor*, included with *WealthBuilder*'s DOS version but not with the Mac. *Smart Investor* can also be bought separately (see below).

Portfolio management. These programs permit you to screen stocks, bonds or mutual funds based on criteria you define and then to manage your portfolio once it's chosen. These programs, however, are not designed for novices and offer relatively little on-screen advice. All packages listed below enable you to obtain the latest prices and research reports by modem (typical cost: $5 to $20 per month), either through the publisher's own service or public ones like CompuServe. All can produce reports and graphs showing your investments' performance. And all permit you to trade securities by modem through discount brokerage houses.

Smart Investor (part of WealthBuilder or $50 separately, DOS only). The best choice for fund watchers, this program lets you sort through Reality's database of more than 17,000 stocks, bonds, funds and CDs. You get your first database disk free. Updates are available monthly by modem for $215 a year (or $119 for everything but individual stocks and bonds). *Smart Investor* also helps you at tax time. For example, the program can figure out the cost basis of shares of a fund in which you have periodically reinvested dividends—essential for calculating gains or losses when you sell.

Captool ($99, DOS only). This is the best choice for serious investors who are primarily interested in individual stocks. It is the only program reviewed here that lets you screen for stocks with high ratios of price to cash flow, which may help you spot companies that are about to raise dividends. It's also the only program that can calculate your stock portfolio's internal rate of return, the best measure of how your investments are doing. The program does not perform sophisticated analysis of funds, though it can track fund prices.

Pulse ($179, DOS only). This package lacks some of the tax and analytical tools that *Smart Investor* and *Captool* provide. Partly as a result, it is simpler to use, a trait many investors find appealing. Moreover, *Pulse* lets you break down your holdings by asset class or any category you designate.

Equalizer ($69, DOS only) and On-Line Xpress ($90, DOS only). These programs' main virtue is that each chops 10% off already discounted commissions from the Schwab and Fidelity brokerage services, respectively, for trades made by modem. But neither program provides significant help in terms of selecting stocks or calculating taxes.

Helping Kids Come of Age Financially

*Economic trends may not be nurturing to the MTV generation. So whatever the age
of your kids, start now to teach them smart money skills.*

Today's kids need financial know-how more than at any period in recent memory. Many will reach adulthood in what forecasters say will be an economy marked by a brutal job market and the burden of the baby boom's Social Security. Indeed, the unemployment rate for 20- to 24-year-olds already runs 10%—higher than for any other adult age group—and an alarming 43% of these jobless youth still live at home. Parents are justifiably concerned that their children will never live as well as they do.

It's up to parents to teach the skills and discipline their kids will need to make the American dream come true. Most kids have a lot to learn. A study by Texas Tech professor Jerry Mason found that high school students know less about financial topics than their counterparts did 30 years ago. Mason thinks schools deserve only part of the blame. "Most parents aren't terrific at managing money," he says, "so kids don't learn money skills at home either." Teenagers shell out a whopping $93 billion a year for food, clothes and entertainment. Teens say they want to save for college, though more than half don't.

Of course, a child's financial education should begin long before it's time to start thinking about college. Experts say children begin to grasp the concept of money as early as age three. Thus parents should start the process before kids begin school, and be prepared to keep it up through college, or even a few years beyond.

Give your child a regular allowance. Managing an allowance is the key to developing good money skills. You can start a weekly stipend as early as age five or six. While child development experts differ on the matter, many recommend that you neither offer the allowance as payment for chores nor withhold it as a punishment. Allowance should be a learning tool that continues without interruption, so the child can learn to budget and save. Insist that your child do chores simply as part of his or her family duty. When you need to discipline the child, take away other privileges. How much allowance you should give depends on your family's financial situation, local living costs and what your child's friends are receiving. But make the amount large enough to be meaningful. One poll found that teens aged 13 to 15 averaged about $15 a week, while those 16 to 19 received nearly $30. Be prepared to raise the amount yearly.

Encourage saving early on. By age eight or nine, children are old enough to save a portion of their allowance. You can encourage the habit by matching whatever your kids put away. You should also help them open a bank account where they can watch interest compound on their savings. You will probably have to co-sign to open the account. And you may have to prime the account with some of your own money to get around the steep minimums that banks require today.

Find ways to describe how money works. Look for opportunities to explain money to your kids. Instead of saying something is too expensive, you might note that a certain toy costs as much as a week's worth of groceries. With children age 12 or 13, you might invite them to help you pay the bills a few times to demonstrate where your money goes.

Gradually give teens more responsibility. The early teens are a good time to switch from a weekly allowance to a monthly one so that your teen will learn to budget money over longer periods of time. You should also increase the allowance to allow him or her to cover most, or all, spending for clothes, entertainment like movies, fast-food meals and so on. As much as possible, let your children spend their money as they want.

Teach basic investing concepts. Owning stock is a great way to begin, says Nancy Dunnan, author of several finance books for teens, including *The Stock Market* (Silver Burdett, $7). Buy your child a couple of shares in a highly visible local company, such as a utility or a brand-name product manufacturer, if there is one nearby. You can then show your child how to follow the company in the newspaper stock tables.

Help kids develop good work habits. In particular, don't let yours waste summer vacation. For ideas, check the guidebooks *Summer Opportunities for Kids and Teenagers* ($20) and *Summer Jobs* ($16, both from Peterson's Guides). Traditional after-school teen jobs, such as working at a fast-food counter or retail store, can also help build responsibility. But monitor the work schedule. A Temple University study found that teens who worked 20 hours or more after school each week achieved grades half a letter lower, on average, than youngsters who worked fewer than 10 hours. Don't let a child sacrifice the chance to get into a good college simply to pay for car and clothing expenses.

Discuss how you'll pay college bills. During junior year in high school, children should begin learning about how you plan to pay for college. Of course, you have to judge whether your teen is mature enough to keep the details of the family budget confidential. In most cases, however, your children will benefit from an undiluted dose of financial reality. When kids understand the limits of the family pocketbook, they often take college and their grades more seriously.

Have a plan for freshman finances. Set up an account at a bank near your child's college so that you can wire money as needed. You may find it convenient to hand over a credit card as well. Be sure to specify what the money and credit card will cover. If your child doesn't live up to his or her

end of the bargain, say no and mean it. But think twice about a job during freshman year. Kids are most likely to drop out of college in their first year, usually because of problems adjusting. Thus it makes sense to spare your freshman a heavy part-time work schedule. One possibility: front-load your support in the first two years and let your child contribute more later.

Think about career possibilities. Research into careers can begin as early as freshman and sophomore years. Students should contact alumni who can explain what their professions are really like, and who may later be helpful in finding a job. Take advantage of internship programs, in which colleges help students land summer jobs related to their field of study. Also look into co-op programs, in which students alternate a year or two of study with one or two semesters of work. Such experience can be key in getting a job.

Set ground rules for boomerangs. You've shelled out $100,000 for Junior's college education and turned his old bedroom into a study. But now he's back on your doorstep, jobless, with plans to stay indefinitely. If you've got a so-called boomerang kid under your roof, avoid returning to the old parent-child pattern. Discuss in advance whether the child will pay rent or a share of the family's costs. If he can't afford to pay anything, he should at least contribute to household chores. You should also set a date—say, in six months—when you both will assess the situation.

Don't pull strings to land your kids a job. Calling old pals and arm twisting them into giving your child an entry-level position won't help in the long run. Likewise, contacting potential employers on your child's behalf will do nothing for your child's self-esteem and may diminish his or her worth in the employers' eyes. Instead, you should offer assistance in revising a resume or rehearsing for an interview. But your child should make the contacts and do the interviewing. The goal, after all, is to gain more independence. That means your kids must be free to succeed or fail on their own.

Today's Consummate Consumer

Bargains abound for consumers these days. Car makers are again loading many new models with free options. Restaurant prices remain moderate as chefs substitute lower priced items. Niche airlines wage regional mini fare wars with the national carriers. Retailers are launching or expanding shop-from-home operations. And the snazziest of the new personal computers are priced within reach. As if that's not rosy enough, there's a bonus. A stronger dollar, which was up about 10% last year against most European currencies, is reducing the prices of many imports. Indeed, this is a very good year to go on a buying binge. Here are some of the most enticing reasons why.

Upstart airlines are undercutting fares. Look for the big boys to play catch-up with feisty new regional airlines such as Newark-based Kiwi International and Reno Air in Nevada. Last year, for example, Southwest inaugurated service from Cleveland to Baltimore, a major USAir hub, causing fares to fall 95% to as low as $19 one way. With smaller airlines offering fare savings of as much as $500 compared with major carriers, the nationals can no longer afford to ignore the competition. With flexibility, you can take advantage of regional specials. For example, *Best Fares Travel Clubs* uses a reservation system that searches for the lowest fare to a given area rather than to a specific airport. The system, called Ultra-fair, also tracks all available discounts, such as companion rates, and special senior citizen and student fares. Membership costs $58 annually and includes a year's subscription to *Best Fares* magazine (call 800-880-1234).

Many new car models are lower priced. Automakers are poised to capture your dollars with some of the best deals in a decade. Take Chrysler's sporty new economy car, the Neon, priced at around $11,500. This is about 10% less than a comparably equipped Honda Civic. And the Neon offers dual air bags as well as a bit more headroom and legroom than the Civic. Even tony Mercedes-Benz is getting competitive with the

debut of the luxury-car maker's C-class sedans, starting at $29,900 and aimed at younger buyers who have been choosing BMW and Lexus models.

The Big Three are continuing their strategy of so-called value pricing to boost new car sales. This Detroit innovation incorporated many popular options into models that didn't quickly move off showroom floors, and then priced the cars *below* their original base. The 1994 Oldsmobile Cutlass Supreme, loaded with air conditioning, AM-FM radio and air bags, is priced just under $17,000. Add those same extras to the old base and the price rises to almost $20,000. Says Christopher Cedergren of the Auto Pacific Group consulting firm: "Cutlass sales should jump 15% to 20% because of the new pricing strategy." He predicts that 50% to 60% of American vehicles will be similarly packaged this year, offering smart buyers savings of 10% or more. To find value priced models, look for ads that heavily tout price and also describe an array of extras.

The best buys in PCs sport CD-ROM. If you are one of the 65 million households that have not yet succumbed, this is the year to bring home a personal computer. It's also a terrific time to trade up. Most experts recommend a multimedia PC, which has a CD-ROM drive along with the necessary sound and graphics cards. Prices have been falling on these machines, which average about $300 more than other models. A fully equipped multimedia PC that cost $2,500 at the end of 1992 could cost half that amount by the end of 1994. Before making a purchase, be sure to find out whether the computer can be equipped with a faster microprocessor. That way, when a chip faster than the current 486 or 586 models comes out, you can easily update your machine.

Multimedia PCs let you run comprehensive programs like Microsoft's *Cinemania* ($80), a compilation of reviews of 20,000 movies. You can also watch video clips of classic film scenes, listen to excerpts of theme songs or peruse a list of every Academy Award winner. Microsoft's *Encarta* encyclopedia ($349) includes video and audio clips of moments in history and a simulation of the earth's and moon's orbit. By the end of the year, the number of CD-ROM titles figures to soar some 33% to 4,000. And Apple Computer gives buyers of its machines a CD-ROM disk that works as a software catalogue. The Software Dispatch (800-937-2828, extension 600) offers more than 80 CD-ROM disk titles at prices equivalent to those of discounters. Users can sample titles on the disk and opt to buy the program by calling a toll-free line. You charge the program on a credit card, and the cataloguer provides an access code that you key in to unlock the software. Then you copy the program to your hard drive. Other companies, such as TestDrive and InfoNow, offer similar catalogues.

Orient your vacation dollars. "Over the next few years," says Earlene Causey, president of the American Society of Travel Agents, "Europe will lose many travelers to the Orient." Not only is the region less expensive than Europe, but the Orient's exotic sights tend to appeal to veteran travelers. For example, Pacific Bestour (800-688-3288) recently featured a six-night tour to Beijing for $998, or about $200 less than in 1993. The price includes round-trip air fare from the West Coast, accommodations at the five-star Shangri-La Hotel (double occupancy) and sightseeing trips to the Great Wall and the Ming Tombs. And watch for vacations in Vietnam to turn chic now that the Treasury Department has relaxed its restrictions on U.S. travelers there. Pearl Cruises (800-556-8850) offers 15-day sails along Vietnam's coastline.

Where to Get the Best Travel Bargains

Want a suite with a view for the price of a puny room overlooking the parking lot? Such deals are available. You simply have to ask.

The travel industry, still struggling to recover from a slump, dearly needs your business. Many airlines and hotels, for example, are operating with more than a third of their seats and rooms empty. "In many areas of travel, it's a buyer's market," says Tim Zagat of the Zagat restaurant and hotel guides. "And few consumers are taking advantage of the values that are available." To help you negotiate the best deals, we asked experts in airlines, cruises, hotels and other travel businesses to map out an insider's strategy. Here is their advice on how to get the most for your money. All it takes is a few key phrases, a willingness to bargain and the understanding that the odds are in your favor.

Shopping for air fares. Be flexible. Don't lock yourself into an airline, an airport or, within reason, a departure date. Try to choose a three-day span for your departure, then ask your travel agent to "do a fare shop" on the computer. That will search out the airlines' lowest fares to your destination. Be sure the selection includes all the airports near the cities you are leaving from and arriving at. You may get substantial savings, for example, by departing from Burbank airport in the Los Angeles area rather than LAX, or by arriving at Newark rather than JFK on your trip to New York City. Also check the fares to a nearby city. Last year, flights from St. Louis to National airport in Washington, D.C. were $198 round trip. But if you flew into Baltimore airport, a 35-minute drive away, they cost $111.

On travel to Europe, ask about flights available through consolidators that buy blocks of tickets from airlines at wholesale prices. About 20% of fliers now go overseas on consolidator tickets, saving as much as 50% of the regular fare. You most likely won't be able to make any ticket changes once you've paid for a consolidator flight, so study

Money Helps

Q. During a trip to Santa Fe, I lost my Abbot Bank of Nebraska Visa card. The bank promises emergency card replacements. When I called Visa, however, I was told that I would have to wait up to two weeks. Abbot Bank was closed for the weekend. I had no cash, and friends had to bail me out. How can I prevent such disasters in the future?
—Ruth Darden, Seattle

A. You were definitely entitled to emergency assistance, whether through Visa or the bank. An Abbot spokesman says emergency replacements are expensive for the bank. So unless you demand it in a rather explicit way, service reps typically don't offer it. If you had shrieked something like, "This is an emergency! If I don't get my card right away, I will have to turn to a career in crime," you would have had a new card within 24 hours. The next time you travel, you should definitely carry some traveler's checks and don't leave home without your ATM (automated teller machine) card. Many banks charge a small fee (typically $1 or less) for transactions through another bank's ATM. But at least the card will give you direct access to funds in your checking and savings accounts.

the restrictions that apply. And before booking any trips within the U.S. or abroad, check prices with at least three travel agents. Think of it as getting a bid from a contractor and go with the one that gives you the best deal.

Negotiating a hotel room. According to Smith Travel Research, which monitors the lodging industry, U.S. hotels are filled to only about 60% capacity these days. So you can negotiate a discount unless you're booking into a large city during a convention or a top-of-the-line resort at high season. Often you can get a minimum of 10% off the published rate and sometimes as much as 50% off the highest-price accommodations. When booking a room, call the hotel directly, not the 800 number, and ask the reservations clerk if there are special rates for the days you plan to stay. If the answer is no, ask for the corporate rate, which is usually about 20% lower than the published rate. You can often get a corporate discount even if you are on a pleasure trip or have no business affiliation with the hotel. When you arrive at the hotel, verify the rate you were quoted over the phone and ask, "Can you do any better?" If you can't get a further discount on the price, ask whether your room can be upgraded to one with more space or a better view or whether you can be moved to the club or concierge floor, where the hotel provides perks such as free breakfast and complimentary shoeshines. Seasoned travelers say they never take the first room they are offered.

Renting a car at an airport. When you arrive, go to the desks of several rental agencies including the one with whom you've made your reservation. Ask them to beat the price you've been quoted or to give you a better car for the same money. You usually can get a better deal. Always ask whether there are club discounts you might qualify for, such as those offered to members of AAA or AARP.

Choosing a cruise. "I haven't seen business this bad since the early 1980s," says Oivind Mathisen of the magazine *Cruise Industry News.* That's good news. Many cruise lines are offering discounts of as much as 50% if you book early. Start negotiations by asking your travel agent to get you the best discount available and an upgrade to a better cabin. To protect yourself in the event of a last-minute fare cut, also ask for a guaranteed further fare reduction or upgrade if the price ultimately goes lower than what you paid.

Booking a tour. When two or more components of your travel, such as air fare and hotel, are sold together it usually is considered a package tour and is nonnegotiable. If a package includes features you don't really want, like sightseeing tours or theater tickets, you should ask your agent to assemble what's known as an "independent package." You and your agent can custom design a tour from an array of choices that might include the same air fare, hotel and car-rental rates as the set package tour. The major difference: you'll pay only for what you want.

Finding a kids' program. Family travel is flourish-ing, and so are children's programs at resorts, hotels and on cruises. Always ask exactly what the price of the program includes and which activities are available only for additional fees. At some resorts you may have to pay as much as $35 extra each time your child goes horseback riding or takes a tennis lesson. When you make your reservation, it doesn't hurt to ask whether a connecting room for the children can be added for half price. Many hotels will agree to that these days.

Today's Top Golf Resort Values

Whether your handicap is nil or astronomical, we'll help you find your money's worth in a golfing vacation.

Each of the estimated 8 million Americans who will take a golfing vacation this year has his or her own idea of what is essential in a resort. But most players who travel to tee off agree that it's crucial to get good value for your dollar. You'll get more than your money's worth, both in golfing pleasure and in vacation amenities, from the 25 top American golf resorts in our rankings. Don't expect low-down bargains, though. Including air fare, figure on spending $2,000 or more per person for a week at most of the blue-chip resorts on our list.

To select these exemplars, we began by scanning a roster of practically every hacker's mecca in the U.S. We narrowed the field to about three dozen semifinalists and graded each on the quality of its golf, the quality of its general resort features and overall value. We identified the 10 criteria, other than price, that travelers say are most important to them in choosing a golf resort. We awarded from one to 10 points in each category, with 100 constituting a perfect score. To determine overall value, we asked each resort to calculate its price for a seven-night stay at high season for two persons. We then measured the golf and resort scores against the prices. Note, however, that we eliminated some excellent places that were simply too

pricey, including the Boulders in Carefree, Ariz., where a week of golf for two costs nearly $5,000.

The overall winner as MONEY's greatest golf resort value is the Marriott at Sawgrass in Ponte Vedra Beach, Fla. This resort south of Jacksonville carded a perfect 60 for its golf and a 32-point resort rating. With price factored in, Sawgrass amassed eight bonus points for a value rating of 100. For runners-up and an enumeration of what all 25 resorts provide in terms of amenities and attractions, see the tables beginning on the next page. Here, in detail, is what we looked for in selecting a great golf resort value:

Plenty of courses. If you're planning to spend more than just a few days at a resort, you'll want the chance to play several tracks. For example, our top choice, Sawgrass, has 99 holes ranging from the 6,857-yard championship TPC Stadium Course to the easier 6,031-yard Oakbridge Course. The more holes a place provides, the less crowded the course is likely to be.

Championship courses. "People care about the style and quality of a golf resort's courses," says Tom Liszewski of Golf Vacations, a Boston travel agency (800-832-4242) that arranges customized

America's 25 Best Golf Resort Values

Our overall value rating considers the quality of a resort's golf and other attractions in relation to its price. A resort could score a maximum of 60 points for its golf and 40 for nongolf attributes. Cost is for two people staying a week at the lowest available high-season room rate and includes daily golf for two with cart and all meals. An asterisk indicates a value rating tie.

RESORT In order of rank	The MONEY Ratings			Accommodations	Activities	Cost
	Overall value	Golf	Resort features			
1 Marriott at Sawgrass Ponte Vedra Beach, Fla. 800-457-4653	100	60	32	350 rooms, 150 villas	HB HC K T W	$2,294
2 PGA National Resort & Spa Palm Beach Gardens, Fla. 800-633-9150	99	57	34	276 rooms, 59 suites, 85 cottages	HC K S T W	$2,215
3 Pinehurst Resort Pinehurst, N.C. 800-487-GOLF	92	59	29	370 rooms, 130 condos	HC K T W	$2,648
4 The Cloister Sea Island, Ga. 800-732-4752	90	51	34	263 rooms	B HB HC K S T W	$2,576
★ Kapalua Bay Hotel & Villas Lahaina, Maui, Hawaii 800-367-8000	90	49	38	194 rooms, 125 villas	HC K T W	$2,769
6 Boyne Highlands Resort Harbor Springs, Mich. 800-GO-BOYNE	87	46	30	225 rooms, 108 condos	B HC K T W	$1,750
★ Grand Cypress Resort Orlando 407-239-1234	87	52	37	750 rooms, 146 villas	B HB HC K S T W	$3,290
8 Amelia Island Plantation Amelia Island, Fla. 800-874-6878	86	47	37	126 rooms, 383 villas	B HB HC K S T W	$2,870
9 The Williamsburg Inn Williamsburg, Va. 800-HISTORY	85	43	37	242 rooms	B HC K T W	$2,484
10 Grand Traverse Resort Grand Traverse, Mich. 800-748-0303	83	47	30	375 rooms, 25 suites, 350 condos	HC K S T W	$2,280
11 Mauna Kea Beach Hotel Kohala Coast, Hawaii 800-882-6060	80	45	40	310 rooms	HB HC K T W	$3,500
12 Eagle Ridge Inn & Resort Galena, Ill. 800-892-2269	79	44	29	80 rooms, 260 rental houses	B HB HC K T W	$2,250
13 The American Club Kohler, Wis. 800-344-2838	77	47	35	236 rooms	HB HC S T	$3,450
★ Doral Resort & Country Club Miami 800-327-6334	77	53	30	650 rooms	B HC S T	$3,590

KEY TO ACTIVITIES: B-BICYCLING, **HB**-HORSEBACK RIDING, **HC**-HEALTH CLUB, **K**-KIDS' PROGRAMS, **S**-SPA, **T**-TENNIS, *TIED WITH THE ABOVE

Golf courses	Special attractions and programs
There are 99 challenging holes here, including two courses designed by Pete Dye, one by Ed Seay, and the most photographed par 3 in the world.	Sawgrass is the site of the Players' Championship Tournament every March. Among the resort's attractions are 2-1/2 miles of beach, marshes, lagoons and waterfalls.
The five championship courses offer something for everyone. Champion has 107 bunkers. Estate features 17 water hazards, and Haig is for high handicappers.	The PGA makes its home here and provides elaborate instruction. The resort has a 26-acre sailing lake, a European-style spa and the largest croquet complex in the Western Hemisphere.
With seven championship courses, Pinehurst has the most in the world. They include four old-style Donald Ross masterpieces. Ross' No. 2 Course is considered one of the best ever built.	Pinehurst was the site of 1991 and 1992 PGA tour events and is host to the 1994 U.S. Senior Open. Its 91-year-old inn is on the National Register of Historic Places.
Four nine-hole courses with some holes bordering the ocean and winding through marshes and over tidal rivers; an 18-hole course is also available.	Formal southern decor and service are among the splendors here. There are indoor practice facilities, a golf fitness program and an annual personal-finance seminar.
You play oceanside and mountain golf among pines, palms and pineapples on three spectacular courses. Plantation, the toughest, has deep valleys, huge mounds, native grasses and 95 bunkers.	According to a University of Maryland study, Kapalua has "the best beach in America." The resort borders a rain forest. It hosts the Lincoln-Mercury Kapalua International PGA tournament.
Heather, a Robert Trent Jones design, and Moor each play about 7,200 yards from the blue tees. The Donald Ross Memorial Course recreates his best 18 holes. There's also a nine-hole course.	Adjacent to Lake Michigan, Boyne has hiking and biking trails through 600 wooded acres. There is summer dinner theater on the premises.
Designed by Jack Nicklaus, the 45 holes feature ledged fairways, dunes and lots of water. The New Course imitates St. Andrews' Old Course, with wide fairways and double greens.	On this 1,500-acre property, next door to Disney World, you will find a 45-acre nature preserve and a pool with grottos and waterfalls. Golf instruction combines video and biomechanics.
Three short, easy, distinctive Pete Dye nine-hole courses include Oysterbay, whose No. 8 hole features a 170-yard carry from the tee over wetlands. The 18-hole Long Point is monstrously tough.	The 1,250-acre resort is perched on cliffs overlooking barrier island white sand beaches. It has 25 tennis courts and a large golf school. Professional tennis tournaments are held here.
Robert Trent Jones' Gold Course winds through valleys. The Green Course, by his son Rees, stretches 7,120 yards from the back tees. The senior Jones also designed the nine-hole course.	Set in historic Colonial Williamsburg, there is classic 18th-century architecture throughout this 173-acre complex. President Reagan hosted the Economic Summit of Industrial Nations here in 1983.
The two courses here feature lakes, terraces and tiers, rolling hills, pot bunkers and wetlands. The Bear, designed by Jack Nicklaus, plays more than 7,000 yards from the blue tees.	The 17-story Tower, another six-story hotel, and 10 restaurants are located on Grand Traverse's 920 acres. It is near wineries and Lake Michigan beaches.
Mauna Kea, designed by Robert Trent Jones on a 5,000-year-old lava flow, has 120 bunkers and ocean views. Hapuna, an Arnold Palmer/Ed Seay design, has wild desert links-style holes.	The hotel has a botanical garden and is decorated with art from Laurance Rockefeller's museum-quality Pacific and Asian collection. Helicopter tours of nearby volcanoes are available.
Three courses—two 18 holes and one nine—feature large undulating greens, elevated tees, rolling terrain, ponds, waterfalls and woods.	Many rooms have fireplaces and four-poster beds. Eagle Ridge offers a wide variety of golf clinics.
Two difficult Pete Dye Scottish-style courses have four sets of tees instead of three. The courses traverse glacier-carved terrain with ravines, riverside holes and native prairie landscaping.	Located in a 500-acre nature preserve with 30 miles of trails, the resort has a log-and-fieldstone clubhouse with fireplace and a modern fitness center.
The five classic Florida courses are lined with palm trees and abundant water; two have water on all 18 holes.	The 2,400-acre resort has a tennis stadium—Arthur Ashe was the resort's tennis pro—and a $40 million spa. The Doral Ryder Open is played here each February.

America's 25 Best Golf Resort Values

RESORT In order of rank	The Money Ratings			Accommodations	Activities	Cost
	Overall value	Golf	Resort features			
15 The Balsams Grand Resort Dixville Notch, N.H. 800-255-0600	76	34	36	232 rooms	B K T W	$2,156
* La Quinta Hotel Golf Resort La Quinta, Calif. 800-598-3828	76	45	35	613 rooms, 27 suites	B K S T	$3,395
17 The Inn at Sem-ahmoo Blaine, Wash. 800-770-7992	75	36	36	200 rooms	HC T	$2,527
18 Salishan Lodge Gleneden Beach, Ore. 800-452-2300	74	36	35	205 rooms	HC T	$2,500
19 The Greenbrier White Sulphur Springs, W.Va. 800-624-6070	74	44	38	541 rooms, 40 suites, 69 cottages	HB S T	$3,836
20 The Broadmoor Colorado Springs 800-634-7711	73	43	35	550 rooms	B HB HC K T	$3,507
21 Horseshoe Bay Resort Horseshoe Bay, Texas 800-531-5105	73	42	28	145 rooms, 5 suites	B HB S T W	$2,540
22 Innisbrook Tarpon Springs, Fla. 800-456-2000	72	50	29	100 suites	B HC K T	$3,650
23 Mauna Lani Bay Kohala Coast, Hawaii 800-367-2323	71	44	39	350 rooms	B HC K T W	$4,210
24 The Homestead Hot Springs, Va. 800-336-5771	68	41	35	518 rooms	HB HC K S T	$3,675
25 The Westin La Paloma Tucson 800-876-3683	65	44	34	456 rooms, 31 suites	B HC K S T	$4,249

KEY TO ACTIVITIES: B-BICYCLING, **HB**-HORSEBACK RIDING, **HC**-HEALTH CLUB, **K**-KIDS' PROGRAMS, **S**-SPA, **T**-TENNIS, *****TIED WITH THE ABOVE

golf trips. "They want a unique design that will be interesting to play, not a flat, standard course with a few bunkers and trees."

Golfing challenge. The best resorts have courses that test the low handicapper while also holding appeal for the 90-plus duffer. We built our ratings around United States Golf Association statistics that have been compiled on the difficulty of golf courses.

Overall cachet. Many golfers love to boast about the courses they have played. So we rated resorts on the bragging rights they confer, awarding points based on factors that influence the reputation of a course. Have major tournaments been played there? Does it feature any well-known holes? Who designed it? Courses laid out by Pete Dye and Robert Trent Jones carry great cachet today. Other course designers whose names are

Golf courses	Special attractions and programs
The Panorama Course, designed by Donald Ross, was built in 1912 on the slopes of Keyser Mountain. It features elevated greens. There is also a nine-hole course.	Award-winning chef Phil Learned prepares five-course dinners every night. The traditional New England inn, open since 1866, is surrounded by 15,000 picturesque acres.
Of the three Pete Dye layouts here, only Dunes and Citrus are normally available to resort guests. Your club pro may be able to get you on the third, called Mountain, which is privately owned.	Since 1926, La Quinta has been a Hollywood getaway. There are 25 pools and 30 tennis courts on 45 gorgeous acres.
The curvy Arnold Palmer/Ed Seay course has wide, bent-grass fairways, many bunkers and weaves through towering woods. It has four sets of tees and plays 7,000 yards from the backs.	The inn is located on 1,000 acres with invigorating views of Cascade peaks. White-water rafting and other outdoor activities are nearby. In summer, daylight lasts until 10 p.m.
Salishan has one Scottish-style course. The front nine wind through ancient cedar, pine and spruce forests. The back nine play along ocean dunes lined with beach grasses.	There's serious dining at this 700-acre coastal resort. Chef Rob Pounding is a medal winner, and the 15,000-bottle wine cellar is one of the world's best, according to *Wine Spectator* magazine.
You can feel the tradition on this famous resort's three courses. The Greenbrier Course, redesigned in 1977 by Jack Nicklaus, is the toughest. Old White was built in 1913.	Since the early 1800s, 23 U.S. Presidents have visited The Greenbrier. Attractions include a $7 million spa, first built in 1910, and a renowned cooking school that guests can attend.
The Broadmoor has the best golf in the Rocky Mountains. The South Course was designed by Arnold Palmer and Ed Seay, the West Course by Robert Trent Jones and the East Course by Donald Ross.	Jack Nicklaus won his first tournament here, the 1959 U.S. Amateur. The U.S. Women's Open will be at Broadmoor in 1995. The pink stucco hotel was built in 1918.
You have a choice of three Robert Trent Jones courses with waterfalls, valleys and four sets of tees. The 6,946-yard Ramrock is considered one of the toughest in Texas.	Exotic birds, sculptures and rock gardens give quirky character to this 4,500-acre development on Lake LBJ in the Texas hill country. The Olympic-size pool is made of black marble.
Innisbrook's three courses pose a variety of challenges: Copperhead plays 7,087 yards; Island features tight fairways; Sandpiper's 27 holes are short but heavily bunkered.	The resort, only minutes from the Gulf of Mexico, is home of the J.C. Penney Classic golf tournament and the excellent Innisbrook Golf Institute.
Both North and South courses are built on lava flows. North is hillier, tougher, greener, with native kiawe trees and roaming goat herds. Both play about 7,000 yards from the back tees.	Mauna Lani was home of the Senior Skins Game at the end of January. It has beaches, waterfalls and views of 13,000-foot mountain peaks. Its July food festival features world-famous chefs.
Three short courses are nestled between mountain ranges. Cascade is the most famous. Donald Ross designed Homestead in 1892; it has the oldest continuously used tee in the U.S.	The 17,000-acre spread in the Allegheny Mountains is the site of several USGA tournaments. The old-fashioned Homestead has a mineral hot-springs spa and serves tea at 4 p.m. daily.
Set in the desert, the three rugged nine-hole layouts designed by Jack Nicklaus have half the grass of a normal golf course. There are lots of cacti and multiple tees.	The $100 million resort in the foothills of the Santa Catalina Mountains has been designed with southwest mission revival architecture. It has a free-form pool with swim-up bar.

likely to be winners at the watercooler include Jack Nicklaus, Dick Wilson, Arnold Palmer and his partner Ed Seay, and Donald Ross, a Scottish designer who built more than 400 courses in the U.S. early in the century.

Superior instruction. Susan Stafford of the highly regarded Roland Stafford Golf Schools says that there are a few key elements to look for in a resort's instructional program. The best resorts will have, at a minimum, a driving area with covered tees in case of bad weather, facilities for a video-taped swing analysis, a low student/teacher ratio (4 to 1 or less), and pros who are members of the Professional Golfers Association or Ladies Professional Golfers Association.

Great facilities. A resort should have extensive

A Gym to Call Your Own

Whether it's telecommuting or shopping by video, today's status symbol is the freedom to stay at home. Small wonder, then, that sales of home gym systems have muscled ahead 16% annually as Americans spent more than $2 billion on exercise equipment. Says Richard Miller, owner of the Gym Source in New York City: "It's hard to beat working out at home. You never have to wait in line, and nobody messes up your equipment."

There is one drawback. A lot of home gyms end up collecting dust, a costly shame. Top-rated treadmills run anywhere from $2,000 to $5,000, while reliable stationary bikes range from $300 to $2,500. To help you get the best workout for your wallet, MONEY asked fitness trainers, equipment makers and retailers for tips on buying exercise equipment. Here's their advice as well as their favorite gear:

Decide goals first, equipment second. If you want to lose weight, you should turn to aerobic gear such as a stationary bicycle or stair climber that can speed your heart rate and metabolism. Aspiring bodybuilders require weight stations or other muscle enhancers. Your best route through the jungle of available gym equipment is to sign on for temporary membership at a health club. That way you can audition a wide variety of machines. Once you've settled on what works for you, shop in specialized fitness stores for durable higher-end equipment. Why? In the long run, it's a better value. Low-priced equipment, often advertised on TV, is more likely to break down than build you up.

Think compact. Unless you're totally gung-ho, buy equipment that doesn't occupy an entire room. Usually stationary bikes and stair climbers make the most efficient use of floor space and are light enough to be shoved into a corner when not in use. Among the better bikes is the Lifecycle 5500 ($1,000; 800-735-3867 for the dealer nearest you). Numerous computerized programs change the pedaling resistance, which helps to keep you motivated.

Choose user-friendly equipment. The more complicated a piece of equipment is to use or adjust, the more maintenance it generally requires. Not much can go wrong with a jump rope, but plenty can with an ill-designed stair climber or treadmill. That's why many experts recommend the Trotter CXT Plus treadmill even though the price is steep ($3,500; 800-876-8837). It features a computerized control panel that monitors numerous factors, from the elevation of the track to the calories burned. All you do is spray a lubricant on the belt and deck every 250 miles or so. Stair climbers favor the Tectrix Personal Climber ($2,100; 800-767-8082) for its sturdy and reliable construction. A simple control panel lets you program and monitor routines of varying difficulty.

Consider low tech. You can create your own gym with the following gear for around $700—less than the cost of an exercise bike. Spalding's SportRope ($25; 800-222-5867) offers a total-body workout in just 20 to 30 minutes. While conventional jump rope exercise works the heart, lungs and legs, SportRope's weighted jumpers also involve the upper body. Swiveling handles and foam grips make them easy to use. Dyna-Band's stretch fitness bands ($10; 800-537-5512) can be tucked in a briefcase. These three-foot strips of latex build muscle with the same principles of resistance used in Nautilus systems. Ivanko Chrome Dumbbells ($425 for five pairs of different weights; 310-514-1155) have contoured handles for an easier grip. Frelonic's Comfort Cushion exercise mat ($33; 508-744-0300) has a special nonskid bottom and shock-absorbing layer.

practice areas, including driving ranges, chipping and putting greens and practice sand traps. It should have a comfortable clubhouse with locker rooms, showers and dining facilities. In addition, the tennis courts, swimming pools and fitness centers at our top 25 resorts are topnotch. Most also offer bicycle rentals, jogging trails and, at least during high season, children's programs. Many have horseback riding too.

Memorable accommodations. The top resorts rent rooms, suites and cottages that reach beyond the generic to make you feel you're in a special place. For example, the American Club in Kohler, Wis. scored a 10 in this category thanks to its sumptuous rooms with a Jacuzzi in every bath. Some accommodations have private spas that simulate natural environments like desert heat and spring rain. Note that all prices in our rankings are based on high-season rates. You can save as much as 50% by planning your trip off season. While the weather may not be as dependable, a light drizzle might not be terribly annoying. And it could give you the perfect excuse for not breaking par.

America's Finest Restaurant Towns

As a service to business and pleasure travelers, we rank the leading places to dine and guide you to their top tables.

The restaurant industry is gripped by two related trends. One is value. Customers, whose busy lives constantly sharpen their appetite for restaurant meals, are demanding it. The second trend is what critics call casualization. The setting of the finest food service—the tradition-steeped establishment with headwaiter, captains and extensive menu selection—has fallen like a gustatory Bastille. And up rose the bistro with staff in work shirts and butcher's aprons, a tight list of offerings and a far friendlier tab.

MONEY's ranking of the 15 top cities appears on the following pages along with recommended restaurants for a variety of occasions. The selection and order of the cities are based on quality and variety of food available, local standards of service and price. To pass responsible judgment on the cities and their restaurants, we turned to Nancy Harmon Jenkins, a respected food critic and a veteran contributor to the *New York Times.* We also recruited chefs, restaurant consultants and other critics. Then we did some eating of our own, of course. The winners:

1. New York. What always made this city the emperor of eating out was its sheer depth and variety. Among its 12,000 full-service restaurants and 25,000 takeouts, you could find more French, Italian, Chinese, seafood, steak places—the list never stops—than anywhere else. The best advice for the visitor to this dizzying feast is to savor the variety that no city on earth can match. The top three recommendations of our New York critic are a fine sample of what real depth has to offer: Vong (East-West trendy); Aureole (American-French); and Gotham Bar & Grill (nouvelle American).

2. San Francisco. Yes, it's the queen of Chinese cookery, more so than ever since a tide of Hong Kong people and money flooded in beginning in the mid-1980s. San Francisco is also the home of the Great American Foodie, the customer so demanding that restaurateurs there are a restless lot. San Francisco's top tier may be relatively thin. But it offers in abundance what most larger cities lack—a staggering cornucopia of mid-range restaurants where everything is modest except the food. LuLu, which our local critic nominates as a best bargain, is a good example. Try anything from LuLu's wood-fired rotisserie and you'll get the point.

The 15 Top Restaurant Towns

Here is MONEY's ranking of the country's 15 finest eating-out cities, plus restaurants recommended by our food critic in each city.

Rank 1993 1990	CITY Critic	Three Top Restaurants Phone number; cost per person/type of food			Best Bargain	Best Family Spot
1 2	**NEW YORK** David Rosengarten	Aureole 212-319-1660 $60/AF	Gotham Bar & Grill 212-620-4020 $55/A	Vong 212-486-9592 $45/TF	Savoy 212-219-8570 $30/MD	Manhattan Plaza Cafe 212-695-5808 $17/A
2 3	**SAN FRANCISCO** Patricia Unterman	Chez Panisse 510-548-5525 $50/CA	Masa's 800-258-7694 $68[2]/F	Ritz-Carlton 415-296-7465 $45/A	LuLu 415-495-5775 $19/CA	Medioevo 415-346-7373 $20/I
3 1	**LOS ANGELES** Charles Perry	Campanile 213-938-1447 $40/CM	Patina 213-467-1108 $40/CF	Rockenwagner 310-399-6504 $35/CF	Joe's 310-399-5811 $20/CF	The Daily Grill[1] 818-986-4111 $24/A
4 4	**CHICAGO** William Rice	Arum's 312-539-1909 $30/T	Spiaggia 312-280-2750 $40/I	Topolobampo 312-661-1434 $28/M	Vivere 312-332-4040 $25/I	Blackhawk Lodge 312-280-4080 $18/A
5 5	**WASHINGTON, D.C.** Phyllis Richman	Galileo 202-293-7191 $46/I	Jean-Louis 202-298-4488 $85[2]/F	Obelisk 202-872-1180 $35/I	El Patio[1] 202-466-7876 $20/SV	Old Glory 202-337-3406 $19/BQ
6 8	**NEW ORLEANS** Gene Bourg	Brigtsen's 504-861-7610 $28/R	Emeril's 504-528-9393 $40/R	Mike's on the Avenue 504-523-1709 $30/SA	L'Economie 504-524-7405 $22/F	The Praline Connection[1] 504-943-3934 $11/R
7 11	**MIAMI** Steven Raichlen	Brasserie Le Coze 305-444-9697 $35/F	Chef Allen's 305-935-2900 $40/R	Mark's Place 305-893-6888 $50/R	Shorty's Bar B. Q.[1] 305-665-5732 $10/BQ	The Forge 305-538-8533 $35/CO
8 6	**SEATTLE** Jonathan Susskind	Kaspar's 206-441-4805 $28/AF	Rover's 206-325-7442 $40/F	Saleh Al Lago 206-524-4044 $30/I	The Yankee Diner[1] 206-643-1558 $10/A	Cucina! Cucina! [1] 206-637-1177 $18/I
9 7	**BOSTON** Rene Becker	Biba 617-426-7878 $41/A	Dali[1] 617-661-3254 $24/SP	L'Espalier 617-262-3023 $56/F	Jae's Cafe & Grill[1] 617-421-9405 $10/K	Pampas 617-661-6613 $19/B
10 13	**HOUSTON** Ann Criswell	Damian's Cucina Italiana 713-522-0439 $30/I	River Oaks Grill 713-520-1738 $26/A	Ruggles 713-524-3839 $22/R	Vincent's[1] 713-528-4313 $18/I	Rio Ranch[1] 713-952-5000 $14/A
11 9	**PHILADELPHIA** Elaine Tait	Deux Cheminees 215-790-0200 $62[2]/F	Dilullo Centro 215-546-2000 $34/I	The Garden 215-546-4455 $35/CO	Le Bar Lyonnais[1] 215-567-1000 $30/F	Le Bus[1] 215-487-2663 $13/A
12 –	**PHOENIX** Barbara Fenzl	Christopher's Bistro 602-957-3214 $30/F	Roxsand 602-381-0444 $30/FA	Vincent Guerithault 602-224-0225 $35/R	L'Ecole 602-990-7639 $15/CO	Tucchetti 602-957-0222 $12/I
13 14	**ATLANTA** Anne Byrn	Ciboulette[1] 404-874-7600 $38/F	The Dining Room 404-237-2700 $56[2]/CO	Hedgerose Heights Inn 404-233-7673 $37/CO	Dawat Indian Cafe[1] 404-623-6133 $8/IN	Houston's[1] 404-351-2442 $12/A
14 15	**SANTA FE** Kimberley Sweet	Cafe Escalera 505-989-8188 $31/MD	Geronimo 505-982-1500 $29/R	Inn of the Anasazi 505-988-3236 $35/R	Diego's[1] 505-983-5101 $10/R	Maria's New Mexican 505-983-7929 $16/R
15 10	**DALLAS** Dotty Griffith	Avner's 214-953-0426 $32/CO	The Conservatory 214-871-3242 $35/A	French Room 214-742-8200 $53/F	Romano's Macaroni Grill[1] 214-265-0770 $18/I	Cayuse[1] 214-521-0114 $20/A

Notes: Except for breakfast and lunch, all prices are for a three-course dinner per person excluding tax, tip or beverage.
For restaurants with more than one location, the phone number of the preferred one is listed.
1 – No or limited reservations   **2** – Four or more courses

Best Breakfast	Best Lunch	Best-Kept Secret	Tips and Tactics
Sarabeths[1] 212-410-7335 $11/A	Aquavit (downstairs) 212-307-7311 $40/SC	Rosemarie's 212-285-2610 $45/I	Bargains outside Manhattan: Poo Thai (718-651-7024/$35) in Queens; Tommaso's (718-236-9883/$35) in Brooklyn
Il Fornaio 415-986-0100 $10/I	Yank Sing[1] 415-362-1640 $15/DS	Helmand 415-362-0641 $20/AG	Try Bradley Ogden's new 1 Market Restaurant (415-777-5577/$35) for great American meat dishes.
Cafe Morpheus[1] 310-657-8484 $7/A	72 Market Street 310-392-8720 $20/CA	Saddle Peak Lodge 818-222-3888 $35/A	Check out Campanile's own La Brea Bakery for wonderful bread. Traffic alert: Allow at least 20 minutes to reach any restaurant.
Seasons[1] 312-649-2349 $14/A	Shaw's Crab House 312-527-2722 $20/S	Printer's Row 312-461-0780 $27/A	Surprises for lunch in the loop include the Berghoff Bar (312-427-3170/$7), a stand-up coffee shop unchanged since Prohibition.
Patisserie Cafe Didier[1] 202-342-9083 $8/F	Citronelle 202-625-2150 $25/CF	Cities 202-328-7194 $25/A	Old Glory is a funky bargain that serves home-style food. Try Citronelle for lunch, but avoid its dinner crowds and higher prices.
Camellia Grill[1] 504-866-9573 $5/A	Bayona 504-525-4455 $20/F	Peristyle 504-593-9535 $27/CO	The shrimp and crab dishes at Kelsey's (504-366-6722/$22) are worth the 15-minute drive over the Mississippi to Algiers.
The Rascal House[1] 305-947-4581 $8/JE	Victor's Cafe 305-445-1313 $25/CU	Big Fish 305-372-3725 $9/S	Miami's hot restaurants live on crowds: To eat at Mark's Place, make a reservation before boarding your flight to Miami.
A. Jay's[1] 206-441-1511 $7/JE	McCormick & Schmick's 206-623-5500 $8/A	Szmania's 206-284-7305 $27/R	For prime seafood, try Anthony's Home Port (206-783-0780/$16) or Ray's Boathouse (206-789-3770/$18).
Charlie's Sandwich 617-536-7669 $6/A	Cafe Louis[1] 617-266-4680 $18/I	Anago Bistro 617-492-9500 $30/MD	Try to dine before the theater; most Boston restaurants close at 10 p.m. You'll find the best late-night eating in Chinatown.
Goode Co. Taqueria[1] 713-520-9153 $5/MA	Quilted Toque 713-942-9233 $15/A	Prego 713-529-2420 $21/I	Generous portions rule in the rejuvenated Houston food scene, making doggy bags de rigueur at most restaurants.
Mayfair Diner[1] 215-624-8886 $5/A	Palladium Restaurant 215-387-3463 $16/CO	Dmitri's[1] 215-625-0556 $15/G	In summer, try the tented piers and resort-like spots with views of the Delaware River like Kat Man Du (215-629-7400/$20).
La Pila 602-252-7007 $5/M	Eddie's Grill 602-241-1188 $9/A	Los dos Molinos[1] 602-243-9113 $12/R	The ubiquitous alfresco dining (including all our selections except for Vincent Guerithault) calls for sunscreen and sunglasses.
OK Cafe[1] 404-233-2888 $5/R	Buckhead Diner[1] 404-262-3336 $15/A	Babette's Cafe[1] 404-523-9121 $20/CO	Check out acclaimed new chefs Jean Banchet at Ciboulette and Guenter Seeger at the Dining Room.
Pasqual's[1] 505-983-9340 $7/R	Old Mexico Grill 505-473-0338 $10/M	Paul's Restaurant 505-982-8738 $25/A	Breakfast getaways just outside town: San Marcos Cafe (505-471-9298/$6) and Harry's Roadside Cafe (505-989-4629/$6)
The Landmark 214-521-5151 $12/R	Baby Routh 214-871-2345 $12/R	Matt's No Place 214-823-9077 $22/R	Don't forget longtime culinary temples: the Mansion on Turtle Creek (214-559-2100-0094/$50), and the Riviera (214-351-0094/$50).

Type of food: A – American **AF** – American-French **AG** – Afghan **B** – Brazilian **BQ** – Barbecue **CA** – California **CF** – California-French **CM** – California-Mediterranean **CO** – Continental **CU** – Cuban **DS** – Dim Sum **F** – French **FA** – French-Asian **G** – Greek **I** – Italian **IN** – Indian **JE** – Jewish **K** – Korean **M** – Mexican **MA** – Mexican-American **MD** – Mediterranean **R** – Regional specialty **S** – Seafood **SA** – Southwest-Asian **SC** – Scandinavian **SP** – Spanish **SV** – Salvadoran **T** – Thai **TF** – Thai-French.

3. Los Angeles. It's still first in Far Eastern ethnic restaurants. That begins with Japanese, where L.A. stands supreme, and includes Thai, Chinese, Korean and Vietnamese. Where else will you find anything quite like Matsuhisa, a Japanese-Peruvian spot that has drawn top billing in the local Zagat Guide for four years running? Or Ginza Sushi-Ko, perhaps the most expensive restaurant in the U.S., where a sushi feast of the rarest ingredients can run as high as $350 per person? If you dote on French and Italian classics, however, you may not be satisfied eating in the handful of first-rate places in L.A. But who ever said that this city was into tradition anyway? Go instead for Californian-Mediterranean at Campanile or Californian-French at Rockenwagner's or Patina.

4. Chicago. If L.A. ties down the salad end of the U.S. food scene, brawny Chicago speaks up for the steak and the stew. Some of the best such fare is at Euro-ethnic spots: Lutnia (Polish), Bohemian Crystal (Czech) and Kenessey's Wine Cellar (Hungarian). The city is also blessed with dozens of newer and more ambitious places led impressively by the 31 restaurants owned and run by Richard Melman, who is considered by critics to be among America's top restaurateurs. His flagship is nouvelle French Ambria.

5. Washington, D.C. Just as the nation's capital took its first leap to serious eating out during the Kennedy Administration, it is taking another, far more ambitious one under the Democrats again. The hottest spot is Red Sage, an extravagant outpost of southwestern food where you might have to wait a month for a table. The latest charmer is the French-accented Citronelle, one of three offshoots of Los Angeles' Citrus. You should telephone a week ahead even for a midweek booking.

The reigning regionals. New Orleans (No. 6). Its Cajun and Creole cuisines are being updated, lightened and opened to Asian and European influences at such standouts as Emeril's, Mike's on the Avenue and Bacco, the latest entry of Ella Brennan's clan, the famed American restaurant dynasty. Miami (No. 7). Aside from great Cuban fare, the local pride is such seafood as snapper, pompano, wahoo and spiny lobster. At the top end, Brasserie Le Coze is the Miami outpost of New York City's seafood star, Le Bernardin. At the bargain end, Big Fish, open only for lunch, offers a real Miami scene of dockhands, downtown lawyers and politicos all digging in.

Among the other cities on our list—Seattle (No. 8), Boston (9), Houston (10), Philadelphia (11), Phoenix (12), Atlanta (13), Santa Fe (14) and Dallas (15)—a consensus of our food-critic sources nominated Atlanta as the one most likely to advance in the ranking over the coming years.

Don't Get Scammed by Scanners

Supermarket scanner errors cost shoppers more than $1 billion annually.
Here's what you can do to stop getting cheated at the checkout.

Like most smart shoppers, you probably scout supermarket specials and compare prices. Yet you have a one-in-10 chance of losing some savings when you hit the checkout counter. The culprit is your neighborhood supermarket's scanner, that laser-shooting, electronic device first installed in stores back in 1973. Scanners err more often than most shoppers realize. And usually the errors are in the store's favor.

The industry argues that scanner error cuts both ways. But a MONEY sampling of 27 supermarket chain stores in 23 states shows that scanner errors hurt shoppers more. In the stores surveyed, our correspondents purchased 10 randomly selected items and were overcharged on at least one item in 30% of the stores. Our reporters found undercharges in only 7% of stores. Some 63% of stores were accurate on all charges. Overcharges occurred more often on sale items. A 1991 study of 21 local markets by New York City's Department of Consumer Affairs also found the odds stacked against the consumer.

How do scanners cheat? When a cashier whisks your groceries over the electronic eye, the scanner reads the bar code, called the Universal Product Code (UPC), on each item and calls up the price from the store's computer. Many supermarket chains have a central database that electronically sends as many as 1,000 to 3,000 weekly price changes to each store. But store personnel may not correctly or immediately update either the shelf tags or the store's own computer listings.

Industry managers contend that stores work hard to ensure accurate scanners. "The push to make sure that shelf price matches scanner price is a high priority," says Edie Meleski at the Food Marketing Institute, an international trade group that represents 1,500 food companies. "Whenever there's an overcharge," continues Meleski, "supermarkets generally give the item to the customer for free. So considering profit margins of less than a penny on the dollar at most stores, any loss like that would prove a strong incentive for supermarket managers to get prices right."

In fact, scanner errors pay off for stores, especially on sale-priced items. "Managers sometimes have bonuses that are tied to their ability to achieve profitability," says Leo Harty of NCR, one of the largest scanner manufacturers. "In some cases, a dishonest person could either change prices or not enter sale prices so consumers pay higher prices." Sale items and limited offer promotions are particularly prone to error because they depend on someone entering changes in the computer. And again, the errors overwhelmingly favor the industry. In the New York City survey, for example, supermarkets wrongly charged regular prices on 10% of their sale items, undercharging consumers on only 1% of such purchases.

The solution, of course, is tougher and better

consumer protection. While a handful of states and cities still have laws requiring stores to mark prices on each grocery item, the overwhelming majority now require only shelf tags, those hard-to-read labels found on supermarket shelving. As a result, when shoppers reach the checkout line with unmarked items, they cannot easily catch errors as prices flash on the cash register, assuming shelf tags were right in the first place. "There is nothing to check prices with, except memory," says Margaret Charters, director of the consumer studies program at Syracuse University. "You can't even challenge a price without holding up yourself and the entire checkout line while someone goes to check the shelf." Around the country, frustrated consumer groups are lobbying to get local governments to require item pricing. Supermarket companies oppose item pricing mainly because it would force them to double the weekly $2,000 or so they now spend on shelf tags for each store.

You can prevent rip-offs at the checkout counter by being vigilant. Here's what to do to get your money's worth:

Test your supermarket's accuracy. On your next trip to the grocery store, buy at least 30 items (about half should be on sale). Write down the price of each item and compare your prices with the register receipt. If you are overcharged on 10% or more of the items, errors are unlikely to be accidental. Products to watch are manager's specials, end-of-aisle displays and limited offer promotions. Overcharges on eggs are particularly common.

Check which day of the week the store announces sale prices. If specials normally start on Mondays and you shop early in the week, pay attention to whether the scanner rings up the latest sale prices.

When you think there's an overcharge, ask for a price check. If the people in line grumble, ask someone to check prices after you pay. Even if you notice an error on your receipt after leaving the store, you can call the manager to report an overcharge. Some chains require stores to give the item free to shoppers who've been charged too much.

Rating Uncle Sam's Hotlines

A recent study by the General Accounting Office (GAO) showed that Social Security's toll-free hotline is less than a ringing success. The GAO's calls went unanswered 56% of the time. We decided to check out the government's so-called consumer help lines. After all, taxpayers spend an estimated $175 million a year to support the numbers listed in the table below. We called each between 20 and 100 times—and were generally underwhelmed. Our advice:

Be prepared to wait . . . and wait. You will probably spend at least five minutes and as much as half an hour on hold to get your question answered. One of the few times we got through on the Social Security line, a recording said we would be able to speak to one of the busy operators in eight minutes.

You may never get a human on the line. The National Highway Traffic Safety Administration's auto safety hotline and the Consumer Product Safety Commission (CPSC) product recall number force you to navigate through a byzantine automated telephone system just to hear the recording you need. Miss an instruction? Tough luck. You have to start all over again. After wading through endless messages on the CPSC's automated system, we kept getting disconnected just before receiving the recall information we wanted about a Baby Bop backpack. A CPSC spokesman says the agency is changing its system.

Call midweek about half an hour after the line opens. To get the most out of the toll-free numbers, never phone on a Monday, which is the busiest day for the lines. When a voice on an automated system tells you how you can reach an operator, do so or at least jot down the instructions (in case you later decide you want to talk to someone). And you should ask to speak to a specialist when you have a technical question for the IRS, FDIC or Small Business Administration. That will at least give you a shot at getting a knowledgeable response.

The Fed's Top 800 Numbers

When we tested these toll-free federal consumer phone lines, we found some far more helpful than others. For example, the tax man was home, but the teacher's aide was out to lunch. The IRS number for ordering free tax forms and publications gets our top rating, though admittedly we called after the busy tax season was over. The U.S. Education Department's student aid hotline was the pits. The hours we cite in the table below are local times, weekdays, except where noted as eastern standard time.

AGENCY	TELEPHONE (800)	HOURS	RATING
IRS (forms, publications)	829-3676	9 A.M. 5 P.M.	Good
Small Business Adm. (answer desk)	827-5722	8:30 A.M. 5 P.M.	Good
IRS (taxpayer assistance)	829-1040	8 A.M. 4:30 P.M.	Fair
IRS (Tele-Tax recordings)	829-4477	24 hours	Fair
Social Security	772-1213	7 A.M. 7 P.M.	Poor
National Highway Traffic Safety Administration	424-9393	8 A.M. 4 P.M.*	Poor
Federal Deposit Insurance Corporation	934-3342	9 A.M. 5 P.M.*	Poor
Health and Human Services (Medicare hotline)	638-6833	8 A.M. 8 P.M.*	Poor
Consumer Product Safety Commission	638-2772	24 hours	Poor
Education Department (student aid information)	433-3243	9 A.M. 5:30 P.M.	A joke

*Eastern standard time

How to Protect Yourself on the Road

Unwary travelers are easy prey for crooks. Here's how to travel smart,
using tactics that reduce your risk of getting ripped off.

Tourists are especially vulnerable to crime because they venture into unfamiliar surroundings loaded with cash and valuables. During one recent 18-month period, a large Las Vegas hotel recorded 800 crimes, half of which were burglaries. According to Richard Mellard, former director of the National Crime Prevention Institute in Louisville, similar epidemics are sweeping resorts and hotels around the country and abroad. "Hotel crimes are cloaked in silence," says Mellard. "The transient population doesn't report them, and the local police are ignorant of at least 60% of actual break-ins."

Crime against travelers has soared to the point that the travel industry now acknowledges the problem. A coalition comprising the American Hotel and Motel Association, the American Society of Travel Agents, the American Association of Retired Persons, the National Crime Prevention Council and American Automobile Association has launched a travel safety campaign. And they came up with some tips, some cautionary advice and a few policy changes. The AAA, for example, no longer lists in its 23 North American tour books lodgings that lack double dead bolts and peepholes on room doors. Your best defense, however, remains your own heightened awareness. Crime victims repeatedly tell police that they were ripped off just when they felt most secure. They often think: "I'm staying at a good hotel, what could happen?" Or: "It's just a short flight; my jewelry is safe in my luggage." Here is expert advice on how to prevent rip-offs, based on interviews with travel and security specialists.

Travel-related scams. Americans lose an annual $40 billion to telemarketing schemes, and one out of seven is travel-related. If a vacation deal looks too good to be true, it probably is. The con artist typically notifies you that you've been chosen for a free or bargain-priced trip. The goal is to learn your credit card number. By the time you realize you're not getting the promised tickets, the company has vanished and strange charges have appeared on your charge card bill. Use a veteran travel agent or reputable travel club to make your arrangements, and turn to them if anything goes awry before or during the trip. When booking a package, check that the tour operator belongs to the United States Tour Operators Association. Its members are backed by a $5 million insurance policy in case the tour company folds.

Long-distance calling cards. Stay alert when using your phone card, especially in airports, train terminals or hotel lobbies. Last year, telephone fraud cost AT&T, Sprint and MCI about $2 billion. Standing far from phone banks, scam artists use telephoto lenses and mirrors to see what digits you punch. Or well-dressed confederates pretending to use the phone near you memorize the card number that you give the operator. When possible, use phones that allow you to slide the card past an electronic eye.

Passports and visas. Carry these documents separate from cash. Notes Gary Sheaffer at the State Department's Bureau of Consular Affairs: "Many passports are inadvertently stolen because travelers carry them in purses or wallets." You should pack the phone numbers of the U.S. embassy, consul or regional security officers in the countries and cities you're visiting. Also carry the 24-hour telephone number of the U.S. mission. You can call the State Department (202-647-4000) for those numbers. Another number at the State Department (202-647-5225) provides a taped recording about trouble spots for travelers around the world.

137

Health insurance. Many people who don't want to pay extra for emergency health insurance discover that lots of countries require cash up front for medical care. Waving your insurance card around won't get you anything. A sample package for an unlimited number of trips in one year costs $95 for $100,000 of coverage. This generally includes emergency evacuation costs, hospital or medical payments, emergency cash and translation services. These companies offer reasonable travel insurance packages: TravMed/Medex Assistance (Lutherville, Md.; 800-732-5309); Worldwide Assistance Services (Washington, D.C.; 800-821-2828) and U.S. Assist (Washington, D.C.; 800-756-5900).

Protecting luggage. The crooked ticketing agent or curbside check-in handler sizes you up as a promising prospect. He then marks your bag with a code that signals handlers to rifle your baggage or steal it outright. Another ploy is to deliberately misroute your bag to an airport where an employee partner waits to pick through it. Be suspicious whenever your bags are misrouted. Most airlines require that any luggage complaint be made either before you depart the airport or within four hours of your flight's arrival. In addition, the most you can recover from the airline is $1,250, provided you back up your claim with receipts. Your ticket also specifies a host of valuables for which the airlines claim no responsibility. Included are jewelry, furs, antiques, electronic equipment and so on. American Express and Diners Club both offer up to $1,250 to cardholders for lost or stolen luggage claims over and above the airline's payment. But in a classic Catch-22, that insurance kicks in only if the airline declares your claim valid and if you have the necessary receipts. You could purchase additional coverage from the airline, which usually costs about $10 for every $1,000 increment up to $5,000. But all exclusions still apply, so don't forget to read the fine print before buying it.

Rental car safety. The FBI's Uniform Crime Report confirms that car theft is among the country's fastest-growing crimes. To help avoid a car-jacking, plan your route before you leave your hotel. Miami Police Officer David Magnusson says: "Carjackers look for people sitting at stoplights with a map out." Have your keys in hand as you approach the car. And make sure no one's lurking around, under or inside the car before you unlock. Once you are on the road, you should remember to keep your car in gear when stopped at a light. That way, you will be prepared to sound your horn or drive away the moment you feel threatened. If you get into a minor traffic accident with another car in an isolated area, drive slowly to a well-lit, populated place before getting out of the car to assess damage. Turn on your four-way flashers as a signal to the other driver that you are not fleeing the scene. Thieves often smack into a car to prompt a driver to pull over, and then they demand your keys. Instead of stopping for a stranded motorist, call the police and request aid. Again, this might be a ploy to demand your keys.

A secure hotel room. A survey by *Corporate Travel* magazine found that nearly a quarter of frequent business travelers had been victims of hotel crimes. Some 40% knew close associates who had been robbed in hotels in the past two years. Yet travelers often experience a false sense of security once they have registered. Experts say you should be particularly alert while checking in and out. That's when your cash and valuables are visible and you're often distracted. Book a room near an elevator or any other busy area, such as a room-service station. The extra noise may be a trade-off for added safety. Refuse a room that doesn't have double dead bolts and a peephole. Call the front desk to verify unexpected deliveries or room service. Before leaving items in the hotel safe, ask about the hotel's insurance coverage. Then get a written, detailed receipt for the items that you have stored.

Above all, always stay attuned to your surroundings when you're on the road, either in the U.S. or abroad. Don't forget that you're navigating on unfamiliar turf where you often don't know the local customs or habits. One security expert sums it up with this motto: "When you go on vacation, make sure that your brain goes with you."

CHAPTER

Your Best Values in Colleges Today

Freud once told a disciple that he decided minor matters by weighing the pros and cons. With vital decisions, however, he thought it best to pay attention to his deep inner needs. You and your son or daughter will have to do both as you pursue your search for the right college, assessing the pluses and minuses of every school you consider. In this chapter, we provide facts, figures and advice that can help you evaluate 1,003 colleges and universities. Parents will want to pay particular attention to our ranking of the country's top 100 colleges (see page 143). Our value-oriented approach to rating schools is unique. We judge them on how much they give you for your money. That's a crucial consideration in light of relentlessly rising college costs. Moreover, our list highlights solid schools you won't find in conventional college rankings.

To find a school that will satisfy a child's inner needs, you must extend your search beyond practical or purely academic considerations. Although a college education may be one of the biggest purchases you'll ever make, the process of selecting a school is more like choosing a mate than buying a home or a car. You expect a college to offer your son or daughter the best possible education. But for most students, college is also the place to discover a calling, make lifelong friends and learn to live independently—in short, to make the difficult transition to adulthood.

Thus the college search may be the last big adventure you undertake together as parent and child. If you're lucky, the experience will probably serve to bring your family closer at the moment that your son or daughter is getting ready to break away. You just have to put your heart into it.

Why College Bills Rise So Fast

A big culprit, it seems, is parents who are willing to pay ever-higher prices.
But take heart; increases may be slowing down at last.

Forget what you learned in Physics 101. When it comes to college costs, what goes up just keeps going up. Tuition soared 126% during the 1980s, more than twice as much as the consumer price index. So far in the 1990s, the news is hardly better, with the cost of higher education rising 16% relative to 9% for inflation. Last year six schools (Bard, Barnard, Brandeis, Hampshire, MIT and Yale) charged more than $25,000 for tuition, fees, room and board, catapulting their four-year costs over the alarming $100,000 barrier. What's going on here? To understand, you have to forget a lot of the explanations you've heard up till now. Start instead with these questions and sometimes surprising answers:

Why do college prices keep going up? Colleges, like businesses, set prices according to what the market will bear. As long as colleges can hike prices with-out driving away too many customers, they will. Even with total costs approaching $25,000, top schools like Harvard, Princeton and Stanford routinely have four or more applicants for every opening. Bruce Johnstone, chancellor of the State University of New York system, takes a skeptical view of the cost controversy. However loudly parents complain about high tuitions, he says, "they tend to vote with their feet, and they are obviously delighted to spend $100,000 on Harvard."

Some schools find that increasing the price can attract *more* applicants. Take Muhlenberg College, a 1,640-student liberal arts school in Allentown, Pa. In the mid-1980s, like many obscure regional private colleges, Muhlenberg saw the number of applications drop. Even more distressing, the quality of its applicants fell as well. To bolster its image, Muhlenberg spent $25 million to build a new library, an arts center and a recreation build-

How a Degree Pays Off

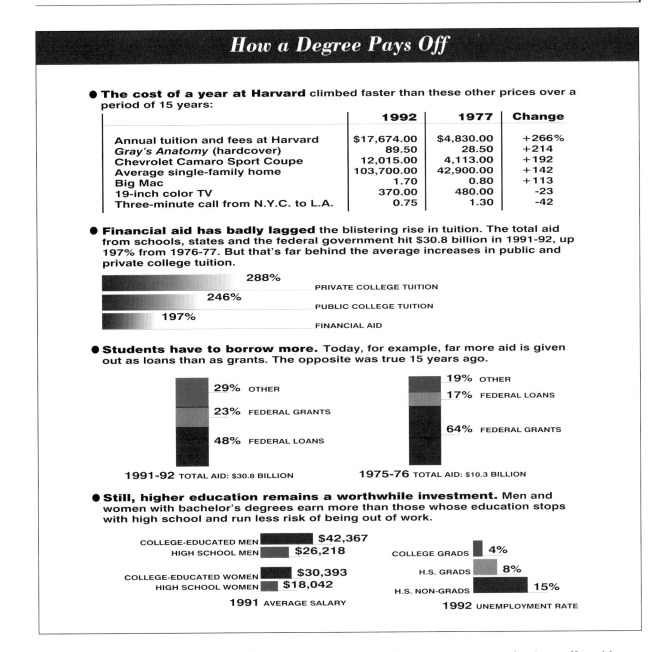

● **The cost of a year at Harvard** climbed faster than these other prices over a period of 15 years:

	1992	1977	Change
Annual tuition and fees at Harvard	$17,674.00	$4,830.00	+266%
Gray's Anatomy (hardcover)	89.50	28.50	+214
Chevrolet Camaro Sport Coupe	12,015.00	4,113.00	+192
Average single-family home	103,700.00	42,900.00	+142
Big Mac	1.70	0.80	+113
19-inch color TV	370.00	480.00	-23
Three-minute call from N.Y.C. to L.A.	0.75	1.30	-42

● **Financial aid has badly lagged** the blistering rise in tuition. The total aid from schools, states and the federal government hit $30.8 billion in 1991-92, up 197% from 1976-77. But that's far behind the average increases in public and private college tuition.

288% PRIVATE COLLEGE TUITION
246% PUBLIC COLLEGE TUITION
197% FINANCIAL AID

● **Students have to borrow more.** Today, for example, far more aid is given out as loans than as grants. The opposite was true 15 years ago.

29% OTHER
23% FEDERAL GRANTS
48% FEDERAL LOANS

1991-92 TOTAL AID: $30.8 BILLION

19% OTHER
17% FEDERAL LOANS
64% FEDERAL GRANTS

1975-76 TOTAL AID: $10.3 BILLION

● **Still, higher education remains a worthwhile investment.** Men and women with bachelor's degrees earn more than those whose education stops with high school and run less risk of being out of work.

COLLEGE-EDUCATED MEN **$42,367**
HIGH SCHOOL MEN **$26,218**
COLLEGE-EDUCATED WOMEN **$30,393**
HIGH SCHOOL WOMEN **$18,042**
1991 AVERAGE SALARY

COLLEGE GRADS **4%**
H.S. GRADS **8%**
H.S. NON-GRADS **15%**
1992 UNEMPLOYMENT RATE

ing. It also expanded its academic offerings, adding a drama major. And it began recruiting students from around the country. To help cover the added outlays, it raised tuition 99% in six years to $13,115 for the 1989-90 academic year. The strategy worked. Applications rose 51%, and Muhlenberg now draws students from 30 states.

Are colleges' rising expenses a factor? Yes, but a much smaller one than administrators want you to think. College price setting is a lot more complicated than simply passing along increased costs. The trustees typically set yearly goals that involve

such things as new courses, faculty staffing, library resources, student counseling programs and, of course, marketing campaigns. Then they figure out how much tuition must be hiked to pay for it all. If the increase seems too high, the year's goals may be scaled back. But the concern is raising enough money for the school's programs, not finding ways to keep the lid on tuition.

Do colleges ever compete on price? Yes, though rarely. Let's go back to Muhlenberg. Toward the end of the 1980s, administrators decided that with the public showing increasing resistance to higher prices, it might be to the school's advantage to be priced below its competition. Thus, over the past four years, Muhlenberg's prices rose an average of only 6% annually, vs. 8% for private colleges. That brought its total cost to $20,795, just under that of such competitors as Bucknell ($22,320), Dickinson ($22,705) and Franklin and Marshall ($23,655). Again, the strategy paid off. Last year's freshman class of 472 was the largest ever.

While other schools have also moderated price increases to stay competitive, drastic discounting is almost unheard of. One exception is 1,000-student Park College in suburban Kansas City, Mo., which last year halved its tuition to $1,770 for someone with an average course load. The gambit seems to be working, with 110 freshman and 190 transfer students enrolled, up from the usual in each category. And there's no sign that the price cuts have hurt the college's reputation. Says admis-

sions director Randy Condit: "People in the area are confident of Park College's quality. Most just say, 'Dang! This is a good deal!'"

What's the outlook for private tuition? These schools will probably hold tuition hikes to two percentage points or so above the inflation rate. With inflation expected to average 3% to 4% during the 1990s, that would mean annual rises of 5% to 6%. Of course, similarly upbeat forecasts have proved wrong in the past. But this time there is evidence that significant numbers of families are finally beginning to balk at the ever-increasing prices. One telling statistic: in a recent College Board study, 30% of students called low tuition a very important factor in selecting a college, up from a low of 17% in 1978.

Where are state school prices headed? The publics averaged 10% tuition increases over the past two years as financially pressed state legislatures slashed appropriations. And they will probably keep hikes within the 5% to 9% range this year. "The college and university presidents I talk to think that tuition is simply at the point where some low-income students cannot afford to come," says James Appleberry, president of the American Association of State Colleges and Universities. But several factors have kept college within reach of middle-income families. One is financial aid, which can knock thousands of dollars off the official price for families who qualify (see "Grab Your Fair Share of Financial Aid" later in this chapter). Moreover, a mere 5% of students attend colleges where annual tuition exceeds $15,000. Indeed, there are only 129 private colleges that charge more than $14,000 a year. There are almost 400 schools that cost $7,000 or less. And don't forget about state colleges and universities. In-state tuition is only $2,030 at our No. 1 school, New College in Sarasota (see right). That amounts to just 4% of the median two-earner family's income, which is hardly a budget buster considering the same family spends 3% of its earnings on restaurants and takeout food. And that fact should add some hope to your happy meals.

Eight Unbeatable Deals

The following schools charge no tuition, which may make them the best deals in higher education. But we didn't include them in our value rankings because of the special circumstances noted below.

• **Berea College** in Berea, Ky. and **College of the Ozarks** in Point Lookout, Mo. both require undergraduate students to pay their way with campus jobs.
• **Cooper Union** in New York City offers majors only in art, architecture and engineering. **Webb Institute of Naval Architecture** in Glen Cove, N.Y. is restricted to naval design and marine engineering.
• The **U.S. Military Academy** at West Point, the **Air Force Academy** in Colorado Springs and the **Naval Academy** in Annapolis require graduates to serve six years of military duty. Grads of the **Coast Guard Academy** in New London, Conn. must serve five years on active duty.

America's Top 100 College Values

Entries in our dean's list of four-year schools all sport prices that are bargains relative to the quality of education they provide students.

Our annual ranking of leading colleges and universities has identified New College of the University of South Florida as America's best college buy. It edged out Rice University, which was our top pick for the previous two years. Rice slipped largely because it hiked tuition and fees 9% to $9,650 for 1993-94, topping the 5% increase (to $7,943) at the Sarasota school. The schools that did best in our analysis charge lower tuitions than institutions of similar quality, as measured by these factors:

Faculty resources. We compared the number of full-time and part-time undergraduates with those of full-time and part-time undergraduate teaching faculty. Average: 14 to 1.

Faculty deployment. The ratio of students to tenured faculty who actually teach courses. Average: 30 to 1.

Core faculty. That's the ratio of students to faculty members holding the highest degrees available in their fields. Average: 19 to 1.

Library resources. Total of all reference materials divided by the number of undergrads and graduate students using the library.

Instructional budget. We used the latest figures reported by colleges to the Department of Education. Average per student: $4,800.

Student services budget. What a school spends on things like counseling and student activities. Average per student: $1,100.

Entrance examination results. This is the percentage of freshmen scoring above 500 on the SAT exams (average: verbal 41%, math 59%), or above 23 on the composite ACT (average: 39%).

Class rank. Percentage of freshmen who finished in the top fifth (average: 44%) or the top quarter (51%) of their high school classes.

High school grade point average. Freshman class' average high school GPA on a four-point scale. Average for all colleges: 2.9.

Freshman retention rate. Percentage of freshmen who become sophomores. Average: 77%.

Graduation rates. Percentage of undergraduate students who earn a degree in four years (average: 46%) and six years (57%).

Advanced study. Percentage of graduates who eventually went on to enroll in professional or graduate schools. Average: 27%.

Default ratio on student loans. Percentage of students who default within two years of leaving, thus identifying colleges whose grads may be ill-prepared for careers. Average: 7%.

Number of graduates who earn doctorates. Based on the National Research Council's count of each college's graduates who went on to earn Ph.D.s between 1981 and 1990.

Business success. This is the tally of the schools attended by the 70,000 top corporate executives listed in *Standard & Poor's Register of Corporations, Directors and Executives.*

Note: Our analysis doesn't adjust tuitions to account for financial aid, because such awards vary widely. To help students searching nationwide for college bargains, we use out-of-state tuitions for public schools. We gathered our data with the help of Orchard House of Concord, Mass., a publisher of college directories. Additional information came from John Minter Associates of Boulder.

The Top 100 Colleges

Here's our honor roll of four-year colleges.
Their prices are bargains when measured against the quality of education they offer.

1	New College of the U. of South Fla.	51	Harvard University (Mass.)
2	Rice University (Texas)	52	University of Virginia
3	Rutgers College (N.J.)	53	Clemson University (S.C.)
4	Trenton State College (N.J.)	54	Columbia University (N.Y.)
5	California Institute of Technology	55	University of the South (Tenn.)
6	U. of Illinois-Urbana/Champaign	56	Hillsdale College (Mich.)
7	U. of North Carolina-Chapel Hill	57	Berry College (Ga.)
8	Northeast Missouri State U.	58	University of South Carolina
9	State U. of N.Y.-Binghamton	59	Miami University (Ohio)
10	Hanover College (Ind.)	60	Ohio University
11	University of Washington	61	MacMurray College (Ill.)
12	Douglass College (N.J.)	62	University of Tulsa (Okla.)
13	Grove City College (Pa.)	63	Emory and Henry College (Va.)
14	St. Mary's College of Maryland	64	Williams College (Mass.)
15	Georgia Institute of Technology	65	Agnes Scott College (Ga.)
16	University of Texas-Austin	66	College of Notre Dame of Maryland
17	Spelman College (Ga.)	67	Davidson College (N.C.)
18	State U. of N.Y.-Albany	68	University of California-Berkeley
19	New Mexico Inst. of Mining & Tech.	69	Grinnell College (Iowa)
20	State U. of N.Y.-Stony Brook	70	Wake Forest University (N.C.)
21	University of Georgia	71	Rosemont College (Pa.)
22	Fisk University (Tenn.)	72	University of Missouri-Columbia
23	Pomona College (Calif.)	73	Drury College (Mo.)
24	Livingston College (N.J.)	74	Dartmouth College (N.H.)
25	Harvey Mudd College (Calif.)	75	College of William and Mary (Va.)
26	University of Kentucky	76	St. Bonaventure University (N.Y.)
27	Auburn University (Ala.)	77	New Jersey Inst. of Technology
28	Yale University (Conn.)	78	Wells College (N.Y.)
29	State U. of N.Y.-Geneseo	79	Chestnut Hill College (Pa.)
30	University of Wisconsin-Madison	80	North Carolina State University
31	State U. of N.Y.-Buffalo	81	U. of California-Los Angeles
32	Mary Washington College (Va.)	82	Michigan Technological U.
33	Baylor University (Texas)	83	Claremont McKenna College (Calif.)
34	University of Iowa	84	St. Mary's U. of San Antonio (Texas)
35	University of Florida	85	Northwestern University (Ill.)
36	Wabash College (Ind.)	86	Stanford University (Calif.)
37	James Madison University (Va.)	87	Creighton University (Neb.)
38	Samford University (Ala.)	88	Bellarmine College (Ky.)
39	Illinois College	89	Indiana University-Bloomington
40	Princeton University (N.J.)	90	Allentown-St. Francis de Sales (Pa.)
41	Trinity University (Texas)	91	Virginia Polytechnic Institute
42	Texas A&M U.-College Station	92	Siena College (N.Y.)
43	Swarthmore College (Pa.)	93	Austin College (Texas)
44	Johns Hopkins University (Md.)	94	Southwestern University (Texas)
45	Washington and Lee University (Va.)	95	Michigan State University
46	Hendrix College (Ark.)	96	Wesleyan College (Ga.)
47	Centenary College of Louisiana	97	Purdue University (Ind.)
48	Centre College (Ky.)	98	University of California-Davis
49	Cook College (N.J.)	99	Salem College (N.C.)
50	Iowa State U. of Science & Tech.	100	Widener University (Pa.)

More Best Values

These tables, drawn from data used in our analysis, rank the best buys among similar types of colleges.

Top state schools ranked by in-state tuition

The 20 best values among public schools when we use in-state tuition and fees in our analysis.

1. UNC-Chapel Hill $1,419
2. New College (Fla.) 2,030
3. North Carolina State 1,600
4. University of Texas-Austin 1,691
5. University of Florida 1,770
6. University of Iowa 2,352
7. Auburn University (Ala.) 1,950
8. Georgia Inst. of Technology 2,277
9. Texas A&M University 1,857
10. University of Washington 2,532
11. New Mexico Tech 1,784
12. Shepherd College (W.Va.) 2,040
13. University of Wyoming 1,648
14. Florida State 1,800
15. University of Kansas 1,917
16. University of Arizona 1,844
17. SUNY-Binghamton 2,989
18. Evergreen State (Wash.) 1,971
19. Iowa State 2,352
20. University of Georgia 2,229

Costly schools that are worth the price

A total of 68 schools charge more than $17,000 in tuition and fees. But only 16, ranked below by the academic strengths we measure, scored high enough in our value analysis to justify their lofty prices.

1. Yale University (Conn.) $18,630
2. Princeton U. (N.J.) 18,940
3. Swarthmore College (Pa.) 18,482
4. Johns Hopkins U. (Md.) 17,900
5. Harvard University (Mass.) 18,745
6. Columbia U. (N.Y.) 17,840
7. Williams College (Mass.) 18,795
8. Dartmouth College (N.H.) 18,340
9. Stanford U. (Calif.) 17,879
10. Bowdoin College (Maine) 18,300
11. Wellesley College (Mass.) 17,725
12. MIT (Mass.) 19,600
13. University of Chicago (Ill.) 18,387
14. Washington U. (Mo.) 17,776
15. Amherst College (Mass.) 19,072
16. Duke University (N.C.) 17,160
20. University of Georgia 2,229

Small liberal arts schools*

1. New College (Fla.)
2. Hanover College (Ind.)
3. St. Mary's College of Maryland
4. Fisk University (Tenn.)
5. Pomona College (Calif.)
6. Wabash College (Ind.)
7. Illinois College
8. Swarthmore College (Pa.)
9. Hendrix College (Ark.)
10. Centenary College of Louisiana

* 1,600 students or fewer

Scientific and technical schools

1. California Institute of Technology
2. Georgia Institute of Technology
3. New Mexico Tech
4. Harvey Mudd College (Calif.)
5. Iowa State University
6. New Jersey Institute of Technology
7. North Carolina State University
8. Michigan Technological University
9. Virginia Polytechnic Institute
10. MIT (Mass.)

More Best Values

Here's how 45 of our top values compare according to their selectivity in admissions, as determined by the schools themselves.

Most selective top values
Students at these schools come from the top 20% of their high school classes, with average grades of B+ or better and SAT scores of at least 1,200 or ACT scores of 29 or above.
1. New College (Fla.)
2. Rice University (Texas)
3. Rutgers College (N.J.)
4. U. of North Carolina-Chapel Hill
5. SUNY-Binghamton
6. Georgia Institute of Technology
7. Pomona College (Calif.)
8. Harvey Mudd College (Calif.)
9. Yale University (Conn.)
10. SUNY-Geneseo
11. Princeton University (N.J.)
12. Trinity University (Texas)
13. Swarthmore College (Pa.)
14. Johns Hopkins University (Md.)
15. Washington and Lee (Va.)

Highly selective top values
Most students at these schools were in the top 40% of their high school classes, with average grades of B or better and SAT scores of 1,100 or above or ACT scores of at least 27.
1. Trenton State (N.J.)
2. U. of Illinois-Urbana/Champaign
3. Northeast Missouri State

4. University of Washington
5. Douglass College (N.J.)
6. Grove City College (Pa.)
7. St. Mary's of Maryland
8. University of Texas-Austin
9. Spelman College (Ga.)
10. SUNY-Albany
11. New Mexico Institute of Mining
12. SUNY-Stony Brook
13. Livingston College (N.J.)
14. University of Wisconsin-Madison
15. SUNY-Buffalo

Selective top values
Most students at these schools ranked in the top 50% of their high school classes, with average grades of B- or better and SAT scores of 950 or higher or ACT scores above 22.
1. Hanover College (Ind.)
2. University of Georgia
3. University of Kentucky
4. Auburn University (Ala.)
5. University of Iowa
6. Samford College (Ala.)
7. Illinois College
8. Hendrix College (Ark.)
9. Centenary College of Louisiana
10. Clemson University (S.C.)
11. Hillsdale College (Mich.)
12. University of South Carolina
13. Ohio University
14. Notre Dame of Maryland
15. Rosemont College (Pa.)

Women's colleges

1. Douglass College (N.J.)
2. Spelman College (Ga.)
3. Agnes Scott College (Ga.)
4. Notre Dame of Maryland
5. Rosemont College (Pa.)
6. Wells College (N.Y.)
7. Chestnut Hill College (Pa.)
8. Wesleyan College (Ga.)
9. Salem College (N.C.)
10. Wellesley College (Mass.)

Historically black colleges

1. Spelman College (Ga.)
2. Fisk University (Tenn.)
3. Howard University (D.C.)
4. Tuskegee University (Ala.)
5. Xavier University of Louisiana
6. Morehouse College (Ga.)

How to Cut Your College Costs in Half

*If your child earns a bachelor's degree in three years instead of four,
you and your Einstein can save far more than one year's tuition.*

Here's the deal. By skipping one year, your child not only saves a year's college bills—more than $25,000 at the most expensive schools—but also starts his or her career a year earlier. Add the $25,000 saved to the $25,000 that a typical grad figures to earn in the first year on a job, and you come up with a nifty gain of $50,000. In effect, you slash 50% from the full price of the costliest college education. At a state school charging $10,000 a year, a degree in three would result in an 88% savings. "A three-year degree can bring private higher education back within the budgets of the hard-pressed middle class," says Frederick Starr, president of Oberlin College in Ohio.

Some kids relish the rapid rush to a degree. At Boston University, for example, students preparing for careers in medicine can earn a combined B.A. and M.D. degree, trimming one to two years off the customary eight-year stint. "We have students who were born wanting to be doctors, got 1,400 or better on their SATs and can't wait to start med school," says Arthur Culbert, associate dean for student affairs at Boston University's school of medicine. "For them, this is the right spot."

Fast-forwarding through college is not for everyone, however. "Poorly prepared kids can't do it," says Starr. Moreover, there's more to the college experience than piling up course credits. "If you're involved in activities such as sports or student government, four years is probably better," says Peg Miller, director of the Virginia State Council on Higher Education.

Almost any college will let students graduate early if they acquire enough credits for a degree. Here's how your child can get them:

Earn college credits in high school. Students can enroll in college-level courses in high school and take the College Board's Advanced Placement (AP) exams (cost: $71 each). Most colleges require a score of at least three points out of a possible five to earn college credit. Ambitious high school students can also take college courses on their own. For example, while a junior at Medford (Ore.) High School, Jorden Leonard studied composition and speech at Southern Oregon State College, earning a total of six credits. During his senior year, he signed up for a couple of courses at SOSC each semester, stockpiling even more credits. "If I don't use the credits to graduate sooner, I'll use them to free up time for a double major," says Leonard, who has his eye on international business and computer science.

Cram extra courses into the schedule. Colleges typically let students earn additional credits for courses completed during the summer and breaks between regular semesters. Students may also carry an extra course or two during regular semesters. By combining the two approaches, along with a few AP credits, a diligent student can compress four years of college into three. Let's say a school requires a total of 36 courses for graduation, or nine a year. Instead of four courses one semester and five the next, a student could take five each semester. Add at least three summer courses and three courses' worth of AP credits, and the student would have successfully met the 36-course requirement in three years.

Enroll in a three-year degree program. If your child is certain to head for graduate school after college, he or she may want to consider a school that lets students pursue a master's degree or doctorate while completing their B.A.s in three years. For a list of schools offering combined study, consult the *College Board Index of Majors and Graduate Degrees* ($17). If your child decides to speed up his or her course of study, try to make certain the child isn't shortchanged educationally just to save money. With careful planning, there is no reason a three-year degree can't be every bit as enriching as one earned in four. "The four-year degree is just an accident of history," says Ernest Boyer, president of the Carnegie Foundation for the Advancement of Teaching. "What's important is what you learn, not how long it takes."

Grab Your Fair Share of Financial Aid

Here are basic rules you must master—plus a preview of reforms that will cut the cost of federal loans starting in the 1994-95 school year.

Last year's deficit-reduction legislation championed by President Clinton includes a money-saving break for college students who qualify for federal financial aid. Such awards typically consist of a combination of grants (which you don't have to pay back), loans (which you do) and work/study jobs. Starting in the 1994-95 school year, the new Federal Direct Student Loan Program will cut in half the fees on all subsidized Stafford student loans. As a result, students who borrow the full amount allowed for four years of college—currently $17,125—will save $685.

The new loan law represents a sharp break with past practices. Since 1965, federal student loans have actually been made by banks and other financial institutions. Lenders have charged as much as 8% of the loan amount in origination and insurance fees. The government has subsidized the loans' interest rates and guaranteed against default. In addition, it has paid the interest while borrowers were still in school. Under the new program, the government will make a portion of these loans directly to students. Direct lending will account for 5% of federal education loans in 1994-95, rising to 60% by 1998-99. Eliminating the costs of subsidizing and insuring the loans will save Uncle Sam $4 billion over those five years.

In turn, the maximum up-front fees for all Stafford loans (including those made by private lenders) will be slashed from 8% to 4%. The lower fees will also apply to the federal PLUS loan, which is made to parents whether or not they qualify for financial aid. (For more on the PLUS and other education loans that are available to all families, see "How to Borrow to Fill the Money Gap" later in this chapter.) The fee cuts will save Stafford and PLUS borrowers some $2 billion over five years. The maximum interest charge on the variable-rate loans will also drop from 9% to 8.25% on the Stafford and from 10% to 9% on the PLUS.

Direct lending, however, won't provide any relief from the daunting forms and formulas involved in financial aid. The time-consuming process begins during the fall of your child's senior year in high school, when you must fill out the Free Application for Federal Student Aid, available from high school guidance counselors and colleges. The form asks for detailed information about your income, savings and investments in the calendar year. You mail the completed form as soon as possible after January 1 to the processing firm listed on the application. In addition, most private colleges will ask you to fill out their own questionnaires.

In analyzing your application, the processing firm will use the federal methodology formula, which calculates what is officially called the "expected family contribution." This is the amount the federal rules assume you can afford to pay toward your child's annual education bills. (To estimate your expected contribution, fill out the worksheet on the right.) If your child won't enter college for another year or more, you have time to

Figure Out Your Family's Expected Contribution

This worksheet can help you estimate how much the federal methodology formula—used in assessing your family's eligibility for federal financial aid—will assume you can afford to spend on college for your son or daughter. (For information about applying for aid, see main text.) Whether or not the figure, officially known as your "expected family contribution," accurately reflects your ability to pay, colleges will use it in determining how much federal assistance to offer your child.

Complete sections 1 and 2 to determine your eligible income and assets. Those figures will be used in section 3 to determine the parents'

expected contribution. Then complete section 4 to calculate the student's share. The sum of the parents' contribution plus the student's is your expected family contribution. If that amount is greater than the college's total annual cost—including tuition, fees, room, board and an allowance for books and transportation—you probably will not qualify for need-based aid. If it is less, you will likely be offered a financial aid package to help make up the difference. Note: this worksheet assumes that there are two parents in the family and that the older is 45. The figures are effective for the 1993-94 school year.

1. PARENTS' INCOME

Enter your adjusted gross income from your tax return. _____

Subtract any child support you paid. _____

Add the sum of all nontaxable income. _____

Add back deductions for IRA and Keogh contributions. _____

Subtract federal, state and Social Security (FICA) taxes. _____

If both parents work, subtract employment expenses: $2,500 or 35% of the lower salary, whichever is less. _____

Subtract your income protection allowance (from Table I). If the result is negative, enter "0" on line A; if it is positive, enter the amount on line A.
A. $ _____

2. PARENTS' ASSETS

If your AGI is $50,000 or less and you do not itemize deductions on your tax return, enter "0" on line B. Otherwise, enter the total value of your investments, including stocks, bonds and real estate other than your home. _____

Enter the sum of all cash, bank and money-market accounts. _____

Subtract $36,600. If the result is negative, enter "0" on line B; if it is positive, multiply by 0.12 and enter the result on line B. _____
B. $ _____

3. PARENTS' CONTRIBUTION

Enter the total of lines A and B. _____

Use this number to find the parents' expected contribution from Table II. Divide that figure by the number of family members attending college, and enter the result on line C. _____

C. $ _____

4. STUDENT'S CONTRIBUTION

Enter the student's AGI as reported on his or her tax return. _____

Subtract federal, state and Social Security (FICA) taxes. _____

Subtract the income protection allowance of $1,750. If the result is negative, enter "0"; if it is positive, multiply by 0.5 and enter here. _____

Add 35% of the student's savings and investments and enter the total on line D. _____

D. $ _____

5. TOTAL FAMILY CONTRIBUTION

Add lines C and D and enter the sum on line E.

E. $ _____

Table I Income protection allowance

Family size (Including student)	Number of family members in college				
	1	2	3	4	5
2	$10,520	$8,720			
3	13,100	11,310	$9,510		
4	16,180	14,380	12,590	$10,790	
5	19,090	17,290	15,500	13,700	$11,910
6	22,330	20,530	18,740	16,940	15,150

Table II Parents' contribution

If line A plus line B equals...	Then the parents' contribution is...
$3,408 or less	Minus $750
$3,409 to $9,400	22% of line A plus line B
$9,401 to $11,800	$2,068 plus 25% of amount over $9,400
$11,801 to $14,200	$2,668 plus 29% of amount over $11,800
$14,201 to $16,600	$3,363 plus 34% of amount over $14,200
$16,601 to $19,000	$4,180 plus 40% of amount over $16,600
$19,001 or more	$5,140 plus 47% of amount over $19,000

Source: The College Board

take several steps to increase your eligibility for aid. For example, if you plan to cash in investments for college bills, sell by December 31 of your child's junior year in high school. Here's why: the government's aid formula assumes that, to meet college bills, parents can tap as much as 47% of after-tax income but no more than 5.6% of assets. (The income and asset figures used in the formula are reduced by allowances in the worksheet.) Since the formula treats capital gains as income, selling an investment early can help cut your family's expected contribution.

Moreover, if you think you'll be eligible for aid, don't save money in your child's name. The formula calls on students to contribute 35% of their assets to college—over six times what is expected of parents. Invest as much as you can afford in a 401(k) or other tax-sheltered retirement plans because the federal formula exempts them in tallying your assets.

After the processing firm finishes its work, the college financial aid office takes over. Let's say that your expected family contribution is $7,000 a year, and your son or daughter will attend a college that costs $13,500 including tuition, fees, room, board and an allowance for books and travel. To help fill the $6,500 gap, the college might offer your child a $1,500 work/study job and a maximum first-year Stafford loan of $2,625. Families with income below roughly $35,000 might also qualify for the two other big sources of federal assistance, Pell Grants and Perkins loans.

Where does the rest of the money you need come from? A few years ago, many colleges would have made up the difference from their own funds. Today, financially pinched colleges usually leave it to you to raise the bulk of the money. Even if the school's policy is to fill 100% of your "unmet need," you may not get any additional aid. That's because many schools use a formula that

Searching for Scholarships

Many parents dream of their child's winning a scholarship to pay for college. Well, it's wake-up time. Thousands of scholarships are given out each year by federal and state government agencies, colleges, corporations and local civic groups, though most are for $500 or less. And if a student approved for need-based financial aid wins a scholarship, his or her college most likely will deduct that amount from the aid package. Your child can get information about scholarships from his or her high school guidance office or the college financial aid office.

Ask your benefits office whether your company offers scholarships to employees' children. You might also check guidebooks such as *The A's and B's of Academic Scholarships* (Octameron, $7) and *The College Financial Aid Annual 1993* (Arco, $22).

Not all scholarships are pittances. Here are four of the most generous national ones, starting with the largest. High school guidance counselors can tell your child more about them.

ROTC. Uncle Sam handed out an estimated $130 million to about 16,000 members of the Reserve Officers Training Corps for 1992-93. Recipients must serve up to eight years in the military.

National Merit Scholarships. Each year, 6,500 top students win awards of $250 to $2,000. Recipients are chosen from among the highest scorers on the PSAT exam.

Coca-Cola Scholars Foundation. The soft drink company annually hands out 50 awards of $20,000 each and 100 of $4,000 each to high school seniors who have demonstrated civic leadership, character and other worthy qualities.

Westinghouse Science Talent Search. Each year, 1,500 entrants submit research projects in science, mathematics or engineering. The top 10 contestants get $10,000 to $40,000, while 30 runners-up win $1,000 each.

can be less generous than the federal methodology to determine how much they expect your family to contribute to your child's college costs. For example, Congress changed the federal formula in 1992 to exclude families' equity in their homes. Yet many private colleges continue to count it when distributing their own funds.

You may be able to negotiate for more help from the college your child wants to attend, states Kalman Chany, author of *The Student Access Guide to Paying for College* (Villard Books, $14). For instance, if you have divorced since you applied for aid or have had to take over the care of an elderly relative, you may succeed in persuading the school to boost your child's award. If your child received a better offer from a comparable college,

the first-choice school might match it.

Direct lending isn't President Clinton's only scheme to ease the college cost burden. During the campaign, he proposed a national service program in which people would take low-paying jobs that benefit the community, working as teacher's aides in inner-city schools, for example. After completing a year or two of such service, they would get credits that they could use for college tuition or to pay off education loans. To keep the costs of such a program under control, however, members of Congress most likely will limit it to no more than 100,000 participants during the first three years. Thus, for the near future, most college grads will have to pay off their loans the old-fashioned way—with income from regular jobs.

How to Borrow to Fill the Money Gap

If your savings for college come up short, you can turn to private lenders or to good old Uncle Sam. Here are the best loan deals.

If financial aid and your savings aren't enough to cover college costs, you may need to go into debt. The loans described in the table on the next page are available to families whether or not they qualify for financial aid. To find out more about them, call the 800 numbers listed and also contact a financial aid officer at the school where your child will enroll. In addition, the college aid officer and your child's high school guidance counselor can alert you to any special loans available from state governments or the college itself.

You should first consider applying for a low-cost Unsubsidized Stafford Loan, which is made by Uncle Sam to the college student. It offers an attractive rate (lately around 6%). Borrowers need not start repaying principal until they graduate or drop out, and some lenders may allow interest payments to be deferred as well. With the subsidized Staffords, which are part of financial aid packages, the government pays the interest while

the student is in school.

If you get an Unsubsidized Stafford and you're still short of money, consider PLUS loans. They cover the full cost of a child's education, minus any financial aid. The terms are similar to those of the Stafford. But the rate and cap on a PLUS loan are slightly higher. And principal payments cannot be deferred except in cases of hardship. As of the 1994-95 school year, maximum up-front fees on both Stafford and PLUS loans were cut to 4% of the loan amount.

Private lenders' rates on college loans are usually one to three percentage points higher than those on Stafford and PLUS loans. On the other hand, several private lenders will let you take as long as 15 to 25 years to repay their loans, compared with Uncle Sam's standard 10-year repayment period. Many private lenders also allow you to defer principal payments while your child is in college. That can translate into sharply lower monthly pay-

The Leading Loans at a Glance

As this rundown of loans shows, students and their parents face a number of relatively attractive options when it comes to borrowing money for college. Overall, though, it's hard to beat the Unsubsidized Stafford and the PLUS loans. The loans are listed from lowest rate to highest.

Name and sponsor	Maximum amount	Credit requirements[2]	Rate	Maximum term	Fees	Principal deferral[8]
Unsubsidized Stafford Loan U.S. Department of Education 800-433-3243	First-year students: $2,625; second year: $3,500; third through fifth year: $5,500 annually[1]	None	91-day T-bill rate plus 3.1 percentage points, adjusted annually; 8.25% cap[3]. Recent rate: 6.22%	10 years[5]	Up to 4%[6]	Yes
PLUS U.S. Department of Education 800-433-3243	Cost of education minus financial aid	No current loan delinquencies of 90 days or longer	One-year T-bill rate plus 3.1 percentage points, adjusted annually; 9% cap[4]. Recent rate: 6.64%	10 years[5]	Up to 4%[7]	No[9]
Extended Repayment Plan Knight Tuition Payment Plans 800-225-6783	Cost of education minus financial aid	Good credit history and ability to repay	7.25% for one year, then 91-day T-bill rate plus 4.5 percentage points, adjusted quarterly; 18% cap. Recent rate: 7.5%	15 years	$55	No
ExtraCredit The College Board 800-874-9390	Cost of education minus financial aid	Good credit history and ability to repay	7.25% for one year, then 91-day T-bill rate plus 4.5 percentage points, adjusted quarterly; 18% cap. Recent rate: 7.5%	15 years	$45	No
Annual Knight Tuition Payment Plans 800-225-6783	Cost of education minus financial aid	Good credit history and ability to repay	91-day T-bill rate plus 4.5 percentage points, adjusted quarterly; 18% cap. Recent rate: 7.5%	10 years	$55 and 3%	Yes
ExtraTime The College Board 800-874-9390	Cost of education minus financial aid	Good credit history and ability to repay	91-day T-bill rate plus 4.5 percentage points, adjusted quarterly; 18% cap. Recent rate: 7.5%	10 years	$45 and 3%	Yes
TERI The Education Resources Institute 800-255-8374	Cost of education minus financial aid	Good credit history and ability to repay. Parents can cosign for students.	Prime rate plus 1.5 to two percentage points, adjusted monthly; no cap. Recent rate: 7.5% to 8%	25 years	5%	Yes
PLATO University Support Services 800-767-5626	$25,000 a year	Annual income of $15,000, a good credit history and ability to repay. Parents can cosign for students.	Greater of 30- or 90-day commercial paper rate plus 4.85 percentage points, adjusted monthly; no cap. Recent rate: 7.99%	15 years	4%	Yes
EXCEL Nellie Mae 800-634-9308	Cost of education minus financial aid	Good credit history and ability to repay. Parents can cosign for students.	Prime rate plus two percentage points, adjusted monthly; no cap. Recent rate: 8%. Or prime rate plus three to four points, adjusted annually; no cap. Recent rate: 9.5%	20 years	5%	Yes
ABLE Knight Tuition Payment Plans 800-225-6783	Cost of education minus financial aid	Good credit history and ability to repay	Prime rate plus 2.5 percentage points, adjusted quarterly; 18% cap. Recent rate: 8.5%	15 years	$55	No

Notes: [1]As of the 1994-95 school year, students who are financially independent of their parents may borrow an additional $4,000 annually during their first and second years, and an additional $5,000 annually during third and fourth years. [2]The Unsubsidized Stafford Loan is made to students; all others are made to parents unless otherwise noted. The credit requirement listed as "ability to repay" depends on debt-to-income ratio and other criteria. [3]For the 1994-95 academic year. Cap is 9% for 1993-94. [4]For the 1994-95 academic year. Cap is 10% for 1993-94. [5]Repayment period can be extended after graduation through the Federal Loan Consolidation program. [6]For the 1994-95 academic year. Fee is 6.5% for 1993-94. [7]For the 1994-95 academic year. Fee is 8% for 1993-94. [8]Repayment of principal begins after student leaves school. [9]Principal payments may be deferred for up to three years in hardship cases.

ments. On a $10,000 TERI loan, for example, you'd face monthly payments of $63 for the first year, compared with $114 on a PLUS loan. The private loans have other appealing features. Knight's Extended Repayment Plan fixes your monthly payment for the life of the loan. As market interest rates rise and fall, your payments remain the same. But your loan's repayment term will lengthen or shorten to reflect the rate changes.

Other advantageous ways to borrow for college include home-equity lines of credit, lately around 7.5%. Interest payments on home-equity loans of as much as $100,000 are generally tax deductible, which isn't the case with other college loans. Note that if you miss your payments you could risk losing your home. And your employer may let you borrow against the balance in your 401(k) savings plan. Federal law requires such loans to be repaid within five years. If you borrow a large sum, your payments will be large too.

Give a College This Safety Checkup

No campus is free of crime. But you can make sure the schools that interest your child are doing everything they can to combat it.

Colleges are beginning to come clean about campus crime. Thanks to a 1990 federal law, the Student Right-to-Know and Campus Security Act, all institutions whose students receive federal financial aid must now issue detailed annual statistics on campus crimes. And many parents are understandably frightened by the latest reported yearly figures for the 2,400 U.S. campuses surveyed by the *Chronicle of Higher Education,* including 30 murders, 993 rapes, 1,822 robberies, 4,669 aggravated assaults, 32,127 burglaries and 8,891 auto thefts.

The data shed welcome light on serious crime, a problem many colleges have long sought to cover up. Yet statistics alone can't tell you what you need to know about campus safety. For one thing, the schools are not required to keep track of petty thefts, such as stolen boom boxes, which safety experts say account for the great majority of all student crime. Nor are the data adjusted for such factors as campus size and location, making many school-to-school comparisons difficult and, in many instances, meaningless. And the fact that one school records far more crimes than a similar institution may simply mean that officials at the first school are doing a better job of encouraging students and faculty to report crimes.

Perform your own campus investigation. To get a more complete picture of the crime problem at the schools your child would like to attend, you have to conduct your own safety review. Begin by asking the admissions office for the federal crime report. Under the law, schools must give a copy to any prospective student who requests it. The report, which can be anything from a letter to a glossy brochure, will include statistics on crimes for the past three years, as well as a description of the college's security policies. And despite the statistical shortcomings noted above, the reports can be helpful. Their descriptions of campus security will give you a basis for questions to ask school officials later on. Moreover, the tone and detail of a report can suggest how willing a school is to deal with its crime problem.

To perform a thorough safety check, you must visit each campus, preferably when classes are in session. Be sure to tour academic buildings, residence halls and other facilities after dark as well as during the day. That way you can see whether walkways, quadrangles, parking lots and other public areas are well lit and whether the campus is patrolled by uniformed guards or university police. At large campuses, make sure commuter buses and vans are readily available, especially after dark.

The Book on Sexual Harassment

For students and parents, one of the top campus concerns these days is sexual harassment. To help you and your child learn more about the problem and how to deal with it, we talked with three highly recognized experts in the field. Ellen Bravo, executive director of the organization 9 to 5, National Association of Working Women in Milwaukee, is co-author (with Ellen Cassedy) of *The 9 to 5 Guide to Combating Sexual Harassment* (John Wiley & Sons, $10). Michele Paludi, a Schenectady, N.Y. psychologist, serves on Governor Mario Cuomo's Task Force on Sexual Harassment and edited *Ivory Power: Sexual Harassment on Campus* (State University of New York Press, $25). Fran Sepler, a St. Paul consultant who specializes in the prevention of sexual harassment, recently developed a sensitivity training program designed for use at the Minnesota state universities system.

Q. How do you define sexual harassment?

BRAVO: Sexual attention that is unwanted, offensive, usually repeated and interferes with your ability to do your work.

SEPLER: The issue can get hazy. For example, some male students call you a "10" as you walk by. You respond by calling them pigs because you feel embarrassed. It's obnoxious, but if it doesn't materially affect your environment to the point that you can't handle your normal activities, it's probably not harassment.

Q. How common is sexual harassment on campus?

PALUDI: The breadth of the problem is difficult to get a handle on. Students who experience it may not label it as sexual harassment, despite the fact that what happened to them fits the legal definition. Research, including my own, suggests that about 30% of female students will come under pressure for sexual favors from professors or instructors. If you include other types of harassment, such as sexist or demeaning comments by professors about students' bodies, the figure rises to 85%. Of course, male students are harassed too, almost always by male professors, but the incidence of such harassment is much lower.

Q. How should schools cope with the problem?

SEPLER: Schools that are really on top of it will have a plan in place for preventing harassment, including awareness programs for faculty, teaching assistants, residence hall advisers and anyone else who deals with students. At the very least, a school should have a clear policy that bans sexual harassment and outlines procedures for dealing with complaints. There should also be a women's resource center or sexual assault program to counsel and assist victims.

Q. How can you judge the climate on campus today?

PALUDI: Most schools issue annual reports on sexual harassment. Call their affirmative action office or sexual harassment committee for a copy. While no one involved is named, the report tells you the number of incidents, how long it took to investigate them and whether they were resolved, including disciplinary action.

SEPLER: You can check through issues of the school newspaper for reports about incidents of harassment and how they were handled.

Q. What should a student do if harassed?

BRAVO: Make sure you've clearly told the aggressor that the behavior offends you. If the harassment doesn't stop, then find out how to file a complaint and file one.

PALUDI: Keep a record of inappropriate touching and lewd comments. That will support your complaint and help you get over the feelings of emotional and physical powerlessness.

Q. How can a student avoid being harassed?

BRAVO: You need to talk to your kids about this. You don't want to make them think there's a lecherous professor behind every classroom door. But you do want them to know that if something seems inappropriate, such as a professor inviting them out alone, they should be on guard. Above all, you want them to know that if they do end up being harassed, you'll always be there to support them. Victims often blame themselves when these things happen. That's a major reason why most harassment incidents go unreported.

Check for basic security features in residence halls, such as devices to keep ground-floor windows from being opened more than a few inches and alarms that prevent students from propping open outside doors.

To gauge the social scene, drive down fraternity row at night and stroll through student hangouts. Are students merely partying, or have they gone over the edge? This is important because alcohol abuse fuels crime. According to the Campus Violence Prevention Center at Towson State University in Maryland, alcohol figures in as much as 90% of violent campus crimes. Both victim and victimizer usually have been drinking.

Check out areas surrounding the campus. Many schools are located near neighborhoods where you wouldn't feel safe walking alone at night. That's not necessarily a problem if the streets closest to the campus are well lit and busy. But if the college is surrounded by a neighborhood that is plagued by gangs, drugs and violence, you may want to scratch the school off your list. Here, as in other aspects of your safety review, there are no hard and fast standards; your own comfort level must be your guide. Then discuss your concerns about campus crime with the college's public safety director and the dean of students or whoever else is in charge. "Don't be afraid to ask any question you want," says Joseph Griffin, director of public safety at Northeastern University in Boston and president of the International Association of Campus Law Enforcement Administrators. "You have a right to straight answers that put a school on record about the situation and the policies for dealing with it."

You may also want to speak with the editor of the student newspaper, the staff at the women's resource center, residence hall advisers and students. Here are key questions to ask:

What are the most common crimes on and near the campus? Theft and vandalism top the list at most schools. Probe for information about problems that may be of particular concern to you, such as hazing, sexual harassment, hate crimes targeted against minorities or homosexuals and rape.

How does the school combat crime? In general, the college should have uniformed security guards or police officers; emergency telephones along walkways, at bus stops and at outlying areas such as athletic fields; and nighttime transportation services. Campus police at the University of Massachusetts at Dartmouth, the University of Washington, the University of Wisconsin at Madison and several other schools patrol on mountain bikes, which enables them to cover their sprawling campuses better than they could on foot or in cars.

What's the school's judicial system? Alcohol violations, fistfights, vandalism and many other minor incidents usually end up being handled by tribunals composed of administrators, faculty and students who hear testimony behind closed doors and hand down sentences. Such panels may also deal with more serious crimes such as date rape when victims are reluctant to press charges against fellow students or when local prosecutors don't think there is enough evidence to take cases to court. Ask the dean of student life how many and what type of cases the school's tribunals handled in recent years. Find out what it takes for a student to get reprimanded, fined, put on probation, suspended or expelled, and how often the college has meted out such punishment.

What's being done to curb alcohol abuse? Does the school co-sponsor educational campaigns with local bars, as well as fraternities, sororities and other student organizations? Does it require students who violate drinking laws to undergo counseling? Does it provide a safe means of transportation home for drunk students? The University of Texas at Austin, for example, hires cabs every weekend to pick up drunken students anywhere in Austin and take them home, free of charge. The cabs are also available to students who were counting on rides from someone who ended up drinking too much. So that the students will always have the phone number handy, they're given stick-

The College Admissions Calendar

The process of choosing and applying to colleges actually begins when your daughter or son enters high school. This calendar, which has been written from your child's perspective, will help him or her organize the four years of picking the right classes, taking tests, gathering information about colleges, visiting campuses and filling out application forms. Meeting these deadlines will force your scholar to think seriously about academic strengths, interests and goals. That, in turn, may help your child find a school where he or she will thrive.

Freshman Year

FALL: As you select your first high school courses, remember that, by graduation day, you must complete most colleges' basic entrance requirements, which typically include three years of math and two or three years of a foreign language. Outside the classroom, you should try to participate in extracurricular activities such as athletics, theatrical productions or the school newspaper. While you're expanding your horizons, you'll also be making yourself a stronger college candidate.

Sophomore Year

FALL: Consider taking either the PLAN test or the PSAT. The PLAN test, a rehearsal for American College Testing's ACT, includes a questionnaire that can help identify your academic strengths and interests. The PSAT is a scaled-down version of the College Board's Scholastic Aptitude Test. Your scores on these exams will not go to colleges without your specific instructions.

SPRING: Most top colleges require scores from College Board achievement tests in English, math and a third subject of your choice. If you want to take an exam in a subject you'll study only this year, do it now while the material is still fresh in your mind. But take the English and math exams in your junior or senior year, as additional classroom study may help boost your scores.

Junior Year

FALL: Colleges like applicants who stretch themselves, so consider enrolling in honors or Advanced Placement courses. AP classes prepare you for exams that can earn you valuable college credits. Even if you took the PSAT as a sophomore, take it again in October. Juniors who get top scores may qualify for one of 6,500 National Merit Scholarship Corporation awards of $250 to $2,000.

WINTER: Consider taking the SAT or the ACT for the first time in December and again later in the school year. Note: this spring the College Board intends to replace the Scholastic Aptitude Test with new verbal and math exams called SAT-I: Reasoning Tests, and change the name of the achievement tests to SAT-II: Subject Tests. The new verbal exam puts more emphasis on critical reading, and the math exam requires students to come up with their own answers for some questions. Currently the exam is entirely multiple choice. The achievement tests are largely unchanged. Ask your school's guidance office for the schedule of test dates and registration deadlines.

SPRING: You should discuss possible college choices with your guidance counselor. Among the factors to weigh are how far from home you would like to go and how much your family can afford to pay. Aim for a preliminary list of about a dozen schools. Write or phone for information such as their brochures, course catalogues and application forms.

SUMMER: Think about topics for your application essays, drawing on any important life experiences, personal beliefs and values or people who have influenced you. Write a draft version to show to parents and teachers for comment. Narrow your list of prospective colleges to six or seven. If you plan to visit schools in September or October, call to make appointments now.

Senior Year

FALL: Ask two or three faculty members who know you well to write college recommendations for you. If you want to try to improve your entrance exam scores, take the appropriate test again. Colleges often consider only a student's highest score. Alert your parents to gather tax returns, bank statements and other information they will need to fill out lengthy financial aid applications. Also remember that it is up to you to make sure your high school submits transcripts by the colleges' application deadlines, usually January 1, January 15, February 1, February 15 or March 1.

WINTER: Mail your applications, allowing adequate time for them to arrive at the colleges by the due dates. File financial aid forms with the appropriate processing firm as soon as possible after January 1, the earliest date permitted. Students whose paperwork arrives at a college financial office early sometimes get better deals than latecomers.

SPRING: Acceptance letters usually arrive during March and April. If a favorite school puts you on its waiting list, write back immediately expressing your eagerness to attend and send the admissions office any better grades or honors you've recently attained. Don't panic if you're not admitted anywhere. Your high school guidance counselor can probably identify a number of solid and suitable schools that still have openings. Apply to several, and chances are you will find yourself in college in the fall.

ers for their ID cards. Officials do not think of the program as a perk but rather as a way to make sure drunk drivers don't kill themselves or others.

Does the school teach crime prevention? At the very least, officials should discuss campus crime with freshmen during orientation. And the more the administration tries to raise students' awareness of safety issues, the better. Rutgers University in New Jersey conducts a Street Smart Survival program. Student participants act as targets for a mock crime—say, a purse snatching committed by a plainclothes police officer. Although students are in on the game, they don't know what the staged incident will be or where it will occur. After the crime has taken place, students discuss their reactions with the officers and learn how they could have handled it differently or avoided it.

All the security guards, alarm systems and shuttle buses in the world won't protect students who don't know how to take care of themselves. There are a number of ways in which you can encourage your children to be safer students. Make sure they attend freshman orientation and pay special attention to safety information. You might also pass along the fact that students commit 80% of campus crimes. "It's difficult to convince young people that not everyone is honest," says Susan Riseling, chief of police at the University of Wisconsin at Madison. And even honest classmates can behave in ways that threaten your child. Dormmates may prop open residence hall doors, disconnect alarms or let strangers into the building. Says Riseling: "Students can be victimized by their own false sense of camaraderie." For that reason, she adds, "just don't bring a shiny new bike or an irreplaceable heirloom to college."

Collegians can avoid a lot of trouble merely by locking their doors whenever they leave their rooms or go to bed at night. And although murder and rape by a stranger are rare on campus, in several cases that have occurred the victim's door was unlocked. Experts agree that by exercising common sense and drinking responsibly, your child can reduce his or her chances of becoming a victim and still have a good time at school.

MONEY's Guide to
1,003 Colleges

You've come to the right place to size up schools. On the following pages, we provide basic statistics for 1,003 public and private four-year colleges and universities that welcome students without regard to religious backgrounds. Not all of these institutions were included in the analysis that determined our 100 best buys (see page 143). Among those excluded were the service academies, highly specialized colleges and schools that require students to work while attending classes. We also did not include colleges where more than 45% of the students attend classes part time. While schools that placed on our top 100 honor roll are highlighted by their ranks to the left of their names, the institutions excluded from our value analysis are indicated by footnotes. All footnotes appear on page 178. Here are explanations of the statistics:

Tuition and fees. We quote the charges for freshmen, including mandatory fees. For public schools, we list the price for nonresident freshmen. In cases where final figures were not available, we used estimates (indicated by footnotes).

Room and board. We list the most popular option, a two-person dorm room and 14 meals a week.

Percent of students receiving financial aid. This is the portion of undergraduates receiving any financial aid, including loans, work/study, and merit and athletic scholarships.

Percent of need met. This statistic applies to students who qualified for financial aid. It's the average percentage of their calculated need that was filled.

Average gift aid per student. This figure represents the total of all scholarships and grants (including those made to athletes) that came from the college's own funds during the academic year, divided by the number of full-time students.

Student/faculty ratio. We list the ratio of students to teaching faculty reported by the schools themselves. Colleges with low ratios tend to have smaller classes. (For our value rankings, we used three different student/faculty ratios that we calculated from our own data.)

Percent who graduate in six years. This is the portion of the class of 1986 who earned degrees by the summer of 1992.

Student academic level. Each year colleges are asked to characterize the academic achievement level of entering freshmen. Colleges put their typical student in one of these numerical categories:

1. Top 20% of high school class, with GPA of B+ or better, SAT scores above 1,200 or ACT scores above 28.

2. Top 40% of class, GPA of B or better, SAT scores between 1,100 and 1,199, ACT scores of 27 to 28.

3. Top half of class, GPA of B- or better, SAT scores between 950 and 1,099, ACT scores of 23 to 26.

4. Top 60% of class, GPA of C or better, SAT scores between 800 and 949, ACT scores of 19 to 22.

5. Grades/scores lower than the above.

	college name and location	Tuition and fees	Room and board	% of students receiving aid	% of need met	Average gift aid per student	Student/ faculty ratio	% who graduate in six years	Student academic level	Telephone
	Adams State (Colo.)	$4,862	$3,260	80	88	$279	20:1	47	3	800-824-6494
	Adelphi (N.Y.)	12,250	6,000	92	N.A.	2,048	13:1	56	3	516-877-3050
	Adrian (Mich.)	10,800	3,540	85	90	2,114	15:1	46	3	800-877-2246
65	Agnes Scott (Ga.)[1]	12,135	5,000	92	99	4,556	8:1	48	2	404-371-6285
	Alabama A&M[2]	3,200	2,350	75	75	406	15:1	33	4	205-851-5245
	Alaska Pacific	7,330	4,150	47	N.A.	929	12:1	27	3	907-564-8248
	Albertson (Idaho)	12,942	3,000	88	80	3,871	13:1	47	3	208-459-5305
	Albertus Magnus (Conn.)	11,570	5,240	70	N.A.	2,350	11:1	65	3	203-773-8501
	Albion (Mich.)	13,676	4,316	77	98	3,584	13:1	64	3	517-629-0321
	Albright (Pa.)	15,010	4,250	86	93	3,384	11:1	78	2	215-921-7512
	Alcorn State (Miss.)[2]	6,616	2,098	95	N.A.	1,292	20:1	38[3]	4	601-877-6147
	Alderson-Broaddus (W.Va.)	9,746	3,180	95	85	2,302	13:1	37	4	304-457-1700
	Alfred (N.Y.)	16,048	5,009	71	89	3,454	11:1	69	3	607-871-2115
	Allegheny (Pa.)	16,700	4,320	74	100	5,486	11:1	72	2	814-332-4351
90	Allentown–St. Francis de Sales (Pa.)	9,330	4,620	90	90	1,964	14:1	61	3	215-282-1100
	Alma (Mich.)	12,041	4,334	95	90	3,904	15:1	70	3	800-321-2562
	Alvernia (Pa.)	8,374	4,000	85	65	528	14:1	40	4	215-777-5121
	American International (Mass.)	9,278	4,500	69	87	1,583	16:1	63	4	413-747-6201
	Amherst (Mass.)	19,072	5,000	45	100	5,265	10:1	97	1	413-542-2328
	Angelo State (Texas)	5,664	3,592	43	N.A.	853	24:1	27	3	915-942-2041
	Anna Maria (Mass.)	10,800	4,836	77	80	2,654	16:1	72	4	508-849-3360
	Antioch (Ohio)	16,042	3,176	96	N.A.	3,354	8:1	40	3	513-767-6400
	Appalachian State (N.C.)	7,540[4,5]	2,540	68	44	895	16:1	59	3	704-262-2120
	Aquinas (Mich.)	10,402	4,124	89	90	2,754	14:1	54	3	616-732-4460
	Arizona State	7,350	4,680	58	85	496	20:1	46	3	602-965-2604
	Arkansas College	8,090	3,536	94	87	3,543	10:1	42	2	800-423-2542
	Arkansas State	3,070	2,330	N.A.	N.A.	N.A.	24:1	34	4	501-972-3024
	Arkansas Tech	3,360	2,490	47	N.A.	328	18:1	45[3]	4	501-968-0343
	Ashland (Ohio)	10,988	4,520	97	95	3,673	16:1	52	4	419-289-5052
	Assumption (Mass.)	11,595	5,670	60	70	2,259	16:1	77	3	508-752-5615
27	Auburn (Ala.)	5,850	3,873	31	80	88[6]	16:1	66	3	205-844-4080
	Auburn–Montgomery (Ala.)	5,400	1,590	N.A.	N.A.	498	22:1	30	3	205-244-3611
	Augsburg (Minn.)	11,389	4,204	90	85	1,283	15:1	40	3	612-330-1001
	Augusta (Ga.)	4,224	No dorms	44	50	112	28:1	18[7]	5	706-737-1405
	Augustana (Ill.)	12,942	4,017	87	100	3,737	13:1	70	3	309-794-7341
	Augustana (S.D.)	10,300	3,229	87	N.A.	2,679	14:1	57	2	605-336-5516
93	Austin (Texas)	10,865	4,134	77	100	1,817	14:1	70	3	903-813-2387
	Austin Peay State (Tenn.)	5,302	2,630	63	61	425[8]	18:1	28	4	615-648-7661
	Babson (Mass.)[9]	16,445	6,715	47	99	2,904	21:1	84	2	800-488-3696
	Baker (Kans.)	8,234	4,050	92	95	2,599	15:1	53[7]	3	800-873-4282
	Baker College of Flint (Mich.)	5,376	1,575[10]	N.A.	50	163	36:1	N.A.	N.A.	313-766-4000
	Baldwin-Wallace (Ohio)	10,980	4,230	67	100	3,093	15:1	66	3	216-826-2222
	Ball State (Ind.)	6,584	3,376	70	N.A.	499	17:1	46[7]	3	317-285-8300
	Barat (Ill.)	9,830	4,300	70	100	1,198	12:1	50	4	708-234-3000
	Barber-Scotia (N.C.)[2]	4,409	2,740	93	65	221	14:1	12	5	704-786-5171
	Bard (N.Y.)	19,014	6,030	70	94	8,073	10:1	77	2	914-758-7472
	Barnard (N.Y.)[1]	17,756	7,736	60	100	4,175	11:1	87	1	212-854-2014
	Barton (N.C.)	7,363	3,316	83	81	639	13:1	46	4	800-345-4973
	Baruch College–City U. of N.Y.	5,050	No dorms	47	56	118	33:1	44	2	212-447-3750
	Bates (Maine)	23,990[11]	N.A.	50	100	3,226	11:1	89	1	207-786-6000
33	Baylor (Texas)	7,070	3,920	66	67	936	16:1	71	N.A.	817-755-1811
	Beaver (Pa.)	12,510	5,150	56	56	3,306	13:1	66	3	215-572-2910
88	Bellarmine (Ky.)	8,172	2,660	90	80	1,559	13:1	70	3	502-452-8131
	Belmont Abbey (N.C.)	9,154	4,556	81	53	2,939	16:1	37	4	800-523-2355
	Beloit (Wis.)	15,430	3,520	83	100	4,517	12:1	71	3	608-363-2500
	Bemidji State (Minn.)	4,690	2,750	75	88	236	20:1	36	3	218-755-2040
	Benedict (S.C.)[2]	5,484	2,892	82	85	N.A.	14:1	N.A.	4	803-253-5143
	Benedictine (Kans.)[12]	9,080	3,750	92	94	1,810	14:1	42	4	913-367-5340
	Bennett (N.C.)[1,2]	6,010	3,030	86	79	509	11:1	34	4	919-370-8624

Footnotes appear on page 178.

College name and location	Tuition and fees	Room and board	% of students receiving aid	% of need met	Average gift aid per student	Student/ faculty ratio	% who graduate in six years	Student academic level	Telephone
Bennington (Vt.)	$24,850[11]	N.A.	65	100	$6,843	7:1	50	2	800-833-6845
Bentley (Mass.)	12,895	$6,540	70	100	936	20:1	74[7]	3	617-891-2244
Berea (Ky.)[13]	183	2,700	100	100	1,029[14]	13:1	56	2	606-986-9341
57 Berry (Ga.)	8,050	3,940	91	95	2,656	15:1	54	N.A.	706-236-2215
Bethany (Kans.)	8,105	3,225	96	77	2,095	13:1	35	3	913-227-3311
Bethany (W.Va.)	13,660	5,000	77	99	3,981	13:1	55	3	800-922-7611
Bethel (Tenn.)	6,200	2,900	98	60	1,733	12:1	31[7]	N.A.	901-352-1000
Birmingham-Southern (Ala.)	11,150	4,400	82	94	2,515	15:1	69	3	205-226-4686
Blackburn (Ill.)[15]	8,120	1,000	90	N.A.	1,575	14:1	45	4	217-854-3231
Black Hills State (S.D.)	3,892	2,611	63	80	56	24:1	36	4	605-642-6343
Bloomsburg U. of Pennsylvania	7,842	2,854	N.A.	N.A.	107	19:1	65	3	717-389-4316
Bluffton (Ohio)	9,225	3,726	95	100	1,763	13:1	55[7]	3	800-488-3257
Boise State (Idaho)	4,168	3,069	47	N.A.	69	19:1	N.A.	4	208-385-1156
Boston College (Mass.)	16,200	6,700	65	85	2,847	15:1	88	2	617-552-3100
Boston University (Mass.)	17,650	6,480	61	89	5,209	15:1	71	2	617-353-2300
Bowdoin (Maine)	18,300	5,855	43	100	4,200	12:1	92	1	207-725-3100
Bowie State (Md.)[2]	5,127	3,747	65	N.A.	N.A.	22:1	18[7]	4	301-464-6570
Bowling Green State (Ohio)	7,726	3,148	50	90	320	20:1	66	3	419-372-2086
Bradford (Mass.)	13,420	6,120	67	100	4,043	12:1	42	4	508-372-7161
Bradley (Ill.)	10,408	4,310	80	81	2,023	16:1	64	3	309-677-1000
Brandeis (Mass.)	19,030	7,100	49	100	5,506	8:1	83	2	617-736-3500
Brescia (Ky.)	6,700	3,100	57	47	961	15:1	49	4	800-264-1234
Brewton-Parker (Ga.)	4,521	2,370	82	60	1,990[4]	14:1	19[4]	5[16]	912-583-2241
Briar Cliff (Iowa)	9,930	3,445	95	N.A.	2,232	12:1	43	4	712-279-5200
Bridgewater (Va.)	10,770	4,530	98	93	3,544	13:1	55	3	703-828-2501
Bridgewater State (Mass.)	7,555	3,966	36	N.A.	284	17:1	26[3]	3	508-697-1237
Brooklyn College–City U. of N.Y.	5,207	No dorms	46	58	87	16:1	38	2	718-951-5051
Brown (R.I.)	19,006	5,612	35	38[17]	3,099	9:1	94	1	401-863-2378
Bryant (R.I.)[9]	12,120	6,079	54	90	2,556	19:1	75	3	401-232-6100
Bryn Mawr (Pa.)[1]	17,510	6,450	44	100	3,768	9:1	86	1	215-526-5152
Bucknell (Pa.)	17,730	4,590	43	97	2,983	14:1	89	2	717-524-1101
Buena Vista (Iowa)	13,065	3,585	98	91	4,739	13:1	61	3	712-749-2235
Butler (Ind.)	12,280	4,140	84	85	4,650	13:1	65	3	317-283-9255
Cabrini (Pa.)	10,222	5,790	77	77	1,731	18:1	55	4	215-971-8552
5 California Institute of Technology	16,110	4,815	75	100	6,527	5:1[18]	80	1	818-356-6341
California Lutheran	12,040	5,200	80	N.A.	2,270	15:1	39[7]	3	805-493-3135
California Polytechnic–Pomona	9,774	4,724	50	N.A.	73	21:1	34	4	909-869-2000
California Polytechnic–San Luis Obispo	9,582	4,625	N.A.	N.A.	975	17:1	49	N.A.	805-756-2311
California State–Bakersfield	9,412	3,710	N.A.	N.A.	N.A.	16:1	N.A.	3	805-664-3036
California State–Chico	9,480	4,413	42	N.A.	N.A.	20:1	50	4	916-898-6321
California State–Fresno	9,400	4,291	38	80[19]	47	18:1	45	N.A.	209-278-6283
California State–Fullerton	9,418	3,476	N.A.	N.A.	N.A.	19:1	44	3	714-773-2370
California State–Long Beach	9,360	4,900	N.A.	60	762	20:1	32	3	310-985-4111
California State–Northridge	9,380	4,450	25	N.A.	58	19:1	32	N.A.	818-885-3700
California State–Sacramento	9,402	4,899	N.A.	N.A.	221	18:1	26[7]	2	916-278-3901
California State–San Bernardino[12]	9,183	4,466	N.A.	N.A.	185	20:1	21[7]	N.A.	714-880-5200
California U. of Pennsylvania	8,158	3,510	N.A.	95	N.A.	19:1	54	3	412-938-4404
Camden College–Rutgers U. (N.J.)	7,620	4,454	49	24	120	17:1	51	2	609-225-6104
Cameron (Okla.)	3,552	2,302	60	85	401	28:1	38	4	405-581-2230
Canisius (N.Y.)	10,270	5,240	80	88	1,781	17:1	59	3	716-888-2200
Capital (Ohio)	12,500	3,910	95	85	3,972	14:1	61	3	614-236-6101
Cardinal Stritch (Wis.)	7,680	3,460	79	95	405	14:1	50	4	414-351-7504
Carleton (Minn.)	18,405	3,750	86	100	3,617	11:1	89	1	507-663-4190
Carnegie Mellon (Pa.)	17,060	5,500	70	100	3,044	8:1	72	1	412-268-2082
Carroll (Mont.)	7,825	3,650	83	90	1,566	13:1	45	2	406-447-4384
Carroll (Wis.)	11,790	3,700	89	92	4,431	15:1	63	3	414-524-7220
Carthage (Wis.)	12,400	3,595	88	99	4,172	15:1	47	3	414-551-6000
Case Western Reserve (Ohio)	15,315	5,590	77	100	6,656	8:1	69	1	800-967-8898
Castleton State (Vt.)	7,576	4,500	75	80	77	15:1	24[3]	3	802-468-5611

Footnotes appear on page 178.

College name and location	Tuition and fees	Room and board	% of students receiving aid	% of need met	Average gift aid per student	Student/faculty ratio	% who graduate in six years	Student academic level	Telephone
Catawba (N.C.)	$9,000	$3,950	82	80	$1,686	14:1	39	4	800-228-2922
Catholic U. (D.C.)	13,614	6,116	58	98	3,208	9:1	74	3	202-319-5305
Cazenovia (N.Y.)	9,417	4,608	88	100	1,521	16:1	10[20]	4	315-655-8005
47 Centenary College of Louisiana	8,406	3,420	22	82	3,361	11:1	58	3	318-869-5131
Central Connecticut State	5,678	4,332	31	100	198	17:1	44	N.A.	203-827-7543
Central Methodist (Mo.)	8,050	3,370	85	N.A.	3,314	14:1	49	3	816-248-3391
Central Michigan	6,780	3,836	60	85	265	20:1	55	3	517-774-3076
Central Missouri State	4,320	2,978	60	49	250	19:1	40	4	816-543-4290
Central State (Ohio)[2]	6,366	4,509	85	90	310	54:1	N.A.	N.A.	513-376-6348
Central U. of Iowa	10,364	3,660	94	96	N.A.	14:1	71	2	800-458-5503
Central Washington	7,325	3,500	81	N.A.	116	20:1	42	3	509-963-3111
48 Centre (Ky.)	11,600	4,120	72	100	2,963	11:1	72	2	606-238-5350
Chadron State (Neb.)	2,830	2,591	85	N.A.	20[21]	21:1	63	3	308-432-4451
Chapman (Calif.)	16,328	5,780	61	100	4,804	12:1	37	3	714-997-6711
Chatham (Pa.)[1]	12,780	5,230	80	N.A.	4,636	9:1	48[7]	2	412-365-1290
79 Chestnut Hill (Pa.)[1]	9,750	4,775	70	90	3,228	9:1	69	2	215-248-7001
Cheyney U. of Pennsylvania[2]	7,592	3,340	85	85	412	14:1	12[7]	3	800-243-9639
Chicago State (Ill.)	5,776	No dorms	80	N.A.	2,394	20:1	N.A.	4	312-995-2513
Christian Brothers (Tenn.)	8,880	3,180	72	N.A.	1,494	12:1	55	3	901-722-0205
Christopher Newport (Va.)	7,860	4,900	34	65	28	18:1	37[7]	4	804-594-7015
Citadel (S.C.)[9, 22]	13,384[23]	3,184	50	80	736	13:1	66	N.A.	800-868-1842
City College–City U. of N.Y.	5,144	No dorms	52	49	144	15:1	31	2	212-650-6977
83 Claremont McKenna (Calif.)	16,400	5,750	63	100	3,852	8:1	81	1	909-621-8088
Clarion U. of Pennsylvania	8,108	2,802	72	N.A.	184	19:1	55	3	814-226-2306
Clark (Mass.)	17,000	4,400	55	55	3,572	11:1	72	N.A.	508-793-7431
Clarkson (N.Y.)	15,383	5,077	85	83	3,037	15:1	73	2	315-268-6479
53 Clemson (S.C.)	7,896	3,088	55	80	629	19:1	70	3	803-656-2287
Cleveland State (Ohio)	6,252	4,161	60	N.A.	208	23:1	25	4	216-687-3755
Coe (Iowa)	12,805	4,280	88	95	3,456	12:1	63	3	319-399-8500
Coker (S.C.)	9,510	4,280	87	72	1,508	10:1	56	3	803-383-8050
Colby (Maine)	18,690	5,540	45	100	3,231	10:1	88	1	207-872-3168
Colby-Sawyer (N.H.)	13,375	5,120	46	83	4,185	12:1	53	4	603-526-2010
Colgate (N.Y.)	18,620	5,400	68	N.A.	N.A.	10:1	85[3]	1	315-824-7401
College of Charleston (S.C.)	5,900	3,300	58	78	292	20:1	46[24]	3	803-953-5670
College of Great Falls (Mont.)[12]	5,000	5,260	80	59	129	16:1	N.A.	3	406-761-8210
College of Misericordia (Pa.)	10,460	5,360	96	N.A.	1,021	13:1	N.A.	4	717-675-4449
College of Mount St. Vincent (N.Y.)	11,250	5,600	82	70	2,390	12:1	61	4	718-405-3267
College of New Rochelle (N.Y.)[1]	10,680	4,760	70	N.A.	N.A.	10:1	35[3]	3	914-654-5452
College of Notre Dame (Calif.)	11,750	5,700	54	33	1,586	10:1	32	3	415-508-3607
66 College of Notre Dame of Maryland[1]	10,650	5,400	85	100	3,346	15:1	75	3	800-435-0300
College of St. Benedict (Minn.)[1]	11,428	4,030	88	94	2,325	13:1	76	3	612-363-5308
College of St. Catherine (Minn.)[1]	11,700	4,210	68	97	1,779	14:1	65	3	612-690-6505

Footnotes appear on page 178.

Luxury degrees

Schools with the highest charges for tuition, fees, room and board

Brandeis University (Mass.)	$26,130
Barnard College (N.Y.)	25,492
MIT (Mass.)	25,400
Hampshire College (Mass.)	25,210
Yale University (Conn.)	25,110
Bard College (N.Y.)	25,044
Tufts University (Mass.)	24,962
Sarah Lawrence College (N.Y.)	24,960
Harvard University (Mass.)	24,880
Bennington College (Vt.)	24,850

College name and location	Tuition and fees	Room and board	% of students receiving aid	% of need met	Average gift aid per student	Student/ faculty ratio	% who graduate in six years	Student academic level	Telephone
College of St. Francis (Ill.)	$9,100	$3,960	86	100	$2,265	15:1	55	3	815-740-3400
College of St. Rose (N.Y.)	9,542	5,288	85	N.A.	N.A.	17:1	55[3]	3	518-454-5150
College of St. Scholastica (Minn.)	11,280	3,588	86	91	2,506	13:1	54	3	218-723-6046
College of Santa Fe (N.M.)[12]	9,830	4,058	85	80	1,030	14:1	85[7]	3	505-473-6131
College of Staten Island–City U. of N.Y.[12]	5,156	No dorms	29	59	64	23:1	43	2	718-390-7557
College of the Atlantic (Maine)	13,287	3,860	59	95	2,102	10:1	36	3	207-288-5015
College of the Holy Cross (Mass.)	17,550	6,300	56	100	3,615	14:1	92	1	508-793-2443
College of the Ozarks (Mo.)[13]	100	1,900	100	100	1,235[4,14]	14:1	70	2	800-222-0525
College of the Southwest (N.M.)	4,000	2,478	15	N.A.	855	8:1	4[3]	4	505-392-6561
75 College of William and Mary (Va.)	12,604	4,188	26	88	124	14:1	90	1	804-221-4223
College of Wooster (Ohio)	15,425	4,300	70	100	4,256	12:1	66	3	216-263-2322
Colorado College	16,062	3,976	56	N.A.	3,757	13:1	79	2	719-389-6344
Colorado School of Mines	11,764	4,050	75	100	1,459	13:1	60	2	303-273-3220
Colorado State	8,180	4,000	N.A.	N.A.	952	13:1	51	3	303-491-6909
Columbia (Ill.)[9]	7,058	3,542[10]	N.A.	N.A.	184	10:1	N.A.	3	312-663-1600
Columbia (Mo.)	7,900	3,524	63	68	1,395	12:1	46[3]	4	800-231-2391
Columbia (S.C.)[1]	9,750	3,770	80	90	1,314	14:1	49	3	803-786-3871
54 Columbia University (N.Y.)	17,840	6,610	60	N.A.	N.A.	7:1	81	1	212-854-2521
Concord (W.Va.)	4,076	3,096	52	98	233	23:1	30	4	304-384-5249
Concordia (Minn.)	9,720	3,480	83	100	1,586	16:1	40[7]	4	218-299-3004
Connecticut	18,130	6,030	41	41	3,584	11:1	94	1	203-439-2200
Converse (S.C.)[1]	12,050	3,700	N.A.	N.A.	3,069	9:1	63	3	803-596-9040
49 Cook College–Rutgers U. (N.J.)	8,549	4,454	48	18	345	15:1	71	2	908-932-3770
Cooper Union (N.Y.)[9]	300	4,100	43	90	433	7:1	81	1	212-353-4120
Cornell (Iowa)	14,228	4,197	75	90	5,083	13:1	59	2	800-747-1112
Cornell University (N.Y.)	18,170	5,963	N.A.	100	2,464	11:1	90	1	607-255-5241
Cornish College of the Arts (Wash.)[9]	9,355	No dorms	80	67	415	7:1	55	N.A.	206-323-1400
87 Creighton (Neb.)	10,252	4,180	73	N.A.	1,705	14:1	65	3	402-280-2703
Culver-Stockton (Mo.)	7,650	3,500	85	95	3,773	21:1	39	3	314-288-5221
Curry (Mass.)	13,395	4,900	60	85	1,777	15:1	55[7]	4	617-333-0500
Dakota State (S.D.)	2,016	2,360	85	59	175	18:1	N.A.	4	605-256-5139
Dakota Wesleyan (S.D.)	7,110	2,550	88	85	1,192	15:1	67[7]	3	800-333-8506
Dana (Neb.)	8,780	3,130	95	83	2,673	11:1	44	4	800-444-3262
Daniel Webster (N.H.)	11,828	4,656	68	80	2,106	14:1	54	3	603-883-3556
74 Dartmouth (N.H.)	18,340	4,860	40	100	2,761	12:1	96	1	603-646-2875
67 Davidson (N.C.)	16,263	4,774	62	100	3,387	12:1	91	1	704-892-2230
Davis and Elkins (W.Va.)	8,980	4,250	65	100	1,414	14:1	31[7]	4	304-636-5850
Defiance (Ohio)	9,950	3,530	95	95	2,168	14:1	48	4	419-783-2330
Delaware State[2]	4,346	3,464	60	N.A.	N.A.	15:1	23[7]	4	302-739-4917
Delaware Valley (Pa.)	11,645	4,785	87	N.A.	2,375	14:1	58	3	215-345-1500
Delta State (Miss.)	4,154	1,770	90	100	428	19:1	50	4	601-846-4018
Denison (Ohio)	16,730	4,220	57	100	3,567	12:1	78	N.A.	800-336-4766
DePaul (Ill.)	10,590	5,500	65	80	1,488	17:1	62	3	312-362-8300
DePauw (Ind.)	13,700	4,640	60	100	2,961	12:1	79	2	800-447-2495
Dickinson (Pa.)	17,775	4,930	60	100	3,851	11:1	85	1	717-245-1231
Dickinson State (N.D.)	4,448	2,018	86	75	168	18:1	35[7]	4	701-227-2175
Doane (Neb.)	9,390	2,830	95	98	2,291	13:1	54	3	402-826-8222
Dominican of San Rafael (Calif.)	12,180	5,680	61	N.A.	4,206	12:1	36	3	415-485-3204
12 Douglass College–Rutgers U. (N.J.)[1]	7,763	4,454	51	22	235	17:1	83	2	908-932-3770
Drake (Iowa)	13,070	4,215	75	95	3,489	16:1	60	3	515-271-3181
Drew (N.J.)	18,058	5,094	58	61	6,176	11:1	80	2	201-408-3739
Drexel (Pa.)	14,572	5,680	N.A.	76	1,570	15:1	54	2	215-895-2400
73 Drury (Mo.)	8,760	3,380	82	95	2,509	14:1	50	3	417-865-8731
Duke (N.C.)	17,160	5,550	38	N.A.	3,353	9:1	95	1	919-684-3214
Duquesne (Pa.)	11,320	5,114	78	94	2,054	16:1	74	2	412-396-6220
D'Youville (N.Y.)	8,720	4,130	90	70	905	14:1	42	3	800-777-3921
Earlham (Ind.)	15,327	4,056	73	95	4,152	11:1	77	2	800-327-5426
East Carolina (N.C.)	7,098	3,150	77	N.A.	225	15:1	50	3	919-757-6640
Eastern Connecticut State	5,162	3,826	50	N.A.	7[21]	17:1	50[7]	3	203-456-5286

Footnotes appear on page 178.

College name and location	Tuition and fees	Room and board	% of students receiving aid	% of need met	Average gift aid per student	Student/faculty ratio	% who graduate in six years	Student academic level	Telephone
Eastern Illinois	$6,296	$2,948	57	N.A.	$105	17:1	63	3	217-581-2223
Eastern Kentucky	4,750	2,896	71	90	81	23:1	30	4	606-622-2106
Eastern Michigan	6,408	4,031	60	95	253	27:1	34[7]	3	313-487-3060
Eastern Montana	5,556	2,310	60	N.A.	N.A.	19:1	5	3	406-657-2158
Eastern New Mexico	5,280	2,485	83	N.A.	N.A.	20:1	63	4	505-562-2178
Eastern Oregon State	2,500	3,400	70	N.A.	N.A.	14:1	22[3]	4	503-962-3672
Eastern Washington	7,068	3,618	45	N.A.	910[4]	16:1	N.A.	3	509-359-2397
East Stroudsburg U. of Pennsylvania	8,062	3,222	85	N.A.	4	20:1	45	3	717-424-3542
East Tennessee State	5,226	2,808	54	N.A.	160	23:1	43[3]	3	615-929-4213
East-West (Ill.)	6,185	No dorms	87	N.A.	N.A.	16:1	8[3]	5	312-939-0111
Eckerd (Fla.)	14,930	3,925	80	92	4,207	14:1	72	3	813-864-8331
Edinboro U. of Pennsylvania	7,929	3,650	80	98	76	17:1	51	4	800-626-2203
Elizabeth City State (N.C.)[2]	6,462	2,862	93	N.A.	124	13:1	34	5	919-335-3305
Elizabethtown (Pa.)	13,600	4,250	76	95	3,035	14:1	56	3	717-361-1400
Elmhurst (Ill.)	9,676	3,924	54	96	938	15:1	55	3	708-617-3400
Elmira (N.Y.)	13,900	4,550	80	94	3,447	16:1	68	3	607-735-1724
Elms (Mass.)[1]	10,974	4,665	84	100	1,911	14:1	80	3	800-255-3567
Elon (N.C.)	8,630	3,660	49	90	958	17:1	54	3	919-584-2370
Embry-Riddle Aeronautical (Fla.)[9]	7,310	3,600	75	N.A.	260[4]	19:1	37[3]	3	800-222-3728
Emerson (Mass.)[9]	14,831	7,288	65	N.A.	N.A.	15:1	65	3	617-578-8600
Emmanuel (Mass.)[1]	11,973	5,800	71	100	2,429	12:1	54	3	617-735-9715
Emory (Ga.)	16,820	5,110	55	95	3,646	8:1	82	2	404-727-6036
63 Emory and Henry (Va.)	8,546	4,230	89	N.A.	1,133	14:1	58	3	703-944-4121
Emporia State (Kans.)	4,737	3,025	70	N.A.	236	19:1	40	4	316-341-5465
Erskine (S.C.)	10,630	3,680	83	85	2,679	12:1	62	3	803-379-8838
Eureka (Ill.)	11,050	3,555	90	92	2,643	12:1	43	4	800-322-3756
Evergreen State (Wash.)	6,964	4,200	55	N.A.	185	20:1	52[7]	3	206-866-6000
Fairfield (Conn.)	14,560	5,900	68	67	2,813	16:1	87	2	203-254-4100
Fairleigh Dickinson (N.J.)[12]	11,091	5,336	67	N.A.	2,008	17:1	54	3	201-460-5294
Fairmont State (W.Va.)	4,228	3,040	63	75	N.A.	24:1	38	4	304-367-4141
Fayetteville State (N.C.)[2]	7,442[5]	2,300	N.A.	N.A.	456	15:1	14	3	919-486-1371
Ferris State (Mich.)	6,432	3,928	65	N.A.	145	17:1	N.A.	4	616-592-2100
Ferrum (Va.)	8,800	4,000	94	90	1,630	14:1	30[3]	4	703-365-4290
22 Fisk (Tenn.)[2]	6,305	3,690	N.A.	50	532	9:1	63	2	615-329-8666
Fitchburg State (Mass.)	7,174	3,750	50	82	199	16:1	52	3	508-345-2151
Flagler (Fla.)	4,920	3,070	80	N.A.	406	19:1	45	3	904-829-6481
Florida A&M[2]	6,691	2,770	66	13	721	13:1	N.A.	4	904-599-3796
Florida Atlantic[12]	6,693[4]	3,910	26	80	606	20:1	48	3	407-367-3040
Florida Institute of Technology	13,035	3,900	70	N.A.	N.A.	14:1	55	2	800-888-4348
Florida International[12]	6,659	4,325	39	90	243	16:1	55	3	305-348-2363
Florida Southern	7,660	4,600	85	87	1,230	15:1	50	3	813-680-4131
Florida State	6,682	3,964	39	100	212	16:1[18]	54	2	904-644-6200

Footnotes appear on page 178.

Steep climbs

These schools approved the biggest increase in tuition and fees for 1993-94. (We used out-of-state tuition for public schools.)

Sheldon Jackson College (Alaska)	32.9%
Texas Southern University	27.7
Idaho State University	27.1
Olivet College (Mich.)	26.6
Kutztown University (Pa.)	25.4
Lander College (S.C.)	22.6
Bloomsburg U. of Pennsylvania	21.4
Indiana U. of Pennsylvania	21.2
California U. of Pennsylvania	20.4
West Chester University (Pa.)	20.4

College name and location	Tuition and fees	Room and board	% of students receiving aid	% of need met	Average gift aid per student	Student/ faculty ratio	% who graduate in six years	Student academic level	Telephone
Fontbonne (Mo.)	$8,090	$4,000	80	92	$2,212	14:1	48	3	314-889-1400
Fordham (N.Y.)	13,350	6,700	84	N.A.	N.A.	17:1	87[7]	2	718-817-1000
Fort Hays State (Kans.)	4,869	2,972	N.A.	83	146	16:1[18]	34	4	913-628-5666
Fort Lewis (Colo.)	6,525	3,320	66	N.A.	49	20:1	33[7]	4	303-247-7184
Framingham State (Mass.)	7,374	3,426	40	N.A.	240	16:1	55	3	508-626-4500
Francis Marion (S.C.)	5,600	3,078	54	N.A.	246	19:1	35	3	803-661-1231
Franciscan U. of Steubenville (Ohio)	9,325	4,200	82	80	1,203	17:1	57[3]	3	614-283-6226
Franklin (Ind.)	10,100	3,870	92	88	4,043	12:1	57	3	317-738-8062
Franklin and Marshall (Pa.)	19,675	3,980	67	67	4,214	11:1	83	2	717-291-3951
Franklin Pierce (N.H.)	12,820	4,450	66	85	2,921	14:1	33	4	800-437-0048
Frostburg State (Md.)	5,296	4,400	65	60	101	18:1	52	3	301-689-4201
Furman (S.C.)	12,712	3,952	69	100	1,638	12:1	81	2	803-294-2034
Gannon (Pa.)	10,250	4,040	86	21	2,064	12:1	53	3	800-426-6668
George Mason (Va.)	10,206	4,750	26	N.A.	286	17:1	44	3	703-993-2400
Georgetown (D.C.)	17,586	6,824	48	100	5,136	11:1	92	1	202-687-3600
George Washington (D.C.)	16,988	5,482	N.A.	N.A.	4,625	14:1	70	2	202-994-6040
Georgia College	4,457	2,739	50	N.A.	135	25:1	30	4	912-453-5004
15 Georgia Institute of Technology	6,732	4,052	60	66	611	20:1	68	1	404-894-4154
Georgian Court (N.J.)	8,700	3,850	56	80	751	10:1	56[7]	3	908-367-4440
Georgia Southern	4,571	2,790	50	N.A.	N.A.	24:1	37	4	912-681-5531
Georgia Southwestern	4,511	2,520	39	N.A.	N.A.	18:1	23	4	912-928-1273
Georgia State[12]	6,452	No dorms	30	N.A.	311	14:1[18]	29	4	404-651-2365
Gettysburg (Pa.)	18,870	4,090	45	98	4,050	12:1	79	2	717-337-6100
Glenville State (W.Va.)	3,900	2,950	72	70	155	18:1	46	4	304-462-4117
GMI Eng. and Mgt. Institute (Mich.)	11,000	3,158	52	100	223	12:1	75	2	313-762-7865
Goddard (Vt.)	13,470	4,520	70	79	3,164	10:1	N.A.	3	800-468-4888
Gonzaga (Wash.)	12,300	4,150	75	90	3,516	14:1	51	3	509-484-6484
Goucher (Md.)	14,525	5,895	69	N.A.	3,111	9:1	71	2	410-337-6100
Graceland (Iowa)	8,680	2,920	87	80	2,874	14:1	27[3]	3	515-784-5196
Grambling State (La.)[2]	3,838	2,612	N.A.	80	242	21:1	50	5	318-274-2435
Grand Valley State (Mich.)	6,378	4,310	68	95	338	23:1	N.A.	3	616-895-2025
Grand View (Iowa)	9,870	3,260	77	N.A.	1,888	17:1	18[3]	3	515-263-2810
Green Mountain (Vt.)	11,200	2,880	51	82	780	14:1	62	4	800-776-6675
Greensboro (N.C.)	7,816	3,680	49	N.A.	N.A.	18:1	45	4	800-346-8226
69 Grinnell (Iowa)	15,368	4,422	74	100	5,383	10:1	83	2	515-269-3600
13 Grove City (Pa.)	4,976	2,894	50	77	417	20:1	77	2	412-458-2100
Guilford (N.C.)	12,610	5,070	78	95	3,159	14:1	62	3	800-992-7759
Gustavus Adolphus (Minn.)	13,465	3,500	76	95	2,065	13:1	76	2	507-933-7676
Hamilton (N.Y.)	18,650	4,850	60	100	4,227	10:1	90	1	315-859-4421
Hamline (Minn.)	13,021	4,100	82	62	2,863	14:1	66	3	612-641-2207
Hampden-Sydney (Va.)[22]	12,974	4,398	62	100	2,323	13:1	68	3	804-223-6120
Hampshire (Mass.)	20,050	5,160	54	N.A.	4,972	13:1	61	2	413-549-4600
Hampton (Va.)[2,12]	7,356	3,350	80	62	367	18:1	65	3	800-624-3328
10 Hanover (Ind.)	7,750	3,200	72	100	944	14:1	62	3	812-866-7021
Hartwick (N.Y.)	16,400	4,550	66	100	5,073	13:1	69	3	607-431-4150
51 Harvard (Mass.)	18,745	6,135	67	100	4,362	8:1	96	1	617-495-1551
25 Harvey Mudd (Calif.)	16,850	6,436	74	100	3,211	8:1	77	1	909-621-8011
Hastings (Neb.)	9,296	3,130	96	82	3,296	13:1	53	3	402-463-2402
Haverford (Pa.)	18,000	5,950	45	100	1,035	11:1	90	1	215-896-1350
Hawaii Pacific	5,900	6,400	32	92	213	20:1	N.A.	3	808-544-0238
Heidelberg (Ohio)	13,123	4,198	85	85	3,063	14:1	69	3	419-448-2330
Henderson State (Ark.)	2,940	2,400	N.A.	80	268	20:1	N.A.	3	501-246-5511
46 Hendrix (Ark.)	8,610	3,060	74	98	1,425	14:1	52	3	501-450-1362
Heritage (Wash.)[12]	5,540	No dorms	68	62	1,355	10:1	N.A.	N.A.	509-865-2244
High Point (N.C.)	7,760	3,700	70	61	696	17:1	45	3	919-841-9216
56 Hillsdale (Mich.)	10,670	4,440	70	85	4,254	13:1	80	3	517-437-7341
Hiram (Ohio)	13,825	4,515	85	100	5,663	12:1	70	3	800-362-5280
Hobart and William Smith (N.Y.)	18,309	5,616	49	97	3,633	13:1	80	2	800-852-2256
Hofstra (N.Y.)	11,080	6,416	N.A.	75	1,379	18:1	58	2	516-463-6700

Footnotes appear on page 178.

College name and location	Tuition and fees	Room and board	% of students receiving aid	% of need met	Average gift aid per student	Student/ faculty ratio	% who graduate in six years	Student academic level	Telephone
Hollins (Va.)[1]	$13,170	$5,300	57	100	$3,158	9:1	68	2	703-362-6401
Hood (Md.)	13,258	5,752	78	100	3,692	13:1	67	3	800-922-1599
Hope (Mich.)	11,542	4,156	78	90	2,506	13:1	73	3	800-968-7850
Howard (D.C.)[2]	7,535	3,834	N.A.	N.A.	N.A.	7:1	44	3	202-806-2752
Hunter College–City U. of N.Y.	5,156	No dorms	40	54	132	17:1	38	2	212-772-4490
Huntingdon (Ala.)	7,640	3,760	85	80	2,368	13:1	48	3	205-834-3300
Idaho State	5,216	2,840	N.A.	N.A.	792	18:1	N.A.	4	208-236-2475
Illinois Benedictine	10,080	3,800	95	95	2,722	15:1	58	3	708-960-1500
39 Illinois College	7,550	3,650	90	93	1,022	15:1	66	3	217-245-3030
Illinois Institute of Technology	13,750	4,500	78	100	3,788	12:1	50	2	312-567-3025
Illinois State	8,203	3,160	75	N.A.	24	22:1	53	4	309-438-2181
Illinois Wesleyan	13,395	3,985	85	100	2,701	13:1	83	2	309-556-3031
Incarnate Word (Texas)	8,250	3,890	67	98	1,489	14:1	73	3	210-829-6005
Indiana State	6,410	3,588	60	N.A.	N.A.	15:1	27[3]	4	812-237-2121
89 Indiana U. at Bloomington	8,630	3,729	70	N.A.	99	19:1	66	2	812-855-0661
Indiana U.–Northwest[12]	5,685	No dorms	51	N.A.	115	16:1	32	4	219-980-6991
Indiana U. of Pennsylvania	7,937	2,834	N.A.	83	360	19:1	59	3	412-357-2230
Indiana U.–Purdue U. at Indianapolis[12]	8,059	3,015	42	48	70	21:1	12[7]	4	317-274-4591
Iona (N.Y.)	10,210	5,200	89	89	1,265	17:1	61	3	914-633-2502
Iowa State	7,386	3,104	N.A.	100	568	19:1	64	2	515-294-5836
Iowa Wesleyan	9,850	3,400	93	80	3,213	14:1	43	4	319-385-6231
Ithaca (N.Y.)	13,837	5,842	55	91	2,485	13:1	68	2	607-274-3124
Jackson State (Miss.)[2]	4,464	1,143	90	90	43	17:1	34	4	601-968-2100
Jacksonville (Fla.)	10,080	4,250	62	N.A.	2,322	15:1	47	3	904-744-3950
Jacksonville State (Ala.)	2,520	2,520	50	N.A.	192	23:1	27	4	205-782-5400
James Madison (Va.)	7,650	4,400	49	80	172	18:1	82	2	703-568-6147
Jamestown (N.D.)	7,270	2,980	97	80	3,810	18:1	49	2	701-252-3467
Jersey City State (N.J.)	3,637	4,700	38	100	26	16:1	33	4	201-200-3234
John Carroll (Ohio)	11,610	5,450	85	73	2,717	14:1	71	2	216-397-4294
Johns Hopkins (Md.)	17,900	6,460	61	100	3,307	10:1	87	1	410-516-8171
Johnson C. Smith (N.C.)[2]	6,338	2,191	85	N.A.	636	15:1	31[7]	4	800-782-7303
Juniata (Pa.)	14,150	4,240	78	100	3,674	13:1	73	3	814-643-4310
Kalamazoo (Mich.)	15,135	4,839	82	100	3,373	12:1	68[7]	2	616-337-7166
Kansas State	6,460	2,840	70	85	267	17:1	48	3	913-532-6250
Kansas Wesleyan	8,020	3,200	96	100	1,561	14:1	68[7]	3	913-827-5541
Kean (N.J.)	3,486	3,970	N.A.	33	27	14:1	45[7]	N.A.	908-527-2195
Keene State (N.H.)	7,945	3,960	49	51	370	19:1	57	4	603-358-2276
Kendall (Ill.)[9]	7,800	4,851	85	90	378	10:1	30[3]	4	708-866-1304
Kennesaw State (Ga.)[12]	2,881	No dorms	18	N.A.	71	30:1	48[3]	4	404-423-6300
Kent State (Ohio)	7,192	3,394	70	60	262	23:1	43	4	216-672-2444
Kentucky State[2]	4,300	2,682	85	83	961	12:1	20	5	502-227-6813
Kentucky Wesleyan	7,600	3,950	92	75	2,077	11:1	46	3	502-926-3111

Footnotes appear on page 178.

Not just for natives

Public schools from our top 100 that report the highest percentage of out-of-state students

New Mexico Tech	**41%**
New College (Fla.)	**40**
Northwest Missouri State	**40**
Auburn University (Ala.)	**37**
Georgia Institute of Technology	**36**
University of Virginia	**33**
University of Wisconsin–Madison	**30**
College of William and Mary (Va.)	**30**
Mary Washington College (Va.)	**30**
Indiana University–Bloomington	**30**

College name and location	Tuition and fees	Room and board	% of students receiving aid	% of need met	Average gift aid per student	Student/ faculty ratio	% who graduate in six years	Student academic level	Telephone
Kenyon (Ohio)	$18,730	$3,700	38	95	$3,937	11:1	86	2	614-427-5776
Keuka (N.Y.)	9,340	4,170	95	93	2,613	15:1	47	3	315-536-5254
King's (N.Y.)	8,350	3,920	N.A.	91	1,664	10:1	42	4	914-944-5650
King's (Pa.)	10,600	4,850	80	84	1,905	17:1	68	3	717-826-5858
Knox (Ill.)	15,132	3,858	87	100	4,561	12:1	78	2	309-343-0112
Kutztown (Pa.)	8,285	2,970	N.A.	N.A.	N.A.	20:1	52[7]	3	215-683-4060
Lafayette (Pa.)	17,950	5,500	58	99	2,383	11:1	89	1	215-250-5100
LaGrange (Ga.)	7,197	3,405	80	N.A.	955	15:1	N.A.	3	706-812-7260
Lake Erie (Ohio)[12]	9,600	4,200	85	N.A.	2,327	13:1	33[3]	4	216-639-7879
Lake Forest (Ill.)	16,175	3,785	57	100	4,899	10:1	75	2	708-735-5000
Lake Superior State (Mich.)	12,472	3,987	67	95	448	20:1	N.A.	4	906-635-2231
Lamar (Texas)	5,552	2,600	58	N.A.	235	25:1	19	5	800-458-7558
Lambuth (Tenn.)	5,070	3,160	75	68	1,385	14:1	58[7]	4	901-425-3223
Lander (S.C.)	4,648	3,110	53	75	208	16:1	39	4	803-229-8307
LaSalle (Pa.)[12]	11,510	5,430	85	85	2,254	13:1	70	2	215-951-1500
Lawrence (Wis.)	16,341	3,555	82	100	6,039	11:1	78	2	414-832-6500
Lawrence Technological (Mich.)	4,530	2,250	65	80	316	20:1	35	2	313-356-0200
Lebanon Valley (Pa.)	13,700	4,600	78	90	3,835	12:1	69	3	717-867-6181
Lehigh (Pa.)	17,750	5,220	50	98	3,279	12:1	90	2	215-758-3100
Lehman College–City U. of N.Y.[12]	5,160	No dorms	51	53	184	17:1	25	2	718-960-8131
Le Moyne (N.Y.)	10,605	4,540	80	95	1,882	13:1	73	3	315-445-4300
LeMoyne-Owen (Tenn.)[2]	4,550	3,600	85	64	198	16:1	60	4	901-942-7302
Lenoir-Rhyne (N.C.)	10,220	3,848	85	80	N.A.	14:1	50	3	704-328-7300
Lesley (Mass.)[1]	11,880	5,125	60	83	2,100	14:1	53[7]	4	617-349-8800
Lewis (Ill.)	9,536	4,270	67	N.A.	1,559	16:1	45	3	815-838-0500
Lewis and Clark (Ore.)	15,051	4,929	75	93	3,201	13:1	66[7]	3	503-768-7040
Lewis-Clark State (Idaho)	4,240	2,300	N.A.	N.A.	358	16:1	36	N.A.	208-799-2210
Limestone (S.C.)	7,300	3,500	N.A.	93	1,529	10:1	24	4	803-489-7151
Lincoln (Pa.)[2]	5,232	3,215	N.A.	N.A.	116[21]	12:1	34	3	215-932-8300
Lincoln Memorial (Tenn.)	5,530	2,680	75	98	1,103	14:1	46	3	615-869-6280
Lindenwood (Mo.)	8,880	4,600	90	80	4,144	14:1	42	3	314-949-4949
Lindsey Wilson (Ky.)	6,080	3,450	93	60	1,790	18:1	26	5	502-384-8100
Linfield (Ore.)	12,700	3,970	85	N.A.	3,117	13:1	68	3	503-472-4121
Livingston College–Rutgers U. (N.J.)	7,845	4,454	46	22	324	17:1	62	2	908-932-3770
Lock Haven (Pa.)	7,906	3,620	80	80	96	19:1	44	3	717-893-2027
Long Island U.–Brooklyn (N.Y.)	10,750	4,720	87	N.A.	1,258	9:1	N.A.	3	718-488-1011
Long Island U.–C.W. Post (N.Y.)	11,500	4,920	75	75	1,639	15:1	38	3	516-299-2413
Long Island U.–Southampton (N.Y.)	12,150	5,792	N.A.	78	3,062	15:1	52	4	516-283-4000
Longwood (Va.)	9,190	3,694	60	90	214	14:1	58	3	804-395-2600
Loras (Iowa)	10,578	3,470	75	98	2,396	13:1	44	3	319-588-7236
Louisiana State and A&M	6,058	2,900	57	98	1,108	18:1	36	3	504-388-1175
Louisiana State–Shreveport	4,460	No dorms	30	N.A.	139	21:1	24	N.A.	318-797-5061
Louisiana Tech	3,624[4]	2,325	66	40	468	25:1	36	3	318-257-3036
Loyola (La.)	10,625	5,190	N.A.	93	2,141	15:1	56	3	504-865-3240
Loyola (Md.)	12,565	6,060	60	95	2,133	15:1	73	2	410-617-2252
Loyola Marymount (Calif.)	13,010	6,000	64	N.A.	N.A.	15:1[25]	64	2	310-338-2750
Loyola U. of Chicago (Ill.)	10,570	5,310	85	85	2,377	N.A.	64	2	312-915-6500
Luther (Iowa)	12,375	3,525	79	96	3,170	13:1	76[7]	3	319-387-1287
Lycoming (Pa.)	13,200	4,100	78	83	3,726	14:1	56	3	717-321-4026
Lynchburg (Va.)	11,600	5,400	67	N.A.	1,793	13:1	56	3	804-522-8300
Lyndon State (Vt.)	7,906	4,600	70	N.A.	730	17:1	42	4	802-626-9371
Lynn (Fla.)	13,200	5,100	48	84	1,025	20:1	65[3]	3	407-994-0770
Macalester (Minn.)	15,107	4,208	73	N.A.	4,187	12:1	75	1	612-696-6357
MacMurray (Ill.)	9,160	3,640	92	94	1,895	12:1	50	4	217-479-7056
Manchester (Ind.)	9,600	3,640	91	75	2,800	14:1	55	3	219-982-5055
Manhattan (N.Y.)	12,800	6,600	68	95	632	15:1	71	3	718-920-0200
Manhattanville (N.Y.)	13,900	7,165	75	N.A.	N.A.	12:1	72[7]	2	914-694-2200
Mankato State (Minn.)	4,725	2,643	70	N.A.	76	20:1	49[7]	4	507-389-1822
Mansfield U. of Pennsylvania	7,812	3,230	77	90	68	18:1	51	3	717-662-4243

Footnotes appear on page 178.

College name and location	Tuition and fees	Room and board	% of students receiving aid	% of need met	Average gift aid per student	Student/ faculty ratio	% who graduate in six years	Student academic level	Telephone
Marian (Ind.)	$9,360	$3,616	74	75	$1,501	12:1	38	3	317-929-0321
Marian of Fond du Lac (Wis.)	8,650	3,840	80	80	1,319	16:1	52	4	414-923-7650
Marietta (Ohio)	13,470	3,770	94	100	4,536	12:1	70	3	614-374-4600
Marist (N.Y.)	10,480	5,800	70	85	1,591	17:1	62	3	914-575-3226
Marlboro (Vt.)	17,461	5,675	65	95	6,079	8:1	55[7]	3	802-257-4333
Marquette (Wis.)	10,850	4,150	80	90	1,594	15:1	74	3	414-288-7302
Marshall (W.Va.)	5,146	3,500	65	N.A.	246	23:1	40[7]	5	304-696-3160
Mars Hill (N.C.)	7,500	3,550	80	N.A.	1,314	13:1	50	3	800-543-1514
Mary Baldwin (Va.)[1]	10,654	7,046	70	100	3,559	11:1	60[3]	3	703-887-7019
Marygrove (Mich.)	7,652	3,706	90	67	723	17:1	40[3]	3	313-862-5200
Marymount (N.Y.)[1]	11,540	6,200	57	N.A.	1,263	12:1	58	3	914-332-8295
Marymount (Va.)	10,804	5,126	84	100	2,404	14:1	44	4	703-284-1500
Maryville (Tenn.)	10,428	4,046	90	N.A.	N.A.	14:1	32[7]	4	615-981-8092
32 Mary Washington (Va.)	7,136	4,844	50	75	180	17:1	68	2	703-899-4681
Marywood (Pa.)	10,550	4,300	80	90	2,196	16:1	55	3	717-348-6234
Massachusetts Institute of Technology	19,600	5,800	55	100	5,228	5:1[18]	89	1	617-253-4791
Mayville State (N.D.)	4,511	2,260	N.A.	95	36	15:1	44	4	701-786-2301
McKendree (Ill.)	7,460	3,440	82	100	971	15:1	46	3	618-537-4481
McMurry (Texas)	6,590	3,130	89	90	1,467	14:1	24	3	915-691-6226
McNeese State (La.)	3,484	2,310	N.A.	53	1,244	22:1[18]	28	4	318-475-5146
Medaille (N.Y.)	8,350	4,300	79	60	144	15:1	33[3]	4	716-884-3281
Medgar Evers College–City U. of N.Y.	2,761	No dorms	63	58	89	18:1	N.A.	3	718-270-6024
Memphis State (Tenn.)	5,640	3,420	N.A.	60	550	20:1	34	3	901-678-2101
Menlo (Calif.)	14,175	6,200	40	85	2,644	16:1	41	4	415-688-3753
Mercer (Ga.)	11,160	3,963	93	90	3,970	12:1	71	3	912-752-2650
Mercyhurst (Pa.)	9,838	3,650	88	92	2,207	16:1	59	3	814-824-2202
Meredith (N.C.)[1]	6,340	3,100	38	85	376	15:1	68	3	919-829-8581
Merrimack (Mass.)	11,825	6,200	65	95	2,235	16:1	62	3	508-837-5100
Mesa State (Colo.)	4,922	3,624	N.A.	60	40	19:1	48	4	303-248-1376
Methodist (N.C.)	8,970	3,550	80	78	460	14:1	63	4	919-630-7027
Metropolitan State (Colo.)	6,045	No dorms	40	N.A.	8	19:1	14	4	303-556-3018
59 Miami (Ohio)	9,170	3,840	66	67	279	21:1	83	2	513-529-2531
95 Michigan State	10,655	3,542	50	N.A.	421	13:1[18]	67	3	517-355-8332
82 Michigan Technological	7,685	3,784	50	85	606	19:1	58	3	906-487-2335
Middlebury (Vt.)	24,400[11]	N.A.	38	100	3,502	11:1	92[3]	1	802-388-3711
Middle Tennessee State	5,132	2,106	60	80	1,118	20:1	40[3]	3	615-898-2111
Midland Lutheran (Neb.)	9,530	2,850	93	90	2,716	15:1	52	4	402-721-5480
Midway (Ky.)[1]	6,660	3,850	87	N.A.	916	12:1	36[20]	4	800-755-0031
Midwestern State (Texas)	15,766	3,059	N.A.	43	572	23:1	23	4	817-689-4321
Millersville U. of Pennsylvania	8,449	3,620	52	N.A.	774	18:1	64	2	717-872-3371
Millikin (Ill.)	11,331	4,168	87	90	3,934	15:1	64	3	217-424-6210
Mills (Calif.)[1]	14,210	6,500	71	N.A.	6,894	11:1	57[3]	3	510-430-2135

Footnotes appear on page 178.

Deep pockets

Schools that gave the most in need-based aid from their own funds, per student who qualified for such aid

Swarthmore (Pa.)	$11,304	Mount Holyoke (Mass.)	9,564
Amherst College (Mass.)	11,256	Pine Manor (Mass.)	9,455
Vassar College (N.Y.)	11,225	Bryn Mawr College (Pa.)	9,434
Bennington College (Vt.)	11,050	Georgetown U. (D.C.)	9,329
Bowdoin College (Maine)	10,486	Barnard College (N.Y.)	9,256
Stanford U. (Calif.)	10,448	Caltech (Calif.)	9,247
Pitzer College (Calif.)	10,303	MIT (Mass.)	9,226
St. Lawrence U. (N.Y.)	10,041	Pepperdine U. (Calif.)	9,140
Brandeis U. (Mass.)	9,834	Harvard U. (Mass.)	9,088
Trinity College (Conn.)	9,775	Scripps College (Calif.)	9,028

	College name and location	Tuition and fees	Room and board	% of students receiving aid	% of need met	Average gift aid per student	Student/ faculty ratio	% who graduate in six years	Student academic level	Telephone
	Millsaps (Miss.)	$11,236	$4,250	64	80	$4,163	14:1	55	3	601-974-1050
	Milwaukee School of Engineering (Wis.)	10,800	3,000	82	82	2,198	15:1	49	2	414-277-7200
	Minot State (N.D.)	4,260	1,912	67	85	62	19:1	N.A.	3	701-857-3350
	Mississippi State	4,433	2,884	N.A.	97	1,160	26:1	52	3	601-325-2224
	Mississippi U. for Women	4,393	2,057	89	95	518	17:1	46	3	601-329-7106
	Missouri Southern State	3,650	2,490	78	75	70	25:1	32	4	417-625-9378
	Missouri Valley	8,650	4,950	69	85	6,998	18:1[18]	14	4	816-886-6925
	Missouri Western State	3,628	2,452	75	90	431	18:1	32	4	816-271-4263
	Molloy (N.Y.)	8,550	No dorms	95	85	887	11:1	62	4	516-678-5000
	Monmouth (Ill.)	13,000	3,800	88	100	2,119	11:1	70	3	800-747-2687
	Monmouth (N.J.)	12,290	5,170	62	87	2,816	15:1	52	3	908-571-3456
	Montana Mineral Science and Technology	5,743	3,210	60	90	494	16:1	57[7]	3	406-496-4178
	Montana State	6,500	3,600	51	95	222	17:1	40[7]	3	406-994-2452
	Montclair State (N.J.)	4,040	4,700	55	65	81	15:1	53	2	800-331-9205
	Moorhead State (Minn.)	4,428	2,601	61	N.A.	80	20:1	48	4	218-236-2161
	Moravian (Pa.)	14,490	4,470	82	N.A.	3,328	13:1	78[4]	2	215-861-1320
	Morehead State (Ky.)	4,800	2,840	70	70	450	20:1[18]	24[3]	N.A.	606-783-2000
	Morehouse (Ga.)[2,22]	8,000	5,224	71	77	1,117	17:1	45[7]	3	800-851-1254
	Morgan State (Md.)[2,12]	5,062	4,640	90	N.A.	N.A.	18:1	25	4	410-319-3000
	Morningside (Iowa)	10,376	3,520	87	85	3,475	15:1	41[7]	3	712-274-5111
	Morris (S.C.)[2]	4,405	2,475	93	N.A.	77	14:1	36	4	803-775-9371
	Morris Brown (Ga.)[2]	7,796	4,438	94	N.A.	N.A.	14:1	39[3]	4	404-220-0145
	Mount Holyoke (Mass.)[1]	18,555	5,520	65	87	5,961	10:1	85[7]	2	413-538-2023
	Mount Marty (S.D.)	7,466	2,980	95	89	2,340	12:1	38	3	800-658-4552
	Mount Mary (Wis.)[1]	8,100	2,868	65	65	787	15:1	62	4	414-259-9220
	Mount Mercy (Iowa)	9,900	3,330	85	88	1,883	15:1	52	3	319-363-8213
	Mount St. Clare (Iowa)	9,280	3,600	95	100	1,895	10:1	20	4	319-242-4153
	Mount St. Mary (N.Y.)	7,990	4,800	80	75	536	13:1	70	3	914-561-0800
	Mount St. Mary's (Calif.)[1]	11,750	4,816	70	N.A.	3,242	12:1	67	3	301-471-9516
	Mount St. Mary's (Md.)	11,725	6,100	N.A.	N.A.	N.A.	15:1	78	3	301-447-5214
	Mount Senario (Wis.)	7,655	3,800	95	N.A.	1,018	12:1	N.A.	4	715-532-5511
	Mount Union (Ohio)	12,320	3,530	90	80	4,321	15:1	53	3	216-821-5320
	Muhlenberg (Pa.)	16,385	4,410	60	93	3,469	13:1	82	2	215-821-3200
	Murray State (Ky.)	4,780	3,022	60	60	619	18:1	41	3	800-272-4678
	Muskingum (Ohio)	13,010	3,740	75	91	4,550	14:1	62	3	614-826-8137
	National–Louis (Ill.)	9,090	4,128	85	N.A.	1,382	13:1	45[7]	3	708-475-1100
	Nazareth College of Rochester (N.Y.)	10,280	4,900	84	99	2,074	14:1	58	3	800-462-3944
	Nebraska Wesleyan	9,186	3,200	90	80	2,537	14:1	60	3	402-465-2218
	Newberry (S.C.)	8,894	3,100	90	100	N.A.	13:1	49	4	800-845-4955
1	New College of the U. of South Florida	7,943	3,677	60	95	1,485	11:1	62[3]	1	813-359-4269
	New England (N.H.)	12,690	5,180	38	82	925	13:1	48	4	603-428-2223
77	New Jersey Institute of Technology	9,037	5,179	60	70	500	15:1	70	2	201-596-3300
	New Mexico Highlands	5,168	2,500	80	N.A.	206	23:1	22	3	505-425-7511
19	New Mexico Institute of Technology	5,646	3,426	N.A.	N.A.	741	13:1	40	2	505-835-5424
	New Mexico State	6,074	2,592	65	85	560	19:1	N.A.	3	505-646-3121
	New School for Social Research (N.Y.)	13,900	7,834	90	N.A.	2,988	9:1	55	2	212-229-5665
	New York Institute of Technology	8,650	5,160	80	N.A.	N.A.	19:1	36	4	800-345-6948
	New York University	17,640	7,065	66	84	2,632	13:1	68	2	212-998-4500
	Niagara (N.Y.)	10,070	4,638	83	87	1,770	16:1	60	3	716-286-8700
	Nicholls State (La.)	3,661	2,550	37	N.A.	1,721	23:1	34	5	504-448-4145
	North Adams State (Mass.)	7,540	4,000	50	42	278	20:1	46	4	413-664-4511
	North Carolina A&T State[2]	7,302[4]	3,130	70	64	646	14:1	37	4	919-334-7946
80	North Carolina State	8,788	3,150	40	97	381	14:1	59	2	919-515-2434
	North Carolina Wesleyan	8,350	4,130	90	77	765	12:1	35[7]	4	919-985-5100
	North Central (Ill.)	11,286	4,212	80	90	2,878	14:1	63	3	708-420-3414
	North Dakota State	5,498	2,590	60	N.A.	169	19:1	46	3	701-237-8643
	Northeastern (Mass.)[12]	12,771	7,080	55	80	1,003	11:1	43	3	617-373-2200
	Northeastern Illinois[12]	5,710	No dorms	37	N.A.	114	20:1	N.A.	4	312-794-2600
8	Northeast Louisiana	3,686	1,980	50	70	554	20:1	29	5	318-342-5252

Footnotes appear on page 178.

College name and location	Tuition and fees	Room and board	% of students receiving aid	% of need met	Average gift aid per student	Student/ faculty ratio	% who graduate in six years	Student academic level	Telephone
Northeast Missouri State	$4,436	$3,080	76	90	$646	16:1	54	2	816-785-4114
Northern Arizona	6,596	3,014	N.A.	69	546	20:1	40	3	602-523-5511
Northern Illinois	7,425	3,116	56	77	138	18:1	52	3	815-753-0446
Northern Kentucky	4,720	2,950	42	80	126	15:1	49	4	606-572-5220
Northern Michigan	4,800	3,800	71	100	430	20:1	39	4	906-227-2650
Northern Montana	5,442	3,470	70	N.A.	N.A.	17:1	30[3]	4	406-265-3704
Northern State (S.D.)	3,764	2,065	71	71	1,193	19:1	95	4	605-622-2544
North Georgia	4,400	2,475	80	N.A.	113	17:1	57	3	706-864-1800
Northland (Wis.)	9,800	3,750	N.A.	N.A.	2,197	16:1	46[7]	3	715-682-1224
North Park (Ill.)	12,190	4,090	89	88	2,808	12:1	56	3	312-583-2700
85 Northwestern (Ill.)	15,804	5,289	60	98	N.A.	8:1	89	1	708-491-7271
Northwestern Oklahoma State	3,844	1,956	70	95	286	18:1	23	4	405-327-1700
Northwestern State U. of Louisiana	4,282	2,154	60	N.A.	429	33:1	21	N.A.	318-357-4503
Northwest Missouri State	3,570	3,000	80	50	294	22:1	41	4	800-633-1175
Northwood Institute–Midland (Mich.)	8,622	4,065	70	93	1,786	26:1	60	3	517-837-4273
Norwich (Vt.)	13,460	5,270	N.A.	90	3,476	14:1	55	3	800-468-6679
Notre Dame (N.H.)	9,506	4,900	90	N.A.	1,628	12:1	70	4	603-669-4298
Oakland (Mich.)	8,210	3,890	20	87	299	19:1	50[7]	3	313-370-3360
Oakland City (Ind.)	7,076	2,840	95	N.A.	N.A.	15:1	85	4	812-749-1222
Oberlin (Ohio)	18,949	5,620	55	100	4,770	13:1	84	2	216-775-8411
Occidental (Calif.)	16,146	5,325	65	99	5,238	12:1	73	2	213-259-2700
Oglethorpe (Ga.)	11,990	4,020	70	88	4,441	14:1	70	2	404-364-8307
Ohio Northern	14,775	3,885	92	94	3,496	13:1	63	3	419-772-2260
Ohio State–Columbus	8,871	5,382	65	90	2,304	14:1	53	3	614-292-3980
60 Ohio University	7,250	3,957	56	77	1,514	17:1	62	3	614-593-4100
Ohio Wesleyan	15,726	5,382	66	100	4,679	13:1	72	2	614-368-3020
Oklahoma City	6,265	3,630	84	N.A.	2,884	21:1	N.A.	3	405-521-5050
Oklahoma Panhandle State	3,296	1,800	42	72	86	22:1	19[3]	4	405-349-2611
Oklahoma State	5,073	3,100	60	76	566	22:1	46	2	405-744-6876
Old Dominion (Va.)	9,464	4,134	N.A.	100	28	18:1	44	3	804-683-3637
Olivet (Mich.)	10,500	3,500	90	N.A.	N.A.	15:1	42[3]	3	616-749-7635
Oregon Institute of Technology	7,620	3,726	70	N.A.	N.A.	15:1	42	4	503-885-1150
Oregon State	7,890	3,444	65	N.A.	N.A.	17:1	N.A.	4	503-737-4411
Otterbein (Ohio)	12,192	4,314	90	90	2,671	13:1	58	3	614-890-0004
Our Lady of the Lake U. of San Antonio (Texas)	7,584	3,496	N.A.	70	1,357	17:1	34	N.A.	210-434-6711
Pace (N.Y.)[12]	10,780	4,660	N.A.	N.A.	2,272	22:1	60	3	212-346-1323
Pacific (Ore.)	13,490	3,815	81	N.A.	3,890	13:1	45	2	800-635-0561
Pacific Lutheran (Wash.)	13,280	4,030	67	83	2,348	14:1	68	2	206-535-7151
Park (Mo.)	3,540	3,780	95	N.A.	428	12:1	33[3]	3	800-745-7275
Pembroke State (N.C.)	6,454	2,580	41	51	128	16:1	38·	4	919-521-6262
Pennsylvania State	10,170	3,790	75	N.A.	1,636	19:1	60	2	814-865-5471
Pennsylvania State–The Behrend College	10,170	3,790	80	N.A.	1,958	18:1	60	3	814-898-6100

Footnotes appear on page 178.

Big on books

Schools with the most titles in their libraries, including periodicals and microfilm, in millions

Harvard University (Mass.)	16.1
Yale University (Conn.)	14.3
U. of California–Los Angeles	12.9
U. of California–Berkeley	12.2
U. of Illinois–Urbana/Champaign	12.0
Cornell University (N.Y.)	11.4
U. of Michigan	11.1
Columbia U. and Barnard (N.Y.)	10.2
U. of Washington	10.2
U. of Texas–Austin	10.1

	College name and location	Tuition and fees	Room and board	% of students receiving aid	% of need met	Average gift aid per student	Student/ faculty ratio	% who graduate in six years	Student academic level	Telephone
	Pepperdine (Calif.)	$17,260	$6,530	70	95	$10,663	14:1	68	2	310-456-4392
	Peru State (Neb.)	2,834	2,624	84	75	399	28:1	28[3]	4	402-872-2221
	Pfeiffer (N.C.)	8,190	3,180	67	88	1,390	16:1	48	4	800-338-2060
	Philadelphia Textiles and Science (Pa.)[9]	10,954	4,982	75	75	2,715	16:1	59	3	215-951-2800
	Phillips (Okla.)	9,310	2,904	88	78	3,013	13:1	36	3	405-237-4433
	Pine Manor (Mass.)[1]	15,915	6,460	44	90	3,278	13:1	53	4	617-731-7104
	Pittsburg State (Kans.)[1]	4,798	2,814	53	N.A.	N.A.	19:1	39[3]	4	316-235-4250
	Pitzer (Calif.)	18,198	5,582	N.A.	100	5,655	10:1	73	2	714-621-8129
	Plymouth State (N.H.)	8,050	3,870	49	97	278	20:1	N.A.	3	603-535-2237
	Polytechnic University (N.Y.)	15,800	4,700	85	80	4,487	14:1	60	2	718-260-3100
23	Pomona (Calif.)	16,900	6,920	52	100	4,983	9:1	88[7]	1	909-621-8134
	Portland State (Ore.)	7,029	4,168	42	72	439	18:1	20	3	503-725-3511
	Prairie View A&M (Texas)[2]	5,617	3,478	88	97	1,309	25:1	25	4	409-857-2618
	Pratt Institute (N.Y.)[9]	13,233	6,456	73	75	2,104	12:1	51[7]	2	718-636-3669
	Presbyterian (S.C.)	11,984	3,416	75	90	2,709	15:1	72	2	803-833-8230
	Prescott (Ariz.)	9,745	No dorms	66	66	2,570	7:1	20	3	602-776-5180
40	Princeton (N.J.)	18,940	5,710	42	100	3,283	6:1	95	1	609-258-3060
	Providence (R.I.)	13,775	5,900	53	95	2,204	14:1	93	2	401-865-2535
97	Purdue (Ind.)	8,850	4,130	43	95	264	17:1	66	3	317-494-1776
	Queens College–City U. of N.Y.	5,235	No dorms	32	60	80	18:1	43	2	718-997-5600
	Quincy (Ill.)	9,742	3,904	89	91	3,092	12:1	65	3	217-228-5215
	Quinnipiac (Conn.)	11,810	5,790	65	100	2,016	15:1	78	3	203-281-8600
	Radford (Va.)	6,684	4,110	43	90	104	24:1	53	3	703-831-5371
	Ramapo College of New Jersey	4,449	4,800	43	62	198	19:1	35	3	201-529-7600
	Randolph-Macon (Va.)	12,230	4,750	71	88	1,822	11:1	62	3	804-752-7305
	Randolph-Macon Woman's (Va.)[1]	13,320	5,780	N.A.	100	3,103	9:1	70	3	800-745-7692
	Reed (Ore.)	19,250	5,230	49	100	4,737	9:1	65	1	503-777-7511
	Regis (Colo.)	11,840	6,600	81	N.A.	4,837	16:1	35	4	303-458-4900
	Rensselaer Polytechnic Institute (N.Y.)	17,325	5,742	76	N.A.	3,386	11:1	75[7]	1	518-276-6216
	Rhode Island School of Design[9]	15,900	6,415	64	70	1,299	12:1	85[7]	2	401-454-6300
	Rhodes (Tenn.)	14,916	4,708	66	96	4,868	12:1	76	2	901-726-3700
2	Rice (Texas)	9,650	5,210	N.A.	N.A.	3,289	9:1	85	2	713-527-4036
	Rider (N.J.)	12,950	5,210	70	85	1,043	16:1	63	3	609-896-5042
	Ripon (Wis.)	14,520	3,810	88	100	5,544	11:1	62	3	800-947-4766
	Roanoke (Va.)	12,625	4,350	72	88	3,495	14:1	52	3	703-375-2270
	Robert Morris (Pa.)	6,670	4,106	64	83	560	22:1	45	4	412-262-8206
	Rochester Institute of Technology (N.Y.)	13,515	5,439	60	90	2,350	12:1	62	3	716-475-6631
	Rockford (Ill.)	11,500	3,800	86	100	3,408	12:1	60[3]	3	815-226-4050
	Rockhurst (Mo.)	9,120	3,840	87	93	3,422	14:1	59	3	816-926-4100
	Rocky Mountain (Mont.)	8,933	3,327	73	80	1,540	16:1	59	3	406-657-1026
	Roger Williams (R.I.)	12,070	5,650	30	80	1,263	19:1	43	4	401-254-3500
	Rollins (Fla.)	15,950	4,925	58	96	3,071	12:1	75	2	407-646-2161
	Rosary (Ill.)	10,550	4,490	70	75	2,102	11:1	65[7]	3	708-524-6800
	Rose-Hulman Inst. of Technology (Ind.)	12,330	3,900	90	85	1,438	13:1	74	1	812-877-1511
71	Rosemont (Pa.)[1]	11,075	5,700	60	94	1,262	10:1	73	3	215-526-2966
	Rowan State (N.J.)	3,983	4,800	55	100	346	17:1	47	3	609-863-5346
	Russell Sage (N.Y.)[1]	11,930	4,860	38	N.A.	2,536	9:1	55	3	800-999-3772
	Rust (Miss.)[2]	4,502	1,998	98	97	879	18:1	37	5	601-252-8000
3	Rutgers College–Rutgers U. (N.J.)	7,809	4,454	62	21	289	17:1	79	1	908-932-3770
	St. Ambrose (Iowa)	9,850	2,830	96	N.A.	2,596	11:1	68	3	800-383-2627
	St. Andrews Presbyterian (N.C.)	9,880	4,360	98	N.A.	1,562	11:1	55[7]	3	800-763-0198
	St. Anselm (N.H.)	12,140	5,200	67	86	2,381	16:1	75	3	603-641-7500
76	St. Bonaventure (N.Y.)	10,026	4,736	80	27	2,515	14:1	70	3	716-375-2400
	St. Cloud State (Minn.)	4,530	2,650	62	100	85	22:1	45	4	612-255-2244
	St. Edward's (Texas)	8,902	3,920	55	77	1,770	17:1	40	3	512-448-8500
	St. Francis (Ind.)	8,300	3,630	85	76	1,589	15:1	N.A.	3	219-434-3279
	St. Francis (N.Y.)	6,700	No dorms	56	46	691	23:1	34	4	718-522-2300
	St. Francis (Pa.)	11,074	4,720	84	85	4,077	15:1	63	3	814-472-3000
	St. John Fisher (N.Y.)	10,275	5,140	87	89	1,545	16:1	55	3	716-385-8064

Footnotes appear on page 178.

College name and location	Tuition and fees	Room and board	% of students receiving aid	% of need met	Average gift aid per student	Student/ faculty ratio	% who graduate in six years	Student academic level	Telephone
St. John's (Md.)	$16,350	$5,450	55	95	$4,256	8:1	61	2	800-727-9238
St. John's (Minn.)	11,428	3,936	72	75	2,028	13:1	71	3	612-363-2196
St. John's (N.M.)	16,300	5,450	55	98	4,746	8:1	64	2	800-331-5232
St. John's (N.Y.)	8,980	No dorms	70	N.A.	760	20:1	65	2	718-990-6240
St. Joseph's (Ind.)	10,830	3,900	73	99	2,924	12:1	58	4	800-447-8781
St. Joseph's (Maine)	9,740	4,850	72	78	2,177	14:1	67	4	800-338-7057
St. Joseph's (Pa.)	12,100	5,700	82	N.A.	2,239	16:1	74	3	215-660-1300
St. Lawrence (N.Y.)	18,190	5,530	70	97	7,357	12:1	84	3	315-379-5261
St. Leo (Fla.)	9,370	4,200	66	95	1,255	17:1	19[3]	3	904-588-8283
St. Louis (Mo.)	10,820	4,610	80	85	1,722[26]	15:1	65	3	314-658-2500
St. Martin's (Wash.)	10,870	4,060	72	N.A.	N.A.	12:1	45	4	206-438-4311
St. Mary's (Calif.)	12,738	6,110	45	70	1,725	16:1	69	3	510-631-4224
St. Mary's (Ind.)	12,507	4,244	44	100	1,903	11:1	79	3	219-284-4587
84 St. Mary's (Texas)	8,586	3,371	82	67	1,052	15:1	67	3	210-436-3126
14 St. Mary's of Maryland	6,700	4,500	50	90	492	14:1	63	2	800-492-7181
St. Mary's of Minnesota	10,380	3,470	60	95	1,392	14:1	61	4	800-635-5987
St. Michael's (Vt.)	12,430	5,600	62	96	2,241	14:1	75	2	802-654-3000
St. Norbert (Wis.)	11,465	4,245	89	90	3,017	15:1	73	3	800-236-4878
St. Olaf (Minn.)	13,560	3,640	60	100	2,140	12:1	81[7]	2	507-646-3025
St. Paul's (Va.)[2]	5,521	3,650	90	95	469	13:1	29	4	804-848-3984
St. Peter's (N.J.)	9,445	4,880	70	85	1,143	17:1	46[7]	4	201-915-9213
St. Thomas (Fla.)	9,680	4,600	82	N.A.	731	15:1	N.A.	4	305-628-6546
St. Thomas Aquinas (N.Y.)	8,150	5,400	68	N.A.	215	17:1	58	4	914-359-9500
St. Vincent (Pa.)	10,318	3,766	75	94	1,650	15:1	70	3	412-537-4540
99 Salem (N.C.)[1]	10,076	6,025	61	90	2,335	10:1	57	3	919-721-2621
Salem State (Mass.)	6,883	3,514	40	N.A.	N.A.	18:1	25[3]	3	508-741-6200
Salem-Teikyo (W.Va.)	9,233	3,952	95	100	603	12:1	N.A.	4	800-283-4562
Salisbury State (Md.)	5,694	4,490	N.A.	50	90	16:1	52	3	410-543-6161
Salve Regina (R.I.)	13,860	6,300	53	52	1,972	14:1	89	2	401-847-6650
38 Samford (Ala.)	7,770	3,738	80	75	2,193	15:1	51	3	800-888-7218
Sam Houston State (Texas)	5,536	2,090	33	80	186	24:1	31	4	409-294-1111
San Diego State (Calif.)	9,122	4,370	N.A.	75	85	19:1	37	N.A.	619-594-6871
San Francisco State (Calif.)	9,664	5,116	40	95	319	21:1	36	4	415-338-2017
San Jose State (Calif.)	9,104	4,956	26	N.A.	263	18:1	5[3]	3	408-924-2000
Santa Clara (Calif.)	12,879	5,903	56	97	1,917	14:1	82	3	408-554-4700
Sarah Lawrence (N.Y.)	18,460	6,500	50	100	3,444	6:1	80	1	914-395-2510
Savannah College of Art and Design (Ga.)[9]	9,180	5,000	60	N.A.	N.A.	19:1	60[3]	2	912-238-2483
Savannah State (Ga.)[2]	4,505	2,305	92	N.A.	N.A.	19:1	38[3]	3	912-356-2181
Schreiner (Texas)	8,610	5,670	65	76	3,520	13:1	29	3	800-343-4919
Scripps (Calif.)[1]	16,550	7,050	50	100	4,707	9:1	73	1	909-621-8149
Seattle Pacific (Wash.)	12,054	4,263	67	94	3,931	15:1	41	3	206-281-2021
Seattle University (Wash.)	12,150	4,050	70	90	2,709	14:1	45[3]	3	206-296-5800

Footnotes appear on page 178.

High on healing

Schools reporting the highest percentage of graduates entering medical school

Johns Hopkins University (Md.)	**27%**
Emory University (Ga.)	**17**
Heidelberg College (Ohio)	**16**
Xavier U. of Louisiana	**15**
Harvard University (Mass.)	**14**
New York University	**14**
Furman University (S.C.)	**13**
University of the South (Tenn.)	**13**
Bennett College (N.C.)	**12**
Columbia University (N.Y.)	**12**

	College name and location	Tuition and fees	Room and board	% of students receiving aid	% of need met	Average gift aid per student	Student/ faculty ratio	% who graduate in six years	Student academic level	Telephone
	Seton Hall (N.J.)	$11,654	$5,958	70	60	$1,485	17:1	61	3	201-761-9332
	Seton Hill (Pa.)	10,440	3,980	73	90	2,759	12:1	55	3	412-838-4255
	Sheldon Jackson (Alaska)	9,250	4,450	91	N.A.	2,365	10:1	17	N.A.	907-747-5221
	Shenandoah (Va.)	9,800	3,900	81	68	1,575	9:1	51	4	703-665-4581
	Shepherd (W.Va.)	4,670	3,500	39	64	227	18:1	74	2	304-876-2511
	Shippensburg U. of Pennsylvania	8,108	3,268	68	75	49[21]	20:1	65	3	717-532-1231
92	Siena (N.Y.)	10,505	4,905	75	N.A.	1,203	16:1	81	2	518-783-2423
	Simmons (Mass.)[1]	15,794	6,740	69	N.A.	3,880	10:1	69	3	617-738-2107
	Simpson (Iowa)	10,825	3,810	95	93	3,526	14:1	61	3	515-961-1624
	Sioux Falls (S.D.)	8,450	3,090	94	98	1,303	15:1	56[3]	4	605-331-6600
	Skidmore (N.Y.)	17,775	5,455	46	97	2,353	11:1	78	2	518-587-7569
	Slippery Rock (Pa.)	7,645	3,364	75	50	1,174	20:1	51	3	412-738-2015
	Smith (Mass.)[1]	18,136	6,100	54	100	5,320	10:1	85	2	413-585-2500
	Sonoma State (Calif.)	9,126	5,455	60	80	40[21]	20:1	26	N.A.	707-664-2778
	South Dakota State	4,183	2,014	80	98	162	17:1	47[7]	4	605-688-4121
	Southeastern Louisiana	3,974[5]	2,120	55	N.A.	27	24:1	24[7]	5	504-549-2123
	Southeastern Oklahoma State	3,544	2,048	70	80	122	19:1	26	4	405-924-0121
	Southeast Missouri State	3,758	3,320	50	20	378	24:1	35	4	314-651-2255
	Southern Arkansas	2,270	2,240	62	N.A.	414	19:1	24	4	501-235-4040
	Southern College of Technology (Ga.)	4,412	2,775	33	90	48	20:1	20	4	404-528-7281
	Southern Connecticut State	7,550	4,452	N.A.	N.A.	200	19:1	40	3	203-397-4450
	Southern Illinois U. at Carbondale	7,552[4]	3,038	88	99	148	17:1	43	4	618-453-4381
	Southern Illinois U. at Edwardsville	5,653[4]	4,388	60	98	32	16:1	32	3	618-692-3705
	Southern Methodist (Texas)	13,580	4,941	63	100	3,668	13:1	69	2	214-768-2058
	Southern Oregon State	6,819	3,300	N.A.	N.A.	45	18:1	43	4	503-552-6411
	Southern Vermont	8,570	4,304	61	100	1,560	18:1	46	4	802-442-5427
	Southwestern (Kans.)	6,500	3,532	87	N.A.	1,530	12:1	19[3]	3	316-221-4150
	Southwestern Oklahoma State	3,563	1,920	N.A.	100	251	19:1	30	4	405-774-3777
94	Southwestern University (Texas)	11,000	4,484	68	100	2,907	12:1	61	2	512-863-1200
	Southwest Missouri State	4,636	2,630	60	N.A.	456	23:1	36	3	417-836-5517
	Southwest State (Minn.)	4,935	2,750	84	82	191	19:1	40	4	507-537-6286
	Southwest Texas State	5,685	2,732	34	85	142	22:1	30	3	512-245-2364
	Spalding (Ky.)	7,896	2,600	90	N.A.	N.A.	15:1	50[3]	3	502-585-9911
17	Spelman (Ga.)[1,2]	7,452	5,250	N.A.	85	320	16:1	60	2	800-982-2411
	Spring Hill (Ala.)	11,425	4,590	70	N.A.	1,840	15:1	61	3	205-460-2130
86	Stanford (Calif.)	17,879	6,535	65	100	5,711	10:1	92	1	415-723-2091
18	State U. of N.Y.–Albany	6,783	4,136	90	100	1,141	18:1	71	2	518-442-5435
9	State U. of N.Y.–Binghamton	6,889	4,960	49	90	76	18:1	78	1	607-777-2171
	State U. of N.Y.–Brockport	6,840	4,630	86	100	69	20:1	43	3	716-395-2751
31	State U. of N.Y.–Buffalo	6,978	4,808	65	85	85	15:1	49	2	716-829-2111
	State U. of N.Y.–College at Buffalo	6,790	4,130	55	65	57	22:1	35	3	716-878-4017
	State U. of N.Y.–Cortland	6,822	4,040	85	N.A.	12	21:1	45	3	607-753-4711
	State U. of N.Y.–Fredonia	6,859	3,980	60	N.A.	26	20:1	58	3	716-673-3251
29	State U. of N.Y.–Geneseo	6,940	3,994	83	75	26[21]	20:1	68	1	716-245-5571
	State U. of N.Y.–New Paltz	6,854	4,240	55	95	1,277	18:1	50	2	914-257-3200
	State U. of N.Y. Oneonta	6,826	4,400	N.A.	55	13	20:1	56	3	607-436-2524
	State U. of N.Y.–Oswego	6,844	4,080	59	90	2	19:1	56	2	315-341-2250
	State U. of N.Y.–Plattsburgh	6,825	4,252	50	60	70	20:1	58	2	518-564-2040
	State U. of N.Y.–Potsdam	6,801	4,210	80	75	130	20:1	54	2	315-267-2180
	State U. of N.Y.–Purchase	6,850	4,104	68	75	60	18:1	38	2	914-251-6300
20	State U. of N.Y.–Stony Brook	6,889	4,400	N.A.	60	626[27]	17:1	53	2	516-632-6868
	Stephen F. Austin State (Texas)	5,595	3,602	55	78	189	21:1	40	4	409-568-2504
	Stephens (Mo.)[1]	13,410	5,040	70	68	3,139	11:1	45	3	314-876-7207
	Stetson (Fla.)	11,995	4,440	80	N.A.	1,540	12:1	57	3	904-822-7100
	Stevens Institute of Technology (N.J.)	16,490	5,290	80	N.A.	N.A.	10:1	75[3]	2	201-216-5194
	Stockton State (N.J.)	3,336	3,974	46	42	76	17:1	47	2	609-652-4261
	Stonehill (Mass.)	11,440	5,996	68	80	1,881	17:1	78	2	508-230-1373
	Suffolk (Mass.)	9,860	5,250	64	74	1,335	14:1	52	4	617-573-8460
	Sul Ross State (Texas)	5,540	2,920	N.A.	17	1,513	20:1	16	4	915-837-8052

Footnotes appear on page 178.

College name and location	Tuition and fees	Room and board	% of students receiving aid	% of need met	Average gift aid per student	Student/ faculty ratio	% who graduate in six years	Student academic level	Telephone
Susquehanna (Pa.)	$15,580	$4,370	60	90	$3,394	14:1	70	3	717-372-4260
43 Swarthmore (Pa.)	18,482	6,300	47	100	5,203	9:1	91	1	215-328-8300
Sweet Briar (Va.)[1]	14,107	5,755	66	100	3,162	8:1	60	2	804-381-6142
Syracuse (N.Y.)	14,705	6,600	62	81	3,385	10:1	64	2	315-443-3611
Tabor (Kans.)	8,050	3,410	100	N.A.	N.A.	16:1	37	3	800-822-6799
Talladega (Ala.)[2]	8,248	2,364	92	N.A.	N.A.	13:1	N.A.	3	205-761-6206
Tarleton State (Texas)	5,540[4]	3,140[4]	45	53	94	21:1	32	4	817-968-9125
Teikyo Marycrest (Iowa)	9,620	3,280	80	85	1,755	15:1	43	3	319-326-9225
Teikyo Westmar (Iowa)	9,780	3,350	100	98	1,239	14:1	42[7]	3	712-546-2070
Temple (Pa.)	9,802	5,210	N.A.	N.A.	939	12:1	43	3	215-204-7200
Tennessee Technological	5,522	2,762	75	90	354	20:1	52	3	615-372-3888
Texas A&I	5,388	2,816	70	75	230	18:1	35	4	512-595-2315
42 Texas A&M U.–College Station	5,937	3,738	59	97	407	22:1	66	2	409-845-3741
Texas Christian	8,950	3,210	58	58	1,876	15:1	65	2	817-921-7490
Texas Lutheran	7,460	3,280	88	99	2,021	15:1	37	4	210-372-8050
Texas Southern[2]	6,780	3,320	N.A.	100	59	19:1	10	N.A.	713-527-7070
Texas Tech	5,628	3,697	50	N.A.	N.A.	18:1	39	3	806-742-3661
Texas Woman's[1]	5,602	2,938	64	100	345	19:1[25]	34	N.A.	817-898-2000
Thiel (Pa.)	10,668	4,820	94	N.A.	2,273	11:1	54	4	412-589-2345
Thomas Aquinas (Calif.)	12,480	5,410	83	100	3,959	10:1	69	1	800-634-9797
Thomas More (Ky.)	9,137	3,780	70	80	1,342	12:1	55[7]	3	606-344-3332
Tougaloo (Miss.)[2]	5,170	1,840	82	99	731	15:1	35	3	601-977-7700
Towson State (Md.)	5,624	4,330	37	N.A.	118	17:1	47	3	410-830-2112
Transylvania (Ky.)	10,670	4,300	82	97	3,729	12:1	70	2	606-233-8242
4 Trenton State (N.J.)	5,934	5,400	46	95	2,609	15:1	72	2	609-771-2131
Trinity (Conn.)	18,480	5,420	46	100	3,918	10:1	88	2	203-297-2180
41 Trinity University (Texas)	11,720	4,640	73	100	2,531	10:1	73	1	210-736-7207
Tri-State (Ind.)	9,552	4,200	74	93	2,751	13:1	58	4	219-665-4100
Tufts (Mass.)	19,269	5,693	39	100	N.A.	13:1	90	1	617-627-3170
Tulane (La.)	18,760	5,730	48	49	6,981	12:1	80	2	504-865-5731
Tusculum (Tenn.)	7,100	3,300	90	90	857	15:1	33	4	615-636-7312
Tuskegee (Ala.)[2]	6,734	3,394	85	92	493	13:1	52	4	205-727-8500
Union (Ky.)	7,000	2,790	89	100	1,569	13:1	43	3	800-489-8646
Union (Neb.)	8,420	2,700	82	82	1,820	12:1	42	3	402-486-2504
Union (N.Y.)	17,877	5,940	45	100	3,446	11:1	86	2	518-388-6112
U.S. Air Force Academy (Colo.)[9]	0	0	N.A.	100	N.A.	8:1	71[3]	1	719-472-2520
U.S. Coast Guard Academy (Conn.)[9]	1,500	0	100	N.A.	N.A.	8:1[18]	64[7]	1	203-444-8501
U.S. International (Calif.)[9]	10,875	4,881	N.A.	93	2,777	15:1	88	3	619-693-4772
U.S. Merchant Marine Academy (N.Y.)[9]	4,090	0	11	90	N.A.	11:1	62	2	516-773-5391
U.S. Military Academy (N.Y.)[9]	0	0	N.A.	N.A.	N.A.	9:1	76	1	914-938-4041
U.S. Naval Academy (Md.)[9]	0	0	N.A.	100	N.A.	7:1	75[3]	1	410-267-4361
U. of Akron (Ohio)	7,580	3,660	N.A.	N.A.	174	20:1	41	4	216-972-7100

Footnotes appear on page 178.

Legions of lawyers

Schools with the highest percentage of graduates entering law school

Columbia University (N.Y.)	25%
Claremont McKenna (Calif.)	21
University of Chicago (Ill.)	18
Emory University (Ga.)	16
Brandeis University (Mass.)	15
Tulane University (La.)	15
University of the South (Tenn.)	15
Harvard University (Mass.)	14
Sarah Lawrence College (N.Y.)	14
Furman University (S.C.)	13
New York University	13

	College name and location	Tuition and fees	Room and board	% of students receiving aid	% of need met	Average gift aid per student	Student/ faculty ratio	% who graduate in six years	Student academic level	Telephone
	U. of Alabama–Tuscaloosa	$5,424	$3,520	43	N.A.	$379	19:1	48[7]	3	205-348-5666
	U. of Alaska–Anchorage[12]	5,106	2,300[10]	58	70	118	22:1	N.A.	4	907-786-1525
	U. of Alaska–Fairbanks[12]	5,190	3,520	70	N.A.	148	14:1	N.A.	3	907-474-7521
	U. of Arizona	7,350	3,968	48	N.A.	1,022	20:1	49	2	602-621-3237
	U. of Arkansas–Fayetteville	4,958	3,225	71	77	530	18:1	39	4	501-575-5346
	U. of Arkansas–Monticello	3,492	2,220	70	74	1,733	20:1	25	4	501-460-1026
	U. of Bridgeport (Conn.)	12,668	6,540	74	100	3,501	8:1	65	4	203-576-4552
68	U. of California–Berkeley	12,034	5,992	51	100	869	17:1	77	1	510-642-3175
98	U. of California–Davis	11,673	5,822	66	60	386	18:1	75	2	916-752-2971
	U. of California–Irvine	11,611	5,083	N.A.	98	449	20:1	65	3	714-856-6703
81	U. of California–Los Angeles	11,612	5,410	89	85	N.A.	17:1	74	1	310-825-3101
	U. of California–Riverside	11,814	5,430	41	N.A.	N.A.	14:1	63	2	909-787-4531
	U. of California–San Diego	11,707	6,562	42	100	439	19:1	66	2	619-534-4831
	U. of California–Santa Barbara	11,676	5,807	36	N.A.	479	18:1	66	2	805-893-2485
	U. of California–Santa Cruz	11,828	5,904	N.A.	N.A.	541	19:1	58	2	408-459-4008
	U. of Central Arkansas	3,274	2,500	62	47	1,369	20:1	30	4	501-450-3128
	U. of Central Florida	6,659	4,145	43	75	203	17:1	46	3	407-823-3000
	U. of Central Oklahoma	3,559	2,150	N.A.	N.A.	68	24:1	22	4	405-341-2980
	U. of Chicago (Ill.)	18,387	6,130	65	100	5,791	5:1[18]	86	1	312-702-8650
	U. of Cincinnati (Ohio)	8,712	4,371	65	65	755	14:1	48	3	513-556-1100
	U. of Colorado–Boulder	12,087	3,830	40	N.A.	N.A.	19:1	66	3	303-492-6301
	U. of Connecticut	11,410	4,878	33	37	614	10:1[18]	68	2	203-486-3137
	U. of Dallas (Texas)	10,200	4,683	90	92	3,249	12:1	55	2	214-721-5266
	U. of Dayton (Ohio)	11,090	4,030	60	100	2,423	15:1	69[7]	3	513-229-4411
	U. of Delaware	10,048	4,030	53	21	671	17:1	71	2	302-831-8123
	U. of Denver (Colo.)	14,562	4,500	50	100	4,371	13:1	66	3	303-871-2036
	U. of Detroit Mercy (Mich.)[12]	10,900	3,500	70	75	2,642	15:1	51	3	313-993-1245
	U. of Dubuque (Iowa)	10,530	3,620	86	N.A.	2,714	15:1	12	3	319-589-3200
	U. of Evansville (Ind.)	11,330	4,170	86	85	3,203	13:1	60	3	812-479-2468
	U. of Findlay (Ohio)	11,024	4,780	85	85	1,498	14:1	45	4	800-548-0932
35	U. of Florida	6,890	4,080	80	83	332	28:1	60	2	904-392-1365
21	U. of Georgia	5,918	3,285	50	95	258	14:1	61	3	706-542-8776
	U. of Hartford (Conn.)	14,260	5,598	63	62	3,642	11:1	54	3	203-768-4296
	U. of Hawaii–Hilo	2,800	2,041	41	N.A.	105	13:1	30	3	808-933-3414
	U. of Hawaii–Manoa	4,358	3,505	14	100	840	11:1	N.A.	N.A.	808-956-8975
	U. of Houston (Texas)	5,550	3,770	N.A.	75	785	20:1	31	3	713-743-1010
	U. of Idaho	5,326	3,404	60	N.A.	330	17:1	42	3	208-885-6326
	U. of Illinois–Chicago	7,504	4,988	60	N.A.	268	11:1	32	4	312-996-0998
6	U. of Illinois–Urbana/Champaign	7,658	4,358	86	N.A.	454	16:1	79	2	217-333-2033
34	U. of Iowa	7,740	3,306	75	N.A.	332	16:1	60	3	319-335-3847
	U. of Kansas	6,535	3,280	33	100	737	16:1	55	3	913-864-3911
26	U. of Kentucky	6,198	2,952	52	N.A.	419	16:1	49	3	606-257-2000

Footnotes appear on page 178.

Glorious mosaics

Schools from MONEY's top 100 with the highest percentage of minority students*

St. Mary's University (Texas)	**70%**
University of California–Los Angeles	**54**
University of California–Berkeley	**52**
Stanford University (Calif.)	**42**
New Jersey Institute of Technology	**41**
University of California–Davis	**39**
Columbia University (N.Y.)	**37**
Pomona College (Calif.)	**36**
California Institute of Technology	**34**
Harvard University (Mass.)	**34**
Livingston College (N.J.)	**34**
Rutgers College (N.J.)	**34**

*Excluding historically black colleges

College name and location	Tuition and fees	Room and board	% of students receiving aid	% of need met	Average gift aid per student	Student/ faculty ratio	% who graduate in six years	Student academic level	Telephone
U. of LaVerne (Calif.)	$12,775	$4,550	74	N.A.	N.A.	17:1	43[3]	3	714-593-3511
U. of Louisville (Ky.)	5,270	3,468	N.A.	67	$758	19:1	30	3	502-588-6531
U. of Maine	8,800	4,580	57	31	698	16:1	55	3	207-581-1561
U. of Maine–Farmington	6,560	3,790	65	N.A.	N.A.	16:1	52	3	207-778-7050
U. of Maine–Fort Kent	6,510	3,600	90	89	219	11:1	44	4	207-834-3162
U. of Maine–Machias	6,535	3,530	65	50	25	16:1	45	4	207-255-3313
U. of Maine–Presque Isle	6,600	3,364	75	N.A.	88	13:1	24	4	207-764-0311
U. of Mary (N.D.)	6,340	2,570	89	82	874	17:1	35[3]	4	701-255-7500
U. of Maryland–Baltimore County	8,594	4,208	46	N.A.	434	17:1	35	2	410-455-2291
U. of Maryland–College Park	8,783	5,003	36	53	470	14:1	64	3	301-314-8385
U. of Maryland–Eastern Shore[2]	7,117	3,580	90	82	930	18:1	29[7]	4	410-651-6410
U. of Massachusetts–Amherst	11,813	3,897	51	85	785	18:1	66	3	413-545-0222
U. of Massachusetts–Boston	10,528	No dorms	53	N.A.	310[4]	16:1	38	3	617-287-6100
U. of Massachusetts–Dartmouth	8,049	4,400	N.A.	100	158	16:1	48[7]	3	508-999-8605
U. of Miami (Fla.)	16,060	6,232	80	N.A.	5,008	8:1	55	2	305-284-4323
U. of Michigan	15,145	4,482	35	80[28]	1,034	11:1	85	1	313-764-7433
U. of Minnesota–Duluth	8,800[4]	3,375	N.A.	61	138	17:1	40	4	218-726-7171
U. of Minnesota–Morris	10,158	3,060	87	100	289	16:1	49	2	612-589-6035
U. of Minnesota–Twin Cities	9,458	3,300	N.A.	N.A.	431	10:1[18]	36	3	612-625-2008
U. of Mississippi	5,116	2,900	63	90	608	19:1	52	3	601-232-7226
U. of Missouri–Columbia	7,178	3,160	60	80	425	15:1	53	2	314-882-7786
U. of Missouri–Kansas City	8,651	4,540	55	80	701	12:1	37	2	816-235-1111
U. of Missouri–Rolla	8,692	3,485	67	85	1,447	15:1	45	2	314-341-4164
U. of Montana	6,009	3,680	55	N.A.	342	19:1	30	4	406-243-4277
U. of Montevallo (Ala.)	4,564	3,030	66	N.A.	394	24:1	67	3	205-665-6030
U. of Nebraska–Kearney	3,093	2,490	N.A.	96	208	22:1	45[7]	3	308-234-8526
U. of Nebraska–Lincoln	5,980	2,915	39	94	491	16:1	52	3	402-472-3620
U. of Nebraska–Omaha	3,765	No dorms	45	N.A.	N.A.	30:1	N.A.	4	402-554-2393
U. of Nevada–Las Vegas[12]	6,005	5,000	N.A.	N.A.	436	25:1	27	3	702-739-3443
U. of Nevada–Reno	5,965	4,070	50	N.A.	556	21:1	N.A.	3	702-784-6865
U. of New England (Maine)	11,200	4,850	87	N.A.	N.A.	14:1	58[3]	3	207-283-0171
U. of New Hampshire	11,966	3,862	61	42	794	18:1	67	3	603-862-1360
U. of New Mexico	6,268	3,021	55	N.A.	355	15:1	32	3	505-277-2446
U. of New Orleans (La.)	5,154	3,476	61	57	115	20:1	15	4	504-286-6595
U. of North Alabama	2,060	2,684	40	55	136	24:1	30	4	205-760-4608
U. of North Carolina–Asheville	6,752	3,270	35	74	227	14:1	34	2	704-251-6481
U. of North Carolina–Chapel Hill	8,461	3,950	38	95	422	9:1[18]	82	1	919-966-3621
U. of North Carolina–Charlotte	7,580	3,300	40	90	163	16:1	49	3	704-547-2213
U. of North Carolina–Greensboro	7,325	2,842	43	80	241	14:1	48	3	919-334-5243
U. of North Carolina–Wilmington	7,642	3,310	38	79	210	16:1	46	3	919-395-3243
U. of North Dakota	5,612	2,580	45	N.A.	114	19:1	46[7]	4	701-777-3821
U. of Northern Colorado	7,400	3,894	57	74	119	20:1	41	3	303-351-2881
U. of Northern Iowa	5,994	2,620	56	70	344	16:1	62	3	319-273-2281
U. of North Texas	5,592	3,579	30	N.A.	N.A.	18:1	32	3	817-565-2681
U. of Notre Dame (Ind.)	15,810	4,020	68	85	1,938	12:1	94	1	219-631-7505
U. of Oklahoma	5,196	3,526	60	80	659	15:1[18]	42	3	405-325-2251
U. of Oregon	9,247	3,550	45	N.A.	383	18:1	54	3	503-346-3201
U. of Pennsylvania	17,838	6,534	43	100	3,365	9:1	90	1	215-898-7507
U. of Pittsburgh (Pa.)	10,708	4,130	N.A.	74	792	16:1	60	N.A.	412-624-7488
U. of Pittsburgh–Bradford (Pa.)	10,700	4,100	74	N.A.	808	14:1	50	4	814-362-7555
U. of Pittsburgh–Greensburg (Pa.)	10,620	3,620	76	65	N.A.	18:1	53	4	412-836-9880
U. of Pittsburgh–Johnstown (Pa.)	10,800	3,704	76	88	43	20:1	74[3]	3	814-269-7050
U. of Portland (Ore.)	11,120	3,940	75	88	2,383	17:1	60	3	503-283-7147
U. of Puget Sound (Wash.)	15,220	4,300	70	85	2,734	13:1	58	2	206-756-3211
U. of Redlands (Calif.)	15,985	5,999	75	98	4,163	13:1	57	3	909-335-4074
U. of Rhode Island	10,606	5,148	65	N.A.	631	16:1	62	3	401-792-9800
U. of Richmond (Va.)	13,540	3,140	54	100	2,423	12:1	83	2	804-289-8640
U. of Rio Grande (Ohio)	6,252	3,555	82	100	527	18:1	60	4	614-245-5353
U. of Rochester (N.Y.)	17,400	6,296	87	N.A.	4,766	12:1	77	2	716-275-3221

Footnotes appear on page 178.

	College name and location	Tuition and fees	Room and board	% of students receiving aid	% of need met	Average gift aid per student	Student/faculty ratio	% who graduate in six years	Student academic level	Telephone
	U. of St. Thomas (Minn.)	$11,712	$4,037	66	91	$1,426	17:1	68	3	612-962-6150
	U. of St. Thomas (Texas)	8,042	3,870	56	N.A.	5,263	17:1[25]	70	2	713-525-3500
	U. of San Diego (Calif.)	12,930	6,520	52	98	2,971	18:1	63	2	619-260-4506
	U. of San Francisco (Calif.)	12,478	6,174	46	82	2,225	17:1	57	3	415-666-6563
	U. of Scranton (Pa.)	11,490	5,456	80	73	1,831	16:1	84	3	717-941-7540
	U. of South Alabama	2,965	2,958	63	N.A.	N.A.	28:1	12[3]	4	205-460-6141
	U. of South Carolina–Coastal Carolina	6,160	3,670	68	62	222	17:1	35	4	800-277-7000
58	U. of South Carolina–Columbia	7,808	3,218	72	N.A.	250	16:1	61	3	803-777-7700
	U. of South Dakota–Vermillion	3,975	2,428	85	81	280	18:1	49	3	605-677-5434
	U. of Southern California	16,800	6,080	N.A.	60	4,870	13:1	66	2	213-740-1111
	U. of Southern Colorado	6,385	3,600	77	N.A.	N.A.	18:1	27	4	719-549-2461
	U. of Southern Indiana	4,825	1,660	45	62	290	20:1	26	4	800-467-1965
	U. of Southern Maine[12]	7,760	4,219	N.A.	N.A.	113	15:1	N.A.	4	207-780-5670
	U. of Southern Mississippi	4,852	2,470	68	N.A.	N.A.	17:1	42	N.A.	601-266-5555
	U. of South Florida	6,758	3,520	68	61	252	15:1	46	3	813-974-3350
	U. of Southwestern Louisiana	4,098[4]	2,110	53	N.A.	N.A.	25:1	27	N.A.	318-231-6467
	U. of Tampa (Fla.)	11,985	4,200	82	N.A.	N.A.	16:1	41	3	813-253-6228
	U. of Tennessee–Chattanooga	5,550	3,360	N.A.	46	1,031	17:1	33	3	615-755-4662
	U. of Tennessee–Knoxville	5,762	3,262	41	52	238	17:1	48	3	615-974-2184
	U. of Texas–Arlington	4,412	4,050	35	80	354	28:1	28	3	817-273-2118
16	U. of Texas–Austin	4,830	4,100	50	78	1,015	20:1	64	2	512-471-7601
	U. of Texas–Dallas[12]	5,530	No dorms	38	90	90[4]	19:1	N.A.	2	214-690-2294
	U. of Texas–El Paso	5,565	3,850	38	N.A.	577	24:1	12[3]	4	915-747-5576
	U. of the District of Columbia[2,12]	2,990	No dorms	15	11	215	14:1	28	N.A.	202-282-3200
	U. of the Pacific (Calif.)	15,800	5,300	64	71	3,477	15:1	64	3	209-946-2211
55	U. of the South (Tenn.)	14,910	3,920	55	100	3,080	11:1	79	2	615-598-1238
	U. of Toledo (Ohio)	4,522	3,401	37	30	752	18:1	47	3	419-537-2696
62	U. of Tulsa (Okla.)	9,995	3,958	75	97	2,985	12:1	44	2	918-631-2307
	U. of Utah	6,741	3,575	N.A.	70	251	15:1	34	3	801-581-7281
	U. of Vermont	15,344	4,763	87	89	1,482	15:1	78	2	802-656-3370
52	U. of Virginia	12,254	3,614	33	86	990	11:1	92	1	804-982-3200
	U. of Virginia–Clinch Valley	6,826	3,400	91	N.A.	1,251	23:1	28	4	703-328-0102
11	U. of Washington	7,134	4,700	33	79	151	11:1	63	2	206-543-9686
	U. of West Florida	6,605	3,760	35	90	300	26:1	33	3	904-474-2230
	U. of Wisconsin–Eau Claire	6,680	2,605	48	N.A.	45	18:1	49	3	715-836-5415
	U. of Wisconsin–Green Bay	6,552	2,381	65	98	184	22:1	38	3	414-465-2111
	U. of Wisconsin–La Crosse	6,256	2,210	48	N.A.	25	19:1	47	3	608-785-8067
30	U. of Wisconsin–Madison	8,200	3,850	39	N.A.	244	12:1	69	2	608-262-3961
	U. of Wisconsin–Milwaukee[12]	8,445	3,380	48	87	164	19:1	35	4	414-229-3800
	U. of Wisconsin–Oshkosh	6,465[4]	2,176	45	88	831	20:1	N.A.	3	414-424-0202
	U. of Wisconsin–Platteville	6,647	2,518	74	N.A.	N.A.	20:1	52[3]	3	608-342-1125
	U. of Wisconsin–Stevens Point	6,770	3,030	46	N.A.	N.A.	19:1	24[3]	3	715-346-2441

Footnotes appear on page 178.

Grants for grades

Schools that award the most in non-need-based scholarships per undergraduate

Buena Vista College (Iowa)	$3,955
Jamestown College (N.D.)	3,493
Bard College (N.Y.)	3,366
Wabash College (Ind.)	3,188
Transylvania University (Ky.)	3,129
Carthage College (Wis.)	2,892
Alma College (Mich.)	2,717
Franklin College (Ind.)	2,714
Case Western Reserve (Ohio)	2,696
Mercer University (Ga.)	2,658

College name and location	Tuition and fees	Room and board	% of students receiving aid	% of need met	Average gift aid per student	Student/ faculty ratio	% who graduate in six years	Student academic level	Telephone
U. of Wisconsin–Stout	$6,623	$2,464	49	N.A.	$11[21]	20:1	43	3	715-232-1411
U. of Wisconsin–Superior	6,529	2,470	80	81	471	12:1	25	3	715-394-8230
U. of Wisconsin–Whitewater	6,224	2,284	N.A.	98	N.A.	20:1	52	3	414-472-1440
U. of Wyoming	5,182	3,343	65	81	566	18:1	44	3	307-766-5160
Upsala (N.J.)	12,500	5,260	89	N.A.	N.A.	16:1	45[7]	3	201-266-7191
Urbana (Ohio)	8,437	4,140	92	75	1,106	14:1	13	4	513-652-1301
Ursinus (Pa.)	14,265	4,900	78	93	5,218	12:1	77	2	215-489-4111
Utah State	5,298	3,105	65	80	1,872	19:1	N.A.	4	801-750-1096
Utica College of Syracuse U. (N.Y.)	11,980	4,734	63	N.A.	2,169	15:1	56	3	800-782-8884
Valley City State (N.D.)	4,531	2,230	81	78	264	15:1	36	4	701-845-7101
Valparaiso (Ind.)	11,720	3,090	76	76	2,453	14:1	74	2	219-464-5011
Vanderbilt (Tenn.)	17,480	6,010	46	90	4,010	8:1	81	2	615-322-2561
Vassar (N.Y.)	18,456	5,750	55	57	5,845	11:1	84	1	914-437-7300
Villa Julie (Md.)	6,880	3,000[10]	80	N.A.	N.A.	15:1	N.A.	3	410-486-7001
Villanova (Pa.)	14,790	5,770	60	65	2,696	12:1	86	2	215-645-4000
Virginia Commonwealth	10,305	3,860	65	100	662	14:1	44	3	804-367-1222
Virginia Intermont	8,270	3,980	78	N.A.	N.A.	8:1	30[3]	4	800-451-1842
Virginia Military Institute[9,22]	10,690[23]	3,690	60	92	1,594	13:1	66	3	703-464-7211
91 Virginia Polytechnic Institute & State	9,680	2,876	53	70	424	17:1	70	2	703-231-6267
Virginia Wesleyan	10,150	4,650	72	50	2,093	16:1	61	3	804-455-3208
Viterbo (Wis.)	8,775	3,360	90	90	1,623	12:1	66	4	608-791-0420
36 Wabash (Ind.)[22]	12,450	4,000	94	100	6,550	11:1	77	2	317-364-4225
Wagner (N.Y.)	12,500	5,250	70	78	1,807	12:1	48	3	718-390-3411
70 Wake Forest (N.C.)	13,000	4,300	63	N.A.	2,435	13:1	85	2	919-759-5201
Walsh (Ohio)	7,710	3,930	85	90	883	19:1	70	3	216-499-7090
Warren Wilson (N.C.)[15]	12,917	2,852	79	81	1,164	11:1	68[3]	3	704-298-3325
Wartburg (Iowa)	11,080	3,375	92	98	2,489	14:1	63	3	319-352-8264
Washburn U. of Topeka (Kans.)[12]	4,562	3,100	N.A.	N.A.	663	17:1	50	4	913-231-1010
Washington (Md.)	13,952	5,318	69	100	3,824	12:1	65	3	410-778-7700
Washington and Jefferson (Pa.)	15,620	3,740	70	90	3,110	12:1	85	3	412-223-6025
45 Washington and Lee (Va.)	13,235	4,260	45	95	1,588	11:1	88	1	703-463-8710
Washington State	7,259	3,832	33	100	320	16:1	55	2	509-335-5586
Washington University (Mo.)	17,776	5,731	55	81	4,066	6:1	85	2	314-935-6000
Waynesburg (Pa.)	8,580	3,380	88	80	2,161	16:1	46	3	412-852-3248
Wayne State (Neb.)	2,826	2,640	58	N.A.	490	18:1	38[7]	4	402-375-7234
Wayne State University (Mich.)[12]	6,350	1,380	N.A.	N.A.	633	8:1	37	3	313-577-3577
Webber (Fla.)	5,750	2,900	80	68	613	16:1	91	3	813-638-2910
Webb Inst. of Naval Architecture (N.Y.)[9]	0	4,800	20	N.A.	N.A.	5:1	67[3]	1	516-671-2213
Weber State (Utah)	4,866	2,490	50	N.A.	N.A.	21:1	35[3]	4	801-626-6743
Wellesley (Mass.)[1]	17,725	5,960	53	100	4,519	10:1	85	1	617-283-2270
78 Wells (N.Y.)[1]	14,100	5,300	84	95	5,367	8:1	69	2	315-364-3264
Wentworth Institute of Technology (Mass.)	9,250	5,950	43	N.A.	617	20:1	N.A.	4	617-442-9010
Wesley (Del.)	9,645	4,100	85	80	947	16:1	53	4	302-736-2400
96 Wesleyan (Ga.)[1]	11,195	4,250	80	90	3,972	14:1	55	3	800-447-6610
Wesleyan University (Conn.)	18,410	4,830	49	100	3,718	11:1	90	1	203-347-9411
Westbrook (Maine)	11,000	4,900	82	85	2,278	10:1	N.A.	4	207-797-7261
West Chester (Pa.)	7,627	3,988	44	N.A.	N.A.	18:1	59	3	215-436-3411
Western Carolina (N.C.)	7,147[4]	2,310	53	87	373	18:1	45	3	704-227-7317
Western Connecticut State	7,720	3,562	33	N.A.	37	16:1	N.A.	4	203-797-4297
Western Illinois	6,244	3,043	70	82	106	18:1	45	3	309-298-3157
Western Kentucky	4,912	2,780	42	75	528	19:1	28[7]	4	502-745-2551
Western Maryland	13,750	5,240	78	95	4,209	13:1	58	3	410-857-2230
Western Michigan	6,710	3,940	63	92	271	19:1	53	3	616-387-2000
Western New England (Mass.)	9,274	5,400	49	73	376	17:1	47	4	413-782-1321
Western State of Colorado	5,918	3,741	70	80	43	20:1	20[7]	3	303-943-2119
Western Washington	7,110	3,956	66	N.A.	85	21:1	49	3	206-650-3440
Westfield State (Mass.)	6,890	3,942	51	67	133	18:1	60	3	413-568-3311
West Georgia	4,911	2,614	63	N.A.	160	25:1	31	4	404-836-6416
West Liberty State (W.Va.)	3,800	2,900	55	60	116	18:1	43	3	304-336-8076

Footnotes appear on page 178.

College name and location	Tuition and fees	Room and board	% of students receiving aid	% of need met	Average gift aid per student	Student/ faculty ratio	% who graduate in six years	Student academic level	Telephone
Westminster (Mo.)	$9,950	$3,800	75	95	$2,999	14:1	57	3	314-642-3365
Westminster (Pa.)	11,770	3,270	82	95	3,368	15:1	70	3	412-946-7100
West Virginia	5,870	4,038	55	92	399	18:1	55	4	800-344-9881
West Virginia Institute of Technology	4,002	3,752	41	N.A.	201	14:1	50	4	304-442-3167
West Virginia Wesleyan	13,400	3,500	82	N.A.	5,105	15:1	57	3	800-722-9933
Wheaton (Mass.)	17,790	6,050	58	93	4,590	14:1	68	3	508-285-7722
Wheeling Jesuit (W.Va.)	10,000	4,370	83	92	2,422	13:1	61	3	304-243-2359
Wheelock (Mass.)	12,640	5,360	69	90	3,014	16:1	69	4	617-734-5200
Whitman (Wash.)	15,805	4,790	80	100	3,832	11:1	69	2	509-527-5176
Whittier (Calif.)	16,181	5,480	76	95	5,409	13:1	47	3	310-907-4238
Whitworth (Wash.)	11,965	4,300	82	93	3,509	15:1	65	2	509-466-3212
Wichita State (Kans.)	6,527	3,005	60	50	254	18:1[18]	N.A.	4	316-689-3085
100 Widener (Pa.)	11,740	4,860	65	97	1,502	12:1	65	3	215-499-4126
Wiley (Texas)[2]	3,450	2,718	99	91	671	15:1	10	N.A.	903-927-3311
Wilkes (Pa.)	10,898	4,830	80	89	1,704	14:1	53	3	717-824-9890
Willamette (Ore.)	13,665	4,420	76	99	3,603	13:1	67	2	503-370-6303
William Jewell (Mo.)	9,720	2,780	92	95	2,090	14:1	57	3	800-753-7009
William Paterson of New Jersey	3,728	4,510	31	45	70	14:1	47	4	201-595-2125
64 Williams (Mass.)	18,795	5,595	50	100	3,463	11:1	95	1	413-597-2211
William Woods (Mo.)[1]	9,960	4,200	85	90	1,927	13:1	41	3	800-995-3159
Wilmington (Ohio)	9,830	3,870	90	N.A.	N.A.	17:1	46	3	513-382-6661
Wilson (Pa.)	11,546	5,084	83	98	3,686	7:1	66	3	717-264-4141
Winona State (Minn.)	4,600	2,800	70	95	73	20:1	48	3	507-457-5100
Winston-Salem State (N.C.)[2]	6,606	2,900	75	89	133	15:1	31	4	919-750-2070
Winthrop (S.C.)	6,110	3,206	48	N.A.	431	17:1	49	3	803-323-2191
Wittenberg (Ohio)	15,726	4,272	60	95	4,189	13:1	70[7]	2	513-327-6314
Wofford (S.C.)	11,480	4,150	73	95	2,828	15:1	73	2	803-597-4130
Worcester Polytechnic Institute (Mass.)	15,290	5,060	75	90	3,566	11:1	77[7]	2	508-831-5286
Wright State (Ohio)	5,868	3,600	49	97	N.A.	20:1	33	4	513-873-2211
Xavier (Ohio)	10,970	4,740	80	90	3,110	16:1	64	3	513-745-3301
Xavier U. of Louisiana[2]	6,650	3,800	88	80	1,096	16:1	43	4	504-483-7388
28 Yale (Conn.)	18,630	6,480	44	100	3,813	7:1[18]	95[7]	1	203-432-1900
York College–City U. of N.Y.[12]	5,134	No dorms	44	65	131	17:1	23	3	718-262-2165
York College of Pennsylvania	4,995	3,350	57	98	340	19:1	79	3	717-849-1600
Youngstown State (Ohio)	5,112	3,675	60	63	247	20:1	31	4	216-742-3150

Notes and explanations:

[1] Women's college
[2] Historically black college
[3] Four-year rate
[4] Estimate
[5] Includes book rental
[6] Figure does not include athletic scholarships
[7] Five-year rate
[8] Includes some private scholarship money
[9] Specialty school. Not included in MONEY's value study.
[10] Room only; meals not included
[11] Comprehensive tuition price includes room and board
[12] School with a large part-time student enrollment. Not included in MONEY's value study.
[13] Work/study college. Not included in MONEY's value study.
[14] Financial aid mainly for room and board
[15] Work program required of all students
[16] Open admissions
[17] Percentage met from university sources. Other sources not included.
[18] Estimate based on faculty that taught one course in fall 1992
[19] Percentage applies only to freshmen
[20] Recently became a four-year college
[21] Based on merit aid only
[22] Men's college
[23] Uniform fees included
[24] Includes students in joint programs with other colleges
[25] Data from 1991
[26] Frost campus only
[27] Includes New York State grants
[28] For nonresidents. State residents have 100% need met.
  N.A.: Not available

Getting Started With Mutual Funds

Investing, it is said, is the triumph of greed over fear. But greed has nothing to do with the need to buy your family a home, send your kids to college or ensure your secure retirement. These are the reasons most Americans put their money at risk in the securities markets. The day is long gone when you could expect to reach such goals on the meager proceeds of a passbook savings account or the eternally bullish advice of your local broker.

The rise of mutual funds ensures you a wealth of alternatives. For all the exaggerations of their sponsors, funds make a big contribution. They provide professional management for small portfolios at an affordable fee. In effect, they have made individual investors the beneficiaries of Wall Street's expertise rather than stooges on the losing end of the smart money's trades. As a result, funds are approaching a historic threshold. Barring a major market correction in 1994, total assets of funds are likely to surge past the $2 trillion now on retail deposit in U.S. banks and S&Ls, reports research firm Strategic Insight.

To meet that booming market, and the varying needs of the new clientele, the number of funds has soared toward 4,000. That's more than the listed issues on the New York and American stock exchanges combined. Such a proliferation of choices makes it likely that there's an ideal fund for you. But it complicates the process of finding it. There were just 477 funds when MONEY pioneered its monthly Fund Watch column in 1977. Now we provide performance data on over 3,095 funds in the rankings that begin on page 188.

Is this the right time to invest? With stocks hovering at record heights, many investors are paralyzed by the fear of getting into the market at the wrong time. The truth, incredible as it seems, is that there's no wrong time as long as you select an appropriate fund or mix of funds and buy in gradually. Consider the following. Suppose that 20 years ago you set up a $5,000 per annum investing program in the S&P 500 index. Assume further that in every one of those 20 years you had the uncanny bad luck to invest that stake on the very day the index hit its annual high. For fun, the American Funds group in Los Angeles calculated the anticipated carnage of such calamitous mistiming. Well, that hapless investor ended up with a huge profit and a cache of over $460,000. That's an annual return of 13.6%, barely less than 14.3% for the S&P itself, assuming that you put in $5,000 at the beginning of each of the 20 years.

Face it, there's no profit in, or prayer of, trying to time the market. The ideal moment to buy is when the market is hitting terrifying new daily lows and everyone else is desperate to sell. But nobody knows how low is low, and no trumpet blows when the turnaround is nigh. The one certainty is that when a bull market does come, it comes in a fevered rush.

What's the risk of being on the sidelines? A study by Ned Davis Research in Venice, Fla. tested the proposition that the real peril is not being in the market but being out of it at the wrong time. An individual who had bought the S&P 500 index in January 1980 and held it during the decade that followed would have enjoyed average annual gains of 17.6%. But if that investor had missed just the 10 biggest market days of those 120 months, his or her average gains would have been cut dramatically to 12.5% a year. And if you had the Job-like misfortune to be out of the market during the 20 biggest market days of the decade, your return would shrink to an annual 9.4%.

Consider one last eye-opening example. Suppose you had the foresight and discipline to put away $1,000 a year from ages 20 to 29, and then stopped, without adding another penny. By age 60 your retirement nest egg (assuming a 9% return) would have grown to a solid $219,717. But had you waited instead until age 30 to begin investing that same $1,000 and kept doing so for the next 30 years, you would have amassed only $148,575. Because of your procrastination, you would have had to put up approximately three times as much money to reap about a third less. Let's hope that disparity solves the question of when to get started. Today is better than tomorrow. Yesterday would have been better than either.

How to Choose the Right Fund for You

Convenience, diversification and professional management have made funds a big hit.
But you still have to decide what kind of investor you are.

At the age of 22, Deborah Clary took her future into her own hands and became an investor. The office manager for a Columbia, S.C. financial planning firm, Clary had absorbed enough theory around the watercooler to know that stocks were the best choice for an unmarried recent college grad whose most immediate financial goal—the down payment for a house—was five to 10 years off. But beyond that, she was a pure neophyte. "I knew just enough to know that I didn't know enough to run out and buy stocks myself," she says. So Clary did what millions of first-time investors do; she bought shares in mutual funds. Clary had the advantage of working with financial pros. But that's hardly a prerequisite for success in mutual funds. To get started, you need three things: a fundamental understanding of what funds can and can't do for you; an awareness of your financial goals and ability to tolerate risk; and a grasp of how to size up funds that may meet your goals.

What Funds Can Offer You

Let's start with a review of the basics, whether you're a new investor or a seasoned veteran. A mutual fund is a corporation whose sole business is to pool money from investors like you and invest it in stocks, bonds, money-market instruments or some combination of the three. When you invest in a fund, you receive shares representing part ownership of the fund's holdings and entitling you to a proportionate slice of whatever income and profits (or losses) those assets generate. By joining forces with other shareholders, you enjoy distinct return-enhancing advantages over those lone wolves who venture into the securities markets on their own. Among a mutual fund's most important attributes are the following:

Affordable professional management. You normally couldn't interest a professional money manager in minding your savings unless you had at least six-figure sums to invest. With funds, however, you usually can get in the door for $1,000 to $3,000. Every fund comes with its own investment management team. These pros work full time tracking the securities markets, monitoring the fund's investments and deciding what and when to buy or sell. In exchange, the management team typically takes 0.5% to 1.5% of the fund's assets each year as an advisory fee.

Ample diversification. On average, stock funds own shares in about 90 companies, while bond funds hold 70 issues. By investing in such a large number and wide range of securities, funds virtually eliminate the risk that an unforeseen plunge in the price of a single stock or bond could take a big chunk out of your money.

Ready access to your cash. Most funds are open-ended. That means they, unlike conventional corporations, don't issue a set number of shares that trade on the stock markets or over the counter. Instead, open-ended funds issue new shares whenever you invest and buy them back whenever you cash in. Thus when you want to buy or sell, you don't have to find another investor to take the other side of the deal. That's a big plus if you invest in markets where securities trade infrequently (e.g., certain small-company stocks or municipal bonds). With funds, you can always buy or cash in your shares at net asset value (plus or minus a sales charge, if the fund has one). Net asset value, or NAV, is the per-share worth of your fund's portfolio. Funds calculate net asset value at the end of each trading day, and it's listed the next morning in the business section of most newspapers.

A variety of ways to make money. If the securities in the fund's portfolio appreciate, the net asset value of your shares rises commensurately. If you redeem your shares at the higher price, you score a capital gain. You also net a gain if your fund sells some of the securities in its portfolio at a profit. (Funds typically pay out all the year's net trading profits in a single capital gains distribution, usually in December.) And if your fund owns bonds or other interest-bearing securities or stocks that pay dividends, the fund will also pay that income to you in the form of monthly, quarterly or semiannual income distributions.

You can elect to have either kind of distribution paid to you in cash, which you might choose to do if you plan to live off the income. But if you're investing to build your wealth, you should order the fund to reinvest the distributions in additional shares for your account. It can make a huge difference. Say you invested $10,000 in the famous Fidelity Magellan fund in 1980 and chose to receive dividends and capital gains in cash. After 13 years, you would have received about $23,750 in payouts and your stake in the fund would have grown to roughly $23,500. If, on the other hand, you had Fidelity reinvest your dividends in the fund, you would have built up principal of nearly $104,000.

What You Need in a Fund

It isn't hard to describe the perfect fund. It offers stellar long-term gains, bountiful dividends and never, ever loses money. Alas, such a paragon doesn't exist. No fund can honestly offer both high returns and safety. Investing always means weighing potential benefits against risks. The cardinal rule: the more safety you demand, the less return you can expect, and vice versa. That means you cannot search intelligently for the best funds without some soul searching first. These questions will help you define what is best for you.

Do you need growth, income or safety? You're a growth investor if your key need is to build capital for a major future expense that lies five or more

years away, such as your kids' college education or your own retirement. The best funds for you invest mainly for capital appreciation. Such funds have a strong record of appreciation over long periods but are also the most prone to harsh short-term setbacks. As a result, you can't consider yourself a growth investor unless you are confident that you can endure painful stretches when your fund is down 20% or more.

If you want your funds to help you pay ongoing expenses, you're an income investor. You should look at funds invested at least partly in bonds and sporting above-average yields (the amount of income they pay out as a percentage of the principal invested). If you need to stash money for an expense you will incur within a few years (e.g., a down payment on a house), what you need from your funds is safety. Your best choices are ultrasafe money-market funds or taxable short-term bond funds. Neither category as a whole has ever lost money over the course of a calendar year. The principal drawback: their yields lately have been achingly low, with taxable money-market funds averaging about 2.7%.

How much risk can you handle? Think of risk as the entry fee you pay to invest. You can choose to take a lot or a little, but you can never avoid it entirely. The payback for assuming risk is potential return. The most aggressive stock funds, for example, have suffered precipitous falls of 20% or so in their worst years. But their long-term average gains of roughly 15% annually make a compelling case for investing in them anyway. Thus risk isn't necessarily bad as long as you don't take on more than you can handle.

When will you need your money? As a rule, the longer you're planning to hold on to your fund shares, the more you can afford to shoot for the stock market's higher returns. Say you had invested in the S&P 500 index at the start of any calendar year in the past 55 years and pulled out after 12 months. According to the research firm Ibbotson Associates in Chicago, you would have made money two out of three times. Had you held on for five years, your odds of making a profit would have improved to four out of five. And if you stood by your stocks for 10 years, you would have finished in the black 96% of the time.

How much could you bear to lose? No matter how impressive a fund's long-term record may be, you won't score big if you bail out when the fund turns temporarily cold. So ask yourself how much you could stand to see your investment plunge in a given year before pulling the ripcord. Bailard Biehl & Kaiser, an investment and financial planning outfit in San Mateo, Calif., uses this rough-and-ready gauge of risk tolerance. "If you're willing to stomach losses of 10% or more in a year, you're an aggressive investor," says BBK strategist Art Micheletti. That suits you for high-risk, high-return funds such as maximum capital gains and small-company growth portfolios. A 5% threshold of pain suggests you're interested in trading off some return for safety in, say, equity income funds that blend yield-rich stocks and bonds. "If you're unwilling to tolerate any losses," says Micheletti, "you're too conservative for virtually any stock fund and all but the safest bond portfolios." Your options are money-market funds or those invested in short-term or intermediate-term bonds.

How much advice do you need? Funds are sold in either of two ways (discussed in greater detail later in this chapter). Many funds are peddled by stockbrokers, independent planners and insurance agents. You get the salesperson's advice in choosing your fund. But the fund will deduct a commission (the load) from your investment either in an up-front fee, typically 4% to 6%, or in some combination of redemption charges and ongoing annual charges. No-loads are sold by fund sponsors directly to investors without commission. The money usually changes hands by mail or by bank wire, though big outfits like Fidelity and Dreyfus have walk-in offices in many cities. Note, however, that not all no-loads are free of commissions. For example, about a third of Fidelity's directly sold funds carry so-called low loads of 2% to 3%, which the company itself pockets. The low load

isn't as onerous as the charges levied by broker-sold funds, but then you don't get any advice for your money either.

For every load fund now on the market, you can almost always find an equally promising alternative among no-loads. Don't believe a fund salesperson who tells you that load funds have an innate advantage because they can afford to hire better stock pickers or because their annual expenses are lower. Neither is necessarily true. There's no difference in performance between load and no-load funds. The only difference is in how they're sold. So whether to go load or no-load hinges entirely on whether you think a salesperson's fund-picking prowess and ongoing advice will be worth the price.

Sizing Up the Best Fund for You

Evaluating your investment needs and tolerance for risk lets you create a sort of composite sketch of funds to look for. Your next step is to identify the products that match that template and have the best prospects for solid returns. Start by getting answers to the following basic questions.

What are a fund's investment goals? Your first clues to its intentions come from its name and its category. Both can be deceiving, however. IDS Managed Retirement, for example, may sound like a sturdy income producer for widows. In fact, it's a moderately aggressive growth and income fund subject to occasional pratfalls of as much as 14% in a quarter. So be sure to confirm your fund's orientation before you invest. Get a copy of the fund's prospectus from its sponsor (in the case of a no-load) or your salesperson (load funds) and refer to the section called Investment Objectives. Check the fund's portfolio statistics, which you'll also find in our rankings of the top performers in six fund groups beginning on page 191. An income fund, for example, should have a yield of at least 4% to 5%, a growth fund less than 3%.

What does a fund's history tell you? The classic investor's mistake is to assume that last year's performance will be repeated this year. No strategy stays hot forever, and last year's success story often becomes this year's dud. To avoid being fooled by a flashy gain, use our performance tables to look for consistency among returns over intervals of one, three and five years. A fund should compare well over each period with the average for its category or investment style, as well as with benchmarks such as the S&P 500 index. Of course, a fund's long-term return may be meaningless if a new manager has recently come on board. So before lending too much credence to a sterling record, check that the person responsible for it is still at the helm. You'll find the manager's name and tenure in references such as Morningstar, available at most large libraries, or call the fund's sponsor and ask.

How well does the fund handle risk? It is one thing to accept the notion that bearing up through market dips will eventually pay off. It's quite another to stand by calmly while a bear market takes 5% out of your life savings week after week. So when you analyze a fund's performance, you must pay particular attention to its returns in falling markets. Ask yourself whether you could stand to lose that much without losing your nerve and selling out, which is often the worst thing you could do.

Checking MONEY's risk-adjusted grades is a quick way to tell whether a fund's recent returns have justified its risk level. For the purposes of the calculation, we define risk as volatility, explained in greater detail in "How to Read Our Tables" on page 190. Note that our grades should not be interpreted as safety ratings. A volatile fund can still get a lower risk score provided that its return amply compensated shareholders for the risks taken by its manager. Our system captures a far more subtle aspect of performance—how deftly the fund's manager negotiated the trade-off between risk and reward. That's the truest measure of how well a fund serves its shareholders.

Thinning Out the Thicket of Marketers

Everyone, it seems, wants to sell you a fund these days. Here's how to determine which of the pitchpeople are just talking through their hats.

No doubt you've found lots of folks eager for your business these days. There's that persistent broker who keeps calling and that smiling sales rep in your bank lobby. You may even encounter pitches for funds in such unlikely places as an airline seat, a utility bill or a newsletter from a professional organization. Here are some timely tips on investing through brokers, banks, discount brokers, no-load families and affinity groups. Where you choose to buy should depend on how much guidance you need as well as how much convenience you demand. Bear in mind that hand-holders also hold out their hands, either for commissions or consulting fees. Personal advice and service will cost you more than doing the fund picking and paperwork on your own.

Brokers for advice at a price. Investors who want advice typically turn to brokers and financial planners, who account for roughly 60% of mutual fund sales. But you have to pay for that service in the form of loads, or sales charges. These usually amount to 4% to 6% of your investment up front or a flat rate in the case of fee-only planners. Of course, there's nothing wrong with paying a load as long as the guidance and returns justify the cost. But avoid any broker or planner who pushes a fund without first learning about your financial situation, investment goals and tolerance for risk. And be sure to read the fund's prospectus and annual report and ask about the adviser's compensation for selling the fund. Some brokerages offer incentives for pushing the house brand.

Banks for convenience. The banks' target market tends to be beginning investors disappointed with returns on CDs or savings accounts. But think twice if you're tempted by higher yields. You are most likely to be offered a nonbank load fund from a limited range of sponsors or a bank-run fund that may be no bargain. None of these investment products are insured by the FDIC. Remember too that the convenience of a bank can be oversold. Many bank-based brokers work for outside firms and often move between different branches, precluding the possibility of long-term stewardship of your money.

No-load funds for independence. If you are willing to research funds on your own, it's probably a waste of money to pay a load and to miss out on the abundant no-load choices marketed directly by fund families. The first step is to write or call a fund group (most have toll-free numbers) and ask for a prospectus, an annual report and an application. You can arrange for telephone switching between funds, redemption by wire, check writing and other services. If you buy a fund on your own, there is no one to stop you from making a mistake or to help you decide to cut your losses. But some

no-load groups including Fidelity, Dreyfus and T. Rowe Price offer free retirement planning workbooks and asset-allocation assistance.

Discount brokers for one-stop shopping. Active investors who trade frequently may prefer to work with a discount broker. A key attraction is the ability to buy and sell funds with a single phone call and without the hassle of multiple applications and other paperwork. Transaction fees start at about $30 for a $5,000 investment. Discounters with fund programs include Charles Schwab (800-526-8600), Jack White & Co. (800-233-3411), Fidelity Brokerage Services (800-544-8666) and Waterhouse Securities (800-934-4410). Schwab and White offer certain no-loads without any charges other than the funds' standard expenses.

Affinity groups for variety. You may get a fund pitch from an organization you belong to or even a company you do business with. There are socially conscious funds with ethical buying criteria. And now corporations are muscling into the fund market. American Airlines pushes its no-load American AAdvantage money fund to its passengers through its inflight magazines and promo-

Could Your Fund Go Bust?

It's a reasonable question. After all, it takes a leap of faith to hand over your savings to a broker you may have met only a few days earlier or to mail cash to a company you know only as a voice at the end of an 800 line. How do you know that the managers you've chosen won't abscond to Rio with your savings or go broke in some debacle?

Relax. Fraud is rare in the fund industry. In the 70 odd years since funds first appeared in the U.S., none has ever gone bankrupt. (It's not uncommon, however, for a laggard performer to be dissolved or merged into a more successful fund.) For starters, funds deal in highly visible assets. The price of large stocks and many bonds becomes known almost the

instant a trade is completed. When the securities markets close each afternoon, your fund checks the prices of the securities it holds and calculates its own share value, transmitting that information to news services for the next morning's papers.

Federal law also provides effective checks and balances. A fund's manager doesn't have direct access to the fund's assets. The cash and securities are held by a custodian, usually a bank, which every day reconciles its books with those of the fund. So a fund employee with a larcenous bent couldn't even get started without fellow conspirators at the custodian. As a final defense, each fund must also submit to an annual audit by independent accountants.

tional cards on food trays. Don't rush to buy a fund simply because it is offered by a group that you know. For example, the American Association of Retired Persons puts its name on a group of

funds managed by Scudder. These funds are just as good as, but no better than, others in that Boston family. Judge a fund not by its name or by who is peddling it but by its long-term track record.

Take a Hard Look at Pesky Fund Fees

Even if you are willing to pay a sales charge for help in selecting a fund, you may balk at less visible fees that can pilfer your profits.

You can't really predict a fund's future returns from its past performance. But history is a very reliable guide to fund expenses, which play a crucial yet often overlooked role in determining how much of your fund's gains actually wind up in your pocket. These expenses include not only any sales charges you pay when buying or redeeming shares but also investment management fees and other obscure levies you are nicked for, year in and year out.

True, up-front sales charges have generally declined during the past decade, with fewer than 1% of funds extracting the maximum 8.5%. But management, marketing and administrative expenses have jumped big time. Annual fees for stock funds overall rose 48% to 1.5% of assets over a recent 10-year period. For taxable bond funds, costs spurted 13% to 1%. Only expenses for tax-exempt bond funds fell, declining 6% to 0.75%. Fund apologists claimed in the 1980s that fees would come down as fund size went up. Well, growth stock funds' assets lately were up 148% over a decade. But average annual expenses actually rose 30% to 1.3% of assets.

Those hikes would have been easier to swallow in the 1980s, when stock funds gained an average of 14% a year and bond funds rose almost 13%. But high expenses can be a real drag in the slow-growth 1990s, when returns are expected to be closer to the historic norms of 10% for stocks and 7% for bonds. If stock returns fall back to 10%, expenses would eat up 15% of fundholders' returns, vs. an average of 7% in the 1980s.

To understand the impact of expenses, compare Ivy International and Harbor International, two similar funds managed by Hakan Castegren. The no-load Harbor, with its 1.28% expenses, rewarded investors with a recent five-year return of nearly 17% annually. But Ivy delivered only 14% a year partly because of its hefty 1.7% expenses. In addition, Ivy investors were socked with a 5.75% initial sales charge. Carefully consider these and other fee-related issues before investing.

Weigh the sales charge, or load. You can avoid commissions altogether by buying your funds directly from a no-load family. That way, every dollar you invest will be working for you from Day One. If you choose to invest through a broker or financial planner, you'll most often be hit with a front load of 4% to 6% when you make your purchase. Beware of funds like Common Sense Growth and IDEX that still grab 8.5% of assets. If your $10,000 investment returns 10% annually over 10 years, you'll wind up with just $23,735 after supinely suffering that 8.5% sales charge. That amount works out to $2,204 less than in a no-load posting the same return.

Newer on the scene are back loads, also known as contingent deferred sales charges. There's no fee to buy the fund. But you'll pay a stiff penalty if you cash out early, usually coughing up 1% to 5% of any withdrawal you make before the end of year five. A growing number of broker-sold fund groups, including Merrill Lynch, now offer you the choice of buying a fund with a front or back load. While choosing among these options may be confusing, experts say there's often little difference. That's because most back loads are accompanied by nettlesome 12b-1 fees (described in detail below), which boost annual expenses. You're probably best off paying a front load if you plan to hold your fund for just a few years and if the charge is 4.5% or less. Back loads tend to be more economical if your time horizon is five years or longer. While you're likely to pay a higher 12b-1 charge at the outset, in most cases it converts to a smaller 0.25% service fee sometime between the seventh and ninth year.

Compare annual expense ratios. That's your fund's costs as a percentage of its average net assets. You'll find this figure, plus a five-year expense projection, in the fee table near the front of every fund prospectus. You should generally avoid a fund if its fees are higher than the median for its investment objective (see the table at right for expense benchmarks for nine key fund types.) If you're torn between two funds of the same type with comparable records, you probably should opt for the one with lower expenses.

Watch out for vexing 12b-1 fees. Named after a Securities and Exchange Commission rule, 12b-1 fees allow funds to recoup their advertising and marketing costs by skimming a bit from current shareholders. These charges now range from 0.1% to 1.25% of assets per year and are included in your fund's expense ratio. Fund companies claim that 12b-1 fees actually benefit investors by allowing funds to gather more assets and thus spread their costs over a bigger base, reducing expenses. But a study by State University of New York (Buffalo) finance professor Charles Trczinka found that funds with 12b-1 fees don't seem to pass economies of scale along to their investors. A new National Association of Securities Dealers rule requires funds to include 12b-1 fees when calculating sales charges. The rule limits annual 12b-1 fees to 0.75% of net assets but allows funds to charge a 0.25% service fee. It also caps total sales charges including 12b-1 at 6.25% to 8.5%.

Don't overlook turnover. You might not think of turnover, or how often your fund trades its portfolio, as an expense. But high turnover can cut into your returns in the same insidious manner as sales charges and 12b-1 fees. That's because the fund pays a brokerage commission on each trade and, in some cases, may actually move a stock's price with a buy or sell decision. Each time your fund turns over its entire portfolio—a 100% turnover rate—it probably costs you 0.5% to 1%, figures Professor Trczinka. Thus, he says a fund with a 200% turnover rate could run you $200 for each $10,000 you've invested. In addition, you'll have to pay capital gains tax on your share of any profits the fund passes along to you. That said, taxed gains are better than no gains, and turnover may be an indication of appropriately active and vigilant professional management, particularly in the more volatile and aggressive fund categories such as small-company growth and technology.

How Fund Fees Stack Up

To ensure that you're not overpaying for a fund, compare its expense ratio with its category below. Why the discrepancy between categories? Because running, say, a small-cap growth portfolio is more manager-intensive and thus justifiably pricier.

Fund objective	Median annual expenses	Range of annual expenses
International stock	1.8%	0.3 to 3.7%
Maximum capital gains	1.4	0.7 to 3.0
Small-company growth	1.3	0.2 to 3.1
Growth	1.2	0.3 to 3.1
High-yield bond	1.2	0.3 to 2.5
Growth and income	1.1	0.2 to 3.1
High-grade corp. bond	0.9	0.3 to 2.0
Long-term muni bonds	0.8	0.1 to 2.6
Money market	0.8	0.3 to 1.6

Your Guide to All

Perhaps the only thing that grew as fast as the mutual fund industry this past year is the number of investors seeking the best possible coverage of fund performance. In response, we've improved our fund report to give you more funds and more information than you can find anywhere else. You'll find returns through the end of 1993 for all 3,095 stock and bond funds tracked by our data supplier, Morningstar. The only funds missing are upstarts that haven't been around long enough to post 12-month returns. And our new data measuring risk and performance make it easier than ever for you to find the safest, steadiest fund winners.

We begin by introducing the 25 winners for the past year, three years and five years in each of six broad categories: **growth, total return, specialty, international, taxable bonds** and **tax-exempt bonds.** Average returns for the categories and the types of funds appear opposite. In general, overseas funds turned in the best performance of all types in 1993, climbing 37.5%, compared with 13.2% for the average stock fund. Gold funds, which we lump together with other specialty portfolios, soared 92.4% in 1993, led by the year's No. 1 gainer, the highly volatile Lexington Strategic Investments, up an amazing 264.9%. (In 1992, that fund lost 60.7%.) Among bond funds, high-yield corporates (a.k.a. junk bonds) outperformed the pack with an 18.9% average total return.

You can find out how your own portfolio of funds performed to the end of 1993 by flipping through the alphabetical listings that start on page 194. We've divided these comprehensive listings into two, easy-to-access sections: one for **major funds** and another for **extra funds**.

The section covering major funds provides a microscopic view of nearly 2,000 funds that are available in most states and accept initial investments of $25,000 or less. They collectively manage nearly 80% of all mutual fund assets, so start looking for your funds here. If you can't find your holdings in the major funds tables, turn to the listings of more than 1,100 extra funds that start on page 219. The extras include single-state muni bond funds, funds available in fewer than half the states, and the less widely held or newer share classes of some major funds.

Among the data in the major funds section that deserve special mention is our **style** analysis. With stock funds, style tells you whether a fund favors stocks of small, medium or large companies and whether it leans toward growth or value stocks or a blend of the two. Growth managers look for steadily expanding companies. Value managers try to identify shares priced cheaply in relation to their assets or their future earnings. Among bond funds, style tells you whether a fund holds bonds of short, intermediate or long terms and whether the bonds carry high or low credit ratings.

3,095 Funds

Our tables also include two new measures. **Risk level**—the probability that a fund will gain less than risk-free Treasury bills—compares funds across the Morningstar database and ranks them on a sliding scale from 1 (for safest) to 12 (for riskiest). Aggressive growth funds and internationals hold the highest risk scores (8 to 12), while short- and intermediate-term bond funds get the lowest (1 to 3).

Our **annual performance analysis** lets you quickly discover how well a fund has done compared with others of its type during each of the past five years. You should check these columns to learn whether a top long-term performer built its record by stringing together consistently high returns or by mixing mediocre years with some spectacular—but erratic—gains.

And in our **expense analysis**, you should pay special attention to the **five-year total per $1,000** column. It tells you the amount of expenses you would pay on an initial $1,000 investment earning 5% annually that you redeemed after five years (a reporting period mandated by the Securities and Exchange Commission). As we have reiterated in previous chapters, stock and bond funds are likely to face difficult market conditions in 1994. Therefore, it's more important than ever that you avoid frittering away your return in excessive fees. So use the following fund tables to help keep your investing costs down and your returns up.

How the Fund Types Stack Up

Use this table to measure your funds' performance against all the funds in their broad general categories (in **bold** type) or against only those of the same type (in regular print).

Category average	Starts on page	% annual gain to Jan. 1, 1994		
		One year	Three years	Five years
GROWTH FUNDS	194	**13.2**	**20.3**	**15.3**
Aggressive growth		17.1	24.8	16.8
Capital growth		11.5	18.2	14.6
TOTAL RETURN	199	**11.7**	**15.6**	**12.4**
Growth and income		10.8	15.7	12.7
Equity total return		12.7	15.0	11.9
Income total return		14.1	17.4	12.8
SPECIALTY	204	**29.7**	**17.3**	**13.4**
INTERNATIONAL	206	**37.5**	**14.0**	**9.4**
Overseas		36.6	14.9	10.1
Foreign regional		43.1	11.4	7.2
TAXABLE BONDS	208	**10.0**	**11.7**	**10.1**
Government bond		8.6	9.8	9.9
Investment-grade corporates		9.7	10.9	10.2
High-yield corporates		18.9	24.2	11.2
Mortgage-backed securities		5.6	8.9	9.8
World income		12.6	8.1	9.2
TAX-EXEMPT BONDS	216	**11.3**	**10.4**	**9.3**

HOW TO READ OUR TABLES

TYPE

We divide our 3,095 funds into 14 types, such as Agg for aggressive growth, depending on each fund's investment objective and the kind of securities it buys. To make it easier to compare your funds with their peers, we've grouped the types into seven broad categories: Growth, Total Return, Specialty, International, Taxable Bonds, Tax-Exempt Bonds and Single-State Munis. All funds are listed alphabetically within their broad category.

ABBREVIATIONS Types: Agg—Aggressive growth; **ETR**—Equity total return; **G&I**—Growth and income; **Gov**—U.S. Government bond; **Gro**—Capital growth; **HYC**—High-yield corporate; **IGC**—Investment-grade corporate; **Intl**—International; **ITR**—Income total return; **MBS**—Mortgage-backed securities; **Muni**—Municipal bond; **Reg**—Foreign regional; **Spec**—Specialty; **WI**—World income

RISK LEVEL

Our risk measure weighs both the likelihood that a fund will underperform a risk-free Treasury bill in any given month and the likely magnitude of such underperformance, based on the fund's three-year record. We then compare each fund's risk with that of all other funds and rate all on an evenly divided scale from 1 to 12. The higher the number, the riskier the fund.

ANNUAL CHARGES

This figure reflects the fund's total operating expenses—including administrative costs, investment management fees and any marketing charges—expressed as a percentage of assets. These expenses come straight out of the shareholders' money, so lean toward funds with below-average expenses: under 0.9% for bond funds and below 1.3% for stock funds.

Fund name	Type	Style	Risk level	% compound annual return to Jan. 1, 1994			Annual performance analysis (percentile ranking by type)[1]					Expense analysis			Net assets (millions)	Phone (800)
				One year	Three years	Five years	1993	1992	1991	1990	1989	% max. sales charge	Annual charges	Five-year total per $1,000		
G R O W T H																
20th Century Giftrust Inv.	Agg	Sm/Gro	12	31.4%	42.1%	29.0%	54	58	85	34	79	None	1.00%	$55	$153.7	345-2021

STYLE

This two-part abbreviation gives you two insights. For stock funds, it tells you the median market value (large, medium or small) of the stocks that the fund owns and whether the manager favors growth stocks with rapidly expanding earnings, bargain-priced value stocks or a blend of both. For fixed-income funds, it notes whether the average weighted maturity of its bonds is short, intermediate or long and whether the bonds' credit quality is high, medium or low.

ABBREVIATIONS Stock fund styles: Bl—Buys stocks that blend growth and value characteristics; **Gro**—Buys companies with rapidly rising earnings; **Lg**—Buys stocks with total market values over $5 billion; **Md**—Buys stocks with total market values between $1 billion and $5 billion; **Sm**—Buys stocks with total market values under $1 billion; **Val**—Buys stocks that are inexpensive in relation to assets or earnings. **Bond fund styles: Hi**—Buys bonds rated AA or better; **M**—Buys bonds rated BBB or better; **Lo**—Buys bonds rated BB or lower; **Int**—Buys bonds with maturities between four and 10 years; **L**—Buys bonds with maturities over 10 years; **Sh**—Buys bonds with maturities under four years.

ANNUAL PERFORMANCE ANALYSIS

In these columns we rank the fund's total return in each of the past five years against all funds of the same type. A score of 99, for example, means that a fund beat 99% of its closest competitors that year. Funds that consistently score above 50 (the median) are likely to provide a higher return in the long run than funds that rise to 80 in one year and then plunge to 20 the next.

FIVE-YEAR TOTAL COST PER $1,000

This column shows you the total amount you would pay—including all annual fees and sales charges—if you invested $1,000 in a mutual fund that earned 5% annually and then redeemed your shares after five years. This SEC-mandated calculation is the fairest way to compare the expense of investing in funds with different cost structures—load vs. no load, front-end vs. back-end load, and so on.

Data provided by Morningstar Inc.

THE TOP-PERFORMING FUNDS

GROWTH

ONE-YEAR WINNERS

Fund name	Type	Style	% 1993 return	Risk level
1. Govett Smaller Companies	Agg	Sm/Gro	58.5	N.A.
2. PBHG Growth	Agg	Sm/Gro	46.6	12
3. Oak Hall Equity	Agg	Sm/Gro	42.1	N.A.
4. American Heritage	Agg	Md/Bl	41.4	11
5. Templeton Capital Accum.	Gro	Md/Val	39.5	N.A.
6. Gabelli Value	Gro	Lg/Bl	39.4	N.A.
7. Thomson Opportunity B[1]	Agg	Sm/Gro	36.2	11
8. Mutual Discovery[1]	Agg	Sm/Val	35.8	N.A.
9. Fidelity Capital App.	Agg	Md/Bl	33.4	9
10. Putnam New Opportunities A	Gro	Sm/Gro	32.7	N.A.
11. Acorn[1]	Agg	Sm/Gro	32.3	10
12. Putnam OTC Emer. Gro. A	Agg	Sm/Gro	32.0	12
13. AIM Aggressive Growth	Agg	Sm/Gro	32.0	12
14. Smith Bar. Shear. Sp. Eq. B	Agg	Sm/Gro	31.9	12
15. 20th Century Giftrust Inv.	Agg	Sm/Gro	31.4	12
16. Merrill Lynch Growth B	Gro	Sm/Gro	31.1	11
17. New Economy	Gro	Md/Gro	31.0	9
18. Dean Witter Developing Gro.	Agg	Sm/Gro	30.8	12
19. Oakmark	Gro	Md/Val	30.5	N.A.
20. Merrill Lynch Phoenix A	Gro	Sm/Gro	29.5	10
21. CGM Capital Development[1]	Gro	Md/Bl	28.7	12
22. Alliance Growth B	Gro	Md/Bl	28.2	10
23. SteinRoe Capital Opp.	Agg	Md/Gro	27.5	12
24. Fidelity Destiny II[2]	Gro	Md/Bl	26.8	10
25. Fidelity Destiny I[2]	Gro	Lg/Bl	26.4	9
Average growth fund			**13.2**	

THREE-YEAR WINNERS

Fund name	Type	Style	% avg. annual return	Risk level
1. American Heritage	Agg	Md/Bl	48.9	11
2. CGM Capital Development[1]	Gro	Md/Bl	44.4	12
3. Thomson Opportunity B[1]	Agg	Sm/Gro	43.2	11
4. Hancock Special Equities A[1]	Agg	Sm/Gro	42.3	12
5. 20th Century Giftrust Inv.	Agg	Sm/Gro	42.1	12
6. PBHG Growth	Agg	Sm/Gro	41.9	12
7. Putnam New Opportunities A	Gro	Sm/Gro	40.8	N.A.
8. Montgomery Small Cap[1]	Agg	Sm/Gro	39.4	N.A.
9. AIM Aggressive Growth	Agg	Sm/Gro	38.0	12
10. Delaware Trend	Agg	Sm/Gro	37.7	12
11. MFS Emerging Growth B[1]	Agg	Sm/Gro	37.5	12
12. Skyline Special Equities[1]	Agg	Sm/Val	37.1	9
13. Heartland Value	Agg	Sm/Val	36.2	10
14. Berger 100	Gro	Md/Gro	35.4	11
15. Parnassus	Gro	Sm/Bl	34.8	11
16. Acorn[1]	Agg	Sm/Gro	34.3	10
17. Keystone Custodian S-4	Agg	Sm/Gro	33.5	12
18. ABT Emerging Growth	Agg	Md/Gro	33.5	12
19. Strong Common Stock[1]	Agg	Sm/Bl	33.4	N.A.
20. Oppenheimer Discovery	Agg	Sm/Gro	33.3	11
21. Kaufmann	Agg	Sm/Gro	33.2	11
22. MetLife-State St. Cap. App. A	Agg	Sm/Gro	32.7	12
23. FPA Capital	Agg	Sm/Val	32.7	12
24. Oberweis Emerging Gro.	Agg	Sm/Gro	32.6	12
25. Vista Capital Growth	Gro	Sm/Bl	32.3	10
Average growth fund			**20.3**	

FIVE-YEAR WINNERS

Fund name	Type	Style	% avg. annual return	Risk level
1. CGM Capital Development[1]	Gro	Md/Bl	29.2	12
2. 20th Century Giftrust Inv.	Agg	Sm/Gro	29.0	12
3. Thomson Opportunity B[1]	Agg	Sm/Gro	28.9	11
4. Berger 100	Gro	Md/Gro	28.3	11
5. 20th Century Ultra Inv.	Agg	Md/Gro	28.1	12
6. Hancock Special Equities A[1]	Agg	Sm/Gro	27.5	12
7. PBHG Growth	Agg	Sm/Gro	27.3	12
8. Kaufmann	Agg	Sm/Gro	26.6	11
9. Fidelity Contrafund	Gro	Md/Gro	26.5	7
10. MFS Emerging Gro. B[1]	Agg	Sm/Gro	26.3	12
11. Alger Small Capitalization	Agg	Sm/Gro	26.1	12
12. Vista Capital Growth	Gro	Sm/Bl	25.8	10
13. AIM Constellation	Agg	Md/Gro	24.9	12
14. ABT Emerging Growth	Agg	Md/Gro	24.9	12
15. AIM Aggressive Growth	Agg	Sm/Gro	24.3	12
16. Delaware Trend	Agg	Sm/Gro	24.2	12
17. Oberweis Emerging Growth	Agg	Sm/Gro	23.9	12
18. Skyline Special Equities[1]	Agg	Sm/Val	23.7	9
19. Fidelity Blue Chip Growth	Gro	Md/Gro	23.6	9
20. American Cap. Emerg. Gro. A	Agg	Md/Gro	23.5	11
21. Brandywine	Gro	Md/Gro	23.1	11
22. Westcore Midco Growth	Gro	Md/Gro	23.0	11
23. MainStay Capital App.	Gro	Md/Gro	22.8	11
24. Keystone Custodian S-4	Agg	Sm/Gro	22.6	12
25. Wasatch Aggressive Equity	Agg	Sm/Bl	22.4	11
Average growth fund			**15.3**	

TOTAL RETURN

ONE-YEAR WINNERS

Fund name	Type	Style	% 1993 return	Risk level
1. Warburg Pincus Gro. & Inc.	G&I	Md/Gro	37.1	7
2. Oppenheimer Main St. I&G	G&I	Sm/Bl	35.4	8
3. Safeco Equity	G&I	Md/Gro	30.9	10
4. IDS Diversified Equity-Inc.	ETR	Md/Bl	29.2	N.A.
5. Fidelity Ast. Manager–Gro.	ETR	Md/Bl	26.3	N.A.
6. MainStay Convertible	ITR	N.A.	24.5	7
7. USAA Invest. Cornerstone	ETR	Lg/Bl	23.7	7
8. Berger 101	G&I	Lg/Bl	23.6	8
9. Fidelity Asset Manager	ETR	Md/Bl	23.3	5
10. Mutual Beacon	G&I	Sm/Val	22.9	6
11. Babson Value	G&I	Lg/Val	22.9	10
12. Mutual Qualified[1]	G&I	Md/Val	22.7	7
13. Strong Total Return	G&I	Md/Gro	22.5	9
14. MetLife-State St. Eq.-Inc. A	ETR	Md/Val	22.4	7
15. Merrill Lynch Basic Value A	G&I	Lg/Bl	22.2	9
16. MetLife-State St. Mgd. A	ETR	Md/Gro	21.9	6
17. Founders Equity-Income	ITR	Md/Bl	21.8	6
18. CGM Mutual	ETR	Lg/Val	21.8	8
19. Franklin Income	ITR	Lg/Val	21.5	6
20. Fidelity Puritan	ETR	Md/Bl	21.4	7
21. Fidelity Equity-Income	ETR	Lg/Val	21.3	8
22. Bond Fund for Growth	ITR	N.A.	21.2	6
23. Oppenheimer Total Return	G&I	Md/Bl	21.2	8
24. Thomson Equity-Income B	ETR	Lg/Val	21.2	8
25. Mutual Shares[1]	G&I	Md/Val	21.0	7
Average total-return fund			**11.7**	

THREE-YEAR WINNERS

Fund name	Type	Style	% avg. annual return	Risk level
1. Oppenheimer Main St. I&G	G&I	Sm/Bl	43.5	8
2. MainStay Convertible	ITR	N.A.	27.9	7
3. Berger 101	G&I	Lg/Bl	27.8	8
4. Fidelity Equity-Income II	ETR	Md/Val	27.6	N.A.
5. Vista Growth & Income	G&I	Md/Val	27.4	7
6. Bond Fund for Growth	ITR	N.A.	26.9	6
7. Pacific Horizon Capital Inc.	ITR	N.A.	26.3	7
8. Fidelity Convertible Secs.	ITR	N.A.	25.9	6
9. Franklin Income	ITR	Lg/Val	25.5	6
10. Dreman High Return	ETR	Lg/Val	24.6	10
11. Quest for Value Opp. A	ETR	Md/Val	24.6	7
12. MainStay Value	G&I	Md/Val	24.2	8
13. Evergreen Foundation	ETR	Md/Val	23.7	N.A.
14. Fidelity Growth & Income	G&I	Md/Bl	23.7	8
15. Liberty Equity-Income	ETR	Md/Val	23.5	7
16. Franklin Convertible Sec.	ITR	N.A.	23.2	7
17. Oppenheimer Total Return	G&I	Md/Bl	23.1	9
18. IDS Diversified Equity-Inc.	ETR	Md/Bl	23.0	N.A.
19. Putnam Conv. Inc.-Growth	ITR	N.A.	22.4	7
20. IDS Managed Retirement	G&I	Lg/Bl	22.4	8
21. Legg Mason Total Return	G&I	Lg/Val	22.4	8
22. Neuberger/Berman Guardian	G&I	Md/Val	22.3	9
23. Safeco Equity	G&I	Md/Gro	22.3	10
24. Babson Value	G&I	Lg/Val	22.3	10
25. Mutual Qualified[1]	G&I	Md/Val	22.2	7
Average total-return fund			**15.6**	

FIVE-YEAR WINNERS

Fund name	Type	Style	% avg. annual return	Risk level
1. Oppenheimer Main St. I&G	G&I	Sm/Bl	28.2	8
2. Vista Growth & Income	G&I	Md/Val	26.6	7
3. IDS Managed Retirement	G&I	Lg/Bl	19.8	8
4. Pacific Horizon Capital Inc.	ITR	N.A.	19.6	7
5. Fidelity Convertible Secs.	ITR	N.A.	19.6	6
6. Berger 101	G&I	Lg/Bl	18.2	8
7. Invesco Industrial Income	ETR	Md/Val	18.1	7
8. Fidelity Growth & Income	G&I	Md/Bl	18.0	8
9. Safeco Equity	G&I	Md/Gro	17.8	10
10. AIM Charter	G&I	Lg/Val	17.8	7
11. CGM Mutual	ETR	Lg/Val	17.5	8
12. MainStay Value	G&I	Md/Val	16.9	8
13. Laurel Stock	G&I	Lg/Bl	16.7	8
14. Pierpont Equity	G&I	Lg/Bl	16.5	8
15. Oppenheimer Total Return	G&I	Md/Bl	16.4	9
16. Warburg Pincus Gro. & Inc.	G&I	Md/Gro	16.3	7
17. Quest for Value Opp. A	ETR	Md/Val	16.3	7
18. Fidelity Advisor–Inc. & Gro.	ETR	Md/Bl	16.3	6
19. Neuberger/Berman Guardian	G&I	Md/Val	16.2	9
20. SteinRoe Prime Equities	G&I	Md/Bl	16.2	8
21. Chubb Growth & Income	G&I	Md/Bl	16.0	8
22. IDS Stock	G&I	Lg/Bl	16.0	7
23. Dreman High Return	G&I	Lg/Val	15.9	10
24. IDS Equity Plus	G&I	Md/Bl	15.9	8
25. Fidelity Asset Manager	ETR	Md/Bl	15.9	5
Average total-return fund			**12.4**	

Notes: [1]Closed to new investors [2]Investment by contractual plan only N.A.: Not available
Risk level requires five-year record. **Source: Morningstar Inc.**, Chicago, Ill.; 800-820-8082

INTERNATIONAL

ONE-YEAR WINNERS

Fund name	Type	Style	% 1993 return	Risk level
1. Dean Witter Pacific Growth	Reg	Md/Gro	94.7	N.A.
2. Merrill Lynch Dragon B[1]	Reg	Lg/Gro	85.8	N.A.
3. Equifund Hong Kong Natl. Fid.	Reg	N.A.	84.3	N.A.
4. Fidelity Emer. Markets	Intl	N.A.	81.8	N.A.
5. Govett Emerging Markets	Intl	Md/Bl	79.7	N.A.
6. T. Rowe Price New Asia	Reg	Md/Gro	78.8	N.A.
7. Newport Tiger	Reg	Lg/Gro	75.2	N.A.
8. 59 Wall St. Pac. Basin Eq.	Reg	N.A.	74.9	N.A.
9. Templeton Devel. Markets	Intl	Md/Val	74.5	N.A.
10. Scudder Latin America	Intl	N.A.	74.3	N.A.
11. Hancock Freedom Pac. Basin	Reg	Lg/Bl	70.5	12
12. Merrill Lynch Devel. Cap.	Intl	Md/Bl	69.0	N.A.
13. Prudential Pacific Gro. B	Reg	Md/Gro	65.1	N.A.
14. G.T. Global Emerg. Mkt. A	Intl	N.A.	64.5	N.A.
15. Fidelity Pacific Basin	Reg	Lg/Bl	63.9	12
16. Lexington Worldwide Emer.	Intl	Md/Gro	63.4	10
17. Merrill Lynch Latin Amer. B	Reg	N.A.	63.0	N.A.
18. Franklin Pacific Growth	Reg	Md/Val	60.6	N.A.
19. G.T. Pacific Growth A	Reg	Lg/Gro	60.6	10
20. Mackenzie Canada	Reg	Sm/Val	60.1	11
21. Scudder Pacific Opp.	Reg	Md/Gro	60.1	N.A.
22. Prudential Glob. Genesis B	Intl	Sm/Gro	59.5	10
23. Montgomery Emerging Mkt.	Intl	N.A.	58.7	N.A.
24. Govett International Equity	Intl	Md/Bl	54.5	N.A.
25. Oakmark International	Intl	Md/Val	53.6	N.A.
Average international fund			**37.5**	

THREE-YEAR WINNERS

Fund name	Type	Style	% avg. annual return	Risk level
1. Equifund Hong Kong Natl. Fid.	Reg	N.A.	42.2	N.A.
2. Newport Tiger	Reg	Lg/Gro	39.2	N.A.
3. Dean Witter Pacific Growth	Reg	Md/Gro	34.8	N.A.
4. T. Rowe Price New Asia	Reg	Md/Gro	33.4	N.A.
5. Smith Barney Intl. Eq. A	Intl	Md/Gro	28.4	10
6. 59 Wall St. Pac. Basin Eq.	Reg	N.A.	28.3	N.A.
7. Lexington Worldwide Emer.	Intl	Md/Gro	28.2	10
8. Merrill Lynch Devel. Cap.	Intl	Md/Bl	28.2	10
9. Fidelity Emer. Markets	Intl	N.A.	27.1	N.A.
10. Keystone Amer. Glob. Opp. A	Intl	Sm/Gro	26.4	11
11. Templeton Global Opp.	Intl	Lg/Val	25.3	N.A.
12. Hancock Freedom Pac. Basin	Reg	Lg/Bl	25.1	12
13. Templeton Smaller Co. Gro.	Intl	Sm/Val	24.0	9
14. Prudential Glob. Genesis B	Intl	Sm/Gro	22.6	10
15. SmallCap World	Intl	Sm/Gro	22.6	N.A.
16. Templeton Growth	Intl	Lg/Val	22.0	8
17. Templeton World	Intl	Lg/Val	21.4	9
18. Founders Worldwide Growth	Intl	Md/Gro	21.1	N.A.
19. National Worldwide Opp.	Intl	Md/Bl	21.0	11
20. Harbor International[1]	Intl	Lg/Val	20.8	10
21. Warburg Pincus Intl. Com.	Intl	Md/Val	20.4	N.A.
22. Ivy International A	Intl	Lg/Val	20.2	11
23. United International Growth	Intl	Md/Gro	19.9	11
24. Fidelity Pacific Basin	Reg	Lg/Bl	19.9	12
25. Olympic International	Intl	Md/Val	19.5	N.A.
Average international fund			**14.0**	

FIVE-YEAR WINNERS

Fund name	Type	Style	% avg. annual return	Risk level
1. Smith Barney Intl. Eq. A	Intl	Md/Gro	19.7	10
2. Lexington Worldwide Emer.	Intl	Md/Gro	18.2	10
3. G.T. Pacific Growth A	Reg	Lg/Gro	17.1	10
4. Harbor International[1]	Intl	Lg/Val	16.8	10
5. Oppenheimer Global A	Intl	Md/Gro	15.9	10
6. Scudder Global	Intl	Lg/Val	15.6	7
7. Templeton Foreign	Intl	Lg/Val	15.5	8
8. EuroPacific Growth	Intl	Lg/Bl	15.3	8
9. Templeton Growth	Intl	Lg/Val	15.2	8
10. Keystone Amer. Glob. Opp. A	Intl	Sm/Gro	15.0	11
11. New Perspective	Intl	Lg/Bl	14.8	8
12. Prudential Glob. Genesis B	Intl	Sm/Gro	14.6	10
13. Ivy International	Intl	Lg/Val	14.1	11
14. G.T. Worldwide Growth A	Intl	Md/Gro	13.8	9
15. Templeton Smaller Co. Gro.	Intl	Sm/Val	13.7	9
16. T. Rowe Price Intl. Dis.	Intl	Sm/Bl	13.4	11
17. SoGen International	Intl	Sm/Bl	13.3	5
18. Templeton World	Intl	Lg/Val	13.0	9
19. Hancock Freedom Pac. Basin	Reg	Lg/Bl	12.3	12
20. Dreyfus Strat. World Inv.	Intl	Md/Gro	12.2	6
21. Managers Intl. Equity	Intl	Lg/Bl	12.1	9
22. T. Rowe Price Intl. Stock	Intl	Lg/Bl	12.1	11
23. Princor World	Intl	Md/Bl	12.0	10
24. Putnam Global Gro. A	Intl	Md/Bl	12.0	10
25. Hancock Freedom Global B	Intl	Lg/Gro	11.9	11
Average international fund			**9.4**	

SPECIALTY

ONE-YEAR WINNERS

Fund name	Type	Style	% 1993 return	Risk level
1. Lexington Strategic Invest.	Spec	Sm/Bl	264.9	12
2. United Svcs. Gold Shares	Spec	Sm/Gro	123.9	12
3. Van Eck Intl. Investors	Spec	Md/Gro	113.4	12
4. Fidelity Select P.M.	Spec	Sm/Gro	111.6	12
5. Keystone Precious Metals	Spec	Sm/Gro	101.9	12
6. Blanchard Precious Metals	Spec	Sm/Gro	100.4	12
7. Vanguard Sp. Gold & Prec.	Spec	Sm/Gro	93.4	12
8. United Services World Gold	Spec	Sm/Gro	89.8	12
9. Thomson P.M./Nat. Res. B	Spec	Md/Gro	89.5	12
10. Bull & Bear Gold Investors	Spec	Sm/Gro	87.6	12
11. Lexington Goldfund	Spec	Md/Gro	87.0	12
12. Benham Gold Equities Index	Spec	Md/Gro	81.2	12
13. IDS Precious Metals	Spec	Md/Gro	80.9	12
14. Van Eck Gold/Resources	Spec	Md/Gro	80.6	12
15. Fidelity Select Amer. Gold	Spec	Md/Gro	78.7	12
16. Lexington Strategic Silver	Spec	Sm/Gro	76.5	12
17. United Gold & Gov.	Spec	Sm/Gro	75.8	12
18. Franklin Gold	Spec	Md/Gro	73.8	12
19. Invesco Strat. Gold	Spec	Sm/Gro	72.6	12
20. Pioneer Gold Shares	Spec	Sm/Gro	70.8	N.A.
21. Smith Bar. Shear. P.M.&Min. A	Spec	Md/Gro	65.4	12
22. Oppenheimer Gold/Spec. Min.	Spec	Md/Gro	61.8	12
23. Scudder Gold	Spec	Sm/Gro	59.4	12
24. USAA Investment Gold	Spec	Md/Gro	58.3	12
25. Dean Witter P.M. & Mining	Spec	Md/Gro	55.9	N.A.
Average specialty fund			**29.7**	

THREE-YEAR WINNERS

Fund name	Type	Style	% avg. annual return	Risk level
1. Fidelity Select Home Finance	Spec	Sm/Val	49.0	12
2. Hancock Freedom Reg. Bank B	Spec	Sm/Val	42.8	9
3. Fidelity Select Broker./Inv.	Spec	Md/Val	42.0	12
4. Fidelity Select Reg'l. Banks	Spec	Md/Val	39.8	12
5. Fidelity Select Fin. Svc.	Spec	Md/Gro	39.5	12
6. Fidelity Select Automotive	Spec	Md/Bl	38.1	9
7. Fidelity Select Soft./Comp.	Spec	Md/Gro	37.8	12
8. Invesco Strat. Fin. Svc.	Spec	Md/Gro	37.8	12
9. Invesco Strat. Leisure	Spec	Sm/Gro	36.8	11
10. PaineWebber Regional Fin. A	Spec	Sm/Val	36.3	10
11. Fidelity Select Devel. Com.	Spec	Sm/Gro	35.6	N.A.
12. Fidelity Select Transport.	Spec	Sm/Bl	35.2	10
13. Seligman Commun./Info A	Spec	Md/Gro	35.1	12
14. Invesco Strat. Technology	Spec	Md/Gro	34.2	12
15. T. Rowe Price Science/Tech.	Spec	Md/Gro	33.2	12
16. Fidelity Select Retailing	Spec	Sm/Bl	32.4	11
17. Fidelity Select Brdcst./Med.	Spec	Lg/Gro	32.2	11
18. Fidelity Select Electronics	Spec	Lg/Gro	31.6	12
19. Fidelity Select Con./Housing	Spec	Md/Bl	30.9	11
20. Fidelity Select Technology	Spec	Md/Gro	30.5	12
21. Alliance Technology A	Spec	Md/Gro	29.4	12
22. Fidelity Select Leisure	Spec	Md/Gro	29.2	10
23. Fidelity Select Computers	Spec	Sm/Bl	27.1	12
24. Fidelity Select Indust. Equip.	Spec	Sm/Gro	26.5	11
25. Cowen Opportunity	Spec	Sm/Bl	26.3	12
Average specialty fund			**17.3**	

FIVE-YEAR WINNERS

Fund name	Type	Style	% avg. annual return	Risk level
1. Fidelity Select Biotech.	Spec	Md/Gro	30.2	12
2. Invesco Strat. Fin. Svc.	Spec	Md/Gro	27.1	10
3. T. Rowe Price Science/Tech.	Spec	Md/Gro	26.8	12
4. Invesco Strat. Technology	Spec	Md/Gro	26.1	12
5. Invesco Strat. Leisure	Spec	Sm/Gro	25.8	11
6. Fidelity Select Home Finance	Spec	Sm/Val	25.1	12
7. Invesco Strat. Health Sci.	Spec	Sm/Gro	24.7	12
8. Fidelity Select Medic. Del.	Spec	Md/Gro	24.5	12
9. Fidelity Select Soft./Comp.	Spec	Md/Gro	24.2	12
10. Fidelity Select Technology	Spec	Md/Gro	23.5	12
11. Fidelity Select Retailing	Spec	Sm/Bl	23.3	11
12. Seligman Commun./Info A	Spec	Md/Gro	23.3	12
13. Medical Research Invest.	Spec	Md/Bl	23.0	10
14. Fidelity Select Electronics	Spec	Lg/Gro	22.8	12
15. Fidelity Select Health Care	Spec	Md/Gro	22.4	11
16. Fidelity Select Reg'l. Banks	Spec	Md/Val	22.4	12
17. Fidelity Select Broker./Inv.	Spec	Md/Val	22.3	12
18. Hancock Freedom Reg. Bank B	Spec	Sm/Val	22.1	9
19. PaineWebber Regional Fin. A	Spec	Sm/Val	22.0	10
20. Fidelity Select Computers	Spec	Sm/Bl	21.0	12
21. Fidelity Select Automotive	Spec	Md/Bl	20.6	9
22. Vanguard Sp. Health Care	Spec	Md/Bl	20.1	9
23. Fidelity Select Transport.	Spec	Sm/Bl	20.0	10
24. Cowen Opportunity	Spec	Sm/Bl	20.0	12
25. Fidelity Select Tele.	Spec	Lg/Gro	19.8	10
Average specialty fund			**13.4**	

Notes: [1]Closed to new investors [2]Investment by contractual plan only N.A.: Not available
Risk level requires five-year record. **Source: Morningstar Inc.,** Chicago, Ill.; 800-820-8082

TAXABLE BONDS

ONE-YEAR WINNERS

Fund name	Type	Style	% 1993 return	Risk level
1. G.T. Global High-Income A	WI	N.A.	51.6	N.A.
2. G.T. Global Strategic Inc. A	WI	L/M	43.9	6
3. Benham Target Mat. 2020	Gov	L/Hi	35.6	N.A.
4. Keystone Amer. Strat. Inc. A	HYC	L/Lo	31.7	8
5. Dean Witter High-Yield Sec.	HYC	Int/Lo	31.5	11
6. Alliance Bond Corp. Bond A	IGC	L/Lo	31.1	5
7. Benham Target Mat. 2015	Gov	L/Hi	30.5	11
8. FT International Income A	WI	Int/Hi	27.0	N.A.
9. Benham Target Mat. 2010	Gov	L/Hi	26.3	9
10. Keystone Custodian B-4	HYC	Int/Lo	26.2	8
11. G.T. Global Gov. Income A	WI	L/Hi	25.5	6
12. Bull & Bear Global Income	WI	L/M	25.0	6
13. Fidelity Capital & Income	HYC	N.A.	24.2	6
14. Northeast Investors	HYC	Int/Lo	23.6	6
15. PaineWebber High-Inc. A	HYC	Int/Lo	22.7	6
16. MetLife-State St. H/I A	HYC	Int/Lo	22.4	7
17. Loomis Sayles Bond	IGC	L/M	22.2	N.A.
18. T. Rowe Price High-Yield	HYC	Int/Lo	21.8	6
19. Fortis Advantage High-Yield	HYC	Int/Lo	21.8	7
20. MainStay High-Yield Corp.	HYC	Int/Lo	21.7	6
21. Benham Target Mat. 2005	Gov	L/Hi	21.6	8
22. Phoenix High-Yield	HYC	Int/Lo	21.5	6
23. Transamerica Sp. H/Y Bond	HYC	Int/Lo	21.4	6
24. Fidelity Global Bond	WI	Int/M	21.3	5
25. Oppenheimer Champion H/Y	HYC	Int/Lo	21.2	2
Average taxable bond fund			10.0	

THREE-YEAR WINNERS

Fund name	Type	Style	% avg. annual return	Risk level
1. Dean Witter High-Yield Sec.	HYC	N.A.	39.9	11
2. Keystone Amer. Strat. Inc. A	HYC	L/Lo	31.3	8
3. PaineWebber High-Inc. A	HYC	Int/Lo	30.8	6
4. Advantage High-Yield Bond	HYC	L/Lo	30.5	N.A.
5. Liberty High-Inc. Bond	HYC	Int/Lo	30.2	7
6. Fortis Advantage High-Yield	HYC	Int/Lo	30.1	7
7. Kemper Diversified Income	HYC	Int/Lo	29.3	6
8. Keystone Custodian B-4	HYC	Int/Lo	28.3	8
9. Kemper Inv. Diver. Inc. Init.	HYC	Int/Lo	28.3	7
10. Putnam High Yield Advantage	HYC	Int/Lo	27.9	6
11. Colonial High-Yield Secs. A	HYC	Int/Lo	27.8	6
12. MFS High-Income A	HYC	Int/Lo	27.7	7
13. Kemper High-Yield	HYC	Int/Lo	27.4	7
14. Franklin Tax-Adv. H/Y	HYC	Int/Lo	27.3	7
15. Fidelity Capital & Income	HYC	N.A.	27.3	6
16. Franklin AGE High-Income	HYC	Int/Lo	26.7	6
17. Kemper Inv. H/Y Init.	HYC	Int/Lo	26.4	7
18. MetLife-State St. H/I A	HYC	Int/Lo	26.2	7
19. AIM High-Yield A	HYC	Int/Lo	25.9	6
20. Fidelity Advisor High-Yield	HYC	Int/Lo	25.8	5
21. Eaton Vance Income Boston	HYC	Int/Lo	25.7	6
22. IDS Extra Income	HYC	Int/Lo	25.7	6
23. Fidelity Spartan High-Income	HYC	N.A.	25.5	N.A.
24. American Cap. H/Y Inv. A	HYC	Int/Lo	25.5	8
25. Merrill Lynch High-Income A	HYC	Int/Lo	25.5	6
Average taxable bond fund			11.7	

FIVE-YEAR WINNERS

Fund name	Type	Style	% avg. annual return	Risk level
1. Fidelity Advisor High-Yield	HYC	Int/Lo	17.2	5
2. Benham Target Mat. 2015	Gov	L/Hi	17.2	11
3. Benham Target Mat. 2010	Gov	L/Hi	16.4	9
4. Alliance Bond Corp. Bond A	IGC	L/Lo	15.9	5
5. Benham Target Mat. 2005	Gov	L/Hi	15.6	8
6. Kemper Diversified Income	HYC	Int/Lo	15.3	6
7. PaineWebber High-Inc. A	HYC	Int/Lo	15.1	6
8. Oppenheimer Champion H/Y	HYC	Int/Lo	15.1	2
9. G.T. Global Strategic Inc. A	WI	L/M	15.1	6
10. Scudder Intl. Bond	WI	Int/M	14.6	6
11. Merrill Lynch High-Income A	HYC	Int/Lo	14.5	6
12. Fidelity Capital & Income	HYC	N.A.	14.0	6
13. Liberty High-Inc. Bond	HYC	Int/Lo	13.9	7
14. Benham Target Mat. 2000	Gov	Int/Hi	13.8	7
15. Kemper Inv. Diver. Inc. Init.	HYC	Int/Lo	13.8	7
16. Scudder Zero Coupon 2000	Gov	Int/Hi	13.7	7
17. American High-Income	HYC	Int	13.4	5
18. Smith B. Sh. Inv. Gr. Bd. B	IGC	L/M	13.3	6
19. Heartland US Government	Gov	Int/M	13.2	3
20. Vanguard F/I L/T Corp. Bond	IGC	L/M	13.2	5
21. Managers Intm. Mortgage	MBS	N.A.	13.1	1
22. Dreyfus 100% US Long-Term	Gov	L/Hi	13.0	5
23. Putnam High Yield Advantage	HYC	Int/Lo	13.0	6
24. AIM High-Yield A	HYC	Int/Lo	12.9	6
25. Vanguard F/I Long-Term US	Gov	L/Hi	12.9	6
Average taxable bond fund			10.1	

TAX-EXEMPT BONDS

ONE-YEAR WINNERS

Fund name	Type	Style	% 1993 return	Risk level
1. Smith B. Shear. Mgd. Muni A	Muni	L/M	16.0	5
2. Van Kampen T/F High-Inc. A	Muni	L/M	15.7	1
3. UST Master L/T T/E Non-Plan	Muni	L/M	15.6	5
4. Transamerica T/F Bond A	Muni	L/M	15.1	N.A.
5. Sierra National Muni	Muni	L/M	15.0	N.A.
6. Vista Tax-Free Income	Muni	L/M	15.0	4
7. Cambridge Municipal Inc. B	Muni	L/M	14.9	N.A.
8. Piper Jaffray Natl. T/E	Muni	L/M	14.6	4
9. Eaton Vance National Muni	Muni	L/M	14.6	4
10. Premier Muni Bond A	Muni	L/M	14.4	3
11. United Municipal Bond	Muni	L/M	14.3	6
12. Principal Pres. Tax-Exempt	Muni	L/Hi	14.3	2
13. Flagship All-Amer. T/E A	Muni	L/M	14.2	4
14. MFS Muni Bond A	Muni	L/M	14.2	5
15. RBB Tax-Free	Muni	L/M	14.2	4
16. Benham Natl. T/F Long-Term	Muni	L/Hi	14.2	6
17. Seligman Tax-Ex. National	Muni	L/Hi	14.1	6
18. Fidelity Spartan Muni Inc.	Muni	L/M	13.9	N.A.
19. Scudder H/Y Tax-Free	Muni	L/M	13.8	4
20. Phoenix Tax-Exempt Bond	Muni	L/M	13.6	5
21. Flagship Intermediate T/E A	Muni	Int/M	13.6	N.A.
22. Eaton Vance Muni Bond	Muni	L/M	13.5	4
23. Nuveen Ins. Muni Bond	Muni	L/Hi	13.5	5
24. Oppenheimer T/F Bond	Muni	L/M	13.5	3
25. Fidelity Insured Tax-Free	Muni	L/Hi	13.5	4
Average tax-exempt bond fund			11.3	

THREE-YEAR WINNERS

Fund name	Type	Style	% avg. annual return	Risk level
1. Transamerica T/F Bond A	Muni	L/M	14.2	N.A.
2. Vista Tax-Free Income	Muni	L/M	14.0	4
3. Sierra National Muni	Muni	L/M	13.4	N.A.
4. Smith B. Shear. Mgd. Muni A	Muni	L/M	13.2	5
5. Flagship All-Amer. T/E A	Muni	L/M	13.1	4
6. UST Master L/T T/E Non-Plan	Muni	L/M	12.8	5
7. Premier Muni Bond A	Muni	L/M	12.7	3
8. Scudder H/Y Tax-Free	Muni	L/M	12.7	4
9. General Municipal Bond	Muni	L/M	12.6	4
10. Strong Muni Bond	Muni	L/M	12.6	4
11. United Municipal Bond	Muni	L/M	12.4	6
12. Vanguard Muni High-Yield	Muni	L/M	12.4	5
13. Fidelity Advisor High-Income	Muni	L/Lo	12.2	1
14. Putnam Tax Exempt Inc. A	Muni	L/M	12.2	5
15. Eaton Vance National Muni	Muni	L/M	12.1	4
16. MFS Muni Bond A	Muni	L/M	12.1	5
17. Benham Natl. T/F Long-Term	Muni	L/Hi	12.1	6
18. RBB Tax-Free	Muni	L/M	12.1	4
19. Quest for Value Natl. T/E	Muni	L/M	12.1	N.A.
20. Vanguard Muni Long-Term	Muni	L/M	12.1	5
21. Nuveen Ins. Muni Bond	Muni	L/Hi	12.0	5
22. Eaton Vance Muni Bond	Muni	L/M	12.0	4
23. Van Kampen Muni Inc. A	Muni	L/M	11.9	N.A.
24. Putnam Muni Income A	Muni	L/M	11.9	N.A.
25. Phoenix Tax-Exempt Bond	Muni	L/M	11.9	5
Average tax-exempt bond fund			10.4	

FIVE-YEAR WINNERS

Fund name	Type	Style	% avg. annual return	Risk level
1. Fidelity Advisor High-Inc.	Muni	L/Lo	12.0	1
2. Vista Tax-Free Income	Muni	L/M	11.8	4
3. UST Master L/T T/E Non-Plan	Muni	L/M	11.4	5
4. General Municipal Bond	Muni	L/M	11.3	4
5. Flagship All-Amer. T/E A	Muni	L/M	11.3	4
6. Premier Muni Bond A	Muni	L/M	11.1	3
7. MFS Muni Bond A	Muni	L/M	11.0	5
8. Smith B. Shear. Mgd. Muni A	Muni	L/M	10.9	5
9. Vanguard Muni Long-Term	Muni	L/M	10.9	6
10. Scudder H/Y Tax-Free	Muni	L/M	10.9	4
11. Vanguard Muni High-Yield	Muni	L/M	10.8	5
12. United Municipal Bond	Muni	L/M	10.8	6
13. Eaton Vance Muni Bond	Muni	L/M	10.7	4
14. Alliance Muni Inc. Natl. A	Muni	L/M	10.6	2
15. Phoenix Tax-Exempt Bond	Muni	L/M	10.6	5
16. Benham Natl. T/F Long-Term	Muni	L/Hi	10.5	6
17. Kemper Municipal Bond	Muni	L/Hi	10.5	5
18. Scudder Mgd. Muni Bonds	Muni	L/Hi	10.5	5
19. Smith Barney Muni Natl. A	Muni	L/M	10.4	3
20. Putnam Tax Exempt Inc. A	Muni	L/M	10.4	5
21. Vanguard Muni Insured Long	Muni	L/Hi	10.4	6
22. Nuveen Ins. Muni Bond	Muni	L/Hi	10.4	5
23. Invesco Tax-Free L/T Bond	Muni	L/M	10.4	5
24. Safeco Muni Bond	Muni	L/M	10.4	5
25. T. Rowe Price T/F High-Yield	Muni	L/M	10.4	1
Average tax-exempt bond fund			9.3	

THE 1,935 MAJOR FUNDS

Fund name	Type	Style	Risk level	% compound annual return to Jan. 1, 1994			Annual performance analysis (percentile ranking by type)					Expense analysis			Net assets (millions)	Telephone (800)
				One year	Three years	Five years	1993	1992	1991	1990	1989	% max. sales charge	Annual charges	Five-year total per $1,000		

G R O W T H

Fund name	Type	Style	Risk level	One year	Three years	Five years	1993	1992	1991	1990	1989	% max. sales charge	Annual charges	Five-year total per $1,000	Net assets (millions)	Telephone (800)
20th Century Giftrust Inv.	Agg	Sm/Gro	12	31.4	42.1	29.0	54	58	85	34	79	None	1.00%	$55	$153.7	345-2021
20th Century Growth Inv.	Gro	Lg/Gro	11	3.8	18.8	18.2	27	12	69	47	82	None	1.00	55	4,642.6	345-2021
20th Century Heritage Inv.	Gro	Md/Bl	10	20.5	21.7	17.2	61	36	35	35	66	None	1.00	55	682.0	345-2021
20th Century Select Inv.	Gro	Lg/Bl	9	14.7	13.0	14.9	49	11	31	54	75	None	1.00	55	5,160.4	345-2021
20th Century Ultra Inv.	Agg	Md/Gro	12	21.8	32.0	28.1	38	29	86	78	60	None	1.00	55	8,019.0	345-2021
20th Century Vista Inv.	Agg	Md/Gro	12	5.4	21.5	18.1	10	23	72	36	82	None	1.00	55	847.3	345-2021
59 Wall St. Small Co.	Agg	N.A.	N.A.	12.2	N.A.	N.A.	22	45	N.A.	N.A.	N.A.	None	1.10	67	40.9	493-8100[5]
ABT Emerging Growth	Agg	Md/Gro	12	17.9	33.5	24.9	31	51	76	55	55	4.75	1.26	123	58.1	553-7838
AIM Aggressive Growth	Agg	Sm/Gro	12	32.0	38.0	24.3	55	63	61	52	36	5.5	1.00	120	215.1	347-1919
AIM Constellation	Agg	Md/Gro	12	17.3	32.0	24.9	30	53	68	56	61	5.5	1.20	118	2,754.1	347-1919
AIM Growth A	Gro	Lg/Gro	11	3.6	12.5	11.7	27	19	36	44	53	5.5	1.17	116	149.8	347-1919
AIM Summit[3]	Gro	Lg/Bl	9	8.3	17.6	16.5	36	26	43	57	57	8.5	0.73	42	705.7	347-1919
AIM Value A	Gro	Md/Bl	9	18.7	25.6	21.6	58	46	43	59	59	5.5	1.12	115	677.0	347-1919
AIM Weingarten	Gro	Lg/Bl	10	1.5	13.7	16.1	23	17	47	67	68	5.5	1.10	114	4,699.0	347-1919
AMCAP	Gro	Lg/Gro	9	11.0	17.7	14.7	42	31	36	46	50	5.75	0.75	97	3,104.5	421-0180
API Growth	Gro	Md/Gro	12	13.1	19.0	11.3	46	22	46	27	27	None	1.98	N.A.	44.2	544-6060
Accessor Equity Market	Gro	Lg/Bl	N.A.	3.4	N.A.	N.A.	27	N.A.	N.A.	N.A.	N.A.	None	1.21	N.A.	8.6	759-3504
Accessor Growth	Gro	Lg/Bl	N.A.	14.2	N.A.	N.A.	48	N.A.	N.A.	N.A.	N.A.	None	1.21	N.A.	7.8	759-3504
Accessor Small Cap	Agg	Sm/Val	N.A.	14.3	N.A.	N.A.	25	N.A.	N.A.	N.A.	N.A.	None	1.55	N.A.	8.6	759-3504
Acorn[1]	Agg	Sm/Gro	10	32.3	34.3	20.1	56	68	43	33	42	None	0.68	35	2,032.7	922-6769
Advantage Growth	Gro	Lg/Bl	9	10.4	18.1	14.2	41	32	38	44	44	4.0(d)	2.06	115	77.4	243-8115
Advantage Special	Agg	Sm/Gro	11	20.2	29.2	19.3	35	52	53	48	38	4.0(d)	2.39	150	26.0	243-8115
Alger Growth	Gro	Md/Gro	11	20.3	24.2	21.5	61	37	43	60	66	5.0(d)	2.19	144	38.0	992-3863
Alger Small Capitalization	Agg	Sm/Gro	12	12.8	21.9	26.1	23	33	51	74	100	5.0(d)	2.10	136	299.8	992-3863
Alliance A	Gro	Lg/Bl	11	25.7	24.5	17.9	72	43	33	46	42	4.25	0.91	110	870.0	227-4618
Alliance Counterpoint A	Gro	Lg/Gro	9	7.2	14.4	13.9	34	26	33	45	64	4.25	1.57	138	67.7	227-4618
Alliance Growth B	Gro	Md/Bl	10	28.2	32.0	22.0	77	36	62	38	51	4.0(d)	2.15	128	105.1	227-4618
Alliance Premier Growth B	Gro	Lg/Gro	N.A.	9.4	N.A.	N.A.	39	N.A.	N.A.	N.A.	N.A.	4.0(d)	2.68	143	152.8	227-4618
Alliance Quasar A	Agg	Sm/Bl	12	16.2	17.1	9.5	28	31	28	24	47	4.25	1.68	138	214.9	227-4618
American Cap. Emerg. Gro. A	Agg	Md/Gro	11	23.9	29.7	23.5	42	43	57	66	48	5.75	1.10	117	550.1	421-5666
American Cap. Enterprise A	Gro	Md/Gro	10	11.0	18.8	16.4	42	33	39	49	58	5.75	0.99	109	781.6	421-5666
American Cap. Pace A	Gro	Md/Bl	9	10.8	15.0	13.0	42	26	31	42	53	5.75	1.06	110	2,450.8	421-5666
American Growth	Gro	Md/Bl	8	24.1	20.1	15.0	69	40	23	40	45	5.75	1.44	158	67.3	525-2406
American Heritage	Agg	Md/Bl	11	41.4	48.9	17.3	71	59	98	11	2	None	2.10	118	133.9	828-5050
American National Growth	Gro	Lg/Gro	10	8.2	12.5	11.4	36	13	35	49	44	5.75	1.07	113	112.2	231-4639
Atlanta Growth	Gro	Md/Bl	N.A.	6.0	N.A.	N.A.	32	N.A.	N.A.	N.A.	N.A.	3.75	2.53	203	8.8	762-0227
Babson Enterprise II	Agg	Sm/Val	N.A.	19.8	N.A.	N.A.	35	56	N.A.	N.A.	N.A.	None	1.83	99	27.7	422-2766
Babson Enterprise[1]	Agg	Sm/Val	9	16.3	27.5	16.4	29	69	38	36	39	None	1.11	64	219.7	422-2766
Babson Growth	Gro	Lg/Val	9	10.3	14.9	10.9	40	34	25	34	39	None	0.86	48	246.8	422-2766
Baird Capital Development	Gro	Sm/Bl	10	11.5	23.1	16.4	43	42	46	38	44	5.75	1.70	138	53.2	792-2473
Baron Asset	Agg	Sm/Gro	11	23.5	23.8	13.9	41	51	29	31	42	None	1.80	92	64.4	992-2766
Beacon Hill Mutual	Gro	Lg/Gro	9	(5.2)	5.6	8.5	9	16	26	68	37	None	2.50	148	4.9	482-0795[21]
Benham Equity Growth	Gro	Md/Val	N.A.	11.4	N.A.	N.A.	43	26	N.A.	N.A.	N.A.	None	0.75	42	91.3	472-3389
Berger 100	Gro	Md/Gro	11	21.2	35.4	28.3	63	33	89	43	93	None	1.69	107	1,524.0	333-1001
Berwyn	Gro	Sm/Val	10	23.0	28.7	13.6	66	53	43	3	28	None	1.40	76	46.0	824-2249
Blanchard American Equity	Gro	Lg/Gro	N.A.	(1.2)	N.A.	N.A.	17	N.A.	N.A.	N.A.	N.A.	None	3.13	N.A.	22.4	922-7771
Boston Co. Cap. App. Retail	Gro	Lg/Val	10	16.5	14.2	10.0	53	26	22	26	45	None	1.16	63	358.3	225-5267
Boston Co. Contrarian Retail	Gro	Sm/Val	10	21.2	23.8	15.3	63	36	41	36	30	None	2.00	108	3.8	225-5267
Boston Co. Spec. Gro. Retail	Gro	Md/Gro	11	20.0	25.1	17.2	60	62	28	45	33	None	1.75	97	87.0	225-5267
Boulevard Blue-Chip Growth	Gro	Lg/Gro	N.A.	(2.2)	N.A.	N.A.	15	N.A.	N.A.	N.A.	N.A.	4.0	0.75	N.A.	31.0	285-3863
Brandywine	Gro	Md/Gro	11	22.6	28.4	23.1	66	45	49	57	61	None	1.10	61	1,476.2	338-1579
Bruce	Gro	N.A.	12	19.4	10.3	8.9	59	36	0	53	26	None	2.12	118	2.7	236-9160[13]
Bull & Bear Special Eq.	Agg	Md/Gro	12	16.4	28.0	13.7	29	76	35	2	68	None	2.62	161	80.7	847-4200
CGM Capital Development[1]	Gro	Md/Bl	12	28.7	44.4	29.2	78	48	100	58	30	None	0.86	49	487.6	345-4048
Calvert Social Inv. Equity	Gro	Md/Bl	8	2.1	10.5	10.4	24	33	21	44	50	4.75	1.13	102	87.0	368-2748
Calvert-Ariel Appreciation	Gro	Sm/Bl	N.A.	8.0	17.6	N.A.	36	41	33	52	N.A.	4.75	1.37	125	215.3	368-2748
Calvert-Ariel Growth[1]	Agg	Sm/Bl	10	8.8	17.3	11.1	16	47	26	36	43	4.75	1.17	113	228.6	368-2748
Cambridge Capital Growth B	Gro	Lg/Bl	N.A.	2.0	N.A.	N.A.	24	N.A.	N.A.	N.A.	N.A.	None	2.24	119	55.7	382-0016
Cambridge Growth B	Gro	Lg/Gro	N.A.	3.9	N.A.	N.A.	27	N.A.	N.A.	N.A.	N.A.	None	2.41	121	34.4	382-0016
Cappiello-Rushmore Emerg. Gro.	Agg	Sm/Gro	N.A.	22.5	N.A.	N.A.	39	N.A.	N.A.	N.A.	N.A.	None	N.A.	82	10.4	343-3355
Cappiello-Rushmore Gro.	Gro	Md/Bl	N.A.	14.4	N.A.	N.A.	49	N.A.	N.A.	N.A.	N.A.	None	N.A.	82	4.2	343-3355
Capstone Fund of the S.W.	Gro	Md/Gro	11	8.2	20.2	16.1	36	33	47	36	61	4.75	2.06	148	15.3	262-6631
Capstone US Trend	Gro	Lg/Bl	9	6.1	13.0	12.8	32	20	34	48	57	4.75	1.13	105	96.5	262-6631
Colonial Growth Shares A	Gro	Md/Bl	10	10.0	17.9	13.6	40	37	33	32	54	5.75	1.16	119	170.0	248-2828
Colonial Small Stock A	Agg	Sm/Val	11	18.8	19.5	7.8	33	62	11	23	23	5.75	1.89	168	25.3	248-2828

Notes: (d): Maximum deferred sales charge [1]Closed to new investors [3]Investment by contractual plan only
[5]Area code 212 [13]Area code 312 [21]Area code 617

Fund name	Type	Style	Risk level	% compound annual return to Jan. 1, 1994			Annual performance analysis (percentile ranking by type)					Expense analysis			Net assets (millions)	Telephone (800)
				One year	Three years	Five years	1993	1992	1991	1990	1989	% max. sales charge	Annual charges	Five-year total per $1,000		
Colonial US Fund for Gro. B	Gro	Md/Bl	N.A.	13.2	N.A.	N.A.	46	N.A.	N.A.	N.A.	N.A.	5.0(d)	2.25%	N.A.	$121.0	248-2828
Columbia Growth	Gro	Lg/Bl	9	13.0	19.3	16.2	46	38	34	48	54	None	0.82	$48	614.2	547-1707
Columbia Special	Agg	Sm/Gro	12	21.6	27.6	19.2	38	50	46	42	52	None	1.13	65	741.0	547-1707
Common Sense Growth	Gro	Md/Bl	9	9.4	17.5	15.0	39	31	38	48	51	8.5	1.18	144	2,065.7	544-5445
Compass Cap. Aggress. Eq.	Agg	Sm/Val	N.A.	6.0	N.A.	N.A.	11	47	N.A.	N.A.	N.A.	3.75	1.38	102	22.3	451-8371
Compass Capital Growth	Gro	Lg/Bl	N.A.	1.6	11.8	N.A.	23	27	30	48	N.A.	3.75	0.98	91	157.8	451-8371
Composite Northwest 50	Gro	Md/Val	11	2.4	15.2	15.8	24	25	43	53	72	4.5	1.08	103	167.8	543-8072
Connecticut Mutual Growth	Gro	Md/Val	9	20.9	22.8	18.1	62	39	36	38	66	5.0	1.07	111	65.6	322-2642
CoreFund Growth Equity B	Gro	Md/Gro	N.A.	5.7	N.A.	N.A.	31	N.A.	N.A.	N.A.	N.A.	4.5	N.A.	91	7.3	355-2673
DG Equity	Gro	Lg/Bl	N.A.	5.6	N.A.	N.A.	31	N.A.	N.A.	N.A.	N.A.	2.0	0.98	N.A.	278.8	748-8500
Dean Witter American Value	Gro	Md/Gro	10	18.7	24.5	19.1	58	25	57	53	46	5.0(d)	1.72	106	1,138.7	869-3863
Dean Witter Capital Growth	Gro	Md/Bl	N.A.	(9.0)	10.3	N.A.	1	18	48	N.A.	N.A.	5.0(d)	1.74	114	684.1	869-3863
Dean Witter Developing Gro.	Agg	Sm/Gro	12	30.8	23.6	15.9	53	22	44	56	28	5.0(d)	1.88	121	266.3	869-3863
Delaware DelCap	Gro	Sm/Gro	11	11.9	17.5	16.0	44	22	42	47	64	5.75	1.33	129	1,040.7	523-4640
Delaware Trend	Agg	Sm/Gro	12	22.4	37.7	24.2	39	65	73	22	78	5.75	1.33	119	280.5	523-4640
Delaware Value	Gro	Sm/Val	9	18.8	26.8	18.5	58	43	49	26	59	5.75	1.72	156	147.4	523-4640
Dreman Contrarian	Gro	Lg/Val	10	9.1	15.4	11.3	38	38	26	42	32	None	1.25	69	17.1	533-1608
Dreman Small Cap Value	Agg	Sm/Val	N.A.	2.2	N.A.	N.A.	5	N.A.	N.A.	N.A.	N.A.	None	1.25	69	5.7	533-1608
Dreyfus Appreciation	Gro	Lg/Gro	9	0.7	13.3	12.7	21	26	38	51	50	None	0.55	63	241.2	242-8671
Dreyfus Cap. Gro. (Premier)	Gro	Lg/Bl	8	14.7	17.4	13.9	49	29	32	52	36	3.0	1.07	87	619.1	242-8671
Dreyfus Growth Opportunity	Gro	Md/Gro	11	2.0	14.0	9.7	23	12	51	41	24	0.54	55	515.0	782-6620
Dreyfus New Leaders	Agg	Sm/Bl	9	17.0	23.0	16.6	30	43	41	43	52	None	1.21	69	330.5	782-6620
Dreyfus Strat. Investing A	Gro	Md/Bl	9	16.7	16.1	15.8	54	10	41	57	60	4.5	1.68	132	276.4	782-6620
Dreyfus Strategic Growth	Agg	Md/Bl	10	24.7	11.9	8.2	43	0	26	51	27	3.0	1.72	N.A.	44.4	782-6620
Dreyfus Third Century	Gro	Md/Bl	9	5.3	14.0	12.5	30	22	38	63	30	None	1.11	60	524.3	782-6620
Dreyfus-Wilshire Lrg. Co. Gro.	Gro	Lg/Gro	N.A.	(0.7)	N.A.	N.A.	18	N.A.	N.A.	N.A.	N.A.	None	N.A.	N.A.	8.2	782-6620
Dreyfus-Wilshire Lrg. Co Val.	Gro	Lg/Val	N.A.	13.3	N.A.	N.A.	47	N.A.	N.A.	N.A.	N.A.	None	N.A.	N.A.	8.0	782-6620
Dreyfus-Wilshire Sm. Co. Gro.	Agg	Sm/Bl	N.A.	8.9	N.A.	N.A.	16	N.A.	N.A.	N.A.	N.A.	None	N.A.	N.A.	7.9	782-6620
Dreyfus-Wilshire Sm. Co. Val.	Agg	Sm/Val	N.A.	18.7	N.A.	N.A.	33	N.A.	N.A.	N.A.	N.A.	None	N.A.	N.A.	16.4	782-6620
Eagle Growth Shares	Gro	Md/Gro	10	1.2	13.8	12.0	22	33	33	9	100	8.5	3.69	207	3.2	749-9933
Eaton Vance Growth	Gro	Lg/Bl	10	(2.5)	12.7	14.0	14	27	39	43	56	4.75	0.89	93	144.5	225-6265
Eaton Vance Special Equities	Gro	Md/Gro	11	1.1	17.8	15.7	22	23	57	61	42	4.75	1.05	97	87.9	225-6265
Eclipse Fin. Asset Equity	Agg	Sm/Val	9	17.0	22.4	13.0	30	60	25	40	30	None	1.12	63	189.3	872-2710
Enterprise Capital App.	Agg	Lg/Gro	10	5.7	21.2	19.9	11	37	56	69	56	4.75	1.75	138	103.7	432-4320
Enterprise Growth	Gro	Lg/Bl	10	10.6	18.6	15.0	41	30	41	50	41	4.75	1.60	130	87.7	432-4320
Equity Strategies[1]	Agg	Sm/Val	12	18.2	10.9	15.0	32	31	4	100	36	None	1.12	62	87.3	443-1021
Evergreen	Agg	Md/Val	11	6.3	17.4	10.4	12	42	35	43	28	None	1.12	63	630.0	235-0064
Evergreen Limited Market	Agg	Sm/Val	10	9.6	22.2	14.6	17	44	47	45	36	None	1.24	69	116.2	235-0064
FAM Value[1]	Agg	Sm/Val	8	0.2	22.8	16.0	1	70	43	54	35	None	1.50	82	226.8	932-3271
FPA Capital	Agg	Sm/Val	12	16.7	32.7	20.3	29	64	62	40	43	6.5	1.06	121	151.9	982-4372
Fasciano	Agg	Sm/Gro	9	8.1	16.3	13.7	15	40	29	61	39	None	1.80	92	16.8	848-6050
Fidelity Advisor Equity Gro.	Gro	Lg/Gro	N.A.	14.9	N.A.	N.A.	50	N.A.	N.A.	N.A.	N.A.	4.75	1.96	148	349.4	522-7297
Fidelity Advisor Gro. Opp.	Gro	Md/Bl	10	22.2	26.1	19.6	65	44	42	52	44	4.75	1.69	135	2,052.0	522-7297
Fidelity Advisor Strat. Opp.	Gro	Lg/Bl	7	20.4	18.7	15.5	61	40	22	40	61	4.75	1.57	128	291.5	522-7297
Fidelity Blue Chip Growth	Gro	Md/Gro	9	24.5	27.0	23.6	69	29	55	63	68	3.0	1.25	98	1,002.6	544-8888
Fidelity Capital App.	Agg	Md/Bl	9	33.4	19.5	12.8	58	55	1	36	45	3.0	0.77	68	1,289.1	544-8888
Fidelity Contrafund	Gro	Md/Gro	7	21.4	29.7	26.5	63	45	55	64	82	3.0	1.13	88	5,834.8	544-8888
Fidelity Destiny I[3]	Gro	Lg/Bl	9	26.4	26.5	19.7	73	44	38	48	46	8.24	0.65	34	3,079.5	752-2347
Fidelity Destiny II[3]	Gro	Md/Bl	10	26.8	27.5	20.6	74	45	41	50	48	8.24	0.84	49	1,196.7	752-2347
Fidelity Disciplined Equity	Gro	Lg/Val	N.A.	13.9	20.6	18.9	48	41	35	53	69	None	1.15	64	788.7	544-8888
Fidelity Emerging Growth	Agg	Md/Gro	N.A.	19.9	29.5	N.A.	35	41	65	N.A.	N.A.	3.0	1.19	88	669.3	544-8888
Fidelity Growth Company	Gro	Md/Gro	10	16.2	23.0	22.2	52	32	48	63	79	3.0	1.11	88	2,497.9	544-8888
Fidelity Low-Priced Stock	Agg	Sm/Val	N.A.	20.2	31.4	N.A.	35	77	41	62	N.A.	3.0	1.12	66	2,037.2	544-8888
Fidelity Magellan	Gro	Md/Bl	8	24.7	23.5	19.3	70	30	41	45	65	3.0	0.99	84	30,387.5	544-8888
Fidelity New Millennium	Gro	Sm/Gro	N.A.	24.7	N.A.	N.A.	70	N.A.	N.A.	N.A.	N.A.	3.0	1.77	N.A.	254.2	544-8888
Fidelity OTC	Agg	Sm/Val	9	8.3	22.9	18.2	15	52	45	55	50	3.0	1.08	92	1,327.6	544-8888
Fidelity Retirement Growth	Gro	Md/Bl	9	22.1	25.3	18.2	65	36	45	33	56	None	1.02	46	2,710.4	544-8888
Fidelity Stock Selector	Gro	Md/Val	N.A.	14.0	24.3	N.A.	48	44	46	N.A.	N.A.	3.0	1.22	64	598.8	544-8888
Fidelity Strat. Opp. Initial[1]	Gro	Lg/Bl	7	21.1	19.3	16.1	62	41	23	41	62	4.75	0.89	93	21.3	544-8888
Fidelity Trend	Gro	Md/Bl	10	19.1	23.8	16.9	59	47	36	27	59	None	0.83	31	1,456.8	544-8888
Fidelity Value	Gro	Md/Bl	9	22.9	23.4	15.0	66	54	25	27	41	None	1.20	55	1,621.9	544-8888
Fiduciary Capital Growth	Gro	Sm/Val	10	14.7	21.4	13.3	50	43	36	30	31	None	1.20	73	47.2	338-1579
First Amer. Equity Index	Gro	N.A.	N.A.	9.8	N.A.	N.A.	39	N.A.	N.A.	N.A.	N.A.	4.5	0.35	64	145.6	637-2548
First Amer. Regional Eq.	Gro	N.A.	N.A.	21.1	N.A.	N.A.	62	N.A.	N.A.	N.A.	N.A.	4.5	0.80	87	61.2	637-2548
First Invest. Made in USA	Gro	N.A.	N.A.	(0.9)	N.A.	N.A.	18	N.A.	N.A.	N.A.	N.A.	6.25	0.69	N.A.	15.6	423-4026
First Investors Spec. Sit.	Agg	Sm/Gro	N.A.	20.5	28.6	N.A.	36	56	46	N.A.	N.A.	6.25	1.41	153	53.6	423-4026
First Union Value B Invest.	Gro	Lg/Val	7	9.3	13.9	12.6	38	32	24	48	49	4.0	1.01	94	187.4	326-3241
First Union Value Trust	Gro	Lg/Val	N.A.	9.7	N.A.	N.A.	39	33	N.A.	N.A.	N.A.	None	0.68	38	456.9	326-2584
Flag Inv. Emerging Growth	Agg	Sm/Bl	12	(0.6)	10.5	7.1	0	11	45	27	53	4.5	1.46	126	28.9	767-3524
Flag Inv. Quality Growth	Gro	Lg/Bl	N.A.	(5.6)	8.5	N.A.	8	28	27	63	N.A.	4.5	1.23	113	53.1	767-3524
Fontaine Capital App.	Agg	Md/Gro	N.A.	14.1	7.0	N.A.	25	20	3	73	N.A.	None	1.50	82	10.8	247-1550
Fortis Adv. Capital App.	Agg	Sm/Gro	12	15.9	26.9	20.5	28	37	64	39	72	4.5	1.68	132	58.4	800-2638
Fortis Capital	Gro	Md/Gro	10	2.8	17.9	15.4	25	30	49	34	72	4.75	1.20	112	255.1	800-2638
Fortis Fiduciary	Gro	Md/Gro	11	2.8	18.8	15.9	25	30	52	31	77	4.75	1.46	125	53.6	800-2638
Fortis Growth	Gro	Md/Gro	12	10.4	23.1	20.1	41	20	68	41	82	4.75	1.09	107	609.4	800-2638
Forum Investors Stock	Gro	Lg/Val	N.A.	(9.6)	2.8	N.A.	0	26	14	52	N.A.	3.75	1.35	102	11.8	879-1900[4]
Founders Discovery	Agg	Sm/Gro	N.A.	16.0	27.5	N.A.	19	53	60	84	N.A.	None	1.69	97	222.0	525-2440
Founders Frontier	Agg	Sm/Gro	11	16.5	23.8	20.4	29	42	45	50	71	None	1.73	92	247.7	525-2440
Founders Growth	Gro	Md/Gro	11	25.5	24.5	19.6	72	26	47	32	80	None	1.42	80	377.0	525-2440
Founders Special	Agg	Lg/Bl	11	16.0	27.2	20.7	28	41	61	45	63	None	1.37	64	449.9	525-2440

Notes: (d): Maximum deferred sales charge   [1]Closed to new investors
[3]Investment by contractual plan only   [4]Area code 207

Fund name	Type	Style	Risk level	One year	Three years	Five years	1993	1992	1991	1990	1989	% max. sales charge	Annual charges	Five-year total per $1,000	Net assets (millions)	Telephone (800)
				\% compound annual return to Jan. 1, 1994			Annual performance analysis (percentile ranking by type)					Expense analysis				
Fountain Square Mid Cap	Gro	N.A.	N.A.	1.4	N.A.	N.A.	22	N.A.	N.A.	N.A.	N.A.	4.5	0.99%	N.A.	$26.3	334-0483
Fountain Square Quality Gro.	Gro	Lg/Bl	N.A.	(1.0)	N.A.	N.A.	17	N.A.	N.A.	N.A.	N.A.	4.5	0.99	N.A.	72.8	334-0483
Franklin Balance Sheet Inv.	Gro	Sm/Val	N.A.	25.6	27.5	N.A.	72	55	34	N.A.	N.A.	1.5	0.00[2]	$151	22.1	342-5236
Franklin CA Growth	Gro	Sm/Bl	N.A.	17.6	N.A.	N.A.	55	27	N.A.	N.A.	N.A.	1.5	0.00[2]	161	4.1	342-5236
Franklin Equity	Gro	Md/Val	11	8.5	12.6	8.7	37	25	26	36	29	4.0	0.69	77	332.4	342-5236
Franklin Growth	Gro	Lg/Bl	8	8.5	12.3	12.3	37	24	26	60	43	4.0	0.66	75	568.7	342-5236
Franklin Small Cap Gro.	Agg	Sm/Gro	N.A.	21.8	N.A.	N.A.	38	N.A.	N.A.	N.A.	N.A.	4.5	0.00[2]	N.A.	12.0	342-5236
Fremont Growth	Gro	Lg/Bl	N.A.	6.4	N.A.	N.A.	33	N.A.	N.A.	N.A.	N.A.	None	0.90	62	42.1	548-4539
FundTrust Aggressive Gro.	Agg	N.A.	9	14.6	18.7	13.4	26	27	40	50	37	1.5	1.70	88	31.9	344-9033
FundTrust Growth	Gro	N.A.	8	13.3	16.6	11.9	47	24	35	42	30	1.5	1.88	87	21.9	344-9033
G.T. America Growth A	Agg	Sm/Val	12	8.3	19.4	19.5	15	81	11	50	86	4.75	1.80	180	127.1	824-1580
GIT Special Growth	Agg	Sm/Gro	10	14.8	15.6	10.4	26	38	19	36	44	None	1.35	76	42.4	336-3063
Gabelli Asset	Gro	Md/Bl	7	21.8	18.3	14.7	64	44	17	42	50	None	1.31	72	924.9	422-3554
Gabelli Growth	Gro	Md/Gro	8	11.3	16.0	16.5	42	26	34	51	76	None	1.39	77	718.4	422-3554
Gabelli Small Cap Growth	Agg	Sm/Bl	N.A.	22.8	N.A.	N.A.	40	62	N.A.	N.A.	N.A.	4.5	1.97	146	211.5	422-3554
Gabelli Value	Gro	Lg/Bl	N.A.	39.4	21.9	N.A.	100	40	14	43	N.A.	5.5	1.53	133	519.4	422-3554
Galaxy Eq. Growth Retail	Gro	Lg/Bl	N.A.	5.4	13.4	N.A.	30	29	30	N.A.	N.A.	None	0.98	52	427.2	628-0414
Galaxy Eq. Value Retail	Gro	Md/Val	8	14.7	15.3	11.6	50	32	22	48	29	None	0.96	52	175.9	628-0414
Galaxy Sm. Co. Eq. Retail	Agg	Sm/Gro	N.A.	22.8	N.A.	N.A.	40	29	N.A.	N.A.	N.A.	None	1.22	63	55.4	628-0414
Gateway Capital	Gro	Lg/Bl	N.A.	5.2	N.A.	N.A.	30	N.A.	N.A.	N.A.	N.A.	None	1.50	82	10.4	354-6339
Gintel	Gro	Sm/Gro	11	2.0	13.7	11.2	24	60	14	41	43	None	1.70	93	144.0	243-5808
Goldman Sachs Capital Gro.	Gro	Md/Bl	N.A.	14.2	23.0	N.A.	48	58	31	N.A.	N.A.	5.5	1.38	134	766.1	762-5035
Govett Smaller Cos.	Agg	N.A.	N.A.	58.5	N.A.	N.A.	100	N.A.	N.A.	N.A.	N.A.	4.95	1.95	N.A.	37.1	634-6838
Gradison-McDonald Estab. Val.	Gro	Md/Val	9	20.8	17.6	11.7	62	36	21	37	27	None	1.28	72	243.3	869-5999
Gradison-McDonald Opp. Val	Agg	Sm/Val	9	11.1	20.0	13.1	20	51	30	41	40	None	1.44	81	82.6	869-5999
Greenspring	Gro	Sm/Val	6	14.6	16.8	10.5	49	46	18	41	16	None	1.43	81	29.3	366-3863
Growth Fund of America	Gro	Lg/Gro	10	14.5	18.6	15.8	49	31	35	46	56	5.75	0.77	99	5,070.6	421-0180
Growth Fund of Washington	Gro	Md/Val	10	12.5	18.7	9.5	45	48	26	15	26	4.75	1.55	128	40.5	972-9274
Guardian Park Avenue	Gro	Md/Val	9	20.3	25.1	16.3	61	53	35	28	43	4.5	0.82	89	540.1	221-3253
Hancock Discovery B	Agg	Sm/Gro	N.A.	6.4	N.A.	N.A.	12	51	N.A.	N.A.	N.A.	4.0(d)	2.81	N.A.	37.3	225-5291
Hancock Growth A	Gro	Md/Gro	11	13.2	19.4	15.3	46	29	41	36	58	5.0	1.58	113	170.6	225-5291
Hancock Sovereign Achiever B	Gro	Lg/Bl	10	8.8	15.1	9.9	37	31	30	36	26	4.0(d)	2.22	142	93.9	225-5291
Hancock Special Equities A[1]	Agg	Sm/Gro	12	19.7	42.3	27.5	34	79	84	48	47	5.0	1.87	162	296.8	225-5291
Harbor Capital Appreciation	Gro	Lg/Gro	11	12.1	24.0	18.4	44	35	55	51	44	None	0.85	51	145.1	422-1050
Harbor Growth	Gro	Md/Gro	12	18.4	18.6	13.9	57	8	50	41	41	None	0.89	50	208.2	422-1050
Harris Insight Equity	Gro	Lg/Val	9	18.3	17.8	14.0	57	33	27	38	51	4.5	0.96	96	47.4	982-8782
Hartwell Emerging Growth A	Agg	Sm/Gro	12	4.4	22.1	21.1	9	28	71	68	62	5.75	1.27	132	198.1	343-2898
Hartwell Growth A	Gro	Lg/Gro	11	9.8	22.1	15.8	39	22	63	22	66	5.75	1.75	156	27.2	343-2898
Heartland Value	Agg	Sm/Val	10	18.8	36.2	17.4	33	100	45	34	15	3.0(d)	1.50	81	173.6	432-7856
Heritage Capital Appreciation	Gro	Md/Gro	9	18.4	20.6	13.0	57	35	34	27	36	4.0	1.56	130	79.2	421-4184
HomeState PA Growth	Gro	N.A.	N.A.	19.1	N.A.	N.A.	58	N.A.	N.A.	N.A.	N.A.	5.0	1.87	N.A.	4.8	232-0224
Hudson Capital Appreciation	Gro	Md/Bl	N.A.	17.8	N.A.	N.A.	56	33	N.A.	N.A.	N.A.	5.5	2.50	181	18.5	221-5588
IAI Emerging Growth	Agg	Md/Gro	N.A.	14.8	N.A.	N.A.	26	65	N.A.	N.A.	N.A.	None	1.25	69	216.2	945-3863
IAI Midcap Growth	Gro	Md/Gro	N.A.	22.8	N.A.	N.A.	66	N.A.	N.A.	N.A.	N.A.	None	1.25	N.A.	34.7	945-3863
IAI Regional	Gro	Md/Bl	8	9.0	15.2	14.9	38	25	35	54	58	None	1.25	69	675.9	945-3863
IAI Value	Gro	Md/Bl	10	22.1	17.8	12.2	64	39	19	30	40	None	1.25	69	28.5	945-3863
IDEX	Gro	Lg/Gro	11	4.1	18.9	19.0	28	19	62	53	83	8.5	1.28	149	358.2	624-4339
IDEX 3[1]	Gro	Lg/Gro	11	5.2	19.4	19.0	30	19	62	51	82	8.5	1.22	146	204.6	624-4339
IDEX II Growth	Gro	Lg/Bl	11	3.6	18.5	19.0	27	21	59	54	85	5.5	1.60	138	549.0	624-4339
IDS Discovery	Agg	Sm/Gro	12	9.5	22.1	19.0	17	42	49	63	51	5.0	1.03	104	506.0	328-8300
IDS Growth[1]	Gro	Lg/Gro	10	8.6	19.9	19.5	37	32	47	62	69	5.0	0.87	96	998.2	328-8300
IDS New Dimensions	Gro	Lg/Gro	9	14.0	21.8	20.2	48	28	50	67	59	5.0	0.92	100	3,658.6	328-8300
IDS Progressive	Gro	Sm/Val	9	12.0	19.0	9.0	44	52	24	16	16	5.0	1.09	106	256.1	328-8300
IDS Strat. Aggressive Eq.	Agg	Md/Gro	11	7.9	17.3	16.3	15	25	47	61	54	5.0(d)	1.75	119	647.7	328-8300
Indep. Cap. Opportunities	Gro	Md/Bl	N.A.	5.0	10.4	N.A.	30	32	18	N.A.	N.A.	4.5	1.82	141	34.5	833-4264
Invesco Dynamics	Agg	Md/Gro	11	19.1	31.1	20.9	33	49	65	52	39	None	1.20	65	304.5	525-8085
Invesco Emerging Growth	Agg	Sm/Gro	N.A.	23.3	N.A.	N.A.	41	71	N.A.	N.A.	N.A.	None	1.54	N.A.	229.4	525-8085
Invesco Growth	Gro	Md/Bl	10	19.0	20.3	17.7	58	24	42	52	58	None	1.04	58	493.3	525-8085
Inv. Svc. Cap. Gro. Inv.	Gro	Md/Bl	N.A.	8.5	16.9	N.A.	37	33	35	43	N.A.	5.75	1.00	110	14.8	245-4770
Ivy Growth A	Gro	Lg/Bl	9	12.2	15.6	13.6	44	27	30	47	50	5.75	1.33	126	260.1	456-5111
JP Growth	Gro	Md/Bl	8	7.7	14.5	14.2	35	28	32	52	58	4.5	0.82	91	37.2	458-4498
Jackson National Growth	Gro	N.A.	N.A.	9.4	N.A.	N.A.	39	N.A.	N.A.	N.A.	N.A.	4.75	0.50	N.A.	31.7	888-3863
Janus	Gro	Lg/Bl	8	10.9	19.2	19.7	42	30	42	54	89	None	0.96	54	9,098.9	525-3713
Janus Enterprise	Gro	Sm/Bl	N.A.	15.6	N.A.	N.A.	51	N.A.	N.A.	N.A.	N.A.	None	1.42	N.A.	241.1	525-3713
Janus Twenty[1]	Gro	Lg/Bl	11	3.4	21.3	22.1	26	22	69	56	98	None	1.11	62	3,751.1	525-8983
Janus Venture[1]	Agg	Sm/Bl	8	9.1	20.1	19.1	16	39	43	62	62	None	1.02	59	1,837.6	525-8983
Kaufmann	Agg	Sm/Gro	11	18.2	33.2	26.6	32	46	78	52	74	None	2.66	157	856.2	237-0132
Kemper Growth	Gro	Lg/Gro	10	1.6	18.6	17.8	23	16	67	64	57	5.75	1.03	111	1,826.7	621-1048
Kemper Inv. Growth Initial	Gro	Lg/Gro	10	4.5	16.8	15.6	29	14	57	52	59	4.0(d)	2.06	118	841.8	621-1048
Kemper Small Cap. Equity	Agg	Sm/Gro	11	16.8	25.5	18.8	29	27	67	54	44	5.75	1.03	124	509.8	621-1048
Kent Expanded Mkt. Eq. Inv.	Gro	Sm/Val	N.A.	16.8	N.A.	N.A.	54	N.A.	N.A.	N.A.	N.A.	4.0	N.A.	N.A.	4.5	633-5368
Kent Value Plus Equity Inv.	Gro	Lg/Val	N.A.	11.8	N.A.	N.A.	44	N.A.	N.A.	N.A.	N.A.	4.0	N.A.	N.A.	3.8	633-5368
Keystone Amer. Omega A	Agg	Md/Gro	11	19.3	24.2	20.0	34	33	51	58	54	5.75	1.47	140	91.3	343-2898
Keystone Custodian K-2	Gro	Md/Gro	10	13.1	20.2	14.9	46	33	41	40	43	4.0(d)	1.89	86	403.4	343-2898
Keystone Custodian S-3	Gro	Md/Gro	11	8.8	17.6	13.1	37	27	42	36	45	4.0(d)	1.74	92	288.8	343-2898
Keystone Custodian S-4	Agg	Sm/Gro	12	25.3	33.5	22.6	44	44	71	53	40	4.0(d)	2.04	80	1,090.1	343-2898
L. Roy Papp Stock	Gro	Md/Bl	N.A.	1.7	15.6	N.A.	23	41	33	61	N.A.	None	1.25	71	39.0	421-4004
Landmark Equity	Gro	Lg/Gro	10	12.3	16.5	11.1	44	31	30	24	45	3.5	1.19	123	198.6	223-4447
Leeb Personal Finance	Gro	Lg/Val	N.A.	2.9	N.A.	N.A.	25	29	N.A.	N.A.	N.A.	None	1.50	N.A.	57.4	543-8721
Legg Mason Special Inv.	Agg	Sm/Bl	9	24.1	25.9	21.5	42	53	34	63	53	None	2.00	115	470.3	822-5544

Notes: (d): Maximum deferred sales charge
[1] Closed to new investors   [2] Manager absorbing costs

Fund name	Type	Style	Risk level	One year	Three years	Five years	1993	1992	1991	1990	1989	% max. sales charge	Annual charges	Five-year total per $1,000[2]	Net assets (millions)	Telephone (800)
Legg Mason Value	Gro	Lg/Val	10	11.3	18.7	10.8	42	38	34	18	35	None	1.84%	$103	$890.2	822-5544
Lindner	Gro	Sm/Val	7	20.0	18.6	12.0	60	40	23	30	38	None	0.80	44	1,455.1	727-5305[14]
Loomis Sayles Growth	Gro	Md/Gro	N.A.	9.2	N.A.	N.A.	38	25	N.A.	N.A.	N.A.	None	1.28	82	31.5	633-3330
Loomis Sayles Small Cap	Agg	Sm/Bl	N.A.	24.7	N.A.	N.A.	43	49	N.A.	N.A.	N.A.	None	1.45	82	61.8	633-3330
Lord Abbett Developing Gro.	Agg	Sm/Gro	12	12.6	19.5	12.8	22	21	53	52	26	5.75	1.31	125	138.0	874-3733
Lord Abbett Equity 1990[1]	Gro	Lg/Bl	N.A.	13.5	15.7	N.A.	47	33	25	N.A.	N.A.	5.5	1.80	N.A.	56.6	874-3733
Lord Abbett Fund. Value	Gro	Md/Val	8	13.5	14.9	14.3	47	39	18	55	53	5.75	1.60	140	32.1	874-3733
Lord Abbett Value App.	Gro	Md/Val	9	14.1	18.2	13.6	48	41	27	45	35	5.75	1.22	121	197.4	874-3733
MA Investors Growth Stock A	Gro	Md/Gro	12	14.5	21.6	18.4	49	30	47	42	71	5.75	0.68	100	1,187.9	225-2606
MFS Capital Growth B	Gro	Lg/Val	8	4.4	13.7	13.3	28	32	29	51	54	5.0(d)	2.14	140	479.5	225-2606
MFS Emerging Growth Class B	Agg	Sm/Gro	12	24.0	37.5	26.3	42	47	88	58	45	4.0(d)	2.21	145	605.0	225-2606
MFS Growth Opportunities A	Gro	Md/Bl	9	16.2	15.3	13.5	52	32	21	46	52	5.75	0.83	107	714.3	225-2606
MFS Managed Sectors B	Gro	Lg/Gro	11	3.7	19.8	15.7	27	25	60	25	76	5.0(d)	2.21	147	258.0	225-2606
MFS Research A	Gro	Md/Gro	8	21.7	21.5	16.3	64	37	32	42	48	5.75	0.90	107	296.1	225-2606
MFS Value A	Gro	Sm/Bl	9	25.3	22.4	14.6	71	49	23	29	40	5.75	1.37	136	134.8	225-2606
MIM Stock Appreciation	Gro	Md/Gro	11	10.4	27.4	20.4	41	28	77	67	28	None	2.50	141	57.7	233-1240
MIM Stock Growth	Gro	Md/Bl	10	2.2	8.4	5.3	24	16	26	42	11	None	2.80	150	9.1	233-1240
Mackenzie American	Gro	Md/Bl	10	22.9	13.1	7.5	66	32	8	22	28	5.75	1.91	160	48.0	456-5111
MainStay Capital App.	Gro	Md/Gro	11	14.0	28.7	22.8	48	37	69	64	48	5.0(d)	1.80	128	304.0	522-4202
Managers Capital App.	Gro	Md/Gro	9	16.7	21.6	16.6	53	45	32	51	39	None	1.19	60	71.2	835-3879
Managers Special Equity	Agg	Sm/Bl	10	17.4	26.9	18.2	30	55	45	36	55	None	1.28	73	92.4	835-3879
Mark Twain Equity	Gro	N.A.	N.A.	0.1	N.A.	N.A.	20	N.A.	N.A.	N.A.	N.A.	3.5	1.32	N.A.	31.4	866-6040
Marshall Stock	Gro	Lg/Bl	N.A.	3.3	N.A.	N.A.	26	N.A.	N.A.	N.A.	N.A.	None	0.94	N.A.	279.1	236-8560
Mathers	Gro	Sm/Gro	4	2.1	4.8	7.0	24	24	8	78	15	None	0.88	49	450.2	962-3863
Mentor Growth	Gro	Sm/Gro	11	15.6	26.2	15.9	51	45	50	30	30	5.0(d)	2.02	127	176.7	825-5353
Merger	Agg	Sm/Val	N.A.	17.7	13.1	N.A.	31	36	9	64	N.A.	None	2.49	147	22.2	343-8959
Meridian	Agg	Sm/Gro	11	13.1	27.3	20.7	23	53	55	69	34	None	1.47	95	140.6	446-6662
Merrill Lynch Fd. Tomorrow B	Gro	Lg/Gro	9	10.3	14.9	12.4	40	27	30	38	53	4.0(d)	1.92	107	410.3	637-3863
Merrill Lynch Fundamental B	Gro	Lg/Gro	N.A.	5.1	N.A.	N.A.	30	N.A.	N.A.	N.A.	N.A.	1.0(d)	2.79	N.A.	47.6	637-3863
Merrill Lynch Growth B	Gro	Sm/Gro	11	31.1	20.9	18.1	83	33	23	53	59	4.0(d)	1.87	101	1,049.2	637-3863
Merrill Lynch Phoenix A	Gro	Sm/Gro	10	29.5	31.0	14.8	80	63	36	7	23	6.5	1.25	134	217.9	637-3863
Merrill Lynch Sp. Value A	Agg	Sm/Bl	11	14.3	27.5	8.6	25	56	51	17	7	6.5	1.28	144	75.1	637-3863
Merriman Cap. Appreciation	Gro	N.A.	N.A.	3.6	9.2	N.A.	27	24	21	65	N.A.	None	1.51	80	38.7	423-4893
Merriman Leveraged Growth	Gro	Lg/Bl	N.A.	3.4	N.A.	N.A.	26	N.A.	N.A.	N.A.	N.A.	None	2.03	165	5.9	423-4893
MetLife-State St. Cap. App. A	Agg	Sm/Gro	12	22.9	32.7	21.6	40	42	73	40	52	4.5	1.50	123	225.8	882-0052
MetLife-State St. Eq. Inv. A	Gro	Lg/Gro	10	12.8	18.6	13.6	46	35	34	34	46	4.5	1.50	123	30.0	882-0052
Midwest Strat. Growth	Gro	Md/Val	10	(1.7)[28]	11.3[28]	6.2[28]	N.A.	33	26	16	35	4.0	2.00	150	3.4	543-8721
Monetta[1]	Agg	Sm/Gro	10	0.5	18.2	16.2	2	36	52	81	28	None	1.45	82	547.1	666-3882
Monitor Growth Invest Share	Gro	Lg/Bl	N.A.	3.3	N.A.	N.A.	26	31	N.A.	N.A.	N.A.	4.0	1.09	101	3.9	253-0412
Monitor Growth Trust Shares	Gro	Lg/Bl	N.A.	3.5	12.2	N.A.	27	32	26	56	N.A.	None	0.84	50	107.4	253-0412
Montgomery Small Cap[1]	Agg	Sm/Gro	N.A.	24.3	39.4	N.A.	42	43	100	N.A.	N.A.	None	1.40	82	257.6	572-3863
Mutual Benefit	Gro	Md/Bl	7	8.7	15.3	13.3	37	36	27	44	52	4.75	1.01	101	50.1	323-4726
Mutual Discovery[1]	Agg	Sm/Val	N.A.	35.8	N.A.	N.A.	62	N.A.	N.A.	N.A.	N.A.	None	1.29	N.A.	463.9	553-3014
Mutual of Omaha Growth	Gro	Sm/Gro	12	8.5	21.3	16.9	37	21	62	37	63	5.75	1.15	108	140.9	225-6292
National Industries	Gro	Lg/Bl	10	1.4	8.2	10.2	22	10	31	62	44	None	1.50	82	32.1	220-8500[10]
National Stock	Gro	Md/Bl	9	13.3	17.7	14.1	47	47	22	41	49	5.75	1.35	128	229.7	356-5535
Nationwide Growth	Gro	Lg/Bl	9	11.3	17.2	11.3	43	29	35	39	25	4.5	N.A.	80	411.4	848-0920
Neuberger/Berman Genesis	Agg	Sm/Val	10	13.9	23.1	12.9	25	54	36	35	31	None	1.65	90	118.3	877-9700
Neuberger/Berman Manhattan	Gro	Md/Bl	10	10.0	19.3	15.0	40	48	30	38	54	None	1.04	59	535.2	877-9700
Neuberger/Berman Partners	Gro	Md/Bl	8	16.5	18.8	14.3	53	48	21	44	41	None	0.84	48	1,233.8	877-9700
Neuberger/Berman Sel. Sect.	Gro	Lg/Val	9	16.3	20.7	16.5	53	54	24	42	55	None	0.92	50	578.1	877-9700
New Economy	Gro	Md/Gro	9	31.0	25.5	18.6	83	47	28	33	59	5.75	0.89	104	1,926.6	421-0180
New USA Mutual	Gro	Md/Gro	N.A.	9.3	N.A.	N.A.	38	N.A.	N.A.	N.A.	N.A.	5.0	1.51	N.A.	293.7	222-2872
New York Venture	Gro	Lg/Val	9	16.1	22.3	19.0	52	39	40	49	65	4.75	0.89	95	874.8	279-0279
Nicholas	Gro	Md/Val	9	5.9	19.2	15.0	32	40	42	45	44	None	0.76	43	3,133.0	272-6133[18]
Nicholas II	Agg	Sm/Val	9	6.4	17.6	12.4	12	43	34	52	32	None	0.67	37	714.2	272-6133[18]
Nicholas Limited Edition[1]	Agg	Sm/Val	9	9.0	22.5	16.2	16	56	39	60	31	None	0.90	52	181.8	272-6133[18]
Nicholas-Applegate Gro. Eq A	Agg	Md/Gro	11	20.3	26.7	21.3	35	42	52	53	60	5.25	1.54	139	98.0	225-1852
North American Growth	Gro	Md/Val	11	10.8	18.1	11.1	42	50	24	21	38	4.0	1.99	143	64.2	872-8037
Northeast Investors Growth	Gro	Lg/Gro	9	2.4	11.7	13.4	24	18	36	58	62	None	1.47	77	39.6	225-6704
Norwest Val. Gro. St. Inv. A	Gro	Md/Bl	9	6.6	17.0	14.9	33	35	36	52	49	4.5	1.20	108	99.9	363-3300[5]
Oak Hall Equity	Agg	Sm/Gro	N.A.	42.1	N.A.	N.A.	72	N.A.	N.A.	N.A.	N.A.	None	1.23	N.A.	17.5	625-4255
Oakmark	Gro	Md/Val	N.A.	30.5	N.A.	N.A.	82	100	N.A.	N.A.	N.A.	None	1.34	92	1,101.9	476-9625
Oberweis Emerging Growth	Agg	Sm/Gro	12	9.7	32.6	23.9	18	50	87	63	41	None	1.81	106	104.2	323-6166
Olympic Small Cap.	Agg	Sm/Bl	11	11.6	23.5	15.6	21	50	44	48	36	None	1.00	57	11.3	346-7301
Oppenheimer	Gro	Lg/Bl	8	15.3	17.2	13.7	51	33	28	45	43	5.75	1.10	114	227.6	525-7048
Oppenheimer Discovery	Agg	Sm/Gro	11	17.8	33.3	21.9	31	55	71	37	56	5.75	1.34	136	617.8	525-7048
Oppenheimer Special A	Gro	Md/Bl	10	2.7	18.8	14.7	25	41	44	50	38	5.75	0.93	104	745.1	525-7048
Oppenheimer Target	Agg	Md/Bl	11	3.9	17.4	13.4	8	44	36	59	33	5.75	1.09	114	377.7	525-7048
Oppenheimer Time	Gro	Md/Gro	10	19.6	19.2	15.0	59	22	39	40	51	5.75	0.99	108	415.3	525-7048
PBHG Growth	Agg	Sm/Gro	12	46.6	41.9	27.3	80	76	47	46	49	None	2.39	169	53.2	809-8008
Pacific Horizon Agg. Growth	Agg	Md/Gro	12	7.3	21.6	21.0	13	23	69	71	60	4.5	1.51	120	186.3	332-3863
Pacifica Equity Value	Gro	Md/Val	N.A.	25.8	18.9	N.A.	72	36	20	N.A.	N.A.	4.5	1.01	99	146.0	662-8417
PaineWebber Blue Chip Gro. B	Gro	Md/Gro	10	12.8	16.6	12.8	46	29	32	30	56	5.0(d)	2.10	137	46.4	647-1568
PaineWebber Growth A	Gro	Md/Gro	10	19.2	22.4	17.9	59	26	47	38	64	4.5	1.22	120	142.9	647-1568
Parnassus	Gro	Sm/Bl	12	17.3	34.8	14.7	55	80	52	9	0	3.5	1.47	112	90.3	999-3505
Pasadena Growth	Gro	Lg/Gro	12	(5.9)	17.7	16.5	8	24	68	45	71	5.5	1.50	137	554.2	882-2855
Pasadena Nifty Fifty	Gro	Lg/Gro	N.A.	(0.5)	20.0	N.A.	18	25	68	N.A.	N.A.	5.5	1.80	148	145.5	882-2855
Pennsylvania Mutual[1]	Agg	Sm/Val	7	11.3	19.4	12.0	20	55	25	43	30	None	0.97	50	1,054.2	221-4268
Peoples S&P MidCap Index	Gro	Md/Bl	N.A.	13.5	N.A.	N.A.	47	39	N.A.	N.A.	N.A.	None	0.09	64	66.1	782-6620

Notes: (d): Maximum deferred sales charge [1]Closed to new investors [5]Area code 212 [10]Area code 303 [14]Area code 314 [18]Area code 414 [28]To Dec. 1; fund since merged

Fund name	Type	Style	Risk level	One year	Three years	Five years	1993	1992	1991	1990	1989	% max. sales charge	Annual charges	Five-year total per $1,000[2]	Net assets (millions)	Telephone (800)
Permanent Port. Agg. Gro.	Agg	Md/Bl	N.A.	21.9	24.0	N.A.	38	61	24	N.A.	N.A.	None	1.14%	$102	$5.0	531-5142
Perritt Capital Growth	Agg	Sm/Val	11	5.3	15.9	5.7	10	38	33	35	9	None	2.30	121	7.2	338-1579
Phoenix Capital App.	Gro	Lg/Bl	N.A.	10.1	20.8	N.A.	40	32	48	100	N.A.	4.75	1.40	121	427.0	243-4361
Phoenix Growth	Gro	Lg/Bl	7	4.3	11.7	13.5	28	26	27	68	50	4.75	1.20	109	2,563.4	243-4361
Phoenix Stock	Agg	Lg/Gro	9	11.6	15.9	12.3	21	40	23	53	37	4.75	1.28	113	143.1	243-4361
Pierpont Capital App.	Agg	Sm/Bl	12	8.6	27.3	15.0	16	59	56	22	48	None	0.90	50	245.6	521-5412
Pioneer Capital Growth	Gro	Sm/Val	N.A.	16.7	27.3	N.A.	54	67	36	N.A.	N.A.	5.75	1.29	134	194.7	225-6292
Pioneer Three	Agg	Sm/Val	9	16.2	23.9	14.8	28	61	31	41	36	5.75	0.84	102	1,040.0	225-6292
Piper Jaffray Emerging Gro.	Agg	Md/Gro	N.A.	18.5	28.1	N.A.	32	39	63	N.A.	N.A.	4.0	1.29	109	197.6	866-7778
Piper Jaffray Sector Perf.	Agg	Md/Bl	10	11.0	20.3	17.2	20	46	35	62	46	4.0	1.28	109	86.1	866-7778
Piper Jaffray Value	Gro	Md/Bl	10	5.1	16.9	17.6	30	24	48	58	74	4.0	1.26	108	248.0	866-7778
Portico MidCore Growth	Gro	Md/Gro	N.A.	10.0	N.A.	N.A.	40	N.A.	N.A.	N.A.	N.A.	None	0.89	N.A.	84.5	228-1024
Portico Special Growth	Gro	Sm/Bl	N.A.	8.0	22.3	N.A.	36	31	58	57	N.A.	None	0.85	50	347.1	228-1024
Preferred Growth	Gro	Md/Gro	N.A.	16.1	N.A.	N.A.	52	N.A.	N.A.	N.A.	N.A.	None	1.00	N.A.	136.3	662-4769
Princor Capital Accumulation	Gro	Lg/Val	9	7.6	17.1	10.5	35	33	37	32	24	5.0	0.84	99	240.0	451-5447
Princor Emerging Growth	Agg	Sm/Bl	10	12.3	25.4	17.3	22	52	49	52	36	5.0	1.56	140	48.7	451-5447
Princor Growth	Gro	Md/Bl	10	7.5	22.9	16.6	35	36	57	52	31	5.0	1.17	112	80.1	451-5447
Prudent Speculator	Agg	Sm/Val	12	9.7	22.0	2.0	18	28	61	0	2	None	3.83	197	4.0	444-4778
Prudential Equity B	Gro	Md/Val	9	21.1	18.4	16.0	63	37	23	46	60	5.0(d)	1.68	104	1,709.1	225-1852
Prudential Growth B	Gro	Md/Bl	10	8.5	11.5	8.9	37	24	23	33	40	5.0(d)	2.16	124	211.8	225-1852
Prudential Growth Opp. B	Agg	Sm/Val	10	18.8	25.6	15.6	33	62	33	42	34	5.0(d)	1.97	124	389.4	225-1852
Prudential Multi-Sector B	Gro	Md/Bl	N.A.	22.6	16.0	N.A.	66	20	26	N.A.	N.A.	5.0(d)	2.09	122	106.4	225-1852
Putnam Investors A	Gro	Lg/Bl	10	17.9	17.8	16.3	56	32	28	49	64	5.75	0.90	111	845.4	225-1581
Putnam New Opportunities A	Gro	Sm/Gro	N.A.	32.7	40.8	N.A.	86	61	68	N.A.	N.A.	5.75	1.31	142	474.8	225-1581
Putnam OTC Emerging Gro. A	Agg	Sm/Gro	12	32.0	28.0	19.5	55	48	35	46	48	5.75	1.39	129	424.8	225-1581
Putnam Vista A	Gro	Md/Gro	9	17.4	23.8	17.3	55	48	37	40	47	5.75	0.96	115	491.2	225-1581
Putnam Voyager A	Agg	Md/Gro	11	18.4	25.0	20.7	32	43	46	58	57	5.75	1.12	120	2,789.2	225-1581
Quest for Value A	Gro	Md/Bl	8	6.6	18.6	13.3	33	49	32	40	35	5.5	1.73	145	244.5	232-3863
Quest for Value Sm. Cap. A	Agg	Sm/Val	N.A.	18.2	28.3	15.5	32	63	43	41	23	5.5	1.94	162	104.5	232-3863
Reich & Tang Equity	Gro	Md/Val	8	13.8	17.9	12.7	48	47	22	42	31	None	1.18	63	110.6	221-3079
Retirement Planning Growth	Gro	Md/Bl	11	11.2	15.0	15.2	42	14	40	45	76	5.0(d)	2.55	136	45.6	279-0279
Rightime Growth	Gro	Md/Val	9	(5.1)	9.1	6.0	9	33	25	25	34	4.75	2.33	167	35.7	242-1421
Robertson Stephens Emer. Gro.	Agg	Sm/Gro	12	7.2	18.4	21.3	13	22	55	78	71	None	1.60	87	173.6	766-3863
Robertson Stephens Val. Plus	Agg	Sm/Val	N.A.	18.6	N.A.	N.A.	33	N.A.	N.A.	N.A.	N.A.	None	1.71	N.A.	71.5	766-3863
Rodney Square Growth	Gro	Md/Bl	10	14.6	19.8	15.2	49	29	41	40	50	4.0	1.43	117	65.0	336-9970
Royce OTC	Agg	Sm/Val	N.A.	23.7	N.A.	N.A.	41	77	N.A.	N.A.	N.A.	None	1.69	107	9.6	221-4268
Royce Premier	Agg	Sm/Val	N.A.	19.0	N.A.	N.A.	33	54	N.A.	N.A.	N.A.	None	1.55	84	43.0	221-4268
Royce Value	Agg	Sm/Val	8	10.7	18.9	11.0	19	54	24	40	29	1.0(d)	1.88	113	187.2	221-4268
Rushmore Nova	Gro	Lg/Bl	N.A.	4.5[28]	6.0[28]	N.A.	N.A.	17	15	34	N.A.	None	1.36	63	0.1	343-3355
Rushmore OTC Index+	Agg	Lg/Gro	12	12.8	21.1	11.0	23	35	46	33	28	None	1.00	49	5.7	343-3355
Safeco Growth	Agg	Sm/Gro	12	22.2	24.4	14.3	39	21	60	38	34	None	0.91	50	161.3	426-6730
Safeco Northwest	Gro	Sm/Val	N.A.	1.2	N.A.	N.A.	22	42	N.A.	N.A.	N.A.	None	1.11	61	41.0	426-6730
STI Classic Cap. Gro. Inv.	Gro	Lg/Bl	N.A.	9.3	N.A.	N.A.	38	N.A.	N.A.	N.A.	N.A.	3.75	1.80	N.A.	161.3	428-6970
SWRW Growth Plus	Gro	Md/Bl	9	9.3	15.5	14.9	38	27	34	45	68	None	1.50	91	19.8	354-6339
Salomon Bros. Capital	Gro	Md/Bl	11	17.0	17.9	15.8	54	27	33	35	75	None	1.34	73	105.0	725-6666
Salomon Bros. Opportunity	Gro	Md/Val	9	12.8	14.8	13.3	46	42	30	20	37	None	1.23	69	118.6	725-6666
Scudder Capital Growth	Gro	Md/Gro	11	20.1	22.5	15.4	60	31	43	18	63	None	0.97	54	1,476.2	225-2470
Scudder Development	Agg	Sm/Gro	12	9.0	22.5	18.1	16	23	70	65	40	None	1.30	70	814.6	225-2470
Scudder Quality Growth	Gro	Lg/Gro	N.A.	0.0	N.A.	N.A.	19	30	N.A.	N.A.	N.A.	None	1.22	69	126.2	225-2470
Scudder Value	Gro	Md/Val	N.A.	11.6	N.A.	N.A.	43	N.A.	N.A.	N.A.	N.A.	None	1.25	N.A.	29.6	225-2470
Security Equity	Gro	Md/Bl	9	14.5	19.6	16.4	49	37	34	45	57	5.75	1.06	113	377.3	888-2461
Security Ultra	Agg	Sm/Bl	12	9.8	23.6	8.9	18	40	56	17	23	5.75	1.31	126	71.4	888-2461
Selected Special Shares	Agg	Sm/Bl	10	10.8	14.6	12.6	19	41	18	51	48	None	1.41	77	55.6	243-1575
Seligman Capital A	Agg	Md/Gro	11	5.0	21.9	19.5	9	47	51	65	53	4.75	1.14	116	205.2	221-2783
Seligman Frontier A	Agg	Sm/Gro	11	26.3	29.9	20.6	45	54	45	47	47	4.75	1.34	119	43.7	221-2783
Seligman Growth A	Gro	Md/Gro	11	6.5	17.9	15.8	33	38	38	44	63	4.75	0.92	103	615.1	221-2783
Sentinel Growth	Gro	Md/Bl	9	3.3	11.4	12.0	26	29	25	56	49	5.0	1.24	123	59.5	282-3863
Sentry	Gro	Md/Bl	8	6.0	13.6	13.9	32	31	28	67	43	None	0.88	50	76.3	533-7827
Sequoia[1]	Gro	Lg/Val	7	10.8	19.3	15.9	41	34	40	47	51	None	1.00	56	1,530.8	245-4500[5]
Seven Seas Matrix Equity	Gro	Md/Bl	N.A.	15.4	N.A.	N.A.	51	N.A.	N.A.	N.A.	N.A.	None	0.60	31	66.1	654-6089[21]
Seven Seas S&P Midcap Index	Gro	Md/Bl	N.A.	12.5	N.A.	N.A.	45	N.A.	N.A.	N.A.	N.A.	None	N.A.	N.A.	34.6	654-6089[21]
Shadow Stock	Agg	Sm/Val	9	15.3	23.8	11.2	27	57	34	30	22	None	1.25	69	36.4	422-2766
Sierra Emerging Growth	Agg	Sm/Bl	N.A.	22.3	25.3	N.A.	39	53	34	N.A.	N.A.	4.5	1.59	N.A.	120.9	222-5852
Sit Growth	Agg	Md/Gro	11	8.5	20.7	18.4	16	23	63	59	57	None	0.80	46	331.0	332-5580
Skyline Special Equities[1]	Agg	Sm/Val	9	22.8	37.1	23.7	40	100	43	47	41	None	1.51	120	221.6	458-5222
Smith Barney Equity A	Gro	Lg/Bl	9	18.5	14.8	13.9	57	20	28	48	58	4.5	0.99	97	92.4	544-7835
Smith Bar. Sh. Agg. Gro. A	Agg	Md/Gro	12	21.1	20.7	18.5	37	30	37	53	66	5.0	1.35	118	188.4	451-2010
Smith Barney Shear. App. A	Gro	Lg/Bl	8	8.1	13.4	13.5	36	29	26	55	55	5.0	1.08	105	1,610.4	451-2010
Smith Bar. Shear. Dir. Val. B	Gro	Md/Val	10	9.4	13.3	10.8	39	34	21	40	41	5.0(d)	1.83	109	155.8	451-2010
Smith B. Shear. Fund. Val. B	Gro	Md/Bl	N.A.	18.8	N.A.	N.A.	58	N.A.	N.A.	N.A.	N.A.	5.0(d)	2.28	132	131.2	451-2010
Smith Bar. Sh. Gro. & Opp. B	Gro	Md/Bl	10	8.5	17.4	10.1	37	44	29	22	31	5.0(d)	2.13	125	135.4	451-2010
Smith Bar. Sh. Sec. Anal. B	Gro	Lg/Bl	10	4.5	13.8	10.9	29	31	31	39	60	5.0(d)	2.17	126	139.5	451-2010
Smith Bar. Shear. Sp. Eq. B	Agg	Sm/Gro	12	31.9	27.7	13.2	55	42	40	21	33	5.0(d)	2.33	133	121.1	451-2010
Sound Shore	Gro	Md/Val	8	12.0	21.5	14.4	44	54	32	32	40	None	1.29	75	56.1	551-1980
SteinRoe Capital Opp.	Agg	Md/Gro	12	27.5	28.6	15.6	48	31	60	14	60	None	1.06	58	164.3	338-2550
SteinRoe Special	Gro	Md/Bl	9	20.4	22.6	19.0	61	42	33	42	72	None	0.97	55	1,117.7	338-2550
SteinRoe Stock	Gro	Lg/Gro	9	2.8	11.9	17.3	25	32	46	57	67	None	0.93	51	378.0	338-2550
Stratton Growth	Gro	Md/Val	8	6.4	11.5	9.9	33	30	21	40	43	None	1.39	73	25.4	634-5726
Strong Common Stock[1]	Agg	Sm/Bl	N.A.	25.2	33.4	N.A.	44	62	54	64	N.A.	None	1.40	78	748.7	368-1030
Strong Discovery	Agg	Sm/Bl	10	22.2	27.8	20.3	39	30	65	58	41	None	1.50	82	272.4	368-1030

Notes: (d): Maximum deferred sales charge [1]Closed to new investors [5]Area code 212 [21]Area code 617 [28]To Dec. 1; fund since merged

Fund name	Type	Style	Risk level	% compound annual return to Jan. 1, 1994			Annual performance analysis (percentile ranking by type)					Expense analysis			Net assets (millions)	Telephone (800)
				One year	Three years	Five years	1993	1992	1991	1990	1989	% max. sales charge	Annual charges	Five-year total per $1,000		
Strong Opportunity	Gro	Md/Bl	9	21.2	23.3	14.5	63	48	31	30	32	None	1.40%	$82	$437.6	368-1030
Sun Eagle Equity Growth	Gro	Lg/Bl	N.A.	14.0	N.A.	N.A.	48	N.A.	N.A.	N.A.	N.A.	None	0.39	N.A.	45.4	752-1823
SunAmerica Emer. Growth A	Agg	Sm/Gro	12	13.9	28.4	13.7	25	61	51	18	40	5.75	1.71	154	41.9	858-8850
SunAmerica Growth A	Gro	Md/Gro	11	10.8	21.1	14.2	41	39	42	22	53	5.75	1.68	147	35.8	858-8850
SunAmerica Value B	Gro	Lg/Gro	11	19.4	19.0	7.3	59	33	29	0	20	4.0(d)	2.49	144	81.0	858-8850
T. Rowe Price Capital App.	Gro	Md/Val	6	15.7	15.4	13.0	51	34	21	52	38	None	1.09	60	514.7	638-5660
T. Rowe Price Growth Stock	Gro	Lg/Bl	9	15.6	17.9	14.5	51	29	33	46	46	None	0.85	46	1,894.6	638-5660
T. Rowe Price Mid-Cap Gro.	Gro	Md/Gro	N.A.	26.2	N.A.	N.A.	73	N.A.	N.A.	N.A.	N.A.	None	1.25	N.A.	55.1	638-5660
T. Rowe Price New Am. Gro.	Gro	Md/Gro	11	17.4	27.9	20.5	55	35	62	28	73	None	1.25	69	606.8	638-5660
T. Rowe Price New Horizons	Agg	Sm/Gro	12	22.0	27.1	18.6	38	45	48	47	44	None	0.97	51	1,626.7	638-5660
T. Rowe Price OTC Sec.	Agg	Sm/Bl	10	18.4	23.2	12.1	32	51	33	28	34	None	1.29	69	205.2	638-5660
T. Rowe Price Sm.-Cap Val.[1]	Agg	Sm/Val	8	23.3	26.0	15.9	40	63	28	44	32	None	1.20	69	430.6	638-5660
T. Rowe Price Spectrum Gro.	Gro	Lg/Bl	N.A.	21.0	19.0	N.A.	62	31	29	N.A.	N.A.	None	0.00	49	535.8	638-5660
TNE Capital Gro. Class A	Gro	Md/Gro	N.A.	7.9	N.A.	N.A.	36	N.A.	N.A.	N.A.	N.A.	5.75	1.00	N.A.	94.5	343-7104
TNE Growth Class A[1]	Gro	Lg/Bl	11	11.3	17.7	15.9	42	8	57	66	40	6.5	1.19	124	1,232.4	343-7104
Templeton Capital Accum.	Gro	Md/Val	N.A.	39.5	N.A.	N.A.	100	30	N.A.	N.A.	N.A.	None	1.00	54	21.2	237-0738
Third Avenue Value	Agg	Sm/Bl	N.A.	23.7	26.3	N.A.	41	63	28	N.A.	N.A.	5.75	1.63	176	118.8	443-1021
Thomson Growth B	Gro	Lg/Gro	9	9.3	16.6	16.9	38	22	41	56	71	None	1.90	103	1,068.9	227-7337
Thomson Opportunity B[1]	Agg	Sm/Gro	11	36.2	43.2	28.9	62	76	66	50	51	1.0(d)	1.90	108	622.2	227-7337
Thomson Target B	Gro	Md/Gro	N.A.	24.5	N.A.	N.A.	69	N.A.	N.A.	N.A.	N.A.	None	2.00	N.A.	334.5	227-7337
Tocqueville	Gro	Md/Bl	6	22.5	17.2	14.0	65	47	11	58	30	None	1.73	98	27.7	698-0800[5]
Torray	Gro	Md/Val	6	6.4	15.6	N.A.	32	54	19	N.A.	N.A.	None	1.25	69	19.1	493-4600[9]
Transamerica Capital App.	Agg	Sm/Bl	12	6.8	17.9	13.1	13	37	40	52	35	5.75	1.41	121	88.9	343-6840
Transamer. Sp. Emer. Gro. B	Agg	Sm/Gro	12	11.8	25.8	20.6	21	48	55	61	49	5.0(d)	2.64	149	219.5	343-6840
UMB Heartland	Agg	Sm/Val	7	6.0	8.6	2.4	11	46	0	48	0	None	1.04	154	24.3	422-2766
UMB Stock	Gro	Lg/Bl	7	10.7	13.9	11.4	41	31	24	50	33	None	0.87	48	21.0	422-2766
USAA Mutual Aggressive Gro.	Agg	Sm/Bl	12	8.1	19.3	11.8	15	12	70	43	30	None	0.87	46	281.4	382-8722
USAA Mutual Growth	Gro	Lg/Gro	8	7.4	14.7	14.0	35	35	27	55	50	None	1.09	59	611.8	382-8722
UST Master Equity	Gro	Md/Bl	9	16.3	22.2	15.4	53	46	34	28	51	4.5	1.08	107	121.8	233-1136
United Accumulative	Gro	Lg/Bl	9	9.0	15.5	12.0	38	42	23	33	51	5.75	0.63	103	1,029.9	366-5465
United New Concepts	Agg	Sm/Gro	11	10.8	29.6	19.3	19	34	88	66	18	5.75	1.18	143	212.2	366-5465
United Svc. Growth	Gro	Sm/Gro	12	12.9	8.3	5.9	46	0	26	26	36	5.75	2.79	138	3.9	873-8637
United Vanguard	Gro	Lg/Gro	10	14.2	14.6	11.5	48	24	27	47	32	5.75	0.96	134	923.1	366-5465
Valley Forge	Gro	Lg/Bl	5	17.1	11.4	8.1	54	34	7	43	21	None	1.40	77	10.0	548-1942
Value Line	Gro	Md/Gro	10	6.8	19.6	17.4	33	27	53	54	58	None	0.80	47	344.1	223-0818
Value Line Lev. Gro. Inv.	Agg	Md/Gro	11	16.2	18.4	16.6	28	22	42	60	53	None	0.95	51	314.9	223-0818
Value Line Spec. Situations	Agg	Sm/Gro	12	13.0	14.6	11.9	23	21	32	55	38	None	1.09	60	95.7	223-0818
Vanguard Explorer	Agg	Sm/Bl	10	15.0	26.7	14.7	27	49	52	45	20	None	0.70	38	809.0	851-4999
Vanguard Index Extended Mkt.	Agg	Sm/Bl	10	14.5	22.2	14.3	26	48	37	39	41	None	0.19	71	869.5	851-4999
Vanguard Index Growth	Gro	Lg/Gro	N.A.	1.5	N.A.	N.A.	23	N.A.	N.A.	N.A.	N.A.	None	0.21	61	45.7	851-4999
Vanguard Small Cap. Stock	Agg	Sm/Bl	11	18.7	26.8	13.0	33	58	40	32	21	None	0.18	70	462.7	851-4999
Vanguard US Growth	Gro	Lg/Gro	9	(1.4)	14.1	16.4	17	23	46	65	71	None	0.49	27	1,877.5	851-4999
Vanguard/Morgan Growth	Gro	Lg/Bl	9	7.3	15.0	12.9	34	35	29	52	41	None	0.48	27	1,167.7	851-4999
Vanguard/Primecap	Gro	Md/Bl	11	18.0	19.7	15.2	56	34	32	49	38	None	0.67	38	800.5	851-4999
Vista Capital Growth	Gro	Sm/Bl	10	20.2	32.3	25.8	61	40	71	42	85	4.75	1.48	117	224.3	348-4782
Vista Equity	Gro	Lg/Bl	N.A.	8.6	14.5	N.A.	37	27	31	N.A.	N.A.	None	0.30	17	120.6	348-4782
Volumetric	Gro	Md/Val	10	2.1	15.1	10.9	24	37	34	44	27	None	2.01	108	11.6	541-3863
Voyageur Growth Stock	Gro	Lg/Bl	11	(5.0)	16.7	14.0	9	28	58	41	55	4.75	1.90	154	32.7	553-2143
WPG Tudor	Gro	Sm/Gro	12	13.4	20.2	15.6	47	25	45	44	45	None	1.24	68	265.0	223-3332
Warburg Pincus Cap. Common	Gro	Md/Gro	9	15.9	16.3	13.6	52	31	25	43	49	None	1.01	59	159.4	257-5614
Warburg Pincus Emer. Common	Agg	Sm/Gro	11	18.1	27.4	17.8	32	48	52	46	38	None	1.20	68	165.5	257-5614
Wasatch Aggressive Equity	Agg	Sm/Bl	11	22.5	24.5	22.4	39	35	46	76	53	None	1.50	82	25.3	345-7460
Wasatch Growth	Gro	Sm/Bl	11	8.0	16.8	17.0	36	27	40	78	45	None	1.49	82	18.0	345-7460
Wasatch Mid-Cap	Gro	Md/Gro	N.A.	(3.0)	N.A.	N.A.	13	N.A.	N.A.	N.A.	N.A.	None	1.73	N.A.	2.5	345-7460
Wayne Hummer Growth	Gro	Md/Bl	7	3.1	13.6	13.8	26	36	28	66	43	None	1.12	68	97.8	621-4477
Weitz Value	Gro	Lg/Gro	7	20.0	20.3	15.0	60	41	27	44	39	None	1.35	87	100.7	232-4161
Westcore MIDCO Growth Inst.	Gro	Md/Gro	11	17.5	27.8	23.0	55	30	67	65	54	None	0.83	80	262.3	392-2673
William Blair Growth	Gro	Md/Gro	9	15.5	21.5	18.1	51	31	44	51	56	None	0.78	46	142.0	742-7272
Winthrop Focus Agg. Growth	Agg	Sm/Val	8	21.8	29.5	17.0	38	58	46	41	30	4.0(d)	1.37	82	73.8	225-8011
Winthrop Focus Growth	Gro	Lg/Bl	9	13.8	14.1	11.7	48	22	27	39	48	4.0(d)	1.24	69	48.6	225-8011
Working Assets Cit. Growth	Gro	Md/Bl	N.A.	0.0	N.A.	N.A.	19	N.A.	N.A.	N.A.	N.A.	4.0	1.75	N.A.	49.2	223-7010
Yacktman	Gro	Lg/Bl	N.A.	(6.6)	N.A.	N.A.	6	N.A.	N.A.	N.A.	N.A.	None	1.19	N.A.	143.6	525-8258
Zweig Appreciation A	Agg	Md/Val	N.A.	15.4	14.0	N.A.	27	42	N.A.	N.A.	N.A.	5.5	1.74	142	236.8	444-2706
Zweig Priority Selection A	Gro	Md/Gro	8	13.7	14.0	14.7	47	13	34	50	71	5.5	1.58	151	60.0	444-2706
Zweig Strategy A	Gro	Md/Val	N.A.	15.0	15.1	N.A.	50	31	22	50	N.A.	5.5	1.47	136	412.7	444-2706

T O T A L   R E T U R N

Fund name	Type	Style	Risk level	One year	Three years	Five years	1993	1992	1991	1990	1989	% max. sales charge	Annual charges	Five-year total per $1,000	Net assets (millions)	Telephone (800)
20th Century Balanced Inv.	ETR	Lg/Bl	8	7.2	13.9	13.6	14	21	91	73	77	None	1.00	55	705.5	345-2021
ABT Growth & Income	G&I	Lg/Bl	9	4.0	11.6	7.9	22	30	43	54	24	4.75	1.23	112	78.8	553-7838
AIM Balanced A	ITR	N.A.	9	15.5	21.9	14.8	63	27	85	51	41	4.75	2.15	156	21.2	347-1919
AIM Charter	G&I	Lg/Val	7	8.9	14.9	17.8	34	25	56	95	65	5.5	1.15	116	1,690.5	347-1919
API Capital Income	ETR	Lg/Bl	8	6.7	11.4	5.8	13	53	44	52	0	None	3.29	183	1.9	544-6060
API Total Return	ETR	Lg/Bl	10	12.3	12.8	6.1	20	48	45	18	32	None	2.27	135	5.0	544-6060
ASM	G&I	Lg/Bl	N.A.	13.3	N.A.	N.A.	44	36	N.A.	N.A.	N.A.	None	0.75	43	17.1	445-2763
Accessor Value & Income	ETR	Lg/Val	N.A.	14.7	N.A.	N.A.	23	N.A.	N.A.	N.A.	N.A.	None	1.21	N.A.	10.1	759-3504
Addison Capital Shares	G&I	Md/Val	9	13.0	16.3	13.4	43	38	45	60	46	3.0	2.13	141	39.9	526-6397
Advantage Income	ITR	Md/Val	6	14.1	14.3	12.1	56	22	24	69	49	4.0(d)	1.84	99	79.2	243-8115
Aetna Fund	ETR	Lg/Val	N.A.	9.7	N.A.	N.A.	17	59	N.A.	N.A.	N.A.	None	0.07	60	54.3	367-7732
Aetna Growth & Income	G&I	Lg/Bl	N.A.	6.6	N.A.	N.A.	28	41	N.A.	N.A.	N.A.	None	0.33	70	50.5	367-7732

Notes: (d): Maximum deferred sales charge [1] Closed to new investors
[5] Area code 212 [9] Area code 301

Fund name	Type	Style	Risk level	% compound annual return to Jan. 1, 1994 — One year	Three years	Five years	Annual performance analysis (percentile ranking by type) — 1993	1992	1991	1990	1989	Expense analysis — % max. sales charge	Annual charges	Five-year total per $1,000	Net assets (millions)	Telephone (800)
Affiliated	G&I	Lg/Val	8	12.8	15.7	12.6	43	53	32	63	39	5.75	0.60%	$89	$4,152.9	874-3733
Alger Income & Growth	G&I	Md/Val	9	7.6	12.4	10.4	30	40	33	57	42	5.0(d)	2.68	182	8.2	992-3863
Alliance Balanced B	ETR	Md/Bl	7	12.6	15.2	14.0	20	27	80	69	76	4.0(d)	2.15	128	38.9	227-4618
Alliance Balanced Shares A	ETR	Lg/Bl	7	9.9	12.3	9.6	17	59	38	60	42	4.25	1.32	127	174.7	227-4618
Alliance Growth & Income A	G&I	Lg/Bl	8	10.0	13.5	12.5	36	33	40	71	42	4.25	1.03	112	459.6	227-4618
Alliance Multi-Mkt. Inc./Gro.	ITR	N.A.	N.A.	8.4	N.A.	N.A.	33	2	N.A.	N.A.	N.A.	1.0	2.32	133	106.3	227-4618
Amana Income	ETR	Md/Val	7	11.6	12.0	10.0	19	44	44	57	55	None	1.58	98	10.4	728-8762
American Balanced	ETR	Lg/Val	6	11.3	15.0	12.7	19	67	46	62	65	5.75	0.74	96	1,642.5	421-0180
American Cap. Comstock A	G&I	Lg/Bl	8	9.1	15.3	14.4	34	38	47	67	51	5.75	0.87	110	982.9	421-5666
American Cap. Equity-Inc. A	ETR	Lg/Bl	7	16.0	17.6	13.5	25	70	50	53	65	5.75	1.01	110	175.5	421-5666
American Cap. Growth & Inc.	G&I	Lg/Bl	9	16.3	18.4	12.7	51	46	44	63	24	5.75	1.15	117	214.4	421-5666
American Cap. Harbor A	ITR	N.A.	6	13.6	15.3	12.8	54	28	29	61	56	5.75	0.99	111	437.9	421-5666
American Leaders A	G&I	Lg/Val	9	11.7	17.8	12.4	40	51	46	71	17	4.5	1.20	107	226.4	245-5051
American Mutual	G&I	Lg/Val	7	14.3	14.5	13.1	46	42	31	71	42	5.75	0.60	89	5,283.1	421-0180
American National Income	ETR	Lg/Bl	7	10.5	13.8	13.7	18	49	55	70	85	5.75	1.18	119	118.8	231-4639
Analytic Optioned Equity	G&I	Lg/Bl	6	6.7	8.7	8.9	28	37	18	79	28	None	1.06	56	78.9	374-2633
Arch Gro. & Inc. Investor	G&I	Lg/Bl	7	9.6	15.3	13.9	35	48	39	72	44	4.5	0.71	85	10.9	551-3731
BNY Hamilton Equity-Income	G&I	Lg/Bl	N.A.	11.9	N.A.	N.A.	41	N.A.	N.A.	N.A.	N.A.	None	1.11	N.A.	105.2	426-9363
Babson Value	G&I	Lg/Val	10	22.9	22.3	13.9	67	61	42	48	29	None	1.01	56	41.5	422-2766
Baird Blue Chip	G&I	Lg/Gro	8	4.6	11.9	12.9	23	28	45	82	45	5.75	1.50	129	64.7	792-2473
Bartlett Cap. Basic Value	G&I	Md/Val	9	11.7	15.7	9.4	40	48	38	52	17	None	1.21	66	98.7	800-4612
Benham Income & Growth	G&I	Lg/Val	N.A.	11.3	18.6	N.A.	39	42	58	N.A.	N.A.	None	0.75	42	221.7	472-3389
Berger 101	G&I	Lg/Bl	8	23.6	27.8	18.2	68	34	92	56	33	None	2.56	145	190.0	333-1001
Berwyn Income	ITR	N.A.	3	16.9	20.5	14.1	68	68	29	66	31	None	1.20	73	29.1	824-2249
Bond Fund for Growth	ITR	L/Lo	6	21.2	26.9	15.2	86	100	45	35	24	3.25	1.75	133	58.2	383-1300[23]
Boston Co. Ast. Alloc. Retail	ETR	Lg/Bl	7	8.0	13.8	12.0	15	63	49	71	53	None	1.27	73	12.8	225-5267
Boulevard Strat. Bal. Inv.	G&I	N.A.	N.A.	4.7	N.A.	N.A.	24	N.A.	N.A.	N.A.	N.A.	4.0	0.71	N.A.	28.5	285-3865
Brundage Story & Rose G & I	G&I	Lg/Bl	N.A.	10.2	11.5	N.A.	37	28	33	N.A.	N.A.	4.0	1.50	82	18.9	545-0103
Bull & Bear Fin. News Comp.	G&I	Lg/Bl	9	12.7	13.2	10.4	42	26	39	52	42	None	1.77	96	5.8	847-4200
Burnham A	G&I	Lg/Val	6	9.4	11.6	11.6	35	41	26	71	37	3.0	1.20	106	121.5	874-3863
CGM Mutual	ETR	Lg/Val	8	21.8	22.1	17.5	32	57	79	71	65	None	0.93	51	850.4	345-4048
Calamos Convertible	ITR	L/Lo	8	17.6	20.1	14.1	71	21	67	52	44	4.5	1.70	133	17.4	323-9943
Calvert Social Inv. Managed	ETR	Md/Bl	6	6.0	10.3	10.1	12	61	33	73	56	4.75	1.28	116	540.2	368-2748
Capital Exchange	G&I	N.A.	9	5.7	13.8	13.6	26	32	51	89	35	4.0	N.A.	N.A.	46.8	225-6265
Capital Income Builder	ETR	Lg/Val	6	15.3	16.8	14.7	24	68	49	79	60	5.75	0.38	100	2,826.1	421-0180
Capital Market Index	G&I	N.A.	N.A.	9.7	N.A.	N.A.	35	N.A.	N.A.	N.A.	N.A.	None	0.34	N.A.	296.9	328-7408
Capstone Cashman Farrell	G&I	Md/Bl	N.A.	22.4[29]	22.1[29]	8.2[29]	N.A.	54	40	32	22	4.75	2.19	159	4.2	262-6631
Cardinal	G&I	Lg/Val	7	5.9	15.5	12.0	26	47	48	60	36	6.0	0.67	120	282.2	848-7734
Carillon Capital	ETR	Sm/Val	6	14.2	15.9	12.4	22	62	50	65	47	5.0	1.09	N.A.	33.9	999-1840
Centurion Growth	G&I	Md/Bl	11	(0.3)	0.5	0.3	12	0	16	45	22	4.75	2.32	227	5.4	947-6984
Chubb Growth & Income	G&I	Md/Bl	8	15.3	18.0	16.0	49	39	49	67	55	5.0	1.00	117	14.3	258-3648
Chubb Total Return	ETR	Md/Bl	7	13.1	16.1	14.4	21	60	56	66	77	5.0	1.00	117	13.8	258-3648
Clipper	G&I	Lg/Val	9	11.3	19.6	14.1	39	62	48	57	36	None	1.13	63	282.0	776-5033
Colonial A	G&I	Md/Val	7	14.5	17.7	12.6	47	54	38	57	32	5.75	1.12	116	519.9	248-2828
Colonial US Equity Index	G&I	Lg/Bl	N.A.	8.5[28]	14.4[28]	12.9[28]	N.A.	37	41	65	49	5.75	1.34	132	50.4	248-2828
Columbia Balanced	ETR	Lg/Bl	N.A.	13.6	N.A.	N.A.	22	65	N.A.	N.A.	N.A.	None	0.70	45	173.4	547-1707
Columbia Common Stock	G&I	Lg/Bl	N.A.	16.4	N.A.	N.A.	51	47	N.A.	N.A.	N.A.	None	0.80	48	96.7	547-1707
Common Sense Gro. & Inc.	G&I	Lg/Bl	8	9.4	15.5	13.7	35	40	46	68	45	8.5	1.09	140	712.5	544-5445
Compass Cap. Equity-Income	ETR	Lg/Bl	N.A.	17.1	16.5	N.A.	26	60	49	73	N.A.	3.75	1.00	89	264.8	451-8371
Composite Bond & Stock	ETR	Lg/Val	6	9.3	13.5	10.4	16	68	40	67	36	4.5	1.15	105	180.6	543-8072
Composite Growth	G&I	Lg/Val	8	6.8	14.7	9.7	29	49	40	61	17	4.5	1.15	104	95.3	543-8072
Connecticut Mutual T/R	ETR	Md/Val	6	15.9	17.7	14.8	24	68	53	67	68	5.0	1.06	108	162.3	322-2642
Copley	G&I	Md/Val	6	10.2	14.9	12.0	36	66	24	72	28	None	1.14	76	77.0	424-8570
CoreFund Equity Index	G&I	Lg/Bl	8	8.7	14.8	12.9	33	39	45	63	47	None	0.64	33	75.3	355-2673
CoreFund Value Equity B	G&I	Md/Bl	N.A.	9.8	N.A.	N.A.	36	N.A.	N.A.	N.A.	N.A.	4.5	N.A.	113	0.9	355-2673
Covenant	G&I	Md/Val	N.A.	4.0	N.A.	N.A.	22	N.A.	N.A.	N.A.	N.A.	4.5	2.50	172	5.1	833-4909
Cowen Income + Growth	ETR	Lg/Val	7	9.2	15.8	11.6	16	75	50	38	71	4.85	1.33	117	37.0	221-5616
Dean Witter Convertible	ITR	N.A.	9	15.7	16.1	9.3	63	23	35	21	36	5.0(d)	1.90	124	208.7	869-3863
Dean Witter Dividend Growth	G&I	Lg/Bl	8	14.2	16.4	14.0	46	36	45	58	53	5.0(d)	1.40	98	6,356.4	869-3863
Dean Witter Equity-Income	ETR	Lg/Bl	8	(3.5)	10.7	10.7	0	77	46	72	62	5.0(d)	2.01	130	167.7	869-3863
Dean Witter Managed Assets	ETR	Lg/Val	6	9.4	13.5	9.6	16	55	50	64	24	5.0(d)	1.80	117	246.8	869-3863
Dean Witter Strategist	ETR	Lg/Bl	8	8.0	15.3	14.1	14	61	62	75	69	5.0(d)	1.62	109	809.6	869-3863
Dean Witter Value Mkt. Eq.	G&I	Md/Bl	10	12.6	18.8	12.8	42	54	47	47	38	5.0(d)	1.71	115	334.5	869-3863
Delaware	ETR	Md/Val	7	9.4	14.2	13.2	16	76	39	66	77	5.75	0.79	102	507.7	523-4640
Delaware Decatur I	ETR	Lg/Bl	9	15.4	15.2	12.2	24	65	41	29	65	8.5	0.72	122	1,540.1	523-4640
Delaware Decatur II	ETR	Lg/Bl	8	14.9	14.4	11.7	23	63	38	41	80	5.75	1.22	121	446.5	523-4640
Depositors Fund of Boston[1]	G&I	N.A.	10	1.9	13.6	12.6	17	37	53	70	43	4.0	N.A.	N.A.	N.A.	225-6265
Diversification[1]	G&I	N.A.	9	6.6	14.3	12.6	28	34	49	71	39	4.0	N.A.	N.A.	N.A.	225-6265
Dodge & Cox Balanced	ETR	Lg/Bl	7	16.0	15.7	14.0	25	70	39	70	69	None	0.61	35	459.3	434-0311[19]
Dodge & Cox Stock	G&I	Lg/Bl	9	18.3	16.8	13.9	56	49	31	63	45	None	0.63	36	427.1	434-0311[19]
Domini Social Equity	G&I	Lg/Bl	N.A.	6.5	N.A.	N.A.	28	52	N.A.	N.A.	N.A.	None	0.75	42	20.3	762-6814
Dreman High Return	G&I	Lg/Val	10	9.4	24.6	15.9	35	72	71	55	29	None	1.25	69	27.9	533-1608
Dreyfus	G&I	Lg/Val	7	6.4	12.9	11.4	28	36	41	67	39	None	0.74	43	3,116.8	782-6620
Dreyfus Balanced	ETR	Md/Bl	N.A.	10.8	N.A.	N.A.	18	N.A.	N.A.	N.A.	N.A.	None	N.A.	N.A.	55.4	782-6620
Dreyfus Cap. Val. A (Prem.)	ETR	Md/Gro	8	12.7	1.7	6.0	20	8	5	71	76	4.5	1.58	127	421.9	782-6620
Dreyfus Growth & Income	G&I	Md/Gro	N.A.	18.6	N.A.	N.A.	56	73	N.A.	N.A.	N.A.	None	N.A.	92	1,158.9	782-6620
EBI Equity	G&I	Md/Bl	8	9.2	15.5	12.6	34	36	50	66	35	None	2.18	118	88.0	554-1156
EBI Flex	ETR	Lg/Val	6	10.5	14.1	11.4	18	61	47	62	51	None	2.17	118	262.9	554-1156
Eaton Vance Equity-Income	ETR	Md/Val	7	7.3	6.6	8.3	14	42	21	52	88	6.0(d)	2.46	153	48.9	225-6265
Eaton Vance Investors	ETR	Lg/Bl	6	11.2	12.8	11.9	19	58	40	70	62	4.75	0.89	94	221.6	225-6265

Notes: (d): Maximum deferred sales charge [1]Closed to new investors [19]Area code 415 [23]Area code 716 [28]To Dec. 1; fund since merged [29]To Nov. 1; fund since merged

Fund name	Type	Style	Risk level	% compound annual return to Jan. 1, 1994			Annual performance analysis (percentile ranking by type)					Expense analysis			Net assets (millions)	Telephone (800)
				One year	Three years	Five years	1993	1992	1991	1990	1989	% max. sales charge	Annual charges	Five-year total per 1,000		
Eaton Vance Stock	G&I	Lg/Gro	8	4.2	10.6	11.9	22	39	31	77	48	4.75	0.95%	$96	$91.4	225-6265
Eclipse Fin. Asset Balanced	ETR	Md/Val	N.A.	17.0	15.9	N.A.	26	69	39	72	N.A.	None	0.40	29	20.5	872-2710
Enterprise Growth & Income	G&I	Md/Bl	8	13.5	15.0	10.4	44	43	34	56	28	4.75	1.50	125	49.5	432-4320
Evergreen American Ret.	G&I	Md/Val	5	14.1	14.9	11.3	46	52	27	74	20	None	1.41	99	36.3	235-0064
Evergreen Foundation	ETR	Md/Val	N.A.	15.7	23.7	N.A.	24	97	70	88	N.A.	None	1.23	78	220.2	235-0064
Evergreen Total Return	ETR	Md/Val	7	12.9	15.2	10.8	21	68	43	48	50	None	1.18	66	1,197.7	235-0064
Evergreen Value Timing	G&I	Md/Bl	8	14.4	17.9	14.5	47	57	38	65	42	None	1.27	77	81.0	235-0064
Exchange Fund of Boston[1]	G&I	N.A.	9	4.6	13.3	11.3	23	29	52	70	32	4.0	N.A.	N.A.	N.A.	225-6265
FPA Paramount[1]	G&I	Md/Bl	7	20.5	18.1	15.5	61	47	35	79	37	6.5	0.89	113	330.5	982-4372
FPA Perennial	G&I	Md/Bl	6	4.6	12.9	12.8	23	55	31	78	43	6.5	1.07	122	85.3	982-4372
Fidelity	G&I	Md/Bl	8	18.4	16.8	14.3	56	43	35	63	48	None	0.66	37	1,517.4	544-8888
Fidelity Advisor Equity Inc.	ETR	N.A.	N.A.	18.3	N.A.	N.A.	27	N.A.	N.A.	N.A.	N.A.	4.75	1.55	104	39.2	522-7297
Fidelity Advisor Inc. & Gro.	ETR	Md/Bl	6	19.7	20.7	16.3	29	66	66	58	74	4.75	1.58	135	1,652.1	522-7297
Fidelity Asset Manager	ETR	Md/Bl	5	23.3	19.8	15.9	34	76	44	84	45	None	1.09	64	7,841.7	544-8888
Fidelity Ast. Manager: Gro.	ETR	Md/Bl	N.A.	26.3	N.A.	N.A.	38	98	N.A.	N.A.	N.A.	None	1.19	66	1,415.4	544-8888
Fidelity Ast. Manager: Inc.	ITR	Lg/Val	N.A.	15.4	N.A.	N.A.	62	N.A.	N.A.	N.A.	N.A.	None	0.65	N.A.	224.5	544-8888
Fidelity Balanced	ETR	Md/Bl	5	19.3	17.7	14.2	29	62	51	66	59	None	0.93	53	4,416.4	544-8888
Fidelity Convertible Secs.	ITR	N.A.	6	17.8	25.9	19.6	72	69	73	55	70	None	0.95	53	1,050.5	544-8888
Fidelity Equity-Income	ETR	Lg/Val	8	21.3	21.7	12.9	31	82	56	24	56	2.0	0.64	57	6,641.9	544-8888
Fidelity Equity-Income II	ETR	Md/Val	8	18.9	27.6	N.A.	28	95	90	N.A.	N.A.	None	0.91	56	4,732.2	544-8888
Fidelity Growth & Income	G&I	Md/Bl	8	19.5	23.7	18.0	59	51	62	50	50	3.0	0.85	76	7,383.4	544-8888
Fidelity Market Index	G&I	Lg/Bl	N.A.	9.6	15.3	N.A.	35	40	45	N.A.	N.A.	None	0.44	75	304.5	544-8888
Fidelity Puritan	ETR	Md/Bl	7	21.4	20.4	14.3	31	84	46	47	59	None	0.74	44	8,652.7	544-8888
Fiduciary Exchange[1]	G&I	N.A.	9	0.3	14.3	14.7	13	30	66	81	50	4.0	0.87	N.A.	N.A.	225-6265
First American Asset Alloc.	ETR	N.A.	N.A.	9.6	N.A.	N.A.	16	N.A.	N.A.	N.A.	N.A.	4.5	0.75	85	58.2	637-2548
First American Balanced	ETR	N.A.	N.A.	12.3	N.A.	N.A.	20	N.A.	N.A.	N.A.	N.A.	4.5	0.75	85	116.9	637-2548
First Investors Blue Chip	G&I	Lg/Bl	N.A.	7.8	13.5	N.A.	31	38	40	67	N.A.	6.25	1.46	144	117.1	423-4026
First Investors Total Return	ETR	Lg/Bl	N.A.	7.2	8.8	N.A.	13	38	40	N.A.	N.A.	6.25	1.36	146	60.2	423-4026
First Prairie Diver. Asset	ITR	Lg/Val	4	10.2	14.4	12.9	40	24	34	78	52	4.5	0.02[2]	142	50.4	346-3621
First Union Balanced B Inv.	ETR	Lg/Val	N.A.	10.4	N.A.	N.A.	18	62	N.A.	N.A.	N.A.	4.0	0.91	88	32.4	326-3241
First Union Balanced Trust	ETR	Lg/Val	N.A.	10.7	N.A.	N.A.	18	63	N.A.	N.A.	N.A.	None	0.66	37	726.3	326-2584
Flag Inv. Val. Builder A	ETR	Lg/Bl	N.A.	11.8	N.A.	N.A.	19	N.A.	N.A.	N.A.	N.A.	4.5	1.35	N.A.	110.2	767-3524
Flex-funds Growth	ETR	Md/Bl	7	7.2	11.5	9.7	14	57	40	81	30	None	1.53	82	26.0	325-3539
Flex-funds Muirfield	ETR	N.A.	7	7.8	14.6	11.8	14	61	57	74	39	None	1.31	77	78.3	325-3539
Fortis Adv. Asset Allocation	ETR	Md/Gro	6	11.3	15.2	13.2	19	57	56	64	68	4.5	1.58	127	108.5	800-2638
Founders Blue Chip	G&I	Lg/Bl	8	14.5	13.6	14.8	47	21	42	76	61	None	1.29	61	309.9	525-2440
Founders Equity-Income	ITR	Md/Bl	6	21.8	16.7	13.6	89	15	29	47	68	None	1.42	95	63.0	525-2440
Fountain Square Balanced	ETR	N.A.	N.A.	1.8	N.A.	N.A.	7	N.A.	N.A.	N.A.	N.A.	4.5	1.00	N.A.	64.0	334-0483
Franklin Convertible Sec.	ITR	L/Lo	7	20.5	23.2	14.6	83	49	59	44	35	4.0	0.25	83	47.3	342-5236
Franklin Corp. Qual. Div.	ITR	N.A.	6	6.6	15.3	10.5	25	51	30	70	20	1.5	1.04	75	35.0	342-5236
Franklin Equity-Income	ETR	Lg/Val	7	17.9	19.6	14.1	27	77	54	40	72	4.0	0.25	83	42.0	342-5236
Franklin Income	ITR	Lg/Val	6	21.5	25.5	15.3	88	46	80	32	36	4.0	0.54	69	4,162.7	342-5236
Franklin Premier Return	G&I	Md/Bl	8	18.5	18.2	11.3	56	57	32	53	20	4.0	0.94	89	22.6	342-5236
Franklin Rising Dividends	G&I	Md/Val	7	(3.5)	13.1	11.7	4	48	53	76	31	4.0	1.31	117	360.2	342-5236
FundTrust Growth & Income	G&I	N.A.	8	12.9	15.1	10.6	43	38	39	56	29	1.5	1.69	82	40.0	344-9033
FundTrust Managed T/R	ETR	N.A.	5	8.9	11.3	9.6	16	58	35	68	43	1.5	1.90	130	24.4	522-7297
Fundamental Investors	G&I	Lg/Bl	8	18.2	19.3	15.4	55	47	45	60	48	5.75	0.65	92	1,926.1	421-0180
Gabelli Convertible Sec.	ITR	N.A.	N.A.	13.1	12.8	N.A.	52	39	0	90	N.A.	4.5	1.42	118	109.5	422-3554
Gabelli Equity-Income	ETR	Lg/Val	N.A.	17.9	Three	N.A.	27	64	N.A.	N.A.	N.A.	4.5	1.75	104	55.5	422-3554
Galaxy Asset Alloc. Retail	ETR	Lg/Bl	N.A.	8.1	N.A.	N.A.	15	58	N.A.	N.A.	N.A.	None	1.01	63	91.3	628-0414
Galaxy Equity-Income Retail	ETR	Lg/Bl	N.A.	8.1	12.4	N.A.	15	61	42	N.A.	N.A.	None	1.06	57	123.9	628-0414
Gateway Index Plus	G&I	Lg/Bl	3	7.4	10.0	11.9	30	35	25	100	31	None	1.03	61	211.3	354-6339
General Securities	ETR	Lg/Bl	6	6.2	15.2	12.9	12	56	69	67	61	5.0	1.32	121	27.4	331-4923
Geo. Putnam Fund of Boston A	ETR	Lg/Val	7	10.9	13.7	12.5	18	62	43	64	71	5.75	0.90	113	838.0	225-1581
Goldman Sachs Select Equity	G&I	Lg/Bl	N.A.	12.8	N.A.	N.A.	43	22	N.A.	N.A.	N.A.	5.0	1.28	N.A.	87.7	762-5035
Hancock Sovereign Bal. B	ETR	Lg/Val	N.A.	10.6	N.A.	N.A.	18	N.A.	N.A.	N.A.	N.A.	4.0(d)	2.09	202	70.8	225-5291
Hancock Sovereign Invest. A	G&I	Lg/Bl	6	5.7	13.9	13.8	26	40	45	86	39	5.0	1.13	109	1,221.7	225-5291
Harbor Value	G&I	Lg/Val	9	8.4	12.2	11.6	32	41	31	62	50	None	0.87	52	59.9	422-1050
Harris Insight Convertible	ITR	N.A.	9	11.6	17.5	8.3	46	47	38	0	30	4.5	0.80	87	6.0	982-8782
Heritage Income-Growth	G&I	Md/Bl	7	11.1	18.5	10.9	39	51	50	49	20	4.0	1.75	135	35.1	421-4184
Homestead Value	G&I	Md/Val	9	18.8	15.9	N.A.	57	51	25	N.A.	N.A.	None	1.25	67	49.1	258-3030
IAI Balanced	ETR	Lg/Gro	N.A.	5.0	N.A.	N.A.	11	N.A.	N.A.	N.A.	N.A.	None	1.25	N.A.	69.6	945-3863
IAI Growth & Income	G&I	Lg/Bl	9	10.0	13.2	11.9	36	32	39	59	50	None	1.25	69	133.4	945-3863
IDS Blue Chip Advantage	G&I	Lg/Bl	N.A.	12.2	15.8	N.A.	41	39	43	N.A.	N.A.	5.0	1.10	N.A.	140.3	328-8300
IDS Diversified Equity-Inc.	ETR	Md/Bl	N.A.	29.2	23.0	N.A.	41	81	49	N.A.	N.A.	5.0	0.96	107	525.5	328-8300
IDS Equity Plus	G&I	Md/Bl	8	14.6	18.8	15.9	47	48	48	67	49	5.0	0.75	139	632.2	328-8300
IDS Managed Retirement	G&I	Lg/Bl	8	15.0	22.4	19.8	48	45	69	76	59	5.0	0.84	100	1,846.4	328-8300
IDS Mutual	ETR	Md/Val	6	14.4	16.0	12.4	23	69	44	58	56	5.0	0.79	91	2,894.6	328-8300
IDS Stock	G&I	Lg/Bl	7	16.6	16.7	16.0	52	39	40	79	50	5.0	0.72	88	2,059.1	328-8300
IDS Strat. Equity	G&I	Md/Bl	8	16.4	19.0	14.0	51	54	42	61	35	5.0(d)	1.58	112	953.0	328-8300
Income Fund of America	ITR	Lg/Val	8	14.0	16.5	13.5	56	35	31	55	62	5.75	0.62	92	10,095.9	421-0180
Indep. Cap. T/R Growth	G&I	Lg/Gro	N.A.	12.2	13.1	N.A.	41	11	52	N.A.	N.A.	4.5	1.46	122	36.6	833-4264
Invesco Industrial Income	ETR	Md/Val	7	16.7	19.9	18.1	25	42	90	70	97	None	0.98	54	3,739.6	525-8085
Investment Co. of America	G&I	Lg/Bl	7	11.6	14.8	14.5	40	39	39	77	49	5.75	0.58	88	18,802.4	421-0180
Inv. Ser. High-Qual. Stock	G&I	Lg/Val	8	10.9	16.4	11.9	38	50	41	73	18	5.75	1.00	136	30.4	245-4761
Ivy Growth with Income A	G&I	Lg/Val	9	16.3	17.6	13.9	51	28	54	75	28	5.75	1.94	156	21.7	456-5111
Jackson National T/R	ETR	N.A.	N.A.	11.9	N.A.	N.A.	19	N.A.	N.A.	N.A.	N.A.	4.75	1.20	N.A.	32.4	888-3863
Janus Balanced	ETR	Md/Gro	N.A.	10.0	N.A.	N.A.	17	N.A.	N.A.	N.A.	N.A.	None	2.05	N.A.	72.4	525-3713
Janus Flexible Income	ITR	N.A.	6	15.6	17.7	10.1	63	35	38	48	14	None	1.00	55	471.2	525-3713
Janus Growth & Income	G&I	Lg/Bl	N.A.	6.7	N.A.	N.A.	28	35	N.A.	N.A.	N.A.	None	1.33	83	518.6	525-3713

Notes: (d): Maximum deferred sales charge [1]Closed to new investors [2]Manager absorbing costs

Fund name	Type	Style	Risk level	% compound annual return to Jan. 1, 1994 — One year	Three years	Five years	Annual performance analysis (percentile ranking by type) 1993	1992	1991	1990	1989	Expense analysis — % max. sales charge	Annual charges	Five-year total per 1,000	Net assets (millions)	Telephone (800)
Kemper Blue Chip	G&I	Lg/Bl	9	3.4	13.9	14.0	21	19	66	81	45	5.75	1.46%	$133	$203.0	621-1048
Kemper Inv. T/R Initial	ETR	Md/Gro	7	8.2	17.2	14.1	15	52	82	68	60	4.0(d)	1.96	116	1,363.3	621-1048
Kemper Retirement I[1]	ETR	Lg/Gro	N.A.	11.4	17.6	N.A.	19	44	84	N.A.	N.A.	5.0	0.92	N.A.	126.8	621-1048
Kemper Retirement II[1]	ETR	Lg/Gro	N.A.	12.5	18.0	N.A.	20	48	81	N.A.	N.A.	5.0	0.95	N.A.	210.4	621-1048
Kemper Retirement III[1]	ETR	Lg/Gro	N.A.	12.8	N.A.	N.A.	22	N.A.	N.A.	N.A.	N.A.	5.0	0.95	N.A.	149.9	621-1048
Kemper Total Return	ETR	Md/Gro	7	11.6	17.0	14.9	19	46	77	80	59	5.75	1.06	113	1,463.4	621-1048
Kent Index Equity Inv.	G&I	Lg/Bl	N.A.	9.6	N.A.	N.A.	35	N.A.	N.A.	N.A.	N.A.	4.0	N.A.	N.A.	3.4	633-5368
Keystone Amer. Eq.-Inc. A	ETR	Lg/Val	7	12.3	13.8	12.8	20	53	47	60	81	5.75	1.83	155	27.3	343-2898
Keystone Custodian K-1	ETR	Lg/Bl	7	10.3	12.3	10.8	17	49	45	62	59	4.0(d)	1.93	107	1,509.8	343-2898
Keystone Custodian S-1	G&I	Lg/Bl	9	9.8	12.3	11.6	36	22	42	64	48	4.0(d)	2.28	112	233.6	343-2898
Kidder Peabody Asset All. B	ETR	Lg/Bl	N.A.	7.6	N.A.	N.A.	14	N.A.	N.A.	N.A.	N.A.	None	1.75	100	107.8	854-2505
Kidder Peabody Equity-Inc. A	ETR	Lg/Gro	8	1.7	13.0	13.7	7	30	89	73	88	5.75	1.35	124	118.5	854-2505
LMH	G&I	Md/Val	10	7.2	11.3	4.7	30	43	26	31	17	None	2.63	142	6.6	847-6002
Landmark Balanced	ETR	Lg/Gro	7	8.5	14.5	10.0	15	59	56	55	34	3.5	1.29	123	265.1	223-4447
Laurel Stock	G&I	Lg/Bl	8	11.8	17.1	16.7	40	41	50	76	58	None	0.90	50	92.5	235-4331
Legg Mason Total Return	G&I	Lg/Val	8	14.1	22.4	12.1	46	58	60	35	25	None	1.95	125	168.0	822-5544
Lepercq-Istel	G&I	Md/Val	7	13.5	12.0	9.8	44	36	25	59	35	None	1.54	89	17.1	338-1579
Lexington Convertible Secs.	ITR	N.A.	9	6.5	20.4	12.5	25	38	91	53	22	None	2.34	137	8.0	526-0056
Lexington Corporate Leaders	G&I	Lg/Bl	8	17.6	15.5	14.3	54	46	28	65	54	None	0.62	N.A.	142.3	526-0056
Lexington Growth & Income	G&I	Lg/Bl	9	13.2	16.7	12.4	44	53	36	51	46	None	1.20	75	133.8	526-0056
Liberty Equity-Income	ETR	Md/Val	7	20.8	23.5	12.3	31	68	82	28	24	4.5	1.01	97	56.1	245-5051
Liberty Financial Gro. & Inc.	G&I	Lg/Val	N.A.	7.9	N.A.	N.A.	31	N.A.	N.A.	N.A.	N.A.	4.5	1.25	N.A.	20.9	872-5426
Lindner Dividend	ITR	Md/Val	4	14.9	21.0	13.1	60	66	41	41	34	None	0.74	42	1,374.3	727-5305[14]
Loomis Sayles Growth & Inc.	G&I	Md/Val	N.A.	11.9	N.A.	N.A.	41	57	N.A.	N.A.	N.A.	None	1.50	82	19.1	633-3330
MFS Total Return A	ETR	Lg/Val	6	15.1	15.5	13.1	24	68	40	60	69	4.75	0.84	92	1,729.3	225-2606
MIM AFA Equity Income	ETR	Md/Val	N.A.	4.9	N.A.	N.A.	11	72	N.A.	N.A.	N.A.	2.60		176	3.8	233-1240
MIM Stock Income	G&I	Lg/Bl	8	(0.7)	7.6	5.4	11	35	28	67	10	None	3.50	138	8.3	233-1240
MIMLIC Asset Allocation	ETR	Lg/Gro	6	4.9	12.3	11.8	11	55	53	78	58	5.0	1.33	120	57.0	443-3677
MIMLIC Investors I	G&I	Lg/Bl	9	1.2	13.5	12.9	15	34	56	76	41	5.0	1.40	123	30.0	443-3677
Mackenzie North American A	ETR	Lg/Val	7	14.2	12.4	8.1	22	59	30	42	39	5.75	1.72	158	38.3	456-5111
MainStay Convertible	ITR	Int/Lo	7	24.5	27.9	15.8	100	39	100	40	21	5.0(d)	1.90	143	67.0	522-4202
MainStay Equity Index	G&I	Lg/Bl	N.A.	5.7	14.1	N.A.	34	42	44	N.A.	N.A.	5.5	0.90	103	63.5	522-4202
MainStay Total Return	ETR	Md/Gro	8	10.5	16.1	13.6	18	49	71	83	44	5.0(d)	1.80	129	513.9	522-4202
MainStay Value	ETR	Md/Val	8	13.5	24.2	16.9	44	71	61	61	35	5.0(d)	1.90	124	267.8	522-4202
Managers Balanced	ETR	Lg/Bl	8	6.8	13.7	11.7	13	53	59	52	75	None	0.52	92	4.6	835-3879
Managers Income Equity	ETR	Lg/Val	8	12.4	17.1	11.5	20	68	56	27	70	None	1.30	68	50.8	835-3879
Massachusetts Investors A	G&I	Lg/Bl	8	10.0	14.7	15.5	36	40	40	75	62	5.75	0.68	95	1,695.9	225-2606
Merrill Lynch Balanced B	ETR	Lg/Bl	7	14.7	13.9	10.8	23	48	47	57	51	4.0(d)	1.87	100	833.2	637-3863
Merrill Lynch Basic Value A	G&I	Lg/Bl	9	22.2	19.7	11.9	65	48	40	44	28	6.5	0.56	95	2,171.5	637-3863
Merrill Lynch Capital A	G&I	Md/Val	6	13.7	14.3	13.1	45	34	37	77	38	6.5	0.55	94	2,232.6	637-3863
Merrill Lynch Strat. Div. B	ETR	Lg/Val	8	7.5	10.0	8.7	14	62	27	43	70	4.0(d)	1.91	103	223.3	637-3863
Merriman Asset Allocation	ETR	N.A.	N.A.	18.5	10.5	N.A.	28	44	21	75	N.A.	None	1.52	83	30.2	423-4893
Merriman Blue Chip	G&I	Lg/Bl	6	2.8	6.5	6.6	19	19	27	84	13	None	1.69	87	16.5	423-4893
MetLife-State St. Eq.-Inc. A	ETR	Md/Val	7	22.4	17.7	12.7	33	76	33	34	76	4.5	1.50	123	39.0	882-0052
MetLife-State St. Managed A	ETR	Md/Gro	6	21.9	16.8	12.5	32	62	39	57	51	4.5	1.25	111	121.9	562-0032
Monitor Inc.-Eq. Tr. Shares	ETR	Lg/Val	N.A.	10.8	13.7	N.A.	18	61	44	40	N.A.	None	0.82	47	131.2	253-0412
Monitrend Summation	G&I	Lg/Bl	8	(5.3)	(1.7)	1.3	0	1	12	71	22	3.5	2.44	161	3.0	251-1970
Mutual Beacon	G&I	Sm/Val	6	22.9	21.1	13.9	67	79	25	56	27	None	0.73	46	1,060.8	553-3014
Mutual Qualified[1]	G&I	Md/Val	7	22.7	22.2	13.4	66	79	30	51	22	None	0.79	47	1,530.2	553-3014
Mutual Shares[1]	G&I	Md/Val	7	21.0	21.1	13.0	62	75	30	52	23	None	0.75	45	3,539.1	553-3014
Mutual of Omaha Income	ITR	N.A.	5	10.2	12.1	11.1	40	20	17	80	44	4.5	0.99	100	300.4	225-6292
NCC Equity Retail	G&I	N.A.	N.A.	(0.7)	N.A.	N.A.	11	37	N.A.	N.A.	N.A.	3.75	0.59	104	8.3	624-6450
National Income & Growth A	ETR	Lg/Bl	6	14.5	16.5	14.9	23	74	44	63	86	5.75	1.33	129	589.9	356-5535
National Total Return	G&I	Lg/Bl	N.A.	13.6[28]	17.3[28]	14.0[28]	N.A.	46	42	61	46	5.75	1.38	127	285.9	356-5535
Nations Equity-Inc. Inv. A	ETR	Lg/Val	N.A.	12.5	N.A.	N.A.	20	67	N.A.	N.A.	N.A.	4.5	1.17	108	36.3	321-7854
Nations Value Investor A	G&I	Lg/Val	N.A.	16.1	16.1	N.A.	50	40	38	80	N.A.	4.5	1.20	108	32.6	321-7854
Nationwide	G&I	Lg/Bl	8	6.8	12.7	14.0	28	29	44	76	57	4.5	0.61	78	755.2	848-0920
Neuberger/Berman Guardian	G&I	Md/Val	9	14.5	22.3	16.2	47	70	51	64	35	None	0.81	46	1,895.8	877-9700
Nicholas Income	ITR	Int/Lo	3	13.0	15.3	9.5	42	0	5	82	66	None	0.60	38	158.7	272-6133[18]
North American Asset Alloc.	ETR	Md/Bl	N.A.	10.1	11.7	N.A.	17	59	34	30	N.A.	4.0	1.99	143	96.1	872-8037
North American Gro. & Inc.	G&I	Lg/Val	N.A.	9.2	N.A.	N.A.	34	43	N.A.	N.A.	N.A.	4.0	1.99	143	37.4	872-8037
Olympic Balanced Income	ETR	Lg/Val	6	12.5	14.0	11.7	20	66	38	66	53	None	1.00	57	33.2	346-7301
Olympic Equity-Income	ETR	Lg/Val	10	15.8	21.1	12.5	24	80	66	11	71	None	1.00	57	79.9	346-7301
Oppenheimer Asset Alloc.	ETR	Md/Bl	6	16.3	12.8	11.2	25	61	26	70	51	5.75	1.10	118	278.8	525-7048
Oppenheimer Equity-Income A	ETR	Lg/Val	7	14.6	12.8	10.9	23	59	32	63	55	5.75	0.82	100	1,857.8	525-7048
Oppenheimer Main St. I&G	G&I	Sm/Bl	8	35.4	43.5	28.2	96	100	100	60	42	5.75	1.46	133	78.7	525-7048
Oppenheimer Str. I&G A	ITR	Lg/Bl	N.A.	7.8	N.A.	N.A.	30	N.A.	N.A.	N.A.	N.A.	4.75	1.46	N.A.	54.9	525-7048
Oppenheimer Total Return	G&I	Md/Bl	9	21.2	23.1	16.4	63	54	54	66	31	5.75	0.96	107	1,176.9	525-7048
Oppenheimer Val. Stock Cl. A	G&I	Lg/Val	8	9.0	14.4	12.4	34	46	37	72	35	5.75	1.22	119	88.4	525-7048
Overland Exp. Ast. Alloc. A	ETR	Lg/Bl	5	12.5	13.4	11.5	20	61	38	89	30	4.5	1.36	111	52.4	552-9612
Overland Express G&I A	G&I	Md/Val	N.A.	5.8	16.8	N.A.	26	59	46	N.A.	N.A.	4.5	0.90	70	15.2	552-9612
Pacific Horizon Capital Inc.	ITR	N.A.	7	20.2	26.3	19.6	82	67	72	50	73	4.5	0.25	45	122.3	332-3863
Pacifica Balanced	ETR	Lg/Val	N.A.	18.6	15.6	N.A.	28	68	34	N.A.	N.A.	4.5	1.05	100	107.4	662-8417
PaineWebber Asset Alloc. B	ETR	Lg/Bl	6	14.7	12.4	9.9	23	52	34	73	32	5.0(d)	2.05	129	92.9	647-1568
PaineWebber Dividend Gro. A	G&I	Lg/Val	8	(2.6)	11.1	11.3	6	32	52	75	41	4.5	1.13	109	327.9	647-1568
Parnassus Income Balanced	ITR	Sm/Val	N.A.	15.9	N.A.	N.A.	64	N.A.	N.A.	N.A.	N.A.	None	0.00[2]	69	9.8	999-3505
Pasadena Balanced Return	ETR	Lg/Gro	8	2.4	14.1	14.5	8	52	75	66	100	5.5	2.10	165	87.8	882-2855
Pax World	ETR	Lg/Bl	6	(1.1)	6.3	10.6	3	41	39	100	75	None	1.00	58	485.6	767-1729
Penn Square Mutual	G&I	Lg/Bl	8	12.9	16.0	13.2	43	44	40	63	42	4.75	0.99	98	251.8	523-8440
Peoples Index	G&I	Lg/Bl	N.A.	9.5	15.3	N.A.	35	41	44	63	N.A.	None	0.65	36	281.4	782-6620

202

Notes: (d): Maximum deferred sales charge [1]Closed to new investors [2]Manager absorbing costs [14]Area code 314 [18]Area code 414 [28]To Dec. 1; fund since merged

Fund name	Type	Style	Risk level	One year	Three years	Five years	1993	1992	1991	1990	1989	% max. sales charge	Annual charges	Five-year total per 1,000	Net assets (millions)	Telephone (800)
Permanent Portfolio	ETR	Md/Gro	6	15.5	8.6	5.5	24	46	13	55	18	None	1.18%	$102	$76.0	531-5142
Philadelphia	G&I	Md/Val	8	17.6	14.2	11.8	54	71	7	48	55	None	1.81	97	98.0	749-9933
Phoenix Balanced	ETR	Lg/Bl	6	6.4	12.7	13.9	13	59	49	90	75	4.75	1.04	99	3,126.0	243-4361
Phoenix Convertible	ITR	N.A.	5	9.9	11.9	11.9	39	38	1	82	55	4.75	1.20	111	252.1	243-4361
Phoenix Total Return	ETR	Lg/Gro	6	10.5	16.2	14.2	18	69	54	81	55	4.75	1.32	118	110.2	243-4361
Pierpont Equity	G&I	Lg/Bl	8	11.0	17.4	16.5	39	44	50	79	52	None	0.90	50	233.9	521-5412
Pilgrim MagnaCap	G&I	Lg/Bl	9	10.8	14.5	12.2	38	42	37	68	36	5.0	1.53	130	202.9	334-3444
Pioneer	G&I	Md/Bl	8	14.2	16.9	12.0	46	57	33	50	38	5.75	0.96	109	2,034.8	225-6292
Pioneer Equity-Income	ETR	Md/Val	N.A.	12.9	20.0	N.A.	21	100	50	N.A.	N.A.	5.75	1.38	146	142.7	225-6292
Pioneer II	G&I	Md/Val	8	18.9	17.8	12.0	57	45	38	46	36	5.75	0.95	107	4,436.0	225-6292
Piper Jaffray Balanced	ETR	Lg/Bl	7	7.2	14.8	11.4	13	70	52	59	50	4.0	1.32	109	61.7	866-7778
Piper Jaffray Growth & Inc.	G&I	Lg/Bl	N.A.	6.1	N.A.	N.A.	27	N.A.	N.A.	N.A.	N.A.	4.0	1.32	109	97.1	866-7778
Portico Balanced	ETR	Md/Bl	N.A.	8.2	N.A.	N.A.	15	N.A.	N.A.	N.A.	N.A.	None	0.75	N.A.	82.1	228-1024
Portico Equity Index	G&I	Lg/Bl	N.A.	9.1	14.9	N.A.	34	39	44	63	N.A.	None	0.50	30	83.8	228-1024
Portico Growth & Income	ETR	Lg/Val	N.A.	6.5	11.2	N.A.	13	55	42	66	N.A.	None	0.85	50	160.7	228-1024
Preferred Asset Allocation	ETR	Lg/Bl	N.A.	10.6	N.A.	N.A.	18	N.A.	N.A.	N.A.	N.A.	None	1.27	N.A.	53.6	662-4769
Preferred Value	G&I	Lg/Bl	N.A.	8.8	N.A.	N.A.	33	N.A.	N.A.	N.A.	N.A.	None	0.96	N.A.	125.6	662-4769
Primary Income	ITR	Lg/Val	N.A.	15.4	12.5	N.A.	62	0	25	82	N.A.	None	0.84	47	3.2	443-6544
Primary Trend	G&I	Md/Bl	8	11.4	9.4	7.0	39	18	28	71	12	None	1.20	61	24.4	443-6544
Principal Pres. Div. Achiev.	G&I	Lg/Bl	9	(5.0)	10.7	10.4	1	30	57	78	31	4.5	1.20	108	25.8	826-4600
Principal Pres. S&P 100 Plus	G&I	Lg/Bl	8	9.7	13.8	12.1	35	35	41	68	40	4.5	1.30	112	37.4	826-4600
Princor Blue Chip	G&I	Lg/Bl	N.A.	2.6	N.A.	N.A.	19	37	N.A.	N.A.	N.A.	5.0	1.38	N.A.	23.8	451-5447
Princor Managed	ETR	Md/Val	7	9.0	16.6	10.7	16	69	60	51	31	5.0	1.27	117	40.0	451-5447
Prudential Equity-Income B	ETR	Md/Val	7	20.4	17.9	13.2	30	63	48	50	61	5.0(d)	2.02	119	526.6	225-1852
Prudential Flex. Cons. B	ETR	Md/Bl	6	13.8	13.8	11.9	22	58	40	76	46	5.0(d)	1.97	122	358.3	225-1852
Prudential Flex. Strategy B	ETR	Lg/Bl	7	12.2	13.4	11.9	20	49	48	69	59	5.0(d)	2.01	121	372.5	225-1852
Prudential IncomeVertible B	ITR	N.A.	7	12.0	12.9	10.4	48	20	20	43	58	5.0(d)	2.09	125	326.6	225-1852
Putnam Conv. Income-Growth	ITR	N.A.	7	17.0	22.4	14.0	69	66	47	27	46	5.75	1.11	115	707.9	225-1581
Putnam Corporate Asset	ITR	N.A.	2	11.9	14.3	10.7	47	27	25	66	32	2.5	0.83	73	142.7	225-1581
Putnam Dividend Growth	G&I	Lg/Val	N.A.	7.3	13.9	N.A.	30	35	46	N.A.	N.A.	5.75	1.36	154	49.8	225-1581
Putnam Equity-Income Class A	ETR	Lg/Val	8	16.5	15.0	10.3	25	53	46	45	46	5.75	1.23	120	333.9	225-1581
Putnam Fund for G/I A	G&I	Lg/Val	7	14.4	15.1	13.5	47	51	27	81	33	5.75	1.07	112	5,211.5	225-1581
Putnam Managed Income	ITR	Md/Val	7	12.4	15.8	12.3	49	33	32	55	50	5.75	1.11	117	551.6	225-1581
Quantitative Boston G&I Ord.	G&I	Lg/Val	8	11.9	15.0	15.6	41	38	41	73	64	1.0(d)	1.76	111	41.5	331-1244
Quest for Value G&I A	G&I	Lg/Bl	N.A.	11.8	N.A.	N.A.	40	43	N.A.	N.A.	N.A.	4.75	1.90	161	28.5	232-3863
Quest for Value Opp. A	ETR	Md/Val	7	8.2	24.6	16.3	15	91	100	35	68	5.5	1.88	170	126.8	232-3863
RBB Balanced	ETR	Lg/Bl	6	13.5	15.1	13.5	21	60	47	77	59	4.75	0.67	N.A.	0.8	888-9723
RIMCO Monument Stock	G&I	Lg/Val	N.A.	18.5	N.A.	N.A.	56	N.A.	N.A.	N.A.	N.A.	3.5	0.69	88	48.9	934-3883
Rea-Graham Balanced	ETR	Sm/Val	7	0.2	6.2	4.0	5	51	26	49	23	4.75	2.31	153	21.6	433-1998
Retirement Planning Conv.	ITR	L/Lo	N.A.	17.3	N.A.	N.A.	70	N.A.	N.A.	N.A.	N.A.	4.75	1.18	118	43.1	279-0279
Rightime	G&I	Lg/Bl	7	8.1	13.5	10.5	32	33	44	79	16	None	2.54	131	172.3	242-1421
Rightime Blue Chip	G&I	Lg/Bl	7	7.3	11.2	10.8	30	32	34	78	31	4.75	2.17	167	223.6	242-1421
Rightime MidCap	G&I	Md/Bl	N.A.	5.8	N.A.	N.A.	26	51	N.A.	N.A.	N.A.	4.75	2.19	164	61.9	242-1421
Rightime Social Awareness	G&I	Lg/Bl	N.A.	(2.3)	10.7	N.A.	7	54	34	N.A.	N.A.	4.75	2.54	172	10.6	242-1421
Rodney Square Gro. & Inc.	G&I	Lg/Bl	7	14.4	15.2	14.1	47	38	38	72	47	4.0	1.50	119	6.3	336-9970
Royce Equity-Income	ETR	Sm/Val	N.A.	13.1	20.7	N.A.	21	96	58	19	N.A.	None	1.00	55	79.5	221-4268
Rushmore Stock Market Index+	G&I	Lg/Bl	9	10.0	12.3	11.1	36	26	39	68	38	None	1.00	56	8.4	343-3355
Safeco Equity	G&I	Md/Gro	10	30.9	22.3	17.8	85	45	41	55	61	None	0.94	53	168.2	426-6730
Safeco Income	ETR	Lg/Val	7	12.6	15.6	10.5	20	72	44	34	57	None	0.90	50	205.6	426-6730
SBSF	G&I	Md/Bl	7	20.4	15.2	14.8	61	39	27	69	58	None	1.16	66	128.2	422-7273
SBSF Convertible Securities	ITR	N.A.	6	20.1	19.5	14.0	82	33	42	47	52	None	1.32	74	68.8	422-7273
Salomon Bros. Investors	G&I	Lg/Bl	9	15.2	17.0	12.7	48	40	43	60	35	None	0.71	38	393.7	725-6666
Schwab 1000	G&I	Lg/Bl	N.A.	9.6	N.A.	N.A.	35	43	N.A.	N.A.	N.A.	None	0.45	25	519.4	526-8600
Scudder Balanced	ETR	N.A.	N.A.	4.1	N.A.	N.A.	10	N.A.	N.A.	N.A.	N.A.	N.A.	N.A.	N.A.	61.2	225-2470
Scudder Growth & Income	G&I	Md/Val	7	15.6	17.5	14.9	49	46	41	70	44	None	0.88	51	1,600.4	225-2470
Second Fiduciary Exchange[1]	G&I	N.A.	10	4.9	11.6	11.1	24	32	40	73	37	4.0	0.86	N.A.	N.A.	225-6265
Security Growth & Income	G&I	Lg/Bl	7	8.2	11.4	10.1	32	34	32	68	33	5.75	1.26	123	80.2	888-2461
Selected American Shares	G&I	Lg/Bl	10	5.5	17.7	13.5	25	36	69	66	32	None	1.09	64	445.4	243-1575
Seligman Common Stock A	G&I	Lg/Bl	9	15.0	18.3	15.1	48	49	44	66	45	4.75	0.90	100	557.9	221-2783
Seligman Income A	ITR	N.A.	6	16.0	21.1	13.4	65	54	49	34	42	4.75	1.06	107	312.1	221-2783
Sentinel Balanced	ETR	Lg/Bl	6	9.6	12.8	11.8	17	57	44	73	58	5.0	1.05	111	232.9	282-3863
Sentinel Common Stock	G&I	Lg/Bl	8	9.3	14.8	13.4	35	36	45	69	46	5.0	0.86	102	915.0	282-3863
Seven Seas S&P 500 Index	G&I	Lg/Bl	N.A.	8.0	N.A.	N.A.	31	N.A.	N.A.	N.A.	N.A.	None	0.15	N.A.	309.8	654-6089[21]
Sierra Growth & Income	G&I	Lg/Bl	N.A.	11.0	13.4	N.A.	39	29	40	67	N.A.	4.5	1.01	N.A.	94.7	222-5852
Signet Select. Val. Eq. Inv.	G&I	Lg/Val	N.A.	1.1	9.8	N.A.	15	37	34	N.A.	N.A.	None	0.62	91	20.1	444-7123
Sit Growth & Income	G&I	Lg/Gro	8	3.1	12.8	13.1	20	34	48	70	54	None	1.42	82	38.7	332-5580
Smith Barney Inc. & Growth A	G&I	Lg/Val	7	16.4	16.4	12.1	51	40	38	52	41	4.5	0.95	94	632.1	544-7835
Smith Barney Shear. Conv. B	ITR	Int/Lo	7	12.5	16.8	9.8	50	40	35	33	28	5.0(d)	2.00	112	77.4	451-2010
Smith Barney Shear. G&I B	G&I	N.A.	N.A.	7.9	N.A.	N.A.	31	N.A.	N.A.	N.A.	N.A.	5.0(d)	N.A.	N.A.	60.4	451-2010
Smith Barney Shear. Pr. Ret. '96[1]	ETR	Lg/Bl	N.A.	7.2	11.7	N.A.	13	61	38	77	N.A.	5.0	0.75	91	93.9	451-2010
Smith Barney Shear. Pr. Ret. '98[1]	ETR	Lg/Bl	N.A.	9.5	N.A.	N.A.	16	59	N.A.	N.A.	N.A.	5.0	0.98	103	140.5	451-2010
Smith Barney Shear. PrmTlRet. B	ETR	Lg/Val	7	11.2	17.3	14.1	19	76	55	74	52	5.0(d)	1.69	N.A.	1,381.9	451-2010
Smith Barney Shear. Strat. Inv. B	ETR	Lg/Val	7	14.6	15.6	13.3	23	58	50	60	71	5.0(d)	2.02	121	321.2	451-2010
Smith Breeden Mkt. Trk. Svc.	G&I	N.A.	N.A.	13.0	N.A.	N.A.	43	N.A.	N.A.	N.A.	N.A.	None	0.40	N.A.	1.6	221-3138
Stagecoach Asset Allocation	ETR	Lg/Bl	4	15.0	14.4	12.6	23	59	41	92	35	4.5	0.90	95	981.8	222-8222
Stagecoach Corporate Stock	G&I	Lg/Bl	8	8.9	14.2	13.2	34	37	42	66	50	None	0.97	51	259.6	222-8222
Stagecoach Growth & Income	G&I	Md/Val	N.A.	8.0	15.2	N.A.	31	56	36	N.A.	N.A.	4.5	0.95	67	107.7	222-8222
Steadman American Industry[1]	G&I	Md/Bl	12	9.1	1.1	(5.6)	34	5	0	0	6	None	13.42	N.A.	2.5	424-8570
Steadman Associated[1]	G&I	Lg/Val	12	10.7	13.3	7.9	38	36	36	15	58	None	4.10	N.A.	8.6	424-8570
Steadman Investment[1]	G&I	Lg/Val	12	2.9	8.2	3.1	19	2	50	37	12	None	4.32	N.A.	3.7	424-8570

Notes: (d): Maximum deferred sales charge [1]Closed to new investors [21]Area code 617

Fund name	Type	Style	Risk level	One year	Three years	Five years	1993	1992	1991	1990	1989	% max. sales charge	Annual charges	Five-year total per $1,000	Net assets (millions)	Telephone (800)
SteinRoe Prime Equities	G&I	Md/Bl	8	12.9	18.0	16.2	43	47	48	71	52	None	0.88%	$54	$104.5	338-2550
SteinRoe Total Return	ETR	Lg/Bl	7	12.3	16.2	13.2	20	62	56	62	61	None	0.81	47	226.9	338-2550
Stellar	ETR	Md/Val	N.A.	13.1	N.A.	N.A.	21	52	N.A.	N.A.	N.A.	4.5	1.39	125	67.7	677-3863
Stratton Monthly Dividend	ETR	Md/Val	6	6.6	16.7	12.7	13	69	67	55	56	None	0.94	60	190.6	634-5726
Strong Investment	ETR	Lg/Bl	5	14.5	12.2	10.1	23	48	36	76	33	None	1.20	66	249.7	368-1030
Strong Total Return	G&I	Md/Gro	9	22.5	18.1	9.4	66	23	50	58	0	None	1.20	70	633.1	368-1030
SunAmerica Bal. Assets B	ETR	Lg/Gro	7	14.2	15.3	12.1	22	55	52	60	55	4.0(d)	1.91	114	134.6	858-8850
T. Rowe Price Balanced	ETR	Lg/Bl	5	13.3	14.0	13.9	21	60	41	89	62	None	1.00	55	322.4	638-5660
T. Rowe Price Dividend Gro.	G&I	Lg/Bl	N.A.	19.4	N.A.	N.A.	58	N.A.	N.A.	N.A.	N.A.	None	N.A.	N.A.	37.3	638-5660
T. Rowe Price Equity Index	G&I	Lg/Bl	N.A.	9.4	14.9	N.A.	35	40	43	N.A.	N.A.	None	0.45	50	158.3	638-5660
T. Rowe Price Equity-Income	ETR	Lg/Val	7	14.8	18.0	11.7	23	80	48	46	41	None	0.95	54	2,763.8	638-5660
T. Rowe Price Growth/Income	G&I	Lg/Val	9	13.0	19.7	12.7	43	60	46	49	31	None	0.83	47	1,128.7	638-5660
T. Rowe Price Spectrum Inc.	ITR	N.A.	N.A.	12.3	13.2	N.A.	49	21	20	N.A.	N.A.	None	0.00	49	568.9	638-5660
TNE Balanced Class A	ETR	Lg/Val	9	14.2	18.9	10.7	22	80	56	34	30	5.75	1.41	134	150.5	343-7104
TNE Growth Opportunities A	G&I	Lg/Bl	8	7.9	15.5	13.5	31	45	45	65	47	5.75	1.17	119	109.7	343-7104
TNE Value Class A	G&I	Lg/Bl	10	17.0	20.2	12.9	53	64	40	43	37	5.75	1.34	126	181.2	343-7104
Templeton American	ETR	Md/Val	N.A.	15.8	N.A.	N.A.	24	63	N.A.	N.A.	N.A.	5.0(d)	2.65	176	34.1	237-0738
Thomson Equity-Income B	ETR	Lg/Val	8	21.2	20.3	10.4	31	62	64	19	33	None	2.10	113	105.8	227-7337
Tower Capital Appreciation	G&I	Lg/Bl	8	14.4	14.6	14.2	46	22	46	70	54	4.5	0.85	89	142.1	999-0124
Transamerica Gro. & Inc. A	G&I	Md/Bl	8	9.7	17.2	14.9	35	49	47	74	41	5.75	1.34	127	122.4	343-6840
Transamerica Sp. Blue Chip	G&I	Md/Bl	8	2.3	12.7	12.1	18	30	53	76	38	5.0(d)	2.76	140	42.9	343-6840
Triflex	ETR	Lg/Bl	7	5.7	10.7	9.3	12	48	46	71	40	5.75	1.15	117	21.1	231-4639
USAA Investment Balanced	ETR	Lg/Val	N.A.	13.7	11.0	N.A.	22	53	26	71	N.A.	None	0.93	51	122.2	382-8722
USAA Investment Cornerstone	ETR	Lg/Bl	7	23.7	15.2	11.1	34	57	30	39	66	None	1.22	65	734.4	382-8722
USAA Mutual Income	ITR	N.A.	4	9.9	12.5	12.2	39	23	19	96	45	None	0.42	24	1,965.9	382-8722
USAA Mutual Income Stock	ETR	Lg/Val	7	11.6	15.3	13.9	19	62	52	63	82	None	0.71	41	1,092.7	382-8722
UST Master Income & Growth	G&I	Md/Bl	8	19.4	22.0	12.7	58	73	38	32	36	4.5	1.15	111	80.0	233-1136
United Continental Income	ETR	Md/Bl	7	13.1	16.3	12.8	21	69	49	48	72	5.75	0.77	126	418.5	366-5465
United Income	ETR	Lg/Bl	8	16.1	19.0	15.2	25	74	56	50	83	5.75	0.64	105	2,987.3	366-5465
United Retirement Shares	ETR	Lg/Gro	6	12.7	15.7	14.2	20	76	41	73	70	5.75	0.80	127	416.6	366-5465
United Svcs. All American	G&I	Lg/Bl	10	10.0	13.8	8.8	36	36	39	48	26	None	1.03	98	11.3	873-8637
United Svcs. Income	ITR	Md/Val	7	17.7	13.3	12.9	72	22	5	33	100	None	1.83	114	14.7	873-8637
Value Line Convertible	ITR	N.A.	7	14.8	18.9	12.4	60	41	45	52	31	None	1.10	63	52.1	223-0818
Value Line Income	ITR	Md/Bl	6	8.3	12.3	12.1	32	1	45	74	61	None	0.93	49	171.0	223-0818
Van Kampen Gro. & Inc. A	G&I	Md/Val	9	14.8	17.2	12.0	47	42	43	56	30	4.65	1.71	137	36.8	225-2222
Vanguard Asset Allocation	ETR	Lg/Bl	6	13.5	15.3	13.8	21	61	48	70	71	None	0.49	29	1,078.1	851-4999
Vanguard Balanced Index	ETR	Lg/Bl	N.A.	10.0	N.A.	N.A.	17	N.A.	N.A.	N.A.	N.A.	None	0.20	62	349.0	851-4999
Vanguard Convertible Secs.	ITR	L/Lo	8	13.5	22.0	14.1	54	59	61	35	44	None	0.74	47	201.2	851-4999
Vanguard Equity-Income	ETR	Lg/Val	8	14.7	16.2	11.8	23	66	48	30	80	None	0.40	25	1,102.8	851-4999
Vanguard Index 500	G&I	Lg/Bl	8	9.9	15.4	14.3	36	41	44	67	53	None	0.19	60	8,083.3	851-4999
Vanguard Ind. Tot. Stk. Mkt.	G&I	Lg/Bl	N.A.	10.6	N.A.	N.A.	38	N.A.	N.A.	N.A.	N.A.	None	0.20	64	486.8	851-4999
Vanguard Index Value	G&I	Lg/Val	N.A.	18.2	N.A.	N.A.	56	N.A.	N.A.	N.A.	N.A.	None	0.20	61	179.9	851-4999
Vanguard Preferred Stock	ITR	N.A.	4	13.0	14.0	13.4	52	23	24	91	51	None	0.59	32	391.9	851-4999
Vanguard Quantitative	G&I	Lg/Val	8	13.8	16.6	15.4	45	39	45	69	54	None	0.45	22	513.1	851-4999
Vanguard STAR	G&I	Lg/Val	7	11.0	15.1	11.7	18	69	46	56	56	None	0.00	21	3,570.2	851-4999
Vanguard/Trustees' Eq. US	G&I	Md/Bl	10	17.2	16.5	11.2	53	38	39	55	27	None	0.65	36	95.8	851-4999
Vanguard/Wellesley Income	ITR	Lg/Val	5	14.6	14.8	13.7	59	24	25	81	57	None	0.36	20	5,872.2	851-4999
Vanguard/Wellington	ETR	Lg/Val	7	13.5	14.9	12.4	21	62	44	58	65	None	0.35	19	7,854.8	851-4999
Vanguard/Windsor II	G&I	Lg/Val	8	13.6	17.9	13.5	45	52	42	51	46	None	0.41	23	7,485.5	851-4999
Vanguard/Windsor[1]	G&I	Md/Val	10	19.4	21.4	11.7	58	63	42	38	23	None	0.38	15	10,537.3	851-4999
Vista Growth & Income	G&I	Md/Val	7	13.0	27.4	26.6	43	60	89	76	100	4.75	1.39	121	964.1	348-4782
Vontobel US Value	G&I	Md/Val	N.A.	6.0	18.8	N.A.	27	60	55	N.A.	N.A.	None	1.96	105	35.2	527-9500
WPG Dividend Income	ETR	Md/Val	7	10.8	15.8	9.8	18	57	61	47	29	None	1.54	104	25.6	223-3332
WPG Growth & Income	G&I	Md/Bl	10	9.5	20.6	15.0	35	57	61	50	46	None	1.26	75	64.2	223-3332
WPG Quantitative Equity	G&I	Lg/Val	N.A.	13.9	N.A.	N.A.	45	N.A.	N.A.	N.A.	N.A.	None	1.47	N.A.	44.7	223-3332
Warburg Pincus Gro. & Inc.	G&I	Md/Gro	7	37.1	19.1	16.3	100	45	18	85	34	None	1.14	113	38.8	257-5614
Washington Mutual Investors	G&I	Lg/Val	8	12.8	15.0	13.5	43	45	34	66	49	5.75	0.70	96	12,563.6	421-0180
Westcore Basic Value Inst.	G&I	Md/Val	10	4.9	14.8	9.7	24	47	46	42	35	None	0.96	84	89.8	392-2673
Westcore Equity-Income Inst.	ETR	Lg/Bl	8	11.3	15.3	13.5	19	53	60	58	80	None	0.99	88	35.4	392-2673
Westcore Modern Val. Equity	G&I	Lg/Val	10	12.4	15.6	13.2	42	27	51	75	33	4.5	0.99	86	31.4	392-2673
Winthrop Focus Gro. & Inc.	G&I	Lg/Bl	7	15.7	14.9	12.9	49	37	34	68	41	4.0(d)	1.25	71	51.5	225-8011
Woodward Equity Index Rtl.	G&I	N.A.	N.A.	9.8	N.A.	N.A.	36	N.A.	N.A.	N.A.	N.A.	N.A.	N.A.	N.A.	341.6	688-3350
Working Assets Citizens Bal.	ETR	Md/Val	N.A.	4.3	N.A.	N.A.	10	N.A.	N.A.	N.A.	N.A.	4.0	1.75	N.A.	40.6	223-7010

S P E C I A L T Y

Fund name	Type	Style	Risk level	One year	Three years	Five years	1993	1992	1991	1990	1989	% max. sales charge	Annual charges	Five-year total per $1,000	Net assets (millions)	Telephone (800)
ABT Utility Income	Spec	Lg/Val	7	8.9	12.4	12.3	9	60	29	43	55	4.75	1.17	109	151.4	553-7838
AIM Utilities A	Spec	Md/Val	7	12.3	14.4	14.6	11	58	33	46	58	5.5	1.13	116	200.6	347-1919
API Special Markets	Spec	Lg/Bl	11	5.8	1.7	0.8	8	50	17	40	16	None	3.77	135	1.2	544-6060
Alliance Technology A	Spec	Md/Gro	12	21.6	29.4	17.4	14	64	54	46	13	4.25	1.67	138	178.4	227-4618
America's Utility	Spec	Md/Val	N.A.	13.3	N.A.	N.A.	11	N.A.	N.A.	N.A.	N.A.	None	1.21	67	129.5	487-3863
American Gas Index	Spec	Md/Val	N.A.	16.6	10.3	N.A.	12	61	18	38	N.A.	None	0.84	47	254.3	343-3355
BT Investment Utility	Spec	N.A.	N.A.	11.0	N.A.	N.A.	10	N.A.	N.A.	N.A.	N.A.	None	1.25	69	38.0	545-1074
Benham Gold Equities Index	Spec	Md/Gro	12	81.2	13.7	9.0	35	44	8	28	49	None	0.75	42	548.0	472-3389
Blanchard Precious Metals	Spec	Sm/Gro	12	100.4	16.9	5.6	42	36	15	24	14	None	3.24	197	65.2	922-7771
Bull & Bear Gold Investors	Spec	Sm/Gro	12	87.6	15.4	7.4	37	37	15	25	33	None	3.01	156	49.3	847-4200
Cappiello-Rushmore Util. Inc.	Spec	Lg/Val	N.A.	6.1	N.A.	N.A.	8	N.A.	N.A.	N.A.	N.A.	None	N.A.	58	11.3	343-3355
Century Shares	Spec	Md/Val	10	(0.4)	18.5	16.8	6	74	38	41	66	None	0.84	47	273.8	321-1928
Colonial Natural Resources A	Spec	Md/Bl	N.A.	33.8	N.A.	N.A.	18	N.A.	N.A.	N.A.	N.A.	5.75	2.06	N.A.	31.2	248-2828
Colonial Utilities A	Spec	Md/Val	6	9.3	18.3	13.1	10	68	34	44	31	4.75	1.23	114	523.9	248-2828

Notes: (d): Maximum deferred sales charge [1]Closed to new investors

Fund name	Type	Style	Risk level	% compound annual return to Jan. 1, 1994			Annual performance analysis (percentile ranking by type)					Expense analysis			Net assets (millions)	Telephone (800)
				One year	Three years	Five years	1993	1992	1991	1990	1989	% max. sales charge	Annual charges	Five-year total per 1,000		
Cowen Opportunity	Spec	Sm/Bl	12	31.6	26.3	20.0	17	55	48	57	29	4.85	2.52%	$146	20.2	221-5616
Dean Witter Natural Res.	Spec	Md/Bl	10	17.5	10.1	9.9	12	57	21	40	51	5.0(d)	1.96	126	134.9	869-3863
Dean Witter P.M. & Mining	Spec	Md/Gro	N.A.	55.9	10.3	N.A.	26	43	13	N.A.	N.A.	5.0(d)	2.89	192	45.2	392-2550[5]
Dean Witter Utilities	Spec	Md/Val	6	12.0	13.1	12.5	11	59	29	49	41	5.0(d)	1.46	106	4,081.7	869-3863
Dreyfus Edison Electric	Spec	Md/Val	N.A.	10.5	N.A.	N.A.	10	57	N.A.	N.A.	N.A.	None	0.75	72	117.8	782-6620
Eaton Vance Nat. Resource	Spec	Md/Bl	10	25.6	11.8	9.0	15	55	21	37	39	6.0(d)	4.45	190	6.1	225-6265
Eaton Vance Total Return	Spec	Lg/Val	7	9.6	13.0	14.1	10	57	33	50	54	4.75	1.32	120	674.9	225-6265
Evergreen Real Estate	Spec	Sm/Bl	N.A.	51.4	23.6	N.A.	24	60	25	28	N.A.	None	2.19	133	131.3	235-0064
Fidelity Advisor Glob. Res.	Spec	Sm/Bl	10	37.9	21.4	17.7	20	62	26	44	53	4.75	3.27	181	40.0	522-7297
Fidelity Real Estate Inv.	Spec	Sm/Bl	8	12.5	23.2	14.2	11	68	43	40	25	None	1.17	68	460.6	544-8888
Fidelity Select Air Transport.	Spec	Md/Bl	12	30.9	24.1	14.6	17	57	42	29	43	3.0	2.12	166	12.8	544-8888
Fidelity Select Amer. Gold	Spec	Md/Gro	12	78.7	17.6	10.4	34	49	12	30	37	3.0	1.50	121	330.4	544-8888
Fidelity Select Automotive	Spec	Md/Bl	9	35.4	38.1	16.8	19	86	42	42	10	3.0	1.66	120	99.9	544-8888
Fidelity Select Biotech.	Spec	Md/Gro	12	0.7	21.7	30.2	7	42	85	100	69	3.0	1.61	117	669.9	544-8888
Fidelity Select Brdcst./Med.	Spec	Lg/Gro	11	38.0	32.2	17.7	20	69	42	20	52	3.0	1.58	166	190.9	544-8888
Fidelity Select Broker./Inv.	Spec	Md/Val	12	49.3	42.0	22.3	24	56	73	31	25	3.0	1.64	152	94.1	544-8888
Fidelity Select Chemicals	Spec	Md/Gro	10	12.7	19.4	13.9	11	59	43	45	30	3.0	1.91	137	23.0	544-8888
Fidelity Select Computers	Spec	Sm/Bl	12	28.9	27.1	21.0	16	70	38	70	15	3.0	1.97	133	25.4	544-8888
Fidelity Select Con./Housing	Spec	Md/Bl	11	33.6	30.9	18.8	18	67	45	39	29	3.0	1.71	143	42.6	544-8888
Fidelity Select Cnsmr. Prod.	Spec	Md/Gro	N.A.	24.6	23.3	N.A.	15	58	43	N.A.	N.A.	3.0	2.50	165	9.3	544-8888
Fidelity Select Def./Aerosp.	Spec	Md/Val	11	28.8	17.8	11.2	16	51	35	44	17	3.0	2.53	166	3.8	544-8888
Fidelity Select Devel. Com.	Spec	Sm/Gro	N.A.	31.7	35.6	N.A.	18	66	59	N.A.	N.A.	3.0	1.54	136	270.3	544-8888
Fidelity Select Elec. Util.	Spec	Md/Val	7	12.8	16.1	14.5	11	59	34	48	46	3.0	1.54	127	25.8	544-8888
Fidelity Select Electronics	Spec	Lg/Gro	12	32.2	31.6	22.8	18	74	41	56	28	3.0	1.51	127	48.9	544-8888
Fidelity Select Energy	Spec	Lg/Val	11	19.1	5.2	9.7	13	49	16	45	68	3.0	1.56	128	85.4	544-8888
Fidelity Select Energy Svc.	Spec	Sm/Bl	12	21.0	(1.4)	9.2	14	54	0	52	92	3.0	1.46	130	65.7	544-8888
Fidelity Select Environ.	Spec	Md/Bl	N.A.	(0.6)	1.8	N.A.	6	50	22	47	N.A.	3.0	1.93	142	52.9	544-8888
Fidelity Select Fin. Svc.	Spec	Md/Val	12	17.6	39.5	19.6	12	87	59	22	33	3.0	1.48	119	149.5	544-8888
Fidelity Select Food/Agri.	Spec	Md/Bl	8	8.8	15.7	18.6	9	56	40	60	62	3.0	1.56	126	97.3	544-8888
Fidelity Select Health Care	Spec	Md/Gro	11	2.4	15.8	22.4	7	36	74	77	67	3.0	1.57	115	573.9	544-8888
Fidelity Select Home Fin.	Spec	Sm/Val	12	27.3	49.0	25.1	16	100	61	33	18	3.0	1.47	119	303.4	544-8888
Fidelity Select Indust. Equip.	Spec	Sm/Gro	11	43.3	26.5	15.1	22	61	35	32	31	3.0	1.89	166	70.0	544-8888
Fidelity Select Indus. Matl.	Spec	Md/Gro	11	21.4	22.8	9.9	14	62	41	30	11	3.0	2.14	143	18.0	544-8888
Fidelity Select Insurance	Spec	Md/Val	10	8.2	21.9	11.6	9	70	42	39	60	3.0	1.87	166	19.0	544-8888
Fidelity Select Leisure	Spec	Md/Gro	10	39.6	29.2	17.1	20	65	39	24	50	3.0	1.62	137	156.8	544-8888
Fidelity Select Medic. Del.	Spec	Md/Gro	12	5.5	17.7	24.5	8	40	70	68	90	3.0	1.93	131	128.9	544-8888
Fidelity Select Paper & For.	Spec	Md/Bl	12	18.6	21.4	9.6	13	61	40	33	10	3.0	2.23	152	11.3	544-8888
Fidelity Select Precious Metals	Spec	Sm/Gro	12	111.6	18.9	11.9	46	33	17	26	52	3.0	1.54	129	392.5	544-8888
Fidelity Select Reg. Banks	Spec	Md/Val	12	11.0	39.8	22.4	10	92	62	26	44	3.0	1.47	116	141.5	544-8888
Fidelity Select Retailing	Spec	Sm/Bl	11	13.0	32.4	23.3	11	70	63	44	48	3.0	1.77	131	52.0	544-8888
Fidelity Select Soft./Comp.	Spec	Md/Gro	12	32.5	37.8	24.2	18	81	48	51	22	3.0	1.49	124	168.1	544-8888
Fidelity Select Technology	Spec	Md/Gro	12	28.6	30.5	23.5	16	59	57	62	29	3.0	1.48	124	143.3	544-8888
Fidelity Select Tele.	Spec	Lg/Gro	10	29.6	25.1	19.8	17	64	38	31	80	3.0	1.48	129	494.2	544-8888
Fidelity Select Transport.	Spec	Sm/Bl	10	29.3	35.2	20.0	17	72	54	25	46	3.0	2.19	166	7.1	544-8888
Fidelity Select Utilities	Spec	Md/Val	6	12.4	14.6	16.0	11	60	31	50	62	3.0	1.31	113	316.6	544-8888
Fidelity Utilities Income	Spec	Md/Val	6	15.6	15.8	14.8	12	60	31	52	43	None	0.87	53	1,640.8	544-8888
Flag Inv. Telephone Inc. A	Spec	Lg/Val	8	18.2	17.9	17.7	13	62	32	41	76	4.5	0.92	95	470.0	767-3524
Flagship Utility Income A	Spec	Md/Val	6	11.0	10.2	6.8	10	59	24	48	12	4.2	1.03	105	34.1	227-4648
Fortress Utility	Spec	Md/Val	6	15.2	16.5	15.0	12	59	34	51	43	1.0	1.07	70	1,012.6	245-5051
Franklin DynaTech	Spec	Lg/Gro	8	7.5	14.9	15.2	9	55	41	53	48	4.0	0.81	83	71.1	342-5236
Franklin Global Health Care	Spec	Sm/Gro	N.A.	6.2	N.A.	N.A.	8	N.A.	N.A.	N.A.	N.A.	4.5	0.00[2]	N.A.	4.6	342-5236
Franklin Global Utilities	Spec	Lg/Val	N.A.	31.5	N.A.	N.A.	17	N.A.	N.A.	N.A.	N.A.	4.5	0.00[2]	N.A.	60.3	342-5236
Franklin Gold	Spec	Md/Gro	12	73.8	13.6	10.9	32	34	20	28	66	4.0	0.62	81	358.2	342-5236
Franklin Utilities	Spec	Lg/Val	7	11.5	14.7	13.8	10	59	33	50	43	4.0	0.55	71	3,664.4	342-5236
G.T. Global Health Care A	Spec	Md/Gro	N.A.	2.6	11.9	N.A.	7	40	56	65	N.A.	4.75	2.09	150	449.8	824-1580
G.T. Global Tele. A	Spec	Lg/Gro	N.A.	47.7	N.A.	N.A.	23	N.A.	N.A.	N.A.	N.A.	4.75	2.22	162	1,219.5	824-1580
Global Utility A	Spec	Lg/Val	N.A.	22.9	18.0	N.A.	14	59	32	60	N.A.	5.25	1.13	127	146.2	225-1852
Hancock Freedom Environ. A	Spec	Md/Bl	N.A.	(0.3)	0.8	N.A.	6	47	22	38	N.A.	5.0	2.12	155	16.9	225-5291
Hancock Freedom Global Rx	Spec	Sm/Gro	N.A.	1.2	N.A.	N.A.	7	67	N.A.	N.A.	N.A.	5.0	2.23	N.A.	17.7	225-5291
Hancock Freedom Global Tech.	Spec	Md/Gro	12	32.1	22.9	12.0	18	56	39	29	29	5.0	2.10	129	40.9	225-5291
Hancock Freedom Gold/Gov. B	Spec	N.A.	6	15.9	10.2	9.6	25	47	21	69	52	4.0(d)	1.63	138	51.9	225-5291
Hancock Freedom Natl. Avia.	Spec	Md/Bl	12	20.9	17.8	13.0	14	54	38	28	63	5.0	1.49	129	82.2	225-5291
Hancock Freedom Reg. Bank B	Spec	Sm/Val	9	20.5	42.8	22.1	14	91	60	26	30	4.0(d)	1.96	126	171.8	225-5291
IDS Precious Metals	Spec	Md/Gro	12	80.9	16.7	7.4	35	44	14	23	31	5.0	1.58	142	67.9	328-8300
IDS Utilities Income	Spec	Md/Val	6	18.8	16.9	15.1	13	60	31	48	47	5.0	0.86	99	798.2	328-8300
Invesco Strat. Energy	Spec	Md/Bl	12	16.7	(0.8)	3.2	12	40	14	31	69	None	1.73	95	50.3	525-8085
Invesco Strat. Environ. Svcs.	Spec	Sm/Bl	N.A.	(4.7)	(3.3)	N.A.	5	35	28	N.A.	N.A.	None	1.85	101	40.6	525-8085
Invesco Strat. Fin. Svc.	Spec	Md/Val	10	18.5	37.8	27.1	13	74	67	42	59	None	1.07	59	384.1	525-8085
Invesco Strat. Gold	Spec	Sm/Gro	12	72.6	13.7	6.6	32	44	11	24	36	None	1.41	78	292.9	525-8085
Invesco Strat. Health Sci.	Spec	Sm/Gro	12	(8.4)	14.4	24.7	3	39	80	79	92	None	1.00	55	560.3	525-8085
Invesco Strat. Leisure	Spec	Sm/Gro	11	35.7	36.8	25.8	19	71	53	37	61	None	1.51	83	351.7	525-8085
Invesco Strat. Technology	Spec	Sm/Gro	12	15.0	34.2	26.1	12	67	69	59	36	None	1.12	62	248.8	525-8085
Invesco Strat. Utilities	Spec	Md/Val	7	21.2	19.8	15.2	14	60	36	38	51	None	1.13	63	181.7	525-8085
Kemper Environmental Svc.	Spec	Md/Bl	N.A.	(3.5)	3.1	N.A.	5	44	33	N.A.	N.A.	5.75	1.62	139	41.6	621-1048
Kemper Technology	Spec	Md/Gro	11	11.7	16.8	14.8	10	50	47	50	41	5.75	0.82	100	626.1	621-1048
Keystone Precious Metals	Spec	Sm/Gro	12	101.9	23.6	11.6	42	40	22	20	41	4.0(d)	2.49	143	188.9	343-2898
Lexington Goldfund	Spec	Md/Gro	12	87.0	11.7	6.5	37	34	12	26	40	None	1.76	96	136.3	526-0056
Lexington Strategic Invest.	Spec	Sm/Bl	12	264.9	5.1	1.5	100	0	3	2	95	5.75	2.78	207	65.9	526-0056
Lexington Strategic Silver	Spec	Sm/Gro	12	76.5	10.1	1.0	33	41	6	13	28	5.75	2.78	207	25.8	526-0056
Liberty Financial Utilities	Spec	Lg/Val	N.A.	15.0	N.A.	N.A.	12	60	N.A.	N.A.	N.A.	4.5	1.20	111	304.5	872-5426

Notes: (d): Maximum deferred sales charge [2]Manager absorbing costs [5]Area code 212

Fund name	Type	Style	Risk level	% compound annual return to Jan. 1, 1994			Annual performance analysis (percentile ranking by type)					Expense analysis			Net assets (millions)	Telephone (800)
				One year	Three years	Five years	1993	1992	1991	1990	1989	% max. sales charge	Annual charges	Five-year total per $1,000[2]		
Liberty Utility	Spec	Md/Val	6	15.1	16.5	14.8	12	59	34	52	39	4.5	1.11%	$102	$959.9	245-5051
MFS Gold & Natural Resource B	Spec	Md/Gro	12	48.7	13.4	5.2	24	52	14	23	27	5.0(d)	2.97	153	24.6	225-2606
MFS Utilities A	Spec	Md/Val	N.A.	20.6	N.A.	N.A.	14	N.A.	N.A.	N.A.	N.A.	4.75	0.65	N.A.	43.4	225-2606
MainStay Nat. Resources/Gold	Spec	Md/Gro	12	42.6	10.9	4.6	21	45	19	23	34	5.0(d)	2.40	170	16.7	522-4202
Medical Research Investment	Spec	Md/Bl	10	26.4	22.5	23.0	16	53	45	56	72	4.75	2.50	173	10.9	262-6631
Merrill Lynch Global Util. B	Spec	Md/Val	N.A.	23.2	15.0	N.A.	14	58	26	N.A.	N.A.	4.0(d)	1.61	96	600.1	637-3863
Merrill Lynch Healthcare A	Spec	Md/Gro	12	(2.6)	13.6	8.9	5	54	48	43	21	6.5	1.85	144	69.7	637-3863
Merrill Lynch Natural Res. B	Spec	Md/Bl	10	17.8	4.8	7.4	13	45	20	48	43	4.0(d)	1.99	108	198.3	637-3863
Merrill Lynch Technology A	Spec	N.A.	N.A.	22.4	N.A.	N.A.	14	N.A.	N.A.	N.A.	N.A.	6.5	1.42	N.A.	139.2	637-3863
MetLife-State St. Glob. En. A	Spec	Sm/Bl	N.A.	32.1	5.0	N.A.	18	57	4	N.A.	N.A.	4.5	1.75	136	35.4	882-0052
Midwest Leshner Fin. Util. A	Spec	Lg/Val	N.A.	8.0	12.6	N.A.	9	58	32	53	N.A.	4.0	1.40	132	47.3	543-8721
Monitrend Gold	Spec	N.A.	12	20.7	(7.4)	(4.7)	14	27	11	34	26	3.5	2.45	161	2.9	251-1970
Oppenheimer Global Bio-Tech	Spec	Sm/Gro	12	(0.7)	19.2	18.7	6	32	100	64	39	5.75	1.72	129	221.4	525-7048
Oppenheimer Global Environ.	Spec	Sm/Bl	12	11.5	0.7	N.A.	10	41	19	N.A.	N.A.	5.75	1.68	144	43.1	525-7048
Oppenheimer Gold/Spec. Min.	Spec	Md/Gro	12	61.8	13.4	7.5	28	43	16	19	56	5.75	1.38	129	166.0	525-7048
PRA Real Estate Securities	Spec	Sm/Bl	N.A.	19.9	20.4	N.A.	13	66	32	25	N.A.	None	1.23	74	141.7	435-1405
PaineWebber Global Energy B	Spec	Md/Val	10	14.8	6.3	8.5	11	48	23	45	49	5.0(d)	2.78	180	24.1	647-1568
PaineWebber Regional Fin. A	Spec	Sm/Val	10	10.3	36.3	22.0	10	84	62	36	36	4.5	2.05	134	56.2	647-1568
Pilgrim Corporate Utilities	Spec	Md/Val	N.A.	(17.7)	(3.9)	(5.3)	0	52	21	36	0	3.0	1.65	100	9.9	334-3444
Pioneer Gold Shares	Spec	Sm/Gro	N.A.	70.8	14.1	N.A.	31	44	12	N.A.	N.A.	5.75	1.75	147	14.1	225-6292
Princor Utilities	Spec	Md/Val	N.A.	8.4	N.A.	N.A.	9	N.A.	N.A.	N.A.	N.A.	5.0	1.00	N.A.	50.4	451-5447
Prudential Glob. Nat. Res. B	Spec	Md/Gro	11	29.6	10.8	7.3	17	54	18	33	38	5.0(d)	3.18	186	44.7	225-1852
Prudential Utility B	Spec	Md/Val	7	15.3	14.4	13.9	12	59	29	42	59	5.0(d)	1.57	98	4,989.0	225-1852
Putnam Energy–Resources	Spec	Md/Bl	11	13.5	9.1	10.7	11	57	21	44	56	5.75	1.18	139	128.3	225-1581
Putnam Health Sciences A	Spec	Lg/Gro	11	0.0	10.0	16.9	6	42	50	67	66	5.75	1.13	120	771.3	225-1581
Putnam Util. G&I A	Spec	Lg/Val	N.A.	14.0	11.8	N.A.	11	57	26	N.A.	N.A.	5.75	1.32	126	678.6	225-1581
Rushmore Prec. Metals Index+	Spec	Md/Gro	N.A.	51.4	3.1	N.A.	24	42	3	20	N.A.	None	1.00	57	10.0	343-3355
Scudder Gold	Spec	Sm/Gro	12	59.4	10.5	4.5	27	44	11	31	20	None	2.17	135	98.9	225-2470
Seligman Commun./Info A	Spec	Md/Gro	12	35.7	35.1	23.3	19	66	54	37	49	4.75	1.67	138	82.5	221-2783
Smith Bar. Shear. P.M.& Min. A	Spec	Md/Gro	12	65.4	14.9	7.1	29	47	14	27	27	5.0	2.50	153	20.1	451-2010
Smith Barney Sh. Tele. Gr A	Spec	Md/Gro	11	35.3	25.1	18.5	19	68	31	34	61	5.0	1.49	125	76.0	573-9410[21]
Smith Bar. Shear. Tel. Inc.[1]	Spec	Lg/Bl	10	15.8	9.9	14.9	12	60	18	48	84	5.0	0.95	51	74.4	573-9410[21]
Smith Barney Shear. Util. B	Spec	Lg/Val	6	11.5	13.3	12.6	10	57	31	53	35	5.0(d)	1.56	96	2,825.0	451-2010
Smith Barney Utility A	Spec	Md/Val	N.A.	11.4	11.6	N.A.	10	57	28	N.A.	N.A.	4.5	0.98	101	128.6	544-7835
Steadman Ocean. Tech./Gro.[1]	Spec	Sm/Val	12	(7.8)	3.8	(4.0)	4	47	36	0	49	None	6.34	N.A.	1.5	424-8570
T. Rowe Price New Era	Spec	Lg/Gro	9	15.3	10.5	8.9	12	53	26	40	40	None	0.82	45	741.6	638-5660
T. Rowe Price Science/Tech.	Spec	Md/Gro	12	24.2	33.2	26.8	15	67	58	48	64	None	1.25	69	467.8	638-5660
Templeton Real Estate Sec.	Spec	Sm/Val	N.A.	33.0	23.0	N.A.	18	55	40	35	N.A.	5.75	1.68	155	70.2	237-0738
Thomson P.M./Nat. Res. B	Spec	Md/Gro	12	89.5	16.3	6.5	38	41	13	21	28	5.0(d)	2.60	138	28.6	227-7337
Transamerica Sp. Nat. Res.	Spec	Sm/Bl	9	23.9	15.1	11.6	15	58	26	34	51	5.0(d)	3.64	202	19.5	343-6840
USAA Investment Gold	Spec	Md/Gro	12	58.3	11.7	3.9	27	45	13	20	31	None	1.57	78	170.8	382-8722
United Gold & Gov.	Spec	Sm/Gro	12	75.8	15.7	7.5	N.A.	N.A.	N.A.	N.A.	N.A.	5.75	1.81	180	42.6	366-5465
United Science & Technology	Spec	Md/Gro	11	8.5	18.4	15.3	9	48	57	46	45	5.75	0.89	130	439.5	366-5465
United Services World Gold	Spec	Sm/Gro	12	89.8	20.5	8.0	38	47	14	18	29	None	2.00	152	152.2	873-8637
United Svcs. Gold Shares	Spec	Sm/Gro	12	123.9	(2.4)	0.1	50	8	5	11	100	None	1.88	101	283.9	873-8637
United Svcs. Real Estate	Spec	Sm/Gro	11	0.2	17.7	7.0	6	55	55	27	15	None	1.40	98	22.3	873-8637
Van Eck Gold/Resources	Spec	Md/Gro	12	80.6	17.7	7.4	35	46	13	20	32	5.75	1.46	138	194.1	221-2220
Van Eck Intl. Investors	Spec	Md/Gro	12	113.4	15.8	11.4	46	27	18	19	80	5.75	1.26	119	615.8	221-2220
Vanguard Sp. Energy	Spec	Md/Bl	10	26.4	10.4	13.8	16	56	16	48	69	None	0.21	30	262.9	851-4999
Vanguard Sp. Gold & Prec.	Spec	Md/Gro	12	93.4	17.6	11.2	39	35	19	27	49	None	0.36	32	477.0	851-4999
Vanguard Sp. Health Care	Spec	Md/Bl	9	11.8	17.2	20.1	10	50	48	69	53	None	0.22	30	580.1	851-4999
Vanguard Sp. Service Econ.	Spec	Md/Bl	11	12.0	18.5	13.1	44	36	34	22	59	None	0.56	39	34.9	851-4999
Vanguard Sp. Technology	Spec	Sm/Gro	12	11.3	23.0	14.8	10	63	49	42	26	None	0.25	33	68.2	851-4999
Vanguard Sp. Utilities Inc	Spec	Lg/Val	N.A.	15.1	N.A.	N.A.	12	N.A.	N.A.	N.A.	N.A.	None	0.45	22	831.4	851-4999

I N T E R N A T I O N A L

Fund name	Type	Style	Risk level	One year	Three years	Five years	1993	1992	1991	1990	1989	% max. sales charge	Annual charges	Five-year total per $1,000[2]	Net assets (millions)	Telephone (800)
20th Century Intl. Equity	Intl	Md/Bl	N.A.	42.6	N.A.	N.A.	45	74	N.A.	N.A.	N.A.	None	1.90	55	601.0	345-2021
59 Wall St. European Eq.	Reg	N.A.	N.A.	27.1	14.3	N.A.	26	74	41	N.A.	N.A.	None	1.50	97	88.7	493-8100[5]
59 Wall St. Pac. Basin Eq.	Reg	N.A.	N.A.	74.9	28.3	N.A.	78	71	52	N.A.	N.A.	None	1.50	97	92.6	493-8100[5]
AIM International Equity	Intl	Md/Gro	N.A.	45.8	N.A.	N.A.	49	56	N.A.	N.A.	N.A.	5.5	1.80	N.A.	370.7	347-1919
Acorn International	Intl	Sm/Bl	N.A.	49.1	N.A.	N.A.	54	N.A.	N.A.	N.A.	N.A.	None	1.40	N.A.	645.8	922-6769
Aetna International Growth	Intl	Lg/Bl	N.A.	30.4	N.A.	N.A.	28	13	N.A.	N.A.	N.A.	None	0.50	87	35.0	367-7732
Alliance Global Canadian	Intl	Md/Bl	11	17.4	2.3	0.9	9	19	0	16	47	5.5	2.69	190	13.8	227-4618
Alliance Global Sm. Cap A	Intl	Sm/Gro	12	20.0	12.7	6.0	13	36	64	0	55	4.25	2.37	173	67.0	227-4618
Alliance International A	Intl	Lg/Val	12	27.5	9.0	5.8	24	33	19	12	68	4.25	1.88	152	183.7	227-4618
Alliance New Europe A	Reg	Lg/Val	N.A.	34.6	11.4	N.A.	34	59	28	N.A.	N.A.	4.25	2.33	169	89.4	227-4618
American Cap. Glob. Eq. A	Intl	Md/Bl	N.A.	20.5	N.A.	N.A.	14	51	N.A.	N.A.	N.A.	5.75	2.93	162	21.1	421-5666
BB&K International Equity	Intl	Md/Bl	12	37.8	7.5	2.8	38	11	3	18	26	None	1.05	85	199.2	571-5800[19]
Babson-Stewart Ivory Intl.	Intl	Md/Gro	11	33.5	14.7	11.7	32	49	37	49	61	None	1.57	86	38.9	422-2766
Bartlett Capital Val. Intl.	Intl	Lg/Val	11	31.3	16.1	N.A.	29	48	54	33	N.A.	None	1.93	108	40.7	800-4612
Bernstein Intl. Value	Intl	Lg/Val	N.A.	34.6	N.A.	N.A.	34	N.A.	N.A.	N.A.	N.A.	None	2.00	N.A.	612.4	756-4097[5]
Blanchard Global Growth	Intl	Md/Bl	7	24.5	12.2	9.2	35	46	34	47	51	None	2.40	147	89.9	922-7771
Boston Co. Intl. Retail	Intl	Lg/Bl	12	24.6	6.0	2.3	19	15	16	20	30	None	1.79	98	4.0	225-5267
Bull & Bear US & Overseas	Intl	Md/Bl	10	26.7	14.8	9.8	22	45	57	52	30	None	3.57	184	11.4	847-4200
Calvert World Val. Glob. Eq.	Intl	Md/Bl	N.A.	22.5	N.A.	N.A.	16	N.A.	N.A.	N.A.	N.A.	4.75	1.50	150	63.0	368-2748
Capstone European	Reg	Lg/Val	11	18.8	8.8	9.5	17	54	49	100	33	4.75	1.97	129	10.5	262-6631
Centerland Kleinwort Intl. B	Intl	Md/Bl	11	28.5	11.5	7.8	25	42	29	32	50	4.5	2.31	N.A.	50.0	237-4218
Colonial Global Equity B	Intl	Md/Val	N.A.	34.3	N.A.	N.A.	33	N.A.	N.A.	N.A.	N.A.	5.0(d)	2.00	N.A.	40.8	248-2828
Colonial Intl. Equity Index	Intl	Lg/Gro	12	30.6	7.6	2.6	28	10	19	19	22	5.75	1.79	149	10.7	248-2828

Notes: (d): Maximum deferred sales charge
[1]Closed to new investors [5]Area code 212 [19]Area code 415 [21]Area code 617

Fund name	Type	Style	Risk level	% compound annual return to Jan. 1, 1994			Annual performance analysis (percentile ranking by type)					Expense analysis			Net assets (millions)	Telephone (800)
				One year	Three year	Five year	1993	1992	1991	1990	1989	% max. sales charge	Annual charges	Five-year total per 1,000		
Columbia International Stock	Intl	Lg/Gro	N.A.	33.4	N.A.	N.A.	32	N.A.	N.A.	N.A.	N.A.	None	1.88%	N.A.	$56.8	547-1707
Compass Cap. Intl. Equity	Intl	N.A.	N.A.	37.3	N.A.	N.A.	37	42	N.A.	N.A.	N.A.	3.75	1.63	$119	22.8	451-8371
CoreFund Intl. Growth B	Intl	N.A.	N.A.	36.9	N.A.	N.A.	37	N.A.	N.A.	N.A.	N.A.	4.5	N.A.	119	0.8	355-2673
Dean Witter European Growth	Reg	Md/Bl	N.A.	38.3	13.3	N.A.	38	59	34	N.A.	N.A.	5.0(d)	2.41	148	459.6	869-3863
Dean Witter Pacific Growth	Reg	Md/Gro	N.A.	94.7	34.8	N.A.	100	68	67	N.A.	N.A.	5.0(d)	2.56	166	689.3	392-2550[5]
Dean Witter World Inv.	Intl	Md/Gro	10	40.8	15.8	10.2	42	26	48	47	33	5.0(d)	2.40	148	301.4	869-3863
Delaware Intl. Equity	Intl	Lg/Val	N.A.	28.2	N.A.	N.A.	24	50	N.A.	N.A.	N.A.	5.75	1.25	122	33.4	523-4640
Dreyfus Glob. Inv A (Prem.)	Intl	Lg/Bl	N.A.	23.9	N.A.	N.A.	18	N.A.	N.A.	N.A.	N.A.	4.5	N.A.	164	74.9	242-8671
Dreyfus Strat. World Inv.	Intl	Md/Gro	6	21.7	11.6	12.2	15	45	44	97	45	3.0	1.61	115	150.5	782-6620
Enterprise Intl. Growth	Intl	Lg/Bl	11	36.1	14.3	8.7	36	52	26	36	35	4.75	2.00	150	19.8	432-4320
Equifund Dutch Natl. Fid. Eq.	Reg	N.A.	N.A.	19.5	6.5	N.A.	17	46	43	N.A.	N.A.	None	2.00	108	6.9	888-9471
Equifund Hong Kong Natl. Fid.	Reg	N.A.	N.A.	84.3	42.2	N.A.	89	89	100	N.A.	N.A.	None	2.00	108	10.0	888-9471
Equifund Ital. Natl. Fid. Eq.	Reg	N.A.	N.A.	11.5	(12.2)	N.A.	9	0	0	N.A.	N.A.	None	2.00	108	0.7	888-9471
Equifund Span. Natl. Fid. Eq.	Reg	N.A.	N.A.	21.6	(4.4)	N.A.	20	1	37	N.A.	N.A.	None	2.00	108	0.8	888-9471
Equifund UK Natl. Fid Eq.	Reg	N.A.	N.A.	3.7	0.7	N.A.	0	47	35	N.A.	N.A.	None	2.00	108	0.2	888-9471
EuroPacific Growth	Intl	Lg/Bl	8	35.6	18.1	15.3	35	64	46	79	54	5.75	1.10	122	5,156.0	421-0180
FT International Equity A	Intl	Md/Bl	12	31.3	9.9	6.8	29	32	18	42	38	4.5	1.58	126	199.3	245-5051
Fidelity Advisor Overseas	Intl	Lg/Bl	N.A.	41.8	13.0	N.A.	44	37	16	N.A.	N.A.	4.75	2.82	181	219.9	522-7297
Fidelity Canada	Reg	Md/Bl	9	25.5	12.8	11.5	24	55	61	75	46	3.0	2.00	135	95.1	544-8888
Fidelity Diver. Intl.	Intl	Md/Val	N.A.	36.7	N.A.	N.A.	36	2	N.A.	N.A.	N.A.	None	1.62	N.A.	255.8	544-8888
Fidelity Emer. Markets	Intl	N.A.	N.A.	81.8	27.1	N.A.	100	78	16	N.A.	N.A.	None	2.39	164	746.3	544-8888
Fidelity Europe	Reg	Lg/Bl	11	27.2	8.9	10.3	26	56	30	78	54	3.0	1.18	97	527.9	544-8888
Fidelity Intl. Gro./Inc.	Intl	Lg/Bl	10	35.1	12.2	10.2	34	42	19	69	40	2.0	1.43	106	1,001.4	544-8888
Fidelity Japan	Reg	Lg/Val	N.A.	20.5	N.A.	N.A.	18	N.A.	N.A.	N.A.	N.A.	3.0	1.73	74	119.8	544-8888
Fidelity Overseas	Intl	Lg/Val	12	40.1	10.4	8.4	41	11	21	58	34	3.0	1.43	110	1,488.0	544-8888
Fidelity Pacific Basin	Reg	Lg/Bl	12	63.9	19.9	6.9	66	48	49	5	21	3.0	1.67	127	489.6	544-8888
Fidelity Worldwide	Intl	Md/Val	N.A.	36.5	16.1	N.A.	36	80	19	N.A.	N.A.	3.0	1.40	110	288.3	544-8888
First Investors Global	Intl	Lg/Bl	11	23.0	11.0	10.6	17	37	42	40	91	6.25	1.83	161	199.8	423-4026
Flag Inv. International	Intl	Md/Val	12	50.6	12.1	7.0	56	15	9	16	54	4.5	1.50	126	15.0	767-3524
Fontaine Global Growth	Intl	Md/Bl	N.A.	10.8	N.A.	N.A.	0	N.A.	N.A.	N.A.	N.A.	None	1.50	82	0.9	247-1550
Fortis Global Growth	Intl	Md/Gro	N.A.	19.5	N.A.	N.A.	12	80	N.A.	N.A.	N.A.	4.75	2.25	162	28.2	800-2638
Founders Worldwide Growth	Intl	Md/Gro	N.A.	29.9	21.1	N.A.	27	61	88	100	N.A.	None	2.01	104	64.5	525-2440
Franklin Intl. Equity	Intl	Lg/Val	N.A.	33.0	N.A.	N.A.	31	59	N.A.	N.A.	N.A.	4.5	0.50	172	19.2	342-5236
Franklin Pacific Growth	Reg	Md/Val	N.A.	60.9	N.A.	N.A.	63	67	N.A.	N.A.	N.A.	4.5	0.50	172	22.5	342-5236
Fremont Global	Intl	Lg/Bl	6	19.6	14.3	11.2	29	54	34	62	47	None	1.01	62	185.2	548-4539
G.T. Europe Growth A	Reg	Lg/Bl	12	28.3	5.9	7.4	27	40	30	45	68	4.75	2.00	153	841.9	824-1580
G.T. Global Emerg. Mkt. A	Intl	N.A.	N.A.	64.5	N.A.	N.A.	76	N.A.	N.A.	N.A.	N.A.	4.75	2.40	169	184.4	824-1580
G.T. Global Gro. & Inc. A	Intl	Lg/Val	N.A.	27.4	15.9	N.A.	23	65	48	N.A.	N.A.	4.75	1.85	142	251.1	824-1580
G.T. Intl. Growth A	Intl	Lg/Bl	10	34.2	12.7	11.2	33	33	33	34	92	4.75	1.90	147	495.1	824-1580
G.T. Japan Growth A	Reg	Md/Gro	12	33.4	0.6	3.1	33	22	13	0	100	4.75	2.20	162	103.2	824-1580
G.T. Latin America Growth A	Reg	N.A.	N.A.	52.9	N.A.	N.A.	54	56	N.A.	N.A.	N.A.	4.75	2.40	169	129.5	824-1580
G.T. Pacific Growth A	Reg	Lg/Gro	10	60.6	18.7	17.1	63	46	50	57	80	4.75	2.00	152	403.6	824-1580
G.T. Worldwide Growth A	Intl	Md/Gro	9	27.6	16.6	13.8	24	68	51	39	90	4.75	2.10	155	183.4	824-1580
Govett Emerging Markets	Intl	Md/Bl	N.A.	79.7	N.A.	N.A.	97	N.A.	N.A.	N.A.	N.A.	4.95	2.50	176	53.4	634-6838
Govett International Equity	Intl	Md/Bl	N.A.	54.5	N.A.	N.A.	62	N.A.	N.A.	N.A.	N.A.	4.95	2.50	176	41.0	634-6838
Hancock Freedom Global B	Intl	Lg/Gro	11	33.9	18.0	11.9	32	54	58	17	77	4.0(d)	2.74	163	19.3	225-5291
Hancock Freedom Pac. Basin	Reg	Lg/Bl	12	70.5	25.1	12.3	73	64	49	18	33	5.0	2.94	187	22.1	225-5291
Harbor International[1]	Intl	Lg/Val	10	45.4	20.8	16.8	49	55	54	48	88	None	1.26	71	2,275.6	422-1050
IAI International	Intl	Md/Val	11	40.2	14.5	9.1	41	26	39	37	39	None	1.91	109	104.3	945-3863
IDEX II Global	Intl	Md/Gro	N.A.	30.9	N.A.	N.A.	28	47	N.A.	N.A.	N.A.	5.5	2.50	173	29.3	624-4339
IDS Global Growth	Intl	Md/Bl	N.A.	39.1	15.7	N.A.	40	47	34	N.A.	N.A.	5.0	1.58	139	244.0	328-8300
IDS International	Intl	Lg/Val	11	32.3	11.7	9.1	30	33	29	59	37	5.0	1.54	125	439.5	328-8300
IDS Strat. Worldwide Gro.	Intl	Lg/Val	12	31.1	10.2	5.4	29	29	23	36	22	5.0(d)	2.75	176	131.2	328-8300
Invesco European	Reg	Lg/Val	11	24.6	7.5	9.2	24	47	39	95	42	None	1.29	71	108.7	525-8085
Invesco Intl. Growth	Intl	Lg/Bl	12	27.9	6.2	3.5	24	6	17	33	32	None	1.36	75	299.2	525-8085
Invesco Pacific Basin	Reg	Md/Bl	12	39.7	11.0	4.4	40	36	51	14	35	None	1.78	97	144.2	456-5111
Ivy International A	Intl	Lg/Val	11	48.2	20.2	14.1	53	56	42	38	64	5.75	1.71	145	750.2	525-3713
Janus Worldwide	Intl	Md/Gro	N.A.	28.4	N.A.	N.A.	25	91	N.A.	N.A.	N.A.	None	1.51	94	567.5	535-2726
Japan	Reg	Md/Gro	12	23.6	2.0	(0.2)	22	30	27	40	21	None	1.29	78	259.7	621-1048
Kemper International	Intl	Md/Bl	11	35.7	12.1	9.1	35	37	22	55	38	5.75	1.36	128	2.4	633-5368
Kent Intl. Equity Inv.	Intl	N.A.	N.A.	29.7	N.A.	N.A.	27	N.A.	N.A.	N.A.	N.A.	4.0	N.A.	N.A.	38.6	343-2898
Keystone Amer. Glob. Opp. A	Intl	Sm/Gro	11	37.7	26.4	15.0	38	100	80	56	8	5.75	2.61	196	121.0	343-2898
Keystone International	Intl	Lg/Bl	12	30.4	15.1	3.9	28	65	35	3	0	4.0(d)	3.14	188	174.9	854-2505
Kidder Peabody Glob. Eq. A	Intl	Lg/Bl	N.A.	30.8	N.A.	N.A.	28	68	N.A.	N.A.	N.A.	5.75	1.63	144	21.2	223-4447
Landmark Intl. Equity	Intl	Md/Bl	N.A.	29.8	N.A.	N.A.	27	47	N.A.	N.A.	N.A.	3.5	1.75	140	92.6	526-0056
Lexington Global	Intl	Md/Val	11	31.9	9.3	8.9	30	42	39	26	56	None	1.50	83	79.7	526-0056
Lexington Worldwide Emer.	Intl	Md/Gro	10	63.4	28.2	18.2	74	70	61	33	64	None	1.89	102	48.3	526-0056
Loomis Sayles Intl. Equity	Intl	Md/Val	N.A.	38.5	N.A.	N.A.	39	36	N.A.	N.A.	N.A.	None	1.50	82	65.3	633-3330
Lord Abbett Global Eq.	Intl	Md/Val	10	26.1	12.5	8.1	22	49	37	40	37	5.75	1.84	151	71.2	874-3733
MFS World Total Return A	Intl	Lg/Bl	N.A.	21.5	15.8	N.A.	15	75	54	N.A.	N.A.	4.75	1.74	164	145.5	225-2606
MFS Worldwide Equity B	Intl	Lg/Gro	8	29.1	12.1	11.3	26	61	18	64	63	5.0(d)	2.62	173	33.6	456-5111
Mackenzie Canada	Reg	Sm/Val	11	60.1	10.8	3.4	62	47	1	25	19	5.75	2.63	192	12.8	456-5111
Mackenzie Global	Intl	Md/Bl	N.A.	29.6	N.A.	N.A.	27	66	N.A.	N.A.	N.A.	5.75	1.95	160	28.3	522-4202
MainStay Global	Intl	Lg/Val	11	24.7	8.8	4.2	20	23	31	41	12	5.0(d)	2.60	170	52.1	835-3879
Managers Intl. Equity	Intl	Lg/Bl	9	38.2	19.4	12.1	39	72	45	48	29	None	1.52	82	218.4	637-3863
Merrill Lynch Devel. Cap.	Intl	Md/Bl	N.A.	69.0	28.2	N.A.	82	59	59	62	N.A.	4.0	1.71	89	703.7	637-3863
Merrill Lynch Dragon B[1]	Reg	Lg/Gro	N.A.	85.8	N.A.	N.A.	90	N.A.	N.A.	N.A.	N.A.	4.0(d)	2.34	N.A.	765.3	637-3863
Merrill Lynch EuroFund B	Reg	Lg/Val	11	30.6	12.1	11.2	30	49	55	82	42	4.0(d)	2.16	114	4,299.2	637-3863
Merrill Lynch Glob. Alloc. B	Intl	Md/Bl	N.A.	19.7	19.2	N.A.	29	71	52	70	N.A.	4.0(d)	1.93	112	34.0	637-3863
Merrill Lynch Global B	Intl	Lg/Gro	9	22.9	13.7	10.1	17	68	40	47	49	4.0(d)	2.52	134		637-3863

Notes: (d): Maximum deferred sales charge [1] Closed to new investors [5] Area code 212

Fund name	Type	Style	Risk level	% compound annual return to Jan. 1, 1994			Annual performance analysis (percentile ranking by type)					Expense analysis			Net assets (millions)	Telephone (800)
				One year	Three years	Five years	1993	1992	1991	1990	1989	% max. sales charge	Annual charges	Five-year total per $1,000		
Merrill Lynch Glob. Conv. B	Intl	N.A.	7	13.5	13.1	6.9	30	88	67	12	78	4.0(d)	3.50%	$181	$29.8	637-3863
Merrill Lynch Latin Amer. B	Reg	N.A.	N.A.	63.0	N.A.	N.A.	65	63	N.A.	N.A.	N.A.	4.0(d)	2.63	141	249.6	637-3863
Merrill Lynch Pacific A	Reg	Md/Bl	12	34.5	13.0	8.5	34	45	61	62	27	6.5	0.91	116	448.4	637-3863
Montgomery Emerging Mkt.	Intl	N.A.	N.A.	58.7	N.A.	N.A.	67	N.A.	N.A.	N.A.	N.A.	None	1.90	104	591.2	572-3863
Morgan Stanley Glob. Eq. A	Intl	N.A.	N.A.	21.7	N.A.	N.A.	15	N.A.	N.A.	N.A.	N.A.	4.75	1.70	N.A.	14.1	282-4404
National Worldwide Opp.	Intl	Md/Bl	11	37.8	21.0	8.3	38	68	61	7	13	5.75	1.88	168	103.5	356-5535
Nations Intl. Eq. Invest A	Intl	Lg/Bl	N.A.	26.9	N.A.	N.A.	23	N.A.	N.A.	N.A.	N.A.	4.5	1.59	N.A.	1.4	321-7854
Nations Intl. Eq. Trust A	Intl	Lg/Bl	N.A.	28.8	N.A.	N.A.	25	21	N.A.	N.A.	N.A.	None	1.30	N.A.	228.8	321-7854
New Perspective	Intl	Lg/Bl	8	27.0	17.4	14.8	23	71	57	72	58	5.75	0.87	102	4,759.3	421-0180
Newport Tiger	Reg	Lg/Gro	N.A.	75.2	39.2	N.A.	79	100	81	44	N.A.	5.0	1.79	145	293.0	776-5455
Nomura Pacific Basin	Reg	N.A.	12	38.2	10.5	7.0	38	37	48	43	39	None	1.51	82	58.8	833-0018
North Amer. Global Growth	Intl	Lg/Bl	N.A.	29.6	11.9	N.A.	26	44	28	N.A.	N.A.	4.0	2.40	163	63.4	872-8037
Oakmark International	Intl	Md/Val	N.A.	53.6	N.A.	N.A.	60	N.A.	N.A.	N.A.	N.A.	None	1.33	N.A.	810.0	476-9625
Olympic International	Intl	Md/Val	N.A.	45.8	19.5	N.A.	49	45	51	N.A.	N.A.	None	1.00	57	9.1	346-7301
One Group Intl. Eq. Fid.	Intl	N.A.	N.A.	29.6	N.A.	N.A.	26	N.A.	N.A.	N.A.	N.A.	None	1.22	N.A.	73.5	338-4345
Oppenheimer Global A	Intl	Md/Gro	10	42.6	16.0	15.9	45	0	69	77	83	5.75	1.32	128	1,517.2	525-7048
Oppenheimer Global G&I	Intl	Md/Bl	N.A.	39.5	14.6	N.A.	40	31	37	N.A.	N.A.	5.75	1.74	146	96.6	525-7048
Pacific European Growth	Intl	Md/Bl	N.A.	51.3	18.6	N.A.	57	53	27	N.A.	N.A.	4.0	1.95	156	121.9	866-7778
PaineWebber Atlas Glob. A	Intl	Md/Bl	10	41.3	12.2	9.4	43	21	23	55	42	4.5	1.48	134	183.8	647-1568
PaineWebber Europe Gro. A	Reg	Md/Val	N.A.	32.6	6.3	N.A.	32	44	20	N.A.	N.A.	4.5	1.99	150	97.8	647-1568
PaineWebber Glob. G&I A	Intl	Md/Gro	N.A.	35.1	13.0	N.A.	34	42	26	82	N.A.	4.5	2.00	134	67.3	647-1568
Phoenix International	Intl	Md/Bl	N.A.	37.6	10.1	N.A.	38	7	26	63	N.A.	4.75	2.02	150	87.4	243-4361
Pierpont Intl. Equity	Intl	Lg/Val	N.A.	26.2	7.6	N.A.	22	13	26	N.A.	N.A.	None	1.39	76	182.7	521-5412
Pioneer Europe	Reg	Md/Val	N.A.	25.1	N.A.	N.A.	23	54	N.A.	N.A.	N.A.	5.75	2.00	159	48.8	225-6292
Preferred International	Intl	Md/Val	N.A.	41.5	N.A.	N.A.	43	N.A.	N.A.	N.A.	N.A.	None	1.60	N.A.	53.4	662-4769
Princor World	Intl	Md/Bl	N.A.	46.3	19.4	12.0	50	59	38	49	28	5.0	1.69	137	63.7	451-5447
Prudential Global B	Intl	Md/Gro	11	47.9	16.3	8.0	52	35	30	27	21	5.0(d)	2.43	138	249.1	225-1852
Prudential Glob. Genesis B	Intl	Sm/Gro	10	59.5	22.6	14.6	69	55	39	24	68	5.0(d)	2.29	182	82.2	225-1852
Prudential Pacific Gro. B	Reg	Md/Gro	N.A.	65.1	N.A.	N.A.	67	N.A.	N.A.	N.A.	N.A.	5.0(d)	3.52	N.A.	247.5	225-1852
Putnam Europe Growth	Reg	Md/Val	N.A.	31.1	13.9	N.A.	30	58	53	N.A.	N.A.	5.75	1.81	187	29.9	225-1581
Putnam Global Gro. A	Intl	Md/Bl	10	31.8	16.0	12.0	30	56	45	50	55	5.75	1.56	138	937.9	225-1581
Quest for Value Global Eq.	Intl	Lg/Bl	N.A.	25.4	13.9	N.A.	21	62	39	N.A.	N.A.	5.5	1.76	145	144.4	232-3863
Retirement Planning Global	Intl	Md/Val	N.A.	15.2	N.A.	N.A.	12	79	N.A.	N.A.	N.A.	4.75	1.38	134	50.8	279-0279
Rodney Square Intl. Equity	Intl	Md/Bl	12	35.0	9.8	6.0	34	7	29	33	36	4.0	1.75	131	18.9	336-9970
Smallcap World	Intl	Sm/Gro	N.A.	30.0	22.6	N.A.	27	81	83	N.A.	N.A.	5.75	1.15	125	2,441.2	421-0180
Scottish Widows Intl.	Intl	Lg/Val	N.A.	33.5	10.3	N.A.	32	29	18	N.A.	N.A.	5.5	2.20	160	39.1	523-5903
Scudder Global	Intl	Lg/Val	7	31.1	17.1	15.6	29	73	42	59	89	None	1.48	87	845.8	225-2470
Scudder Global Small Co.	Intl	Sm/Gro	N.A.	38.2	N.A.	N.A.	39	55	N.A.	N.A.	N.A.	None	1.50	82	196.6	225-2470
Scudder International	Intl	Lg/Bl	10	36.5	14.1	11.4	36	45	29	51	61	None	1.26	71	2,060.9	225-2470
Scudder Latin America	Intl	N.A.	N.A.	74.3	N.A.	N.A.	90	N.A.	N.A.	N.A.	N.A.	None	2.00	N.A.	259.7	225-2470
Scudder Pacific Opp.	Reg	Md/Gro	N.A.	60.1	N.A.	N.A.	62	N.A.	N.A.	N.A.	N.A.	None	1.75	N.A.	266.7	225-2470
Sierra International Growth	Intl	Lg/Val	N.A.	32.3	10.6	N.A.	30	14	36	N.A.	N.A.	4.5	1.80	N.A.	80.8	222-5852
Sit International Growth	Intl	Lg/Bl	N.A.	48.4	11.5	N.A.	53	66	N.A.	N.A.	N.A.	None	1.85	101	51.1	332-5580
Smith Barney Intl. Eq. A	Intl	Md/Gro	10	52.8	28.4	19.7	59	57	96	41	74	4.5	1.35	128	226.1	544-7835
Smith Barney Shear. Euro B	Reg	N.A.	11	23.0	4.3	7.0	21	45	22	97	38	5.0(d)	3.38	151	33.0	451-2010
Smith Barney Sh. Glob. Opp. A	Intl	Lg/Bl	10	18.0	7.6	5.5	10	31	31	43	38	5.0	1.99	145	33.6	451-2010
SoGen International	Intl	Sm/Bl	5	26.2	17.3	13.3	37	63	33	63	51	3.75	1.31	107	1,208.0	334-2143
Strong International Stock	Intl	Lg/Bl	N.A.	47.8	N.A.	N.A.	52	N.A.	N.A.	N.A.	N.A.	None	2.00	N.A.	80.6	368-1030
T. Rowe Price Euro. Stock	Reg	Lg/Bl	N.A.	27.2	8.8	N.A.	26	50	37	N.A.	N.A.	None	1.39	81	265.8	638-5660
T. Rowe Price Intl. Dis.	Intl	Sm/Bl	11	49.8	15.0	13.4	55	20	29	38	100	None	1.50	82	329.0	638-5660
T. Rowe Price Intl. Stock	Intl	Lg/Bl	11	40.1	16.2	12.1	41	42	39	51	52	None	1.04	58	3,746.1	638-5660
T. Rowe Price Japan	Reg	Md/Bl	N.A.	20.6	N.A.	N.A.	19	36	N.A.	N.A.	N.A.	None	1.50	82	87.2	638-5660
T. Rowe Price New Asia	Reg	Md/Gro	N.A.	78.8	33.4	N.A.	82	81	65	N.A.	N.A.	None	1.36	79	1,650.4	638-5660
TNE International Equity A	Intl	Lg/Val	N.A.	29.3	N.A.	N.A.	26	N.A.	N.A.	N.A.	N.A.	5.75	1.50	N.A.	79.6	343-7104
Templeton Developing Markets	Intl	Md/Val	N.A.	74.5	N.A.	N.A.	90	17	N.A.	N.A.	N.A.	5.75	2.28	160	1,095.5	237-0738
Templeton Foreign	Intl	Lg/Val	8	36.8	17.5	15.5	37	56	45	69	71	5.75	1.12	122	3,063.9	237-0738
Templeton Global Opp.	Intl	Lg/Val	N.A.	38.1	25.3	N.A.	38	82	84	N.A.	N.A.	5.75	1.50	124	370.3	237-0738
Templeton Growth	Intl	Lg/Val	8	32.7	22.0	15.2	31	72	79	50	49	5.75	1.03	117	4,323.4	237-0738
Templeton Smaller Co. Gro.	Intl	Sm/Val	9	31.8	24.5	13.7	30	70	100	29	37	5.75	1.29	138	1,283.5	237-0738
Templeton World	Intl	Lg/Val	9	33.6	21.4	13.0	32	68	75	28	49	5.75	1.02	115	4,792.3	237-0738
Thomson International B	Intl	Lg/Bl	11	33.5	14.7	10.4	32	33	50	30	65	None	2.70	138	174.0	227-7337
USAA Investment Intl.	Intl	Lg/Bl	11	39.8	16.6	11.0	41	55	33	49	35	None	1.68	92	102.0	382-8722
USAA Investment World Gro.	Intl	Lg/Bl	N.A.	24.0	N.A.	N.A.	19	N.A.	N.A.	N.A.	N.A.	None	2.00	N.A.	76.2	382-8722
UST Master International	Intl	Lg/Val	11	36.5	9.4	7.9	36	19	14	49	50	4.5	1.50	127	44.2	233-1136
United International Growth	Intl	Md/Val	11	46.5	19.9	11.0	50	51	48	35	25	5.75	1.18	144	436.3	366-5465
United Svcs. European Income	Reg	Lg/Gro	12	11.7	1.6	(5.3)	9	40	33	8	0	None	2.35	165	2.7	873-8637
Van Eck International Growth	Intl	Lg/Val	N.A.	33.9	N.A.	N.A.	33	N.A.	N.A.	N.A.	N.A.	4.75	0.32	151	1.3	221-2220
Van Eck World Trends	Intl	Lg/Bl	11	22.3	8.0	5.6	16	22	31	54	24	4.75	1.75	138	29.8	221-2220
Vanguard Intl. Equity Euro.	Reg	Lg/Val	N.A.	29.1	12.0	N.A.	28	54	49	N.A.	N.A.	None	0.30	77	546.1	851-4999
Vanguard Intl. Eq. Pacific	Reg	Lg/Bl	N.A.	35.5	7.1	N.A.	35	28	45	N.A.	N.A.	None	0.31	77	542.4	851-4999
Vanguard Intl. Growth	Intl	Lg/Val	11	44.7	12.6	9.4	48	33	11	41	55	None	0.59	32	1,808.3	851-4999
Vanguard/Trustees' Eq. Intl.	Intl	Md/Bl	11	30.5	9.4	7.7	28	21	24	40	58	None	0.42	24	980.8	851-4999
Vontobel EuroPacific	Intl	Md/Gro	11	40.8	17.8	9.5	42	46	47	40	16	None	1.98	107	116.9	527-9500
WPG International	Intl	Md/Bl	N.A.	37.2	9.4	N.A.	37	34	1	32	N.A.	None	2.06	124	14.7	223-3332
Warburg Pincus Intl. Common	Intl	Md/Val	N.A.	51.3	20.4	N.A.	57	38	52	64	N.A.	None	1.46	81	378.1	257-5614
Yamaichi Global	Intl	Lg/Bl	11	33.6	14.3	6.5	32	46	35	17	26	4.75	1.89	147	34.9	257-0228

T A X A B L E   B O N D S

Fund name	Type	Style	Risk level	One year	Three years	Five years	1993	1992	1991	1990	1989	% max. sales charge	Annual charges	Five-year total per $1,000	Net assets (millions)	Telephone (800)
111 Corcoran Bond	IGC	Int/Hi	N.A.	11.6	N.A.	N.A.	31	N.A.	N.A.	N.A.	N.A.	4.5	0.70	82	41.7	422-2080
20th Century Long-Term Bond	IGC	Int/M	5	10.2	11.0	10.6	26	18	27	78	88	None	0.98	55	171.4	345-2021
20th Century US Gov.	Gov	Sh/Hi	1	4.2	6.7	7.5	7	55	29	64	10	None	0.99	55	511.2	345-2021

Notes: (d): Maximum deferred sales charge **Source:** Morningstar Inc., Chicago, Ill.; 800-820-8082

Fund name	Type	Style	Risk level	% compound annual return to Jan. 1, 1994			Annual performance analysis (percentile ranking by type)					Expense analysis			Net assets (millions)	Telephone (800)
				One year	Three years	Five years	1993	1992	1991	1990	1989	% max. sales charge	Annual charges	Five-year total per 1,000		
AIM Adjustable Rate Gov.	MBS	Int/Hi	N.A.	4.2	N.A.	N.A.	35	33	N.A.	N.A.	N.A.	3.0	0.53%	$61	$79.0	347-1919
AIM Gov. Securities A	Gov	Int/Hi	1	7.1	8.7	9.4	16	70	35	74	15	4.75	1.00	100	140.6	347-1919
AIM High-Yield A	HYC	Int/Lo	6	18.4	25.9	12.9	59	47	46	66	56	4.75	1.15	108	535.3	347-1919
AIM Income A	IGC	L/M	5	15.4	13.5	11.5	45	33	28	66	85	4.75	0.96	100	250.0	347-1919
AIM Ltd. Mat. Treas. Ret.	Gov	L/Hi	1	4.4	6.8	7.8	8	65	25	72	9	1.0	0.46	37	343.6	347-1919
API Global Income	WI	N.A.	6	5.3	4.5	5.4	15	46	43	43	79	None	1.33	113	8.6	544-6060
Advantage Gov. Sec.	Gov	L/Hi	3	18.7	14.3	12.6	50	97	42	70	16	4.0(d)	1.32	76	191.2	243-8115
Advantage High-Yield Bond	HYC	L/Lo	N.A.	18.9	30.5	N.A.	60	97	56	54	N.A.	4.0(d)	1.42	82	45.9	367-7732
Aetna Bond	IGC	Int/Hi	N.A.	10.8	N.A.	N.A.	28	27	N.A.	N.A.	N.A.	None	0.05[2]	26	245.9	227-4618
Alliance Bond Corp. Bond A	IGC	L/Lo	5	31.1	20.6	15.9	100	79	29	75	82	4.25	1.48	109	545.5	227-4618
Alliance Bond US Gov. A	Gov	Int/Hi	3	9.7	10.4	10.3	23	68	46	66	19	4.25	1.10	87	163.2	227-4618
Alliance Mortgage Strat. B	MBS	N.A.	N.A.	5.4	N.A.	N.A.	44	N.A.	N.A.	N.A.	N.A.	3.0(d)	2.54	127	863.8	227-4618
Alliance Mort. Secs. Inc. A	MBS	Sh/Hi	1	10.1	11.1	11.0	80	67	76	100	34	4.25	1.01	92	21.5	227-4618
Alliance Multi-Mkt. Inc.	WI	Sh/Hi	N.A.	3.3	3.1	N.A.	11	56	20	N.A.	N.A.	1.0(d)	2.20	98	431.6	227-4618
Alliance Multi-Mkt. Strat. B	WI	Sh/Hi	N.A.	10.1	N.A.	N.A.	24	42	N.A.	N.A.	N.A.	3.0(d)	2.79	169	1,195.2	227-4618
Alliance N. Amer. Gov. Inc. B	WI	N.A.	N.A.	17.8	N.A.	N.A.	38	N.A.	N.A.	N.A.	N.A.	3.0(d)	3.13	154	954.9	227-4618
Alliance S/T Multi-Mkt. A	WI	Sh/Hi	N.A.	7.8	5.8	N.A.	19	55	38	53	N.A.	4.25	1.14	89	149.8	227-4618
Alliance World Income	WI	Sh/Hi	N.A.	7.1	4.7	N.A.	18	60	19	N.A.	N.A.	None	1.52	87	187.5	227-4618
American Cap. Corp. Bond A	IGC	L/M	3	11.7	12.3	9.5	32	41	25	83	23	4.75	1.05	100	71.7	421-5666
American Cap. Fed. Mort. A	MBS	Sh/Hi	1	3.1	5.3	7.8	27	12	25	80	71	2.25	0.91	72	98.8	421-5666
American Cap. Glob. Gov. B	WI	N.A.	N.A.	14.5	N.A.	N.A.	32	54	N.A.	N.A.	N.A.	4.0(d)	2.19	143	3,513.4	421-5666
American Cap. Gov. A	Gov	Int/Hi	3	8.2	10.3	10.9	19	72	48	70	28	4.75	0.97	99	22.6	421-5666
Amer. Cap. Gov. Target '97[1]	Gov	Int/Hi	N.A.	13.4	16.7	N.A.	34	87	100	N.A.	N.A.	3.0	1.63	N.A.	441.2	421-5666
American Cap. H/Y Inv. A	HYC	Int/Lo	8	19.1	25.5	7.9	61	40	44	51	6	4.75	1.09	105	259.0	421-5666
American Cap. US Inc. B	Gov	N.A.	N.A.	5.7	N.A.	N.A.	12	N.A.	N.A.	N.A.	N.A.	4.0(d)	1.50	N.A.	742.7	421-0180
American High-Income	HYC	Int/M	5	17.0	21.0	13.4	54	22	25	85	72	4.75	0.87	97	3.7	421-0180
Arch Gov. & Corp. Inv.	IGC	Int/Hi	3	9.0	10.0	9.5	22	20	21	78	72	4.5	0.93	94	13.5	551-3731
Arch US Gov. Investor	Gov	Int/Hi	1	8.8	9.4	9.8	21	64	39	84	10	4.5	0.95	97	1,572.3	551-3731
Asset Management Adj. Rate	MBS	L/Hi	N.A.	4.7	N.A.	N.A.	39	29	N.A.	N.A.	N.A.	None	0.44	44	235.7	527-3713
Asset Management Intl.-Term	Gov	Sh/Hi	1	5.7	8.1	8.9	12	74	30	75	13	None	0.50	28	218.0	527-3713
Asset Management Intm. Mort.	MBS	L/Hi	2	6.9	10.3	9.9	56	70	83	35	57	None	0.43	34	93.0	527-3713
Asset Management Mort. Secs.	MBS	L/Hi	1	6.9	9.3	10.5	55	52	70	88	80	None	0.53	30	169.6	527-3713
BB&K Intl. Fixed-Inc.	WI	N.A.	N.A.	14.8	11.9	N.A.	32	78	58	N.A.	N.A.	None	0.64	89	57.7	571-5800[19]
BJB Global Income A	WI	Int/Hi	N.A.	11.5	N.A.	N.A.	26	N.A.	N.A.	N.A.	N.A.	None	1.00	N.A.	70.8	435-4659
BNY Hamilton Intm. Gov.	Gov	Int/Hi	N.A.	8.1	N.A.	N.A.	19	N.A.	N.A.	N.A.	N.A.	None	0.80	N.A.	165.3	426-9363
Babson Bond L	IGC	Int/M	3	11.1	11.3	11.0	30	37	20	87	82	None	0.99	54	36.4	422-2766
Babson Bond S	IGC	Sh/M	1	8.4	9.8	9.7	20	29	18	88	67	None	0.67	37	166.5	422-2766
Baird Adjustable Rate Income	MBS	N.A.	N.A.	4.4	N.A.	N.A.	36	N.A.	N.A.	N.A.	N.A.	3.25	N.A.	N.A.	5.5	792-2473
Baird Quality Bond	IGC	L/M	N.A.	10.4	N.A.	N.A.	27	N.A.	N.A.	N.A.	N.A.	4.0	0.00[2]	N.A.	128.1	792-2473
Bartlett Cap. Fixed-Income	IGC	Int/M	2	6.9	9.3	9.3	15	29	19	78	79	None	1.00	55	1,252.7	800-4612
Benham Adjustable Rate Gov.	MBS	Sh/Hi	N.A.	3.5	N.A.	N.A.	30	37	N.A.	N.A.	N.A.	None	0.45	33	376.5	472-3389
Benham European Gov. Bond	WI	L/Hi	N.A.	12.3	N.A.	N.A.	28	N.A.	N.A.	N.A.	N.A.	None	0.87	50	1,314.4	472-3389
Benham GNMA Income	MBS	Int/Hi	1	6.4	9.8	10.7	52	67	77	89	74	None	0.56	32	25.9	472-3389
Benham L/T Treasury & Agency	Gov	L/Hi	N.A.	17.6	N.A.	N.A.	47	N.A.	N.A.	N.A.	N.A.	None	N.A.	42	29.9	472-3389
Benham S/T Treas. & Agency	Gov	Sh/Hi	N.A.	5.3	N.A.	N.A.	10	N.A.	N.A.	N.A.	N.A.	None	0.00[2]	42	83.7	472-3389
Benham Target Mat. 1995	Gov	Sh/Hi	6	6.9	9.7	10.7	15	69	26	100	10	None	0.62	35	296.8	472-3389
Benham Target Mat. 2000	Gov	Int/Hi	7	15.5	14.5	13.8	40	81	42	83	30	None	0.64	37	149.7	472-3389
Benham Target Mat. 2005	Gov	L/Hi	8	21.6	17.2	15.6	58	90	51	52	48	None	0.64	35	67.8	472-3389
Benham Target Mat. 2010	Gov	L/Hi	9	26.3	18.5	16.4	72	90	45	39	72	None	0.70	39	87.6	472-3389
Benham Target Mat. 2015	Gov	L/Hi	11	30.5	19.7	17.2	85	78	49	13	100	None	0.64	35	51.0	472-3389
Benham Target Mat. 2020	Gov	L/Hi	N.A.	35.6	18.2	N.A.	100	51	43	100	N.A.	None	0.70	37	400.5	472-3389
Benham Treasury Note	Gov	Sh/Hi	2	7.8	9.3	9.8	18	72	38	73	17	None	0.53	30	203.7	756-4097[5]
Bernstein Gov. Short Dur.	Gov	Sh/Hi	N.A.	4.5	7.0	N.A.	8	63	28	72	N.A.	None	0.68	39	714.8	756-4097[5]
Bernstein Intm. Duration	IGC	Int/Hi	N.A.	10.2	11.3	N.A.	26	29	26	83	N.A.	None	0.66	38	511.3	756-4097[5]
Bernstein Short Duration Plus	IGC	Sh/Hi	1	5.3	7.9	8.2	9	23	13	88	59	None	0.66	37	98.2	225-1852
Blackrock Gov. Income A	MBS	N.A.	N.A.	2.1	N.A.	N.A.	20	6	N.A.	N.A.	N.A.	3.0	1.05	93	634.8	922-7771
Blanchard Flexible Income	Gov	N.A.	N.A.	13.8	N.A.	N.A.	55	N.A.	N.A.	N.A.	N.A.	None	0.20[2]	N.A.	652.9	922-7771
Blanchard S/T Global Inc.	WI	Sh/Hi	N.A.	8.5	N.A.	N.A.	20	66	N.A.	N.A.	N.A.	None	1.44	96	5,274.8	421-0180
Bond Fund of America	IGC	Int/M	2	14.2	15.4	11.8	40	64	37	64	63	4.75	0.73	86	9.1	421-0180
Boston Co. Intm. Gov. Retail	Gov	Int/Hi	3	9.1	9.3	9.2	22	44	37	62	13	None	1.38	69	57.9	225-5267
Boston Co. Mgd. Inc. Retail	IGC	Int/M	2	14.5	13.4	9.9	42	43	26	67	37	None	1.07	60	2.8	225-5267
Boston Co. S/T Bond Retail	IGC	Sh/Hi	1	3.6	7.2	7.7	3	13	16	90	52	None	0.99	54	74.7	225-5267
Boulevard Managed Income	IGC	Sh/M	N.A.	3.8	N.A.	N.A.	4	N.A.	N.A.	N.A.	N.A.	3.0	0.64	N.A.	44.0	285-3863
Brundage Story & Rose S/I	IGC	Int/Hi	N.A.	8.3	9.3	N.A.	20	25	16	N.A.	N.A.	None	0.50	28	61.2	545-0103
Bull & Bear Global Income	WI	L/M	6	25.0	18.6	9.4	51	100	76	23	42	None	1.95	N.A.	22.4	847-4200
Bull & Bear US Government	Gov	L/Hi	4	10.3	10.2	9.7	25	62	44	65	11	None	1.91	101	28.4	847-4200
CGM Fixed-Income	IGC	L/Lo	N.A.	18.9	N.A.	N.A.	57	N.A.	N.A.	N.A.	N.A.	None	0.85	47	53.6	345-4048
Calvert Income	IGC	L/M	3	12.2	12.5	11.3	34	33	29	69	95	4.75	1.00	104	67.8	368-2748
Calvert Social Inv. Bond	IGC	L/Hi	3	11.7	11.3	11.1	32	27	22	89	85	4.75	0.79	88	13.7	368-2748
Calvert US Government	Gov	L/Hi	2	8.7	8.9	9.7	20	63	34	66	24	4.75	1.11	113	126.2	368-2748
Cambridge Government Inc. B	Gov	N.A.	N.A.	4.1	N.A.	N.A.	7	N.A.	N.A.	N.A.	N.A.	None	1.54	89	478.6	421-0180
Capital World Bond	WI	L/Hi	6	16.7	10.7	9.6	33	56	64	52	72	4.75	1.19	119	106.0	262-6631
Capstone Government Income	Gov	Sh/Hi	3	3.3	4.5	3.9	5	48	9	14	0	None	1.07	51	208.9	848-7734
Cardinal Gov. Obligations	MBS	Int/Hi	1	4.4	7.9	9.3	36	51	53	88	61	4.5	0.76	84	14.2	258-3648
Chubb Government Securities	Gov	N.A.	4	8.6	10.6	11.0	20	79	47	72	26	5.0	1.00	104	11.2	248-2828
Colonial Adj. Rate US Gov. A	MBS	Sh/Hi	N.A.	3.9	N.A.	N.A.	33	N.A.	N.A.	N.A.	N.A.	3.25	0.50	N.A.	1,735.9	248-2828
Colonial Federal Sec. A	Gov	L/Hi	4	11.1	11.7	10.7	33	69	44	59	22	4.75	1.20	109	424.8	248-2828
Colonial High-Yield Secs. A	HYC	Int/Lo	6	19.7	27.8	12.2	63	61	50	53	51	4.75	1.29	118	162.8	248-2828
Colonial Income A	IGC	Int/M	3	12.1	13.2	9.9	33	43	31	60	49	4.75	1.15	108	610.5	248-2828
Colonial Strategic Income A	HYC	N.A.	5	15.0	17.4	10.6	60	28	44	40	29	4.75	1.19	113		248-2828

Notes: (d): Maximum deferred sales charge [1]Closed to new investors [2]Manager absorbing costs
[5]Area code 212 [19]Area code 415

Fund name	Type	Style	Risk level	% compound annual return to Jan. 1, 1994			Annual performance analysis (percentile ranking by type)					Expense analysis			Net assets (millions)	Telephone (800)
				One year	Three years	Five years	1993	1992	1991	1990	1989	% max. sales charge	Annual charges	Five-year total per $1,000[2]		
Colonial US Government A	Gov	Int/Hi	1	5.7	7.2	8.4	11	60	27	76	12	4.75	1.10%	$105	$1,189.7	248-2828
Columbia Fixed-Income Sec.	IGC	Int/Hi	3	10.5	11.7	11.5	27	37	25	89	90	None	0.65	37	304.1	547-1707
Columbia US Govt Sec.	Gov	Sh/Hi	1	5.9	8.1	8.5	12	66	34	70	9	None	0.73	42	36.7	547-1707
Common Sense Government	Gov	Int/Hi	3	8.2	10.1	10.5	19	74	45	67	26	6.75	0.95	117	368.7	544-5445
Compass Cap. Fixed-Income	IGC	L/Hi	N.A.	11.0	11.4	N.A.	29	35	23	83	N.A.	3.75	0.87	85	264.1	451-8371
Compass Cap. Intl. Fixed-Inc	WI	N.A.	N.A.	15.3	N.A.	N.A.	33	65	N.A.	N.A.	N.A.	3.75	1.30	108	46.7	451-8371
Compass Cap. Short/Intm.	IGC	Int/Hi	N.A.	6.9	8.6	N.A.	15	26	13	89	N.A.	3.75	0.88	83	269.2	451-8371
Composite Income	IGC	Int/M	2	10.9	11.8	10.1	29	33	27	89	42	4.0	1.05	101	102.4	543-8072
Composite US Government	Gov	Int/Hi	2	8.1	9.6	10.3	19	69	42	75	22	4.0	1.00	97	266.9	543-8072
Comstock Partners Strategy O[1]	Gov	N.A.	6	20.5	10.3	11.3	55	11	34	40	58	4.5	1.07	122	512.3	782-6620
Connecticut Mutual Gov. Sec.	Gov	L/Hi	2	9.6	10.2	10.8	23	68	43	75	25	4.0	0.96	94	78.9	322-2642
Connecticut Mutual Income	IGC	Sh/M	1	8.0	9.5	8.9	19	26	18	80	59	2.0	0.63	73	48.7	322-2642
CoreFund Intm. Bond B	IGC	Int/Hi	N.A.	4.6	N.A.	N.A.	7	N.A.	N.A.	N.A.	N.A.	4.5	0.75	96	7.9	355-2673
DG Government Income	IGC	Int/Hi	N.A.	9.6	N.A.	N.A.	24	N.A.	N.A.	N.A.	N.A.	2.0	0.74	N.A.	93.9	748-8500
DG Limited-Term Gov. Inc.	IGC	Sh/Hi	N.A.	6.0	N.A.	N.A.	12	N.A.	N.A.	N.A.	N.A.	2.0	0.62	N.A.	117.5	748-8500
Dean Witter Diver. Inc.	Gov	N.A.	N.A.	9.6	N.A.	N.A.	23	N.A.	N.A.	N.A.	N.A.	5.0(d)	0.85	116	162.3	869-3863
Dean Witter Federal Sec.	Gov	L/Hi	4	8.5	9.7	10.1	20	71	40	61	27	5.0(d)	0.74	101	1,133.0	869-3863
Dean Witter Global S/T Inc.	WI	N.A.	6	6.0	5.2	N.A.	16	61	29	N.A.	N.A.	3.0(d)	1.55	84	305.6	869-3863
Dean Witter High-Yield Sec.	HYC	N.A.	11	31.5	39.9	7.2	99	79	100	0	0	5.5	0.67	95	550.9	869-3863
Dean Witter Intm. Income	IGC	N.A.	N.A.	7.8	10.1	N.A.	18	24	25	59	N.A.	5.0(d)	1.64	112	259.7	869-3863
Dean Witter Premier Income	Gov	N.A.	N.A.	0.6	N.A.	N.A.	0	9	N.A.	N.A.	N.A.	3.0	1.56	114	90.6	392-2550[5]
Dean Witter S/T US Treas.	Gov	N.A.	N.A.	4.5	N.A.	N.A.	8	63	N.A.	N.A.	N.A.	None	0.80	N.A.	696.7	392-2550[5]
Dean Witter US Government	Gov	Int/Hi	1	6.5	7.9	8.6	14	66	29	69	14	5.0(d)	1.17	85	12,599.5	869-3863
Dean Witter World Income	WI	Int/Hi	N.A.	9.9	4.6	N.A.	23	65	0	61	N.A.	5.0(d)	1.86	119	275.4	869-3863
Delaware Delchester	HYC	Int/Lo	6	16.5	25.1	11.6	53	39	49	59	54	4.75	1.02	104	954.2	523-4640
Delaware Treas. Res. Intm.	Gov	Sh/Hi	1	5.3	7.9	8.4	10	65	35	74	7	3.0	0.88	78	1,130.6	523-4640
Delaware US Government	Gov	Int/Hi	2	7.8	9.7	9.9	18	71	44	71	15	4.75	1.26	109	237.8	523-4640
Dodge & Cox Income	IGC	Int/Hi	N.A.	11.3	12.3	N.A.	30	36	28	85	N.A.	None	0.60	35	165.9	434-0311[19]
Dreman Fixed-Income	IGC	Sh/Hi	1	6.1	7.7	8.4	12	15	12	97	56	None	0.75	42	5.0	533-1608
Dreyfus 100% US Intm.	Gov	Int/Hi	3	10.9	11.1	11.0	27	77	44	70	21	None	0.60	53	258.1	648-9048
Dreyfus 100% US Long-Term	Gov	L/Hi	5	16.5	14.0	13.0	43	80	56	61	33	None	0.69	54	230.1	648-9048
Dreyfus 100% US Short-Term	Gov	Sh/Hi	2	6.9	8.9	9.2	15	76	35	56	20	None	0.05	62	191.8	648-9048
Dreyfus A Bonds Plus	IGC	L/M	5	15.0	13.9	12.1	43	39	30	72	89	None	0.89	49	655.8	782-6620
Dreyfus GNMA	MBS	N.A.	1	7.2	9.3	9.8	57	50	67	83	42	None	0.94	53	1,843.8	782-6620
Dreyfus Investors GNMA	MBS	Int/Hi	1	8.6	9.6	9.2	68	58	56	67	0	None	0.00[2]	78	56.5	782-6620
Dreyfus Short-Intm. Gov.	Gov	Sh/Hi	1	7.2	9.2	9.8	16	76	37	78	15	None	0.39	43	537.3	782-6620
Dreyfus Short-Term Income	IGC	Sh/M	N.A.	9.0	N.A.	N.A.	22	N.A.	N.A.	N.A.	N.A.	None	0.00[2]	N.A.	280.4	782-6620
Dreyfus Strat. Income	IGC	L/M	4	15.1	14.3	12.4	43	45	31	76	87	3.0	0.86	131	372.8	782-6620
EBI Income	Gov	Int/Hi	3	7.4	8.2	8.3	17	58	33	65	7	None	2.25	122	46.2	554-1156
Eaton Vance Gov. Oblg.	Gov	Int/Hi	1	9.3	9.6	10.2	22	62	41	72	22	4.75	1.41	121	564.0	225-6265
Eaton Vance High-Income	HYC	Int/Lo	7	16.4	23.8	9.4	52	42	38	46	55	6.0(d)	2.09	137	400.5	225-6265
Eaton Vance Income Boston	HYC	Int/Lo	6	18.0	25.7	11.8	57	45	47	52	67	4.75	1.03	104	99.3	225-6265
Eaton Vance S/T Global Inc	WI	N.A.	N.A.	10.8	6.0	N.A.	25	51	33	N.A.	N.A.	3.0(d)	2.06	105	380.8	225-6265
Eaton Vance S/T Treasury	Gov	N.A.	N.A.	2.4	N.A.	N.A.	2	45	N.A.	N.A.	N.A.	None	0.60	33	41.5	225-6265
Enterprise Government Sec.	Gov	L/Hi	1	9.3	10.6	10.2	22	99	34	74	10	4.75	1.30	115	104.7	432-4320
Enterprise High-Yield Bond	HYC	L/Lo	6	17.3	22.1	9.9	55	36	27	60	48	4.75	1.30	115	43.3	432-4320
Executive Inv. High-Yield	HYC	Int/Lo	6	17.1	23.3	10.2	55	46	31	58	47	4.75	1.33	133	13.3	423-4026
FPA New Income	IGC	Int/M	1	10.2	13.3	12.1	26	62	31	90	76	4.5	0.75	86	115.3	982-4372
FT International Income A	WI	Int/Hi	N.A.	27.0	N.A.	N.A.	55	48	N.A.	N.A.	N.A.	4.5	1.17	123	224.6	245-5051
Federated ARMs Institutional	MBS	Int/Hi	4	4.3	7.8	9.1	36	19	78	41	100	None	0.51	29	2,708.1	245-5000
Federated Bond	IGC	Int/Hi	4	13.3	11.7	11.5	37	39	17	92	86	None	0.81	49	106.3	245-5000
Federated GNMA Institutional	MBS	Int/Hi	2	6.5	9.4	10.7	52	52	75	92	89	None	0.66	29	1,966.8	245-5000
Federated Inc. Institutional	MBS	Int/Hi	1	5.9	8.4	9.6	48	42	62	92	55	None	0.51	29	1,743.7	245-5000
Federated Intm. Gov. Inst.	Gov	Sh/Hi	1	7.1	9.0	9.7	16	73	37	74	17	None	0.50	28	949.3	245-5000
Federated S/I Gov. Inst.	Gov	Sh/Hi	1	4.2	6.6	7.8	7	62	24	74	11	None	0.50	27	891.7	245-5000
Fidelity Advisor Gov. Inv.	MBS	L/Hi	2	9.3	9.7	9.8	73	51	58	65	45	4.75	0.82	79	69.3	522-7297
Fidelity Advisor High-Yield	HYC	Int/Lo	5	19.9	25.8	17.2	63	72	31	100	65	4.75	1.12	112	482.6	522-7297
Fidelity Advisor Short F/I	IGC	Sh/M	1	8.9	10.0	9.2	22	35	16	77	64	1.5	0.93	74	648.7	522-7297
Fidelity Capital & Income	HYC	N.A.	6	24.2	27.3	14.0	77	100	20	76	39	None	0.91	44	2,629.4	544-8888
Fidelity Deutsche Mark Perf.	WI	N.A.	N.A.	(1.2)	1.9	N.A.	3	57	22	70	N.A.	0.4	2.26	74	5.8	544-8888
Fidelity Ginnie Mae	MBS	Int/Hi	1	5.8	8.7	10.1	47	57	59	93	73	None	0.80	44	931.9	544-8888
Fidelity Global Bond	WI	Int/M	5	21.3	12.4	11.4	44	67	53	53	86	None	1.15	75	609.7	544-8888
Fidelity Gov. Secs.	Gov	L/Hi	2	11.7	11.8	11.5	29	83	47	75	19	None	0.69	39	749.1	544-8888
Fidelity Intermediate Bond	IGC	Int/Hi	2	11.4	10.6	10.2	31	22	19	86	74	None	0.61	36	1,820.6	544-8888
Fidelity Invest. Grade Bond	IGC	L/M	2	15.6	14.2	12.3	45	40	31	78	81	None	0.68	39	1,053.3	544-8888
Fidelity Mortgage Securities	MBS	Int/Hi	1	6.2	8.1	9.7	50	31	59	91	70	None	0.64	44	399.2	544-8888
Fidelity S/T World Inc.	WI	Sh/M	N.A.	11.9	N.A.	N.A.	27	71	N.A.	N.A.	N.A.	None	1.05	66	394.9	544-8888
Fidelity Short-Intm. Gov.	Gov	Sh/Hi	N.A.	5.0	N.A.	N.A.	9	58	N.A.	N.A.	N.A.	None	0.61	71	162.6	544-8888
Fidelity Short-Term Bond	IGC	Sh/M	1	8.5	9.9	9.2	20	33	18	77	65	None	0.77	48	2,239.6	544-8888
Fidelity Spartan Ginnie Mae	MBS	Int/Hi	N.A.	6.0	8.8	N.A.	49	55	61	N.A.	N.A.	None	0.31	41	621.9	544-8888
Fidelity Spartan Gov. Inc.	Gov	L/Hi	2	9.6	9.6	10.6	15	75	43	73	29	None	0.65	41	415.3	544-8888
Fidelity Spartan High-Income	HYC	N.A.	N.A.	21.1	25.5	N.A.	67	63	29	N.A.	N.A.	None	0.70	44	643.0	544-8888
Fidelity Spartan Inv. Gr. Bd.	IGC	L/M	N.A.	15.1	N.A.	N.A.	44	N.A.	N.A.	N.A.	N.A.	None	0.65	N.A.	129.9	544-8888
Fidelity Spartan Long-Term	Gov	L/Hi	N.A.	16.7	14.0	N.A.	44	84	53	N.A.	N.A.	None	0.65	41	84.6	544-8888
Fidelity Spartan Ltd. Mat.	Gov	Int/Hi	1	6.0	7.8	8.6	12	66	31	73	11	None	0.65	41	1,508.7	544-8888
Fidelity Spartan S/I Gov.	Gov	Int/Hi	N.A.	5.1	N.A.	N.A.	10	N.A.	N.A.	N.A.	N.A.	None	0.02[2]	N.A.	65.1	544-8888
Fidelity Spartan S/T Bond	IGC	Sh/M	N.A.	8.4	N.A.	N.A.	20	N.A.	N.A.	N.A.	N.A.	None	0.20[2]	N.A.	1,526.9	544-8888
Fidelity Sterling Perf.	WI	N.A.	N.A.	2.4	(1.5)	N.A.	9	10	23	100	N.A.	0.4	1.50	86	3.6	544-8888
Fidelity Yen Performance	WI	N.A.	N.A.	13.1	10.0	N.A.	29	62	62	53	N.A.	0.4	1.50	86	2.6	544-8888
First American Intm.-Term	IGC	N.A.	N.A.	6.9	N.A.	N.A.	15	N.A.	N.A.	N.A.	N.A.	4.5	0.70	82	67.8	637-2548

Notes: (d): Maximum deferred sales charge [1]Closed to new investors [2]Manager absorbing costs [5]Area code 212 [19]Area code 415

Fund name	Type	Style	Risk level	% compound annual return to Jan. 1, 1994			Annual performance analysis (percentile ranking by type)					Expense analysis			Net assets (millions)	Telephone (800)
				One year	Three years	Five years	1993	1992	1991	1990	1989	% max. sales charge	Annual charges	Five-year total per 1,000		
First American Ltd.-Term Inc.	IGC	N.A.	N.A.	4.1	N.A.	N.A.	5	N.A.	N.A.	N.A.	N.A.	3.0	0.60%	$62	$119.8	637-2548
First American Mortgage Sec.	MBS	N.A.	N.A.	8.2	N.A.	N.A.	65	N.A.	N.A.	N.A.	N.A.	4.5	0.70	82	32.0	637-2548
First Investors Fund Income	HYC	Int/Lo	7	18.1	25.3	8.5	58	36	48	49	21	6.25	1.33	144	425.9	423-4026
First Investors Government	Gov	L/Hi	3	4.0	8.3	9.2	7	66	44	74	18	6.25	1.15	137	302.2	423-4026
First Investors High-Yield	HYC	Int/Lo	7	17.1	23.2	7.4	55	49	29	50	20	6.25	1.68	156	189.9	423-4026
First Investors Inv. Grade	IGC	Int/M	N.A.	11.8	N.A.	N.A.	32	36	N.A.	N.A.	N.A.	6.25	0.75	135	49.0	423-4026
First Union F/I B Inv.	IGC	Sh/Hi	N.A.	8.3	9.4	N.A.	20	25	17	88	N.A.	4.0	0.90	88	22.5	326-3241
First Union F/I Trust	IGC	Sh/Hi	N.A.	8.7	N.A.	N.A.	21	27	N.A.	N.A.	N.A.	None	0.69	38	383.4	326-2584
First Union Mgd. Bond Tr.	IGC	Int/M	N.A.	10.6	N.A.	N.A.	28	19	N.A.	N.A.	N.A.	None	0.70	39	115.4	326-2584
Flag Inv. T/R US Treas. A	Gov	L/Hi	6	13.7	11.5	10.8	35	56	49	55	23	4.5	0.77	87	224.8	767-3524
Flag Investors Intm.-Term	IGC	Int/M	N.A.	9.0	N.A.	N.A.	22	20	N.A.	N.A.	N.A.	1.5	0.70	54	112.0	767-3524
Flex-funds Bond	IGC	Int/Hi	1	8.2	8.8	8.7	19	0	21	90	54	None	1.00	55	13.1	325-3539
Flex-funds S/T Global Inc.	WI	Sh/Hi	N.A.	0.4	N.A.	N.A.	6	N.A.	N.A.	N.A.	N.A.	None	0.81	N.A.	17.4	325-3539
Fontaine Global Income	WI	Sh/Hi	N.A.	15.6	N.A.	N.A.	34	N.A.	N.A.	N.A.	N.A.	None	1.25	69	0.4	247-1550
Fortis Adv. Gov. Total Ret.	Gov	Int/Hi	2	8.7	7.2	9.0	21	58	15	86	18	4.5	1.25	111	90.1	800-2638
Fortis Advantage High-Yield	HYC	Int/Lo	7	21.8	30.1	11.1	69	29	77	45	31	4.5	1.33	115	73.4	800-2638
Fortis US Gov. Sec.	Gov	Int/Hi	2	8.3	9.2	10.1	19	65	39	80	19	4.5	0.72	86	654.7	800-2638
Fortress Adj. Rate US Gov.	MBS	Int/Hi	N.A.	3.5	N.A.	N.A.	30	29	N.A.	N.A.	N.A.	None	1.01	57	919.7	245-5051
Fortress Bond	IGC	Int/Lo	7	16.3	24.9	12.3	48	100	100	0	6	1.0	0.96	67	125.6	245-5051
Forum Investors Bond	IGC	Int/Lo	N.A.	13.3	12.0	N.A.	37	27	23	93	N.A.	3.75	0.75	75	29.3	879-1900[4]
Founders Government Sec.	Gov	L/Hi	5	9.4	9.8	9.4	22	62	42	46	22	None	1.15	65	32.4	525-2440
Fountain Sq. Quality Bond	IGC	N.A.	N.A.	7.5	N.A.	N.A.	17	54	N.A.	N.A.	N.A.	4.5	0.74	N.A.	43.5	334-0483
Fountain Sq. US Gov.	Gov	Sh/Hi	N.A.	6.2	N.A.	N.A.	13	N.A.	N.A.	N.A.	N.A.	4.5	0.74	N.A.	35.1	334-0483
Franklin AGE High-Income	HYC	Int/Lo	7	17.6	26.7	10.9	56	35	59	54	37	4.0	0.56	71	2,014.8	342-5236
Franklin Adj. Rate Sec.	MBS	Int/Hi	N.A.	4.5	N.A.	N.A.	37	46	N.A.	N.A.	N.A.	2.25	0.00[2]	N.A.	120.8	342-5236
Franklin Adj. US Gov.	MBS	N.A.	1	1.4	4.6	6.7	14	23	15	80	26	2.25	0.36	66	1,818.4	342-5236
Franklin German Gov. Bond	WI	Int/Hi	N.A.	5.2	N.A.	N.A.	14	N.A.	N.A.	N.A.	N.A.	3.0	0.87	N.A.	14.7	354-4111
Franklin Glob. Gov. Income	WI	Int/Lo	6	19.5	10.8	9.1	41	52	59	44	76	4.0	0.69	83	194.9	342-5236
Franklin Intl. H/I Currency	WI	Sh/Hi	N.A.	(2.6)	1.9	N.A.	0	43	49	65	N.A.	3.0	1.81	119	22.9	354-4111
Franklin Intl. Glob. Curr.	WI	Sh/Hi	6	6.0	5.8	7.2	16	66	29	57	73	3.0	1.67	119	61.8	354-4111
Franklin Intl. Hard Curr.	WI	Sh/Hi	N.A.	4.6	5.0	N.A.	13	61	32	68	N.A.	3.0	1.75	121	38.0	354-4111
Franklin Inv. Grade Inc.	IGC	Sh/Hi	1	9.1	10.5	9.4	22	23	25	83	52	4.0	1.04	97	36.0	342-5236
Franklin Short-Intm. Gov.	Gov	Sh/Hi	1	7.7	8.8	9.1	18	73	31	76	9	2.25	0.56	58	272.8	342-5236
Franklin Tax-Adv. H/Y	HYC	Int/Lo	7	17.2	27.3	12.6	55	40	63	50	68	4.0	0.77	81	66.9	342-5236
Franklin T/A US Gov.	MBS	N.A.	1	8.5	10.1	10.7	67	60	69	89	64	4.0	0.59	76	549.4	342-5236
Franklin US Government	MBS	N.A.	1	6.9	9.3	10.4	55	63	60	97	63	4.0	0.52	68	14,202.6	342-5236
Fund for US Gov. Sec. A	Gov	Int/Hi	1	4.9	7.8	9.3	9	62	37	76	23	4.5	0.87	92	1,954.1	245-5051
FundTrust Income	IGC	N.A.	4	10.1	10.9	9.0	26	31	22	70	48	1.5	1.51	70	63.7	344-9033
Fundamental US Gov. Strat.	Gov	L/Hi	N.A.	8.1	N.A.	N.A.	19	N.A.	N.A.	N.A.	N.A.	None	1.27	N.A.	61.4	322-6864
G.T. Global Gov. Income A	WI	L/Hi	6	25.5	13.3	12.0	52	60	57	46	99	4.75	1.60	127	706.9	824-1580
G.T. Global High-Income A	WI	N.A.	N.A.	51.6	N.A.	N.A.	100	N.A.	N.A.	N.A.	N.A.	4.75	1.05	N.A.	138.5	824-1580
G.T. Global Strategic Inc. A	WI	L/M	6	43.9	19.1	15.1	86	58	66	45	94	4.75	1.84	140	289.1	824-1580
GIT Government	Gov	Int/Hi	4	9.4	9.5	9.4	23	62	39	61	14	None	1.52	83	9.9	336-3063
GIT Maximum Income	HYC	Int/Lo	6	15.0	17.4	9.0	48	10	11	69	62	None	1.52	84	7.5	336-3063
Galaxy High-Quality Retail	IGC	L/Hi	N.A.	12.8	11.5	N.A.	36	28	21	N.A.	N.A.	None	0.74	42	161.9	628-0414
Galaxy Intm. Bond Retail	IGC	Int/M	5	5.5	9.4	9.1	10	31	22	77	72	None	0.81	41	445.5	628-0414
Galaxy S/T Bond Retail	IGC	Sh/Hi	N.A.	6.4	N.A.	N.A.	13	20	N.A.	N.A.	N.A.	None	0.83	N.A.	84.5	628-0414
Gateway Gov. Bond Plus	Gov	Int/Hi	4	5.1	7.5	8.7	10	34	47	64	23	None	0.85	56	20.5	354-6339
Goldman Sachs Global Inc.	WI	N.A.	N.A.	12.6	N.A.	N.A.	28	80	N.A.	N.A.	N.A.	4.5	1.30	117	673.1	762-5035
Government Income Sec.	Gov	Int/Hi	1	4.7	7.9	9.3	9	69	35	75	23	1.0	0.97	62	3,887.8	245-5051
Govett Global Gov. Income	WI	L/Hi	N.A.	16.8	N.A.	N.A.	36	N.A.	N.A.	N.A.	N.A.	4.95	1.75	140	116.4	634-6838
Gradison-McDonald Gov. Inc.	Gov	Int/Hi	2	7.5	9.2	9.9	17	70	39	71	20	2.0	0.91	71	272.3	869-5999
Guardian US Gov.	Gov	L/Hi	N.A.	9.6	11.0	N.A.	23	77	49	63	N.A.	4.5	1.48	N.A.	27.6	221-3253
Hancock Freedom Glob. Inc. B	WI	L/Hi	6	8.9	5.8	7.2	21	44	47	52	82	4.0(d)	1.94	123	197.2	225-5291
Hancock Ltd.-Term Gov. A	Gov	Int/Hi	1	7.2	7.9	8.6	16	53	33	65	16	3.0	1.50	120	268.3	225-5291
Hancock Sovereign Bond A	IGC	L/M	2	11.3	11.9	10.9	30	38	25	81	76	4.5	1.41	120	1,535.1	225-5291
Hancock Sovereign US B	Gov	L/Hi	3	9.2	9.6	10.3	22	61	41	68	27	4.0(d)	1.48	103	244.1	225-5291
Hancock Strategic Income A	Gov	N.A.	6	13.2	17.6	7.7	53	20	59	28	0	4.5	1.58	133	322.7	225-5291
Harbor Bond	IGC	L/M	2	12.4	13.6	12.5	34	46	33	88	86	None	0.70	46	164.4	422-1050
Harbor Short Duration	IGC	Int/Hi	N.A.	4.4	N.A.	N.A.	6	11	N.A.	N.A.	N.A.	None	0.90	85	129.4	422-1050
Harris Insight Mgd. F/I	IGC	Int/Hi	N.A.	9.9	N.A.	N.A.	25	16	N.A.	N.A.	N.A.	4.5	0.60	77	80.7	982-8782
Heartland US Government	Gov	Int/M	3	17.8	14.9	13.2	47	100	51	78	15	3.0(d)	1.20	59	65.2	432-7856
Heritage Inc. Ltd. Maturity	Gov	Sh/Hi	N.A.	1.8	5.3	N.A.	0	47	27	N.A.	N.A.	2.0	0.88	N.A.	94.0	421-4184
Heritage Income Diversified	IGC	Int/M	N.A.	9.3	14.1	N.A.	23	51	44	N.A.	N.A.	4.0	1.13	105	41.5	421-4184
Homestead Short-Term Bond	IGC	Sh/M	N.A.	6.7	N.A.	N.A.	14	24	N.A.	N.A.	N.A.	None	0.75	41	34.5	258-3030
Hyperion Short Duration I	MBS	N.A.	N.A.	0.3	N.A.	N.A.	6	13	N.A.	N.A.	N.A.	3.0	0.49	N.A.	66.2	383-3336
Hyperion Short Duration II	MBS	N.A.	N.A.	(0.5)	N.A.	N.A.	0	0	N.A.	N.A.	N.A.	3.0(d)	1.59	N.A.	95.8	383-3336
IAI Bond	IGC	L/Hi	6	12.3	12.1	11.8	34	24	27	83	100	None	1.10	61	134.0	945-3863
IAI Government	Gov	Int/Hi	N.A.	8.5	N.A.	N.A.	20	65	N.A.	N.A.	N.A.	None	1.10	61	42.8	945-3863
IAI Reserve	IGC	Sh/M	1	3.4	4.8	6.3	2	0	1	90	54	None	0.85	47	96.4	945-3863
IDEX II Flexible Income	IGC	L/Lo	6	13.8	16.4	9.0	39	61	47	20	19	7.0	1.50	146	29.3	624-4339
IDEX II Income Plus	HYC	L/Lo	2	13.3	16.0	12.5	43	13	4	89	100	4.75	1.17	109	72.4	624-4339
IDS Bond	IGC	L/M	4	15.4	15.5	12.3	45	58	36	71	66	5.0	0.70	88	2,515.6	328-8300
IDS Extra Income	HYC	Int/Lo	6	19.8	25.7	11.3	63	52	38	62	37	5.0	0.81	94	1,587.7	328-8300
IDS Federal Income	MBS	Int/Hi	1	8.8	8.7	9.4	69	52	36	86	29	5.0	0.77	N.A.	1,024.7	328-8300
IDS Global Bond	WI	L/Hi	N.A.	17.9	13.7	N.A.	38	82	64	54	N.A.	5.0	1.31	122	255.2	328-8300
IDS Selective	IGC	L/M	3	13.1	13.0	11.5	37	45	26	81	76	5.0	0.73	89	1,769.5	328-8300
IDS Strat. Income	IGC	L/M	5	15.7	14.0	11.4	46	50	25	75	60	5.0(d)	1.60	113	761.2	328-8300
IDS Strat. Short-Term Inc.	IGC	Int/Hi	N.A.	5.0	6.0	N.A.	8	8	3	83	N.A.	5.0(d)	1.76	119	175.9	328-8300
ISI Total Return US Treas.	Gov	L/Hi	5	13.6	11.4	10.8	35	55	49	55	23	4.45	0.78	86	232.1	955-7175

Notes: (d): Maximum deferred sales charge
[2]Manager absorbing costs [4]Area code 207

Fund name	Type	Style	Risk level	One year	Three years	Five years	1993	1992	1991	1990	1989	% max. sales charge	Annual charges	Five-year total per $1,000[2]	Net assets (millions)	Telephone (800)
				% compound annual return to Jan. 1, 1994			Annual performance analysis (percentile ranking by type)					Expense analysis				
Indep. Cap. T/R Bond	IGC	L/M	N.A.	14.1	13.5	N.A.	40	37	30	N.A.	N.A.	4.5	$1.22	$109	$35.6	833-4264
Intermediate Bd. Fund Amer.	IGC	Int/Hi	2	9.0	9.8	9.5	22	24	18	87	63	4.75	0.82	95	1,726.8	421-0180
Invesco High-Yield	HYC	Int/Lo	5	15.8	17.9	10.2	51	24	6	75	65	None	0.97	55	304.0	525-8085
Invesco Intm. Gov.	Gov	Sh/Hi	3	5.9	8.7	9.1	12	68	40	73	12	None	0.97	54	39.6	525-8085
Invesco Select Income	IGC	L/Lo	2	11.3	13.4	10.6	30	56	30	72	50	None	1.15	63	161.1	525-8085
Invesco US Gov. Sec.	Gov	L/Hi	5	10.3	10.5	10.2	25	66	45	62	19	None	1.40	70	39.0	525-8085
Inv. Ser. US Gov. Bond	Gov	N.A.	1	4.8	7.9	9.3	9	65	37	74	21	5.75	0.96	121	44.5	245-4770
Inv. Trust US Gov. Sec. B	Gov	Int/Hi	1	7.4	8.9	9.8	17	66	38	72	21	5.0(d)	1.70	105	1,302.6	426-5520
JP Income	IGC	L/M	2	10.3	10.2	9.9	27	26	17	80	79	4.5	0.87	94	23.4	458-4498
Jackson National Income	IGC	N.A.	N.A.	11.9	N.A.	N.A.	32	N.A.	N.A.	N.A.	N.A.	4.75	1.00	N.A.	30.2	888-3863
Janus Intm. Govt Sec.	Gov	Int/Hi	N.A.	2.4	N.A.	N.A.	2	58	N.A.	N.A.	N.A.	None	1.00	36	64.6	525-3713
Janus Short-Term Bond	IGC	Sh/M	N.A.	6.1	N.A.	N.A.	12	N.A.	N.A.	N.A.	N.A.	None	1.00	36	75.8	525-3713
J. Hancock S/T Strat. Inc. B	WI	Sh/M	N.A.	3.6	4.5	N.A.	11	63	28	N.A.	N.A.	3.0(d)	2.12	111	142.9	225-5291
Kemper Adj. Rate US Gov.	MBS	Int/Hi	3	4.9	8.1	8.6	40	47	58	49	43	3.5	0.21	83	218.5	621-1048
Kemper Diversified Income	HYC	Int/Lo	6	20.9	29.3	15.3	66	42	67	58	81	4.5	1.06	107	307.8	621-1048
Kemper Global Income	WI	Int/Hi	N.A.	10.2	6.6	N.A.	24	49	45	73	N.A.	4.5	1.52	125	95.6	621-1048
Kemper High-Yield	HYC	Int/Lo	7	20.3	27.4	12.2	65	38	56	57	47	4.5	0.82	88	1,955.6	621-1048
Kemper Income/Capital Pres.	IGC	L/M	3	11.7	12.4	10.4	32	36	28	80	53	4.5	0.82	88	569.4	621-1048
Kemper Inv. Diver. Inc. Init.	HYC	Int/Lo	7	19.9	28.3	13.8	63	37	65	51	78	4.0(d)	1.93	118	264.0	621-1048
Kemper Inv. Gov. Init.	Gov	Int/Hi	5	4.8	8.6	8.9	9	55	51	61	15	4.0(d)	1.75	107	3,881.9	621-1048
Kemper Inv. H/Y Init.	HYC	Int/Lo	7	19.2	26.4	10.4	61	33	54	52	38	4.0(d)	1.81	109	979.6	621-1048
Kemper Inv. S/I Gov. Init.	Gov	Sh/Hi	N.A.	4.7	7.0	N.A.	9	62	27	61	N.A.	4.0(d)	1.87	110	285.3	621-1048
Kemper Inv. S/T Glob. Init.	WI	Sh/Hi	N.A.	1.0	1.1	N.A.	7	22	N.A.	N.A.	N.A.	4.0(d)	1.98	110	118.3	621-1048
Kemper S/T Glob. Inc.	WI	Sh/Hi	N.A.	2.1	1.1	N.A.	9	24	42	N.A.	N.A.	3.5	1.22	88	118.0	621-1048
Kemper US Gov. Sec.	MBS	Int/Hi	3	6.3	9.3	10.3	51	30	92	82	75	4.5	0.64	79	6,750.7	621-1048
Kent Fixed Income Inv.	IGC	N.A.	N.A.	8.2	N.A.	N.A.	19	N.A.	N.A.	N.A.	N.A.	4.0	N.A.	N.A.	3.9	633-5368
Kent Ltd. Mat. Inv.	IGC	N.A.	N.A.	3.0	N.A.	N.A.	1	N.A.	N.A.	N.A.	N.A.	4.0	N.A.	N.A.	1.4	633-5863
Keystone Amer. Cap. Pres. A	MBS	N.A.	N.A.	5.0	N.A.	N.A.	41	15	N.A.	N.A.	N.A.	3.0	0.74	75	44.2	343-2898
Keystone Amer. Cap. Pres.II B	MBS	Sh/Hi	N.A.	4.1	N.A.	N.A.	35	2	N.A.	N.A.	N.A.	3.0(d)	1.50	82	140.9	343-2898
Keystone Amer. Gov. A	Gov	L/Hi	2	8.6	10.4	10.3	20	83	42	69	16	4.75	1.83	100	48.9	343-2898
Keystone Amer. I/T A	IGC	Int/Hi	4	9.3	11.3	9.1	23	38	25	77	34	4.75	1.52	100	18.5	343-2898
Keystone Amer. Strat. Inc. A	HYC	L/Lo	8	31.7	31.3	10.9	100	51	50	31	48	4.75	1.80	136	106.4	343-2898
Keystone Amer. World Bond A	WI	N.A.	6	17.2	10.8	8.7	37	49	73	49	60	4.75	2.20	160	8.3	343-2898
Keystone Australia Income A	WI	Int/Hi	N.A.	17.6	9.3	N.A.	37	35	71	58	N.A.	4.75	2.50	174	9.8	343-2898
Keystone Custodian B-1	IGC	L/Hi	4	8.9	9.1	9.2	22	5	20	81	75	4.0(d)	2.00	108	459.1	343-2898
Keystone Custodian B-2	IGC	L/M	5	13.8	14.0	8.3	39	51	30	37	14	4.0(d)	1.89	107	1,006.2	343-2898
Keystone Custodian B-4	HYC	Int/Lo	8	26.2	28.3	9.4	83	44	45	39	32	4.0(d)	2.06	116	981.1	343-2898
Kidder Peabody Adj./R Gov. A	MBS	Int/Hi	N.A.	4.4	N.A.	N.A.	37	N.A.	N.A.	N.A.	N.A.	2.25	N.A.	N.A.	203.3	854-2505
Kidder Peabody Glob. F/I	WI	N.A.	N.A.	14.4	N.A.	N.A.	58	N.A.	N.A.	N.A.	N.A.	2.25	1.14	N.A.	191.1	854-2505
Kidder Peabody Gov. Inc. A	MBS	L/Hi	2	6.1	8.6	8.8	49	51	57	28	60	2.25	1.13	86	81.1	854-2505
Kidder Peabody Interm F/I A	IGC	L/Hi	N.A.	7.9	N.A.	N.A.	18	N.A.	N.A.	N.A.	N.A.	2.25	1.08	95	55.1	854-2505
Landmark US Gov. Inc.	Gov	N.A.	3	6.1	8.4	9.0	13	64	38	66	17	1.5	0.80	73	82.7	223-4447
Laurel Intm. Income	IGC	Int/Hi	N.A.	7.7	N.A.	N.A.	18	20	N.A.	N.A.	N.A.	None	0.60	33	58.7	235-4331
Legg Mason Gov. Intm.	Gov	Int/Hi	1	6.6	9.0	9.9	14	70	40	77	20	None	0.90	48	350.9	822-5544
Legg Mason Inv. Grade Inc.	IGC	L/M	3	11.3	11.3	10.6	30	28	23	79	81	None	0.85	47	68.4	822-5544
Lexington GNMA Income	MBS	Sh/Hi	3	8.1	9.6	10.7	64	37	78	76	97	None	1.04	56	133.6	526-0056
Liberty Fin. US Gov.	MBS	N.A.	1	5.8	8.6	9.5	47	46	65	91	40	4.5	0.76	92	938.0	872-5426
Liberty High-Inc. Bond	HYC	Int/Lo	7	17.4	30.2	13.9	56	39	85	58	50	4.5	1.18	107	446.3	245-5051
Limited Term (Fund)	IGC	Sh/Hi	N.A.	7.3	N.A.	N.A.	16	22	N.A.	N.A.	N.A.	1.0	0.91	65	240.8	245-5051
Loomis Sayles Bond	IGC	L/M	N.A.	22.2	N.A.	N.A.	69	87	N.A.	N.A.	N.A.	None	1.00	55	59.3	633-3330
Loomis Sayles Glob. Bond	WI	Int/Hi	N.A.	14.6	N.A.	N.A.	32	56	N.A.	N.A.	N.A.	None	1.50	82	19.5	633-3330
Loomis Sayles US Gov. Sec.	Gov	Int/Hi	N.A.	15.8	N.A.	N.A.	41	89	N.A.	N.A.	N.A.	None	1.00	55	16.4	633-3330
Lord Abbett Bond-Debenture	HYC	Int/Lo	6	16.0	23.0	12.6	51	32	38	69	70	4.75	0.84	92	936.9	874-3733
Lord Abbett Global Inc.	WI	Int/Hi	6	10.6	10.3	10.9	24	75	60	52	100	4.75	1.22	111	265.5	874-3733
Lord Abbett US Gov.	Gov	Int/Hi	4	9.0	10.9	11.0	21	76	51	74	20	4.75	0.87	93	3,960.8	874-3733
MFS Bond A	IGC	Int/M	3	13.9	12.7	11.6	39	24	29	83	83	4.75	0.88	95	520.7	225-2606
MFS Gov. Mortgage A	MBS	L/Hi	4	6.5	8.6	8.5	52	48	56	0	66	4.75	1.48	121	540.2	225-2606
MFS Gov. Securities A	Gov	L/Hi	3	9.6	10.3	10.2	23	77	40	65	17	4.75	0.68	113	392.8	225-2606
MFS Gov. Ltd. Maturity A	Gov	Sh/Hi	2	7.0	7.3	7.5	18	68	18	48	12	2.5	1.29	78	329.6	225-2606
MFS High-Income A	HYC	Int/Lo	7	19.4	27.7	11.2	62	38	61	49	44	4.75	1.03	104	619.7	225-2606
MFS Income & Opp. A	IGC	L/Lo	6	13.2	14.2	9.3	37	16	47	52	24	4.75	2.05	151	60.2	225-2606
MFS Intm.-Income B	Gov	N.A.	4	9.3	7.7	7.6	22	39	30	62	1	5.0(d)	2.17	138	483.7	225-2606
MFS Limited Maturity A	IGC	Int/M	N.A.	6.2	N.A.	N.A.	12	N.A.	N.A.	N.A.	N.A.	2.5	0.59	N.A.	93.7	225-2606
MFS World Gov. A	WI	N.A.	6	18.4	10.8	11.5	39	58	55	64	83	4.75	1.53	164	433.9	225-2606
MIM Bond Income	IGC	Int/Lo	6	3.0	8.3	5.6	1	28	22	49	17	None	2.70	148	3.7	233-1240
MIMLIC Fixed-Inc. Secs.	IGC	L/M	3	11.3	11.5	10.7	30	32	24	82	78	5.0	1.00	102	14.5	443-3677
MIMLIC Mort. Secs. Inc.	MBS	Int/Hi	4	6.7	9.5	10.2	54	46	81	76	69	5.0	1.25	115	27.1	443-3677
Mackenzie Adj. Rate Gov. A	MBS	Sh/Hi	N.A.	3.5	N.A.	N.A.	30	23	N.A.	N.A.	N.A.	1.0	0.82	76	25.1	456-5111
Mackenzie Fixed-Income	IGC	L/Lo	5	15.4	12.4	11.1	45	35	19	65	95	4.75	1.49	125	135.4	456-5111
MainStay Gov.	Gov	L/Hi	4	5.9	7.6	8.4	12	51	37	60	18	5.0(d)	1.70	116	1,223.6	522-4202
MainStay High-Yield Corp.	HYC	Int/Lo	6	21.7	25.1	11.4	69	64	25	68	32	5.0(d)	1.70	121	872.0	522-4202
Managers Bond	IGC	L/M	2	11.6	12.8	12.0	31	37	31	87	86	None	1.15	53	43.5	835-3879
Managers Intm. Mortgage	MBS	N.A.	1	11.5	13.3	13.1	89	100	100	91	91	None	0.75	45	265.5	835-3879
Managers Short & Intm. Bond	IGC	L/Hi	1	8.4	10.9	10.3	20	65	14	85	70	None	0.86	49	106.9	835-3879
Managers Short Government	Gov	L/Hi	1	3.9	6.2	7.0	6	51	26	62	7	None	0.88	43	92.1	835-3879
Mark Twain Fixed-Income	IGC	L/Hi	N.A.	10.8	N.A.	N.A.	29	N.A.	N.A.	N.A.	N.A.	3.5	1.05	N.A.	41.5	866-6040
Marshall Government Income	Gov	Sh/Hi	N.A.	6.0	N.A.	N.A.	12	N.A.	N.A.	N.A.	N.A.	None	0.85	N.A.	54.6	236-8560
Marshall Intm. Bond	IGC	Int/Hi	N.A.	6.9	N.A.	N.A.	15	N.A.	N.A.	N.A.	N.A.	None	0.70	N.A.	308.2	236-8560
Marshall Short-Term Inc.	IGC	Sh/Hi	N.A.	3.7	N.A.	N.A.	3	N.A.	N.A.	N.A.	N.A.	None	0.50	N.A.	86.0	236-8560
Merrill Lynch Adj. Rate B	MBS	Sh/Hi	N.A.	2.9	N.A.	N.A.	25	7	N.A.	N.A.	N.A.	3.0(d)	1.40	80	513.6	637-3863

Notes: (d): Maximum deferred sales charge

Fund name	Type	Style	Risk level	% compound annual return to Jan. 1, 1994			Annual performance analysis (percentile ranking by type)					Expense analysis			Net assets (millions)	Telephone (800)
				One year	Three years	Five years	1993	1992	1991	1990	1989	% max. sales charge	Annual charges	Five-year total per $1,000		
Merrill Lynch Fed. Sec. A	Gov	Int/Hi	1	7.1	8.8	10.1	16	65	38	80	23	4.0	0.79%	$83	$1,731.3	637-3863
Merrill Lynch Glob. Bond B	WI	N.A.	6	11.9	11.3	11.0	27	78	64	58	80	4.0(d)	0.82	96	897.6	637-3863
Merrill Lynch H/I A	HYC	N.A.	6	17.2	25.5	14.5	55	58	41	75	67	4.0	0.54	72	901.0	637-3863
Merrill Lynch Hi.-Qual. A	IGC	N.A.	3	12.6	11.8	11.2	35	22	26	83	85	4.0	0.59	71	409.0	637-3863
Merrill Lynch Intm.-Term A	IGC	N.A.	2	11.7	11.0	10.8	32	22	22	90	77	2.0	0.59	54	193.7	637-3863
Merrill Lynch S/T Glob. B	WI	Sh/Hi	N.A.	5.9	2.7	N.A.	16	42	22	N.A.	N.A.	3.0(d)	1.58	82	1,664.6	637-3863
Merrill Lynch World Inc. A	WI	N.A.	4	13.9	14.2	11.8	30	75	100	48	81	4.0	0.77	87	479.0	637-3863
Merriman Flex. Bond	IGC	L/Hi	4	14.5	10.7	9.3	42	10	16	78	52	None	1.54	82	13.2	423-4893
MetLife-State St. Gov. Sec. A	Gov	Int/Hi	3	9.5	10.5	10.4	23	71	46	69	18	4.5	1.24	111	111.4	882-0052
MetLife-State St. Hi.-Inc. A	HYC	Int/Lo	7	22.4	26.2	11.2	71	57	34	50	57	4.5	1.15	106	605.1	882-0052
Midwest Intm.-Term Gov.	Gov	Int/Hi	3	10.2	10.5	9.8	25	72	43	61	12	1.0	0.99	65	89.5	543-0407
Midw. Leshner Fn. Trea. T/R A	Gov	L/Hi	6	10.0	10.0	9.6	24	58	46	41	26	4.0	1.25	106	39.2	543-8721
Midwest US Gov.	MBS	N.A.	3	8.3	9.1	9.1	66	48	54	60	25	4.0	1.20	103	37.2	543-8721
Midwest US Long Mat.	Gov	L/Hi	N.A.	17.2	11.9	N.A.	45	68	35	N.A.	N.A.	4.0	0.71	83	10.0	543-8721
Monitor F/I Inv. Shares	IGC	Int/M	N.A.	10.1	N.A.	N.A.	26	24	N.A.	N.A.	N.A.	2.0	0.99	78	2.6	253-0412
Monitor F/I Trust Shares	IGC	Int/M	N.A.	10.3	10.9	N.A.	27	26	23	85	N.A.	None	0.74	46	110.3	253-0412
Monitor Mort. Sec. Inv.	MBS	Int/Hi	N.A.	7.7	N.A.	N.A.	62	N.A.	N.A.	N.A.	N.A.	2.0	0.61	75	8.3	253-0412
Monitor Mort. Sec. Trust	MBS	Sh/Hi	N.A.	12.9	N.A.	N.A.	100	N.A.	N.A.	N.A.	N.A.	None	0.76	42	94.3	253-0412
Monitor S/I F/I Trust Sh.	IGC	Sh/M	N.A.	7.4	9.1	N.A.	17	24	17	90	N.A.	None	0.71	41	126.3	253-0412
Monitrend Gov. Income	Gov	N.A.	6	11.8	6.0	6.1	30	0	21	44	4	3.5	1.10	93	1.5	251-1970
Montgomery Sh. Dur. Gov.	Gov	Int/Hi	N.A.	8.0	N.A.	N.A.	19	N.A.	N.A.	N.A.	N.A.	None	0.22	N.A.	25.4	572-3863
Mutual of Omaha Amer.	Gov	Int/Hi	4	9.1	10.2	10.5	22	69	45	65	25	4.5	1.16	108	90.1	225-6292
NCC Fixed-Inc. Retail	IGC	N.A.	N.A.	10.2	N.A.	N.A.	26	33	N.A.	N.A.	N.A.	3.75	0.57	96	6.3	624-6450
National Bond	HYC	Int/Lo	N.A.	21.4[28]	31.2[28]	11.4[28]	N.A.	83	65	55	6	4.75	1.37	123	571.0	356-5535
National Federal Sec.	Gov	Int/Hi	N.A.	9.4[28]	11.7[28]	10.7[28]	N.A.	83	63	46	22	4.75	1.12	104	291.5	356-5535
National Multi-Sect. F/I A	Gov	N.A.	N.A.	15.2	18.3	N.A.	61	36	44	87	N.A.	4.75	1.40	124	176.9	356-5535
Nations Gov. Sec. Tr. A	Gov	Int/Hi	N.A.	7.8	N.A.	N.A.	18	62	N.A.	N.A.	N.A.	2.5	1.00	74	47.9	321-7854
Nations Mgd. Bond Tr. A	IGC	Int/Hi	N.A.	10.7	10.6	N.A.	28	31	17	86	N.A.	None	0.64	69	212.4	321-7854
Nations S/I Gov. Inv. A	Gov	Int/Hi	N.A.	7.8	N.A.	N.A.	18	65	N.A.	N.A.	N.A.	2.5	0.66	62	178.1	321-7854
Nationwide Bond	IGC	L/Hi	4	10.7	11.8	10.9	28	37	25	89	67	4.5	0.65	80	150.4	848-0920
Nationwide US Gov. Inc.	Gov	L/Hi	N.A.	8.8	N.A.	N.A.	21	N.A.	N.A.	N.A.	N.A.	5.0(d)	1.00	65	38.4	848-0920
Neuberger/Berman Ltd. Mat.	IGC	Sh/Hi	1	6.8	7.9	8.7	14	15	12	91	70	None	0.65	36	356.2	877-9700
Neuberger/Berman Ultra Sh.	IGC	Sh/Hi	1	3.2	4.7	6.4	2	3	0	90	58	None	0.65	36	104.3	877-9700
North Amer. Inv. Qual. Bond	IGC	Int/Hi	N.A.	9.2	N.A.	N.A.	23	40	N.A.	N.A.	N.A.	4.0	0.56	106	14.6	872-8037
North Amer. US Gov.	MBS	Int/Hi	2	8.1	9.3	9.5	64	54	57	63	42	4.0	0.64	106	163.9	872-8037
Northeast Investors	HYC	Int/Lo	6	23.6	22.4	10.8	75	40	12	65	51	None	1.34	44	496.3	225-6704
Norwest Adj. US Gov. Inv. A	MBS	Sh/Hi	N.A.	5.3	N.A.	N.A.	43	N.A.	N.A.	N.A.	N.A.	2.5	0.38	46	87.2	363-3300[5]
Norwest Gov. Income Inv. A	Gov	Int/Hi	1	7.9	10.5	10.7	18	75	50	79	16	4.5	0.60	77	21.5	363-3300[5]
Norwest Inc. Investor A	IGC	Int/Hi	4	8.9	11.8	10.9	22	37	31	94	60	4.5	0.60	77	5.2	363-3300[5]
Oppenheimer Champion H/Y	HYC	Int/Lo	2	21.2	22.6	15.1	67	33	22	89	78	4.75	1.24	118	110.1	525-7048
Oppenheimer Gov. Sec.	MBS	N.A.	1	7.8	9.2	10.3	62	27	77	91	72	4.75	0.98	99	178.8	525-7048
Oppenheimer High-Yield	HYC	Int/Lo	4	20.5	20.8	12.2	65	20	17	78	66	4.75	0.97	96	1,131.4	525-7048
Oppenheimer Inv. Gr. Bond A	IGC	L/M	3	10.3	11.7	10.2	27	28	29	72	71	4.75	1.02	105	114.9	525-7048
Oppenheimer Mort. Inc. A	MBS	N.A.	1	7.8	8.8	9.7	62	28	65	88	49	4.75	1.40	120	91.6	525-7048
Oppheimer Str. Inv. Gr. Bd. A	IGC	Int/M	N.A.	10.5	N.A.	N.A.	27	N.A.	N.A.	N.A.	N.A.	4.75	1.20	N.A.	30.2	525-7048
Oppenheimer Strat. S/T Inc.A	IGC	Sh/M	N.A.	8.2	N.A.	N.A.	19	N.A.	N.A.	N.A.	N.A.	3.5	1.18	N.A.	2.6	525-7048
Oppenheimer Strat. Inc. A	HYC	N.A.	N.A.	19.2	15.6	N.A.	78	21	22	99	N.A.	4.75	1.08	108	2,885.7	525-7048
Oppenheimer US Gov.	Gov	Int/Hi	2	7.9	9.3	9.5	18	60	44	64	17	4.75	1.17	109	374.2	525-7048
Overland Express S/T Gov.	Gov	N.A.	N.A.	3.1	N.A.	N.A.	4	N.A.	N.A.	N.A.	N.A.	3.0	0.77	68	58.8	552-9612
Overland Express US Gov. A	Gov	L/Hi	4	10.7	11.3	11.9	26	65	56	79	30	4.5	0.69	70	49.1	552-9612
Overland Exp. Var. Rate A	MBS	Sh/Hi	N.A.	4.9	5.9	N.A.	40	25	15	N.A.	N.A.	3.0	0.86	70	2,082.9	552-9612
Pacific Horizon US Gov.	MBS	N.A.	1	6.9	9.8	10.5	55	66	73	90	59	4.5	0.91	65	162.1	332-3863
Pacifica Asset Preservation	IGC	Sh/M	N.A.	4.5	6.1	N.A.	6	11	4	N.A.	N.A.	None	0.75	41	158.5	662-8417
Pacifica Government Income	Gov	Int/Hi	N.A.	9.2	9.8	N.A.	22	63	44	N.A.	N.A.	4.5	0.79	87	172.9	662-8417
PaineWebber Glob. Inc. B	WI	N.A.	5	13.4	8.1	9.4	30	55	44	63	76	5.0(d)	1.96	127	1,188.9	647-1568
PaineWebber High-Inc. A	HYC	Int/Lo	6	22.7	30.8	15.1	72	78	57	67	47	4.0	0.96	92	357.9	647-1568
PaineWebber Income B	IGC	L/M	5	12.5	15.2	11.2	34	55	43	58	55	5.0(d)	1.94	129	32.5	647-1568
PaineWebber Inv. Grade A	IGC	L/M	2	13.4	13.5	11.8	38	44	30	80	78	4.0	0.98	94	209.2	647-1568
PaineWebber US Govt Inc. A	MBS	N.A.	2	6.5	9.2	10.0	52	49	72	82	62	4.0	0.92	89	666.8	647-1568
Parnassus Inc. Fixed-Inc.	IGC	L/Hi	N.A.	11.0	N.A.	N.A.	29	N.A.	N.A.	N.A.	N.A.	None	0.00[2]	55	4.1	999-3505
Permanent Port. Treas. Bill	Gov	Sh/Hi	1	2.3	3.5	5.1	1	43	4	63	3	None	0.71	75	153.7	531-5142
Permanent Port. Vers. Bd.	IGC	Sh/M	N.A.	3.8	N.A.	N.A.	4	18	N.A.	N.A.	N.A.	None	0.82	82	35.1	531-5142
Phoenix High-Qual. Bond	IGC	Int/M	N.A.	13.4[29]	13.3[29]	10.2[29]	N.A.	43	23	71	76	4.75	0.75	89	68.9	243-4361
Phoenix High-Yield	HYC	Int/Lo	6	21.5	21.0	11.7	68	37	9	82	48	4.75	1.10	104	182.3	243-4361
Phoenix US Govt Securities	Gov	Int/Hi	3	7.9	10.0	10.0	18	84	39	68	16	4.75	0.75	88	57.1	243-4361
Pierpont Bond	IGC	Int/M	1	9.4	9.8	10.0	24	28	16	98	63	None	0.81	45	103.2	521-5412
Pilgrim Adj. Rate Secs. I[1]	MBS	Sh/Hi	N.A.	6.1	N.A.	N.A.	49	59	N.A.	N.A.	N.A.	4.0(d)	0.76	N.A.	63.0	334-3444
Pilgrim Adj. Rate Secs. I-A	MBS	Sh/Hi	N.A.	6.4	N.A.	N.A.	51	N.A.	N.A.	N.A.	N.A.	4.0(d)	0.76	N.A.	177.9	334-3444
Pilgrim Adj. Rate Secs. II	MBS	Sh/Hi	N.A.	7.0	N.A.	N.A.	56	68	N.A.	N.A.	N.A.	3.0	0.76	96	61.0	334-3444
Pilgrim Adj. Rate Secs. III	MBS	Sh/Hi	N.A.	7.0	N.A.	N.A.	56	69	N.A.	N.A.	N.A.	5.0	0.61	N.A.	34.0	334-3444
Pilgrim Adj. US Gov. I[1]	MBS	Sh/Hi	N.A.	3.2	N.A.	N.A.	28	46	N.A.	N.A.	N.A.	4.0(d)	0.61	N.A.	674.5	334-3444
Pilgrim Adj. US Gov. I-A	MBS	Sh/Hi	N.A.	2.9	N.A.	N.A.	25	N.A.	N.A.	N.A.	N.A.	4.0(d)	0.61	N.A.	378.0	334-3444
Pilgrim Adj. US Gov. II	MBS	Sh/Hi	N.A.	4.2	N.A.	N.A.	35	N.A.	N.A.	N.A.	N.A.	3.0	0.61	96	99.5	334-3444
Pilgrim GNMA	MBS	Int/Hi	2	4.7	8.0	8.9	39	64	44	59	59	3.0	1.12	89	84.3	334-3444
Pilgrim High-Yield	HYC	Int/Lo	6	18.5	21.3	10.5	59	33	19	65	58	3.0	2.04	136	18.8	334-3444
Pilgrim S/T Multi-Mkt. Inc.	WI	Sh/Hi	10	1.5	(4.4)	(8.5)	8	0	1	0	0	3.5	1.60	100	31.6	334-3444
Pilgrim S/T Multi-Mkt. Inc. II	WI	Sh/Hi	N.A.	1.6	N.A.	N.A.	8	19	N.A.	N.A.	N.A.	4.0(d)	2.50	140	9.0	334-3444
Pioneer Bond	IGC	L/Hi	2	11.4	11.6	10.7	31	37	22	84	72	4.5	1.09	102	117.6	225-6292
Pioneer Short-Term Inc.	IGC	Sh/Hi	N.A.	5.8	N.A.	N.A.	11	N.A.	N.A.	N.A.	N.A.	2.5	0.50	N.A.	53.8	225-6292
Pioneer US Government	Gov	Int/Hi	1	9.1	9.3	9.7	22	73	31	72	15	4.5	1.00	98	109.4	225-6292

Notes: (d): Maximum deferred sales charge [1]Closed to new investors [2]Manager aborbing costs
[5]Area code 212 [28]To Dec. 1; fund since merged [29]To Nov. 1; fund since merged

Fund name	Type	Style	Risk level	% compound annual return to Jan. 1, 1994			Annual performance analysis (percentile ranking by type)					Expense analysis			Net assets (millions)	Telephone (800)
				One year	Three years	Five years	1993	1992	1991	1990	1989	% max. sales charge	Annual charges	Five-year total per $1,000		
Piper Jaffray Gov. Income	Gov	N.A.	5	10.0	11.0	10.4	24	55	59	70	10	4.0	1.07%	$100	$162.4	866-7778
Portico Bond IMMDEX	IGC	L/Hi	N.A.	11.0	11.6	N.A.	29	34	25	89	N.A.	None	0.50	30	260.5	228-1024
Portico S/T Bond Mkt.	IGC	Sh/M	N.A.	6.4	8.9	N.A.	13	28	16	86	N.A.	None	0.53	30	142.5	228-1024
Preferred Fixed-Income	IGC	Int/Hi	N.A.	10.0	N.A.	N.A.	26	N.A.	N.A.	N.A.	N.A.	None	1.05	N.A.	39.9	662-4769
Preferred S/T Gov. Sec.	Gov	Sh/Hi	N.A.	5.3	N.A.	N.A.	11	N.A.	N.A.	N.A.	N.A.	None	0.78	N.A.	28.9	662-4769
Premier GNMA A	MBS	L/Hi	1	8.2	10.0	10.6	65	52	75	94	55	4.5	0.78	101	198.2	242-8671
Primary US Government	Gov	Int/Hi	N.A.	8.0	8.6	N.A.	19	48	41	68	N.A.	None	0.75	42	1.4	443-6544
Principal Pres. Government	Gov	Int/Hi	4	10.2	10.7	10.4	25	74	44	71	15	4.5	1.00	100	52.0	826-4600
Princor Bond	IGC	L/M	3	12.8	12.9	11.3	35	42	27	71	84	5.0	0.90	96	85.0	451-5447
Princor Gov. Sec. Income	MBS	Int/Hi	4	9.2	10.6	11.3	72	48	88	80	88	5.0	0.89	100	236.7	451-5447
Princor High-Yield	HYC	Int/Lo	6	11.4	17.2	7.0	37	11	17	60	46	5.0	1.37	123	19.2	451-5447
Prudential Adj. Rate Secs. A	MBS	N.A.		1.8	N.A.	N.A.	18	N.A.	N.A.	N.A.	N.A.	1.0	0.67	79	167.2	225-1852
Prudential GNMA B	MBS	Sh/Hi	2	4.3	7.3	8.5	36	44	46	62	55	5.0(d)	1.57	97	331.9	225-1852
Prudential Government Plus B	Gov	Int/Hi	4	6.8	9.1	9.3	15	70	40	61	18	5.0(d)	1.69	102	2,426.6	225-1852
Prudential Gov. Intm.	Gov	Sh/Hi	2	7.2	8.8	9.2	16	69	36	66	15	None	0.80	44	351.7	225-1852
Prudential High-Yield B	HYC	Int/Lo	6	16.5	21.7	9.9	53	30	28	65	45	5.0(d)	1.37	89	3,663.8	225-1852
Prudential Int. Glob. Inc. A	WI	Int/Hi	5	15.8	8.8	8.6	34	67	28	42	94	3.0	1.34	104	336.8	225-1852
Prudential S/T Glob. Asts. A	WI	N.A.	N.A.	4.3	N.A.	N.A.	13	57	N.A.	N.A.	N.A.	0.99	1.49	82	127.8	225-1852
Prudential S/T Glob. Inc. B	WI	N.A.	N.A.	7.2	5.0	N.A.	18	48	39	N.A.	N.A.	3.0(d)	1.98	104	375.8	225-1852
Prudential Struc. Mat. A	IGC	Sh/M	N.A.	7.0	8.9	N.A.	15	27	15	95	N.A.	3.25	0.83	77	115.2	225-1852
Prudential US Government B	Gov	Int/Hi	6	10.8	10.3	9.9	27	63	42	42	28	5.0(d)	1.82	107	166.9	225-1852
Putnam Adj. Rate US Gov. A	MBS	Sh/Hi	1	0.4	3.8	5.9	7	22	0	67	23	3.25	1.12	94	193.9	225-1581
Putnam Amer. Gov. Inc.	Gov	Int/Hi	4	6.0	7.1	8.4	12	68	19	63	23	4.75	0.91	98	3,426.6	225-1581
Putnam Diversified Income A	Gov	N.A.	3	15.9	17.2	12.2	64	36	31	86	17	4.75	1.21	115	1,004.8	225-1581
Putnam Federal Income	Gov	Int/Hi	4	4.9	8.6	9.7	9	67	44	67	26	4.75	1.11	106	600.6	225-1581
Putnam Global Gov. Inc.	WI	L/Hi	6	13.6	11.0	11.3	30	69	63	61	84	4.75	1.46	123	553.7	225-1581
Putnam High Yield A	HYC	Int/Lo	6	18.5	25.4	12.4	59	51	40	72	40	4.75	0.92	105	3,275.7	225-1581
Putnam High Yield Advantage	HYC	Int/Lo	6	21.0	27.9	13.0	67	47	54	68	35	4.75	1.14	107	719.1	225-1581
Putnam Income A	IGC	Int/M	3	11.9	13.3	11.2	33	52	29	70	76	4.75	0.97	99	814.9	225-1581
Putnam US Gov. Income A	MBS	Int/Hi	1	5.6	8.0	9.3	46	53	44	85	59	4.75	0.88	101	4,672.9	225-1581
Quest for Value Global Inc.	WI	Sh/Hi	N.A.	12.6	N.A.	N.A.	28	33	N.A.	N.A.	N.A.	3.0	1.70	129	23.3	232-3863
Quest for Value Inv. Qual.	IGC	L/M	N.A.	13.6	12.0	N.A.	38	48	15	N.A.	N.A.	4.75	1.17	118	61.0	232-3863
Quest for Value US Gov.	Gov	L/Hi	1	6.7	8.6	9.6	15	70	34	79	17	4.75	1.15	108	188.8	232-3863
RBB Government Securities	Gov	Int/Hi	N.A.	9.2	N.A.	N.A.	22	71	N.A.	N.A.	N.A.	4.75	0.67	81	62.4	888-9723
RBB High-Yield Bond	HYC	N.A.	N.A.	(0.5)	N.A.	N.A.	0	16	N.A.	N.A.	N.A.	4.75	1.25	113	0.2	888-9723
RIMCO Monument Bond	IGC	Int/Hi	N.A.	10.7	N.A.	N.A.	28	N.A.	N.A.	N.A.	N.A.	3.5	0.50	70	51.1	934-3883
Retirement Planning Bond	MBS	N.A.	2	3.7	6.7	7.1	31	24	48	35	14	5.0(d)	2.45	134	57.7	279-0279
Rightime Government Sec.	Gov	L/Hi	6	7.5	7.0	6.2	17	92	0	0	26	4.75	2.00	152	33.9	242-1421
Rodney Sq. Divers. Income	IGC	Int/Hi	N.A.	7.9	N.A.	N.A.	18	28	N.A.	N.A.	N.A.	3.5	0.65	75	41.0	336-9970
Rushmore US Gov. Intm.	Gov	Int/Hi	6	11.9	11.7	11.3	30	76	48	58	28	None	0.80	45	21.4	343-3355
Rushmore US Gov. L/T	Gov	L/Hi	7	15.3	12.6	12.1	40	69	50	46	42	None	0.80	45	29.8	343-3355
Safeco High-Yield Bond	HYC	Int/Lo	5	16.9	18.3	10.2	54	20	8	77	59	None	1.07	58	34.2	426-6730
Safeco Intm.-Term US	Gov	Int/Hi	2	10.8	10.3	9.6	27	72	37	62	11	None	0.96	54	14.6	426-6730
Safeco US Government Secs.	MBS	Int/M	2	7.1	9.5	10.0	57	55	70	69	61	None	0.92	52	62.0	426-6730
Schwab S/I Gov.	Gov	Sh/Hi	N.A.	7.7	N.A.	N.A.	17	68	N.A.	N.A.	N.A.	None	0.60	33	279.3	526-8600
Scudder GNMA	MBS	Int/Hi	2	6.0	9.3	10.1	49	58	72	88	59	None	0.93	55	653.9	225-2470
Scudder Income	IGC	L/Hi	3	12.7	12.2	11.5	35	28	27	89	80	None	0.93	51	522.6	225-2470
Scudder Intl. Bond	WI	Int/M	6	15.8	15.1	14.6	34	81	95	70	83	None	1.25	69	1,332.0	225-2470
Scudder S/T Global Income	WI	Sh/M	N.A.	6.7	N.A.	N.A.	17	73	N.A.	N.A.	N.A.	None	1.00	55	1,042.4	225-2470
Scudder Short-Term Bond	IGC	Sh/Hi	1	8.2	9.3	10.2	19	18	18	97	83	None	0.75	42	3,181.8	225-2470
Scudder Zero Coupon 2000	Gov	Int/Hi	7	16.0	14.6	13.7	42	84	63	47	48	None	1.00	55	34.2	225-2470
Security Inc. Corp. Bond A	IGC	L/M	3	13.7	12.9	11.0	39	45	23	81	62	4.75	1.03	101	123.3	888-2461
Security Inc. US Gov. A	MBS	L/Hi	2	11.8	10.1	10.4	92	33	61	84	45	4.75	1.10	106	10.9	888-2461
Select. US Gov. Income	Gov	L/Hi	3	7.9	8.9	8.7	18	62	38	70	4	None	1.44	79	10.7	243-1575
Seligman H/Y Bond A	HYC	Int/Lo	6	19.2	23.2	12.5	61	55	22	69	65	4.75	1.23	115	55.6	221-2783
Seligman Secured Mtg. Inc.	MBS	L/Hi	N.A.	5.8[29]	8.6[29]	7.5[29]	N.A.	26	54	46	9	4.75	1.47	113	14.5	221-2783
Seligman US Gov. Sec. A	Gov	L/Hi	3	7.5	9.0	8.5	17	66	39	57	7	4.75	1.13	103	57.7	221-2783
Sentinel Bond	IGC	Int/M	3	12.4	12.6	11.5	34	35	28	84	78	5.0	0.83	99	83.6	282-3863
Sentinel Gov. Secs.	Gov	Int/Hi	2	9.3	10.6	10.7	22	78	44	73	19	5.0	0.94	101	137.6	282-3863
Seven Seas S/T Term Gov.	Gov	Sh/Hi	N.A.	4.2	N.A.	N.A.	5	N.A.	N.A.	N.A.	N.A.	None	0.60	N.A.	29.9	654-6089[21]
Seven Seas Yield Plus	IGC	Sh/M	N.A.	2.7	N.A.	N.A.	0	N.A.	N.A.	N.A.	N.A.	None	0.36	N.A.	1,088.4	654-6089[21]
Sierra Corporate Income	IGC	Int/M	N.A.	16.4	15.5	N.A.	48	51	36	N.A.	N.A.	4.5	1.24	N.A.	483.6	222-5852
Sierra S/T Glob. Government	WI	N.A.	N.A.	6.8	N.A.	N.A.	17	N.A.	N.A.	N.A.	N.A.	3.5	0.73	N.A.	235.6	222-5852
Sierra US Government	Gov	Int/Hi	N.A.	6.8	9.3	N.A.	15	70	42	74	N.A.	4.5	0.91	N.A.	863.7	222-5852
Signet Sel. US Gov. Inv.	MBS	Int/Hi	N.A.	7.2	9.4	N.A.	57	48	72	N.A.	N.A.	None	0.57	79	122.2	444-7123
Sit US Gov. Secs.	Gov	Sh/Hi	1	7.4	8.5	9.5	17	63	34	84	14	None	0.89	55	40.8	332-5580
Skyline Monthly Income	HYC	Int/Lo	3	12.8	16.8	10.8	41	24	6	77	83	None	1.07	96	24.5	458-5222
Smith Barney Global Gov. A	WI	N.A.	N.A.	19.2	N.A.	N.A.	40	57	N.A.	N.A.	N.A.	4.0	1.31	114	107.9	544-7835
Smith Barney Inc. Return A	IGC	Sh/Hi	1	4.0	6.9	8.1	5	20	9	93	66	1.5	0.50	43	54.4	544-7835
Smith Barney Mo. Pymt. Gov. A	MBS	N.A.	2	6.5	9.4	10.6	53	55	74	83	92	4.0	0.51	69	54.3	544-7835
Smith Barney Sh. A/R Gov. A	MBS	N.A.	N.A.	3.1	N.A.	N.A.	27	N.A.	N.A.	N.A.	N.A.	None	1.50	82	426.0	451-2010
Smith B. Sh. Div. St. Inc. B	Gov	N.A.	N.A.	12.8	12.5	N.A.	51	15	18	100	N.A.	4.5(d)	1.59	98	2,334.5	451-2010
Smith B. Shear. Glob. Bd. B	WI	Int/Hi	5	11.9	10.3	9.3	27	66	66	47	80	4.5(d)	2.22	119	74.1	451-2010
Smith B. Shear. Gov. Secs. B	Gov	Int/Hi	5	10.5	10.6	10.7	26	63	48	59	28	4.5(d)	1.51	90	895.1	451-2010
Smith Barney Shear. H/I B	HYC	Int/Lo	7	19.0	24.3	9.9	61	52	30	57	37	4.5(d)	1.66	100	471.1	451-2010
Smith B. Sh. Inv. Gr. Bd. B	IGC	L/M	6	18.0	16.2	13.3	54	40	41	63	98	4.5(d)	1.57	94	496.1	451-2010
Smith B. Sh. Ltd. Mat. Treas.	Gov	Int/Hi	N.A.	8.3	N.A.	N.A.	19	98	N.A.	N.A.	N.A.	1.25	0.65	58	52.4	451-2010
Smith B. Shear. Mgd. Govt A	MBS	N.A.	3	9.1	10.7	10.4	72	48	90	88	20	4.5	0.92	101	449.0	451-2010
Smith B. Sh. S/T World Inc. A	WI	Sh/Hi	N.A.	1.2	1.2	N.A.	7	46	16	N.A.	N.A.	3.0	1.40	94	59.4	451-2010
Smith B. Shear. W/W Prime A	WI	N.A.	N.A.	(0.3)	N.A.	N.A.	4	47	N.A.	N.A.	N.A.	None	1.75	95	87.3	451-2010

Notes: (d): Maximum deferred sales charge [21]Area code 617 [29]To Nov. 1; fund since merged

Fund name	Type	Style	Risk level	% compound annual return to Jan. 1, 1994			Annual performance analysis (percentile ranking by type)					Expense analysis			Net assets (millions)	Telephone (800)
				One year	Three years	Five years	1993	1992	1991	1990	1989	% max. sales charge	Annual charges	Five-year total per $1,000[2]		
Smith Barney US Gov. A	MBS	L/Hi	3	6.4	9.6	10.6	52	55	80	80	84	4.0	0.50%	$68	$481.3	544-7835
Smith Breeden Intermediate	Gov	L/Hi	N.A.	10.4	N.A.	N.A.	25	N.A.	N.A.	N.A.	N.A.	3.5	0.43	N.A.	10.5	221-3138
Smith Breeden Short I	MBS	Sh/Hi	N.A.	4.3	N.A.	N.A.	36	N.A.	N.A.	N.A.	N.A.	2.75	0.43	N.A.	112.3	221-3138
Stagecoach Ginnie Mae	MBS	N.A.	N.A.	7.1	N.A.	N.A.	57	59	N.A.	N.A.	N.A.	4.5	0.61	70	305.7	222-8222
Stagecoach US Gov. Alloc.	Gov	L/Hi	6	17.4	13.0	11.4	46	58	52	51	21	4.5	1.00	98	288.2	222-8222
Stagecoach Variable Rate	MBS	Sh/Hi	N.A.	4.3	N.A.	N.A.	36	5	N.A.	N.A.	N.A.	3.0	0.89	79	29.7	222-8222
Starburst Gov. Income	Gov	N.A.	N.A.	7.0	N.A.	N.A.	15	N.A.	N.A.	N.A.	N.A.	4.5	0.98	96	97.0	239-1930
State St. Research Gov. A	Gov	L/Hi	3	9.9	10.8	10.8	24	74	47	72	19	4.5	1.05	100	866.1	882-0052
SteinRoe Gov. Income	Gov	L/Hi	3	7.1	9.3	9.9	16	69	43	68	22	None	0.95	55	61.8	338-2550
SteinRoe Income	IGC	Int/M	3	13.2	13.1	10.5	37	46	26	79	43	None	0.82	50	163.2	338-2550
SteinRoe Intm. Bond	IGC	Int/M	2	8.9	10.5	10.3	22	35	21	84	79	None	0.67	39	328.7	338-2550
Strong Advantage	IGC	Sh/M	1	8.1	9.0	8.6	19	41	8	81	59	None	0.90	55	349.9	368-1030
Strong Gov. Securities	Gov	L/Hi	1	12.8	12.9	11.4	33	93	50	70	10	None	0.80	64	213.0	368-1030
Strong Income	IGC	L/M	6	16.8	13.6	6.7	50	48	20	17	0	None	1.20	72	127.0	368-1030
Strong S/T Bond	IGC	Sh/M	1	9.3	10.2	8.8	23	27	19	74	51	None	0.80	52	1,391.1	368-1030
Sun Eagle Gov. Sec.	Gov	Sh/Hi	N.A.	5.1	N.A.	N.A.	10	N.A.	N.A.	N.A.	N.A.	None	0.44	N.A.	33.4	752-1823
Sun Eagle Intm. Fixed-Inc.	IGC	Int/M	N.A.	8.9	N.A.	N.A.	22	N.A.	N.A.	N.A.	N.A.	None	0.39	N.A.	49.4	752-1823
SunAmerica Fed. Sec. B	MBS	N.A.	2	1.6	6.8	8.4	16	30	66	84	48	4.0(d)	1.85	125	100.5	858-8850
SunAmerica High-Income A	HYC	Int/Lo	6	16.2	24.8	11.7	52	64	36	71	35	4.75	1.77	130	25.8	858-8850
SunAmerica US Gov. Secs B	Gov	L/Hi	1	4.0	6.4	7.3	6	64	22	72	4	4.0(d)	1.82	114	1,174.5	858-8850
T. Rowe Price Adj Rate US	MBS	Sh/Hi	N.A.	2.7	N.A.	N.A.	24	22	N.A.	N.A.	N.A.	None	0.40	14	291.4	638-5660
T. Rowe Price GNMA	MBS	Int/Hi	2	6.1	9.1	10.3	49	52	72	87	75	None	0.79	48	925.4	638-5660
T. Rowe Price Global Gov.	WI	Int/Hi	N.A.	11.1	8.5	N.A.	25	65	46	N.A.	N.A.	None	1.20	66	55.8	638-5660
T. Rowe Price High-Yield	HYC	Int/Lo	6	21.8	22.3	9.9	69	25	22	62	46	None	0.87	49	1,620.3	638-5660
T. Rowe Price Intl. Bond	WI	Int/Hi	7	20.0	13.1	10.2	42	62	75	60	42	None	1.02	60	726.1	638-5660
T. Rowe Price New Income	IGC	Int/M	3	9.5	9.9	10.1	24	13	22	92	76	None	0.84	48	1,597.7	638-5660
T. Rowe Price S/T Glob. Inc.	WI	Sh/Hi	N.A.	7.8	N.A.	N.A.	19	N.A.	N.A.	N.A.	N.A.	None	1.00	55	84.4	638-5660
T. Rowe Price S/T Bond	IGC	Sh/Hi	1	6.5	7.6	8.2	14	14	10	91	61	None	0.73	42	693.0	638-5660
T. Rowe Price US Intm.	Gov	Sh/Hi	N.A.	7.9	9.6	N.A.	18	70	42	72	N.A.	None	0.80	44	173.9	638-5660
T. Rowe Price US Long-Term	Gov	L/Hi	N.A.	12.9	11.6	N.A.	33	66	48	59	N.A.	None	0.80	44	61.7	638-5660
TNE Adj. Rate US Gov. A	MBS	Sh/Hi	N.A.	4.0	N.A.	N.A.	34	34	N.A.	N.A.	N.A.	3.0	0.60	62	740.0	343-7104
TNE Bond Income Class A	IGC	Int/M	2	12.0	12.4	11.3	33	33	29	85	74	4.5	1.03	102	179.6	343-7104
TNE Global Government Cl. A	WI	N.A.	6	12.6	8.6	8.1	28	65	40	49	71	4.5	2.66	157	19.4	343-7104
TNE Government Securities A	Gov	Int/Hi	6	8.9	10.1	9.7	21	74	42	53	19	4.5	1.20	110	190.8	343-7104
TNE High-Income Class A	HYC	Int/Lo	6	16.5	22.6	10.5	53	31	34	57	63	4.5	1.50	123	30.2	343-7104
TNE Ltd.-Term US Gov. Cl. A	Gov	Int/M	N.A.	6.4	8.6	8.6	14	65	38	81	N.A.	3.0	1.13	92	573.3	343-7104
Templeton Income	WI	Int/Hi	5	10.4	9.4	9.3	24	65	62	48	88	4.5	1.01	107	212.2	237-0738
Thomson Income B	IGC	Int/M	5	7.1	8.8	6.8	16	32	12	58	33	None	1.90	103	251.5	227-7337
Thomson Short-Intm. Gov.	Gov	Sh/Hi	N.A.	2.8	N.A.	N.A.	3	37	N.A.	N.A.	N.A.	None	1.60	82	121.4	227-7337
Thomson US Government B	Gov	Int/Hi	4	7.1	8.4	8.8	16	41	47	58	18	None	1.80	97	522.1	227-7337
Thornburg Limited-Term US	MBS	Int/Hi	1	6.2	8.7	9.1	50	63	50	72	29	2.5	1.01	76	201.3	847-0200
Tower Total Return Bond	IGC	L/M	N.A.	8.2	N.A.	N.A.	19	N.A.	N.A.	N.A.	N.A.	4.5	0.77	N.A.	58.6	999-0124
Tower US Government Income	Gov	Int/Hi	1	7.7	9.0	9.6	18	59	42	72	16	4.5	0.68	82	88.2	999-0124
Transamerica Adj. US A	MBS	Int/Hi	N.A.	4.0	N.A.	N.A.	33	53	N.A.	N.A.	N.A.	3.5	0.50	75	32.7	343-6840
Transamerica Government Sec.	Gov	Int/Hi	5	8.2	10.3	10.2	19	69	50	73	14	4.75	1.44	110	697.3	343-6840
Transamerica Intm. Gov.	Gov	Int/Hi	1	6.8	8.7	9.2	15	72	34	75	11	1.0(d)	0.51	71	4.0	343-6840
Transamerica Invst. Quality	IGC	Int/M	5	9.1	10.9	10.6	23	22	28	87	78	4.75	1.31	114	109.5	343-6840
Transamerica Sp. Gov. Inc.	Gov	Int/Hi	5	7.6	9.0	9.0	17	62	39	65	12	5.0(d)	2.00	125	292.6	343-6840
Transamerica Sp. H/Y Bond	HYC	Int/Lo	6	21.4	22.7	10.4	68	18	29	71	32	5.0(d)	2.24	129	153.8	343-6840
UMB Bond	IGC	N.A.	1	8.4	9.4	9.5	20	26	16	88	71	None	0.83	93	1,590.1	421-0180
US Government Securities	Gov	Int/Hi	1	10.4	10.7	10.7	26	80	40	77	16	4.75	0.87	48	90.5	422-2766
USAA Investment GNMA	MBS	N.A.	N.A.	7.1	N.A.	N.A.	57	47	N.A.	N.A.	N.A.	None	0.35	21	283.3	382-8722
UST Master I/T Mgd. Non-Plan	IGC	Int/Hi	N.A.	8.5	N.A.	N.A.	20	N.A.	N.A.	N.A.	N.A.	4.5	1.05	84	44.6	233-1136
UST Master Mgd. Inc. Non-Plan	IGC	L/Hi	5	12.6	11.6	11.9	35	21	25	91	99	4.5	1.04	102	113.6	233-1136
United Bond	IGC	L/M	5	13.2	13.1	10.6	37	33	31	69	66	5.75	0.64	104	657.5	366-5465
United Government Securities	Gov	L/Hi	4	10.0	11.3	10.5	24	77	51	61	15	4.25	0.71	82	193.5	366-5465
United High-Income	HYC	Int/Lo	7	17.7	23.6	8.1	57	35	36	53	21	5.75	0.75	123	1,044.5	366-5465
United High-Income II	HYC	Int/Lo	6	17.3	21.2	10.3	55	29	23	73	39	5.75	0.81	128	389.5	366-5465
Value Line Adj. Rate US	MBS	Sh/Hi	N.A.	6.1	N.A.	N.A.	49	N.A.	N.A.	N.A.	N.A.	None	0.75	58	44.3	223-0818
Value Line Aggressive Income	HYC	Int/Lo	6	19.0	19.1	10.8	61	10	13	77	60	None	1.15	65	38.9	223-0818
Value Line US Government	Gov	Int/Hi	1	9.8	10.8	10.9	24	70	49	80	17	None	0.60	36	459.6	223-0818
Van Eck S/T World Income C	WI	Sh/Hi	N.A.	(4.5)[28]	N.A.	N.A.	0	N.A.	N.A.	N.A.	N.A.	None	1.16	106	15.0	221-2220
Van Eck World Income	WI	Int/Hi	7	4.9	6.6	9.5	14	41	83	62	99	4.75	1.32	116	264.4	221-2220
Van Kampen High-Yield A	HYC	Int/Lo	7	17.7	23.0	8.5	57	38	31	60	19	4.65	1.42	121	260.8	341-2911
Van Kampen S/T Glob. Inc. A	WI	Sh/M	N.A.	7.3	7.4	N.A.	18	72	38	N.A.	N.A.	3.0	1.18	100	208.7	225-2222
Van Kampen US Government A	MBS	Int/Hi	2	8.0	9.9	10.6	63	49	79	81	73	4.65	0.77	90	3,690.3	225-2222
Vanguard Bond Index	IGC	Int/Hi	2	9.6	10.6	10.8	24	31	21	91	85	None	0.18	61	1,400.8	851-4999
Vanguard F/I GNMA	MBS	Sh/Hi	1	5.8	9.7	10.8	47	56	87	91	85	None	0.31	16	7,328.2	851-4999
Vanguard F/I H/Y Corp.	HYC	Int/Lo	6	18.1	20.3	10.8	58	22	18	72	58	None	0.35	19	2,532.4	851-4999
Vanguard F/I Intm.-Term	Gov	Int/Hi	N.A.	11.4	N.A.	N.A.	28	82	N.A.	N.A.	N.A.	None	0.29	15	998.4	851-4999
Vanguard F/I L/T Corp. Bond	IGC	L/M	5	14.4	14.9	13.2	41	51	36	79	95	None	0.31	18	3,386.8	851-4999
Vanguard F/I Long-Term US	Gov	L/Hi	6	16.7	13.8	12.9	44	79	53	54	39	None	0.29	15	887.5	851-4999
Vanguard F/I S/T Corp.	IGC	Sh/M	1	6.9	9.1	9.6	15	32	15	94	71	None	0.29	15	3,421.4	851-4999
Vanguard F/I S/T Fed.	Gov	Sh/Hi	1	6.9	8.4	9.2	15	69	32	74	15	None	0.29	15	1,923.9	851-4999
Vanguard F/I Short-Term US	Gov	Sh/Hi	N.A.	6.3	N.A.	N.A.	13	74	N.A.	N.A.	N.A.	None	0.29	15	677.2	851-4999
Venture Income (+) Plus	HYC	Int/Lo	7	17.4	20.4	6.8	56	74	0	51	31	4.75	1.81	147	57.9	279-0279
Vista Bond	IGC	Int/Hi	N.A.	10.4	10.9	N.A.	27	31	21	N.A.	N.A.	4.5	0.31	17	61.1	348-4782
Vista Short-Term Bond	IGC	Sh/Hi	N.A.	4.5	6.1	N.A.	6	10	5	N.A.	N.A.	None	0.31	17	70.7	348-4782
Vista US Government Income	Gov	Int/Hi	4	10.3	10.3	10.7	25	67	42	69	26	4.5	0.75	85	92.9	348-4782
WPG Government Securities	Gov	Sh/Hi	1	9.0	10.2	10.7	21	83	39	72	24	None	0.79	44	329.9	223-3332

Notes: (d): Maximum deferred sales charge [28]To Dec. 1; fund since merged

Fund name	Type	Style	Risk level	% compound annual return to Jan. 1, 1994			Annual performance analysis (percentile ranking by type)					Expense analysis			Net assets (millions)	Telephone (800)
				One year	Three years	Five years	1993	1992	1991	1990	1989	% max. sales charge	Annual charges	Five-year total per $1,000		
Warburg Pincus Fixed-Inc.	IGC	Int/M	3	10.2	11.2	9.1	26	27	25	62	57	None	0.75%	$42	$81.2	257-5614
Warburg Pincus Global F/I	WI	Int/M	N.A.	19.1	11.7	N.A.	40	61	61	N.A.	N.A.	None	0.12	25	61.9	257-5614
Warburg Pincus Intm. Mat.	Gov	Int/Hi	2	7.9	9.8	10.0	18	73	43	72	16	None	0.60	33	77.6	257-5614
Wasatch Income	IGC	Sh/Hi	5	4.0	7.4	9.4	4	12	17	100	92	None	0.99	55	3.7	345-7460
Wayne Hummer Income	IGC	Int/M	N.A.	10.6	N.A.	N.A.	28	N.A.	N.A.	N.A.	N.A.	None	N.A.	N.A.	35.1	621-4477
Westcore S/T Gov. Inst.	Gov	Sh/Hi	1	4.4	7.0	8.3	8	63	28	81	10	None	0.62	71	25.3	392-2673
William Blair Income	IGC	Int/Hi	N.A.	7.8	10.4	N.A.	18	31	24	N.A.	N.A.	None	0.79	49	198.9	742-7272
Winthrop Focus Fixed-Income	IGC	N.A.	2	9.6	10.4	10.8	24	31	19	95	85	4.0(d)	0.75	50	40.5	225-8011
Wm. Penn Quality Income	IGC	L/Hi	3	13.0	13.2	11.7	36	39	30	89	66	4.75	0.31	64	25.3	523-8440
Wm. Penn US Gov. Income	Gov	L/Hi	3	11.6	10.8	11.2	29	90	31	73	26	4.75	1.05	103	49.7	523-8440
Working Assets Citizens Inc.	IGC	Int/Hi	N.A.	10.0	N.A.	N.A.	26	N.A.	N.A.	N.A.	N.A.	2.0	1.75	N.A.	16.0	223-7010
Zweig Government Sec. A	Gov	L/Hi	4	10.1	9.6	9.4	25	56	40	55	19	4.75	1.34	121	62.1	444-2706

T A X - E X E M P T S

Fund name	Type	Style	Risk level	One year	Three years	Five years	1993	1992	1991	1990	1989	% max. sales charge	Annual charges	Five-year total per $1,000	Net assets (millions)	Telephone (800)
20th Century T/E Intm.	Muni	Int/M	1	9.1	8.8	7.8	43	55	43	46	26	None	0.85	34	98.4	345-2021
20th Century T/E Long-Term	Muni	L/M	5	12.2	10.6	9.5	69	58	62	43	61	None	0.86	34	70.6	345-2021
AIM Municipal Bond A	Muni	L/M	5	11.7	11.3	9.8	65	69	74	33	61	4.75	0.92	95	296.7	347-1919
AIM T/F Intermediate Shares	Muni	L/M	1	9.0	9.0	8.4	43	60	42	51	47	1.0	0.38	49	99.8	347-1919
Alliance Muni Inc. Natl. A	Muni	L/M	2	13.3	11.9	10.6	78	80	60	61	66	4.25	0.84	89	386.3	227-4618
Alliance Muni Ins. Natl. A	Muni	L/Hi	3	13.1	11.3	10.1	77	65	64	54	62	4.25	0.87	88	185.8	227-4618
American Cap. Muni Bond A	Muni	L/M	3	11.2	10.6	9.6	61	67	61	36	76	4.75	0.90	95	334.7	421-5666
Amer. Cap. T/E H/Y Muni A[1]	Muni	L/Lo	1	10.2	10.0	9.2	52	69	49	43	69	4.75	1.07	103	407.6	421-5666
Amer. Cap. T/E Insured A	Muni	L/Hi	2	9.0	8.8	8.3	42	60	37	46	52	4.75	1.20	110	76.6	421-5666
Babson Tax-Free Income L	Muni	L/Hi	5	12.3	11.0	9.6	70	64	64	46	51	None	1.00	55	34.3	422-2766
Benham Natl. T/F Intm.	Muni	Int/Hi	3	10.1	9.6	8.8	52	54	58	54	45	None	0.72	40	78.2	472-3389
Benham Natl. T/F Long-Term	Muni	L/Hi	6	14.2	12.1	10.5	85	71	71	52	60	None	0.72	40	62.5	472-3389
Bernstein Diversified Muni	Muni	L/Hi	N.A.	8.3	8.3	N.A.	37	50	44	54	N.A.	None	0.69	39	459.6	756-4097[5]
Boston Co. T/F Bond Retail	Muni	L/Hi	4	10.9	10.2	9.3	58	63	58	44	63	None	1.03	42	19.1	225-5267
Bull & Bear Municipal Inc.	Muni	L/M	5	10.6	10.1	8.6	56	46	78	14	52	None	1.61	87	23.0	847-4200
Calvert T/F Res. Long-Term	Muni	L/M	5	11.1	10.3	9.1	60	61	59	26	62	4.75	0.81	89	52.9	368-2748
Calvert T/F Res. Ltd.-Term	Muni	Sh/M	1	4.0	5.2	5.8	2	39	8	49	31	2.0	0.68	59	624.6	368-2748
Cambridge Municipal Income B	Muni	L/M	N.A.	14.9	N.A.	N.A.	92	N.A.	N.A.	N.A.	N.A.	None	1.21	92	51.5	382-0016
Chubb Tax-Exempt	Muni	L/M	4	12.3	10.7	9.8	70	70	49	31	83	5.0	1.00	104	15.6	258-3648
Colonial High-Yield Muni. B	Muni	L/M	N.A.	8.6	N.A.	N.A.	40	N.A.	N.A.	N.A.	N.A.	5.0(d)	2.00	128	120.4	248-2828
Colonial Tax-Exempt A	Muni	L/M	2	10.7	10.2	9.0	57	63	59	49	42	4.75	1.03	103	3,380.2	248-2828
Colonial Tax-Exempt Ins. A	Muni	L/Hi	3	11.0	10.0	9.1	59	57	59	48	55	4.75	1.09	106	243.5	248-2828
Common Sense Muni Bond	Muni	L/M	2	11.2	10.3	9.0	61	65	55	40	47	4.75	1.14	107	95.4	544-5445
Compass Cap. Muni Bond	Muni	L/Hi	N.A.	11.4	9.5	N.A.	63	54	42	59	N.A.	3.75	1.01	78	32.8	451-8371
Composite Tax-Exempt Bond	Muni	L/M	4	12.6	11.0	9.5	72	69	55	52	42	4.0	0.79	87	251.1	543-8072
DG Municipal Income	Muni	N.A.	N.A.	12.7	N.A.	N.A.	74	N.A.	N.A.	N.A.	N.A.	2.0	0.76	N.A.	28.5	748-8500
Dean Witter Sel. Muni Reinv.	Muni	L/M	5	12.0	11.0	9.5	67	68	62	33	58	None	1.12	N.A.	86.6	869-3863
Dean Witter Tax-Exempt Secs.	Muni	L/M	4	10.6	10.8	9.8	56	69	68	41	71	4.0	0.48	66	1,568.5	869-3863
Delaware Tax-Free Insured	Muni	L/Hi	2	8.4	9.1	8.6	38	58	54	44	59	4.75	0.98	93	96.2	523-4640
Delaware Tax-Free USA	Muni	L/M	3	11.3	11.1	9.6	62	74	66	15	70	4.75	0.89	94	767.0	523-4640
Dreyfus Insured Muni Bond	Muni	L/Hi	4	12.5	10.5	9.5	71	59	55	57	50	None	0.94	53	289.6	782-6620
Dreyfus Intermediate Muni	Muni	Int/Hi	2	11.5	10.4	9.4	63	67	53	53	50	None	0.70	39	1,834.6	782-6620
Dreyfus Municipal Bond	Muni	L/M	2	12.6	11.0	9.7	72	64	61	48	58	None	0.69	38	4,497.7	782-6620
Dreyfus Short-Intm. T/E	Muni	Sh/M	1	6.6	7.2	7.0	23	51	26	52	24	None	0.73	42	535.9	782-6620
Eaton Vance Muni Bond	Muni	L/M	4	13.5	12.0	10.7	80	68	76	56	72	4.75	0.76	87	114.0	225-6265
Eaton Vance Natl. L/M T/F	Muni	Int/M	N.A.	8.8	N.A.	N.A.	41	N.A.	N.A.	N.A.	N.A.	3.0(d)	1.50	79	139.7	225-6265
Eaton Vance National Muni	Muni	L/M	4	14.6	12.1	9.6	89	77	59	8	44	6.0(d)	1.77	117	2,131.3	225-6265
Enterprise Tax-Exempt Inc.	Muni	L/Hi	2	10.8	9.9	8.8	57	60	52	40	49	4.75	1.25	113	41.0	432-4320
Evergreen S/I Muni	Muni	Int/M	N.A.	7.2	N.A.	N.A.	28	68	N.A.	N.A.	N.A.	None	0.40	48	66.0	235-0064
Fidelity Advisor High-Income	Muni	L/Lo	1	13.4	12.2	12.0	79	85	63	100	100	4.75	0.95	99	494.6	522-7297
Fidelity Aggressive Tax-Free	Muni	L/M	1	13.2	11.4	10.2	77	70	59	62	59	None	0.65	38	961.8	544-8888
Fidelity High-Yield T/F	Muni	L/M	2	12.7	10.4	10.2	73	65	44	76	80	None	0.56	31	2,196.3	544-8888
Fidelity Insured Tax-Free	Muni	L/Hi	4	13.5	11.0	9.9	79	61	58	57	58	None	0.62	36	466.1	544-8888
Fidelity Ltd.-Term Muni	Muni	L/M	1	11.7	10.4	9.2	65	62	54	56	39	None	0.60	38	1,260.5	544-8888
Fidelity Municipal Bond	Muni	L/M	4	12.8	11.2	10.0	74	69	61	55	59	None	0.49	28	1,289.3	544-8888
Fidelity Spartan Muni Inc.	Muni	L/M	N.A.	13.9	11.7	N.A.	83	65	68	N.A.	N.A.	None	0.36	29	900.0	544-8888
Fidelity Spartan S/I Muni	Muni	Sh/M	1	6.9	7.4	7.0	26	49	31	48	22	None	0.55	36	1,030.9	544-8888
First Investors Insured T/E	Muni	L/Hi	2	9.9	9.4	8.7	50	61	45	43	57	6.25	1.16	128	1,497.1	423-4026
First Prairie T/E Insured	Muni	L/Hi	5	10.8	10.7	10.0	57	72	60	66	65	4.5	0.00[2]	45	10.2	537-4938
First Prairie T/E Intm.	Muni	Int/M	2	10.1	9.7	9.1	52	55	60	64	53	4.5	0.00[2]	45	30.5	537-4938
First Union Ins. T/F B Inv.	Muni	L/Hi	N.A.	13.3	N.A.	N.A.	78	N.A.	N.A.	N.A.	N.A.	4.0	0.49	88	105.6	326-3241
Flag Investors Mgd. Muni A	Muni	L/Hi	N.A.	11.4	9.7	N.A.	63	51	51	N.A.	N.A.	4.5	0.90	94	53.5	767-3524
Flagship All-Amer. T/E A	Muni	L/M	4	14.2	13.1	11.3	86	82	85	40	83	4.2	0.65	90	189.6	227-4648
Flagship Intermediate T/E A	Muni	Int/M	N.A.	13.6	N.A.	N.A.	80	N.A.	N.A.	N.A.	N.A.	4.2	0.39	N.A.	28.7	227-4648
Flagship Ltd.-Term T/E A	Muni	Int/M	1	9.1	9.3	8.5	43	67	42	51	42	2.5	0.70	68	696.5	227-4648
Fortis Tax-Free National	Muni	L/M	4	12.3	11.4	9.7	70	68	71	34	52	4.5	0.92	105	80.8	800-2638
Fortress Muni Income	Muni	L/M	2	11.1	10.0	9.5	60	61	51	50	73	1.0	1.09	69	485.3	245-5051
Forum Taxsaver Bond	Muni	L/M	N.A.	10.5	9.9	N.A.	55	68	44	57	N.A.	3.75	0.60	67	17.9	879-1900[4]
Franklin Fed. I/T T/F Inc.	Muni	N.A.	N.A.	12.8	N.A.	N.A.	74	N.A.	N.A.	N.A.	N.A.	2.25	0.05	N.A.	47.8	342-5236
Franklin Federal T/F Income	Muni	L/M	2	11.3	11.3	9.7	61	73	73	36	54	4.0	0.51	67	6,957.7	342-5236
Franklin H/Y T/F Income	Muni	L/M	2	13.3	11.6	9.9	78	69	65	31	62	4.0	0.52	68	3,201.7	342-5236
Franklin Insured T/F Income	Muni	L/M	2	11.8	10.8	9.8	66	70	55	50	64	4.0	0.53	68	1,769.5	342-5236
GIT Tax-Free High-Yield	Muni	L/Hi	5	11.8	10.1	8.6	66	62	45	34	34	None	1.09	62	42.2	336-3063
Galaxy T/E Bond Retail	Muni	L/Hi	N.A.	11.9	N.A.	N.A.	67	71	N.A.	N.A.	N.A.	None	0.42	N.A.	143.8	628-0414
General Municipal Bond	Muni	L/M	4	13.2	12.6	11.3	77	75	87	65	81	None	0.80	42	1,320.6	782-6620

Notes: (d): Maximum deferred sales charge
[1]Closed to new investors [4]Area code 207 [5]Area code 212

Fund name	Type	Style	Risk level	% compound annual return to Jan. 1, 1994			Annual performance analysis (percentile ranking by type)					Expense analysis			Net assets (millions)	Telephone (800)
				One year	Three years	Five years	1993	1992	1991	1990	1989	% max. sales charge	Annual charges	Five-year total per 1,000		
Great Hall National T/E	Muni	L/Lo	1	11.5	10.9	9.9	63	76	55	48	69	4.5	1.01%	$92	$74.4	934-6674
Hancock Managed T/E B	Muni	L/Hi	5	11.6	10.6	9.5	64	62	61	43	65	4.0(d)	1.23	94	258.3	225-5291
Hancock Tax-Exempt Inc.	Muni	L/M	4	11.5	10.7	9.4	64	64	63	45	54	4.5	1.26	112	543.2	225-5291
IAI Tax-Free	Muni	L/M	N.A.	12.6	N.A.	N.A.	72	N.A.	N.A.	N.A.	N.A.	None	0.95	N.A.	8.3	945-3863
IDEX II Tax-Exempt	Muni	L/M	3	8.6	8.7	8.4	39	50	51	37	71	4.75	1.00	100	30.7	624-4339
IDS High-Yield T/E	Muni	L/M	2	9.7	10.1	9.4	48	66	61	32	80	5.0	0.61	83	6,788.4	328-8300
IDS Insured Tax-Exempt	Muni	L/Hi	4	12.9	11.2	10.0	75	69	58	42	69	5.0	0.65	N.A.	525.2	328-8300
IDS Tax-Exempt Bond	Muni	L/M	5	13.1	10.0	9.6	77	52	43	51	84	5.0	0.64	84	1,329.0	328-8300
ISI Managed Municipal	Muni	L/Hi	N.A.	11.4	9.7	N.A.	63	52	50	N.A.	N.A.	4.45	0.90	93	88.4	955-7175
Invesco Tax-Free L/T Bond	Muni	L/M	5	11.9	11.1	10.4	67	67	67	58	84	None	1.03	57	342.2	525-8085
Jackson Natl. Tax-Exempt	Muni	N.A.	N.A.	12.5	N.A.	N.A.	71	N.A.	N.A.	N.A.	N.A.	4.75	0.90	N.A.	29.8	888-3863
Kemper Municipal Bond	Muni	L/M	5	13.2	11.5	10.5	77	66	69	52	79	4.5	0.48	71	4,071.8	621-1048
Kent Med/Tm T/E Bond Inv.	Muni	N.A.	N.A.	8.3	N.A.	N.A.	37	N.A.	N.A.	N.A.	N.A.	4.0	0.00[2]	N.A.	2.8	633-5368
Keystone Amer. T/F Income A	Muni	L/Hi	2	10.6	10.0	8.8	56	62	55	35	50	4.75	1.31	110	127.8	343-2898
Keystone Tax-Exempt	Muni	L/M	4	10.4	9.6	8.6	54	57	51	33	52	4.0(d)	1.81	101	826.8	343-2898
Keystone Tax-Free[1]	Muni	L/M	4	11.1	9.8	9.0	60	57	50	52	54	4.0(d)	1.67	76	1,556.9	343-2898
Legg Mason T/F I/T Income	Muni	Int/Hi	N.A.	10.2	N.A.	N.A.	52	N.A.	N.A.	N.A.	N.A.	2.0	0.20	37	54.6	822-5544
Lexington Tax-Exempt Bond	Muni	L/Hi	3	10.9	9.1	8.3	59	50	43	51	35	None	1.50	82	14.5	526-0056
Liberty Fin. Ins. Muni	Muni	L/Hi	N.A.	12.5	N.A.	N.A.	71	52	N.A.	N.A.	N.A.	4.5	0.60	N.A.	45.2	872-5426
Liberty Fin. T/F Bond	Muni	L/M	N.A.	11.1	10.4	N.A.	60	68	55	52	N.A.	4.5	0.55	74	270.5	872-5426
Liberty Muni Securities	Muni	L/M	3	10.3	10.4	9.5	53	64	67	40	70	4.5	0.83	89	766.0	245-5051
Loomis Sayles Muni Bond	Muni	L/M	N.A.	11.6	N.A.	N.A.	64	72	N.A.	N.A.	N.A.	None	1.00	55	4.9	633-3330
Lord Abbett T/F Inc. Natl.	Muni	L/Hi	4	12.9	11.4	10.2	75	67	66	59	59	4.75	0.87	91	713.8	874-3733
MFS Muni High-Inc. A[1]	Muni	L/Lo	1	9.7	9.4	8.4	48	61	47	5	72	4.75	1.14	102	808.7	225-2606
MFS Muni Ltd. Maturity A	Muni	Int/M	N.A.	8.0	N.A.	N.A.	35	N.A.	N.A.	N.A.	N.A.	2.5	0.68	N.A.	91.2	225-2606
MFS Muni Bond A	Muni	L/M	5	14.2	12.1	11.0	86	72	70	47	95	4.75	0.58	80	2,188.9	225-2606
MFS Muni Income B	Muni	L/M	3	10.5	9.9	8.5	55	60	56	10	56	5.0(d)	2.11	129	528.9	225-2606
Mackenzie L/T Municipal	Muni	Int/Hi	N.A.	7.6	N.A.	N.A.	31	42	N.A.	N.A.	N.A.	3.0	0.85	82	114.3	456-5111
Mackenzie National Muni	Muni	L/Hi	5	11.6	9.6	8.8	64	52	48	42	56	4.75	1.10	105	41.8	456-5111
MainStay Tax-Free Bond	Muni	L/M	5	10.4	9.9	8.3	54	64	51	25	34	5.0(d)	1.20	91	500.2	522-4202
Managers Short Municipal	Muni	Sh/Hi	1	3.9	4.6	5.3	1	32	0	38	29	None	0.64	33	4.6	835-3879
Merrill Lynch Muni Inc. B	Muni	L/M	4	10.6	9.7	8.4	56	58	51	31	38	2.0(d)	1.16	64	158.1	637-3863
Merrill Lynch Muni Ins. A	Muni	L/Hi	5	13.0	11.4	10.2	76	69	62	57	60	4.0	0.42	64	2,234.0	637-3863
Merrill Lynch Muni Ltd. A	Muni	Int/M	1	4.4	5.8	6.1	5	43	17	44	29	0.75	0.41	30	887.7	637-3863
Merrill Lynch Muni Natl. A	Muni	L/M	4	12.7	11.3	9.8	73	67	67	41	54	4.0	0.55	70	1,379.2	637-3863
MetLife-State St. T/E A	Muni	L/M	5	12.1	11.1	9.5	68	71	60	28	60	4.5	1.20	111	297.6	882-0052
Midwest T/F Intm.-Term	Muni	L/M	1	10.9	9.2	8.2	59	59	34	43	35	1.0	0.99	68	108.9	543-8721
Mutual of Omaha T/F Inc.	Muni	L/Hi	4	13.0	11.4	10.3	76	67	66	61	66	4.5	0.87	93	530.2	225-6292
National Secs. T/E Bonds	Muni	L/M	N.A.	12.0[29]	10.8[29]	9.2[29]	N.A.	66	60	55	59	4.75	0.96	94	112.0	356-5535
Nations Muni Inc. Inv. A	Muni	L/M	N.A.	12.3	N.A.	N.A.	71	N.A.	N.A.	N.A.	N.A.	2.5	0.66	66	30.3	321-7854
Nationwide Tax-Free Inc.	Muni	L/M	4	12.7	11.0	9.8	73	72	50	43	65	5.0(d)	0.98	64	252.0	848-0920
Neuberger/Berman Muni	Muni	Int/Hi	2	9.5	8.5	8.1	47	53	33	54	44	None	0.57	28	104.1	877-9700
Norwest Tax-Free Inc. Inv. A	Muni	L/M	N.A.	9.5	8.7	N.A.	47	56	37	41	N.A.	4.5	0.60	77	31.6	363-3300[5]
Nuveen Ins. Muni Bond	Muni	L/Hi	5	13.5	12.0	10.4	80	74	69	52	59	4.75	0.68	86	713.6	351-4100
Nuveen Municipal Bond	Muni	L/M	2	8.6	9.3	8.4	40	65	49	39	75	4.75	0.66	80	2,597.9	351-4100
Oppenheimer Insured T/E Bond	Muni	L/Hi	4	13.1	11.3	10.2	77	73	56	45	75	4.75	0.95	118	63.7	525-7048
Oppenheimer Intm. T/E Bond	Muni	L/M	3	10.0	10.4	9.7	51	71	60	44	80	3.5	1.16	101	71.9	525-7048
Oppenheimer T/F Bond	Muni	L/M	3	13.5	11.7	10.1	80	73	63	41	58	4.75	0.94	97	606.9	525-7048
Overland Exp. Muni Inc A	Muni	L/Hi	N.A.	13.1	N.A.	N.A.	76	76	N.A.	N.A.	N.A.	3.0	0.09	43	97.6	552-9612
PaineWebber Muni H/I A	Muni	L/M	4	12.2	11.7	10.1	69	74	75	36	61	4.0	0.87	106	84.8	647-1568
PaineWebber Natl. T/F Inc. A	Muni	L/M	4	12.3	10.5	9.4	70	61	53	50	55	4.0	0.88	88	441.3	647-1568
Phoenix Tax-Exempt Bond	Muni	L/M	5	13.6	11.9	10.6	80	81	56	47	76	4.75	0.74	87	63.4	243-4361
Pierpont Tax-Exempt Bond	Muni	Int/Hi	3	8.6	8.7	8.3	40	51	51	56	44	None	0.74	43	474.0	521-5412
Pioneer Municipal Bond	Muni	L/M	4	11.1	10.3	9.4	60	66	54	48	62	4.5	0.85	90	80.9	225-6292
Piper Jaffray Natl. T/E	Muni	L/M	4	14.6	11.7	10.2	89	65	62	59	50	4.0	0.95	90	75.0	866-7778
Premier Muni Bond A	Muni	L/M	3	14.4	12.7	11.1	87	77	80	61	64	4.5	0.74	N.A.	596.2	242-8671
Principal Pres. Insured T/E	Muni	L/Hi	4	13.2	10.3	9.3	77	61	39	44	61	4.5	1.10	104	20.4	826-4600
Principal Pres. Tax-Exempt	Muni	L/Hi	2	14.3	10.9	9.7	86	66	42	46	57	4.5	0.90	93	67.0	826-4600
Princor Tax-Exempt Bond	Muni	L/M	3	12.4	11.4	10.1	71	73	62	37	72	5.0	0.91	102	177.5	451-5447
Prudential Muni H/Y B	Muni	L/M	2	10.9	10.4	9.2	59	63	61	17	75	5.0(d)	1.14	72	1,175.9	225-1852
Prudential Muni Ins. B	Muni	L/Hi	5	11.4	10.3	9.3	63	61	58	44	60	5.0(d)	1.12	72	838.2	225-1852
Prudential Muni Modified B	Muni	L/M	3	10.5	9.5	8.7	55	57	49	45	51	5.0(d)	1.46	100	60.8	225-1852
Prudential National Muni B	Muni	L/M	5	12.1	11.0	9.3	68	65	66	42	35	5.0(d)	1.15	72	870.2	225-1852
Putnam Muni Income A	Muni	L/M	N.A.	12.0	11.9	N.A.	67	87	65	52	N.A.	4.75	1.00	110	855.3	225-1581
Putnam Tax Exempt Inc. A	Muni	L/M	5	13.4	12.2	10.4	79	80	67	32	73	4.75	0.74	93	2,438.5	225-1581
Putnam Tax-Free H/Y B	Muni	L/M	1	12.5	11.6	9.4	72	81	59	11	49	5.0(d)	1.45	99	1,424.1	225-1581
Putnam Tax-Free Ins. B	Muni	L/Hi	5	11.2	9.8	8.9	61	54	53	33	62	5.0(d)	1.74	117	448.9	225-1581
Quest for Value Natl. T/E	Muni	L/M	N.A.	13.0	12.1	N.A.	76	79	70	N.A.	N.A.	4.75	0.12	79	116.5	232-3863
RBB Tax-Free	Muni	L/Hi	4	14.2	12.1	10.2	85	78	60	43	50	4.75	0.18	56	6.6	888-9723
Safeco Muni Bond	Muni	L/M	5	12.8	11.8	10.4	74	67	79	51	65	None	0.53	30	567.6	426-6730
Schwab L/T T/F Bond	Muni	L/Hi	N.A.	13.3	N.A.	N.A.	78	N.A.	N.A.	N.A.	N.A.	None	0.45	N.A.	52.5	526-8600
Scudder H/Y Tax-Free	Muni	L/M	4	13.8	12.7	10.9	83	83	76	43	68	None	1.01	54	316.5	225-2470
Scudder Medium-Term T/F	Muni	Int/Hi	1	10.9	10.7	8.8	59	68	63	47	18	None	0.00[2]	N.A.	1,014.2	225-2470
Scudder Mgd. Muni Bonds	Muni	L/Hi	5	13.3	11.5	10.5	78	69	64	53	78	None	0.64	35	925.9	225-2470
Security Tax-Exempt A	Muni	L/M	4	12.4	10.4	8.3	70	55	59	45	0	4.75	0.82	92	32.5	888-2461
Seligman Tax-Ex. National	Muni	L/Hi	6	14.1	11.1	9.8	85	60	56	40	61	4.75	0.86	93	135.3	221-2783
Sentinel Tax-Free Income	Muni	L/M	N.A.	12.7	11.3	N.A.	73	69	63	N.A.	N.A.	5.0	0.50	99	112.5	282-3863
Sierra National Muni	Muni	L/M	N.A.	15.0	13.4	N.A.	92	77	93	N.A.	N.A.	4.5	0.86	N.A.	411.0	222-5852
Sit Tax-Free Income	Muni	L/M	1	10.4	9.1	8.6	54	59	35	60	46	None	0.80	44	368.3	332-5580
Smith Barney Muni Natl. A	Muni	L/M	3	13.4	11.8	10.4	79	71	69	54	63	4.0	0.53	69	442.6	544-7835

Notes: (d): Maximum deferred sales charge   [1]Closed to new investors
[4]Area code 207 [5]Area code 212

Fund name	Type	Style	Risk level	% compound annual return to Jan. 1, 1994			Annual performance analysis (percentile ranking by type)					Expense analysis			Net assets (millions)	Telephone (800)
				One year	Three years	Five years	1993	1992	1991	1990	1989	% max. sales charge	Annual charges	Five-year total per 1,000		
Smith B. Sh. Ltd. Mat. Muni	Muni	Int/M	N.A.	7.2	N.A.	N.A.	28	58	N.A.	N.A.	N.A.	1.25	0.65%	$58	$94.0	451-2010
Smith B. Shear. Mgd. Muni A	Muni	L/M	5	16.0	13.2	10.9	100	72	84	32	66	4.5	0.73	84	1,867.7	451-2010
Smith B. Shear. T/E Inc. B	Muni	L/M	2	11.7	10.5	9.1	65	67	54	30	54	4.5(d)	1.38	90	1,153.7	451-2010
Starburst Muni Income	Muni	N.A.	N.A.	10.4	N.A.	N.A.	54	55	N.A.	N.A.	N.A.	4.5	0.77	93	42.9	239-1930
SteinRoe High-Yield Muni	Muni	L/M	2	10.4	8.5	8.9	54	41	41	65	81	None	0.73	38	355.8	338-2550
SteinRoe Intm. Muni	Muni	L/Hi	2	10.9	9.7	9.0	58	58	49	63	43	None	0.72	44	261.3	338-2550
SteinRoe Managed Munis	Muni	L/Hi	4	11.0	10.4	9.8	60	63	60	56	71	None	0.64	36	788.9	338-2550
Strong Insured Muni Bond	Muni	L/Hi	N.A.	12.9	N.A.	N.A.	75	100	N.A.	N.A.	N.A.	None	0.40	63	62.6	368-1030
Strong Muni Bond	Muni	L/M	3	11.8	12.5	9.8	66	93	75	24	31	None	0.60	49	425.7	368-1030
Strong S/T Muni Bond	Muni	Sh/M	N.A.	6.8	N.A.	N.A.	25	55	N.A.	N.A.	N.A.	None	0.50	46	208.0	368-1030
SunAmerica T/Ex Ins. A	Muni	L/Hi	1	7.8	7.7	7.6	33	52	27	45	49	4.75	1.01	113	181.3	858-8850
T. Rowe Price T/F High-Yield	Muni	L/M	1	12.9	11.4	10.4	75	73	59	58	70	None	0.81	45	974.4	638-5660
T. Rowe Price T/F Income	Muni	L/M	5	12.7	11.4	9.8	73	72	63	41	55	None	0.61	34	1,517.4	638-5660
T. Rowe Price T/F S/I	Muni	Sh/Hi	1	6.3	6.7	6.6	21	46	22	43	29	None	0.63	35	524.9	638-5660
TNE Tax-Exempt Inc. Cl. A	Muni	L/M	5	12.6	11.1	9.7	73	68	58	29	68	4.5	0.92	95	224.6	343-7104
Tax-Exempt Bond Fund Amer.	Muni	L/M	4	11.7	10.6	9.5	65	69	54	45	58	4.75	0.71	85	1,382.7	421-0180
Thomson Tax-Exempt B	Muni	L/Hi	5	12.4	9.9	9.1	71	57	42	32	71	None	1.90	97	83.1	227-7337
Thornburg Intm. Muni	Muni	Int/M	N.A.	12.4	N.A.	N.A.	71	75	N.A.	N.A.	N.A.	3.5	0.60	N.A.	101.0	847-0200
Thornburg Ltd.-T Muni Natl.	Muni	Int/M	1	8.8	8.4	7.9	41	59	29	49	39	2.5	1.01	83	719.2	847-0200
Transamerica Sp. H/Y T/F	Muni	L/Lo	2	11.6	11.0	9.2	64	64	71	14	55	5.0(d)	2.17	128	113.2	343-6840
Transamerica T/F Bond A	Muni	L/M	N.A.	15.1	14.2	N.A.	93	89	100	N.A.	N.A.	4.75	0.66	92	138.1	343-6840
USAA Tax-Exempt I/T	Muni	Int/M	2	11.5	10.4	9.4	63	65	53	52	56	None	0.42	25	1,638.6	382-8722
USAA T/E Long-Term	Muni	L/M	3	12.5	11.2	10.1	72	66	65	50	72	None	0.39	22	2,021.5	382-8722
USAA T/E Short-Term	Muni	Sh/M	1	5.6	6.4	6.5	15	45	20	41	35	None	0.43	27	953.2	382-8722
UST Mst. T/E I/T Non-Plan	Muni	L/Hi	2	10.8	9.8	9.0	58	65	44	50	51	4.5	0.64	80	315.9	233-1136
UST Mst. L/T T/E Non-Plan	Muni	L/M	5	15.6	12.8	11.4	97	77	69	56	84	4.5	0.86	91	89.1	233-1136
UST Mst. S/T T/E Sec. Non-Pl.	Muni	N.A.	N.A.	5.5	N.A.	N.A.	14	N.A.	N.A.	N.A.	N.A.	4.5	N.A.	78	53.7	233-1136
United Municipal Bond	Muni	L/M	6	14.3	12.4	10.8	86	73	76	38	77	4.25	0.57	73	1,057.7	366-5465
United Muni High-Income	Muni	L/Lo	1	11.5	11.2	10.3	63	78	61	59	74	4.25	0.71	81	334.8	366-5465
United Svcs. Tax-Free	Muni	L/Md	5	11.8	9.6	8.6	66	55	42	43	44	None	0.32	78	20.5	873-8637
Value Line T/E High-Yield	Muni	L/Md	4	11.5	10.5	9.3	63	60	64	50	45	None	0.60	32	294.0	223-0818
Van Kampen Ins. T/F Inc. A	Muni	L/Hi	4	12.3	10.8	9.8	70	73	48	57	58	4.65	0.83	90	1,202.9	225-2222
Van Kampen Muni Inc. A	Muni	L/Md	N.A.	12.2	11.9	N.A.	69	74	81	N.A.	N.A.	4.65	0.86	92	586.4	225-2222
Van Kampen T/F High-Inc. A	Muni	L/Md	1	15.7	7.9	7.3	98	0	28	6	61	4.65	1.08	103	605.5	341-2911
Vanguard Muni High-Yield	Muni	L/Md	5	12.6	12.4	10.8	72	76	88	42	77	None	0.20	13	1,943.8	851-4999
Vanguard Muni Insured Long	Muni	L/Hi	6	13.0	11.5	10.4	76	70	66	57	71	None	0.20	13	2,194.9	851-4999
Vanguard Muni Intermediate	Muni	Int/Hi	3	11.5	10.8	9.9	63	68	63	59	64	None	0.20	13	5,114.3	851-4999
Vanguard Muni Limited-Term	Muni	Sh/Hi	1	6.3	7.4	7.4	20	49	37	57	42	None	0.20	13	1,739.6	851-4999
Vanguard Muni Long-Term	Muni	L/Md	6	13.4	12.1	10.9	79	71	76	54	82	None	0.20	13	1,121.5	851-4999
Vanguard Muni Short-Term	Muni	Sh/Hi	1	3.8	5.2	5.9	0	36	15	50	31	None	0.20	13	1,456.8	851-4999
Venture Muni (+) Plus	Muni	L/Md	1	8.3	9.5	8.4	37	65	59	0	76	5.0(d)	2.43	129	167.7	279-0279
Vista Tax-Free Income	Muni	L/Md	4	15.0	14.0	11.8	92	98	81	59	65	4.5	0.12	45	83.4	348-4782
Voyageur Natl. Ins. T/F	Muni	L/Hi	N.A.	11.6	N.A.	N.A.	64	N.A.	N.A.	N.A.	N.A.	4.75	0.00[2]	48	21.8	553-2143

Mutual Fund Terms That You Should Know

• **Capital gains distribution.** The payout to a mutual fund's shareholders of the profits realized from the sale of stocks or bonds.

• **Dividend.** Distribution of income generated by stocks and bonds in a fund to its holders.

• **Ex-dividend.** Interval between announcement and payment of a fund's next dividend. An investor who buys shares during that interval is not entitled to the dividend. A stock that has gone ex-dividend is marked with an "x" in newspaper listings.

• **Expense ratio.** Amount, as percentage of total investment, that shareholders pay for fund operating expenses and management fees.

• **Load.** Commission or sales charge for buying fund shares through a broker, financial planner or insurance agent. Some funds that sell directly to the public also charge loads. A charge when you sell shares is a back-end load or exit fee.

• **Management fee.** Charge against investor assets for managing the portfolio of a fund. The fee is a fixed percentage of the fund's asset value, typically 1% or less per year, and is disclosed in the fund's prospectus.

• **Net asset value (NAV).** Value of a fund share. It's computed daily by taking the closing prices of all securities in the portfolio, adding the value of all other assets, subtracting the fund's liabilities, and dividing by fund shares outstanding.

• **Prospectus.** Document that a fund supplies to prospective shareholders, identifying its management company, outlining its investment objectives and assessing the risks involved.

• **Turnover rate.** Figure in a fund's prospectus that indicates how actively the fund traded securities in the past 12-month period. The higher the turnover, the greater the fund's brokerage costs.

• **12b-1 fees.** Named after a SEC rule that permits them, these assessments against fund assets are levied by many funds to help pay for promotion expenses. Such fees are usually included in the fund's expense ratio.

THE 1,160 EXTRA FUNDS

GROWTH

Fund name	Type	One year	Three years	Telephone (800)
44 Wall Street Equity	Agg	26.4	23.3	543-2620
AAL Capital Growth	Gro	6.1	13.4	553-6319
AARP Capital Growth	Gro	16.0	19.5	253-2277
AHA Diversified Equity	Gro	10.9	18.4	445-1341
AMCORE Vintage Equity	Gro	5.5	N.A.	438-6375
Advisors A	Agg	4.7	16.8	451-2010
Alliance B	Gro	1.8	N.A.	227-4618
Alliance Growth A	Gro	29.0	32.7	227-4618
Alliance Premier Growth A	Gro	10.0	N.A.	227-4618
Alliance Quasar B	Agg	11.2	14.8	227-4618
AmSouth Equity	Gro	18.4	15.9	451-8379
AmSouth Regional Equity	Gro	9.5	22.7	451-8379
Ambassador Gro. Stock Fid.	Gro	13.9	N.A.	892-4366
Ambassador Sm. Co. Gro.	Agg	13.1	N.A.	892-4366
American Cap. Emer. Gro. B	Agg	23.1	N.A.	421-5666
American Cap. Enterprise B	Gro	10.0	N.A.	421-5666
American Capital Pace B	Gro	9.7	N.A.	421-5666
American Performance Equity	Gro	10.5	10.4	762-7085
Anchor Capital Accumulation	Gro	(1.9)	7.1	748-2400[24]
Arch Emerging Growth Trust	Gro	23.6	N.A.	551-3731
Armstrong Associates	Gro	15.1	13.4	720-9101[6]
Bascom Hill Investors	Gro	2.9	14.7	767-0300
Brandywine Blue	Gro	27.2	14.2	338-1579
Calamos Growth	Gro	4.4	14.2	323-9943
Caldwell & Orkin Agg. Gro.	Agg	14.9	N.A.	237-7073
California Inv. S&P MidCap	Gro	13.5	N.A.	225-8778
Cambridge Capital Growth A	Gro	3.5	N.A.	382-0016
Cambridge Growth A	Gro	4.8	N.A.	382-0016
CharterCapital Blue Chip	Gro	1.9	11.9	257-1842[18]
Colonial Growth Shares B	Gro	9.1	N.A.	248-2828
Colonial Small Stock B	Agg	17.9	N.A.	248-2828
Colonial US Fund for Gro. A	Gro	14.2	N.A.	248-2828
Commonwealth Growth	Gro	3.8[28]	N.A.	359-5964
Conestoga Growth	Gro	8.0	19.1	344-2716
CoreFund Growth Equity A	Gro	5.3	N.A.	355-2673
Cornerstone Growth	Gro	5.8	11.1	728-0670
Crabbe Huson Equity	Gro	26.0	25.6	541-9732
Crabbe Huson Special	Gro	34.5	28.1	541-9732
DFA US 6-10 Small Company	Agg	13.7	N.A.	395-8005[12]
DFA US 9-10 Small Company	Agg	21.0	29.2	395-8005[12]
Elfun Trusts	Gro	9.0	15.2	242-0134
Emerald Equity	Gro	4.3	N.A.	637-6336
Endowments	Gro	9.6	13.7	421-9360[19]
Excel Value	Gro	(7.8)	0.7	783-3444
Exeter Equity	Gro	2.1	N.A.	525-3863
FBL Growth Common Stock	Gro	26.9	17.0	247-4170
FFB Equity	Gro	6.6	11.7	437-8790
FFB Lexicon Cap. App. Eq.	Gro	7.2	N.A.	833-8974
FFB Lexicon Select Value	Gro	13.5	N.A.	833-8974
FMB Diver. Eq. Consumer	Gro	0.7	N.A.	453-4234
FMB Diver. Eq. Inst.	Gro	0.7	N.A.	453-4234
Fairmont	Gro	15.6	22.8	262-9936
Federated Growth	Gro	6.6	16.1	245-5000
Federated Mini-Cap	Agg	15.3	N.A.	245-5000
Fidelity Advisor Inst. Eq. Gro.	Gro	15.7	28.0	522-7297
Financial Horizons Growth	Gro	9.1	16.2	533-5622
First American Special Eq.	Gro	19.0	19.0	637-2548
First American Stock	Gro	15.1	14.6	637-2548
First Eagle Fund of America	Gro	23.9	23.0	451-3623
First Omaha Equity	Gro	10.9	N.A.	662-4203
GAM North America	Gro	(2.1)	9.4	888-4200[5]
Hawthorne Sea	Gro	(1.6)	7.9	272-4548
HighMark Special Gro. Eq.	Gro	13.9	17.1	433-6884
Hilliard Lyons Growth	Gro	4.1	N.A.	444-1854
Hodges	Gro	6.2	N.A.	388-8512
IAA Growth	Gro	6.3	11.6	557-3222[11]
IBM Small Company Index	Agg	11.3	22.1	426-9876
Investors Research	Gro	6.6	11.0	732-1733
Jensen	Gro	(7.3)	N.A.	221-4384
Kemper Inv. Growth Premier	Gro	5.7	N.A.	621-1048
Kemper Inv. Sm. Cap. Eq.	Agg	16.5	N.A.	621-1048
Kemper Inv. Sm. Cap. Init.	Agg	15.5	N.A.	621-1048
Kent Expanded Mkt. Inst.	Agg	17.1	N.A.	343-2138
Kent ValuePlus Equity Inst.	Gro	12.0	N.A.	343-2138
Lazard Special Equity	Agg	10.3	20.8	228-0203
Lutheran Opportunity Growth	Agg	23.9	N.A.	328-4552
MAS Emerging Growth	Agg	18.3	24.7	354-8185
MAS Equity	Gro	6.7	17.2	354-8185
MAS Select Equity	Gro	6.4	18.1	354-8185
MAS Select Value	Gro	12.0	21.1	354-8185
MAS Small Cap. Value	Agg	21.2	34.6	354-8185
MAS Value	Gro	14.3	21.7	354-8185
MSB	Gro	20.7	16.0	551-1920[5]
Merrill Lynch Tomorrow A	Gro	11.4	16.1	637-3863
Merrill Lynch Growth A	Gro	32.4	22.2	637-3863
Merrill Lynch Phoenix B	Gro	28.2	29.7	637-3863
Merrill Lynch Spec. Value B	Agg	13.1	26.2	637-3863
Moran Equity	Gro	3.8	11.5	852-0658
Morgan Keegan So. Cap.	Gro	5.2	18.2	366-7426
Morgan Stanley Inst. Emer.	Agg	0.0	14.1	548-7786
Morgan Stanley Inst. Eq.	Gro	4.3	N.A.	548-7786
NY Life Inst. Growth Eq.	Gro	9.6	24.6	695-2126
Nations Capital Gro. Tr. A	Gro	7.8	N.A.	321-7854
New Century Capital	Gro	13.8	16.2	244-7055
Nicholas-Applegate Gro. Eq. B	Agg	19.2	N.A.	225-1852
ONE Fund Growth	Gro	16.9	N.A.	578-8078
Omni Investment	Gro	16.3	20.2	223-9790
One Group Blue Chip Fid.	Gro	(2.2)	10.3	338-4345
One Group Disc. Value Fid.	Gro	13.2	17.6	338-4345
One Group Large Co. Val. Fid.	Gro	4.7	N.A.	338-4345
One Group Sm. Co. Gro. Fid.	Agg	12.7	20.9	338-4345
PFAMCo Capital App.	Gro	17.7	N.A.	800-7674
PFAMCo Mid Cap. Growth	Gro	15.8	N.A.	800-7674
PFAMCo Small Cap. Growth[1]	Agg	24.4	N.A.	800-7674
PFAMCo Small Cap. Value	Agg	13.7	N.A.	800-7674
PIC Institutional Growth	Gro	0.8	N.A.	331-3186
Pimco Growth Stock	Gro	5.9	14.7	800-0952
PNC Fin. Common Tr. Equity	Gro	6.2[28]	N.A.	585-5148[7]
PNC Growth Equity Inst.	Gro	13.7	12.3	441-7762
PNC Small Cap. Val. Eq. Inst.	Agg	18.7	N.A.	422-6536
PNC Value Equity Inst.	Gro	18.0	N.A.	441-7762
PaineWebber Blue Chip Gro. A	Gro	13.8	N.A.	647-1568
PaineWebber Growth B	Gro	18.3	N.A.	647-1568
Papp America-Abroad	Gro	0.0	N.A.	421-4004
Paragon Gulf South Growth	Gro	7.9	N.A.	777-5143
Paragon Value Growth	Gro	7.5	19.1	777-5143
Parkstone Small Cap. Inst. C	Agg	21.9	27.9	451-8377
Pelican	Gro	20.1	18.8	330-7500[21]
Performance Eq. Cnsmr. Svc.	Gro	11.7	N.A.	737-3676
Performance Equity Inst.	Gro	12.0	N.A.	737-3676
Pillar Equity Agg. Growth A	Agg	13.2	N.A.	932-7782
Pillar Equity Growth A	Gro	6.1	N.A.	932-7782
Pinnacle	Gro	3.3	12.8	633-4080[15]
Progressive Aggressive Gro.	Agg	20.3	3.5	275-2382
Progressive Value	Gro	21.9	0.5	275-2382
Prudential Equity A	Gro	22.1	20.0	225-1852
Prudential Growth Opp. A	Agg	19.8	26.7	225-1852
Prudential Inst. Gro. Stock	Gro	12.9	N.A.	824-7513
Prudential Multi-Sector A	Gro	23.2	17.0	225-1852
Putnam Voyager B	Agg	17.6	N.A.	225-1581
Quantitative Boston Num. Ord.	Agg	28.9	N.A.	331-1244
RSI Ret. Tr. Emer. Gro.	Agg	21.0	29.1	772-3615
Rainbow	Gro	(4.6)	8.6	983-2980[5]
Regis Sterling Equity	Gro	9.6	N.A.	638-7983
Rembrandt Growth Trust	Gro	5.0	N.A.	443-4725
Rembrandt Small Cap. Trust	Agg	2.8	N.A.	443-4725
Rembrandt Value Trust	Gro	6.7	N.A.	443-4725
Reynolds Blue Chip Growth	Gro	(5.2)	8.8	338-1579
Reynolds Opportunity	Gro	0.1	N.A.	338-1579
Riverside Capital Equity	Gro	16.9	N.A.	874-8376
SEI Inst. Capital App.A	Gro	9.2	16.7	342-5734
SEI Inst. Capital Growth	Gro	13.1	25.3	342-5734
SEI Inst. Small. Cap. Gro. A	Agg	13.3	N.A.	342-5734
STI Classic Cap. Gro. Trust	Gro	9.9	N.A.	428-6970
Sagamore Growth	Gro	3.5	N.A.	321-7442
Schafer Value	Gro	24.0	27.5	343-0481
Schroder US Equity	Gro	12.6	21.2	344-8332
Seafirst Blue Chip	Gro	13.4	13.5	323-9919
Shawmut Gro. Equity Trust	Gro	5.4	N.A.	742-9688
Shawmut Small Cap. Eq. Tr.	Agg	7.8	N.A.	742-9688

Notes: [1]Closed to new investors [2]Manager absorbing costs [5]Area code 212 [6]Area code 214 [7]Area code 215 [11]Area code 309 [12]Area code 310 [15]Area code 317 [18]Area code 414 [19]Area code 415 [21]Area code 617 [24]Area code 802 [28]To Dec. 1; fund since merged

Fund name	Type	% compound annual return to Jan. 1, 1994 One year	Three years	Telephone (800)
Smith Barney Agg. Gro. B	Agg	20.2	N.A.	451-2010
Smith Barney App. B	Gro	7.4	N.A.	451-2010
Smith Barney Val. A	Gro	19.8	21.8	451-2010
Smith Barney Sm. Cap. B	Agg	(0.6)[30]	N.A.	451-2010
Society Erngs. Momentum Eq.	Gro	(3.3)	6.5	362-5365
Society OH Regional Equity	Gro	16.6	27.1	362-5365
Society Relative Value Eq.	Gro	10.1	14.3	362-5365
Southeastern Asset Sm.-Cap.	Agg	19.8	17.4	445-9469
Southeastern Asset Value	Gro	22.2	27.0	445-9469
Special Portfolios Stock	Gro	10.2	23.8	800-2638
State Bond Common Stock	Gro	1.8	11.0	333-3952
State Bond Progress	Gro	1.9	14.4	333-3952
State Farm Growth	Gro	0.6	13.4	766-2029[11]
State St. Research Growth C	Gro	8.9	13.0	882-0052
Thomson Growth A	Gro	10.1	17.4	227-7337
Thomson Opportunity A[1]	Agg	37.1	44.2	227-7337
Thomson Target A	Gro	25.5	N.A.	227-7337
Transamer. Sp. Emer. Gro. A	Agg	12.8	N.A.	343-6840
Universal Capital Growth	Gro	8.4	N.A.	932-3000[22]
WPG Growth	Agg	14.9	24.2	223-3332
Wall Street	Gro	13.2	23.4	443-4693
Westwood Eq. Institutional	Gro	17.2	14.6	253-4510
Woodward Gro./Value Retail	Gro	13.8	N.A.	688-3350
Woodward Intrinsic Val. Rtl.	Gro	14.9	N.A.	688-3350
Woodward Opp. Retail	Agg	24.2	N.A.	688-3350
Wright Junior Blue Chip Eq.	Agg	7.9	15.2	232-0013
Zweig Appreciation B	Agg	13.8	N.A.	444-2706
Zweig Priority Selection B	Gro	12.7	N.A.	444-2706
Zweig Strategy B	Gro	14.2	N.A.	444-2706

TOTAL RETURN

Fund name	Type	One year	Three years	Telephone (800)
AARP Growth & Income	G&I	15.7	16.9	253-2277
AHA Balanced	ETR	11.6	14.6	445-1341
Alliance Balanced A	ETR	11.1	15.2	227-4618
Alliance Balanced Shares B	ETR	9.0	N.A.	227-4618
Alliance Growth & Income B	G&I	9.2	N.A.	227-4618
AmSouth Balanced	ETR	14.4	N.A.	451-8379
Ambassador Ind. Stock Fid.	G&I	9.1	N.A.	892-4366
American AAdvantage Bal.	ETR	14.8	15.1	967-3509[27]
American AAdvantage Equity	G&I	16.1	18.1	967-3509[27]
American Cap. Comstock B	G&I	6.5	N.A.	421-5666
American Cap. Equity-Inc. B	ETR	14.9	N.A.	421-5666
American Cap. Harbor B	ITR	12.7	N.A.	421-5666
Atlas Growth & Income	G&I	10.4	15.6	933-2852
Avondale Total Return	ETR	7.2	10.2	761-3777[27]
BB&T Growth & Inc. Stock	G&I	9.4	N.A.	228-1872
BT Inst. Equity 500 Ind.	G&I	9.8	N.A.	545-1074
Bailard Biehl Kaiser Diver.	ETR	21.6	13.8	882-8383
Bascom Hill Balanced	ETR	4.3	12.2	767-0300
Bridges Investment	G&I	6.2	11.3	397-4700[16]
Calamos Small/Mid Cap. Conv.	ITR	15.2	21.6	323-9943
Calamos Strategic Income	ITR	12.1	12.8	323-9943
Caldwell	ETR	10.9	14.5	338-9477
California Inv. S& P 500	G&I	9.7	N.A.	225-8778
Capitol Equity A	G&I	6.5	13.5	342-5734
Colonial B	G&I	13.8	N.A.	248-2828
Concorde Value	G&I	10.5	17.3	387-8258[6]
CoreFund Balanced A	ETR	8.9	N.A.	355-2673
CoreFund Value Equity A	G&I	11.5	17.7	355-2673
Crabbe Huson Asset Alloc.	ETR	18.2	17.2	541-9732
DFA US Large Company	G&I	9.6	15.3	395-8005[12]
Elfun Diversified	ETR	8.9	11.9	242-0134
Elite Growth & Income	G&I	11.9	15.7	423-1068
FBL Blue Chip	G&I	11.9	14.0	247-4170
FBL Managed	ETR	18.9	14.1	247-4170
FBP Contrarian Balanced	ETR	9.3	16.9	525-3863
Federated Max-Cap	G&I	9.5	15.2	245-5000
Federated Mid-Cap	G&I	5.8	N.A.	245-5000
Federated Stock	G&I	12.5	17.6	245-5000
Fidelity Advisor Inst. Eq. Inc.	ETR	18.8	21.0	522-7297
Fidelity US Equity Index	G&I	9.8	15.3	544-8888
Fiduciary Total Return	G&I	11.1	16.8	338-1579
First Priority Equity Trust	G&I	2.4	N.A.	433-2829
General Elec. S&S Program	G&I	11.5	15.9	242-0134
Geo. Putnam of Boston B	ETR	10.1	N.A.	225-1581
Gintel ERISA	G&I	5.4	11.1	243-5808
Golden Rainbow	ETR	13.0	N.A.	227-4648
Hancock Sovereign Bal. A	ETR	11.4	N.A.	225-5291
HighMark Income-Equity	ETR	12.8	17.2	433-6884

Fund name	Type	% compound annual return to Jan. 1, 1994 One year	Three years	Telephone (800)
IBM Large Company Index	G&I	9.5	14.9	426-9876
Invesco Total Return	ETR	10.4	14.9	525-8085
Invesco Value Equity	G&I	10.4	16.3	525-8085
Kemper Inv. T/R Premier	ETR	9.3	N.A.	621-1048
Kent Index Equity Inst.	G&I	9.7	N.A.	343-2138
Lutheran Brotherhood	G&I	8.7	15.1	328-4552
MAS Balanced	ETR	10.4	N.A.	354-8185
Mariner Total Return Equity	G&I	11.2	16.5	634-2536
Maxus Equity	G&I	24.5	24.4	292-3434[8]
Maxus Income	ITR	8.7	11.2	292-3434[8]
Merrill Lynch Balanced A	ETR	15.9	15.1	637-3863
Merrill Lynch Basic Value B	G&I	20.9	18.5	637-3863
Merrill Lynch Capital B	G&I	12.5	13.2	637-3863
Merrill Lynch Strat. Div. A	ETR	8.7	11.2	637-3863
Morgan Stanley Inst. Bal.	ETR	12.1	12.5	548-7786
Morgan Stanley Inst. Val. Eq.	G&I	15.1	16.2	548-7786
Muhlenkamp	G&I	17.3	25.9	860-3863
N.Y. Life Inst. Indexed Eq.	G&I	9.4	15.0	695-2126
N.Y. Life Inst. Multi-Asset	ETR	8.8	11.2	695-2126
N.Y. Life Inst. Value Eq.	G&I	14.6	23.6	695-2126
National Income & Growth B	ETR	13.8	N.A.	356-5535
Nations Bal. Assets Tr. A	ETR	9.9	N.A.	321-7854
Nations Equity Inc. Trust A	ETR	12.7	N.A.	321-7854
New Century I	ITR	15.3	13.4	244-7055
ONE Income & Growth	ETR	16.8	N.A.	578-8078
Old Dominion Investors'	ETR	11.3	14.4	539-2396[25]
One Group Equity Index Fid.	G&I	9.1	N.A.	338-4345
One Group Inc. Equity Fid.	ETR	11.4	13.7	338-4345
Oppenheimer Strat. Inc. B	ITR	6.7	N.A.	525-7048
PFAMCo Balanced	ETR	5.7	N.A.	800-7674
PFAMCo Diversified Low P/E	G&I	16.4	N.A.	800-7674
PFAMCo Enhanced Equity	G&I	3.8	N.A.	800-7674
PFAMCo Equity-Income	ETR	8.5	N.A.	800-7674
PNC Balanced Investor	ETR	11.7	15.2	441-7762
PNC Fin. Common Tr. Asset	ETR	7.7[28]	N.A.	585-5148[7]
PNC Index Equity Inst.	G&I	9.5	N.A.	422-6538
PaineWebber Asset Alloc. A	ETR	15.7	N.A.	647-1568
PaineWebber Div. Gro. B	G&I	(3.3)	N.A.	647-1568
PaineWebber Div. Gro. D	G&I	(3.3)	N.A.	647-1568
Paragon Value Equity-Inc.	G&I	11.0	16.4	777-5143
Parkstone Balanced Inst. C	ETR	11.4	N.A.	451-8377
Parkstone Equity Inst. C	G&I	13.0	18.5	451-8377
Parkstone H/I Eq. Inst. C	ETR	12.7	15.5	451-8377
Payson Balanced	ETR	16.0	N.A.	879-0009[4]
Pillar Balanced Growth A	ETR	7.9	N.A.	932-7782
Pillar Equity-Income A	G&I	10.3	N.A.	932-7782
Prudential Equity-Income A	ETR	21.4	18.9	225-1852
Prudential Flex. Conserv. A	ETR	14.7	14.7	225-1852
Prudential Flex. Strategy A	ETR	13.1	14.3	225-1852
Prudential IncomeVertible A	ITR	12.8	13.8	225-1852
Prudential Inst. Balanced	ETR	15.8	N.A.	824-7513
Prudential Inst. Stock Ind.	G&I	9.2	N.A.	824-7513
Putnam Fund for Gro./Inc. B	G&I	13.5	N.A.	225-1581
Quantitative Boston Gro. A	G&I	11.5	N.A.	331-1244
RSI Ret. Tr. Core Equity	G&I	10.3	12.5	772-3615
RSI Retire. Tr. Value Equity	G&I	8.1	13.4	772-3615
Regis Sterling Balanced	ETR	9.9	N.A.	638-7983
Rembrandt Balanced Trust	ETR	7.0	N.A.	443-4725
Riverfront Income Equity	ETR	12.1	N.A.	424-2295
Rochester Tax-Managed	G&I	5.7	14.2	383-1300[23]
SEI Index S&P 500 Index	G&I	9.8	15.3	342-5734
SEI Inst. Balanced A	ETR	8.0	12.4	342-5734
SEI Inst. Equity-Income A	ETR	13.2	17.6	342-5734
SEI Inst. Value A	G&I	2.5	11.7	342-5734
Sagamore Total Return	ETR	8.4	N.A.	321-7442
Seafirst Asset Allocation	ETR	10.2	11.2	323-9919
Shawmut G&I. Eq. Tr.	G&I	9.6	N.A.	742-9688
Signet Sel. Val. Eq. Trust	G&I	1.3	9.9	771-7131[25]
Smith Barney G&I A	G&I	8.5	N.A.	451-2010
Smith Barney Prem. T/R A	ETR	11.8	N.A.	451-2010
Smith Breeden Mkt. Tracking	G&I	13.2	N.A.	221-3138
Star Relative Value	G&I	13.7	N.A.	677-3863
State Bond Diversified	G&I	9.6	13.4	333-3952
State Farm Balanced	ETR	3.3	14.9	766-2029[11]
State Street Investment C	G&I	10.2	14.5	882-0052
Stock & Bond A	ETR	10.5	12.0	245-5000
Thomson Equity-Income A	ETR	22.1	N.A.	227-7337
Transamerica G&I B	G&I	8.7	N.A.	343-6840
Vanguard Institutional Index	G&I	10.0	15.5	345-1172
Vista Equity Income	ETR	(2.1)[30]	N.A.	648-4782

Fund name	Type	% compound annual return to Jan. 1, 1994 One year	Three years	Telephone (800)
Westcore Bal. Inv. Inst.	ETR	6.0	N.A.	392-2673
Westwood Bal. Institutional	ETR	16.8	N.A.	253-4510
Wright Quality Core Equities	G&I	1.0	14.9	232-0013
Wright Sel. Blue Chip Eq.	G&I	2.1	13.3	232-0013

SPECIALTY

Fund name	Type	One year	Three years	Telephone (800)
Cohen & Steers Realty Shrs.	Spec	18.8	N.A.	437-9912
Colonial Natural Res. B	Spec	32.8	N.A.	248-2828
Colonial Utilities B	Spec	8.5	N.A.	248-2828
Excel Midas Gold Shares	Spec	98.8	22.6	783-3444
Global Utility B	Spec	22.0	N.A.	225-1852
Hancock Free. Reg. Bank A	Spec	21.1	N.A.	225-5291
Merrill Lynch Global Util. A	Spec	24.1	15.8	637-3863
Merrill Lynch Healthcare B	Spec	(3.5)	12.3	637-3863
Merrill Lynch Nat. Res. A	Spec	19.0	5.9	637-3863
Merrill Lynch Technology B	Spec	20.9	N.A.	637-3863
New Alternatives	Spec	2.9	9.5	466-0808[20]
PaineWebber Glo. Energy A	Spec	15.9	N.A.	647-1568
PaineWebber Reg. Fin. B	Spec	9.6	N.A.	647-1568
Progressive Environmental	Spec	10.2	1.7	275-2382
Prudential Utility A	Spec	16.3	15.3	225-1852
Putnam Util. G&I B	Spec	13.3	N.A.	225-1581
SIFE Trust	Spec	9.3	28.3	524-7433
Smith Barney P.M./Minerals B	Spec	63.9	N.A.	451-2010
Smith Barney Tele. Gro. B	Spec	34.4	N.A.	573-9410[21]
Smith Barney Shear Util. A	Spec	12.1	N.A.	451-2010
Thomson P.M./Nat. Res. A	Spec	90.9	N.A.	227-7337
United Services Glo. Res.	Spec	18.5	6.6	873-8637

INTERNATIONAL

Fund name	Type	One year	Three years	Telephone (800)
Alliance Global Small Cap B	Intl	19.1	11.9	227-4618
Alliance International B	Intl	22.2	6.7	227-4618
Alliance New Europe B	Reg	33.7	N.A.	227-4618
Ambassador Intl. Stock Fid.	Intl	32.5	N.A.	892-4366
American AAdvantage Intl.	Intl	42.8	N.A.	967-3509[27]
American Cap. Glo. Equity B	Intl	19.5	N.A.	421-5666
Brinson Global	Intl	11.1	N.A.	448-2430
Capstone Nikko Japan	Reg	25.3	(3.9)	262-6631
Colonial Global Equity A	Intl	33.9	N.A.	248-2828
CoreFund Intl. Growth A	Intl	37.7	14.0	355-2673
DFA Continental Small Co.	Reg	25.3	(1.3)	395-8005[12]
DFA Japanese Small Co.	Reg	14.2	(3.3)	395-8005[12]
DFA Large Cap. Intl.	Intl	25.8	N.A.	395-8005[12]
DFA Pacific Rim Small Co.	Reg	92.6	N.A.	395-8005[12]
DFA United Kingdom Sm. Co.	Reg	30.1	8.9	395-8005[12]
Eaton Vance Greater China	Reg	80.7	N.A.	225-6265
Elfun Global	Intl	31.9	17.1	242-0134
G.T. Global G&I B	Intl	26.8	N.A.	824-1580
GAM Europe	Reg	22.6	4.9	888-4200[5]
GAM Global	Intl	74.7	22.7	888-4200[5]
GAM International	Intl	80.0	28.9	888-4200[5]
GAM Pacific Basin	Reg	51.0	20.6	888-4200[5]
Galaxy Intl. Eq. Rtl.	Intl	32.4	N.A.	628-0413
International Equity	Intl	45.7	13.5	344-8332
Kent Intl. Equity Inst.	Intl	30.8	N.A.	343-2138
MAS Intl. Equity	Intl	42.7	18.6	354-8185
Mariner European Eq. Index	Reg	24.2	N.A.	634-2536
Mariner North America	Intl	28.4	N.A.	634-2536
Merrill Lynch Consult. Intl.	Intl	21.9	N.A.	637-3863
Merrill Lynch Dragon A[1]	Reg	87.2	N.A.	637-3863
Merrill Lynch EuroFund A	Reg	31.9	13.2	637-3863
Merrill Lynch Glo. Alloc. A	Intl	20.9	20.4	637-3863
Merrill Lynch Global A	Intl	24.1	14.9	637-3863
Merrill Lynch Glo. Conv. A	Intl	14.7	14.3	637-3863
Merrill Lynch Latin Amer. A	Intl	64.3	N.A.	637-3863
Merrill Lynch Pacific B	Reg	33.0	12.0	637-3863
Morgan Stanley Glo. Eq. B	Intl	21.1	N.A.	282-4404
Morgan Stanley Inst. Activ.	Intl	30.7	N.A.	548-7786
Morgan Stanley Inst. Asian	Reg	105.7	N.A.	548-7786
Morgan Stanley Inst. Emer.	Intl	85.8	N.A.	548-7786
Morgan Stanley Inst. Intl.[1]	Intl	46.9	15.8	548-7786
NY Life Inst. EAFE Index	Intl	29.0	7.6	695-2126
Nations Intl. Equity Inv. B	Intl	25.8	N.A.	321-7854
PFAMCo International Equity	Intl	30.6	6.8	800-7674
PNC International Eq. Inst.	Intl	36.9	N.A.	441-7762
PaineWebber Atlas Global B	Intl	41.8	N.A.	647-1568
PaineWebber Europe Gro. B	Reg	31.6	N.A.	647-1568
PaineWebber Glo. G&I B	Intl	34.1	N.A.	647-1568

Notes: [1]Closed to new investors Area codes: [4]207; [5]212; [6]214; [7]215; [8]216; [11]309; [12]310; [16]402; [20]516; [21]617; [22]708; [23]716; [25]804; [27]817
[28]To Dec. 1; fund since merged [30]Three months to Dec.1 [31]1993 to Nov. 1; fund since merged

Fund Name	Type	% compound annual return to Jan. 1, 1994 One year	Three years	Telephone (800)
Parkstone Intl. Dis. Inst. C	Intl	33.9	N.A.	451-8377
Parkstone Intl. Dis. Inv. A	Intl	(2.1)[30]	N.A.	451-8377
Prudential Global A	Intl	48.8	17.2	225-1852
Prudential Global Genesis A	Intl	58.3	23.0	225-1852
Prudential Inst. Intl. Stock	Intl	37.6	N.A.	824-7513
Prudential Pacific Growth A	Reg	66.5	N.A.	225-1852
Putnam Global Growth B	Intl	30.8	N.A.	225-1581
Quantitative Boston For. Ord.	Intl	32.5	8.0	331-1244
RSI Ret. Trust Intl. Equity	Intl	30.4	10.5	772-3615
Rembrandt Intl. Equity Tr.	Intl	26.3	N.A.	443-4725
SEI International	Intl	22.8	9.5	342-5734
Smith Barney Glo. Opp. B	Intl	17.1	N.A.	451-2010
Society Intl. Growth	Intl	35.9	11.8	362-5365
Thomson International A	Intl	34.4	N.A.	227-7337
Warburg Pincus Intl. Eq.	Intl	52.4	N.A.	257-5614
Wright Intl. Blue Chip Eq.	Intl	28.2	13.0	232-0013

TAXABLE BONDS

Fund Name	Type	One year	Three years	Telephone (800)
AAL Bond	IGC	8.8	10.4	553-6319
AAL US Gov. Zero Cpn. 2001	Gov	1.2	9.4	553-6319
AAL US Gov. Zero Cpn. 2006	Gov	7.6	12.1	553-6319
AARP GNMA & US Treasury	Gov	6.0	8.9	253-2277
AARP High-Quality Bond	IGC	11.0	10.8	253-2277
AHA Full Mat. Fixed-Income	IGC	11.6	11.4	445-1341
AHA Ltd. Mat. Fixed-Income	IGC	5.3	7.5	445-1341
AMCORE Vintage F/I	IGC	9.0	N.A.	438-6375
Accessor Interm. F/I	IGC	9.5	N.A.	759-3504
Accessor Mortgage Sec.	MBS	7.3	N.A.	759-3504
Accessor Short-Intm. F/I	IGC	5.6	N.A.	759-3504
Alliance Bond US Gov. B	Gov	9.0	N.A.	227-4618
Alliance Mortgage Strat. A	MBS	6.4	N.A.	227-4618
Alliance Mort. Sec. Inc. B	MBS	9.4	N.A.	227-4618
Alliance Multi-Mkt. Strat. A	WI	10.9	N.A.	227-4618
Alliance N. Am. Gov. Inc. A	WI	18.6	N.A.	227-4618
Alliance S/T Multi-Market B	WI	7.0	5.0	227-4618
AmSouth Bond	IGC	9.9	10.8	451-8382
AmSouth Limited Maturity	IGC	7.2	8.4	451-8382
Ambassador Bond Fiduciary	IGC	11.2	N.A.	892-4366
Ambassador Intm. Bond Fid.	IGC	8.1	N.A.	892-4366
Amer. AAdvantage Ltd.-Term	IGC	6.9	8.6	967-3509[27]
American Cap. Corp. Bond B	IGC	10.8	N.A.	421-5666
American Cap. Fed.Mort. B[1]	MBS	2.3	N.A.	421-5666
American Cap. Global Gov. A	WI	15.2	N.A.	421-5666
American Cap. Gov. B	Gov	7.3	N.A.	421-5666
American Cap. H/Y Inv. B	HYC	18.2	N.A.	421-5666
American Cap. US Income A	Gov	6.6	N.A.	421-5666
American Performance Bond	IGC	10.4	10.6	762-7085
American Perf. Intm. Bond	IGC	8.7	9.5	762-7085
Atlas US Gov. & Mortgage	MBS	7.6	10.3	933-2852
BB&T Intm. US Gov. Bond	Gov	10.0	N.A.	228-1872
BB&T S/I US Gov. Income	Gov	6.8	N.A.	228-1872
BFM Inst. Core Fixed Income	IGC	4.6	N.A.	754-5560[5]
BFM Inst. Short Duration	IGC	5.7	N.A.	754-5560[5]
Bond Port. for Endowments	IGC	12.2	13.9	421-9360[19]
CUFUND Adjustable-Rate	MBS	4.2	N.A.	538-9683
CUFUND Short-Term Mat.	MBS	4.5	N.A.	538-9683
California Inv. US Gov.	Gov	15.8	13.7	225-8778
Cambridge Gov. Inc. A	Gov	4.6	N.A.	382-0016
Capitol Fixed-Income A	IGC	11.3	10.4	342-5734
Colonial Federal Sec. B	Gov	11.3	N.A.	248-2828
Colonial High-Yield Sec. B	HYC	18.8	N.A.	248-2828
Colonial Income B	IGC	11.2	N.A.	248-2828
Colonial Strategic Income B	HYC	14.1	N.A.	248-2828
Colonial US Government B	Gov	4.9	N.A.	248-2828
Conestoga Fixed-Income	IGC	8.7	10.2	344-2716
Conestoga Limited Maturity	IGC	6.5	8.8	344-2716
CoreFund Intm. Bond A	IGC	6.4	N.A.	355-2673
Crabbe Huson Income	IGC	3.7	8.6	541-9732
Crabbe Huson US Gov. Inc.	Gov	4.9	7.8	541-9732
DFA Five-Year Government	Gov	8.3	10.0	395-8005[12]
DFA Global Fixed-Income	WI	11.6	10.2	395-8005[12]
DFA Intm. Gov. Fixed-Income	Gov	11.6	12.0	395-8005[12]
DFA One-Year Fixed-Income	IGC	4.4	6.1	395-8005[12]
Elfun Income	IGC	9.7	10.8	242-0134
Elite Income	IGC	9.2	8.5	423-1068
Emerald US Government Sec.	Gov	9.1	N.A.	637-6336
Evergreen US Gov. Sec.	Gov	(1.8)[30]	N.A.	235-0064
FBL High-Grade Bond	IGC	7.7	10.2	247-4170
FBL High-Yield Bond	HYC	13.4	15.8	247-4170

Fund Name	Type	% compound annual return to Jan. 1, 1994 One year	Three years	Telephone (800)
FFB Lexicon Fixed-Income	IGC	11.4	N.A.	833-8974
FFB Lexicon Intm.-Term Gov.	Gov	7.4	N.A.	833-8974
FFTW US Short-Term F/I	IGC	3.1	4.6	762-4848
FFTW Worldwide F/I Hedged	WI	12.9	N.A.	762-4848
FFTW Worldwide Fixed-Inc.	WI	15.9	N.A.	762-4848
FMB Intm. Gov. Consumer	Gov	8.7	N.A.	453-4234
FMB Intermediate Gov. Inst.	Gov	8.7	N.A.	453-4234
Federated ARMs Inst. Svc.	MBS	4.0	N.A.	245-5000
Federated GNMA Inst. Svc.	MBS	6.3	N.A.	245-5000
Federated High-Yield	HYC	17.4	27.2	245-5000
Federated Inc. Inst. Svc.	MBS	5.7	N.A.	245-5000
Federated Intm. Inst. Svc.	Gov	6.8	N.A.	245-5000
Federated S/I Gov. Inst. Svc	Gov	4.2	N.A.	245-5000
Federated S/T Inc. Inst. Svc.	IGC	5.2	N.A.	245-5000
Federated S/T Income Inst.	IGC	5.5	8.4	245-5000
Fidel. Adv. Inst. Ltd./T Bond	IGC	12.5	11.5	522-7297
Fidelity Institutional S/I	Gov	5.9	8.3	843-3001
Fidelity US Bond Index	IGC	10.2	11.5	843-3001
Financial Horizons Gov. Bond	Gov	9.0	11.0	533-5622
First American Fixed-Income	IGC	9.7	10.3	637-2548
First American Gov. Bond	Gov	5.8	7.2	637-2548
First Omaha Fixed-Income	IGC	11.1	N.A.	662-4203
First Omaha Short/Intm. F/I	IGC	6.4	N.A.	662-4203
First Priority F/I Trust	IGC	8.7	N.A.	433-2829
Franklin Inst. Adj. Rate Sec.	MBS	4.4	N.A.	342-5236
Franklin Inst. Adj. US Gov.	MBS	1.9	N.A.	321-8563
Franklin T/A Intl. Bond	WI	12.6	7.1	342-5236
G.T. Global Gov. Income B	WI	24.7	N.A.	824-1580
G.T. Global High-Income B	WI	50.6	N.A.	824-1580
G.T. Global Strat. Inc. B	WI	43.1	N.A.	824-1580
General Electric S&S L/T	IGC	9.8	10.8	242-0134
Goldman Sachs A/R Gov.	MBS	3.8	N.A.	621-2550
Goldman Sachs S/T Gov.	Gov	5.0	7.0	621-2550
Hancock Sovereign USA	Gov	9.4	N.A.	225-5291
Hawthorne Bond	IGC	8.8	N.A.	272-4548
HighMark Bond	IGC	7.5	9.4	433-6884
IBM US Treasury Index	Gov	10.2	N.A.	426-9876
Investors Prf. Fund Income	MBS	4.1	8.2	543-8072
Jamestown Bond	IGC	8.9	9.5	525-3863
Kemper Inv. Diver. Inc. Prem.	HYC	21.1	N.A.	621-1048
Kemper Inv. Gov. Premier	Gov	5.6	N.A.	621-1048
Kemper Inv. H/Y Premier	HYC	20.1	N.A.	621-1048
Kemper Inv. S/I Gov. Premier	Gov	5.4	N.A.	621-1048
Kemper Inv. S/T Global Prem.	WI	1.6	N.A.	621-1048
Kent Fixed-Income Inst.	IGC	8.4	N.A.	343-2138
Kent Limited Maturity Inst.	IGC	3.4	N.A.	343-2138
Keystone Inst. Adj. Rate	MBS	5.3	N.A.	343-2898
Lutheran Brotherhood H/Y	HYC	20.9	25.5	328-4552
Lutheran Brotherhood Inc.	IGC	10.1	11.7	328-4552
MAS Fixed-Income	IGC	13.8	14.5	354-8185
MAS Fixed-Income II	IGC	12.6	12.9	354-8185
MAS High-Yield Sec.	HYC	24.6	28.6	354-8185
MAS Limited Duration F/I	IGC	6.0	N.A.	354-8185
MAS Mortgage-Backed	MBS	8.2	N.A.	354-8185
MAS Select Fixed-Income	IGC	13.9	14.7	354-8185
MAS Special Purpose F/I	IGC	14.8	N.A.	354-8185
Madison Bond	IGC	6.1	8.2	767-0300
Megy Income	WI	17.2	N.A.	832-7733[17]
Merrill Lynch Adj. Rate A	MBS	3.4	N.A.	637-3863
Merrill Lynch Fed. Sec. B	Gov	6.6	N.A.	637-3863
Merrill Lynch Global Bond A	WI	12.7	12.2	637-3863
Merrill Lynch High-Income B	HYC	16.7	24.6	637-3863
Merrill Lynch High-Qual. B	IGC	11.5	10.9	637-3863
Merrill Lynch Inst. Intm.	Gov	7.4	9.2	637-3863
Merrill Lynch Intm.-Term B	IGC	11.2	N.A.	637-3863
Merrill Lynch S/T Global A	WI	6.4	3.3	637-3863
Merrill Lynch World Inc. B	WI	13.1	N.A.	637-3863
Morgan Grenfell F/I	IGC	13.4	N.A.	932-7781
Morgan Stanley Inst. F/I	IGC	9.1	N.A.	548-7786
Morgan Stanley Inst. Glo. F/I	WI	15.8	N.A.	548-7786
Morgan Stanley Inst. H/Y	HYC	22.4	N.A.	548-7786
NY Life Institutional Bond	IGC	9.7	10.0	695-2126
NY Life Inst. Indexed Bond	IGC	9.6	10.4	695-2126
NY Life Inst. S/T Bond	IGC	5.7	7.6	695-2126
National Multi-Sector F/I B	IGC	14.0	N.A.	356-5535
Nations S/I Gov. Trust A	Gov	8.0	N.A.	321-7854
Nations S/I Gov. Inv. B	Gov	7.2	N.A.	321-7854
ONE Fund Income	IGC	11.2	N.A.	578-8078
One Group Income Bond Fid.	IGC	8.5	10.1	338-4345
One Group Ltd. Vol. Fid.	IGC	6.9	8.8	338-4345

Fund Name	Type	% compound annual return to Jan. 1, 1994 One year	Three years	Telephone (800)
Oppenheimer Strat. Inv. B	IGC	9.7	N.A.	525-7048
Oppenheimer Strat. Inc. B	HYC	18.1	N.A.	525-7048
PFAMCo Mgd. Bond & Inc.	IGC	11.0	N.A.	800-7674
Pimco Foreign	WI	16.4	N.A.	800-0952
Pimco High-Yield	HYC	18.7	N.A.	800-0952
Pimco Long Term US Gov.	IGC	18.6	N.A.	800-0952
Pimco Low Duration	IGC	7.8	9.6	800-0952
Pimco Low Duration II	IGC	6.6	N.A.	800-0952
Pimco Short-Term	IGC	4.6	5.0	800-0952
Pimco Total Return	IGC	12.5	13.9	800-0952
Pimco Total Return III	IGC	12.7	N.A.	800-0952
PNC Fin. Common Tr. F/I	IGC	11.2[28]	12.2[28]	585-5148[7]
PNC Intm. Gov. Inst.	Gov	8.0	N.A.	441-7762
PNC Managed Income Inst.	IGC	11.7	10.8	441-7762
PaineWebber Global Inc. A	WI	14.2	N.A.	647-1568
PaineWebber High-Income B	HYC	22.0	N.A.	647-1568
PaineWebber High-Income D	HYC	22.2	N.A.	647-1568
PaineWebber Income A	IGC	13.5	N.A.	647-1568
PaineWebber Inv. Grade B	IGC	12.6	N.A.	647-1568
PaineWebber Inv. Grade D	IGC	12.8	N.A.	647-1568
PaineWebber US Gov. Inc. B	MBS	5.8	N.A.	647-1568
PaineWebber US Gov. Inc. D	MBS	5.9	N.A.	647-1568
Paragon I/T Bond	IGC	9.2	10.3	777-5143
Paragon Short-Term Gov.	IGC	5.6	7.4	777-5143
Parkstone Bond Inst. C	IGC	9.8	10.3	451-8377
Parkstone Intm. Gov. Inst. C	Gov	7.5	8.8	451-8377
Parkstone Ltd. Mat. Inst. C	IGC	6.9	8.3	451-8377
Parkstone US Gov. Inst. A	Gov	7.5	N.A.	451-8377
Perf. I/T F/I Cnsmr. Svc.	IGC	10.5	N.A.	737-3676
Performance I/T F/I Inst.	IGC	10.8	N.A.	737-3676
Perf. S/T F/I Cnsmr. Svc.	IGC	4.6	N.A.	737-3676
Performance S/T F/I Inst.	IGC	4.4	N.A.	737-3676
Pillar Fixed-Income A	IGC	10.9	N.A.	932-7782
Pillar I/T Government A	Gov	8.2	N.A.	932-7782
Pillar Short-Term Inv. A	IGC	2.9	N.A.	932-7782
Piper Jaffray Inst. Gov.	Gov	15.6	14.7	866-7778
Prudential Adj. Rate Sec. B	MBS	2.0	N.A.	225-1852
Prudential GNMA A	MBS	5.0	7.8	225-1852
Prudential Gov. Plus A	Gov	8.0	10.1	225-1852
Prudential High-Yield A	HYC	17.3	21.9	225-1852
Prudential Intm. Glob. Inc. B	WI	15.1	N.A.	225-1852
Prudential S/T Glob. Ast. B	WI	6.1	N.A.	225-1852
Prudential S/T Glob. Inc. A	WI	8.2	6.1	225-1852
Prudential Struc. Mat. B	IGC	6.2	N.A.	225-1852
Prudential US Government A	Gov	11.7	11.2	225-1852
Putnam Adj. Rate US Gov. B	MBS	(0.1)	N.A.	225-1581
Putnam US Gov. Income B	MBS	4.9	N.A.	225-1581
RSI Ret. Trust Actively Mgd.	Gov	11.2	11.6	772-3615
RSI Ret. Trust I/T	Gov	7.6	9.4	772-3615
RSI Retire. Trust S/T Inv.	IGC	2.4	3.7	772-3615
Regis Sterling S/T F/I	IGC	5.7	N.A.	638-7983
Rembrandt S/I Gov. F/I Tr.	Gov	6.0	N.A.	443-4725
Rembrandt Taxable F/I Trust	IGC	9.8	N.A.	443-4725
Reynolds US Gov. Bond	Gov	8.8	N.A.	338-1579
Riverfront US Gov. Income	Gov	7.3	N.A.	424-2295
Riverside Capital F/I	IGC	8.9	N.A.	874-8376
SEI Cash+ GNMA A	MBS	6.5	9.8	342-5734
SEI Cash+ I/T Gov. A	Gov	7.0	8.8	342-5734
SEI Cash+ S/T Gov. A	Gov	4.7	7.0	342-5734
SEI Cash+ S/T Gov. B	Gov	3.5	6.4	342-5734
SEI Index Bond Index	IGC	9.3	9.9	342-5734
SEI Inst. Bond A	IGC	15.1	13.3	342-5734
SEI Inst. Ltd. Vol. A	IGC	8.8	9.9	342-5734
STI Classic Inv. Grade Tr.	IGC	10.8	N.A.	428-6970
Sagamore Bond	IGC	13.4	N.A.	321-7442
Schwab L/T Gov. Bond	Gov	(1.6)[30]	N.A.	526-8600
Seafirst Bond	IGC	6.4	8.4	323-9919
Shawmut Fixed-Inc. Trust	IGC	9.4	N.A.	742-9688
Shawmut Intm. Gov. Trust	Gov	7.1	N.A.	742-9688
Shawmut Ltd.-Term Inc. Tr.	IGC	4.6	N.A.	742-9688
Signet Select. US Gov. Tr.	MBS	7.4	9.4	771-7131[25]
Smith Barney Dvr. Str. Inc. A	HYC	13.3	N.A.	451-2010
Smith Barney Shearson H/I A	HYC	19.6	N.A.	451-2010
Smith Barney Mgd. Gov. B	MBS	8.6	N.A.	451-2010
Smith Barney S/T Wld. Inc. B	WI	0.6	N.A.	451-2010
Smith Breeden Inst. Intm.	Gov	10.8	N.A.	221-3138
Smith Breeden Inst. Short	MBS	4.7	N.A.	221-3138
Society Intm. Gov. Oblg.	Gov	8.2	9.8	362-5365
Society S/I Fixed Income	IGC	6.1	7.6	362-5365
Special Portfolios Cash	IGC	4.8	6.2	800-2638

Notes: [1]Closed to new investors [5]Area code 212 [7]Area code 215 [12]Area code 310 [19]Area code 415 [25]Area code 804 [27]Area code 817 [28]To Dec. 1; fund since merged [30]Three months to Dec. 1

Fund name	Type	% compound annual return to Jan. 1, 1994 One year	Three years	Telephone (800)
State Bond US Government	Gov	6.3	9.0	333-3952
State Farm Interim	IGC	6.8	8.4	766-2029[11]
Thomson Income A	IGC	8.3	N.A.	227-7337
Thomson S/I Government A	Gov	3.4	N.A.	227-7337
Thomson US Government A	Gov	8.0	N.A.	227-7337
Thornburg Limited Term Inc.	IGC	9.8	N.A.	847-0200
Transamerica Adj. US B	MBS	3.3	N.A.	343-6840
Transamerica Gov. Income	Gov	8.0	9.3	343-6840
Trust for Fed. Intm.-Gov.	Gov	5.3	8.3	821-7432
Trust for Fed. Sec. Short-Gov.	Gov	(0.8)	5.5	821-7432
Trust for Crd. Un. Gov. Sec.	Gov	4.6	N.A.	621-2550
Trust for Crd. Un. Mort. Sec.	MBS	5.9	N.A.	621-2550
Van Eck S/T World Income A	WI	(2.0)[28]	N.A.	221-2220
Van Eck S/T World Income B	WI	(2.7)[28]	N.A.	221-2220
Van Kampen S/T Glob. Inc. B	WI	6.5	N.A.	225-2222
Van Kampen US Gov. B	MBS	7.0	N.A.	225-2222
Vanguard Admiral I/T US	Gov	11.3	N.A.	851-4999
Vanguard Admiral L/T US	Gov	16.6	N.A.	851-4999
Vanguard Admiral S/T US	Gov	6.4	N.A.	851-4999
Voyageur US Gov. Sec.	Gov	10.5	11.5	553-2143
Weitz Fixed-Income	IGC	8.0	8.2	232-4161
Westcore Bonds Plus	IGC	8.3	10.2	392-2673
Westcore I/T Bond Inst.	IGC	9.9	12.3	392-2673
Westcore Long-Term Bond	IGC	15.9	14.6	392-2673
Westwood Intermediate Inst.	IGC	10.7	N.A.	253-4510
Woodward Bond Retail	IGC	11.3	N.A.	688-3350
Woodward Intm. Bond Retail	IGC	8.4	N.A.	688-3350
Wright Current Income	MBS	6.5	9.5	232-0013
Wright Gov. Obligations	Gov	15.9	13.4	232-0013
Wright Near Term Bond	Gov	7.9	9.1	232-0013
Wright Total Return Bond	IGC	11.0	11.1	232-0013
Zweig Government Sec. B	Gov	9.5	N.A.	444-2706

TAX-EXEMPTS

Fund name	Type	One year	Three years	Telephone (800)
AAL Municipal Bond	Muni	12.2	10.1	553-6319
AARP Ins. T/F Gen. Bond	Muni	12.7	11.2	253-2277
Alliance Muni. Inc. Natl. B	Muni	12.5	N.A.	227-4618
Alliance Muni. Ins. Natl. B	Muni	12.0	N.A.	227-4618
American Cap. Muni Bond B	Muni	9.8	N.A.	421-5666
Amer. Cap. T/E H/Y Muni B	Muni	9.2	N.A.	421-5666
American Cap. T/E Ins. B	Muni	8.0	N.A.	421-5666
Atlas National Muni Bond	Muni	13.4	11.8	933-2852
Cambridge Municipal Inc. A	Muni	15.6	N.A.	382-0016
Colonial Tax-Exempt B	Muni	9.9	N.A.	248-2828
Colonial Tax-Exempt Ins. B	Muni	10.2	N.A.	248-2828
Elfun Tax-Exempt Income	Muni	12.0	10.9	242-0134
Evergreen Ins. Natl. T/F	Muni	16.0	N.A.	235-0064
Fidelity Advisor Is L/T T/E	Muni	9.8	9.0	522-7297
Financial Horizons Muni	Muni	13.0	11.2	533-5622
First American Muni Bond	Muni	8.2	8.1	637-2548
Intermediate Muni Inst.	Muni	9.7	9.2	245-5000
Kent Medium Term T/E Inst.	Muni	8.5	N.A.	343-2138
Lutheran Brotherhood Muni	Muni	13.0	11.4	328-4552
Merrill Lynch Muni Inc. A	Muni	10.9	10.0	637-3863
Merrill Lynch Muni Ins. B	Muni	11.7	10.4	637-3863
Merrill Lynch Muni Ltd. B	Muni	3.9	N.A.	637-3863
Merrill Lynch Muni Natl. B	Muni	11.6	10.4	637-3863
Morgan Grenfell Muni Bond	Muni	12.2	N.A.	932-7781
Muni for Temporary Intm.	Muni	8.9	9.0	821-7432
Nations Muni Inc. Trust A	Muni	13.5	N.A.	321-7854
One Group Intm. T/F Fid.	Muni	9.7	9.1	338-4345
PNC Tax-Free Inc. Investor	Muni	13.0	11.1	441-7762
PaineWebber Muni H/I B	Muni	11.3	N.A.	647-1568
PaineWebber Natl. T/F B	Muni	11.5	N.A.	647-1568
PaineWebber Natl. T/F D	Muni	11.8	N.A.	647-1568
Parkstone Muni Bond Inst. C	Muni	9.2	8.6	451-8377
Prudential Muni High-Yield A	Muni	11.4	10.9	225-1852
Prudential Muni Insured A	Muni	11.8	10.8	225-1852
Prudential Muni Modified A	Muni	10.2	9.7	225-1852
Prudential Natl. Muni A	Muni	12.6	11.4	225-1852
Putnam Municipal Inc. B	Muni	11.3	N.A.	225-1581
Putnam Tax Exempt Inc. B	Muni	12.7	N.A.	225-1581
Rembrandt T/E F/I Trust	Muni	8.6	N.A.	443-4725
SEI T/E Intm. Muni	Muni	8.6	8.2	342-5734
Short-Term Municipal Inst.	Muni	4.0	5.5	245-5000
State Bond Tax-Exempt	Muni	9.7	9.4	333-3952
State Farm Municipal Bond	Muni	9.8	9.5	766-2029[11]
T. Rowe Price Ins. Intm.	Muni	12.6	N.A.	638-5660
Thomson Tax-Exempt A	Muni	13.1	N.A.	227-7337
Transamerica T/F Bond B	Muni	14.3	N.A.	343-6840
Van Kampen Muni Income B	Muni	11.3	N.A.	225-2222
Wright Insured Tax-Free	Muni	9.9	9.4	232-0013

SINGLE STATE TAX-EXEMPTS

Fund name	Type	One year	Three years	Telephone (800)
Eaton Vance AL Tax-Free	AL	12.4	N.A.	225-6265
Franklin AL T/F Income	AL	12.2	11.1	342-5236
MFS AL Municipal Bond A	AL	12.1	10.6	225-2606
Eaton Vance AR Tax-Free	AR	13.8	N.A.	225-6265
MFS AR Municipal Bond A	AR	11.9	N.A.	225-2606
Dean Witter M/S Muni AZ	AZ	11.7	N.A.	869-3863
Eaton Vance AZ Tax-Free	AZ	15.0	N.A.	225-6265
First Inv. M/S Ins. T/F AZ	AZ	14.9	11.7	423-4026
Flagship AZ Double T/E A	AZ	13.0	11.8	227-4648
Franklin AZ T/F Income	AZ	11.2	11.1	342-5236
GIT AZ Tax-Free	AZ	12.0	10.1	336-3063
Merrill Lynch AZ Muni A	AZ	13.3	N.A.	637-3863
Merrill Lynch AZ Muni B	AZ	12.8	N.A.	637-3863
Nuveen AZ Tax-Free Value	AZ	13.7	N.A.	351-4100
Prudential Muni AZ A	AZ	12.0	10.7	225-1852
Prudential Muni AZ B	AZ	11.5	10.4	225-1852
Putnam AZ Tax Exempt Inc.	AZ	12.0	N.A.	225-1581
Smith B. Shear. AZ Muni A	AZ	13.1	10.8	451-2010
Tax-Free Trust of AZ	AZ	11.0	10.7	437-1020
Voyageur AZ Ins. Tax-Free	AZ	12.6	N.A.	553-2143
Westcore AZ Intm. T/F	AZ	10.5	N.A.	392-2673
Alliance Muni Inc. CA A	CA	12.9	11.1	227-4618
Alliance Muni Inc. CA B	CA	12.1	N.A.	227-4618
Alliance Muni Ins. CA A	CA	13.1	11.1	227-4618
Alliance Muni Ins. CA B	CA	8.5	N.A.	227-4618
Atlas CA Muni Bond	CA	13.5	11.3	933-2852
Benham CA Muni High-Yield	CA	13.1	11.1	472-3389
Benham CA T/F Insured	CA	13.4	11.3	472-3389
Benham CA T/F Intm.-Term	CA	10.6	9.2	472-3389
Benham CA T/F Long-Term	CA	13.7	11.2	472-3389
Benham CA T/F Short-Term	CA	5.8	N.A.	472-3389
Bernstein CA Muni	CA	8.1	8.1	756-4097[5]
Boston Co. CA T/F Retail	CA	11.0	9.6	225-5267
California Inv. T/F Income	CA	14.8	11.9	225-8778
California Muni	CA	16.8	10.8	322-6864
Calvert CA Muni Intm.	CA	8.9	N.A.	368-2748
Colonial CA Tax-Exempt A	CA	10.5	9.8	248-2828
Colonial CA Tax-Exempt B	CA	9.7	N.A.	248-2828
Dean Witter CA T/F Income	CA	10.5	9.5	869-3863
Dean Witter M/S Muni CA	CA	13.2	N.A.	869-3863
Dreyfus CA Intm. Muni	CA	14.3	N.A.	782-6620
Dreyfus CA Tax-Exempt	CA	11.8	9.6	782-6620
Eaton Vance CA Ltd. Mat. T/F	CA	9.3	N.A.	225-6265
Eaton Vance CA Muni	CA	11.5	9.0	225-6265
Evergreen Sh.-Intm. Muni CA	CA	7.8	N.A.	235-0064
Fidelity CA T/F High-Yield	CA	12.9	10.6	544-8888
Fidelity CA T/F Insured	CA	13.4	11.2	544-8888
Fidelity Spartan CA Muni H/Y	CA	13.5	11.3	544-8888
First Inv. M/S Ins. T/F CA	CA	13.2	11.4	423-4026
Franklin CA Ins. T/F Inc.	CA	13.0	10.8	342-5236
Franklin CA Intm.-Term T/F	CA	11.5	N.A.	312-5236
Franklin CA T/F Income	CA	9.5	9.9	342-5236
Fremont CA Intm. T/F	CA	9.8	9.3	548-4539
General CA Muni Bond	CA	13.6	11.0	242-8671
Hancock Tax-Exempt CA	CA	12.5	10.7	225-5291
IDS CA Tax-Exempt	CA	11.4	10.2	328-8300
Kemper State T/F Inc. CA	CA	13.4	11.0	621-1048
Lord Abbett CA T/F Inc.	CA	13.8	12.1	874-3733
MFS CA Muni Bond A	CA	12.9	11.1	225-2606
Mackenzie CA Muni	CA	11.6	9.6	456-5111
MainStay CA Tax-Free	CA	12.7	N.A.	522-4202
Merrill Lynch CA Muni A	CA	12.6	10.7	637-3863
Merrill Lynch CA Muni B	CA	12.1	10.1	637-3863
Muir CA Tax-Free Bond	CA	11.8	N.A.	648-3448
Muni For CA Inv. CA Intm.	CA	6.5	8.0	821-7432
National's CA T/E Bonds	CA	9.4	9.2	356-5535
Nuveen CA Ins. T/F Value	CA	12.3	11.0	351-4100
Nuveen CA Tax-Free Value	CA	11.4	10.6	351-4100
Oppenheimer CA Tax-Ex.	CA	13.4	10.8	525-7048
Op'heimer Main St. CA T/E A	CA	12.8	10.8	525-7048
Overland Exp. CA T/F Bond A	CA	12.9	11.2	552-9612
Pacific Horizon CA T/E	CA	12.4	10.7	332-3863
Pacifica CA Tax-Free	CA	11.9	10.3	662-8417
PaineWebber CA T/F Inc. A	CA	11.9	10.1	647-1568
PaineWebber CA T/F Inc. B	CA	11.1	N.A.	647-1568
PaineWebber CA T/F Inc. D	CA	11.4	N.A.	647-1568
Parnassus Income CA T/E	CA	13.6	N.A.	999-3505
Premier CA Muni Bond A	CA	13.5	10.9	242-8671
Prud. CA Muni CA Inc. A	CA	14.2	11.8	225-1852
Prudential CA Muni B	CA	11.6	10.2	225-1852
Putnam CA T/E Inc. A	CA	13.0	10.9	225-1581
Putnam CA T/E Inc. B	CA	12.1	N.A.	225-1581
Quest for Value CA T/E	CA	13.0	10.9	232-3863
Safeco CA Tax-Free Inc.	CA	13.2	11.2	426-6730
Schwab CA Long-Term T/F	CA	12.6	N.A.	526-8600
Scudder CA Tax-Free	CA	13.8	12.0	225-2470
Seligman T/E CA High-Yield	CA	9.9	10.0	221-2783
Seligman T/E CA Quality	CA	12.6	10.8	221-2783
Sierra CA Municipal	CA	13.7	10.8	222-5852
Smith Barney Muni CA A	CA	12.1	10.9	544-7835
Smith B. Shear. CA Muni A	CA	12.8	10.8	451-2010
Smith B. Shear. CA Muni B	CA	12.1	N.A.	451-2010
Smith B. Sh. Intm. Mat. CA A	CA	11.5	N.A.	451-2010
Stagecoach CA T/F Bond	CA	13.8	N.A.	222-8222
State St. Research CA T/F C	CA	12.5	11.1	882-0052
T. Rowe Price CA Tax-Free	CA	12.5	11.2	638-5660
Tax-Exempt Fund of CA	CA	12.9	10.4	421-0180
Thornburg Ltd.-T. Muni CA	CA	8.2	7.8	847-0200
Transamerica CA T/F Inc. A	CA	13.6	11.7	343-6840
Transamerica CA T/F Inc. B	CA	12.8	N.A.	343-6840
USAA Tax-Exempt CA Bond	CA	12.8	10.6	382-8722
United Svcs. Near-Term T/F	CA	9.8	8.7	873-8637
Van Kampen CA Ins. T/F A	CA	14.5	11.5	225-2222
Vanguard CA T/F Ins. Long	CA	12.8	11.0	851-4999
Eaton Vance CO Tax-Free	CO	13.1	N.A.	225-6265
Flagship CO Double T/E A	CO	12.9	11.2	227-4648
Franklin CO T/F Income	CO	12.8	11.6	342-5236
Hanifen Imhoff CO BondShrs.	CO	8.1	8.5	525-9989
Seligman Tax-Exempt CO	CO	11.1	9.4	221-2783
Tax-Free Fund of CO	CO	11.1	10.4	872-2652
Voyageur CO Tax-Free	CO	13.6	11.6	553-2143
AIM Tax-Exempt Bond of CT	CT	12.0	10.8	347-1919
Colonial CT Tax-Exempt A	CT	12.9	N.A.	248-2828
Colonial CT Tax-Exempt B	CT	12.0	N.A.	248-2828
Dreyfus CT Intm. Muni	CT	12.7	N.A.	782-6620
Eaton Vance CT Tax-Free	CT	12.4	N.A.	225-6265
Fidelity Spartan CT Muni H/Y	CT	12.5	10.5	544-8888
First Inv. M/S Ins. T/F CT	CT	14.1	11.2	423-4026
Flagship CT Double T/E A	CT	12.3	10.9	227-4648
Franklin CT T/F Income	CT	12.3	10.4	342-5236
Lord Abbett T/F Inc. CT	CT	13.7	N.A.	874-3733
Premier State Muni CT A	CT	12.6	10.8	242-8671
ABT FL High-Inc. Muni	FL	14.9	N.A.	553-7838
ABT FL Tax-Free	FL	12.3	11.2	553-7838
Dean Witter M/S Muni FL	FL	12.5	N.A.	869-3863
Dreyfus FL Intm. Muni	FL	12.7	N.A.	782-6620
Eaton Vance FL Ltd. Mat. T/F	FL	9.9	N.A.	225-6265
Eaton Vance FL Tax-Free	FL	12.9	11.4	225-6265
Emerald FL Tax-Exempt	FL	14.1	N.A.	637-6336
Fidelity Spartan FL Muni Inc.	FL	14.5	N.A.	544-8888
First Inv. M/S Ins. T/F FL	FL	14.2	12.1	423-4026
Flagship FL Double T/E A	FL	13.3	11.8	227-4648
Franklin FL T/F Income	FL	12.0	11.1	342-5236
Kemper State T/F Inc. FL	FL	13.5	N.A.	621-1048
Keystone Amer. FL T/F A	FL	11.3	11.0	343-2898
Lord Abbett T/F Inc. FL	FL	13.2	N.A.	874-3733
MFS FL Muni Bond A	FL	14.4	N.A.	225-2606
Merrill Lynch FL Muni A	FL	12.5	N.A.	637-3863
Merrill Lynch FL Muni B	FL	12.0	N.A.	637-3863
Nuveen FL Tax-Free Value	FL	12.6	N.A.	351-4100
Premier State Muni FL A	FL	11.9	11.1	242-8671
Prudential Municipal FL A	FL	13.4	11.9	225-1852
Putnam FL T/E Inc. A	FL	11.1	11.0	225-1581
Putnam FL T/E Inc. B	FL	10.2	N.A.	225-1581
Seligman Tax-Exempt FL	FL	13.5	11.1	221-2783
Vanguard FL Ins. Tax-Free	FL	13.4	N.A.	851-4999
Voyageur FL Ins. Tax-Free	FL	12.4	N.A.	553-2143
Eaton Vance GA Tax-Free	GA	12.1	N.A.	225-6265
Flagship GA Double T/E A	GA	11.6	10.4	227-4648
Franklin GA T/F Income	GA	11.9	10.9	342-5236
MFS GA Muni Bond A	GA	12.4	10.8	225-2606
Prudential Muni GA A	GA	12.9	10.7	225-1852
Prudential Muni GA B	GA	12.5	10.4	225-1852

Notes: Type is state abbreviation. [5]Area code 212 [11]Area code 309 [28]To Dec.1; fund since merged

Fund Name	Type	% compound annual return to Jan. 1, 1994: One year	Three years	Telephone (800)
Seligman Tax-Exempt MI	MI	11.5	10.9	221-2783
Colonial MN Tax-Exempt A	MN	10.7	9.1	248-2828
Colonial MN Tax-Exempt B	MN	9.9	N.A.	248-2828
Eaton Vance MN Tax-Free	MN	11.6	N.A.	225-6265
Fidelity MN Tax-Free	MN	11.9	9.3	544-8888
First Inv. M/S Ins. T/F MN	MN	11.3	10.5	423-4026
Fortis Tax-Free MN	MN	11.5	10.3	800-2638
Franklin MN Ins. T/F Inc.	MN	11.0	10.1	342-5236
Great Hall MN Insured T/E	MN	11.5	10.2	934-6674
IDS MN Tax-Exempt	MN	11.4	10.2	328-8300
Merrill Lynch MN Muni B	MN	12.1	N.A.	637-3863
Norwest MN Tax-Free Inv. A	MN	11.4	9.2	363-3300[5]
Piper Jaffray MN T/E	MN	12.0	10.5	866-7778
Premier State Muni MN A	MN	11.9	10.6	242-8671
Prudential Muni MN A	MN	10.9	9.1	225-1852
Prudential Municipal MN B	MN	10.5	8.7	225-1852
Putnam MN T/E Income A	MN	11.6	9.9	225-1581
Seligman Tax-Exempt MN	MN	13.5	9.5	221-2783
State MN Tax-Free Inc.	MN	10.2	9.1	333-3952
Voyageur MN Insured	MN	13.7	11.3	553-2143
Voyageur MN Intm. Tax-Free	MN	7.8	7.9	553-2143
Voyageur MN Tax-Free	MN	12.6	10.5	553-2143
Arch MO T/E Bond Investor	MO	11.2	10.5	551-3731
Eaton Vance MO Tax-Free	MO	13.5	N.A.	225-6265
Flagship MO Double T/E A	MO	13.5	11.5	227-4648
Franklin MO T/F Income	MO	13.3	11.4	342-5236
GIT MO Tax-Free	MO	11.2	9.6	336-3063
Lord Abbett T/F Income MO	MO	14.0	N.A.	874-3733
Seligman Tax-Exempt MO	MO	11.4	10.0	221-2783
Voyageur MO Ins. Tax-Free	MO	14.2	N.A.	553-2143
MFS MS Municipal Bond A	MS	12.6	N.A.	225-2606
111 Corcoran NC Muni Secs.	NC	12.4	N.A.	422-2080
Eaton Vance NC Tax-Free	NC	11.5	N.A.	225-6265
Flagship NC Triple T/E A	NC	11.3	10.6	227-4648
Franklin NC T/F Income	NC	11.7	10.7	342-5236
MFS NC Muni Bond A	NC	10.3	9.4	225-2606
Merrill Lynch NC Muni B	NC	13.6	N.A.	637-3863
Premier State Muni NC A	NC	13.8	N.A.	242-8671
Prudential Municipal NC A	NC	9.9	10.0	225-1852
Prudential Municipal NC B	NC	11.3	10.4	225-1852
Seligman Tax-Exempt NC	NC	13.0	10.6	221-2783
Voyageur ND Tax-Free	ND	10.8	N.A.	553-2143
Compass Cap. NJ Muni Bond	NJ	11.6	N.A.	451-8371
Dean Witter M/S Muni NJ	NJ	12.3	N.A.	869-3863
Dreyfus NJ Intm. Muni Bond	NJ	12.4	N.A.	782-6620
Dreyfus NJ Municipal Bond	NJ	12.9	11.2	782-6620
Eaton Vance NJ Ltd. Mat. T/F	NJ	8.9	N.A.	225-6265
Eaton Vance NJ Tax-Free	NJ	12.6	N.A.	225-6265
FFB NJ Tax-Free Income	NJ	12.6	N.A.	437-8790
Fidelity Spartan NJ Muni H/Y	NJ	12.7	11.3	544-8888
First Inv. M/S Ins. T/F NJ	NJ	13.1	11.4	423-4026
Franklin NJ T/F Income	NJ	11.0	10.8	342-5236
Lord Abbett T/F Inc. NJ	NJ	14.2	12.3	874-3733
Merrill Lynch NJ Muni A	NJ	11.8	10.4	637-3863
Merrill Lynch NJ Muni B	NJ	11.1	9.9	637-3863
Nuveen NJ Tax-Free Value	NJ	12.6	N.A.	351-4100
Prudential Municipal NJ A	NJ	12.6	11.4	225-1852
Prudential Municipal NJ B	NJ	12.1	11.1	225-1852
Putnam NJ Tax Ex. Inc. A	NJ	12.5	10.8	225-1581
Putnam NJ Tax Ex. Inc. B	NJ	11.5	N.A.	225-1581
Seligman NJ Tax-Exempt	NJ	12.4	10.8	221-2783
Smith Barney Shear NJ Muni A	NJ	13.0	11.5	451-2010
Smith Barney Shear NJ Muni B	NJ	12.4	N.A.	451-2010
T. Rowe Price NJ Tax-Free	NJ	14.0	N.A.	638-5660
Vanguard NJ T/F Ins. Long	NJ	13.3	11.3	851-4999
Flagship NM Double T/E A	NM	13.9	N.A.	227-4648
Thornburg NM Intm. Muni	NM	10.4	N.A.	847-0200
Alliance Muni Inc. NY A	NY	12.8	11.9	227-4618
Alliance Muni Inc. NY B	NY	11.7	N.A.	227-4618
BNY Hamilton Intm. NY T/E	NY	8.0	N.A.	426-9363
Bernstein NY Municipal	NY	8.4	8.6	756-4097[5]
Boston Co. NY T/F Ret.	NY	9.0	9.1	225-5267
Colonial NY Tax-Exempt A	NY	12.2	11.1	248-2828
Colonial NY Tax-Exempt B	NY	11.4	N.A.	248-2828
Dean Witter NY T/F Income	NY	11.2	10.9	869-3863
Dreyfus NY Ins. T/E Bond	NY	11.0	10.9	782-6620
Dreyfus NY T/E Intm. Bond	NY	11.4	10.7	782-6620
Dreyfus NY Tax-Exempt Bond	NY	12.5	11.3	782-6620
Eaton Vance NY Ltd. Mat. T/F	NY	9.3	N.A.	225-6265
Eaton Vance NY Tax-Free	NY	13.5	12.4	225-6265
Empire Builder Tax-Free	NY	12.2	10.3	845-8406
Fidelity NY T/F High-Yield	NY	12.4	11.6	544-8888
Fidelity NY T/F Insured	NY	12.3	11.1	544-8888
Fidelity Spartan NY Muni H/Y	NY	13.0	12.3	544-8888
First Investors NY Ins. T/F	NY	9.8	10.0	423-4026
Flagship NY Tax-Exempt A	NY	15.5	N.A.	227-4648
Fortis Tax-Free NY	NY	10.8	10.9	800-2638
Franklin NY Ins. T/F Inc.	NY	14.0	N.A.	342-5236
Franklin NY Intm. T/F Inc.	NY	10.2	N.A.	342-5236
Franklin NY T/F Income	NY	11.9	12.2	342-5236
Galaxy NY Muni Bond Retail	NY	12.3	N.A.	628-0414
General NY Muni Bond	NY	14.1	12.7	782-6620
Hancock Tax-Exempt NY	NY	13.8	12.3	225-5291
IDS NY Tax-Exempt	NY	11.6	11.2	328-8300
Investors Preference NY T/F	NY	12.2	N.A.	543-8072
Kemper State T/F Inc. NY	NY	13.0	11.9	621-1048
Landmark NY Tax-Free Inc.	NY	12.0	10.7	223-4447
Lebenthal NY Muni Bond	NY	13.7	N.A.	221-5822
Lord Abbett T/F Inc. NY	NY	12.6	11.7	874-3733
MFS NY Muni Bond A	NY	12.7	11.9	225-2606
Mackenzie NY Municipal	NY	10.2	10.2	456-5111
MainStay NY Tax-Free	NY	12.1	N.A.	522-4202
Mariner NY Tax-Free Bond	NY	14.3	12.5	634-2536
Merrill Lynch NY Muni A	NY	11.7	11.5	637-3863
Merrill Lynch NY Muni B	NY	11.2	11.3	637-3863
New York Muni	NY	12.4	13.3	322-6864
Nuveen NY Ins. T/F Value	NY	13.1	12.1	351-4100
Nuveen NY Tax-Free Value	NY	13.0	12.4	351-4100
Oppenheimer NY T/E A	NY	13.5	11.8	525-7048
PaineWebber NY T/F Inc. A	NY	12.7	11.8	647-1568
PaineWebber NY T/F Inc. B	NY	11.8	N.A.	647-1568
Premier NY Muni Bond A	NY	14.1	12.9	242-8671
Prudential Municipal NY A	NY	13.0	12.1	225-1852
Prudential Municipal NY B	NY	12.6	11.8	225-1852
Putnam NY T/E Opp.	NY	9.2	9.7	225-1581
Putnam NY Tax Ex. Inc. A	NY	13.2	12.7	225-1581
Putnam NY Tax Ex. Inc. B	NY	12.4	N.A.	225-1581
Quest for Value NY T/E	NY	13.7	12.7	232-3863
Rochester Fund Municipals	NY	14.6	12.9	383-1300[23]
Rochester Ltd.-Term NY Muni	NY	10.1	N.A.	383-1300[23]
Scudder NY Tax-Free	NY	12.9	12.5	225-2470
Seligman Tax-Exempt NY	NY	13.2	12.0	221-2783
Smith Barney Muni NY A	NY	13.0	12.3	544-7835
Smith B. Shear NY Muni A	NY	10.8	11.0	451-2010
Smith B. Shear NY Muni B	NY	10.3	N.A.	451-2010
State St. Research NY T/F C	NY	13.4	12.1	882-0052
T. Rowe Price NY Tax-Free	NY	13.3	12.0	638-5660
USAA Tax-Exempt NY Bond	NY	13.5	12.0	382-8722
UST Master NY Intm.-Term	NY	9.3	8.5	233-1136
Value Line NY Tax-Exempt	NY	13.9	12.6	223-0818
Vanguard NY Ins. Tax-Free	NY	13.0	11.9	851-4999
Vista NY Tax-Free Income	NY	13.8	12.4	348-4782
Warburg Pincus NY Muni	NY	9.7	8.9	257-5614
Carnegie T/E OH Gen. Muni	OH	10.2	9.5	321-2322
Colonial OH Tax-Exempt A	OH	11.0	10.2	248-2828
Colonial OH Tax-Exempt B	OH	10.2	N.A.	248-2828
Eaton Vance OH Tax-Free	OH	12.9	N.A.	225-6265
Fidelity OH T/F High-Yield	OH	12.0	10.7	544-8888
First Inv. M/S Ins. T/F OH	OH	13.1	11.5	423-4026
Flagship OH Double T/E A	OH	11.6	10.6	227-4648
Franklin OH Ins. T/F Income	OH	12.5	10.7	342-5236
Gradison-McDonald OH T/F Inc.	OH	13.2	N.A.	869-5999
IDS OH Tax-Exempt	OH	11.1	10.7	328-8300
Merrill Lynch OH Muni B	OH	13.8	N.A.	637-3863
Midwest OH Ins. Tax-Free	OH	12.5	10.8	543-8721
Monitor OH T/F Inv. Share	OH	7.8	N.A.	253-0412
Monitor OH T/F Trust Shrs.	OH	8.1	7.7	253-0412
Nuveen OH Tax-Free Value	OH	13.0	11.5	351-4100
OH Muni Income Fortress	OH	13.3	10.9	245-5051
One Group OH Muni Fiduc.	OH	11.6	N.A.	338-4345
Premier State Muni OH A	OH	12.3	11.3	242-8671
Prudential Municipal OH A	OH	11.9	10.9	225-1852
Prudential Municipal OH B	OH	11.4	10.6	225-1852
Putnam OH T/E Income A	OH	11.1	10.6	225-1581
Scudder OH Tax-Free	OH	12.3	11.0	225-2470
Seligman Tax-Exempt OH	OH	11.7	10.5	221-2783
Society OH Tax-Free Bond	OH	12.6	10.4	362-5365
Vanguard OH T/F Ins. Long	OH	12.7	11.4	851-4999
Columbia Municipal Bond	OR	10.7	9.6	547-1707
Crabbe Huson OR Muni	OR	8.9	8.7	541-9732
Eaton Vance OR Tax-Free	OR	13.4	N.A.	225-6265
Franklin OR T/F Income	OR	10.9	10.7	342-5236
Seligman Tax-Exempt OR	OR	10.9	9.8	221-2783
Tax-Free Trust of OR	OR	10.1	9.6	872-6734
Dean Witter M/S Muni PA	PA	12.6	N.A.	869-3863
Delaware Tax-Free PA	PA	11.0	11.0	523-4640
Eaton Vance PA Ltd. Mat. T/F	PA	9.3	N.A.	225-6265
Eaton Vance PA Tax-Free	PA	12.5	N.A.	225-6265
Fidelity Spartan PA Muni H/Y	PA	12.6	11.4	544-8888
First Inv. M/S Ins. T/F PA	PA	14.3	11.5	423-4026
Flagship PA Triple T/E A	PA	11.2	10.9	227-4648
Franklin PA T/F Income	PA	11.7	11.6	342-5236
Keystone Amer. PA T/F A	PA	14.2	12.4	343-2898
Legg Mason PA Tax-Free Inc.	PA	12.5	N.A.	822-5544
Lord Abbett T/F Income PA	PA	14.6	N.A.	874-3733
Merrill Lynch PA Muni A	PA	13.5	11.8	637-3863
Merrill Lynch PA Muni B	PA	12.7	11.2	637-3863
Nuveen PA Tax-Free Value	PA	13.5	N.A.	351-4100
Oppenheimer PA Tax-Ex.	PA	13.2	10.9	525-7048
PNC PA Tax-Free Inc. Inst.	PA	12.6	N.A.	441-7762
Pennsylvania Muni Inc. Inv.	PA	12.3	11.0	245-5000
Premier State Muni PA A	PA	12.7	11.6	242-8671
Prudential Municipal PA A	PA	12.5	11.5	225-1852
Prudential Municipal PA B	PA	12.0	11.2	225-1852
Putnam PA Tax Exempt Inc.	PA	12.3	11.6	225-1581
SEI T/E PA Municipal	PA	8.5	8.6	342-5734
Scudder PA Tax-Free	PA	13.1	11.5	225-2470
Seligman PA Tax-Exempt	PA	12.9	11.2	221-2783
Sentinel PA Tax-Free	PA	9.7	9.8	282-3863
Van Kampen PA T/F Inc. A	PA	13.2	11.7	225-2222
Vanguard PA T/F Ins. Long	PA	12.7	11.7	851-4999
Wm. Penn PA Tax-Free Inc.	PA	10.2	9.9	523-8440
Franklin PR T/F Income	PA	11.0	10.7	342-5236
Biltmore SC Municipal Bond	SC	12.0	N.A.	763-7277
Eaton Vance SC Tax-Free	SC	13.4	N.A.	225-6265
MFS SC Municipal Bond A	SC	11.3	9.9	225-2606
Seligman Tax-Exempt SC	SC	11.7	10.5	221-2783
Eaton Vance TN Tax-Free	TN	14.5	N.A.	225-6265
Flagship TN Double T/E A	TN	11.8	10.8	227-4648
MFS TN Municipal Bond A	TN	10.5	9.5	225-2606
Amer. Cap. TX Muni Sec. A	TX	12.4	N.A.	421-5666
Franklin TX T/F Income	TX	11.6	10.7	342-5236
Kemper State T/F Income TX	TX	13.6	N.A.	621-1048
Lord Abbett T/F Inc. TX	TX	12.8	11.5	874-3733
MFS TX Municipal Bond	TX	14.4	N.A.	225-2606
Merrill Lynch TX Muni A	TX	13.7	N.A.	637-3863
Merrill Lynch TX Muni B	TX	13.1	N.A.	637-3863
Premier State Muni TX A	TX	13.6	12.2	242-8671
Putnam TX Tax Exempt Inc.	TX	12.6	N.A.	225-1581
Eaton Vance VA Tax-Free	VA	11.6	N.A.	226-6265
First Inv. M/S Ins. T/F VA	VA	12.9	11.5	423-4026
Flagship VA Double T/E A	VA	12.4	11.3	227-4648
Franklin VA T/F Income	VA	12.4	11.2	342-5236
GIT VA Tax-Free	VA	12.5	9.9	336-3063
MFS VA Municipal Bond A	VA	10.5	9.6	225-2606
Nations VA Intm. Muni Inv. A	VA	9.9	8.8	321-7854
Nuveen VA Tax-Free Value	VA	12.0	N.A.	351-4100
Premier State Muni VA A	VA	13.9	N.A.	242-8671
Rushmore VA Tax-Free	VA	11.8	10.2	343-3355
Signet Sel. VA Muni Inv.	VA	12.4	9.8	444-7123
Signet Sel. VA Muni Trust	VA	12.4	9.9	771-7131[25]
T. Rowe Price VA Tax-Free	VA	12.5	N.A.	638-5660
Tax-Exempt Fund of VA	VA	11.2	10.1	421-0180
USAA Tax-Exempt VA Bond	VA	12.7	11.0	382-8722
Calvert T/F Res. VT Muni	VT	10.7	N.A.	368-2748
Tax-Free Fund of VT	VT	5.2	N.A.	675-3333
Lord Abbett T/F Inc. WA	WA	13.6	N.A.	874-3733
Heartland WI Tax-Free	WI	10.8	N.A.	432-7856
MFS WV Muni Bond A	WV	11.4	10.0	225-2606

Notes: Area codes: [1]212, [2]516, [3]808, [23]716 Type is state abbreviation.

Index